A S U R V E Y O F

WESTERN CIVILIZATION VOLUME TWO

A SURVEY OF

WESTERN CIVILIZATION VOLUME TWO

RICHARD D. GOFF
GEORGE H. CASSAR
ANTHONY ESLER
JAMES P. HOLOKA
JAMES C. WALTZ

WEST PUBLISHING COMPANY

St. Paul   New York   Los Angeles   San Francisco

LIBRARY OF CONGRESS CATALOGING-IN-PUBLICATION DATA

A Survey of Western Civilization.

Includes bibliographies and index.
1. Civilization, Occidental—History. 2. Civilization—History. I. Goff, Richard D.
CB245.S95   1987   909'.09821
86-24601
ISBN 0-314-26135-4 (v. 1)
ISBN 0-314-26137-0 (v. 2)

Copyediting: Elaine Linden
Design: Janet Bollow
Cartographic Research and Compilation: Robert Ward, James Vaughn
Cartographic Design and Production: Patricia Isaacs, assisted by Rebecca Miller and Julie L. Mortenson
Photo Research: Monica Suder, assisted by Lindsay Kefauver
Composition: Parkwood Composition Service, Inc.
Cover Design: Imagesmyth, Inc.
Cover Art: Camille Pissarro, *Le Pont Boieldieu à Rouen, temps mouillé,* 1896, oil on canvas, Art Gallery of Ontario, Toronto, Gift of Reuben Wells Leonard Estate, 1937. Used with permission.

ACKNOWLEDGMENTS

(The following list contains sources for all chapter-opening paragraphs.)

383 Louis XIV, "Lessons in Kingship," from his *Memoirs,* translated by H. H. Rowen, in *From Absolutism to Revolution* (New York: Macmillan, 1963), pp. 26–27.

401 A. Burnaby, *Travels through the Middle Settlements in North America,* 2nd ed. (Ithaca, N.Y.: Cornell University Press, 1960), pp. 110–114.

417 M. J. de Caritat, Marquis de Condorcet, "Equisse d'un Tableau Historique des Progress de l' Esprit Human," in O. E. Fellows and N. L. Torrey, eds., *The Age of Enlightenment: An Anthology* (New York: Appleton-Century-Crofts, 1942), pp. 623, 626.

435 The Duc de Niverais, cited in N. Mitford, *Frederick the Great* (Harmondsworth: Penguin Books, 1970), pp. 190–193.

453 Thomas Wood, *The Passing of France,* pp. 137–48 passim; *The Winning of Canada,* pp. 138–39. Both in G. M. Wrong and H. H. Langton, eds. *Chronicles of Canada,* vols. 10, 11 (Toronto: Glasgow, Brook, 1914–1921).

475 Abbe Edgeworth, *Memoirs* (London: Hunter, 1815).

488 Excerpted selection, pp. 404–5, from "The French Revolution" in *Pageant of Europe,* Revised Edition, by Raymond Phineas Stearns (Orlando: Harcourt Brace Jovanovich, Inc.: 1961).

497 Michael J. Thornton, *Napoleon After Waterloo* (Stanford: Stanford University Press, 1968), p. 1.

519 Emile Zola, *Germinal,* translated by Stanley and Eleanor Hochman (New York: New American Library, 1970), p. 42.

537 Frederich Hecker, "The Rising People of Baden 1848," in *Revolution from 1789 to 1906: Documents,* R. W. Postgate, ed. (New York: Harper, 1962), p. 257–58.

555 Comte A. de la Garde Chambonas, Comte Fleury, ed. (London: Chapman and Hall, 1902), pp. 1–3, 12, 29.

573 From *The Reminiscences of Carl Schurz,* quoted in J. P. Scott and A. Baltzly, *Readings in European History Since 1814* (New York: Crofts, 1930), p. 160.

591 Wilhelm Stieber, *The Chancellor's Spy: The Revelations of the Chief of Bismarck's Secret Service* (New York: Grove Press, 1979), pp. 211–12.

598 Giuseppe Bandi, quoted in Denis Mack Smith, ed., *Garibaldi* (Englewood Cliffs: Prentice-Hall, 1969), pp. 134–35.

602 From *Documents of German History,* edited by Louis L. Snyder (New Brunswick, N.J.: Rutgers University Press, 1985), pp. 215–16. Copyright © 1985 by Rutgers, the State University. Reprinted by permission of Rutgers University Press.

611 Count Serge Witte, *Memoirs* (New York: Doubleday, 1920), pp. 250–53.

617 From *The Militant Suffragettes,* by Antonia Raeburn (London: Michael Joseph, 1973), p. 183. Reprinted by permission of A. D. Peters & Co. Ltd.

628 Bertrand Russell, "Introducing the Ideas and Beliefs of the Victorians," in *Ideas and Beliefs of the Victorians* (New York: E. P. Dutton, 1966), p. 22.

644 From *The Horizon History of the British Empire* (New York: The American Heritage Publishing Company, 1973), pp. 9, 11. Copyright © 1973 Time-Life Books Inc.

658 Rudyard Kipling, "The White Man's Burden," from *Rudyard Kipling's Verse: Definitive Edition,* by Rudyard Kipling (New York: Doubleday, Doran, 1940), pp. 321–22. Reprinted by permission of the National Trust and Doubleday & Company, Inc.

667 Cited in William Hohenzollern, by Emil Ludwig (London: Putnam, 1928) pp. 285–86.

683 Erich Maria Remarque, *All Quiet on the Western Front* (New York: Fawcett Crest, 1970), p. 70.

690 Ralph H. Lutz, *Fall of the German Empire, 1914–1918,* vol. 2 (Stanford: Stanford University Press, 1969) pp. 196–97.

694 Erich von Ludendorff, *Ludendorff's Own Story,* vol. 2 (New York: Harper and Brothers, 1920) pp. 334–35.

705 H. G. Wells, *The Outline of History* (New York: Garden City Publishing Co., 1920), pp. 1168–70.

719 Roland N. Stromberg, *After Everything: Western Intellectual History Since 1945* (New York: St. Martin's Press, 1975), pp. 119–20.

737 Benjamin de Casseres, in *Avant Garde Art,* T. B. Hess and J. Ashbery, eds. (New York: Collier Books, 1967), p. 132.

753 Benito Mussolini, *The Political and Social Doctrines of Fascism,* translated by Jane Soames (London: Hogarth Press, 1933), p. 9.

 (continued following index)

CONTENTS

LIST OF MAPS

PREFACE

We have designed this textbook to promote interest in and comprehension of western civilization among students attending two- and four-year colleges and universities. Most of these students are majors in other disciplines who are fulfilling distributional requirements for graduation and are unlikely to take additional courses in history.

Our textbook provides a unique combination of characteristics designed to work effectively in this situation. The overall format—moderate length, color, boxed inserts, maps, section time charts, and chapter-opening vignettes—will attract these students to the subject matter. The relative brevity of the text gives the instructor the opportunity to assign supplementary readings. An instructor's guide and a set of map transparencies provide additional aid for the instructor.

In creating this text, we have particularly concentrated on pedagogical elements that will enable average students to apprehend and retain the principal historical points in each chapter. These elements include short chapters that keep the amount of information under control, a clear expository style, an introductory transition from the opening vignette to the body of the chapter, short subtopics to facilitate notetaking, time bars to reinforce a sense of chronology, and a summary to fix the impression of salient points. A short list of sources at the end of each chapter includes well written monographs, as well as engaging novels and drama, and relevant television programs and films from which students might also profit. A student study guide is also available at the professor's discretion.

We have had four governing principles in presenting the subject matter. First, we wish to help American students from diverse backgrounds to appreciate more clearly their place in western civilization, including the role played by their ethnic forebears and the rising importance of their nation. Therefore, in addition to the traditional comprehensive survey of western civilization in the Mediterranean lands and west-central Europe, we have treated eastern Europe, the Muslim role in transmitting and influencing western culture, the Jewish experience, the impact of western societies on the nonwestern world, and especially the modifications of western civilization in the Americas.

Second, our presentation stresses the last two centuries, when most of the technology, institutions, and ideology that directly affect the modern student took shape. Such an approach is more apt to hold the student's interest.

Third, we have selected for emphasis those elements that best encapsulate the western experience in a text of moderate length. We have concentrated on economic, institutional, and political history, while also treating social, cultural, and intellectual developments.

Finally, we have stressed concepts and causal forces rather than a parade of details. Although average students initially find it more difficult to grasp ideas than to remember discrete facts, with help from their professors they can understand causation and accommodate competing ideological stances. They will, as a result, gain more insight into the subject and retain a more meaningful understanding of western civilization.

Acknowledgments

An enterprise of this magnitude and complexity depends on the dedication and perspiration of many people. We were fortunate that West Publishing Company secured the services of many reviewers, whose insights and information materially strengthened this book. They include

Frank Holt,
University of Houston

Richard Golden,
Clemson University

Jerry Brookshire,
Middle Tennessee State University

Nancy Rachels,
Hillsborough Community College

Donald Higgins,
Glendale Community College

Nelson Diebel,
Moraine Valley Community College

Patrick Foley,
Tarrant County Junior College

Manuel Gonzales,
Diablo Valley College

Charles Bussey,
Western Kentucky University

Jack Censer,
George Mason University

Rizalino Oades,
San Diego State University

Karl Roider,
Louisiana State University

Marshall True,
University of Vermont

Glenn Bugh,
Virginia Polytechnic Institute

Richard Huch,
University of Minnesota-Duluth

Janet Polasky,
University of New Hampshire

Orazio Ciccarelli,
University of Southern Mississippi

Gary Ferngren,
Oregon State University

Patricia Bradley,
Auburn University-Montgomery

Arthur Smith,
California State University-Los Angeles

Frederick Dumin,
Washington State University

Stuart Persell,
California State University-San Bernardino

Bullitt Lowry,
North Texas State University

Rev. Charles E. Ronan, S.J.,
Loyola University of Chicago

Merle Rife,
Indiana University of Pennsylvania

Marc Cooper,
Southwest Missouri State University

Andrew Mikus,
Glendale Community College

Alfred Cornebise,
University of Northern Colorado

Julius Ruff,
Marquette University

Sandra Dresbeck,
Western Washington University

Thomas Kennedy,
University of Arkansas

Paul Devendittis,
Nassau Community College

Robert Linder,
Kansas State University

Marcus Orr,
Memphis State University

Henry Steffens,
University of Vermont

Our colleagues at Eastern Michigan University, Della Flusche, Walter Moss, Ira Wheatley, and Reinhard Wittke were generous with information and advice. We are particularly indebted to Lester Scherer, who read and improved significant portions of the manuscript. Robert Ward and James Vaughn provided the initial cartographic sketches. Jo Ann Holoka materially assisted her husband on the myriad tasks he undertook during this project. We are also especially indebted to Nancy Snyder, who not only put the entire text on the computer and entered the masses of revisions and corrections, but took care of innumerable practical chores to bring our project to fruition.

Finally, we wish to gratefully acknowledge the wizardry of the West Publishing Company staff, who transformed a proposal by five professors into an attractive textbook. Clark Baxter, with the assistance of Nancy Crochiere and Maureen Rosener, was the guiding and sustaining spirit. With assistance by cartographer Patricia Isaacs, our production editor, Mark Jacobsen, with patience and resourcefulness pulled the whole project together.

A   S U R V E Y   O F

WESTERN CIVILIZATION VOLUME TWO

PART FOUR

FROM ABSOLUTISM TO REVOLUTION

The seventeenth and eighteenth centuries were an age of intellectual rationalism and revolutionary change in western civilization. Essential elements in these charges included royal absolutism, intellectual enlightenment, and violent revolution.

In the seventeenth century, monarchs such as France's Louis XIV claimed unprecedented powers over their subjects. Strong Habsburg and Hohenzollern rulers enhanced the positions of Austria and Prussia and Russia's Peter the Great made his country one of the great European powers.

By the eighteenth century, in Latin America and British North America, colonists were developing novel forms of western civilization. Under the influence of the cultural variety of Amerindians and African slaves, they adapted European customs and devised more helpful or appropriate ones.

The most significant intellectual current in the seventeenth and eighteenth centuries was the emphasis on human reason that activated the scientific revolution and the Enlightenment. Early modern science, which had its birth in the heliocentric theory of Copernicus, reached a climax in the work of Isaac Newton in the 1600s. Such scientific achievement prompted thinkers of the succeeding Enlightenment period—Voltaire, Rousseau, and others—to ground radical sociopolitical theories in human reason.

Enlightenment principles strengthened the political trends of constitutionalism and enlightened despotism. Governments in which the power of monarchs was limited by constitutional guarantees of subjects' rights emerged in Great Britain and the Netherlands. In Austria, Prussia, and Russia a number of celebrated enlightened despots claimed to use their powers to reform society for the benefit of the governed.

Great changes were also taking place outside Europe, as British, French, and Dutch imperialists joined the Spanish and Portuguese overseas. With the spread of western power across North America, Asia, and Australia, Great Britain attained mastery of the largest empire in the world. Between 1776 and 1830, however, successful rebellions against European overlords added most American colonies to the list of independent western nations.

The greatest revolution of the age occurred in France, Europe's most powerful nation. Between 1789 and 1799, the French shattered the traditional power structures. Domestic turmoil and foreign intervention, however, produced rampant radicalism, a reign of terror, and dictatorship.

Out of the chaos of the French Revolution came Napoleon Bonaparte. This successful revolutionary general not only became emperor of the French but again and again defeated great-power coalitions to impose his will on much of Europe.

Politics

1618–48
The Thirty
Years' War

1660–85
Stuart
Restoration

1682–1725
Peter
the Great
of Russia

1624–43
Cardinal
Richelieu

1643–1715
Louis XIV

1688
The
"Glorious
Revolution"

Economics & Society

Growth of
mercantilism

1670
Hudson's
Bay Company

Development
of a
global/colonial
economy

Colonization
of North
America
underway

1619–83
Jean Colbert

1679
Habeus
Corpus Act
(England)

Science & Technology

1564–1642
Galileo
Galilei

1683
Anton
von Leeuwenhoek
discovers
bacteria

1709
First
production
of industrial
coke

1561–1626
Francis
Bacon

1628
First
crude
steam
engine

1687
Isaac Newton's
*Mathematical
Principles of
Natural Philosophy*

1718
First
observation
of smallpox
inoculation

Religion & Thought

1651
Thomas
Hobbes'
Leviathan

1685
Edict of
Nantes

Growing
religious
toleration
in British
North America

1596–1650
René
Descartes

1646–1716
Gottfried
Wilhelm
von
Leibnitz

1690
John Locke's
*Two Treatises
of Civil
Government*

Arts & Literature

1577–1640
Peter Paul
Rubens

1622–73
Jean
Baptiste
Molière

1667–74
Milton's
*Paradise
Lost*

1719
Daniel
Defoe's
*Robinson
Crusoe*

Age of
Baroque
and
Classicism

1606–69
Rembrandt
van Rijn

1665
Bernini's
High Altar,
St. Peter's
Basilica, Rome

1685–1750
Johann
Sebastian
Bach

1725	1750	1775	1800	1825	1850

1739–63
Colonial struggles in Western Hemisphere and India

1775–83
American War for Independence

1799
Napoleon overthrows The Directory

1809–26
Independence movements in Latin America

1740–86
Frederick the Great

1756–63
Seven Years' War

1789
French Revolution begins

1815
Waterloo; Congress of Vienna

Industrial Revolution begins in Great Britain

1776
Adam Smith's *The Wealth of Nations*

1789
French Declaration of Rights of Man

Increased importation of black slaves to North America

1764
Cesare Beccaria's *Crimes and Punishments*

1787–91
U.S. Constitution and Bill of Rights

1740
Development of crucible steel-making process

1769
James Watt patents the steam engine

1803
John Dalton's table of atomic weights

1746–51
Benjamin Franklin's experiments with electricity

1770
James Hargreaves' spinning jenny

John Wilkinson improves iron production techniques

1739
David Hume's *Treatise on Human Nature*

1754
Voltaire's *Candide*

1743–94
Marquis de Condorcet

1793
Worship of God outlawed in France

1751–72
Diderot's *Encyclopedia*

1762
Rousseau's *The Social Contract*

1781
Kant's *Critique of Pure Reason*

1801
Concordat between Napoleon and the Pope

1726
Jonathon Swift's *Gulliver's Travels*

1742
George Handel's *Messiah*

1786
Mozart's *The Marriage of Figaro*

1770–1827
Ludwig von Beethoven

Age of Neoclassicism and Rococo

1749–1832
Johann Wolfgang von Goethe

THE RISE OF ROYAL ABSOLUTISM (1648–1725)

To assign the right of decision to subjects and the duty of deference to sovereigns is to pervert the order of things. The head [of the state] alone has the right to deliberate and decide, and the functions of all the other members consist only in carrying out . . . commands . . . [In a well-run state] all eyes are fixed upon [the monarch] alone, all respects are paid to him alone, everything is hoped for from him alone; nothing is undertaken, nothing is expected, nothing is done, except through him alone. His favor is regarded as the only source of all good things; men believe that they are rising in the world to the extent that they come near him or earn his esteem; all else is cringing, all else is powerless. . . .

In these words, begun for his son and heir around 1661, Louis XIV expressed the ideal of absolute monarchy. Louis himself was the most successful embodiment of royal absolutism in government and a model for the other kings of Europe.

Louis spoke for the dominant political theory of his age when he condemned a state in which "subjects" have a right to share in political decision making. Democracy was scarcely more than a glimmer in the eyes of a few radicals when Louis came to the throne of France in the middle of the seventeenth century. During his immensely long reign, monarchs who exercised "absolute sovereignty" over their peoples also came to power in Austria, Prussia, Russia, and elsewhere. The result was what has been described as Europe's "splendid century" of kings and queens. This period of royal magnificence produced some spectacular art; it also, however, saw some terrible wars and real suffering among the peoples of Europe.

The present chapter recounts the rise to power of these royal absolutists and outlines the consequences of their strong government for the evolution of the nation-state in Europe. It also describes the impact of absolutism on society, art, and international relations in the seventeenth and earlier eighteenth centuries.

CONTENTS

Louis XIV. This royal portrait by Hyacinthe Rigaud, 1701, shows the king as he looked in his later years. Pose, costume, and opulent setting all combine to project the splendid image of the Sun King to which all absolute monarchs aspired. Louvre Museum, Paris.

ABSOLUTIST THEORY

The emergence and widespread acceptance of belief in the absolute power of kings and queens was rooted in two conflicting circumstances. In the broadest perspective, absolute monarchy was part of a long-term trend toward more efficient central government in the nation-states of Europe. The strong kings of the medieval era and the new monarchies of the Renaissance represented earlier stages of this political evolution. The absolute monarchies that rose in the seventeenth century and became "enlightened" in the eighteenth were the next stage in the growth of governmental power. The powerfully centralized governments of the nineteenth and twentieth centuries would be the climax of this trend.

Origins of Absolutism

During the seventeenth century, however, Europeans embraced strong government as a reaction to the political breakdowns that had beset them during the last hundred years without thinking of themselves a part of a continuing long-term trend toward powerful rulers. The religious wars of the sixteenth century, particularly destructive between the 1560s and the 1590s, had also been civil wars in France and the Netherlands. The Holy Roman Empire had been torn by religious dissent in the mid-1500s and ravaged by the Thirty Years' War between 1618 and 1848. England had experienced decades of domestic strife between Parliament and king in the 1600s, climaxing in the temporary overthrow of the monarchy during the

"kingless decade" of the 1650s. Finally in mid-century, France had fallen once more into anarchy during the upheaval known as the Fronde.

These revolts actually strengthened the appeal of the emerging absolute monarchies of the later 1600s. The widespread bloodshed and destruction that resulted from these civil struggles led many propertied Europeans and long-suffering peasants to long for a return to peace and order. The best guarantee many could imagine for the restoration of order was a strong hand on the tiller—a powerful monarch at the head of state.

Absolute Sovereignty

Supporting this widely felt need for strong government were a number of theoretical arguments drawn from ancient, medieval, and modern political thought. Older arguments drew on scripture, which seemed to assert more than once that God sanctified the authority of secular rulers. Medieval kings had insisted on their "divine right" to rule, a view that absolute monarchs like Louis XIV accepted as gospel. Medieval and early modern lawyers and legal scholars had also drawn on the example of the Roman emperors. Like the Caesars of old, these experts asserted, modern kings had a right to demand loyal obedience from their people.

More recent defenders of royal power went still farther. Thus the sixteenth-century political theorist Jean Bodin rejected the medieval idea that each subdivision of society—church, state, classes, guilds, and other groups—had its own rights and obligations in a balanced society. Bodin urged that the state must have a single, absolute authority that could im-

pose order on all estates, classes, and conditions of men. The English philosopher Thomas Hobbes agreed. In his *Leviathan* (1651), Hobbes insisted that people were naturally selfish, ambitious, and aggressive. To avoid an anarchic "war of all against all," an all-powerful central government was therefore necessary. For Bodin, Hobbes, and other political thinkers of the age, the only available wielders of this absolute sovereignty were the monarchical governments of the great nations of Europe.

Mercantilism and Bullionism

The growing power of Europe's monarchies was especially enhanced by their ability to foster and control the economic development of the nations. The policy of government intervention in the economic affairs of their people was not new in the age of absolutism, but such intervention increased markedly during the seventeenth and eighteenth centuries. For the age of royal absolutism was also the great age of mercantilism in economic life and of the bullionist theory of the wealth of nations.

Mercantilism was a system of economic regulation by the royal government that emphasized commerce and the role of the merchant in society. The first goal of mercantilist policy was to expand production in every area—land and mineral wealth, old and new handicraft industries. The object was to achieve a surplus of production over consumption. This surplus could then be traded with foreign nations—again with the object of achieving a surplus, in this case a favorable balance of trade.

Such a favorable trade balance would mean that the nation exported

more than it imported. The surplus of exported goods would have to be paid for in gold and silver coins—that is, in bullion. Mercantilists were therefore also bullionists, supporters of the theory that the real wealth of any nation is measured in the amount of precious metals it accumulates. To keep this flow of gold coming into the country through expanded productivity and a favorable trade balance thus became the prime goal of European mercantilism.

To achieve these ends, mercantilistic royal governments regulated their economies in many ways. They pro-

vided subsidies and other supports for new industries. They regulated some industries to keep the quality of their products competitive in foreign markets. They granted monopolies to powerful merchant companies to trade in certain areas or in particular products. They established high tariffs to protect local producers from foreign competitors.

Mercantilist administrators also integrated overseas colonies into this system. Colonial producers in the Americas and elsewhere were expected to contribute raw materials and agricultural products otherwise un-

View of Versailles. This painting of 1668 shows Louis XIV's newly rebuilt palace, with the king himself arriving in pomp and circumstance at lower right. Note the geometrical layout of the palace and grounds, as well as the vast extent of both buildings and gardens.

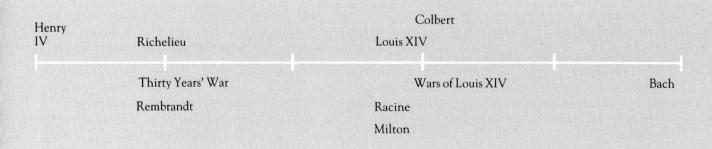

| 1600 | 1625 | 1650 | 1675 | 1700 | 1725 |

Henry
IV
       Richelieu

Colbert
Louis XIV

       Thirty Years' War   Wars of Louis XIV   Bach

       Rembrandt   Racine

Milton

available in Europe. They were to purchase surplus manufactured goods from the European "mother country." Colonials were forbidden to compete with producers at home, and were expected to trade only with the mother country, never with rival imperial powers. Producers in Europe were also, in some cases, prevented from growing agricultural products which were important to colonial economies. Each overseas empire was to be a closed system in economic competition with all others.

ABSOLUTISM IN FRANCE: THE AGE OF LOUIS XIV

Absolutism took different forms in different parts of Europe, but all of them were based in one way or another on that of France.

In the later 1500s, France was ravaged by a succession of wars of religion pitting Catholics against Protestants and rival factions of nobles against one another. The next century, saw two royal minorities: Louis XIII (1610–1643) inherited the throne at the age of nine, Louis XIV (1643–1715) at age five. With children on the throne, greedy or ambitious courtiers and nobles exploited

the country and feuded with one another. Wars took place between the crown on one side and both the rival armies of the nobles and the garrisoned strongholds of the Protestants on the other. At midcentury, finally, came the breakdown of order called the Fronde (1648–1652). This revolt, led by rebellious nobles, also involved peasants and urban poor, who were suffering from famine and the final agonies of the Thirty Years' War.

The Rise of French Absolutism: Richelieu

Through the first decades of the seventeenth century, a series of strong royal ministers labored to strengthen the French monarch to restore order to the nation. As early as the 1590s, Henry IV had ended the wars of religion and brought the house of Bourbon to the throne. He and his first minister, Sully, worked to strengthen the economy and to balance the budget. The breakdown of central authority during the early years of Louis XIII's reign was initially a serious setback. The appointment of the powerful Cardinal Richelieu as chief minister of state, however, gave France a strong political leader for the next two decades, from 1624 to 1643.

Richelieu advanced the cause of royal absolutism, both by weakening

the enemies of central power and by strengthening the royal administration. He fought a series of wars to deprive France's Protestants of the 100 fortified towns they had been granted by Henry IV. Richelieu also compelled the nobles to dismantle their fortified chateaus, another source of potential defiance of royal authority. To advance that authority into the provinces, finally, Cardinal Richelieu greatly expanded the duties of formerly minor officials called *intendants*—officials Louis would also find very useful.

Louis's minority accession in 1643, fortunately, also brought Richelieu's handpicked successor, Cardinal Mazarin, who was able to continue the process of building up the royal bureaucracy. The Sicilian Mazarin had a difficult time keeping ambitious aristocrats in line. Nevertheless, he did carry on the tradition of state building for another decade and a half.

Other motives were involved in these efforts to strengthen the central government. Richelieu and Mazarin were not selfless statesmen, but men as ambitious as those whose divisive ambitions they crushed. Richelieu built a palace in Paris so splendid that it was converted to a royal residence after his death, and Mazarin's greed was notorious. Nevertheless, while advancing their own interests, Ri-

THE RISE OF ROYAL ABSOLUTISM

chelieu and Mazarin were also constructing a centralized national government eminently suited to an absolute monarch.

Developed Absolutism: Louis XIV and Colbert

In the second half of the century, Louis's France found a king large enough to take charge of the absolute

monarchy Richelieu and Mazarin had forged. Louis, who began to rule independently in 1661, was a strong, handsome man, a good Catholic, and a profound believer in his own divine right to rule, He was a hardworking ruler and had considerable tolerance for the endless round of public ceremonies that were required of an absolute sovereign. For most of his reign of more than seventy years, he showed

both political shrewdness and an unswerving concern to increase the power of the French monarchy.

Louis, as had Richelieu, undermined rival sources of power and strengthened royal administration. To weaken his rivals, Louis lured the once rebellious aristocracy to his court at the magnificent new palace of Versailles outside Paris. There France's nobility gradually became dependent

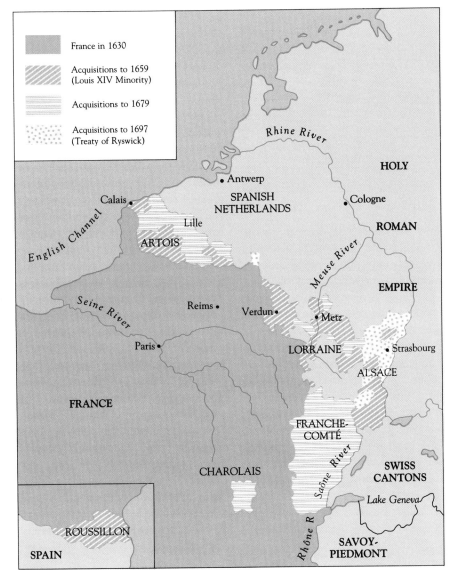

MAP 48
Expansion of France under Louis XIV. Like other absolute monarchs, Louis XIV expanded his domains through war. He focused most of his efforts on the Netherlands and the Rhine Valley. Opposed by strong coalitions, even the Sun King's powerful armies were unable to acquire much new territory. Nevertheless, he succeeded in advancing the French frontier to the southern Rhine.

LOUIS XIV STARTS THE DAY RIGHT

After he had risen, and had been helped into his dressing gown by the Great Chamberlain or the First Gentleman of the Chamber, the other courtiers who had the right to attend the *lever* were gradually admitted, in four successive "waves." Meanwhile, the great noblemen who held posts in the royal Household carried out their functions of aiding the King to dress. The Master of the wardrobe pulled off the King's nightshirt by the right sleeve, and the first Valet of the wardrobe pulled it by the left sleeve. The honor of presenting the King with his shirt belonged to Monsieur (Louis' oldest son), failing him to a *prince du sang*, and failing him to the Great Chamberlain; the first *Valet de chambre* held out the right sleeve, the First Valet of the Wardrobe the left. To the Master of the Wardrobe fell the honor of helping His Majesty to pull on his breeches. And so the ceremony went on. *

This description of a small part of the daily round of ceremony and ritual that attended the life of the Sun King tells us much about life at Versailles and about the central role of the absolute monarch. Every detail of Louis XIV's day was filled with ritual of this sort, performed with a reverence usually reserved for religious ceremonies. The people who performed such menial chores, furthermore, were great noblemen and princes of royal blood (princes du sang). Such idolatry of the royal person further strengthened the godlike royal image of an absolute monarch.

*John Lough, *An Introduction to Seventeenth Century France* (New York: David McKay, 1969), p. 163.

on the king for honors, promotions, and revenues. Louis also bought and sold offices in the formerly independent chartered towns. He compelled the French law courts, called *parlements*, to rubber-stamp all royal decrees; their occasional resistance in earlier centuries was no longer tolerated. Louis also followed the policy of Richelieu and Mazarin in dealing with the Estates General, France's closest approximation of the English Parliament, never convening this body during his three-quarters of a century on the throne.

To impose his own will on the nation, Louis used the *intendants* as his chief agents in the provinces. These bureaucrats, middle-class appointees entirely dependent on the king, had many functions. They kept an eye on the nobles and the provincial cities, provided some police protection for the countryside, and supervised markets. They also collected taxes and recruited soldiers, two crucial functions of the absolutist state.

At the top of this administrative system was a structure of royal councils and powerful royal ministers of state. The two most important ministers were the war minister, the marquis de Louvois, and the minister of finances, Jean Colbert. Louis himself met regularly with his ministers, actively governing Europe's most powerful state.

Colbert was the chief architect of France's elaborate mercantile system. Under his discretion, Louis's government built roads and canals and regulated wages, prices, and the quality of goods. The government protected local industry with high tariffs and granted monopoly rights to powerful combines likely to advance French trade abroad. France's expanding overseas empire was also incorporated into the mercantile system. The government furnished military protection and subsidies for the colonies, but required them to trade exclusively with France and to transport goods only in French ships. Colbert thus became the most persistent and successful practitioner of paternalistic mercantilism.

Louvois, by contrast, encouraged Louis to advance French interests by force of arms. In so doing, he contributed to the four long and costly wars, four massive conflicts fought between 1667 and 1713, that were the reign's least successful ventures. Louis fought the Dutch to punish France's greatest trade rivals and made war on the Holy Roman Empire over territory which both claimed. His most costly military involvements, however, were his struggles to put a Bourbon on the throne of neighboring Spain. Much of the rest of Europe, led by the Dutch and the English, resisted this ploy, which could have made the Bourbon dynasty masters of the continent. After many years of fighting, a Bourbon did gain the Spanish throne, but only by agreeing that the French and Spanish dynasties should remain separate. France, meanwhile, paid dearly in blood and treasure for the king's ambition.

Louis XIV called himself the "Sun King," the center of the political universe, supposedly describing his position as France's absolute sovereign with the famous phrase: *l'état, c'est*

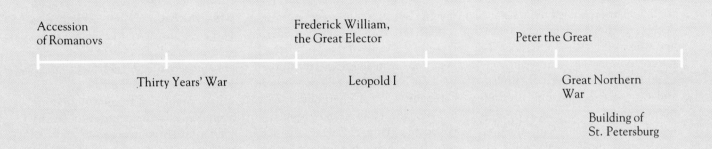

| 1600 | 1625 | 1650 | 1675 | 1700 | 1725 |

Accession of Romanovs

Frederick William, the Great Elector

Peter the Great

Thirty Years' War

Leopold I

Great Northern War

Building of St. Petersburg

moi—"I am the state." His palace at Versailles was a magnificent symbol of this immense power. A third of a mile long, surrounded by vast gardens and housing 10,000 people, Versailles was the embodiment of the grandeur of Europe's most admired ruler.

ABSOLUTISM IN GERMANY

Among the German states of central Europe, two monarchies would dominate the region from the seventeenth through the nineteenth centuries. They would also feud with each other over much of that time. One was the ancient Habsburg Austrian line that ruled the Holy Roman Empire, the other the rapidly rising Hohenzollern dynasty of Prussia.

Both these central European powers moved toward royal absolutism in the seventeenth and early eighteenth centuries. Both sought to follow Louis XIV in strengthening their administrative and military machinery and in building impressive royal courts. Both depended rather more on a powerful and relatively independent aristocracy than Louis did. But the absolutist Habsburg and Hohenzollern

dynasties differed strikingly from each other in the degree of success they achieved.

Austrian Absolutism and Habsburg Revival

The Thirty Years' War left the power of the Habsburg dynasty in German-speaking central Europe shattered. The electors of the Holy Roman Empire, now eight, still elected Austrian Habsburgs emperor, but the emperor's actual authority over the separate German states, never great, had been all but destroyed by the war. In the later seventeenth century, however, Habsburg power revived surprisingly, forging a new multinational empire that stretched along the Danube River into the Balkans.

The Habsburg emperor who built this new empire was Leopold I (1658–1705). A contemporary of Louis XIV, Leopold was an unaggressive, extremely religious prince who had none of the Sun King's self-confidence or skill at public relations. Nevertheless, with the help of some of the greatest generals of the age, Leopold built up the Austrian army, with which he was able to turn back the last great Ottoman Turkish invasion of central Europe and to drive the Turks out of Hungary in the 1680s. With these

extensive lands to the east and with its older holdings in Bohemia (modern Czechoslovakia) to the north, Austria had a new empire to rule. Further, this resurgence of Austrian fortunes enabled the Habsburgs to renew their claims to authority in the German States and to great-power status in Europe as a whole.

Under Leopold also, the Habsburg monarchy attempted to strengthen its hold on these non-German speaking lands through centralized absolutist institutions. Leopold and his heir, Charles VI (1705–1740), prepared official documents declaring the unity of all the Austrian Habsburg lands. These included not only Austria, Bohemia, and Hungary but also other territories acquired over centuries, including parts of the Netherlands and Italy.

The Austrian attempt at absolutist centralization, however, was undermined by the fact that Leopold and his successors depended, not so much on the bourgeoisie, as Louis XIV had done, but on the aristocracy, including the non-German nobility of Hungary and Bohemia. To win their support, the Habsburgs allowed these aristocrats to increase their traditional control over their own peasant populations, thus reinforcing their independent power base.

389

Other divisive forces in the Austrian domains included the resistance of the provincial assemblies, or *diets*, and the deep ethnic divisions between the Germans and their Slav, Czech, Magyar, Hungarian, Italian, and other subject peoples. In addition, Charles in his later years allowed the bureaucracy and the army to decline, further weakening the Habsburg monarchy.

Prussian Absolutism and Hohenzollern Power

Royal absolutism in Prussia got off to a stronger start than it did in Austria in the seventeenth century. The architect of early Prussian absolutism was one of the most famous members of the ruling Hohenzollern dynasty, Frederick William (1640–1688), known as the "Great Elector." Frederick William and his successors built an impressive north German power center on an alliance with the Prussian Junker aristocracy and on such basic absolutist institutions as an efficient civil service and a strong army.

The problems the Hohenzollerns faced in the wake of the Thirty Years' War were as great as those confronted by their Habsburg rivals in southern Germany. The Hohenzollern electors—of the Holy Roman Empire—governed a string of territorially scattered lands stretching across northern Germany. These included Prussia, on the Polish frontier in the east, the central territory of Brandenburg, and Cleves in the Rhineland, in western Germany. The dynasty had first to connect these regions by adding new territories between them. At the same time, they had to impose centralized absolutist rule on all these fiercely independent lands. Finally, they had to build an effective army to protect Prussia, which was located on a plain lacking natural frontiers.

Frederick William took great strides toward these goals. He began to build a small but powerful army. This not only enabled him to acquire new territories, but also gave him a weapon with which to suppress resistance to Hohenzollern absolutism in the states thus captured. The Great Elector also encouraged the development of an extremely efficient bureaucracy, another potent tool to use in imposing a single, centralized authority on the Hohenzollern domains.

To run both his army and his administration, Frederick William and his successors depended on the businesslike Prussian aristocracy known as Junkers. In return for increased authority over the peasant population, the Prussian nobility were willing to support the monarchy. Far from resisting royal power, the Junkers thus established a tradition of state service. They would be the backbone of Hohenzollern power from the Great Elector's day to World War I.

Frederick William had established the fact of Prussian power in north Germany. He remained only an elector, however, not a king; and Brandenburg-Prussia, as it was then known,

MAP 49
Expansion of Prussia to 1740. With their original center of power in Brandenburg, the Hohenzollern monarchs expanded their realm across north Germany. By 1740 they had reached the Baltic to the north and east and had aquired possessions in the Rhine valley to the west. They were now in a position to challenge the Austrian Hapsburgs for domination of the German states.

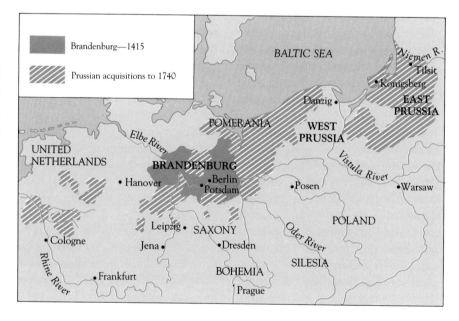

was only a second-class European power. Both these handicaps were overcome by the Hohenzollern rulers who came after him.

Elector Frederick III (1688–1713) earned the title of King Frederick I in 1701 by shrewdly timed military support for the Habsburg emperor. Frederick also began the transformation of Berlin from a provincial city into a great German capital.

King Frederick William I (1713–1740), finally, used the strength of the Prussian army to achieve recognition of Prussia as one of Europe's great powers. As militaristic as Frederick I had been cultured, Frederick William identified wholly with his army. It was easy to laugh at him for his "barracks mentality" and his pleasure in drilling his troops. Nevertheless, Frederick William did cut court expenses drastically and discipline his bureaucrats as he did his soldiers. Perhaps most important, he more than doubled the size of his army, making it the fourth largest and one of the most efficient in Europe.

The disciplined, growing kingdom of Prussia would find brilliant new leadership in the second half of the eighteenth century under Frederick the Great. But the absolutism of the earlier Hohenzollerns, had already transformed a scattering of German principalities into a new European power.

ABSOLUTISM IN RUSSIA: PETER THE GREAT

Strong government was not new to Russia when Peter the Great came to the throne in 1689. Moscovy, as the nation was earlier known, had an autocratic tradition that reached back hundreds of years.

The Romanovs and Russian Autocracy

This autocratic heritage, coupled with a widely felt need for order after a period of anarchy, led to the election of a new royal house early in the seventeenth century. Pretenders to the throne, popular revolts, and foreign invasions by the neighboring states of Poland and Sweden had produced fifteen years of chaos known in Russian history as the "Time of Troubles" (1598–1613). An unstable alliance of aristocrats, townsmen, and cossacks eventually defeated both domestic rebels and foreign invaders. Thereafter, a meeting of the Zemsky Sobor representing all major elements in the population except the serfs selected a new tsar to govern the nation. Their choice, Michael Romanov, was a sickly, pliable young man who was not expected to be a strong ruler. The Romanov dynasty would, however, rule Russia from 1613 down to the revolution of 1917.

The first three Romanov tsars were not strong rulers, but even so they claimed to wield the "full autocracy" of their fifteenth- and sixteenth-century predecessors. They also presided over some expansion of a bureaucracy that was to be a hallmark of Russian government. This period of revival also saw foreign trade grow once more and witnessed the culmination of Russia's great eastward expansion across Siberia to the Pacific.

But the early Romanovs were unable to solve the nation's economic problems, including a decrease in both agricultural production and government revenues. Domestic disorders also continued through the first three-quarters of the seventeenth century, including endless peasant and cossack rebellions and a great schism or split in the Russian Orthodox church.

At the beginning of the 1680s, then, Russia remained a growing but ramshackle autocracy on the eastern edge of Europe. The potential power inherent in its vast size and in autocratic tradition could best be realized by transforming Russian along the political and economic lines already laid down in western Europe. This transformation was finally undertaken by the most famous and controversial of Russian monarchs, Peter the Great.

Peter the Great and the Transformation of Russia

Peter I (1682–1725) came to the Russian throne at the age of ten in 1682 and took control of the country (from an older sister, who had ruled as regent) in 1689. For the next thirty-five years, he was a human whirlwind, shaking up backward, traditional Russia as it had never been shaken up before and would not be again until the twentieth century.

Peter was huge, nearly seven feet tall, ill educated, uncouth, and often brutal. At the same time, he was open to new ideas, practical, and immensely hardworking and energetic. What education he had he gained from Moscow's foreign colony of artisans and advisers who had come to work in backward Russia where their skills were much needed. Peter's orientation toward westerners and western Europe was to be crucial to the direction Russia would take in coming decades.

Like many absolute monarchs, Pe-

Peter the Great. The most powerful of Russian czars, and the first to use the title of emperor, Peter looks every inch a king in this contemporary likeness. Contrast the relative simplicity of Peter's costume with the sumptuous clothing and setting with which Louis XIV surrounded himself. While the Sun King's France was already the arbiter of European fashion, Russia was still a relatively rude and uncultivated place by contemporary standards in Peter's day.

ter was deeply concerned with foreign policy and military matters. Many of his reforms were intended to strengthen his army or improve his international position. He tried to secure the latter by war as well, defeating two powerful rivals, Sweden and Poland. In the long and bloody Great Northern War (1700–1721) with Sweden's dashing King Charles XII, Peter seized territory on the Baltic Sea on which he proceeded to build a new capital for Russia—St. Petersburg. Peter built this "window on the west" on a swamp at a cost of many thousands of lives; but by moving the capital away from isolated Moscow, he opened Russia further to western European trade and cultural influences.

Peter plunged into his domestic reforms with the same drive and determination that he brought to the Great Northern War or to expanding Russian territory. These efforts to transform Russian society are perhaps Peter's main claim to a central place in Russian history. As a dedicated autocrat working within an established Muscovite autocratic tradition, Peter attempted to strengthen his hold on key elements of the population. Russia's ancient hereditary aristocracy thus lost their position to an expanding "service nobility," who earned their ranks by service in the army or the state bureaucracy. The Russian Orthodox church, historically subservient to the tsars, became almost a branch of the government when its traditional head, the patriarch, was replaced by the procurator, a civil servant appointed by the tsar. The peasant masses, including many serfs, were made even more subordinate to the landowning nobility. In addition, peasants were made liable for high taxes and for forced labor on Peter's major building projects.

Voted emperor for his victory in the Great Northern War, Peter also strengthened his authority in other ways. He created an elaborate system of central bureaus and imposed a structure of provincial and district administration on Russia. To import western European skills and efficiency, he hired more foreign experts and encouraged the new service nobility to study abroad.

In typical absolutist style, Peter's government did its best to foster economic growth. Government initiatives led to increased agricultural and mineral production, encouraged new industries, and improved the status of Russia's small middle class. Peter was particularly eager to improve Russia's primitive transportation network, building many roads, bridges, and major canals.

Some of Peter's reforms—like his insistence on western clothing and shaven faces instead of long robes and beards—outraged traditional Russian mores. Russia's peasantry certainly suffered under his relentless demands. Many of his changes, including much of the new governmental structure, did not long outlive him. Nevertheless, Peter did set his country on a new path. From his time, Russia was recognized as one of Europe's great powers. Equally important, his efforts to transform old Muscovy into a modern state began Russia's long push toward modernization. This drive for modernization and world power would reach its climax only in the present century.

SOCIETY AND STRUGGLE IN THE AGE OF ABSOLUTISM

The society over which Europe's absolute monarchs presided was as undemocratic and hierarchic as any in western history. Society under the absolutists was organized according to a system of estates or social classes based more on social prestige and noble titles than on mere wealth. Each class, institution, and even family or household, furthermore, had its own traditional hierarchy. Hereditary aristocrats and high churchmen usually stood at the top of this structure, though royal officials, successful businessmen, and professional people also enjoyed high status.

Aristocrats sneered at the very idea of a middle-class gentleman as a contradiction in terms. Yet it was possible in some places to work one's way up the social ladder, either through business or the royal administration. In western Europe, the commercial middle classes often grew richer under the mercantilist economic policies of royal absolutists; and even in Peter's Russia, merchants sometimes benefited from his reforms. An efficient royal administrator could sometimes rise to the top, particularly if he could point to even a recently-acquired noble title or coat of arms.

MAP 50

Expansion of Russia to 1796. Beginning in Muscovy in the northern part of Russia's European heartland, the Tsars extended their authority across Eurasia to the Pacific. In the eighteenth century Peter the Great and Catherine the Great pressed south to the Black Sea and west towards the European heartland. Russia had now emerged as one of the great powers of Europe.

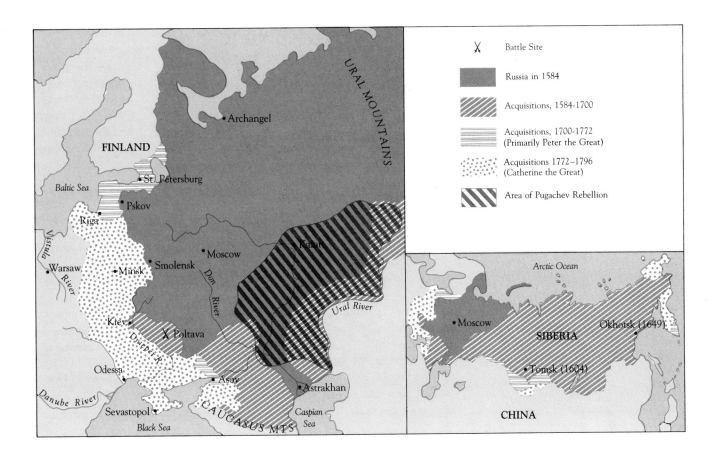

PETER THE GREAT, NATION-BUILDER OR ANTICHRIST?

(1)

This monarch had brought our country to a level with others: he taught us to recognize that we are a people. In brief, everything that we look upon in Russia has its origin in him, and everything which is done in the future will be derived from this source. *

(2)

Ah, this is why he hobnobs with Germans, this is why he . . . robbed Jesus Christ of his primacy and took the title of patriarch. This is why he shaves his beard, why he has donned a short coat . . . this is why he has levied new taxes and assessments upon the Christian world. . . . There have been seven Antichrists. According to the Holy Writ, an eight is to be born. And now he has come in the person of Peter. *

These drastically conflicting evaluations of Peter the Great's place in Russian history reflect two contemporary points of view. For those like Ivan Nepleuv, who shared Peter's vision of a modernized and westernized Russia, the emperor's reign was a great step forward. To those who valued old Russian traditions, particularly Russia's ancient Orthodox Church, the iron-fisted reformer could look like the Antichrist himself.

Whether he was the founder of modern Russia or the destroyer of Russia's soul, Peter's central place in this great debate shows once more how great the impact of an absolute monarch could be.

*Ivan Nepleuv, *Memoirs*, in Vasili Klyuchevsky, Peter the Great "The Opposition of the Traditionalists," in Marc Raeff, ed. *Peter the Great Changes Russia* (Lexington, Mass.: D.C. Heath, 1972), pp. 175–176.

The preeminence of the aristocracy, however, remained generally recognized. The nobility failed in efforts to reassert their medieval independence in revolts like the Fronde in France. Nevertheless, hardworking Prussian Junkers, Russian service nobility who served Peter well, and even the courtier nobility of France were rewarded with the highest positions and the greatest social prestige.

The Splendid Century

Life at the top of this society has earned for the seventeenth century its designation as "the splendid century." Court life at Versailles or at the Schonbrunn palace in Vienna or Peter the Great's new capital of St. Petersburg was enormously expensive and often not particularly comfortable, but it was undeniably magnificent. Absolute monarchs moved in splendor, surrounded by extravagant ceremonials and elaborate rules of precedence. Consultations with their ministers of state might be the core of a monarch's day, but there was plenty of time for banquets, balls, hunting, cards, conversation, opera, theatre, and other entertainments. The palaces were the largest and most ornate, the costumes the most expensive, that Europe had ever seen.

There was vanity and self-indulgence in all this, but there was political realism as well. Absolutism required stately magnificence to maintain its public image of glory and splendor, its political claim to supremacy.

The Lower Orders

The lower orders or classes of society lived under much less enviable conditions. The urban poor and the masses of rural peasantry were the ones who benefited least from the royal absolutism.

Most Europeans were peasants, and they suffered from many misfortunes in the seventeenth century. Some of these were natural calamities, including famines, a return of the plague, and the so-called little ice age, a half-century of cold winters and short growing seasons. But other peasant problems were caused by the policies of their absolutist rulers. Rising taxes to pay for royal grandeur, long and bloody wars to advance royal ambitions, and even a resurgence of serfdom in eastern Europe all hurt Europe's country population.

The urban poor, often migrants from the countryside, had their share of miseries. These included the difficulty of finding work in cities still dominated by the guilds, repeated economic depressions, and particular helplessness in the face of famine and plague.

Under such pressures, Europe's lower orders reacted with sometimes irrational violence. Peasant rebellions, in nations as different as Louis XIV's France and Peter the Great's Russia, were one form of social protest. Waves of witch hunting, sweeping from the German states to Britain's New England colonies, were probably in part expressions of social frustration. In the seventeenth century, gin and rum also began to provide a very unhealthy escape from urban wretchedness in particular.

Popular festivals and social organizations still existed for the masses. Western European peasants tended to be better off than eastern Europeans, and free peasants than serfs. Altogether, however, it is hard to see that the masses of Europeans had much reason to be grateful for the age of absolutism.

War in the Age of Absolutism

The tendency of absolute monarchs to advance their interests by force of arms made warfare a common feature of European life under the absolutists. The wealth and power these monarchs brought to military affairs in fact led to the creation of larger and more powerful armies than Europe had ever seen before.

This royal militarism took some odd forms. Prussia's King Frederick William I prided himself particularly on his "giants," a regiment composed entirely of strapping soldiers more than six feet tall, whom the king much enjoyed drilling. As a child, Russia's Peter the Great organized his aristocratic playmates into military units, trained with real weapons—and worked his own way up from the ranks, beginning as a humble private.

The Great Elector Mounts a Siege. This seventeenth-century engraving depicts Prussian artillery in action against the besieged city of Stettin in 1678. Note the elaborate design of the artillery emplacements, the troops marching into position, and Frederick William himself issuing orders at lower right.

But war was a serious business for wielders of absolute sovereignty. Indeed, much of the effort they put into expanding government, revenues, and national wealth seems to have been ultimately intended to strengthen the armies with which monarchs could try to dominate the international stage. Certainly, large portions of the money collected in taxes went to pay for royal armies and royal wars.

Seventeenth-century armies put new emphasis on discipline and training. Supplies, uniforms, and superior artillery were more readily available than ever before. The arts of military fortification and siegecraft were brought to a high level: It was said of Louis XIV's military engineer, Vauban, that no city he defended could ever be taken, no city he attacked would ever stand. Military commanders planned sweeping campaigns across the map of Europe, and

Bernini's Baldachino in St. Peter's. This huge bronze and gilt canopy over the tomb of St. Peter in St. Peter's Cathedral, Rome, well illustrates the splendor at which baroque art aimed. Standing more than ninety feet high, the baldachino features twisted columns and curving shapes, color, and movement, all typical of baroque.

soldiers marched in step from camp to battlefield.

Many of these troops were dragooned into the king's service, and many of their officers were young noblemen who had purchased commissions rather than earning them through military skill. But some were crack troops, like many in the Prussian army, and some ranks in the French army were promoted on a merit basis. In size, the military machines of the absolute monarchs were awesome. Louis XIV had 400,000 men in his later years, far more troops than the Roman Empire had at its height. Emphasis on military engineering, a relatively efficient supply system, and such innovations as the bayonet all contributed to the power of Louis's military machine.

From one point of view, these militaristic policies served Europe's crowned heads well. With his huge armies, Louis XIV rounded out France's frontiers and put a Bourbon on the throne of Spain, even if not on Louis's terms. Leopold of Austria used military force to create a new Habsburg empire on the Danube. The Hohenzollerns manipulated their powerful army to win a place among the great powers for Prussia, and Peter the Great's hard-won victories in the Great Northern War made Russia a major power.

These wars, however, brought immense suffering to the peoples of Europe. Crushing taxes, military conscription, marauding armies, and heavy casualties were all part of their cost. Even the greatest victories of Peter the Great or Louis XIV cost many lives and drained their nations economically.

MAXIMS

(1)

Self-esteem is the greatest of flatterers.

We are never so well off or so badly off as we imagine.

We are all strong enough to bear the misfortunes of others.

In the distress of our best friends we always find something that does not displease us.

Absence destroys small passions, and increases great ones; the wind extinguishes tapers, but kindles fires. *

(2)

Women run to extremes; they are either better or worse than men.

Children are overbearing, supercilious, passionate, envious, inquisitive, egotistical, idle, fickle, timid, intemperate, liars, and dissemblers; they laugh and weep easily . . . they bear no pain but like to inflict it on others; already they are men. *

These brief maxims and pithy sayings reflect the wit of two shrewd literary observers of the seventeenth-century scene: the Duc de la Rochefoucauld and Jean de la Bruyère. Some of them, at least, seem to have that feel of eternal truth at which classicism aimed. Such satirical sayings and cynical worldliness also lent an air of sophistication much admired in some court circles.

*La Rochefoucauld, *Maximes*, ed. Roger Charbonnel (Paris: Larousse, n.d.), pp. 17, 26, 36; Crane Brinton, ed., *The Portable Age of Reason Reader* (New York: Viking, 1956), pp. 537–540.

The Arts: Baroque and Classicism

Europe's artists, often found Europe's absolute rulers generous patrons, and the arts flourished at their courts. Architects, sculptors, painters, composers, poets, and playwrights were in fact essential to absolute monarchy, for artists provided the lavish life style and the magnificent public image that distinguished the splendid century.

Two styles in particular dominated the arts in the seventeenth century: baroque and classicism. Both reflected the larger political, social, and cultural currents of the age.

The baroque style dominated such arts as architecture, painting, sculpture, and music for much of the seventeenth century. *Baroque* derived from the Portuguese *barroco*, meaning a misshapen or deformed pearl, and some critics saw baroque art as a warping of the Renaissance art from which it grew.

Baroque artists did in fact emphasize or exaggerate certain features of Renaissance art. These included size and magnificence in building, color and movement in painting, and the mixing of various forms, as in the mixture of music and drama in the first operas. The huge, colorful, crowded pictures of the Flemish painter Peter Paul Rubens and the melodies of Claudio Monteverdi, the inventor of opera, were masterpieces of baroque art.

This new style in the arts exactly

The Building of St. Petersburg. Seventeenth-century absolutists demonstrated—and further enhanced—their power by building or refurbishing palaces and even capital cities. Here, Peter the Great supervises the construction of his new capital city of St. Petersburg (Leningrad today). Peter, who had worked with his hands in his own youth, was a hard taskmaster, but the city he built is considered by many to be the most beautiful in Russia today.

suited the new era. Counter-Reformation popes seized on the new style for churches in the later sixteenth century. The result was the emotionally moving, even awe-inspiring, grandeur of churches like St. Peter's in Rome. Absolute monarchs, who wanted to impress their subjects with their own grandeur, began to build baroque palaces in the seventeenth century. Louis XIV's palace at Versailles, with its huge gardens, many fountains, great hall of mirrors, and other splendors, used the baroque style very effectively to glorify the Sun King.

Classicism, important in architecture, painting, and literature, was another widely admired style. It was perhaps especially important as an influence on writing in the seventeenth century. Classicism in general stressed classical Greek and Roman models and rules for the arts, especially regularity, balance, and order. An outstanding example was the French classical tragedy that was so popular at the court of Louis XIV. The plays of Jean Racine, for instance, had plots derived from classical mythology and were written in regular, rhythmic verse. Their themes, heroes, and heroines also had a classic nobility: powerful characters torn between such exalted emotions as duty, honor, and love. The aristocrats of that age of courtly magnificence liked to see themselves as just such noble characters.

These styles served some of the greatest writers and artists of the age. The Dutch painter Rembrandt van Rijn used light and sometimes color with baroque effectiveness in emotionally moving canvasses. The English poet John Milton wrote great religious poems like *Paradise Lost* in classically regular verse, but with language filled with baroque color and grandeur. The French comic playwright Jean Moliere used classical dramatic forms to satirize all classes of French society. The baroque grandeur of Versailles and the stately classicism of Racine's noble tragedies had a special appeal to the kings and aristocrats of the age of absolutism.

SUMMARY

The age of royal absolutism in Europe was an important stage in the growth of powerful governments in the western nations. Reacting against a period of civil wars and social upheaval, Europeans accepted autocratic rulers who could bring domestic order in the seventeenth and early eighteenth centuries.

These new state builders claimed absolute sovereignty over their subjects. To carry out their will, they developed larger and sometimes more efficient administrative systems than their predecessors. These bureaucracies particularly imposed the mercantile system of government regulation on production, trade, and other aspects of the economy.

Absolutism reached its height in the France of Louis XIV, the Sun King. Louis's lavish court, administrative system of *intendants*, huge armies, and impressive power were the envy of his royal rivals. In central Europe, the ancient Austrian Habsburg dynasty used absolutist methods to recover from their loss of power in the Thirty Years' War. At the same time, the Prussian Hohenzollerns thrust their way into the front rank of the nations with the help of absolutist techniques and an impressive bureaucracy and army. In east Europe, the heavy-fisted autocrat Peter the Great won great-power status for Russia by a violent exercise of royal will.

The society over which the absolutist monarchs presided was splendid at its top level, among the aristocracy. The middle-class merchant community, though socially excluded from the elite, often benefited economically from mercantilist policies. Much misery existed among peasants and the urban poor, however, and the wars of the absolute rulers were costly in lives and human suffering. Nevertheless, the artists who built the palaces and entertained the upper classes produced baroque and classical masterpieces of great power. The next chapter will look at the spread of modified forms of this highly developed western society to the European colonies beyond the seas.

SELECTED SOURCES

Adam, Antoine. *Grandeur and Illusion: French Literature and Society, 1600–1715.* Translated by Herbert Tint. 1972. Good survey of the intellectual history of the age, particularly useful on classicism.

Carsten, F. L. *The Origins of Prussia.* 1954. Older but still recommended history of the period through the reign of the Great Elector.

*Dumas, Alexandre. *The Three Musketeers.* 1982. Famous novel of swashbuckling seventeenth-century soldiers. There are also film versions.

Goubert, Pierre. *Louis XIV and Twenty Million Frenchmen.* Translated by Ann Carter. 1970. An analysis of French society under the Grand Monarch.

Kitson, Michael. *The Age of Baroque.* 1966. Beautifully illustrated history of art in Europe in the seventeenth and eighteenth centuries.

Lougee, Carolyn C. *Le Paradis des Femmes: Women, Salons, and Social Stratification in Seventeenth Century France.* 1976. Women in the intellectual and social elite.

Massie, Robert. *Peter the Great.* 1980. Highly readable, Pulitzer prize-winning account.

*Rabb, Theodore K. *The Struggle for Stability in Early Modern Europe.* 1975. Brief but sweeping survey of the "crisis of the seventeenth century," to which absolutism provided a partial solution.

*Wolf, John B. *Louis XIV.* 1968. Monumental biography of the Sun King.

Wolf, John B. *Emergence of the Great Powers 1685–1715.* 1951. Older standard history of Europe and European international relations in the age of Louis XIV and Peter the Great.

*Available in paperback.

WESTERN SOCIETY IN THE NEW WORLD IN THE EARLY EIGHTEENTH CENTURY

*[British] America is formed for happiness, but not for empire: in a course of
1200 miles I did not see a single object that solicited charity; but I saw
insuperable causes of weakness, which will necessarily prevent its being a potent
state; . . . it appears to me very doubtful . . . whether it would be possible to
keep in due order and government so wide and extended an empire; . . . fire and
water are not more heterogeneous than the different colonies in North-America.
. . . nothing can exceed the jealousy . . . they possess in regard to each other.
. . . In short, such is the difference of character, of manners, of religion, of
interest of the different colonies, that . . . were they left to themselves, there
would be a civil war, from one end of the continent to the other; while the
Indians and Negroes would, with better reason, impatiently watch the opportunity
of exterminating them all together. . . . [there] will never take place a permanent
union or alliance of all the colonies, . . .*

The good Reverend Andrew Burnaby, traveling in British North America
in the middle of the eighteenth century, was not the only European who
had difficulty reading the future of an area so different from Europe. To a
person coming from a more unified culture, the multitudinous diversity of
British North American society must have appeared to be a prescription for
perpetual disorder. Burnaby would undoubtedly have made the same
comments if he had been traveling in Latin America, which had its own
diversities and its own divergences from Europe. By the early eighteenth
century, western civilization was no longer confined to the continent of
Europe and to its immediate environs. Three million inhabitants of
European descent and millions of mixed ancestry now lived in Latin
America and British North America. Far from Europe and living in the
presence of Amerindian cultures and African slaves, they were developing
forms of western civilization that departed more and more from those of
Europe.

Western Civilization in the New World. The Chiesa de la Merced in Cuzco, Peru represents
the establishment of the Catholic church in the Americas by the Spanish and the Portuguese.
The Catholic Church was the most monumental European institution transferred to the Western
Hemisphere, eventually encompassing millions of people in a huge area. Whether great urban
cathedrals, city churches such as this one, or rural mission stations, the Spanish and the
Portuguese built thousands of edifaces to express their faith.

401

European settlers arriving in the western hemisphere naturally expected to live in much the same way as they did in their homelands. However, faced first with fighting for survival in the new environment and later finding unique opportunities for prosperity, they rapidly dropped or modified those European customs that turned out to be inappropriate or obstructive, and evolved more suitable practices. This chapter begins with Latin America, the first western culture to markedly differ from the standards of Europe. It then takes up the more radical version of western culture that evolved later in British North America.

LATIN AMERICA

By 1700, Europeans from the Iberian Peninsula had been living in the western hemisphere for more than two centuries. Coming into control of three quarters of the hemisphere, an area some forty times larger than Iberia, European settlers found extremes of climate from steaming jungles to icy wastes. Isolated in small groups by great distances and often by impassable terrain, they found themselves surrounded and outnumbered by Amerindians and African slaves, whose grudging labor was the foundation of their economy.

The Land of Three Races

The unique multiracial situation that developed in Latin America marked the greatest difference between western civilization in Latin America and

in Europe. As a result of economic conditions and religious policies, whites in Latin America were always a distinct minority. Through the years, only a small number of settlers crossed the Atlantic. Ordinary Iberians had little incentive to immigrate, because only a few privileged aristocrats could own land, and the Amerindians and black slaves provided all the labor. In addition, Spain's policy dictated that only "reliable" Catholic Spaniards would go to America. This excluded foreigners, Jews, Jewish converts to Catholicism, and those with some Moorish ancestry. Despite these regulations, other Europeans, including some Protestants and Jews, made their way there. By downplaying their religion and their origin, they sometimes became important landholders, merchants, and officials.

Gender also played a key role. Most of the white immigrants were men; owing to custom and circumstance, few white women migrated to Latin America. The white men, especially those living among the numerous highland Amerindians, took concubines and wives from the subject races. Amerindians remained in the majority in some areas of the former Aztec, Maya, and Inca empires and were the largest single racial group in Latin America as a whole throughout the colonial period. By the eighteenth century, however, mestizo descendants from white-Amerindian unions were the largest racial group in some areas. White males living among the black slaves had also produced an extensive mulatto population throughout the Caribbean and Brazil. Black-Amerindian unions were less common.

The realities of multiracial living brought about a more relaxed attitude

about race in Latin America than in Europe or British North America. The status of the large and increasing mestizo population had to be worked out, much of it by a rough color code. A few individuals with some Amerindian ancestry, if they were from wealthy and accomplished families, became accepted members of the white ruling class; others became a part of the small middle class. The great majority, particularly those who were predominantly Amerindian, were part of the laboring masses.

Although American practice to some degree worked in favor of those of mixed ancestry, it worked against the pure Amerindian. After a short period during which some Amerindians were enslaved, the Spanish crown and the Catholic church consistently held that the Amerindians were free subjects of the crown, to be treated as dependent minors. They could be parceled out to work for the benefit of whites, but only on a limited basis, and were to receive religious and vocational instruction. In actuality, white masters, often working through the Amerindian village chiefs, generally neglected their obligations. They forced the Amerindians under their control to work in mines and factories, on ranches and farms, and as porters and construction laborers. Often separated from their families, Amerindians frequently labored under brutal conditions that brought premature death. They sometimes rose in revolt, but the uprisings were always crushed. Some individuals such as Bartolomé de las Casas campaigned for the welfare of the Amerindian, but neither good intentions nor royal decrees from afar made much headway. By the eighteenth century, some of the more brutal systems of forced labor were on the decline, except in the Andes. Instead, the mass of Amerindians and mestizos had become peons. Bound to the land by debts for shelter, food, and clothing that they could never pay off, they and their descendants were forced to work for their masters in perpetuity.

Blacks as a group fared even worse than the Amerindians. Most Amerindians at least lived a family life in their villages, practicing many aspects of their traditional culture. Blacks were shipped to America as individuals, torn away from their native culture, and put to grueling labor in a strange new land. Most of them were males and thus even denied the comfort of family life. Under the law, they held a dual status. They were human beings, and therefore entitled to humane treatment. However, they were also chattel, like livestock. They could own no property, had no right to keep their families together, and had to obey all commands of their master. In practice, most masters treated their slaves as chattel rather than as human beings. Many slaves were simply worked to death or to incapacity and then replaced by new slaves supplied by the efficient slave-trading companies.

There were a few ways out of slavery. Portugal in particular had provided relatively liberal laws for Brazilian slaves to buy their freedom, and masters found few legal obstacles to freeing a slave if they chose to do so. However, few slaves could accumulate the price of freedom, and few masters chose to free them. Those blacks and mulattoes who did gain their freedom legally found that, unlike the situation in British North America, their race was not an ab-

solute barrier to rising in society. In areas where few lower-class Iberians were present, many blacks possessed valuable skills as artisans and mechanics that whites needed. Particularly in Brazil, where in some areas slaves and free blacks overwhelmingly outnumbered whites, even a small amount of white ancestry gave some mulattoes the social status of whites.

Slaves in the Caribbean sporadically rose in revolt, but always unsuccessfully. Running away into unsettled areas was often more effective. Sometimes, such as with the Maroons in the interior of Jamaica, runaways banded together to successfully hold out against whites. Brazilian slaves often fled into the vast interior; there, during the seventeenth century, blacks set up the state of Palmares, which lasted thirty years before it was destroyed.

European Economic Theory and American Reality

In the early eighteenth century, when mercantilism was still the reigning economic theory, the Spanish government continued to closely regulate the Spanish American economy. As earlier, the crown permitted a group of companies, first in Seville and later in Cadiz, to monopolize the commerce with Spanish America. The companies acted under the regulations of the *Casa de Contratación*, the government bureau that managed the details of the economic life of the colonies and collected the crown's share of taxes and monopolies. The *Casa* still sent out two annual convoys under the protection of the royal navy to the colonies. The convoys called only at three Caribbean ports, through

which all trade with Spain had to pass. A single convoy returned to Spain carrying the exports of Spanish America. The Portuguese were not as rigid, allowing merchants from ports other than Lisbon to trade with Brazil and to send their ships directly there instead of joining the convoys passing in and out of Lisbon.

The convoy arrangement, practical when cargoes from Spanish American production were predominantly gold and silver in need of careful protection, was strangling Spanish American commerce by the eighteenth century. In the first place the fleets often did not have the cargo space to carry away all the products awaiting export. Second, continuing to have the convoy ports only in the Caribbean made it extremely difficult for South American producers to get their goods to Spain. To cite an extreme problem, except for a period in the seventeenth century, ranchers in Argentina could not import or export through their Atlantic port of Buenos Aires. Instead, porters and mules had to haul, say, hides, hundreds of miles across the plains and up into the high country of Bolivia, then down through the passes of the Andes to the Pacific coast. Here the hides were loaded into ships and carried to the Isthmus of Panama, then overland by pack train to Portobello on the Caribbean, one of the three convoy ports. Finally, if cargo space was available, they were placed on a ship to Spain.

The problem of imports was perhaps worse. Following mercantilist doctrine, colonists were not supposed to produce items, such as metalware, textiles, and wine, that competed with the products of the mother country. By the eighteenth century production in Spain was in such decline that most of the products destined for America came from elsewhere in Europe, at high prices and in inadequate amounts. From early times, the desperate colonists had welcomed British, Dutch, and French smugglers; in addition, they ignored the prohibitions on competing with Spanish goods. They began to produce their own textiles, metalware, and wine, combining such production with Amerindian skills in weaving, pottery, and basketry. These colonial products were mostly of the cruder make, however, and the upper classes, though small in number, continuously demanded a supply of products that could not be satisfied by the convoy or even by Spain itself.

Spreading the Catholic Faith

The Roman Catholic church, responsible for meeting the spiritual needs of the millions living in the huge area across the ocean, of necessity created a widespread colonial organization. The Spanish monarchy had secured from the papacy the right to nominate all clerical officials in America as high as the rank of archbishop, giving the crown another large arena for patronage. Since the church, like the state, reflected the class structure of the time, nearly all the top ecclesiastical appointments, numbering eventually ten archbishops and thirty-eight bishops, went to Spanish aristocrats. Most of the clergy that served in America were also Spaniards.

The church had many responsibilities in America but its main charge was, as it saw it, to save the souls of multitudes of heathens doomed to hell. The religious orders (the regular clergy) of Franciscans and Dominicans ac-

companied the early conquistadores and converted millions of Amerindians, by persuasion and sometimes with the aid of force. Later, in the more remote areas, the regular clergy, now joined by the Jesuits, replaced the conquistadores as the frontiersmen, setting up missions in previously unconquered territories. With the help of army detachments, they rounded up the nearby Amerindians and brought them in to live around the mission, to work to maintain themselves and the clergy, and to receive Christian instruction and baptism. Once the area had been secured, the orders set up new missions farther in the interior and repeated the process.

Behind the regular clergy came the secular or diocesan clergy and the religious orders of nuns, whose responsibility was to sustain and consolidate the faith in the settled areas. They organized local parishes, built up a system of education from the primary grades through universities, and founded hospitals, orphanages, and poor houses. Bishops, rich laity, and the government erected cathedrals and other religious edifices, many outstanding for their architectural and artistic beauty.

Spain was perhaps the nation in Europe most devoutly loyal to the Catholic church, and religious practice in its American colonies reflected this zeal. As in Spain, Roman Catholicism was the only faith tolerated; under the watchful eye of the Holy Office (the Inquisition), blasphemy was subject to fines and corporal punishment. Unrepentant Protestant, Jewish, and atheist heretics faced exile or burning at the stake, although executions were infrequent compared with Europe, and the Amerindians

were not subject to its jurisdiction. Spanish America became a bastion of Catholicism, in the jungles of the Amazon and the extreme south, where the Amerindians were unconquered.

Despite an impressive record of accomplishment in transplanting a major aspect of western culture to the New World, many abuses and problems bedeviled the Catholic church in America. The church had accumulated enormous wealth by the eighteenth century, and the huge size of the church organization made corruption inevitable. As a result of these and other factors, the American Catholic church was burdened with idle clerics who congregated for luxurious and sometimes debauched living in the cities. Up to one-half of city property was owned by the church, much of it by the religious orders. The orders often used their money to compete with the laity in banking and commerce, taking advantage of their special exemptions from taxation and economic regulation.

Perhaps the greatest problem for the church was in the countryside. Many dedicated clerics served their mestizo and Amerindian parishioners faithfully, devoting themselves to teaching, vocational instruction, and spiritual guidance. On the other hand, rural parishes were often left impoverished by the church hierarchy, so that many had no priests or were staffed by incompetent, uneducated, or avaricious individuals. Many Amerindians and blacks learned only the external, ceremonial aspects of their new faith, which they combined with their traditional religion. Some parish priests exacted high fees for administering the sacraments and saying mass. The clergy at the missions sometimes exploited Amerindian labor as brutally as the secular land-lords. Ironically, some orders attempted to protect the Amerindians from enslavement and other forms of mistreatment by exploiting black slaves instead and bidding others to do the same.

Ruling America

The class structure and government of eighteenth century Latin America were as intertwined in the colonies as they were in Iberia and the rest of continental Europe. Like Europe, Latin America was governed by a small class of aristocrats and gentry, separated from the rest of society by hereditary privileges and certain immunities from the operations of the law. Through the years the crown had granted control over property in the New World to adventuresome conquistadores and to certain favored aristocrats. By the eighteenth century Peninsulars (aristocrats from Spain who returned there) and Creoles (aristocrats of Spanish descent born and residing in America), who comprised approximately 2 percent of the population, owned virtually all the property of value—mines, ranches, plantations, and manufacturing establishments. Below the aristocracy, mestizos and lower-class Iberian immigrants filled some of the need for merchants and artisans, occupations largely ignored or scorned by the upper class. More than 90 percent of the population—the blacks, mulattoes, Amerindians, and most of the mestizos—toiled for the few.

The administration of Spanish America, until the Bourbon reforms of the mid-eighteenth century, reflected in general the traditional process of royal government in Spain. In

---

THE WEALTH OF MEXICO CITY

The streets of Christendom must not compare with . . . the richness of the shops which do adorn them. . . . where a man's eyes may behold in less than an hour many millions' worth of gold, silver, pearls and jewels. . . .

[The] churches . . . are the fairest that ever my eyes beheld, the roofs and beams being . . . all daubed in gold, and many altars with sundry marble pillars, and others brazil-wood stays standing above one another with tabernacles for several saints richly wrought with golden colors. . . .

. . . the inward riches belonging to the altars are infinite, . . . such as copes, canopies, hanging altar cloths, candlesticks, jewels belonging to the saints, and crowns of gold and silver, and tabernacles of gold and crystal.

. . .

Both men and women are excessive in their appearance, using more silks than stuffs and cloth. Precious stones and pearls further much their vain os-tentation; a hat-band and rose made of diamonds in a gentleman's hat is common, and a hat-band of pearls is common in a tradesman; [even] a black or a tawny young maid and slave . . . will be in fashion with her neck-chain and bracelets of pearls, and her ear-bobs of some considerable jewels.*

This seventeenth century account of Mexico City, as seen by an English priest, portrays the world of the elite classes in urban Latin America. In an era where life was short even for the rich, ostentatious display of their wealth for themselves and for their church is understandable. Sudden abundance also caused families to use their wealth to compete for social standing and political power. The slaves referred to are undoubtedly domestic servants, adorned by their masters as another sign of family wealth.

*Thomas Gage, The English-American: A New Survey of the West Indies, (London: R. Coates, 1648), pp. 89–92 passim.

Spain the monarchy was limited to a degree by the traditional privileges of the nobility and churchmen. The core of royal power lay in its control over, and support from, the cabildos, the councils of the municipal city-states into which Spain was divided. Historical circumstances, however, gave the monarchs even greater power in America. The popes had awarded the New World to the Spanish monarchs as their personal possession. Here there would be little competition from aristocrats and clerics. The Spanish crown quickly set up cabildos in Spanish America to underpin royal authority.

The monarchs soon realized that the Spanish settlements were swallowed up in the huge American landscape and too distant from Spain for regular, effective control. The American cabildos there soon came under the control of the local elites and often ignored royal wishes. The monarchs therefore added a complex system of controls centered in Spain and fanning out over the islands, jungles, plains, and highlands of the sprawling region. Power passed by appointment from the crown to the Council of the Indies, which had the authority to act in the name of the king on matters dealing with broad economic policy, justice, military affairs, and supervi-

Mexico City, 1673. Like Tenochtitlán, conquered 150 years earlier, the city is built in the middle of Lake Texcoco on an artificial earthen base interwoven with canals. The new Mexico City is clearly a Mediterranean city architecturally. The approaches to the causeways are protected by turreted fortifications. Historical Pictures Service.

sion of the Church. Next came the viceroys, who represented the king in New Spain (Mexico and Central America) and Peru (South America). The viceroys, paid well by the crown, had great power over local appointments, administration, finance, and the military forces. Their authority was subject to review, however, by the audiencias, ongoing judicial-consultative bodies in their area of jurisdiction, and by inspectors sent out from Spain.

Below the viceroy were the regional presidents and captains-general, the provincial governors, and finally a network of local officials operating in the rural areas. These local officials supervised the Indian villages, and it was here that extreme abuses often occurred. The local officials were usually either the local landlords or worked with the landlords. They frequently violated Amerindian legal rights, impinged on water rights, seized Amerindian land, exploited labor, and exacted fraudulent taxes.

Whereas the government of Latin America, as in Europe, reflected the class structure, it also divided the white minority in America into factions. The Council of the Indies, immersed in court politics, gave many government positions in America to Peninsulars, thus rebuffing the resident Creoles. Of the 170 viceroys who governed Spanish America during the colonial period, only four were Creoles. Creoles did have some seats in the audiencias and throughout the sixteenth century considered themselves Spanish. By the early eighteenth century, however, some Creoles were beginning to think of themselves as Spanish Americans and resented the political dominance of the Peninsulars. As a group the Creoles had become an idle class without the responsibility or the power that traditionally accompanies an aristocracy.

Class feelings in Latin America were strong: The Creoles were jealous and contemptuous of the lower-class persons arriving from Iberia. They also looked down on the mestizos who were working their way up into the middle class and into some of the lesser offices, especially in the towns.

An Amalgamation of Cultures

Iberian education and culture dominated Latin America in general and was, of course, the exclusive milieu of the ruling elite. The church controlled the classroom from the primary grades through the university curriculum. Education was reserved for the upper and middle classes, who considered it unnecessary and even dangerous for the masses below to be educated. As a result, Latin America, like most of Europe, was 90 percent illiterate. Few women were taught to read and write; most were trained in domestic and social skills.

Advanced study was a strong feature of Spanish American education. By the beginning of the eighteenth century ten major universities of uneven quality were functioning in Spanish America, although the Portuguese colony of Brazil had none. As was traditional, the overwhelming majority of university students studied theology and law, although at the University of Mexico, a person could also study medicine, rhetoric, and certain Amerindian languages.

Intellectual and artistic developments in Latin America closely followed the pattern in Iberia. Latin American scholars worked primarily within the frame of reference of Aquinas and the scholastics. Innovative thought was discouraged by the Inquisition and its index of banned writings. Meanwhile, most Spanish American writers simply added to the stream of standard Spanish chivalric romances, poetry, and devotional literature demanded by the small reading public.

A few writers made unique contributions to the body of western literature. Some writers in Spanish America filled old bottles with new wine, employing traditional epic and romance formats to portray the struggles between the Spaniards and the Amerindians. The most notable was the sixteenth century epic *La Araucana* by Alonso de Ercilla y Zúñiga, which celebrated the heroic resistance of the Araucanian Amerindians of Chile. The greatest poet of Latin America may well have been Sor Juana Inés de la Cruz, a beautiful and highly intelligent young woman with an interest in science, mathematics, and writing. Refused admission to the University of Mexico because she was a woman (although she offered to wear men's clothes) she went into a convent at sixteen and there wrote exquisite drama and love poetry while continuing her studies in other subjects. Her superiors later put a stop to her writing; she sold her enormous library and devoted herself to charity until she died at forty-four.

A great demand both in Europe and America also existed for histories of the conquest, such as that written by one of Cortes's soldiers, Bernal Díaz del Castillo. Perhaps the most intriguing book on the conquest was the *Royal Commentaries of the Incas*, written by the mestizo Garcilaso de la Vega, son of a Spanish father and a princess of the royal line of the Incas. Garcilaso shows the mind of the mestizo caught between two cultures, as he idealizes both the conquering Spanish and the conquered Incas. The European and Latin American publics were also interested in books describing the hemisphere's strange new flora and fauna, such as the *General and Natural History of the Indies*, by Gonzalo Fernández de Oviedo.

The enormous impact of European culture on Latin America by no means meant the elimination of Amerindian and African influence in Latin America. Amerindian culture remained the heart of daily life in many of the rural villages, whereas Amerindian foods, textiles, basketry, metalworking, building materials and techniques, and artistic motifs were integrated into the daily lives of the European immigrants. Black slaves, although cut off from their home culture, nevertheless permanently implanted African foods, music, art forms, and religious practices in the Caribbean and Brazil.

Antonio de Mendoza, Viceroy of New Spain, 1535–1551. The embodiment of the authority of the Spanish crown, the viceroys exercised great power in the New World. Their ability to act, however, was to some degree circumscribed by competing colonial institutions and by inspectors sent out by the crown itself.

BRITISH NORTH AMERICA

Settlers on the Atlantic seaboard of British North America, operating in a different geographical and historical

Slavery in British North America. This 1700 woodcut for a tobacco label depicts the results of the 1619 decision at Jamestown. In Virginia, white planters take their ease in the shade, while black slaves toil in the tobacco fields under a hot sun.

context, departed further from European culture than did Latin Americans. British North America east of the Appalachians was more than a century younger than Latin America. It was one-tenth the size, with a temperate climate and relatively fertile soil, and in the early eighteenth century mustered one million compared to ten million Latin Americans.

Races and Racism

As in Latin America, European arrivals in British North America had to come to terms with the presence of the Amerindians, with fundamentally different results. Unlike some sections of Latin America, the Amerindians were too few in numbers in the Atlantic seaboard of North

America to provide an instant work force. By the eighteenth century, the Europeans had liquidated them or driven them west, seizing the seaboard for whites. The small number of Amerindians and, until the eighteenth century, of many imported Africans, meant that British North America, unlike Latin America, would be a white offspring of Europe, without a large class of mestizos and mulattoes.

The status of blacks in British North America was both better and worse than in Latin America. Despite the regimentation and brutality inevitable in slave labor, particularly on the rice plantations of South Carolina, slaves in British North America enjoyed a higher standard of living and lived longer than in much of Latin America. Slaves also enjoyed more chance for a family life as the percentage of women rose through generations of natural increase.

As a minority race, however, blacks were in a more difficult position than in Latin America. Northern Europeans who settled in British North America manifested strong attitudes of racism toward the nonwhite minorities under their control. Those few Amerindians who lived among whites were treated contemptuously, facing segregation and other forms of oppression. European settlers did not

want to share their opportunities for property and power with the growing number and percentage of blacks. Whites accordingly made it difficult for slaves to gain their freedom and for free blacks to acquire property, especially land. British America had many white artisans and mechanics, and such avenues to prosperity and status were unavailable to blacks. Most free blacks therefore found themselves faced with a precarious existence, carrying out the most menial tasks. In contrast to Brazil, racial bias was so strong in British North America that a small percentage of black ancestry made an individual legally black.

The Genesis of a New Society

Although British North America more closely resembled Europe racially than did Latin America, the virtual ab-

sence of commodities of great value in British North America led to a more radical departure from the European economic social order than had occurred in Latin America. British North America did not produce the spices and silks of Asia, the precious metals of Spanish America, or the sugar of the Caribbean and Brazil. Trapping fur-bearing animals was a lucrative enterprise in the north, but on the whole British North America produced only food and a few staples of secondary value.

The absence of valuable products soon upset traditional patterns of landholding. As in Iberia, the English monarchs during the seventeenth century had given extensive land grants to their political favorites, as individuals or as incorporated companies. However, those grantees who created companies and sent workers over to produce profitable commodities soon found the ventures unremunerative.

New York Harbor, 1717. This view from Brooklyn across the East River to Manhattan is predominantly rural, with little foretaste of the megalopolis to come. Still, the scene gives an impression of modest prosperity. Shipping was a major component of the versatile economy of the northern colonies of British North America.

Frustrated by the virtual absence of traditional products of great wealth, the English government and the aristocratic grantees rapidly abandoned the company/worker format. In its stead they began to encourage a flow of settlers to make a profit from rents and passage rights. Unlike Spain, the English government, presiding over a religiously fragmented nation, did not restrict settlement to nationals of the state church. The British government, grantees, and colonial officials encouraged continental Protestants to settle, and some colonies even tolerated Catholics and Jews. As this became known in Europe, hundreds of thousands of settlers—individuals, families, and religious groups—migrated to British North America beginning in the eighteenth century, quadrupling the population between 1700 and 1740.

Landholding patterns in British North America quickly developed differently from those of Europe and Latin America. The government and the grantees, and many of the settlers had presumed that European society would be replicated; the aristocrats would own the land, the settlers would rent and work it. Conditions in British America soon changed from this outlook. Absentee landlords found it difficult to collect rent, and there was competition to attract settlers among the grantees and between the grantees and the crown. In many instances, settlers simply seized crown and grantee lands and claimed "squatter's rights"—ownership on the basis that they had not been challenged for years and had improved the property by erecting buildings and tilling the soil. As a result, the crown and the grantees found it easier and more profitable to simply sell the land at prices that most settlers could afford. By the

early eighteenth century, most colonists in British North America owned property or paid a nominal rent, and thus for the most part were financially independent. This was a new form of western civilization, for in Europe and Latin America the land was held by a few families and worked by masses of laborers.

British North America also differed sharply from Europe in suffering from a chronic labor shortage, which in turn both raised and depressed the status of labor. Employers on farms and in shops found that neither standard wages nor indentures were sufficient to hold white workers, who could easily obtain their own property. In most of British North America, where production was based on small farms, the labor shortage continued and laborers commanded high wages. Along the coast of the southern colonies, however, the rice, indigo, and tobacco planters solved their shortage of white field hands by importing more and more black slaves.

Although there were many more European women present in British North America than in Latin America, they were still in short supply. This circumstance marginally improved their condition compared with Europe. In the colonies, as in Great Britain, the common law defined a married woman as the subject of her husband, and the property she owned before marriage as his. However, the general scarcity of women in the colonies enabled some of them to insist on prenuptial agreements that gave them some control over their property while married. Because male assistants were scarce, wives often helped their husbands to run small businesses of all kinds and sometimes inherited and operated the businesses when their husbands died.

Compared with the situation in Latin America and Europe, classes were more fluid in British North America. The colonists still retained the strong sense of class that they brought from Europe, with the "middling sort" and "lower sort" deferring to those seen as the "better sort." This attitude, however, was by no means translated into the servility found in Europe, and even the habit of deference was increasingly diluted over time by a sense of individual worth stemming from economic independence. In a land without aristocrats, wealth and merit rather than inherited title rapidly became the chief index of social status.

Unlike both Latin America and Europe, it was possible for large numbers of whites in British North America to move up in social class. No aristocratic class monopolized property and opportunity, so it was relatively easy to obtain property, especially land. Laborers who later acquired their own farms or shops moved into the middle class. Those of the middle class who accumulated extensive land or commercial property—or who rose to distinction as professionals, particularly some lawyers and clergy—became the gentry. This gentry dominated society and politics in British North America, although they were looked on as country bumpkins by European aristocrats.

The Colonial Economy and British Mercantilism

By the eighteenth century, British North America had progressed far beyond a subsistence economy and had developed an extensive international trade shaped by the commandments of mercantilism. The colonists were required to send products on the

"Enumerated Articles" list—furs, lumber, molasses, naval stores (turpentine, pitch, tar, masts, spars), tobacco, rice, and indigo—to Great Britain, or through Great Britain before transshipment to other destinations. The northern colonies had built an extensive merchant marine to carry their grains, meat, and fish to the West Indies and the Mediterranean. New Englanders also engaged in the "carrying trade," hauling cargoes from port to port all over the world. Colonists north and south had begun to produce iron and iron products, but since they competed with British iron, the British government soon regulated their production. Like Latin American colonials, the colonists in British North America often were forced to sell too low and buy too high and as a result turned to smuggling.

Although operating under the principles of mercantilism, the English government placed fewer controls on its colonies than did Spain. It restricted trade with the colonies to English and colonial (after 1707 also Scottish) ships, but it did not limit the trade to a few companies. Fearing no attacks on the colonies' relatively cheap exports, it allowed individual ships to sail in and out of any port in the colonies and in England. The government allowed products not on the Enumerated Articles list to be sold anywhere in the world in peacetime without regulation.

A New Religious Configuration

Religious and ethnic diversity was another characteristic that increasingly distinguished British North America from the states of continental Europe and from Latin America. Not only did the groups from the British Isles

---

A CHEERLEADER FOR BRITISH NORTH AMERICA

He is an American who leaving all behind him all his ancient prejudices and manners, receives new ones from the new mode of life he has embraced, the new government he obeys, and the new rank he holds . . . Here individuals of all nations are melted into a new race of men, whose labors and posterity will one day cause great changes in the world. Americans are the western pilgrims, who are carrying along with them that great mass of arts, sciences, vigor, industry which began long since in the east; they will finish the great circle . . . Here the rewards of his industry follow with equal steps the progress of his labor; his labor is founded on the basis of nature, self-interest . . . without any part being claimed, either by a despotic prince, a rich abbot, or a mighty lord. Here religion demands but little of him; a small voluntary salary to the minister, and gratitude to God; . . . From involuntary idleness, servile dependence, penury, and useless labor, he has passed to toils of a very different nature, rewarded by ample subsistence. [*]

This enthusiastic comment by Hector St. John de Crevecoeur was typical of the messages he addressed to eighteenth century Europeans concerning the characteristics of the new culture in British North America. Although written later in the century, his remarks quite clearly pertain to a society that had already formed earlier. From an old Norman family, Crevecoeur immigrated to Canada and then settled on a farm in New York in 1765. Although imprisoned and exiled by the rebels during the War for Independence, he remained loyal to his adopted land. Only briefly returning to the United States, he worked throughout the rest of his life, in retirement in France, to explain the North American world to the people of Europe.

[*]Hector S. John de Crevecoeur, *Letters from an American Farmer* (New York: Fox, Duffield, and Company, 1904), pp. 90–91.

---

populate the colonies, but settlers from the Continent too: Germans, French, Dutch, and Swedes. Before 1750 there were English-speaking Anglicans, Congregationalists, Presbyterians, Catholics, Baptists, and Quakers. From continental Europe came Dutch, German, and French Reformed; German, Dutch and Swedish Lutherans; German Moravians, Mennonites, Dunkers and Schwenkfelders; and Portuguese-speaking Jews.

This religious diversity had not been anticipated in the seventeenth century when most of the British colonies were originally established and initially settled. The traditional idea that a political unit should have a common religion to bind the inhabitants together led the large Congregationalist majorities in New Hampshire, Massachusetts, and Connecticut to set up state churches. The Congregationalists drove out other religionists, in 1656 even hanging four Quakers who dared to return after being banished. The Anglican church was established in some colonies; there the Anglicans had enough supporters to harass dissenters, but not enough to suppress them.

Despite the fact that established churches were in place in most colonies by the eighteenth century, ef-

A New Farm in British North America. This archetypal scene depicts a clearing being hacked out of the forest. Already, there is a comfortable house, an outbuilding, a fence, a well, cattle, and oxen. Despite the rude conditions and the backbreaking labor, farm families like these were often better off than they would have been in Europe.

forts to enforce religious uniformity failed in British North America. The English Act of Toleration in 1689 acknowledged England's religious divisions by giving some religious rights to Congregationalists, Presbyterians, and Baptists. This new law helped these three dissenting groups in the Anglican colonies. About the same time, the English government forced the Congregationalist colonies to allow Anglicans to worship without penalty.

Conditions in the New World did more than English laws to encourage diversity. Most colonies needed settlers and unofficially tolerated thousands of new arrivals fleeing religious persecution, unemployment, and war who were adherents of other religions. Often the new dissenters settled in such numbers that it was impractical for the established churches to control them or drive them away. In the southern backwoods, where the non-Anglicans were in the great majority, colonial officials were often forced to ignore the requirements of

the state church simply to survive. Even in New England, minorities were becoming too large to control: In the 1750s, dissenting Baptists were permitted to contribute to their own churches the money they had been forced to pay to the Congregationalist church.

Some colonies were founded to protect dissenters, further encouraging religious diversity. Catholics, banned in England and most colonies, were tolerated in Maryland through part of its history. Catholics and all Protestant groups had full rights in Pennsylvania. Rhode Island went farther, granting full religious freedom to Christians, Jews, and Muslims. Thus, although complete religious freedom was advocated only by a few reformers in Europe in the early eighteenth century, British North America moved steadily in that direction in practice.

Missionary activity was feeble compared with Latin America. Because Protestants, unlike Catholics, were cool to missionary work in that

era, churches in British North America made only sporadic efforts to convert the Amerindian and African populations. Protestants, unlike Catholics, had no religious orders dedicated to the mission field, so evangelistic work depended at first on the enthusiasm of individuals. Later in the eighteenth century the Anglican missionary organization, The Society for the Propagation of the Gospel, and members of the Moravian Brethren worked among the Amerindians. Still, few Amerindians and only about 1 percent of the Africans would have called themselves Christians in 1750.

Limited Government and a New Political Process

As the Iberian monarchies had imposed their tradition of expensive, centralized government on Latin America, the English government set up its particular brand of frugal, partially decentralized government in their colonies. In England, the lesser gentry had long represented the royal government in local affairs, sparing the crown the expense of a large set of appointed officials. The English government applied this principle to most of its colonies, simply sending over a governor to work with an assembly representing the gentry that controlled local government. The governor of a colony had the power to appoint from the ranks of the colony's gentry a few executive officials and a council, which also served as the upper house of the colonial legislature and performed certain judicial functions. The governor could control the procedures of the assembly and veto its acts. His position was severely weakened, however, because the British government—to save expense—had given the assembly the power to pay his salary from taxes laid by the assembly on the colonists. Unlike Latin America, the colonists paid no tax money or royal "fifths" to the crown. Nevertheless, many colonial gentry, like many Creoles, chafed at what they saw as excessive power wielded by outsiders.

Underneath the traditional governmental apparatus, a new political process, quite unlike anything in Europe, was evolving. Because of the widespread incidence of property holding in British North America, many white males had access not only to social standing but to political power as well. In Great Britain, one of the few nations having some semblance of government by consent, only adult males who owned property that brought in forty shillings annual rent and who belonged to the state church could vote. This requirement restricted political participation to about 5 percent of the adult males. When these requirements were brought over to British North America from England, however, they produced radically different effects in a population where landholding was increasingly widespread. The colonial assemblies frequently translated the "forty shilling freehold" into 50 to 100 acres of unimproved land or half that amount improved, or land valued at forty to fifty pounds. This practice allowed an estimated one-half of the adult white male colonists to vote in the early eighteenth century, and the proportion continued to rise. Many colonists also met the much higher requirements for holding office. However, despite such widespread enfranchisement, only about 10 percent of the eligible voters took advantage of the opportunity. Most of the potential voters had little appreciation for voting practice or its potential. The New England tradition of the local town meeting was a major exception. By and large, however, colonial voters served as no more than a check, occasionally turning out an incompetent gentleman officeholder.

A Young, Raw Culture

By the lights of most of the European elite, British North America was as much of a wasteland in intellectual and cultural matters as it was in geography. The French scientist the Comte de Buffon and his followers at one time claimed that all species, including humans, degenerated in the New World environment. Certainly, it was true that all class levels gave their attention to exploiting the land's resources and correspondingly little time or interest to financing the development of scholarship, arts, or letters.

In fact, however, a significant start toward a popular rather than an elite culture had been made. Impelled by the Protestant belief that it was important to read the Bible, and that education might help a person to advance, many men and women in British North America were interested in learning to read and write. The resources and density of population of the New England towns and the Atlantic seaports facilitated establishing schools. In these locales perhaps two-thirds of the males and one third of the females were literate by early in the eighteenth century, a far higher percentage than anywhere else in the western world. In the rural areas, private academies were beginning to spread literacy. Higher education lagged far behind the great learning centers of Europe and Latin America, but a beginning had been made. By the early eighteenth century, three private colleges, beginning with Harvard in 1636, offered a traditional curriculum designed to train ministers. Seven more colleges would soon be founded.

SUMMARY

By the eighteenth century, the Iberian monarchies had performed the remarkable feat of firmly implanting western civilization throughout an area twice the size of Europe. Because of the divisive geography and the presence of other races and cultures, the impact of western culture varied widely according to region, ranging from strong in Mexico and Peru to nonexistent in the Amazon and the southern tip of South America. The impact also varied widely by class, the upper classes consciously clinging to their Iberian background and the lower orders still strongly influenced by their native Amerindian and African cultures. The Iberians established Roman Catholicism as the only faith throughout the colonies, although many Amerindian converts had only a rudimentary understanding of their new religion. The Iberian languages were somewhat less widespread, although they were spoken by all races in the urban and commercial centers. Three key characteristics of Iberia—paternalistic government, aristocratic social and economic privilege, and mercantilist economics—were substantially replicated in Latin America. Latin Americans also inherited the intellectual, literary, and artistic outlook of Spain and Portugal. While Iberian culture predominated in Latin America, however, its ongoing interaction with Amerindian and African cultures modified its characteristics, creating a new form of western civilization.

By the early eighteenth century the residents of North America had developed another distinct culture inside Western Civilization, one that on the whole departed more substantially from Europe than did Latin America. In a few characteristics British North America did approximate Europe more closely than did Latin America: The area was overwhelmingly European racially and linguistically, and Amerindians and Amerindian culture played an insignificant role. The African impact was also less profound, although it would grow in time. On the other hand, British North America was fast departing from continental European and Latin American standards on a broad spectrum of economic, social, and political characteristics. It exhibited, in a more accelerated form, a trend towards social and political liberalization that was also getting under way in Great Britain.

Europeans visiting British North America were naturally impressed by the differences rather than the similarities. They commented on the strange landscape, the raw look of both cities and farms, and the lack of monuments or any sign of a living, visible past. They were discomfited by the restless moving about of the population and the cacophony of ethnic groups and religious sects. Above all, Europeans were struck by the individualism at all levels of society and by the absence of servility among the middle and lower orders of whites. Europeans attributed these characteristics to the general prosperity of the population, to education, and to the weakness of the class system. Most of these visitors went home dismayed by the brawling confusion and the social dislocation, but a few enthusiasts thought they had seen in this place the future of western civilization.

SELECTED SOURCES

*Bailyn, Bernard. *Origins of American Politics.* 1970. Insightful examination of the colonial roots of American political theory and practice.

*Bannon, John Francis. *The Colonial World of Latin America.* 1982. A useful introduction to Spanish America and Brazil.

Boxer, Charles R. *Four Centuries of Portuguese Expansion, 1415–1825.* 1969. Treats Brazil within the context of the Portuguese Empire.

*Bridenbaugh, Carl. *Myths and Realities: Societies of the Colonial South.* A well-written survey of the British North American colonies that most resembled the Caribbean and Brazil.

*Commager, Henry Steele, and Elmo

Giordanetti. *Was America a Mistake?* 1967. A fascinating collection of eighteenth-century attacks on, and defenses of, the New World.

*Gibson, Charles. *Spain in America.* 1968. An authoritative interpretation by a renowned scholar.

*Hofstadter, Richard. *America at 1750: A Social Portrait.* 1971. Incomplete at Hofstadter's death, an insightful presentation of the society in British North America.

*Leonard, Irving A. *Baroque Times in Old Mexico: Seventeenth-Century Persons, Places, and Practices.* 1959. A colorful insight into the society and culture of Latin America.

*Martin, Luis. *Daughters of the Conquistadores: Women of the Viceroyalty of Peru.* 1983. An informative survey, with applications to all of Latin America.

Williams, Selma. *Demeter's Daughters.* 1976. A survey of the various roles of women in British North America, stressing the stories of individuals.

*Available in paperback.

THE AGE OF REASON

If we limit ourselves to showing the advantages which have been extracted from the sciences . . . the most important of them perhaps is to have destroyed prejudice and reestablished . . . human intelligence formerly compelled to bend to the false directions forced upon it by . . . absurd beliefs . . . the terrors of superstition and the fear of tyranny.

We may observe that the principles of philosophy, the maxims of liberty, the knowledge of the true rights of men and of their real interests have spread in too great a number of nations, and control in each of them the opinions of too many enlightened men, for them ever to be forgotten again.

This optimistic account of "the progress of the human spirit" in the eighteenth century sums up some of the deepest convictions of that age: the liberating impact of science and reason on the human mind, the importance of human rights, and the inevitable triumph of freedom in the world. The author of these impassioned sentiments, the marquis de Condorcet (1743–1794), was an enlightened aristocrat and a disciple of Voltaire, the most famous philosopher of the era. A strong believer in freedom and progress, Condorcet was an admiring student of the American experiment in free government across the Atlantic. Ironically, he died a victim of the political terror that accompanied the struggle for survival of the French Revolution. Yet this tract, written shortly before his tragic death, indicates that Cordorcet died still confident that in the long run, the political promise of that age of intellectual enlightenment would be realized. The following pages discuss the scientific revolution from which the age of reason sprang. Thereafter, they focus on the Enlightenment itself, in Europe and in the European colonies overseas, and conclude with a summary of developments in the arts during this innovative period.

CONTENTS

Voltaire. This is one of many portraits and sculptural representations of the most celebrated intellectual and social critic of the French Enlightenment. As famous for his wit as for his radical critique of society, Voltaire is shown here with the smile that could make even kings nervous.

THE SCIENTIFIC REVOLUTION

No current of western thought is more characteristic of the modern period than is the scientific approach to understanding the world around us. Whereas earlier centuries depended on philosophy or religion to explain the universe, the modern age has turned increasingly to science for such explanation. The work of the makers of this scientific revolution is thus of great importance in the history of the shaping of the modern mind.

Origins of the Scientific Revolution

One of the major obstacles to scientific progress was the inherited thought of ancient and medieval times. The theories of Greek scientists like the astronomer Ptolemy and the wide-ranging philosopher Aristotle, although inadequate as explanations of the natural world, were accepted as the final word. This attitude was reinforced by the medieval Christian church, which used fundamentally religious ideas to explain the physical world, setting up formidable roadblocks to scientific analysis. More recently, Renaissance scholars and Reformation religious leaders had focused attention on literary, moral, and spiritual values, dismissing the material world as unimportant.

At the same time, the wisdom of the ancients also helped to stimulate attempts to explain the material world. The rediscovery and translation of some Greek scientists stimulated early modern Europeans to think in new ways about the universe. The new scientists who had read Archimedes on physics, for example, discovered a purely mechanical explanation for the behavior of the material world, an approach they found strongly appealing. The ancient Greek atomic theory, which asserted that the universe was made of tiny particles of matter, also provided a useful framework for modern scientific thinking. The very fact that the "wise ancients" had disagreed among themselves made it easier for the scientific revolutionaries to challenge their famous predecessors.

More recent trends also encouraged the rise of modern science. Among these, two oddly contrasting developments were particularly important: technology and magic. Technological developments like the printing press, the magnetic compass, and the widespread use of gunpowder increased respect among Europeans for practical knowledge. In fields as diverse as gunnery, metallurgy, ship-building, and surgery, early modern technicians commonly replaced older ideas with new knowledge. The ancients, they pointed out, were not always right, at least about practical matters.

A wide range of sixteenth-century studies that today would be called magical also helped create an exciting intellectual environment in which the scientific revolutionaries flourished. The common belief in astrology, which claimed to explain earthly affairs by the motions of stars and planets, contributed to the interest in astronomy. Alchemy stressed a mystical search for ultimate truth, but it also used laboratory equipment and chemical experiments. Mystical studies of Neoplatonism and of the Jewish religious book called the Kabbala emphasized the importance of numbers in understanding the way the world works, a mathematical approach that modern science would follow up with great success.

In this stimulating intellectual world, the scientific revolution was born.

The New Scientists

The most famous makers of the scientific revolution were a group of sixteenth- and seventeenth-century innovators in astronomy and physics. These great names included Copernicus, Kepler, Galileo, and Isaac Newton. Scientists in such fields as biology and chemistry also contributed to the expanding knowledge of the material world.

Nicholas Copernicus (1473–1543), who revealed the basic structure of the solar system to the modern world, is sometimes called the Columbus of the scientific revolution. A Polish churchman with a purely theoretical understanding of astronomy, Copernicus questioned the orthodox view of the ancient Alexandrian astronomer Ptolemy that the Earth stood at the center of the cosmos. Copernicus's book *On the Revolutions of the Heavenly Spheres* (1543) declared that the Sun was the true center, with stars and planets orbiting around it. The Earth, Copernicus dared to suggest, was merely a planet moving around that solar center.

The German astronomer Johannes Kepler (1571–1630), offered a much more detailed and exact account of the laws of planetary motion. In particular, he was able to correct the assumption, made by both Ptolemy and Copernicus, that the planets move

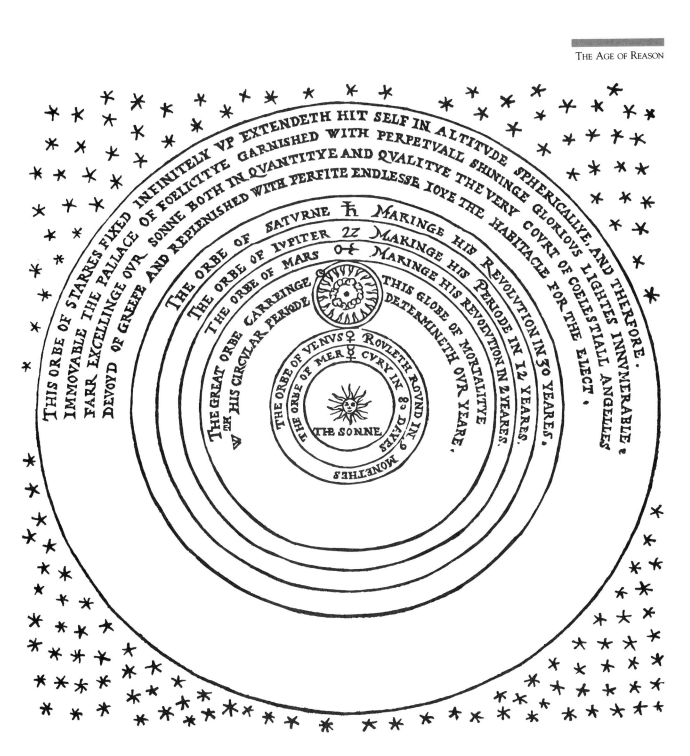

in circles around the Sun, demonstrating that their paths are in fact ellipses, with the Sun at one of the two foci. Kepler's years of precise observation of the night sky as assistant to the Danish astronomer Tycho Brahe

and his elaborate mathematical calculations of planetary orbits were a great step forward. In a more general sense, they showed the value of both observation and mathematics for scientific explanations.

The Copernican View of the Universe. This schematic presentation was the work of the Englishman, Thomas Digges, some thirty years after Copernicus's book appeared in 1543. The Sun is shown in the center, the Earth as the third planet out from it, and the Moon revolving around the Earth.

Galileo Galilei, (1564–1642) a brilliant Italian student of astronomy and physics, made major contributions to both fields. His researches into the laws of falling bodies challenged Aristotle's views. By experiment, he demonstrated that larger objects did not fall faster than smaller ones as Aristotle had said, and even established the mathematical formula for the accelerating speed at which all bodies fall. Like Kepler, Galileo supported Copernicus's Sun-centered theory of the universe against Ptolemy's Earth-centered model. By using a telescope, recently developed in the Netherlands, for astronomical observations, Galileo discovered sunspots, the moons of Jupiter, and the geography of the Moon. In his later years, the pugnacious Italian was summoned before the Inquisition because of his controversial views, but his ideas long outlived the power of his persecutors.

Finally, Isaac Newton (1642–1727) tied the achievements of his predecessors together with his crucial formulation of the law of gravity. His *Mathematical Principles of Natural Philosophy* (1687) asserted that every particle of matter in the universe attracts every other particle with a force that varies with the size of the objects

The Trial of Galileo. This painting by an unknown artist shows the trial of the scientist Galileo by the religious court of the Inquisition. This was actually a rare case of overt persecution of the scientific revolutionaries by ecclesiastical authority. Nevertheless, Galileo's trial, climaxing in his forced recantation of the Copernican worldview, has become symbolic of resistance to the new scientific understanding of the nature of the physical universe.

and the distance between them. Newton's discovery, a century and a half after Copernicus, of a single force affecting everything from planets in space to falling bodies on Earth made Newton the most honored of all the makers of the scientific revolution.

Newton made many other contributions to the scientific revolution besides his formulation of the law of gravity. He explored the nature of light and the laws of optics empirically, using a prism to show that ordinary sunlight is in fact composed of all the colors of the spectrum. He redefined the general laws of motion in terms of inertia (of motion as well as of position) and of action and reaction (for every action, he asserted, there is an equal and opposite reaction). He was a pioneer explorer of the mysteries of calculus. In his long life of service to science, Newton thus vigorously embodied the range as well as the depth of the scientific revolution.

The new scientists constructed a new, coherent, and increasingly accurate picture of the physical universe. It was the beginning of an unparalleled surge of scientific progress which, with many additions and corrections, has continued to the present day.

The Scientific World View

In the course of the sixteenth and seventeenth centuries, scientists and philosophers of science also evolved both a new method of investigation and a new view of the nature of things. The result was a broadly scientific world view that has become one of the central features of modern western thought.

The best minds of the medieval era

THE FIRST HUMAN EYE TO LOOK UPON THE MOUNTAINS OF THE MOON

About ten months ago, a report reached my ears that a certain Fleming had constructed a spyglass by means of which visible objects, though very distant from the eye of the observer, were distinctly seen as if nearby . . . I succeeded in constructing for myself so excellent an instrument that objects seen by means of it appeared . . . over thirty times closer than when regarded with our natural vision . . .

Now let us review the observations made during the past two months . . . Let us speak first of [the] surface of the moon . . . I distinguish two parts of this surface, a lighter and a darker . . . the darker part discolors the moon's surface like a kind of cloud, and makes it appear covered with spots . . . From observations of these spots repeated many times, I have been led to the opinion and conviction that the surface of the moon is not smooth, uniform, and precisely spherical, as a great number of philosophers believe it (and the other heavenly bodies) to be, but is uneven, rough, and full of cavities and prominences, being not unlike the surface of the earth, relieved by chains of mountains and deep valleys . . .*

Vivid reports like this account of Galileo's discoveries made the new "natural philosophy" an increasingly exciting subject as the scientific revolution proceeded. Such concrete discoveries could also have broader theoretical implications. The discovery of mountains and valleys on the moon, for example, challenged the orthodox belief that all the universe except the Earth was perfect and unblemished by irregularities. This view was harder to defend after Galileo's observation of lunar "geography" and sunspots.

*Galileo Galilei, "The Starry Messenger" in Stillman Drake, ed. and trans. *Discoveries and Opinions of Galileo* (New York: Doubleday, 1957), pp. 28–29, 31.

---

had been religious thinkers like Thomas Aquinas, who had tried to understand the physical world as they did the spiritual one, through revealed truth and abstract reasoning. Typically beginning with some religious authority like the Bible or with the writings of a classical scholar like Aristotle or Ptolemy, they used an elaborate system of logic to demonstrate the truth of explanations of the material world. The result was a vision of the world in which religion had a central place, but that included many factual errors about how the universe actually works.

The new scientific world view took explicit shape in the seventeenth century, the century after Copernicus, especially in the writings of the English philosopher Sir Francis Bacon (1561–1626) and the French thinker René Descartes (1596–1650).

Bacon firmly rejected ancient authority as the infallible source of all truth. He also had no use for the abstract, logical hairsplitting of medieval religious thinkers. Instead of blind acceptance of authority or abstract logic, Bacon urged the use of empirical methods—the direct observation and collection of data. This emphasis on empiricism, beginning with observable data and building general

Leonardo
da Vinci

Galileo

Kepler   Descartes

Copernicus

Bacon

Newton

truths on this foundation, became one of the hallmarks of the scientific method.

Descartes also openly expressed his doubt of the authorities, but he offered another road to certainty. Not empirical observation but rational understanding as clear as that of a geometrical theorem was for Descartes the guarantor of truth. The French philosopher's famous assertion "I think, therefore I am," was the first link in a chain of rational proofs that accounted philosophically for the existence, progressively, of humanity, of God, and of God's universe. A medieval religious thinker like Thomas Aquinas, by contrast, would have *begun* with the revealed truth of God's existence and reasoned his way from this to more modest truths about humanity and the individual. Descartes' emphasis on rational processes which he thought were as convincing as mathematical reasoning, like Bacon's stress on empiricism, was fundamental to the scientific world view.

On the basis of empirical observation and mathematical reasoning, seventeenth-century scientists and philosophers constructed a new scientific method to guide the further search for truth. The new approach began with a hypothesis, a scientific

guess about the cause or operation of some natural phenomenon. The scientific approach then required investigators to collect data on the actual behavior of the natural objects concerned. This evidence was then used to test and modify the original hypothesis. Scientists then accepted the result as a scientific law of nature— a new truth added to the store of understanding of the way the world works.

The accumulation of such laws of nature led scientific philosophers to a new vision of the world. The universe came to be seen as an immense and intricate machine operating according to mathematically formulated laws. Many believed that all matter was composed of atoms, tiny particles whose mass, motion through space, and encounters with other atoms explained everything that happens in nature.

To expand our understanding of this "world machine," Bacon in particular pleaded for large, state-supported research institutions. By applying the scientific knowledge thus accumulated, he accurately predicted more than three and a half centuries ago, the human race would acquire a greater mastery of the material environment than humanity has ever had before.

THE ENLIGHTENMENT

Bacon's great fame, like that of Newton and the other builders of the scientific world view, came not in the sixteenth or seventeenth century, but in the eighteenth. It was then that the age of reason reached its climax in the great intellectual movement known as the Enlightenment, a ferment of new ideas important in the growth of modern social, economic, and political thought.

Sources of the Enlightenment

The sources of the enlightenment itself included several major cultural trends of the early modern centuries. Among these were Renaissance humanist reverence for the classics, reaction against the religious intolerance of the Reformation, the impact of the age of discovery on the European mind, and above all the influence of the scientific revolution.

Classical education, with its study of the literature of the Greeks and Romans, contributed to the air, rationality, and cool philosophical tone of much of the writing of the Enlightenment. It also provided models and mentors. French radicals and American revolutionaries alike, for instance, could see themselves as heirs to that "republican virtue" which had flourished in Rome before the Caesars rose.

The wars of religion which had climaxed the reformation spawned a bigotry on the part of both Catholics and Protestants which continued into the eighteenth century. The leaders of the Enlightenment reacted strongly against the official persecutions and mob violence produced by these religious prejudices. The new movement demanded not only an end to sectarian intolerance, but a more secular society in general.

Expanded contacts with other cultures resulting from the age of discovery and the establishment of European empires overseas also affected the Enlightenment. Eighteenth-century European thinkers were impressed by a wide range of non-European cultural achievement, from the ancient learning of Confucian China to the native wisdom of pre-literate Amerindian cultures. Enlightenment Europeans did not yet know much about these nonwestern societies: nevertheless, they pioneered a broader form of toleration, a recognition that no single continent or culture had a monopoly on truth.

The new science, with its continuing success and growing popularity, profoundly shaped the thought of the Enlightenment. New discoveries in a broad spectrum of scientific fields—biology and chemistry as well as physics and astronomy—kept the physical sciences in the forefront of western intellectual life. Scientific societies like the British Royal Society were founded to bring scientists and interested laymen together and to further

support the advancement of science. Popular books explained the scientific world view to a larger public. Enlightenment Europeans dabbled in science as Renaissance Europeans had patronized the arts, and faith in the scientific approach grew steadily.

The Enlightenment, although influenced by new thinking about the physical universe, had broader concerns. The intellectual leaders of the new movement began to apply the scientific method, so successful in explaining the natural world, to the social world as well. They used reason as a scalpel to dissect and expose traditional social institutions that had outlived their time. They sought scientific laws governing human society like those Copernicus and Newton had discovered ruling nature.

This application of science to society was the foundation of the great Enlightenment critique of European political, economic, social, and religious institutions, which challenged the inefficiency, injustice, and intolerance of the old regime, as society in this period later came to be called. Some Enlightenment thinkers began to dream of a perfect society of the future, designed according to scientific principles, in which human beings might live a better life. This scientific analysis of society was also crucial in establishing the modern social sciences, including political science and economics.

The Critics: The Philosophes

The critical aspect of the new movement centered in France, and its leaders were known by the French term *philosophes.* The philosophes were not philosophers in the professional or traditional sense—systematic think-

ers about large abstract issues. Rather, they were philosophizers, social critics who depended on rational analysis to suggest solutions for the concrete problems of their times.

The philosophes found an audience for their views in two important social groups: the aristocracy and the bourgeoisie. The influence of Enlightenment popularizers would even reach the lower classes toward the end of the eighteenth century, but it was the educated classes who were first touched by the Enlightenment critique.

A few of Europe's traditional elite, the hereditary aristocracy, were eager to keep up with the latest advanced ideas. These enlightened aristocrats mingled with the philosophes in a distinctive central Enlightenment institution, the salon. At these elegant social gatherings, literary readings, serious talk, and sparkling wit were the main attractions. Discussions of science and art were staples, but some thoroughly subversive social ideas also circulated in the salons. Hostesses like the internationally known Madame Geoffrin (1699–1777) thus played a crucial role in the intellectual life of the time. The middle class—wealthier, better educated, and more self-confident than ever before—was attracted to the new ideas in even larger numbers. Reading pamphlets and books written by the philosophes, its members found in them expressions of some of their own social discontents. Middle class men and women would provide the leadership for the political upheaval that would follow this intellectual assault on the old order of society.

Among the most influential of the philosophes were the French writers Voltaire, Rousseau, and Diderot. All three were ardent spokesmen for reform and expert propagandists for their causes.

Francois Marie Arouet (1694–1778), under the pen name of Voltaire, was the leader of the philosophes and the most famous intellectual of his age. Voltaire's career spanned most of the century and produced many volumes of innovative history, philosophical fiction, drama, poetry, popular science, pamphlets and essays on social questions, and much more. His comic novel *Candide* (1754) exposed to scathing ridicule many groups and attitudes, from snobbish aristocrats and hypocritical churchmen to the military establishment and establishment philosophy. Voltaire particularly attacked organized religion for its intolerance, superstition, and closed-minded attitude to the new ideas.

In contrast to the witty Voltaire, Jean-Jacques Rousseau (1712–1778), was an emotional, deeply serious critic of the social order who insisted on the superiority of pure nature over artificial society. A pioneer of modern educational theory, he opposed rote learning and championed the development of the individual's innate capacities. He was also a passionate spokesman for a more democratic form of government.

Denis Diderot (1713–1784), one of the most aggressive and colorful of the philosophes, achieved his greatest fame as the editor of one book: the multivolume *Encyclopedia* (1751–1772). This vast compendium of knowledge, twenty years in the making, set out not only to inform but also to change people's way of thinking by approaching political and religious institutions in a thoroughly analytical and critical spirit. So critical was Diderot, in fact that his work was condemned as impious, seditious, and immoral, and he himself spent some time in prison. The *Encyclopedia* also disseminated the achieve-

The Salon of Mme Geoffrin. This painting, done after the fact in the early nineteenth-century, shows a gathering of French aristocrats and intellectuals during the reign of Louis XVI, the last Bourbon ruler before the Revolution. Neither Mme Geoffrin, the white-haired lady on the right, nor the elegant room, carpeting, paintings, and costumes of the guests look at all revolutionary. Nevertheless, radical ideas as well as high culture were staples of salon conversation during the later eighteenth century.

ments of eighteenth-century science and technology, printing many pictures of the intricate machines that had been developed by the eve of the Industrial Revolution.

Other issues that agitated enlightened minds in the eighteenth century included organized religion and the position of women in society. Many philosophes became deists or advocates of "natural religion," and some few even drifted into atheism. Deists believed in a rational God who had created the world the scientists studied, had set it working according to natural laws, and had thereafter ceased to intervene or involve himself in human affairs. In addition to the existence of God, believers in natural religion accepted a few other basic religious propositions—human brotherhood, perhaps even the immortality of the soul—but rejected any more detailed sectarian creed. Protestants and Catholics, Muslims and Buddhists, might all have access to God as they understood him. Out-and-out atheism, was rare in the eighteenth century, but by 1800 a famous scientist was able to tell Napoleon that he had no need of the "hypothesis" of God's existence to explain the universe.

Both the seventeenth and eighteenth centuries saw an undercurrent of intellectual debate about the equality of the sexes and the position of women in society. Some of the learned women of the literary salons of the age of Louis XIV had insisted that women were by nature the equals of men, made subservient by artificial laws and institutions. Such eighteenth-century thinkers as Diderot agreed and demanded reforms to give women the same legal rights as men. Perhaps the most eloquent

A MEDIEVAL SOLUTION TO THE PROBLEM OF EARTHQUAKES

The University of Coimbra had pronounced that the sight of a few people ceremoniously burned alive before a slow fire was an infallible prescription for preventing earthquakes; so when the earthquake had subsided after destroying three-quarters of Lisbon, the authorities . . . could find no surer means of avoiding total ruin than by giving the people a magnificent auto-da-fe.

They therefore seized a Basque, convicted of marrying his godmother, and two Portuguese Jews who had refused to eat bacon with their chicken; and after dinner Dr. Pangloss and his pupil, Candide, were arrested as well, one for speaking and the other for listening with an air of approval . . . They were then marched in procession . . . to hear a moving sermon followed by beautiful music in counterpoint. Candide was flogged in time with the anthem; the Basque and the two men who refused to eat bacon were burnt; and Pangloss was hanged . . . The same day another earthquake occurred and caused tremendous havoc.[*]

Voltaire seized on the historic Lisbon earthquake of 1755 as a focus for this assault on the medieval views and practices of the Inquisition, lampooned here in a passage from Candide. *The "crimes" mentioned included violation of dietary and marriage laws (though a godmother is, of course, no blood relation) and the too-free speech for which the philosophes themselves were often punished. To the enlightened eighteenth-century mind, much of the organized religion of the time seemed this superstitious and fanatical.*

[*]Voltaire, *Candide or Optimism,* trans. by John Butt (Baltimore: Penguin Books, 1947), pp. 36–37.

advocate of female emancipation, however, was Mary Wollstonecraft (1759–1797), whose *Vindication of the Rights of Women* (1792) was a milestone on the road to sexual equality. Writing at the time of the French Revolution, Wollstonecraft dared to demand a revolt against the tyranny of men and the recognition of women as in every way their equals.

The System Builders: Political and Economic Thought

Building on the critical spirit of the Enlightenment, some leading thinkers of the period offered positive insights and prescriptions for a better society. The political and economic theories of the intellectual leaders of the age of reason in fact provided the western world with some of the fundamental social ideas of the next two centuries.

The Enlightenment challenge to the inefficiency and injustice of government under the old regime is well illustrated by the Italian Cesar Beccaria's (1735–1794) pioneering ideas on reforming the prevailing system of justice. Eighteenth-century courts and prisons were notorious for imposing arbitrary and often savage punishments. Beccaria's famous book, *Crimes and Punishments* (1764) emphasized that criminal codes should be clear,

425

NATURAL RIGHTS AND THE SOCIAL CONTRACT ACCORDING TO JOHN LOCKE

All men are naturally in . . . a state of perfect freedom to order their actions . . . as they think fit, within the bounds of the law of nature . . .

[They are in] a state also of equality . . . there being nothing more evident, than that creatures . . . born to all the same advantages of nature, and the use of the same faculties, should also be equal one amongst another without subordination or subjection. . . .

Men being, as has been said, by nature all free, equal, and independent, no one can be . . . subjected to the political power of another without his own consent . . . by agreeing with other men to join and unite into a community. . . . And all this to be directed to no other end but the peace, safety, and public good of the people.*

Belief in human freedom and equality and in government by "consent of the governed" expressed in a social contract or constitution, voiced by John Locke in the seventeenth century, was taken up enthusiastically by enlightened minds in the eighteenth. In the late 1700s, these doctrines would be enshrined in the "Declaration of the Rights of Man and the Citizen" produced by the French Revolution and in the Bill of Rights appended to the Constitution of the United States.

*John Locke, Two Treatises of Government in T. V. Smith and Marjorie Grene, ed. From Descartes to Locke (Chicago: University of Chicago Press, 1940), pp. 456, 470, 474–475.

penalties applied equally to all classes of society, and punishments swift and sure. These views would influence legal and prison reform in a number of countries and remain influential today.

On the political side, the Enlightenment fostered the radical new doctrines of natural rights, constitutional government, and even popular sovereignty. On the economic side, advanced thinkers argued for the existence of natural laws governing the economy and for the freedom of the marketplace.

John Locke (1632–1704), the philosopher of the English revolution of the seventeenth century, was the first influential thinker to claim that all people have inborn natural rights.

These, he said, included freedom, equality, and the right to private property. Locke also insisted that the only legitimate government was one created by a "social contract" or constitution that the people themselves had agreed to. The closest approximation of this ideal in the eighteenth century was the constitutional monarchy of Great Britain. Many continental thinkers admired the British parliamentary system, though they depended on enlightened absolute monarchs to enact social reform on their side of the Channel.

Ideas emphasizing limited governmental power circulated on the continent as well in the eighteenth century. The baron de la Brede et de Montesquieu (1689–1755) thus pro-

posed that government power should be divided among several institutions, rather than concentrated in a single set of hands. This, he said, would create a system of checks and balances that would prevent tyranny. This approach would later be built into the Constitution of the United States.

Jean-Jacques Rousseau's most influential work, The Social Contract, went even farther, urging the principle of popular sovereignty. In this book, Rousseau made an impassioned plea for government by consent of the governed, the "general will" of the people. Rousseau's ideas would be very influential during the time of the French Revolution.

In economic thought also, the Enlightenment produced startling challenges to the autocratic status quo, particularly to the reigning economic theory of mercantilism. In France, a group of economic theorists called physiocrats claimed that land and agriculture were the true sources of national wealth, rather than bullion and trade, as the mercantilists insisted. The physiocrats also urged free trade and opposed government regulation of the economy—the heart of the mercantile system. They thus became early spokesmen for laissez-faire, the belief that economic affairs in general should be allowed to follow natural laws rather than be determined by government decrees.

The most influential spokesman for the free market was the English economic thinker Adam Smith (1723–1790). Smith's extremely influential book The Wealth of Nations (1776) asserted that a natural law of supply and demand underlay all economic processes. If the economy is left free of government regulation, it will re-

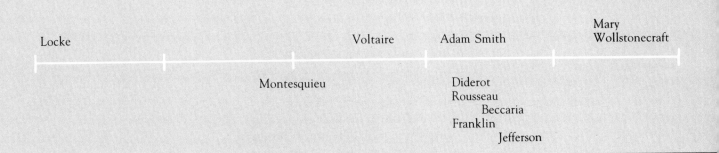

| 1675 | 1700 | 1725 | 1750 | 1775 | 1800 |

Locke   Voltaire   Adam Smith   Mary Wollstonecraft

Montesquieu   Diderot
Rousseau
Beccaria
Franklin
Jefferson

spond naturally to public demand, supplying what the people want at a price people are willing to pay. The result of such free market policies, Smith believed, would be a steady growth in the wealth of all nations. The free trade and free enterprise systems of a number of western nations would reflect these convictions in later centuries.

THE ENLIGHTENMENT OUTSIDE EUROPE

The Enlightenment was an international phenomenon, centered in France but flourishing in other European nations and spreading to those of European heritage living beyond the seas. The new views attracted followers particularly in the British settlements in North America and in the Spanish colonies of Central and South America.

The Enlightenment in British America

Some of the most important ideas of the Enlightenment found a congenial home in the thirteen British colonies of North America, and both scientific and social thought flourished.

Perhaps stimulated by the new environment in which they found themselves, English colonial investigators made significant contributions to the fields of biology, physics, astronomy, and other sciences. Scientific subjects were taught in the colonial universities, from Harvard and Yale in the north to William and Mary in the south. In the New World as in the Old, educated persons dabbled in science. They met in societies dedicated to the study of the natural philosophy, and more than a dozen colonists were elected to the British Royal Society in London.

Colonial enthusiasm for science is perhaps most vividly illustrated in the colorful career of Benjamin Franklin (1706–1790), the many-sided Philadelphia printer who would become one of the founders of the new United States. Franklin's most famous scientific investigations established that lightning "bolts" were really discharges of electrical energy. His technological contributions included such practical inventions as the Franklin stove and the lightning rod. The founder of a philosophical society, a journal, and an academy that subse-

quently became a major university, Franklin was also elected to the Royal Society.

The political, economic, and social ideas of the Enlightenment also found a natural home in the British colonies. The colonists, with their elected legislative assemblies, had more political freedom than most Europeans. Merchants and farmers who had come to find greater economic opportunity in the New World embraced freedom of enterprise. Even religious toleration, for which French philosophes like Voltaire fought so hard, was relatively widespread in British North America.

Enlightenment ideas in the colonies perhaps had their greatest expression in the colonies in the writings of Thomas Jefferson (1743–1826), a Virginia planter who, like Franklin, was a latter-day Renaissance man. An avid student of the physical sciences and an architect of note, Jefferson corresponded with leaders of the European Enlightenment on subjects ranging from science to economics. He was a strong believer in religious toleration and in greater social equality. He opposed black slavery, though he could conceive of no practicable solution except gradual emancipation and emigration. His broader com-

THE DREAM OF FREEDOM SPREADS TO THE AMERICAN COLONIES

We hold these truths to be self-evident: that all men are created equal; that they are endowed by their Creator with certain inalienable rights; that among these are life, liberty, and the pursuit of happiness; that to secure these rights, governments are instituted among men, deriving their just powers from the consent of the governed. . . . *

Compare Thomas Jefferson's statement of the theory of natural rights and constitutional government with the earlier version proposed by John Locke. Compare it also with the ideals expressed in the slogan of the French revolution: Liberty, Equality, Brotherhood. Over the next two centuries, these beliefs would become the basis for new governments all across the western world.

*Thomas Jefferson, The Declaration of Independence in Saul K. Padover, ed. *Thomas Jefferson on Democracy* (New York: New American Library, 1946), p. 13.

mitment to political rights and popular sovereignty still lives in the words of the American Declaration of Independence and Bill of Rights.

The War of Independence itself was in many ways a struggle to realize the ideals advocated by the European Enlightenment, from opposition to mercantilism to government by consent of the governed. The new American nation would incorporate in its Constitution many of these same ideas, including natural rights, checks and balances, and popular sovereignty.

The Enlightenment in Spanish America

The scientific revolution and the Enlightenment reached colonial Latin America also. Particularly with the rule of the enlightened Bourbon dynasty in Spain in the later eighteenth century, the spirit of reform in Spanish America experienced a considerable growth.

The ideas of Copernicus and Newton, Bacon and Descartes were taught in Latin America's two dozen universities, some of which, like those at Mexico City and Lima, Peru, were much older than Harvard and Yale. Some Spanish American colonists, like the British settlers to the north, corresponded with European scientific societies and made important contributions to astronomy, biology, geology, and what amounted to Indian anthropology, as well as to other sciences. The Inquisition was still capable of occasionally persecuting those who advocated the Copernican theory, but in the eighteenth century even the Jesuits were teaching Newton's ideas in the colonies.

Spanish America was strongly influenced by the social theories of the Enlightenment. Colonial newspapers expressed concern over political abuses, voiced demands for economic and social change, and spread the ideas of the philosophes. Similar views were discussed by middle-class mestizo groups in colonial "economic clubs" and by aristocrats in traditional social gatherings called *tertulias*. No representative assemblies existed in the Latin American colonies, but enlightened Bourbon administrators encouraged social reform.

Bourbon reforms would not be enough, however. Enlightenment belief in reason and social progress and willingness to challenge authority and demand political and economic reform would also contribute to the outbreak of the Latin American wars of independence in the early nineteenth century.

ART IN THE AGE OF ENLIGHTENMENT

The arts in the eighteenth century were less innovative than the scientific and social thought of the age. Nevertheless, there were new developments in literature, music, painting, and architecture, including both new styles and new and larger audiences for the arts.

A wider audience was particularly important for the long-term future of the arts. Aristocratic patrons and small, elite groups continued to dominate much of the artistic life of the eighteenth century, and encourage sophisticated traditional styles. But there was a growing middle-class interest in the arts as well, which demanded more contemporary subjects and forms. The music of the period, too, reached larger numbers of people than ever before in opera houses and concert halls.

Aristocratic Art: Neoclassicism and Rococo

Europe's eighteenth-century aristocracy, classically educated and living elegantly, sought art to satisfy both these tastes. Neoclassicism responded to its appreciation of Greek and Roman culture, rococo to its concern for elegance.

Neoclassicism was in essence a refinement of the classical styles of the seventeenth century, which required the artist to adhere to the rules and models of the ancients. The forms of poetry, as in the preceding century, were those used by Greek and Roman poets. Subjects for painting often came from ancient history and myth. Balance and symmetry prevailed in architecture and rationality in neoclassical literature. The sophisticated rhymed couplets of Alexander Pope (1688–1744), and the formally posed portraits of Sir Joshua Reynolds (1723–1792) embodied the neoclassical spirit.

Rococo art, by contrast, was light, elegant, and informal—a decorative style of architecture, sculpture, and painting designed to create a pleasant atmosphere for members of the ruling class to live their lives. Named for the stone and seashell (*rocaille* and *coquille*) motifs used in its room decorations, the rococo style was far less

The Swing. Jean-Honoré Fragonard's famous painting of aristocrats at play is typical of the rococo style. Its subject is frivolous and a bit risqué—the husband pushing the young lady in the swing is presumably unaware of the young man in the bushes. The Wallace Collection, London.

splendid than baroque art, and less stiff and formal than classical design. It offered pleasant paintings of well-dressed ladies and gentlemen, decorations for the walls of aristocratic boudoirs, and sexy china shepherdesses to titillate the fancy of the "beautiful people" of the eighteenth century.

Bourgeois Art and the Novel

The increasing wealth, education and aggressiveness of Europe's rising middle class also exerted an influence on the art of the century. The bourgeoisie demanded contemporary subjects from everyday life, the expression of sentiment, and often a clear moral message in art and literature.

Interest in the "common people" was expressed in paintings of peasants or working people, who were often depicted in close-knit family groups or in ordinary household occupations. Dignity, piety, and warmth were common themes. The English artist William Hogarth (1697–1764), by contrast, produced satirical printed etchings of lowlife in London, with subjects like *The Harlot's Progress* or *Gin Lane,* which sold many copies.

It was in prose fiction, however, that bourgeois taste had its most creative impact, producing the first modern novels. *Robinson Crusoe* by Daniel Defoe (1661–1731) showed the middle-class spirit of industry, inventiveness, and piety at work transforming a desert island into a microcosm of the material world Crusoe had left behind. Henry Fielding (1707–1754) wrote a number of broadly humorous novels, including *Tom Jones,* recounting a young man's colorfully ris-

The Kitchen Maid. Jean-Baptiste Chardin's depiction of a humble servant at work reflects a very different attitude than that of Fragonard's picture, above. Paintings like this attributed a dignity and value to the respectable bourgeoisie and even the hard-working lower orders of society that was often lacking among Europe's rulers in the eighteenth-century. National Gallery of Art, Washington, D.C.

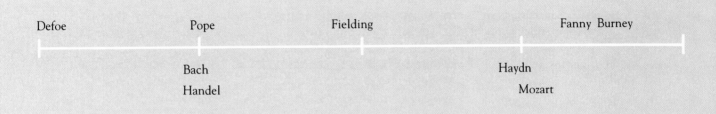

| 1700 | 1725 | 1750 | 1775 | 1800 |

Defoe   Pope   Fielding   Fanny Burney

Bach

Handel   Haydn

Mozart

que adventures in a world of hard-drinking country squires and city sharpers. Despite their exaggerated characters and situations, novels like Fielding's dealt with a down-to-earth world that was thoroughly familiar to middle-class readers. Such books pleased the hard-headed, literal-minded citizens who would in the next century displace an effete aristocracy as Europe's new master class.

Another important audience for eighteenth-century fiction was bourgeois women. Not so highly educated as the aristocratic ladies of the salons, respectable, middle-class women nevertheless influenced the evolution of the novel by encouraging fictional expression of their own interests. Samuel Richard's widely popular *Pamela, or Virtue Rewarded* appealed to these interests with a story of a servant girl who resists her master's efforts to seduce her and is finally rewarded by an honest offer of marriage. Fanny Burney (1752–1840), one of many women novelists, made her literary reputation with her first book, *Evalina, or A Young Lady's Entrance into the World* (1778), detailing a girl's discovery of high society with an ironic eye and a shrewd sense of character. Fictional works like these and the shorter stories appearing in many women's magazines stressed feeling and

morality, qualities that would also be important in middle-class fiction—and middle-class character—of the next century.

A Century of Musical Genius

Perhaps the greatest artistic achievements of the eighteenth century came in music. Composers, continuing to develop older forms, including sacred music and opera, created the orchestra and developed new instruments like the piano and new musical forms such as the classical symphony. Eighteenth-century music, like bourgeois literature and Enlightenment thought, reached beyond the patronage of an aristocratic elite to the larger audiences who flocked to opera houses and concert halls.

The German states, particularly Austria, produced a series of brilliant composers who decisively shaped classical music during this period. From Bach to Mozart, it was one of the great ages in the history of music.

Johann Sebastian Bach (1685–1750) spent a quietly brilliant life creating religious music for German church congregations. Yet his baroque compositions are so rationally and intricately constructed that, formally at least, they seem to embody the very spirit of the age of reason.

George Frederick Handel (1685–1759), Bach's contemporary, emigrated to the England of the Hanoverian kings, where he produced huge oratorios, including his famous *Messiah* (1742), and other dramatic combinations of instrumental music and choral song. Handel's music, though commissioned by England's elite, reached large audiences, as it does today. The operas of Christoph Willibald von Gluck (1714–1787), meanwhile, transformed the traditional opera from a baroque showcase for virtuoso performances and musical fireworks into a more structured and coherent form of musical drama. Opera houses also multiplied in European cities during this century as princes and wealthy cities vied for the prestige of sponsoring these spectacular and widely popular entertainments.

Two other Germans dominated the musical scene in the second half of the century. Joseph Haydn (1732–1809) enjoyed the patronage of Austrian royalty throughout his long and immensely productive musical life. He left a huge number of oratorios, operas, symphonies, and other compositions to enrich the classical tradition. Wolfgang Amadeus Mozart (1756–1791), a child prodigy who dazzled courtly audiences with his playing, in later life tried to break the common pattern of dependence on aristocratic patronage. He earned a precarious living composing operas, symphonies, and other works at a feverish rate, and died in debt at the age of thirty-five. Haydn and Mozart between them developed the modern orchestra and gave definitive form to the symphony. Mozart's operas, arguably his greatest achievements, including the often-performed *Marriage of Figaro* (1786), combined comic and tragic themes, intricate composition and lovely melody in works of singular beauty that transcend the age.

SUMMARY

The period in the history of European thought that is sometimes called the age of reason grew out of the scientific revolution of the sixteenth and seventeenth centuries and reached its climax in the eighteenth-century Enlightenment. It was an age in which new theories and discoveries about the natural world inspired new notions about the sort of social world one ought to live in.

The scientific revolution began with Copernicus's theory that the stars and planets revolve, not around the Earth as they seem to, but around the Sun, and climaxed with Newton's formulation of a law of universal gravitation binding the entire cosmos together. Meanwhile, seventeenth-century philosophers like Bacon and Descartes developed the scientific method, emphasizing an empirical and rationalistic approach.

In the eighteenth century, the intellectual leaders of the Enlightenment used rational analysis for another purpose: to criticize existing social institutions and to propose new principles on which to base a new and more just society. French philosophes like Voltaire, Rousseau, and Diderot attacked the abuses of the old regime with shrewdness, satirical wit, and passion. Thinkers like John Locke and Adam Smith urged a new order based on political and economic freedom, natural rights, and the natural laws of human society. The Enlightenment spread beyond Europe to the European colonies in the Americas, where they sowed the seeds of coming revolutions.

The cultural life of Europe in the eighteenth century also included a variety of artistic achievements, in particular, neoclassical and rococo art, which reflected the predominance of an aristocratic elite, and the novel, which catered to the tastes of the rising middle class. In the history of the arts, as in the history of ideas, the western world was on the threshold of great changes as the eighteenth century drew toward a close.

SELECTED SOURCES

*Artz, Frederick B. *The Enlightenment in France.* 1968. A brief survey of the movement in the land of the philosophes.

*Fielding, Henry. *Tom Jones: A Foundling.* Many editions. Panorama of eighteenth-century England, with rousing adventures.

*Franklin, Benjamin. *The Autobiography of Benjamin Franklin.* Many editions. Engaging life of a colonial who made good—and shared in the main currents of Enlightenment life and thought.

*Galilei, Galileo. *Dialogue Concerning the Two Chief World Systems—Ptolemaic and Copernican.* 1967. Readable discussion of the rival views, by a scientist with an eye to the larger audience.

*Kitson, Michael. *The Age of the Baroque.* 1966. An art book with substantial sections on rococo and neoclassicism; excellent illustrations.

*Koyre, Alexander. *From the Closed World to the Infinite Universe.* 1968. Expanding knowledge of the universe, from Copernicus through Newton.

*Roberts, Kenneth. *Northwest Passage.* 1981. Brilliant fictional recreation of an American artist's life, from Indian encampments to the slums of Hogarth's London.

*Rousseau, Jean-Jacques. *Confessions.* 1953. Intriguing autobiography by one of the more emotional spirits of the age of reason.

*Shaffer, Peter. *Amadeus.* 1984. Recent play—and film—about Mozart, exploring larger questions of artistic mediocrity and genius.

*Voltaire, Francois Marie Arouet de. *Candide or Optimism.* Many editions. Satirical novel highlighting foibles and hypocrites of eighteenth-century European and colonial life.

*Available in paperback.

CONSTITUTIONALISM AND ENLIGHTENED DESPOTISM

Impetuous, vain, presumptuous, scornful, restless, but also attentive, kind and easy to get on with. A friend of truth and reason. He prefers great ideas . . . likes glory and reputation but cares not a rap what his people think of him. . . . He knows himself very well but the funny thing is that he is modest about what is good in him and boastful about his shortcomings. Well aware of his faults, but more anxious to conceal than to correct them. Beautiful speaking voice. . . . I think that, both as a matter of principle and character, he is against war. He'll never allow himself to be attacked, as much from vanity as from prudence—he will find out what his enemies are planning and attack them suddenly before they are quite ready. Woe to them if they are not strong, and woe to him if a well-organized league should force him into a sustained effort of great length.

This portrait of Frederick the Great of Prussia by a French contemporary would apply to almost any enlightened despot of the period. Enlightened despotism, the dominant trend in European politics in the second half of the eighteenth century, is a term assigned to absolute monarchs who, encouraged by the philosophes, exercised their power to make basic rationalist reforms. What made these rulers different from their predecessors was the claim that they used their authority for the benefit of their people. Among other activities, enlightened despots reformed judicial procedures, codified and simplified laws, granted religious toleration, supported scientific research, promoted better public health, and extended popular education.

Another movement, one that preceded enlightened despotism by a century, was the appearance of constitutional government. As a forerunner of democracy, seventeenth-century constitutionalism sought to strike a balance between the authority of the state and the rights of its subjects. In an age when absolutism prevailed nearly everywhere in Europe, the Netherlands and England dealt with the question of sovereignty by establishing a constitutional state. This chapter first surveys the development of constitutional rule in the Netherlands and England, then examines three monarchs who espoused enlightened principles and one who did not.

Joseph II of Austria. Joseph was the most radical but least effective of the enlightened despots, lacking the political acumen that marked Frederick the Great's happy blend of idealism and realism. He worked relentlessly to bring social justice and effective government to his land, but he was rejected by his own subjects. Nevertheless, Joseph was a symbol of energetic reform, and therein may lie his chief historical significance.

CONTENTS

CONSTITUTIONALISM

A unique feature of the seventeenth century was the emergence of constitutional governments in the Netherlands and in England. Constitutionalism is a doctrine or system in which government authority is limited by enforceable rules of law. Various checks and balances prevent the concentration of power so that basic rights of individuals and groups are protected. A nation's constitution may be written, as would be the case of the United States, or unwritten, that is, based on parliamentary statutes, judicial decisions, and traditional laws and practices, such as in Great Britain. What makes constitutionalism function, whether written or unwritten, is recognition by the various branches of government that they must operate within a legal framework. A constitutional state may take the form of a republic or a monarchy. Early constitutional systems restricted the franchise and the holding of public office to a privileged few who could meet stringent property qualifications. In a modern-day democracy, by contrast, most adults can participate directly or indirectly through their elected representatives in the process of government.

CONSTITUTIONALISM IN THE UNITED PROVINCES OF THE NETHERLANDS

During the sixteenth century, the Dutch created the first major constitutional state. In 1581, the United Provinces of the Netherlands, as the provinces that had become independent of Spain termed themselves, formally renounced their allegiance to the Spanish King, Philip II. They embodied their justification in the Act of Abjuration, often termed "the Dutch Declaration of the Rights of Man," a statement that was the model for declarations during subsequent revolutions and independence movements in other lands. The opening comment read: "The people were not created by God for the sake of the Prince . . . but, on the contrary, the Prince was made for the good of the people." The document argued that when a ruler ignored the law that defined his relationship with his subjects, he could be justly deposed.

When the Dutch threw off the Spanish yoke, they considered electing a ruler, but in the end created a republic. Although the Dutch enjoyed more individual rights than citizens elsewhere, their government in the seventeenth century was dominated by an elite of merchants and bankers. The constitutions of the Dutch Republic, the common name for the United Provinces, set up a political system in which the provinces retained a large measure of sovereignty. Each province had its own army, assembly, and elected stadtholder (governor). The federal assembly, the States-General, which sat at the Hague, was composed of delegates from the seven provinces. Its members could do nothing on their own authority. They had to refer all matters to their respective provinces and await directives on how to vote. Often the opposition of a single province was enough to deter action. If a decision was reached, it was not binding on the member states unless it involved foreign affairs and defense.

Operating under such a slow and inefficient system, the republic would probably have collapsed had it not been for the steadying influence of the leadership of the House of Orange. The descendants of William the Silent were men of exceptional ability, and through the office of stadtholder helped to unite the country. Maurice (1584–1625) was stadtholder of five provinces and his successors became stadtholders in six. Since the days of William the Silent and the wars of independence, they had enjoyed enormous prestige, which enabled them to exercise an authority that exceeded that of the office they held. Gradually, they assumed direction of foreign affairs and general supervision of internal administration and were regarded, both at home and abroad, as the rulers of the Dutch Republic. In 1747, the office of stadtholder, then under William IV (1711–1751) became hereditary and the country ceased to be a republic in fact if not in name. It was formally converted into a kingdom by Napoleon and continued as a monarchy after his overthrow in 1815.

THE DECLINE OF ROYAL ABSOLUTISM IN ENGLAND

In the seventeenth century, England reversed the trend toward absolute monarchy and established a semi-popular parliamentary government. The process of change was accompanied by chronic political instability. Puritan resistance to the Elizabethan religious settlement had merged with fierce parliamentary opposition to Stuart absolutism to produce one of the most violent and tumultuous periods England has ever known. Before constitutional rule was achieved, England suffered through a civil war, beheaded one king, experienced a military dictatorship, then restored the monarchy, and finally, in a bloodless revolution, overthrew another king. Since we have already described the earlier events, we begin this narrative with the Restoration of 1660.

The Stuart Restoration, 1660–1688

The Cromwellian experiment having failed, England was ready to restore the monarchy. Living in exile on the continent, Prince Charles, son of Charles I, carefully prepared the way for a Stuart restoration. He promised that if chosen king, he would respect the authority of Parliament and grant a pardon to all rebels, except those lawfully designated to be punished. Proclaimed king by a newly elected Parliament, Charles II (1660–1685) arrived in London on May 29, 1660, amid hysterical jubilation. Charles wanted above all to keep his throne. Patient, shrewd, and manipulative, he operated within the established framework of government, concealing his Catholic bias and desire for absolute authority.

England entered the Restoration period with two major problems unresolved. One was the state's position regarding Catholics and non-Anglican Protestants. Along with the monarchy, the Church of England had been restored as it existed in the reign of Charles I. The Anglican and royalist majority in Parliament, anxious to guard against a revival of Puritan power, enacted a series of repressive

measures between 1661 and 1665 known as the Clarendon Code. The new legislation excluded all but Anglicans to municipal or national office and provided harsh penalties for dissenters who attended services held by non-conforming ministers. Charles was interested less in religious toleration than he was in removing restrictions against Catholics. In 1672, he issued a Declaration of Indulgence, suspending all laws against Catholics and dissenters. Parliament's dread of Catholicism, however, was so intense that Charles was compelled to revoke the declaration. To fortify its victory, Parliament passed the Test Act, which required all officeholders to take communion according to Anglican rites. This forced Charles's brother, James, who had publicly avowed his Catholicism, to resign his admiralship of the navy.

The second problem facing England after 1660 was the relationship between the monarchy and Parliament, which the Restoration settlement had not defined. Charles's ideal political system, an absolute monarchy patterned after the Bourbons, was irreconcilable with the national temper. Treading warily, Charles employed different techniques to increase his power at the expense of Parliament. One way was to become financially independent of Parliament. Parliament had voted the king a grant for life, but this proved insufficient to support his court. As Charles had no wish to become indebted to or involved in strife with Parliament as his father had done, he managed to obtain the necessary funds by other means. He sold Dunkirk to France and married a Portuguese princess who brought a large dowry. For a substantial sum of money, he

entered into the secret Treaty of Dover with Louis XIV, in which he pledged to support the French in a war against the Dutch.

Charles also attempted to influence the actions of Parliament. He appointed members of Parliament as his major advisers, foreshadowing the later cabinet system. The king also sought support for his policies in Parliament through favors and bribes, a practice that led to the development of political parties. Those who were inclined to allow the monarchy relatively broad powers and defended the Anglican church came to be called Tories (Irish robbers) by their opponents. The other faction, derisively nicknamed Whigs (Scottish cattle thieves), favored the subordination of the crown to Parliament and toleration for dissenters. The two groups were not yet true parties, for they lacked organization and discipline.

James II (1685–1688) had little in common with his brother, whom he succeeded in 1685. An arrogant and obstinate man with no sense of political reality, James alienated practically every segment of the population during his brief reign. Having crushed a rebellion shortly after his accession, he kept his army encamped on the outskirts of London and demanded the repeal of the Test Act and Clarendon Code that barred Catholics from office. Parliament, protesting the presence of troops, refused the king's request, whereupon he dismissed it in November 1685. In defiance of the laws, James appointed Catholics to positions in the government, the universities, the army and even the Anglican church. In 1687, James issued a Declaration of Indulgence, which gave religious freedom to all denominations. Because it removed restrictions against the hated Catholics, it thoroughly alienated the Tories while failing to win over the dissenters as he had hoped. He tried seven Anglican bishops for sedition, but they were acquitted by a jury, news of which caused wild public rejoicing. To contemporary English people, it seemed as if James was bent on making Catholicism the estab-lished religion of the country and on reviving the absolutism of his father and grandfather.

The prospect of a Catholic becom-ing the next king of England crystal-lized discontent into an active op-position that ended James's rule. The English people had hitherto tolerated the royal government's tyranny, for James was elderly and without a male heir and it was supposed that on his death the crown would pass to Mary, his eldest daughter by an earlier mar-riage. She was a Protestant and mar-ried to William III of Orange (1672–1702), stadtholder of the Dutch Re-public. In 1688, however, James's second wife, a Catholic, gave birth to a son, apparently assuring a Cath-olic dynasty. To forestall such an

King James II. The narrow-mindedness, rigid temperament, and lack of imagination are not apparent in this portrait of the last Stuart mon-arch. These characteristics, which affected James's mode of governing, dissipated the good will of his subjects and not only brought about his own downfall but also led to permanent changes in the British political system.

United Provinces declare their independence from Spain

Stuart Restoration

The "Glorious Revolution"

Act of Settlement

Maurice of Orange

Bill of Rights

War of the Spanish Succession

Louis XV of France

event, a group of prominent Tories and Whigs, usually bitter political rivals, united and offered the crown to Mary and her husband, William, to rule jointly. In November 1688, William landed with his army in England and was welcomed as a deliverer by the great majority of people. Deserted even by those he considered loyal, James fled to France. The overthrow of James II, known to history as the Glorious Revolution, had brought about a change of rulers with a minimum of bloodshed. The events of November 1688 marked the final triumph of Parliament over the monarchy. By arrogating to itself the authority both to depose and appoint a monarch, Parliament dealt a powerful blow to the concept of the divine right of kings to govern as they saw fit.

The Triumph of Parliament

The Revolution of 1688 brought in its wake major constitutional changes, in the form of legislative enactments. Early in 1689, William III (1689–1702) and Mary II (1689–1694) accepted the throne from Parliament on terms that were later embodied in a formal statute known as the Bill of Rights. This important document asserted and extended the rights of English people and laid down the principles of parliamentary supremacy. Another law eased restrictions against the dissenters in recognition of their opposition to James II. The Toleration Act of 1689 granted freedom of worship to non-Anglican Protestants, but continued to bar them from civil and military office. It conferred no privileges on Catholics, Unitarians, or Jews. The act, with all its limitations, marks the first step toward religious toleration in England.

Speaker of the House of Lords Offering William III and Mary the Crown. Initially, Parliament wanted Mary as sole sovereign, the successor by hereditary right. Mary, however, refused to reign alone. For his part, William would not accept the subordinate position of a prince consort. He insisted on being king for life; otherwise he would remain in his own land. Thus it was that Parliament proclaimed William and Mary joint sovereigns, the actual administration resting with William alone.

THE BILL OF RIGHTS

And thereupon the said lords spiritual and temporal and Commons . . . for the vindication and assertion of their ancient rights and liberties declare:

1. That the pretended power of suspending laws, or the execution of laws, by regal authority, without consent of parliament, is illegal.

2. That the pretended power of dispensing with laws, or the execution of laws, by regal authority, as it hath been assumed and exercised of late, is illegal . . .

4. That levying money for or to the use of the Crown by pretense of prerogative, without grant of parliament, for longer time or in other manner than the same is or shall be granted, is illegal.

5. That it is the right of the subjects to petition the king, and all commitments and prosecutions for such petitioning are illegal.

6. That the raising or keeping a standing army within the kingdom in time of peace, unless it be with consent of parliament, is against law.

7. That the subjects which are Protestants may have arms for their defense suitable to their conditions, and as allowed by law.

8. That election of members of Parliament ought to be free.

9. That the freedom of speech, and debates or proceedings in parliament, ought not to be impeached or questioned in any court or place out of parliament.

10. That excessive bail ought not to be required, nor excessive fines imposed nor cruel and unusual punishments inflicted . . .

13. And that for redress of all grievances, and for the amending, strengthening, and preserving of the laws, parliament ought to be held frequently. . . .

The said lords spiritual and temporal, and commons assembled at Westminster, do resolve that William and Mary, prince and princess of Orange, be, and be declared, king and queen of England, France, and Ireland, and the dominions thereunto belonging, to hold the crown and royal dignity of the said kingdoms and dominions to them the said prince and princess during their lives.*

Like the two earlier safeguards of English liberty, the Magna Carta and the Petition of Right, the Bill of Rights was predominantly specific and negative and did not deal in broad generalities of political theory. Nevertheless, the Bill established the essential constitutional principles underlying limited monarchy and remains the closest to a formal constitution that the British possess. The Bill of Rights also served as an inspiration for republican forms of government. The first ten amendments to the U.S. constitution (1791) and much of the French Declaration of the Rights of Man (1789) owe a debt to the English declaration of 1689.

*Cited in Edward P. Cheyney, *Readings in English History*, Ginn, (Boston and New York: 1922) pp. 545–547.

Finally, Parliament planned the order of succession to the English throne. In 1694, Mary had died of smallpox, leaving William without an heir to the throne. Mary's younger sister Anne was still alive, but her last surviving child died in 1701. To ensure the exclusion of the Catholic Stuarts, Parliament created the Act of Settlement in 1701. The bill prescribed that if Anne succeeded William and died without an heir, the crown would go to the closest Protestant blood relation, Sophia of Hanover, and then to her Protestant descendants.

William, who ruled alone after Mary's death in 1694, was more interested in defending the Dutch Republic against the attacks of Louis XIV of France than in governing England. He generally followed the dictates of Parliament, as he constantly required English resources and money, and left his ministers in charge of internal administration. William's hostility to France changed the direction of England's foreign policy. Under his leadership, England joined the coalition (League of Augsburg) against France, marking the start of a series of wars between the two nations that was to continue for more than a century. William's skill in directing the war effort frustrated Louis XIV's plans to dominate Europe and in the process made England a great power.

Anne (1702–1714), the last of the Protestant Stuarts, faced serious difficulties abroad. In an unsuccessful attempt to prevent Louis XIV from placing a French Bourbon prince on the Spanish throne, England became involved in the long and bitterly contested War of the Spanish Succession (1701–1713). The most outstanding accomplishment of Anne's reign was the formal union of England and Scotland in 1707. The Act of Union created the United Kingdom of Great Britain, with one ruler, one parliament, and one flag—the "Union Jack" combining the Scottish cross of St. Andrew and the English cross of St. George. At Anne's death, the crown passed to the elector of Hanover, George, son of the deceased Sophia.

Significant as they were, the events of 1688–1689 did not constitute a democratic revolution. An oligarchy of wealthy interests, largely landowning gentry elected by a very limited suffrage, governed the House of Commons. The House of Lords was composed of hereditary peers and high Anglican prelates. Thus from 1689 until at least 1832, when the Great Reform Bill was passed, the aristocracy controlled the government.

The Development of Cabinet Government

The Glorious Revolution had given Parliament predominance in the British government but had not reduced the monarch to a mere figurehead. The king retained strong executive powers. He was commander of the armed forces, directed foreign policy, created peerages, and appointed officials to ecclesiastical positions as well as to posts in the government and royal household. In theory, the monarch could also veto legislation enacted by Parliament, but the last royal

veto was in 1707. Through personal loyalties, patronage, and the granting of honors and favors, the crown could and did exert considerable influence over Parliament.

As chief executive, the king was responsible for the day-to-day conduct of state business. Yet final authority rested with Parliament. How could Parliament control the executive branch of government while assuring the smooth and efficient transaction of state affairs?

The solution lay with the evolution of the cabinet system. Its origins dated back to the privy council, a body of officials and dignitaries chosen by the king to advise him on matters of policy. On coming to the throne in 1689, William III, acknowledging that his chief advisers should be acceptable to the legislature, selected them from the two leading parties. He soon realized, however, that the wheels of government operated more smoothly if his cabinet was restricted to men who controlled a majority in the House of Commons. In establishing this precedent, William continued to regard his cabinet ministers as responsible only to the crown. He assumed, as did his successor, Anne, that it was the ruler's role to administer the daily affairs of the state and formulate broad policy. Both regularly presided over cabinet meetings, participated in policy discussions, and occasionally acted without reference to their advisers.

The presence on the throne of the early Hanoverians, George I (1714–1727) and George II (1727–1760), encouraged the trend toward cabinet government. George I could neither speak nor understand English and soon stopped attending cabinet meetings, a practice that reduced the crown's

influence in shaping policy. George II was also disinterested in the intricacies of British politics and followed his father's example.

The absence of the first two Hanoverians from cabinet meetings opened the way for one of the most influential ministers, Sir Robert Walpole, to conduct the discussions and serve as intermediary between the king and cabinet. For some twenty years, from 1721 to 1742, he dominated English politics, enjoying the good will of both kings and leading the Whig party in the House of Commons. Walpole is generally recognized as the first "prime" minister, although he persistently disclaimed the title. Thereafter, it became traditional for the king to appoint as head of the cabinet the acknowledged leader of the strongest party in the Commons. In this way, the cabinet exercised executive power in the king's name but in response to the wishes, and subject to the approval, of Parliament. When Walpole was defeated in the House of Commons in 1742, he resigned at once. His action established the principle that a ministry must resign when it ceased to command the confidence of the lower House.

George III (1760–1820) attempted to subvert the growing power of cabinet government during the early decades of his reign. Born and educated in Great Britain, George believed in the supremacy of Parliament. Still, he wanted to be a "patriotic king," making the cabinet responsible to him and ruling above political parties in accordance with his perception of national welfare. By 1770, George had secured control of Parliament after a decade during which he destroyed the power of the Whig opposition and created his own party,

Sir Robert Walpole Presiding over a Cabinet Meeting. A master orator and unrivaled manager of men, Walpole sought to keep the peace, to encourage trade, and to avoid any dispute that might disturb the collaboration of the king and Parliament. Walpole held a low opinion of human nature, believing that most men can be bought. By patronage, bribery, pressure of all kinds, and hard work, he not only controlled his own Whig party but often enticed some Tories into supporting him as well. His tactics, however unsavory, ensured adoption of policies that gave Great Britain twenty years of quiet government.

known as the King's Friends (mostly Tories), with the help of royal favors and pensions. Over the next dozen years George imposed his personal rule through a docile cabinet headed by Lord North. For England his statesmanship was ruinous, resulting in the loss of most of Great Britain's North American colonies and a huge increase of the national debt. The unpopularity of George's policies, coupled with his periodic lapses into insanity, eroded royal influence and enabled the cabinet to regain the initiative. Ever since, the task of governing Great Britain has belonged to the prime minister and his cabinet colleagues, subject to the approval of Parliament.

ENLIGHTENED DESPOTISM

A new form of absolutism, which came to be called enlightened despotism, emerged on the continent after 1740. Enlightened despotism owed its appearance partly to the writings of the Enlightenment philosophes but mostly to the mid-eighteenth-century wars, which drove some of the crowned heads of Europe to reconstruct their states in anticipation of the next conflict. Enlightened despots believed that their own interests could best be served by adopting national reforms. Measures designed to promote the development of the economy increased the wealth of their subjects but also provided the treasury with more revenues to finance larger armies. By curbing the power of the nobility and clergy, building up a trained and salaried officialdom, and remodeling administrative practices, these monarchs strengthened the central government and increased its efficiency. Other reforms, which resulted in religious toleration, more progressive legal and judicial systems, better health services, a higher level of popular education, solidified internal political support for their rule.

Many of these kinds of reforms had been done by kings before. The difference between the new monarchs and the old absolutists was primarily in attitude and style. Enlightened despots said little about divine or hereditary rights to their thrones. However, holding little faith in the ability of the masses to govern themselves, they firmly believed that a paternalistic monarchy was the best form of government. Their duty, so they claimed, was to act in the interest of their subjects, but in reality few measured up to the image they created of themselves. They ignored the philosophes' cry for social equality and individual rights and generally were loathe to effect any social or political change that might sooner or later turn out to be at their expense. They were more enlightened than their predecessors, but they were still despots. Lesser rulers included Leopold of Tuscany (1765–1790), Charles III of Spain (1759–1788) and Gustav III of Sweden (1771–1792). Of the major rulers, the three most often associated with that title, correctly or not, were Frederick the Great of Prussia (1740–1786), Joseph II of Austria (1780–1790), and Catherine the Great of Russia (1762–1796).

Frederick the Great of Prussia

During the second half of the eighteenth century, Frederick II gained the reputation as the ideal enlightened despot. Possessing an excellent mind, he had from boyhood shown a liking for art, literature, music, and philosophy. He wrote poetry and essays and his treatises on government were sought out by monarchs who wished to emulate his rule. He fervently admired the French philosophes and entertained Voltaire at his court.

Frederick's brilliance lay not so much in actual innovation as in mastering the details of the system he inherited. He worked extremely hard at being king, since he believed that "as the first servant of the state" (as he described himself), his duties were proportionate to his rank. Rising before dawn, he labored at his desk until evening, when he turned to cultural pursuits. No aspect of his government escaped his attention. He visited each part of his kingdom annually, studying problems, talking to citizens, and correcting abuses. He kept a close check on his administrators by corresponding frequently with them and by sending out royal agents to report on their activities. During Frederick's reign, the Prussian civil service attained a level of honesty and efficiency that was unsurpassed in Europe.

Frederick's economic and agricultural policies were designed to achieve national self-sufficiency. Wedded to mercantilist principles, he imposed protective tariffs to foster the development of infant industries, opened new mines, and was careful to protect Prussia's natural resources. As the greatest landlord in Prussia, Frederick devoted special attention to agriculture. The state introduced and supervised scientific farming techniques and the cultivation of new crops such as potatoes and turnips, reclaimed vast areas of farmland, and encouraged the immigration of thousands of farmers.

The most enduring of Frederick's contributions to Prussia were probably his improvements in the administration of justice, his codification of the law, and his policy of religious toleration. He reduced bribery by paying judges adequate salaries, established uniform legal fees, simplified court procedures, and abolished the use of torture to extract confessions except in cases of murder and treason. A new legal code, not completed until 1794, eliminated regional differences and made the laws simpler and more equitable. Personally indifferent to religion, Frederick was the most tolerant ruler in Europe, saying, "All religions shall be tolerated in my states; here everyone may seek salvation in his own way." Jews, however, still faced civil disabilities.

On the other hand, Frederick failed to make significant progress in many areas. He talked at length about the value of a strong educational system, but his improvements were few and unimportant. He did little to change the social order as he found it. Believing in the hierarchical concept of society, he rigidly defined the legal status of the different classes. Because he depended on the aristocracy for service in the army and bureaucracy, he refrained from abolishing serfdom, although he recognized that the institution was an abomination. He permitted only limited freedom of speech and of the press.

In foreign affairs, Frederick's use of power politics was inconsistent with the humanitarian and pacific ideals of the philosophes. A considerable part of Frederick's reign was consumed by two major wars. Frederick had inherited from his father, Frederick William I, a well-filled treasury and perhaps the finest army in Eu-

Frederick II and Voltaire in the Study of the Royal Palace of Sans Souci in Potsdam. Having finally attracted the French intellectual to his side after repeated invitations, Frederick appointed him a court chamberlain and gave him a generous pension. But the relationship between the Prussian monarch and Voltaire was always difficult, in large measure because both were too prickly and self-centered. After two years, Voltaire left Prussia, and in his memoirs, published after his death, poured out his wrath in a scurrilous account of the private life of his former patron.

rope. Although Frederick William had been content merely to build and parade the Prussian army, Frederick was ready to use it for a suitable cause.

Frederick II did not have to wait long to try out his army. Five months after he became king, the Habsburg emperor Charles VI (1711–1740) died. Lacking a male heir, Charles succeeded in obtaining the signature of all the states of Europe, except Bavaria, to the Pragmatic Sanction. This document guaranteed that his daughter Maria Theresa would assume the crown with her territories intact.

Charles had barely been laid to rest when Frederick, without a declaration of war and in defiance of the Pragmatic Sanction, seized the rich Austrian province of Silesia.

This act of aggression by the young Prussian king, who ironically had just published a treatise assailing as immoral the principles of Machiavelli, provoked the long and bloody War of the Austrian Succession (1740–1748). France, Spain, Bavaria, and Saxony joined Prussia, lured by the hope of despoiling Habsburg territory. Great Britain took the side of

Maria Theresa, motivated by its bitter colonial rivalry with France and by a desire to see the Austrian (former Spanish) Netherlands, with which it enjoyed a lucrative trade, remain in friendly hands. The fighting broadened into a worldwide conflict, involving the fate of the Habsburg lands in Europe and a colonial struggle in the western hemisphere and India. Habsburg armies fended off Prussia's allies but were unable to eject Frederick from Silesia. The war ended in a stalemate in 1748. The Treaty of Aix-la-Chapelle restored conditions as they had existed before the conflict, except that Prussia retained Silesia. The pact proved to be merely a truce, for Maria Theresa would not reconcile herself to the loss of her province.

During the next eight years of uneasy peace, a "diplomatic revolution" occurred in which the chief antagonists in the first war changed sides in readiness for the second. In 1756, Austria and France buried their age-long enmity and signed a secret treaty, to which Russia, Sweden, and Saxony also subscribed, agreeing to divide most of Frederick's kingdom among themselves. Spain later entered the alliance against Prussia. Only Great Britain, already at war again with France in the colonies, supported Frederick.

Facing a powerful enemy coalition, Frederick struck before France and Russia were ready to take the field, opening the Seven Years' War (1756–1763). Absorbed in the struggle overseas, Great Britain furnished Frederick with subsidies but little military help. For five years, Frederick held his badly coordinated enemies at bay as he trampled back and forth across his ravaged kingdom. His rapid night marches, ability to elude a pursuing army and then strike unexpectedly at another, management of battles against heavy odds, and indomitable spirit astounded Europe and earned him the title of "the Great." By 1762, his ever-dwindling army was exhausted, he was short of funds, and much of his territory was under the heel of the invaders. Frederick was rescued from his predicament when the Russian Tsarina Elizabeth (1741–1762) died and was briefly replaced by the erratic Peter III (1762). Peter was a fanatical admirer of Frederick and promptly withdrew from the war. Thereafter, Frederick managed to hold his own until his enemies wearied of the struggle. The Treaty of Hubertusburg made no significant changes in the prewar boundaries and confirmed Frederick's possession of Silesia.

Frederick participated in no more major wars, although in 1772 he collaborated with Russia and Austria in partially dismembering Poland. He took as his share West Prussia, which linked East Prussia with the main body of the Hohenzollern state. Under Frederick, Prussia had more than doubled in size and population (see Map 51). With its efficient government, sound economy, and superb army, Prussia was the dominant power in central Europe at Frederick's death.

Joseph II of Austria

The most sincere but the least successful of the enlightened despots was Joseph II of Austria, son of Maria Theresa. Joseph became coruler with his mother in 1765, but she retained final authority until her death in 1780. In the eighteenth century, Austria was

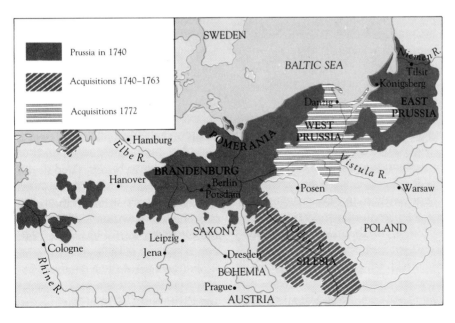

MAP 51

Expansion of Prussia under Frederick II. In two wars against Austria, Frederick secured Silesia and through diplomacy added another large block of land at the expense of Poland, linking Brandenburg and East Prussia. The powerful state created by Frederick was the most striking political achievement of that era.

445

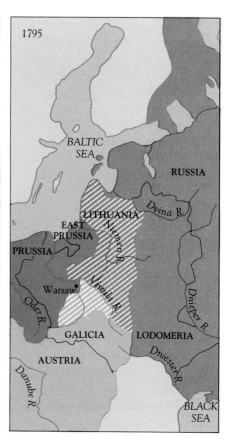

MAP 52

Partitions of Poland. Indefensible borders and internal chaos, largely the result of a highly decentralized government, made Poland easy prey for covetous neighbors. In 1772, Russia, Prussia, and Austria each took a substantial bite, depriving Poland of one-third of its territory and half of its population. In the second partition, in 1793, Russia and Prussia annexed more Polish territory while Austria, preoccupied with a war against revolutionary France, got nothing. Two years later, Russia, Prussia, and Austria divided what remained of Poland. It was not until after World War I that Poland was restored as an independent state.

a loosely-knit empire of diverse peoples and traditions, without a common purpose or will. Although Maria Theresa had enacted some reforms, she was on the whole a cautious monarch, content to follow established practice and careful, whenever possible, not to offend vested interests. Joseph was impatient of custom and less willing to compromise. A disciple of the philosophes, his object was to sweep away archaic institutions and create a new state based on the highest ideals of justice and reason.

Joseph saw that the central administration of the state needed to be tightened if he hoped to enforce his program of reform. To that end, he suppressed provincial assemblies and

other vestiges of local independence, established new administrative districts staffed by his own bureaucrats, and made German the official language.

Joseph's religious policies reflected his tolerance for all faiths and his desire to subordinate the Catholic church to the state. Although a practicing Catholic, Joseph held that "each of my subjects must be reinstated in the possession of his natural rights." One of his first acts was to grant citizenship and religious toleration to Protestants and Orthodox Christians. Jews were granted similar rights and most of the disabilities against them removed. Joseph sought in various ways to eliminate the political influence of the pope and the church. He decreed that no papal bull be published in Austria without the express permission of the government. Bishops were made to swear allegiance to the state, education was freed of church control, and civil marriages were legalized. All monasteries deemed unproductive were dissolved. The wealth of these confiscated properties went to support schools, hospitals, and charitable institutions. Rome naturally protested the assaults on its authority, but in spite of the pope's visit to Vienna, Joseph would concede nothing.

In economic and social matters, Joseph was undoubtedly motivated by the welfare and happiness of his subjects. Joseph was an admirer of the physiocratic theories of economic freedom, but he never completely abandoned the prevailing mercantilist views. He did, however, relax tariff imports, terminate monopolies, and eliminate the power of the guilds to regulate manufacturing.

Joseph expressed his humane concerns by a number of acts. He issued a new penal code that forbade torture and reduced the number of crimes subject to capital punishment. He reorganized the judicial system, making laws more uniform and rational, lessening the influence of local landlords, and establishing equal punishment for the same offenses regardless of the culprit's social standing. Attendance in schools increased but Joseph's hope for universal and compulsory education never materialized. He applied an equitable tax on land, sweeping away the much-cherished exemption previously enjoyed by the privileged classes. Perhaps his most revolutionary move was to abolish serfdom. This legislation entitled the serfs to leave

the land, marry whomever they pleased, and choose their own occupations.

Joseph's rapid efforts to reconstruct Austrian society came to grief. Convinced that he was on the right course, he allowed nothing to stand in his way, riding roughshod over cherished traditions and ingrained prejudices. "Joseph always wishes to take the second step before he has taken the first," was the perceptive judgment of Frederick the Great. The aristocracy chafed at the loss of privileges; the Catholic church resented its diminished status in the state; and Hungary and the Austrian Netherlands revolted against the emperor's plans to make German the official language and to suppress provincial self-government. Joseph died in 1790 at the age of forty-nine, a broken and disillusioned man. Shortly before his death, he summed up his career in an epitaph he composed for himself: "Here lies a prince whose intentions were pure and who had the misfortune to see all his plans miscarry." Indeed, most of his reforms were reversed by his cautious brother and successor, Leopold II (1790–1792). The outcome might have been different if Joseph had enjoyed the support of a large and vigorous middle class such as existed in France.

Catherine the Great of Russia

Catherine II owed her reputation for enlightenment to skillful self-advertising, not to her record of accomplishment. A German princess who went to Russia at the age of fifteen to marry the heir to the throne, she assumed power in 1762 following the murder of her half-demented hus-

band, Peter III. Catherine fancied herself an intellectual. She wrote plays and essays, immersed herself in the literature of the Enlightenment, and corresponded regularly with a number of philosophes, expressing sympathy with many of the ideas they supported. Being a foreigner and a usurper, however, she recognized that she could not afford to alienate the aristocracy who had engineered the palace revolution that deposed Peter. Consequently, her good intentions were rarely translated into deeds.

Catherine did begin her reign auspiciously, summoning a legislative commission to codify the laws of Russia. The 564 deputies, chosen from every class except the serfs, assembled in 1767. Drawing heavily from Montesquieu's *Spirit of Laws*, Catherine prepared a set of *Instructions* to guide their deliberations. The *Instructions* proclaimed equality before the law, denounced capital punishment and torture, and called into question the institution of serfdom. The commission met sporadically for a year and a half, but from the outset it split along class lines. In particular, the peasant deputies clashed with the gentry, who refused to make any concessions for the benefit of the serfs. Catherine used the outbreak of a war against the Ottoman Empire in 1768 as a pretext to disband the commission. The commission failed to accomplish its work, but from Catherine's point of view it had served some purpose. It gave her considerable information about the nation and enhanced her image in the west.

The antagonisms that had simmered in the legislative commission exploded in a great serf uprising in 1773. The lot of the serfs, who comprised about half the peasant population of Russia, had been deteriorating steadily. The landlord's authority over them was practically absolute. Serf owners could transfer them from the land to work in factories or mines, sell them singly or in families, order or forbid their marriage, and punish them at will. Pretending to be Peter III, Emelian Pugachev, an illiterate cossack, sounded the call to arms in September 1773, promising freedom from serfdom, taxation, and military service for the people. Tens of thousands of serfs and servile workers flocked to Pugachev's banner. The rebels threatened Moscow before they were dispersed. Pugachev, betrayed by his own men, was taken to Moscow in an iron cage and publicly executed.

After this outbreak, Catherine dismissed any further thought of rural reform and closed ranks with the nobility. The line that separated serfdom from the chattel slavery, to which blacks in the United States were subjected, became almost indistinguishable. Catherine allowed landlords greater authority over their serfs. Huge grants of land to her favorites converted relatively free crown peasants into serfs. Serfdom was extended into new areas such as the Ukraine. In 1785, Catherine drew up a charter for the nobility, confirming earlier privileges and exemptions and adding certain new ones. Members of the aristocracy were exempt from personal taxes, military service, corporal punishment, and trial by judges whose status was inferior to their own. Under Catherine, the nobility reduced its responsibilities while increasing its privileges.

The Pugachev rebellion also caused Catherine to introduce a new system of local government. Frightened by the collapse of authority under the strain of the revolt, the empress proposed to strengthen provincial government through a process of decentralization. She divided the country into fifty provinces, which in turn were divided into districts. At the provincial level, the governor and his associates were appointed, but in the districts, the officials were mostly elected by the aristocracy.

In other domestic areas, Catherine carried out such reforms as she felt were politically feasible. She founded hospitals and orphanages, assisted artists and writers, and established schools and academies for the upper class. A believer in laissez-faire principles, Catherine abolished internal

A Flattering Portrait of Catherine the Great as an Equestrian. Her awareness that she was not beautiful prompted Catherine to surround herself with young and handsome men. The older she grew, the younger were her favorites. The empress had twenty-one known lovers, the last after she had turned sixty. As each lover dropped from favor, she rewarded him with a title, estate, serfs, and money, which were said to be based on his sexual performance.

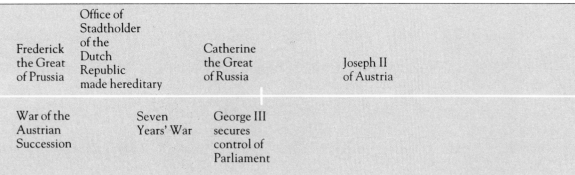

tolls and monopolies and fostered a series of commercial treaties with other countries. Hundreds of new factories sprang up all over Russia. These were built mostly on the estates of the nobility, where serf labor could be used. Some peasants benefited from the new policy by becoming active in cottage industries.

Catherine pursued an expansionist and unscrupulous foreign policy. "If I could live for two hundred years," she remarked to a friend, "all of Europe would be brought under Russian rule." Catherine's drive for warm water ports provoked two wars with the Ottoman Empire. In these wars, she gained the north shore of the Black Sea and vague rights to protect the Christian subjects of the sultan—rights that her successors used as a justification for repeated intervention in Turkey's domestic affairs. Through three partitions of Poland (1772, 1793, and 1795; see Map 52), she acquired about two-thirds of the once huge Polish state, pushing Russia's western boundary deep into central Europe. Catherine's conquests, for which she is called "the Great," made Russia a major European power.

Catherine's Polish acquisitions included a very large Jewish population, which her successors sought both to reduce and assimilate. The resulting oppression accelerated a Jewish drift back to western Europe and in the later nineteenth century, a massive migration to the United States.

Unreformed France

Among the great states, France alone cannot claim to have produced an enlightened ruler. Although raised to believe in the principle of divine right monarchy, Louis XV (1715–1774) was not cast in the same mold as Louis XIV. Indolent, fickle, and devoted to the pleasures of the flesh, Louis lacked the interest or patience to oversee the details of government in the manner of his predecessor. While seeking new ways to alleviate his boredom, he permitted the current woman of his interest to influence state policy. His succession of mistresses, the most prominent of whom were Mme. de Pompadour and Mme. du Barry, encouraged his spendthrift habits and misused their power, rewarding and enriching their friends and wreaking vengeance on their enemies. In thirty years, eighteen foreign secretaries and fourteen controller-generals served in Louis's

administration. Louis's haphazard and irresponsible conduct of policy dragged France into lengthy and unprofitable wars. France did not attain its goals in the War of the Austrian Succession, and not only sustained a shattering defeat in Europe during the Seven Years' War but also lost most of its vast overseas possessions to Great Britain. The immense cost of prosecuting these wars, added to the profligate extravagance at the court, cut deeply into the nation's finances.

In the last decade of his reign, Louis XV was shaken enough by his own unpopularity and by the growing financial crisis of the nation to attempt, in concert with his chief minister, René Maupeou, a few essential reforms. Their most controversial action was to propose shifting some of the national tax burden to the hitherto untaxed nobility and clergy. Louis's edicts were challenged by the regional parlements, or supreme law courts, as an infringement of the natural rights of French people, in particular those of the privileged classes. Because of the weakness of the central government under Louis, the parlements, made up of judges with noble status, had acquired a virtual veto power and frequently used it to

449

hinder royal programs or to interfere with legislation. When Maupeou with the king's support initiated new reforms, the parlements challenged them. Tired of their obstructionism, Louis abolished the parlements and created new law courts with restricted authority. The reforms had barely begun to take effect when Louis died of smallpox in 1774. His successor lacked the strength and determination to continue the struggle against the privileged classes.

SUMMARY

Although absolute monarchy was already established as a dominant trend in early modern Europe, two states, the Dutch Republic and England, evolved in an opposite direction—toward constitutional rule. The Dutch replaced Spanish tyranny with a loose association of provinces, each retaining its individual sovereignty. Although republican in form, the government was in fact controlled by an oligarchy of wealthy merchants and a hereditary succession of powerful stadtholders. In England, the Glorious Revolution destroyed once and for all the Stuart quest for divine right absolutism and laid the foundation for a constitutional monarchy. In the eighteenth century, the development of cabinet government, in which executive power was exercised by ministers responsible to the House of Commons, progressively reduced the king to essentially a ceremonial role.

In the second half of the eighteenth century, Europe produced a new breed of kings—enlightened despots—who were influenced by the ideas of the French philosophes. These monarchs were no more willing than Louis XIV to sacrifice personal power or national glory, but they claimed that they used their authority for the benefit of the people. The three most often cited as enlightened monarchs were Frederick the Great of Prussia, Joseph II of Austria, and Catherine the Great of Russia. To varying degrees, these monarchs rooted out irrational customs and vested interests, made administrative improvements, adopted progressive economic measures, curbed the power of the nobility, and proclaimed religious toleration and equality of all before the law. However, these benevolent monarchs were primarily interested in strengthening the state as a military instrument, and indulged in ruthless territorial aggrandizement.

Equally significant was the absence of enlightened despotism in France. Louis XV was indifferent to affairs of state, and without a firm directing hand the French government moved in fits and starts, pulled in different directions by the passing influence of short-lived advisers. As a consequence, political abuses multiplied and the nation's financial crisis deepened. Few people at the time realized that these danger signals foretold the advent of a cataclysm that would bring down the old regime.

SELECTED SOURCES

*Bernard, Paul P. *Joseph II.* 1968. A concise and balanced treatment of the ill-fated monarch.

*Chimes, Stanley B. *English Constitutional History.* 1967. Succinct account by an eminent scholar, particularly good on seventeenth- and eighteenth-century developments.

*De Madariaga, Isabel. *Russia in the Age of Catherine the Great.* 1981. Meticulously researched biography, sympathetic to Catherine.

*Fraser, Antonia. *Royal Charles: Charles II and the Restoration.* 1979. A lively and thoughtful biography.

*Gagliardo, John G. *Enlightened Despotism*. 1967. A good introduction to the subject.

Gooch, G. P. *Louis XV: The Monarchy in Decline*. 1956. A highly respected study.

*Haley, Kenneth H. D. *The Dutch in the Seventeenth Century*. 1972. A richly illustrated book, emphasizing Dutch accomplishments.

Jones, James R. *Country and Court: England, 1658–1714*. 1978. An excellent treatment of the period.

Miller, J. *James II: A Study in Kingship*. 1977. An even-handed and scholarly volume in which James II is depicted as personally honest but sadly lacking in political acumen.

*Pushkin, Alexander. *The Captain's Daughter*. Various editions. A colorful Russian novel, set against the Pugachev rebellion.

*Plumb, J. H. *England in the Eighteenth Century*. Various editions. A good short account.

*Plumb, J. H. *The First Four Georges*. 1956. Well written and informative.

Ritter, Gerhard. *Frederick the Great*. 1968. A useful assessment by a leading German scholar.

*Thackeray, William M. *The Story of Henry Esmond*. Various editions. A fictional aristocrat caught in intrigue and rebellion during the reign of George II. Also a motion picture.

*Available in paperback.

The Struggle to Dominate the Colonial World (1650–1830)

The separating distance was growing less and less. A hundred paces now! Would that grim line of redcoats never fire! Seventy-five!! Fifty!! Forty!! . . . "Ready!—Present!—Fire!!! . . . the British volleys crashed forth, from right to left, battalion by battalion, all down that thin red line.

The stricken front rank of the French fell before these double-shotted volleys almost to a man. When the smoke cleared off the British had . . . closed up some twenty paces . . . reloading as they came. And now, taking the French in front and flanks, they fired as fast as they could, but steadily and under perfect control. The French on the other hand, were firing wildly, and simply crumbling away under that well-aimed storm of lead . . . In a vain, last effort to lead them on their officers faced death and found it. Montcalm, . . . told he had only a few hours to live, replied, "So much the better, I shall not see the surrender of Quebec."

Wolfe, with three bullet wounds, also lay dying. "They run; see how they run!" a subordinate shouted. "Who run?" Wolfe demanded, like a man roused from sleep. "The enemy, sir. Egad, they give way everywhere!" Wolfe, turning on his side, murmured, "Now, God be praised, I will die in peace."

On September 13, 1759, on the Plains of Abraham outside the fortress-city of Quebec in New France (Canada), the British army led by James Wolfe defeated the French forces of Louis de Montcalm and delivered French North America to Great Britain. Coupled with victories over the French in the Caribbean and India, the conquest of New France gave Great Britain colonial supremacy and dominance of the global trade network. This world-wide confrontation between Great Britain and France had been building throughout the eighteenth century as the great age of seaborne discovery was coming to a close. Late in the eighteenth century and early in the nineteenth, however, successful independence movements throughout the western hemisphere indicated that Latin and British Americans had developed to the point where they could stand alone.

A Major Setback to Imperialism. On October 19, 1781, at Yorktown, Virginia, victorious rebel colonial forces, in conjunction with French army and navy units, force the surrender of Cornwallis's British army, opening the way for independence. In this detail from John Trumbull's somewhat overdramatized painting, General O'Hara, representing Cornwallis, formally capitulates to General Washington. Yale University Art Gallery.

The West Meets the Pacific. Captain Cook's reception by the peoples of the Pacific varied as widely as the different cultures he visited. Overawed by his huge vessel, most groups received him peacefully, but he eventually lost his life in Hawaii. Here Cook lands in the New Hebrides in 1774. A salvo of greeting—and intimidation—stuns a few Hebrideans, but most, although excited, stand their ground. Cook holds out a palm frond as a symbol of peace.

NEW EXPLORATION, NEW COMPETITION

In the late seventeenth and eighteenth centuries, Europeans continued to expand their knowledge of far-off areas of the world, mostly through sea exploration. The voyages of exploration were motivated by the usual commercial and competitive factors, joined in this era by an increased interest in increasing scientific knowledge. As the explorers uncovered areas of the world that Europeans had not known before, traders and warriors bent on seizing control of these areas followed close behind.

Charting the Pacific

Europeans explored the Indian ocean and other regions, but by the eighteenth century they were concentrating their attention on the Pacific.

In their endeavors they were materially aided by the new chronometer, which for the first time allowed navigators to calculate the correct longitude in determining a ship's location. Led by the greatest explorer of the age, Captain James Cook of Great Britain, European ships stopped at Tahiti, Hawaii, and other islands of the central and south Pacific. Following up on earlier sightings and shipwrecks, Dutch and British explorers, chiefly Abel Tasman and Cook, found a land mass large enough to be classified as a continent, later named Australia. Although western Australia was a desert, the east appeared to have a moderate climate suitable for European settlement.

Fortunately for most of the inhabitants of the central and south Pacific, European explorers found few resources they wished to garner or control and left the area relatively unexploited for several generations. Farther south, explorations eliminated the possibility of a rich continent suggested by Ptolemy, but Europeans began to detect a continental land mass frozen in the Antarctic ice. More important, they found sources of future wealth in the whales and seals of that region, whose oil and pelts were in great demand, particularly in China.

Led by Cook, Europeans also explored the North Pacific and its North American and Asian shorelines, finding more whales and seals, as well as sea otters, a new source of wealth. In 1728 the Russian explorer Vitus Bering found that Asia and North America were separated by a body of water. Cook later penetrated this strait, discovering an ice-filled sea and ending the last glimmer of hope for an open waterway through the Arctic. By 1779, when Cook was killed in a skirmish with the Hawaiians, little was left of the globe for Europeans to explore by sea, although the interior of some of the continents still remained unknown to them.

Contesting for North America

During the seventeenth century, impelled by a search for riches, the French penetrated farther into North America from their foothold in the St. Lawrence Valley (see Map 53). Moving by bateaux (heavy canoes) along rivers, lakes, and portages the French moved westward through the Great Lakes. Turning south, Father Jacques Marquette and Louis Joliet, followed by the Sieur de La Salle, descended the Mississippi.

Through these and other such expeditions France claimed the enormous Mississippi-Missouri-Ohio basin extending from the Appalachians to the Rocky Mountains and from the Great Lakes to the Gulf coast between Florida and Mexico, which they named Louisiana. The French later found that the lower Mississippi was a valuable area for the deerskin trade and for planting sugar.

The French were primarily interested in beaver pelts, however, and

Map 53
North America in 1700, 1763, 1783, 1803. The four maps illustrate the changing fortunes of the European nations as they struggled to control the North American continent. In the overall pattern, the Spanish and the British added to their holdings at the expense of the French, followed by the creation and expansion of a new nation, the United States of America. An increasing number of powers laid claim to the northwest coast.

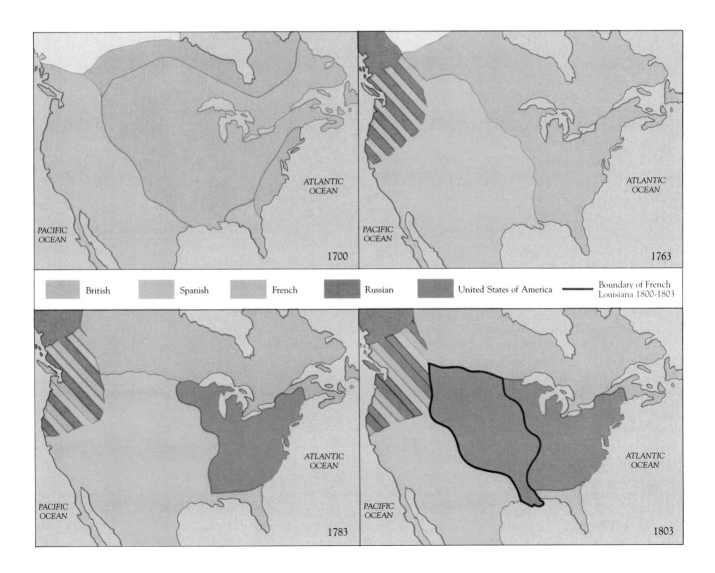

| British | Spanish | French | Russian | United States of America | —— Boundary of French Louisiana 1800-1803 |

these were to be found chiefly to the west and northwest of the Great Lakes. During the eighteenth century French voyageurs moved to the foothills of the Rocky Mountains, setting up a series of fur-trading posts. Not to be outdone, the English established the Hudson's Bay Company in 1670 to obtain a share of the far northern fur trade.

During the eighteenth century several nations competed vigorously for control of the remote but lucrative pelt-laden Pacific coast of North America. The Spanish, temporarily invigorated by the leadership of its new Bourbon dynasty, pushed northward out of Mexico. Initially led by Father Junípero Serra, they moved up the Pacific coast into California, establishing a string of missions and presidios (military posts) from San Diego (1769) and Los Angeles (1781) as far north as San Francisco (1776) and Solano (1823). Spanish sea captains explored the coastline farther to the north, extending Spanish claims as far as Alaska.

The Spanish were soon challenged by the Russians, who had moved into Alaska, looking for sea otter and seal pelts. Ignoring the claims of the Spanish, they moved eastward along the Alaskan coast and then turned south. By the early nineteenth century the Russians had pushed their claims well down the coast. Mounting a direct challenge to the Spanish, in 1812 they established Fort Ross, forty miles north of the San Francisco presidio.

Meanwhile, other nations were pressing their interests in the area. In the 1790s, Great Britain claimed the northwest coast by virtue of George Vancouver's voyages and Alexander Mackenzie's expedition through the Rocky Mountains from the east. A decade later the United States of America asserted its own claims to the area, based on naval explorations in the area and on the expedition of Meriwether Lewis and William Clark through the Rockies. British and U.S. fur traders soon followed, setting up competing trading posts.

By the early nineteenth century, the Pacific coast of North America, virtually unknown a century before, was the center of the overlapping claims of four nations. By 1826, however, tensions had abated; Russia gave up its claims south of Alaska and Spain surrendered its interests north of California. By treaty, Great Britain and the United States jointly occupied Oregon, the area between.

THE DEVELOPING GLOBAL ECONOMY

As explorers were completing European knowledge of the world's waterways, the seaborne commerce developing around the globe brought ever-increasing prosperity to Europe. By the middle of the eighteenth century, European commercial prosperity had long since left the Mediterranean basin and had centered on the Atlantic coast. Five European states—Portugal, Spain, the Netherlands, Great Britain, and France—had added an extensive colonial commerce to their trade on the continent. Including the smaller colonial trading interests of Hamburg and the Baltic states of Denmark, Sweden, and Prussia, eighteenth century overseas commerce now rivaled in value the traditional trade patterns inside Europe. Two-thirds of Great Britain's trade now involved areas outside Europe.

Three major trade patterns dominated overseas commerce. The oldest began with the Spanish importing gold and silver from Spanish America. The Spanish sent much of these precious metals to Great Britain, France, and the Netherlands to buy manufactured products for Spain and the Spanish colonies. The Dutch, French, and British then carried this bullion to China and India to exchange for silk and cotton textiles, tea, and spices which they brought back and sold to the wealthy.

Plantation agriculture in the western hemisphere and Asia formed the second, and by the eighteenth century most valuable, international trading pattern. Europeans had transformed the Atlantic face of the Americas into a plantation belt that extended 5,000 miles from Chesapeake Bay in North America south through the Caribbean islands and down through the northern coast of Brazil. Planters there produced a variety of valuable fibers, foodstuffs, drugs, and forest products desired in Europe. Sugar imports alone equaled in value the entire Asian trade; the British, French, Portuguese, and Danish governments considered their sugar colonies their most valuable possessions. In addition, the Dutch shipped in a variety of commodities from their rapidly developing East Indian plantation system. A subpattern included North Americans shipping furs, lumber, and naval stores to Great Britain and France.

Owing to the growing commerce in American plantation products, the third major pattern, the slave trade, became increasingly lucrative. The grueling work under tropical or semi-

tropical conditions and the constant expansion of plantation areas required a continual flow of fresh labor, and from the earliest times slavers supplied blacks from Africa. As plantation agriculture flourished, the slave trade grew increasingly efficient. During the eighteenth century an average of 60,000 blacks were being imported each year into the western hemisphere. The Portuguese, Dutch, and French had successively taken over the largest share of the slave trade, but by the mid-eighteenth century the British and New Englanders dominated the slaving business outside of Portuguese-supplied Brazil.

The three colonial trade patterns brought immense profits to a few European seaports. Great Britain was the world's foremost overseas trading nation after 1763, and London the world's greatest port, growing rich on Caribbean sugar, Indian cotton, and many other products. Liverpool and Glasgow were fast rising to commercial prominence through trade in slaves, furs, and tobacco. The overseas trade of France rivaled that of Great Britain in value until 1763, with

Profits in Human Misery. By the eighteenth century the Atlantic slave trade had reached its peak, and great wealth devolved on the European states active in the trade. The brutal inhumanity of the slave ships is graphically portrayed here.

The Prosperity Brought by Imperialism. This eighteenth century scene represents one of many busy docks that line the Thames River at London. By this time, London was trading more with the colonies than with the continent.

Bordeaux and Nantes prospering from the slave trade, sugar, and Asian goods. Amsterdam, enjoying immense profits from the slave and spice trades, continued to be one of the greatest commercial centers in Europe, although the overall value of Dutch trade had slipped behind that of Great Britain and France. Lisbon and Cadiz were still prosperous cities although the colonial trade supremacy of the Iberian states had faded.

The merchants of the great eighteenth-century trading centers exerted increasing economic and political power. As a group, they possessed superior management and marketing skills, a knack for cooperating with the banking interests to secure capital and credit, and a sharp eye for technological improvements. Their interests and needs increasingly influenced politics and diplomacy, including decisions on peace and war. Merchants spurred the Industrial Revolution, plowing some of their profits into new manufacturing enterprises. Ironically, by the nineteenth century, the new class of industrial entrepreneurs would supplant the merchants in economic and political power.

THE SHOWDOWN FOR COLONIAL SUPREMACY

As overseas trade became more lucrative, the states of eighteenth century Europe, particularly Great Britain and France, increased their efforts

THE STRUGGLE TO DOMINATE THE COLONIAL WORLD

to control it. In so doing, they diverted more and more of their economic and military resources from traditional contests on the continent to new struggles overseas. By mid-century fighting in India and the western hemisphere had taken on a life of their own, quite different from the tempo of wars and diplomacy in Europe.

Static Colonial Empires

During the eighteenth century, the overseas dominions of Spain, Portugal, and the Netherlands expanded only marginally. Except for its movement north along the Pacific coast, Spain was too weak economically and militarily to do more than doggedly hold on to its sprawling possessions. The Portuguese, meanwhile, having lost most of their Asian empire to the Dutch, concentrated on expanding their "second empire" in Brazil. The Portuguese increased their production of tobacco and sugar in the tropical north, importing ever-larger numbers of slaves from their African possessions. The real boom in the Brazilian economy, however, came at the beginning of the eighteenth century when the Portuguese discovered gold and diamonds in the interior. In the early nineteenth century, as the gold rush faded, the Portuguese turned their attention to producing coffee in the temperate uplands of southern Brazil.

About 1650 it appeared that the Dutch, among the several newcomers to colonization, were destined to carve out the greatest overseas empire, but it proved otherwise. Despite having the largest seventeenth-century merchant marine and navy, the Dutch fell victim to their homeland's small size and vulnerable location. The Dutch lost three naval wars with the English in the late seventeenth century while at the same time fighting for their lives in a series of wars against Louis XIV. Despite these problems, the Dutch in the eighteenth century still held their sugar islands in the Caribbean, slave-trading posts on the African coast, settlements at the southern tip of Africa, cinnamon and tea plantations on Ceylon, and clove and nutmeg production in Indonesia. After 1677, they slowly took control of the pepper and coffee areas in Java and gained footholds in the spice islands. During much of their expansion, the Dutch employed the classic divide-and-conquer technique, already used to great effect by the Spanish and other Europeans on the Amerindians and soon to be employed by the British and French in India. The Dutch supported one Indonesian sultan against a rival ruler, exacting monopolies and land grants as a price and eventually taking over their ally as well.

The Opening of the French-British Conflict

Compared with the relatively static colonial regimes of the Spanish, Portuguese, and Dutch, the British and French aggressively expanded their overseas power. In so doing, they became embroiled with each other in more than a century (1689–1815) of intermittent international warfare for colonial and continental supremacy.

In the late seventeenth century, Louis XIV was as aggressive overseas as he was in Europe, acquiring additional possessions in the Caribbean and trading posts in India. French expansion into the North American interior particularly alarmed their rivals. With the St. Lawrence and its approaches already strongly fortified, the French moved westward and southward. By 1702 they had constructed a series of forts in an enormous C-shaped arc, extending west across the southern Great Lakes, southwest to the Mississippi, south down the Mississippi to its mouth, and east along the Gulf coast to Mobile Bay. As a result, the Spanish found the French threatening Cuba and Mexico, and the English found themselves pinned to the Atlantic seaboard.

Both the Spanish and English moved to curtail French expansion in North America. Acting defensively, the Spanish set up several posts in Texas to protect Mexico and one at Pensacola to shield Florida and Cuba. After 1713, however, the new Bourbon dynasty in Spain became an ally of France and aided the French later by attacking settlements in the southern British colonies. The English, on the other hand, took the offensive during the 1690s and in the War of the Spanish Succession. They repeatedly attacked and finally conquered Nova Scotia, which had threatened New England from the northeast. They also picked up the island of Newfoundland, a prime base for fishing. British successes in the Caribbean enabled them to crack Spain's trade monopoly with Spanish America by wringing from the Spanish an *asiento* to sell goods at the huge annual commercial fair at Cartagena, Colombia.

Until 1740, a precarious balance of power prevailed in Europe, but British-Spanish and British-French rivalry intensified abroad. Great Britain's continual smuggling into Spain's

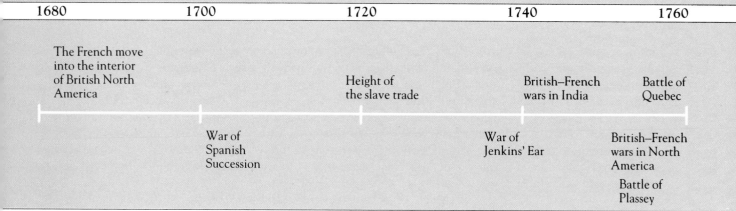

| 1680 | 1700 | 1720 | 1740 | 1760 |

The French move into the interior of British North America

Height of the slave trade

British–French wars in India

Battle of Quebec

War of Spanish Succession

War of Jenkins' Ear

British–French wars in North America

Battle of Plassey

American colonies led to Spanish retaliation in 1739, and then to fighting in the Caribbean, popularly called "The War of Jenkins' Ear." In 1740 war broke out in Europe over the succession to the Austrian throne and ended in 1748 with treaties that provided for the status quo in India and the western hemisphere.

The Triumph of Great Britain

Despite treaty provisions in Europe, recurrent undeclared warfare in the colonies had taken on a life of its own. Beginning in the 1740s, the British and French were entering into the critical phase of a worldwide struggle for colonial and commercial supremacy. The contest was fought over the next four decades in India, the Caribbean, and North America. In this struggle the two nations not only used their own military power but also subsidized an assortment of allies: Frederick the Great and other European rulers, colonial settlers, Amerindian tribes, and Indian princes.

In India, both the British and French trading companies were interested in expanding their power beyond their original collection of coastal trading posts (see Map 54). The In-

dian subcontinent produced valuable spices and textiles, and its huge population was at once a source of cheap labor and an opportunity for profitable taxation. It was also a prospective captive market for European goods, that could replace the drain of European silver going to pay for Indian products. The India companies of various European nations were interested in controlling blocks of territory, where masses of labor could be efficiently organized to produce a higher output of spices and textiles. This arrangement had long been typical of European colonization in the western hemisphere, and the Dutch were doing the same in Indonesia.

By the middle of the eighteenth century the French and British India companies saw opportunities to expand. The Moghul dynasty of Muslim emperors was rapidly dissolving under numerous rebellions and outside attacks by both Hindu and Muslim princes. The opportunity was now present for each national trading company to support certain rajahs against other princes. In repayment for this support, the Indian allies would help destroy the competing trading company. Once it had eliminated its European rivals, the surviving company could then exploit rivalries among the Indian potentates and ex-

pand their economic and political controls over India.

The French moved first. A surprise attack by a French naval squadron in 1746 conquered the key British East India Company post at Madras. However, the French had to restore the post at the treaty of peace in 1748. Shortly afterwards French governor Josef Dupleix began to interfere in the neighboring princely states, planning to build up French supremacy in India under the mantle of the crumbling Moghul empire. By 1751 the French and British India companies, backed by rival Indian factions, were at war, although their governments were officially at peace. During the fighting a pattern emerged that was repeated in the Caribbean and in North America. The French, with better planning, stronger leadership, and more reliable allies, initially gained the upper hand in India. However, as time passed the superior British navy cut off reinforcements to the French while bringing in troops and supplies. The British found better leaders, trained better-disciplined Indian auxiliaries (sepoys), and eventually won the contest. In 1761, the British took the key French post at Pondicherry, effectively eliminating the French as rivals for control of India.

As they had in India, the French

and British in North America began fighting during peace in Europe. In the early 1750s, the French, as in India, took the initiative, building up their military forces in New France (Canada) and constructing a new string of forts southward from the Great Lakes to the upper Ohio Valley. Fort Duquesne (Pittsburgh), built in 1753 just over the mountains from British settlements in Pennsylvania and Virginia, became a provocative threat. Paralleling their initial successes in India, in 1754 and 1755 the French and their Amerindian allies defeated two expeditions mounted against Fort Duquesne.

By 1756, a general conflict had broken out in Europe, merging with the world war in progress for colonial supremacy. As in India, the British fleet was powerful enough to cut off New France, the heart of French power in North America, from supplies and reinforcements, while at the same time transporting land forces to attack the French. With France heavily involved on the continent, the British methodically conquered New France. They captured Fort Duquesne and Louisbourg, the key to the St. Lawrence, in 1758. In 1759 James Wolfe defeated the main French army

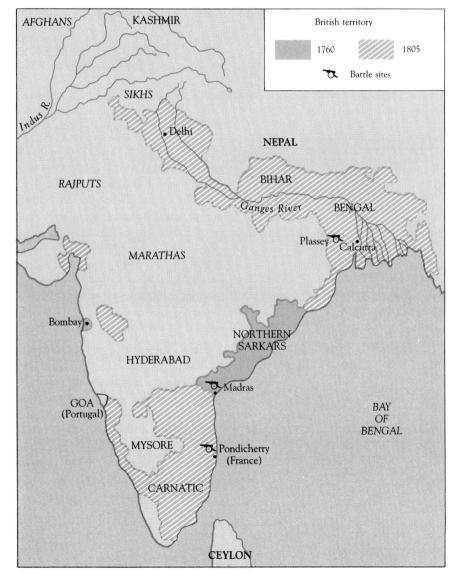

MAP 54
British Expansion in India, 1760–1805. The British takeover of India began in earnest in the 1750's, following a pattern of opportunity. By 1760, the British had taken control of part of the east coast, while at the same time smashing the power of their main European rival, the French. Clive's victory over Indian forces at Plassey in 1757 led to a major stage of expansion. Beginning in 1765, the British took control of the heavily populated Ganges river valley and most of the spice-producing areas of southern India. After 1805 the British would continue to take over the subcontinent, also seizing Ceylon and its tea plantations.

The Key Conflict for Imperial Supremacy. This print depicts the battle on September 13, 1759 between British invading forces and French defenders on the Plains of Abraham outside Quebec, Canada. British troops secretly entered the ravine on the left at night and gained the heights, surprising the French in the morning.

in front of Quebec, and his successors captured Montreal in 1760. Meanwhile, British naval expeditions wrested away nearly all of the French islands in the Caribbean and seized Havana from the Spanish.

At the conclusion of the fighting in 1763 Great Britain controlled the largest European colonial empire and the most profitable network of overseas trade, while the colonial empire of France had been almost totally destroyed. In the Treaty of Paris in 1763 the Spanish received Louisiana west of the Mississippi, giving it, with its earlier holdings, approximately 40 percent of North America. The British, however, laid claim to the largest and by far the richest share of France's former possessions. Great Britain took over New France, thus taking full control of the rich beaver trade. In addition, Great Britain received Louisiana east of the Mississippi and Spanish Florida. A few fishery islands off the coast of Newfoundland were

all that remained of the French empire in North America. The French were allowed to take back their West Indian islands and trading posts in India, but these colonial remnants no longer constituted a threat to British predominance overseas.

REVOLT AND INDEPENDENCE IN BRITISH NORTH AMERICA

The British did not long enjoy their victory over France. A major challenge arose from an unexpected source—their own colonists in North America.

Colonial Unrest and Colonial War

After 1763, the British government took the position that the colonists had not borne their proportionate

share of the costs of the war against the French and should defray the costs of future defense. It also believed that the colonists had been allowed to drift out of the proper mercantilist relationship with the mother country. Too many trade regulations were being thwarted, and some American manufactured goods were competing with those in Great Britain. Consequently, the British government required the colonists to quarter British garrisons and to pay new taxes created by Parliament and enforced by the king. The government also imposed new trade regulations and tightened up on the enforcement of those already in place. Finally, the government prohibited settlement across the Appalachian Mountains, fearing that settlers would harm the deerskin and fur trades and provoke unnecessary wars with the Amerindians.

Many colonists in British North America were shocked by the new policies. They had become used to autonomy in managing their colonial affairs and some of them had come to believe that autonomy was their constitutional right. The Stamp Act in particular, an internal tax rather than a trade regulation, appeared to many colonists to symbolize a radical, even unconstitutional, interference with their tradition of colonial self-government. Because of the new restrictions and exactions, discontent and hostility spread quickly among the colonists in much of British North America during the 1760s. At first the colonists mostly confined their actions to securing the repeal of the new laws and regulations. Colonial lawyers and journalists (those, incidentally, most affected by the stamp tax) turned a significant portion of the informed public against the British policies. The most effective technique was to refuse to sell American products to British merchants and to refuse to buy British goods. As the colonists had hoped, financially beset British businessmen on several occasions persuaded Parliament to repeal the offending taxes or regulations.

By the late 1760s and early 1770s, more radical colonists were questioning the fundamental constitutional relationship between the colonies and Great Britain. Some denied that Parliament could legitimately regulate and tax property inside a colony or even create trade regulations for the colonial empire as a whole. They argued that the king was only a symbol of unity and had no constitutional authority to enforce Parliament's policies. By 1774, a number of disruptive incidents instigated by the colonists had provoked the British government into a series of repressive acts. In response anti-Parliament colonials set

STAMP ACT DISTURBANCES IN BOSTON

This [the presence of Peter Oliver, the stamp distributor for Massachusetts] occasioned murmuring among the people, and an inflammatory piece in the next Boston Gazette. A few days after, early in the morning, a stuffed image was hung upon a tree, ... Labels affixed denoted it to be designed to the distributor of the stamps. . . . The majority of the [Governor's] council . . . advised not to meddle with it . . . an attempt to remove it would bring on a riot. . . .

Forty or fifty tradesmen, decently dressed, preceded; and some thousands of the mob followed down King street to Oliver's dock, near which Mr. Oliver had lately erected a building, which it was conjectured, was designed for a stamp office. This was laid to the ground in a few minutes. From hence the mob proceeded [to Oliver's house], . . . they endeavored to force themselves into it, and being opposed, broke the windows, beat down the doors, entered, and destroyed part of his furniture, and continued in riot until midnight, before they separated.

The next day . . . . Several of the council gave it as their opinion, Mr. Oliver being present, that the people, not only of the town of Boston, but of the country in general, would never submit to the execution of the stamp act, let the consequence of an opposition to it be what it would.

It was also reported that the people of Connecticut had threatened to hang their distributor on the first tree after he entered the colony; and that, to avoid it, he had turned aside to Rhode-Island.

Despairing of protection, and finding his family in terror and great distress, Mr. Oliver came to the decision to resign his office before another night. . . .*

Shortly afterwards the mob attacked the homes of the registrar of the admiralty and the comptroller of the customs and utterly destroyed the home of Lieutenant Governor Thomas Hutchinson, who was believed to be in favor of the stamp tax. A gentleman of high family and loyal to the king during the War for Independence, Hutchinson gives a restrained, even sardonic, version of the events. All the elements of a combustible situation are present: resentment toward a perceived high-handed act by a far-away government; inflammatory journalism; division among the local authorities, some of them undoubtedly conniving in the disruption; ruffians with a nose for violence; and a helpless target.

*Thomas Hutchinson, The History of the Colony and Province of Massachusetts Bay, ed. Lawrence Shaw Mayo, III. (Cambridge: Harvard, 1936), pp. 86–88.

up the Continental Congress, composed of representatives from the older thirteen colonies (but not the new colonies of Florida and Quebec). The congress met in Philadelphia and created a tight new economic boycott enforced by organizations of local

toughs. Most provocative of all, the congress encouraged the colonies to organize, equip, and train companies of independent local militia.

In April 1775, seven years of warfare were inaugurated when British troops clashed with militia companies

463

at Lexington and Concord, Massachusetts. British authority collapsed in the thirteen colonies as royal governors fled and colonial assemblies prepared for further resistance. Despite the outbreak of fighting, most colonists were still loyal to Great Britain and respected the crown as a symbol of unity. However, George III rejected a moderate appeal sent to him by the colonists calling for local autonomy inside the British imperial system. The fighting continued and sentiment crystallized around complete separation. On July 4, 1776, the delegates of the Continental Congress signed and published a Declaration of Independence stating the reasons for their action.

During the war each side enjoyed distinct advantages and suffered from major problems. From a traditional point of view the British were clearly superior. They had a winning tradition, a well-trained army, money to buy supplies and allies, and a navy that could land troops wherever desired, giving them the military initiative. However, it can now be seen that Great Britain was also faced with a difficult new context for conducting war. The struggle was a war of attrition conducted across an ocean against large numbers of military and civilian opponents spread across an area four times the size of Great Britain. Communication across the Atlantic was so slow that often orders arrived that no longer had any relevance. Supplies and reinforcements frequently were late and inadequate. The British won battles, but the enemy continued to resist, and the British did not have enough troops or colonial allies to garrison a hostile countryside. The rebel commander, George Washington, although losing battles, kept his army intact as a rallying point for continued resistance.

On the other side, the rebels, although favored by distance, area, time, and sporadic aid from France, faced huge problems of their own. They were divided in a civil war between rebels and loyalists. Despite Benjamin Franklin's admonition "We must all hang together or we will all hang separately," the rebel leaders quarreled incessantly. In addition, the rebels were beset by Amerindians, and they had to depend on inadequate contributions and loans to finance the war effort. They had few fighting men who were willing to abandon cover and fight the British in the open or assault fortifications. Slowly and painfully, the rebels had to build up a regular army that could fight in the open and stiffen the resolve of the militia.

Both sides attempted to overcome their problems as the war progressed, but by 1777 neither had made significant headway. The British controlled only a strip from Philadelphia to New York and had surrendered an army at Saratoga, while Washington and other rebel commanders found difficulty in keeping a fighting force assembled. As time passed, the question for both sides was whether their supporters would be willing to sustain the sacrifices necessary to outlast the other side and win the war of attrition.

Beginning in 1778, events in the Old World transformed the war that was underway in the New. The French, who had been rebuilding their army and particularly their navy, watched with interest as Great Britain drained itself in a colonial war in North America. Capitalizing on the jealousy and fear of other European powers toward the British, France succeeded in isolating Great Britain diplomatically. In 1778, France, after hearing the news of the British defeat at Saratoga, declared war on Great Britain, followed later by Spain and the Netherlands. What had been a colonial war in North America became another world war, this time fought primarily outside Europe in India, the Caribbean, and North America. The French gave effective aid to the rebels in 1781, when a French army and fleet combined with Washington's army to capture Cornwallis's army at Yorktown, Virginia.

By 1781, unable to reconquer the rebel colonies, the British government chose to surrender them and concentrate their forces elsewhere. After concluding a separate peace with the Americans in 1782, the British were able to defend their Caribbean and Indian possessions. At the Peace of Paris in 1783 Great Britain recognized the independence of the United States of America, ceding to the new nation the area south of Canada and east of the Mississippi, except for Florida and the Gulf coast, which went to Spain.

The United States of America

During the first half century of its independence the United States expanded and prospered. The population increased five-fold, and the key aspects of the colonial economy—foodstuffs, fishing, and the maritime trade—continued to flourish. Americans were also making a small beginning in manufacturing. There was one enormous innovation in the economy, however, brought about by a simple technological invention. The cotton gin made it possible for Americans to grow abundant supplies of short-fibered cotton for mass producing cheap cotton clothing. The enormous demand in Europe soon made cotton the most valuable American commodity: As some enthusiastic southerners put it, "Cotton is king!" The huge size of the new nation also placed a premium on improving transportation and communication. Americans, with heavy financial backing from British investors, were in the forefront of creating or improving canals, roads, and steamboats and eventually railroads and the telegraph.

Society and politics in the United States were characterized by an acceleration of trends already under way in the colonial period. The percentage of those owning property continued to rise, along with the standard of living. The passage of time, plus the libertarian influence of the Enlightenment, eased religious animosities and began to create an atmosphere of positive toleration. Ethnic and religious hostilities persisted, but they were somewhat weakened as individuals of different backgrounds began to associate and to intermarry. Most white Americans learned to read and write, women rapidly closing the literacy gap between themselves and men. Many colleges sprang up, mostly sectarian and primarily for men. Some schools reflected the influence of the Enlightenment as they introduced courses in mathematics, science, foreign languages, history, and other subjects.

Politics also continued to develop from colonial trends. For most of this period, men of property still dominated politics, and the officers of the new nation all came from the ranks of the upper class. However, the organized political party and the rapid

abolition of state religious and property qualifications for voting was quickly placing political power into the hands of the mass of white males.

The greatest political achievement of the gentry was the Constitution of 1787 and the Bill of Rights of 1791. Reflecting the heterogeneous nature of American society, they set up a federal republic where the national government controlled diplomacy, war, peace, interstate and international commerce, the army and navy, and Indian affairs. The states retained control of the bulk of everyday affairs, including civil and criminal law, education, health and safety, and the militia. The Bill of Rights promised an open, liberal society that would tolerate freedom of religion, speech, and the press. Further, it guaranteed procedural protections and a fair trial for those accused of crime. Whites did not interpret these provisions as applying to blacks or to Amerindians under their control.

Despite the growing freedom and prosperity for whites in the United States, unresolved problems threatened the unity of the republic. Sectional economic competition had become acute by the 1820s. Many northerners favored a protective tariff to build up American industry and create a home market for agriculture. Most southerners, on the other hand, wanted free trade so they could keep their costs of production down and sell their cotton, rice, and tobacco abroad without fear of foreign tariff retaliation.

The economic competition between sections was soon intensified by another issue, black slavery. Although slavery was on its way out in the north, the cotton economy had fixed it firmly into the social and ide-

ological fabric of the southern states. An increasing number of individuals, mostly in the north, wanted either to barricade slavery in the south for economic reasons, or to eradicate it for moral reasons.

As a new nation, the United States of America found that it was not a truly independent state. Insignificant as a military power, after 1792 it was soon caught up in the final phase of the long struggle between Great Britain and France. On the Atlantic, the United States was caught in a contradictory situation. Americans were making great sums of money supplying the belligerents. At the same time many American ships were seized and some crewmen were impressed to serve on foreign ships or clapped into foreign jails. Beyond the Appalachians, the Spanish and British intrigued with the Amerindians and pressured the settlers, making the government fearful of losing the west to conquest or secession. The United States tried diplomacy, undeclared naval war, several forms of embargo, and a formal war with Great Britain (the War of 1812) to protect its commerce. However, only the end of the struggle between Great Britain and France in 1815 brought interference with U.S. trade to an end. In the west, on the other hand, the United States was spectacularly successful. Military forces crushed the Amerindians, who would never again be a major obstacle to white expansion on the continent. By exploiting hostilities among European nations, applying military pressure on Spain, and enjoying simple luck, the United States added Florida and Louisiana to the national domain, doubling its territory and bringing it to the Rocky Mountains. It held a strong claim to Oregon as well, with excellent prospects for reaching the Pacific.

THE CONTINUED GROWTH OF THE BRITISH EMPIRE

At the same time that Great Britain was losing a major part of her empire in North America, it was expanding in other parts of the world. In the South Pacific, the British established a penal colony at Botany Bay (now Sydney) on the east coast of Australia in 1788, soon to be followed by other penal settlements up and down the coast. No other European power considered Australia to be worth contesting, and Great Britain thus added an entire continent to its dominions. Great Britain began to absorb nearby

New Zealand early in the nineteenth century.

To the British, however, gaining control of India was of far greater importance than developing Australia. The process of conquest began in 1757 when Robert Clive defeated a large Indian army at Plassey, obtaining the province of Bengal in northeast India for the British East India Company. After a pause, British expansion picked up again in the 1780s. The British East India Company continually intervened in the incessant quarrels of the Indian princes, employing its efficient and better-equipped forces to seize province after province. By the 1820s, the British were in effective control of the subcontinent. They had defeated their major Indian opponents and maintained direct rule over the Indus valley and most of east and

south India, while overawing most of the remaining princes.

Besides taking over India and Australia, the British made one more major expansion of their colonial empire, seizing some colonies of the Dutch. During the 1790s, revolutionary France had made the Netherlands a satellite. This gave the British, persistent foes of Revolutionary and Napoleonic France, an opportunity to conquer Dutch possessions that threatened British trade routes to India and east Asia. By 1815, the British had achieved their objective, taking over South Africa, Mauritius Island (from the French), and Ceylon. By the 1820s the British had established a major base at Singapore at the tip of the Malay Peninsula and thus controlled the trade route to east Asia. Thus, despite the loss of her Atlantic

Triumph in India. This scene depicts the aftermath of the battle of Plassey, June 23, 1757, which opened India to British conquest. Robert Clive meets with Mir Jaffar, whose treachery to the *nawab* Siraj secured the British victory. The practice of divide and conquer was a successful imperialist technique in India and elsewhere. National Portrait Gallery, London.

The Spanish
move into
California

First
Settlement
of Australia

Independence movements
in Latin America

Independence movement
in British North America

Cook voyages the Pacific

The British
accelerate
conquest
of India

Claims to northwest
coast of North
America settled

---

seaboard colonies, Great Britain in the early nineteenth century continued to be the greatest European colonial power.

REVOLT AND INDEPENDENCE IN LATIN AMERICA

At the beginning of the nineteenth century, only Spain, with her huge possessions in the western hemisphere, might have disputed Great Britain's position as the greatest European colonial master. The Spanish empire in America, however, along with Portugal's, soon crumbled under the twin pressures of upheavals at home and revolt in the colonies.

The Long Struggle for Freedom

For centuries, Spanish and Portuguese colonists had chafed under economic deprivations, and many Creoles had resented the political power of the peninsulars sent over to govern. Some Creoles were impressed by the principles and success of the North American independence movement and by the reforms of the French Revolution and Napoleon; they hoped to create comparable liberal institutions in Latin America, at least for the upper classes. Some of the more radical wanted to disestablish the Roman Catholic church and tax or even confiscate its property. Few gave much thought to the needs of the masses of workers and peasants.

As it turned out, the revolutionary era was inaugurated not by Creoles but by mulatto freemen and black slaves. In the 1790s, after fighting broke out between whites and mulattoes in the French Caribbean colony of Saint Dominique (Haiti), the masses of black slaves rose and drove out white authority. Toussaint L'Ouverture, the rebel leader, trained a disciplined army and fended off attacks by other European nations and revolts by mulatto factions. He abolished slavery before the republican government of France belatedly terminated it in all French possessions. Napoleon, however, flirting with thoughts of restoring the old French empire in the western hemisphere, decided to restore white rule in Haiti and the old plantation system in the French Caribbean. He sent an army to Haiti, but the climate, yellow fever, and black resistance destroyed the French in a struggle punctuated by racial massacres. L'Ouverture, captured by treachery, died in a French prison. In 1804, however, Jean Jacques Dessalines proclaimed the independence of the new nation of Haiti with himself as emperor. The success of the black slaves of Haiti disturbed conservative nations in general and slaveholding nations in particular. Haiti was shunned in diplomatic circles for decades.

The main movement for Latin American independence began in 1807–1808. Napoleon took control of Portugal, sending the monarchy in flight to Brazil, and deposed the Bourbon monarchy in Spain, plunging Spain into intermittent civil war. Throughout Spanish America, royal authority weakened. In Argentina, it collapsed in 1810 without a fight; Argentinians formally proclaimed independence in 1816. Rebels in Venezuela pronounced their liberation in 1811 and fighting began in 1812. Rebel forces were led by Simón Bolívar, a Venezuelan aristocrat who had taken an oath to free his country from Spain. For seven years Bolívar's fortunes fluctuated from splendid victories to humiliating defeats and exile. Finally Bolívar decisively defeated the Spanish in Colombia in 1819 and in Venezuela in 1821, receiving the title of "Liberator" from the trium-

467

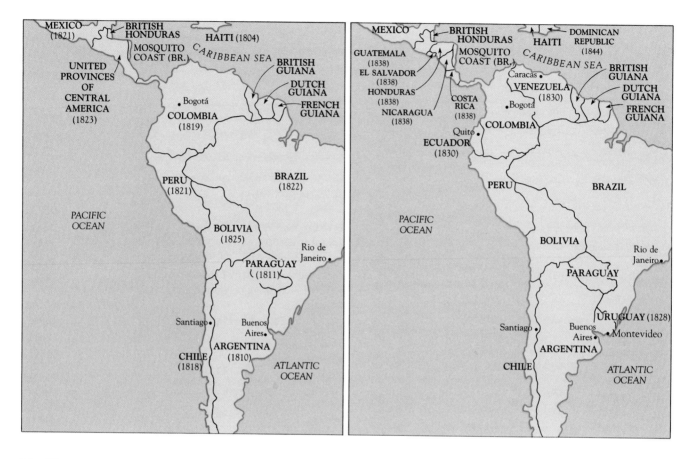

MAP 55

The Independent Nations in Latin America 1828, 1845. The independence movement in Latin America produced two waves of new nations. During the first separation from Spain and Portugal, ten new nations were founded. Some of these new nations contained incompatible regional interests, however, and a series of new nations appeared as a result of secession movements in Central America, Colombia, Brazil, and Haiti. Only the Spanish colonies of Cuba and Puerto Rico remained of the great Iberian empires in the Western Hemisphere.

phant rebels. Meanwhile, José de San Martín, a military professional, made a spectacular surprise crossing of the high Andes passes from Argentina into Chile in 1817, driving out the Spanish by 1818. With the aid of the British and Chileans, he built a navy and landed in 1821 in Lima, Peru, the heart of the Spanish authority in South America. Bolívar moved south in 1822 through Ecuador to join San Martín against the remaining Spanish army. San Martín returned to Argentina, and Bolívar crushed the last remnants of Spanish authority at Ayacucho, Peru, in 1824.

The Spanish were not the only threat to the South American revolutionaries. Conservative nations in Europe had smashed a liberal revo-

lution in Spain in 1822 and restored the deposed monarch. Some of these nations considered sending troops to Latin America to eradicate rebellion against monarchy there as well. The British government opposed this plan, however, realizing that independence had opened up an entire continent to British trade and investment. Great Britain could block any expedition to America with its navy, so the invasion scheme was dropped. The United States also voiced its opposition, in the 1823 Monroe Doctrine, but the outlook of that weak nation was irrelevant to the powerful European states.

Unlike Spanish South America, where independence had essentially been a struggle among elements of the

European-descended upper classes, Mexico's initial path to independence contained a strong element of class revolution and even race warfare. From 1808 to 1810, confused maneuvering took place among various Creole groups and the peninsulars. In 1810, the upper classes were confronted by an uprising of mestizo and Amerindian peasants initially led by Father Miguel Hidalgo under the banner of the dark-skinned Virgin of Guadalupe. Hidalgo's demands for civil rights for the peasants alarmed the upper classes; liberal and conservative Creoles joined to crush this specter of lower-class power, and the revolutionary movement dissolved into guerrilla warfare. The 1820 liberal revolution in Spain, however, prompted conservative Creoles to rebel. Agustín de Iturbide, a military adventurer, drew up the Plan of Iguala, which called for independence and promised something for all the elite groups in Mexico, without basic social and economic change. Iturbide received such overwhelming support that the Spanish were forced to concede the independence of Mexico in 1821. Social revolution had not disappeared from Mexican history, however, as events in the twentieth century were to show.

Compared with the wars and revolutionary movements in Spanish

The Liberator. This portrait of Simón Bolívar represents a remarkable life. Active on a dozen battlefields, he persisted for years through many adversities to liberate one-third of the continent of South America from Spanish rule.

BOLÍVAR PONDERS A SUITABLE GOVERNMENT FOR SPANISH AMERICA

. . . the diversity of racial origin will require an infinitely firm hand and great tactfulness to manage this heterogeneous society, whose complex mechanism is easily . . . disintegrated by the slightest controversy. . . .

. . . it is a marvel that the [federal] prototype in North America endures so successfully and has not been overthrown at the first sign of adversity or danger. . . . But . . . never . . . compare the position and character of two states as dissimilar as the English-American and Spanish-American. We [are] not prepared for such good, . . . Our moral fiber [does] not . . . possess the stability necessary to derive benefits from a wholly representative government; . . .

This I recommend . . . the study of the British Constitution . . . for that body of laws appears destined to bring about the greatest possible good for the peoples that adopt it; but . . . I only refer to its republican features; and indeed can a political system be labeled a monarchy when it recognizes popular sovereignty, division and balance of powers, civil liberty, freedom of conscience and press, and all that is politically sublime? . . . [it serves] as a model for those who aspire to the enjoyment of the rights of man and who seek all the political happiness which is compatible with frailty of human nature.

Writing in 1819 when the future of the independence movement was still in doubt, Bolívar went on to recommend a house of representatives elected by a restricted franchise, and a hereditary senate of especially trained and educated members. He also suggested an elected chief executive reelectable for long terms or elected for life, and an independent judiciary. Influenced by his readings in Enlightenment thought and by the limitations placed on him as a Creole, Bolívar was in some respects a radical, demanding equality before the law, even for the masses. However, his upper-class background and the realities of war and political revolution made him moderate concerning the nature of government. He favored limiting political power to the middle and upper classes for the foreseeable future until the masses were educated and their economic condition uplifted. By 1826, the final divisive struggle for independence and the rampant factionalism after independence had made Bolívar more conservative. He created a government for Bolivia which resembled the authoritarian constitutions of Napoleon.

*Address to the Second National Congress of Venezuela, comp. Vincente Lecuna, trans. Lewis Bertrand, ed. Harold A. Bierck, Jr., Selected Writings of Bolívar (New York: Colonial Press, 1951), Vol. 1, pp. 174–197 passim.

America, Brazilians won their independence relatively easily. While the Portuguese royal family was in exile in Brazil it set up a complete government. It opened Brazil to free trade, encouraged immigration and industrial production, and formally confederated Brazil with Portugal into a joint kingdom. When Napoleon was finally defeated in 1815, King John VI chose to stay in Brazil and rule Portugal through a council of regents.

After putting down a rebel republic in northern Brazil, he rushed to Portugal in 1820 to deal with a liberal uprising that coincided with the revolt in Spain, leaving his son Pedro as regent. The Portuguese legislature, however, began to strip Brazil of its status and repeal John's reforms. The exasperated Brazilians persuaded Pedro to support a break with Portugal and to proclaim an independent Empire in 1822. Portugal capitulated to the inevitable, recognizing the independence of Brazil in 1825.

By 1825, the only colonies remaining in the western hemisphere south of Canada were the Caribbean islands (except the island of Santo Domingo, which was controlled by Haiti) and a few small enclaves on the coasts of Central and South America (see Map 55).

The New Nations of Latin America

By the 1830s nineteen new nations had formed in Latin America. Although each had its distinct social and political personality, the similarities, a colonial heritage, far outweighed their differences. They were basically dependent on the export and sale of agricultural and mineral raw materials, but they had to import manufactured goods at an unfavorable balance of trade. Their own output of these products was low and their outmoded productive techniques, still dependent on cheap hand labor, were on a level with central and eastern Europe. Their transportation network was rudimentary and their financial situation precarious. Still, Latin America had abundant untapped resources and such potential for profit that many Europeans began to invest there. Welcomed by the new nations with investment incentives, European businessmen combined labor-saving technology with cheap labor, first to create enormously profitable plantations and mines, and later factories, roads, railroads, telegraph networks, and petroleum refineries.

The social and political characteristics of the Latin American states were also by and large carried over from colonial days. The rich property holders and the church continued to wield economic and political power in Spanish America, now joined by the new national military establishments. Independence brought little relief for the masses, who continued to work for the elite. Like the bulk of the European peasantry, the peons received a pittance for pay, and for the most part they continued to be denied access to decent housing, adequate food, proper sanitation, and rudimentary education.

The constitutions of Spanish America, influenced by revolutionary France and the United States, set up liberal republics with elected offices, civil liberties, equality before the law, and varying degrees of religious toleration. In practice, however, a liberal republic ill fitted a society composed of a tiny elite and a mass of impoverished and uneducated peons. Political and civil rights were not extended to the masses, and politics became a kaleidoscopic struggle among opportunistic individuals and cliques.

The broadest trend in the politics of Latin America was the struggle between conservative and liberal parties, and in this arena some outstanding statesmen drew up eloquent manifestos of political principles. The conservatives stood for retaining the prerogatives and powers of the upper classes and the church, whereas the liberals wished to break down these privileges so that the small, mostly mestizo, middle class could share economic and political power. Despite the contributions made by many dedicated individuals, politics was often accompanied by fraud and corruption, and elections were frequently overturned by the armed forces, who installed dictators.

SUMMARY

From the late seventeenth to the early nineteenth century Europeans continued to expand their knowledge of, and controls over, more of the world. They charted the Pacific and discovered Australia, but the greatest interest was in the interior and northwest coast of North America, where several European nations competed for beaver, seal, and otter pelts. The fur trade, however, was only a minor part of an emerging global economy that combined the products of Asia and the Americas and the labor of Africa into enormous wealth for the seafaring powers of Europe in general and their Atlantic port cities in particular.

While the Spanish, Portuguese, and Dutch were struggling to retain what they had accumulated before 1700, the French and British rapidly expanded their colonial empires. The two nations fought each other in North America and India with increasing intensity throughout the first half of the eighteenth century, with the British emerging triumphant in 1763. France lost its huge North American empire to Great Britain and Spain and was reduced to impotence in India and the Caribbean. Great Britain was now by far the greatest colonial power in the world.

After 1763 the British tightened their controls on their North American colonists and subjected them to British taxes. The colonists resisted and both sides escalated the contest. In 1775, fighting broke out; compromise failing, the colonists declared their independence in 1776 and a war of attrition ensued. France and other nations entered the war against Great Britain, and in 1783 the British recognized the independence of the United States of America. The British subsequently claimed and settled Australia, expanded their control in India, and gained control of the approaches to India and East Asia from the Dutch and French.

In the first three decades of the nineteenth century colonists in part of the Caribbean and throughout mainland Latin America fought for and won independence. The black population of Haiti led the way, followed by Argentina. Bolívar and San Martín led a series of spectacular military expeditions that finally drove the Spanish out in 1824. The Mexican elite maneuvered between the twin threats of Spanish control and mass social revolution, and secured independence in 1821. The Brazilians attained their freedom without a significant struggle.

Among the new nations, the United States differed substantially from its neighbors to the south. A liberal federal republic, the United States enjoyed, in spite of a number of national problems, a vibrant economy and both population and territorial growth. Most of its white citizens owned property, were literate, and participated in politics. The Latin American nations, also liberal republics in form, maintained their colonial culture where a small elite controlled the masses and a stagnant but potentially rich economy. Factions of this elite struggled for political power, taking it legally or illegally, as circumstances dictated. Whether any of the new nations of the western hemisphere would rise to prominence in western civilization remained to be seen.

SELECTED SOURCES

Allen, Hervey. *The Forest and the Fort.* 1943. Gripping story about life on the Pennsylvania frontier during the French and Indian war. Colonists, British, French, Amerindians all are locked in devastating conflict. First of a trilogy.

Dorn, Walter. *Competition for Empire.* 1940. Still an accurate, lively account.

Eccles, William J. *France in America.* 1972. The best study, concise and well-written.

Gardner, Brian. *The East India Company: A History.* 1971. An engagingly written survey of the rise and fall of the greatest trading company in British history.

Halperin-Donghi, Tulio. *The Aftermath of Revolution in Latin America.* 1973. An insightful look into economic, social, and political conditions during the nineteenth century.

Jensen, Merrill. *The Founding of a Nation: A History of the American Revolution, 1763–1776.* 1968. A long, but well-written survey which stresses the complexity of the period.

Lynch, John. *The Spanish-American Revolutions, 1808–1826.* 1973. The best synthesis of a sprawling subject.

Maclean, Alistair. *Captain Cook.* 1972. A narrative of Cook's voyages, based on the explorer's journals.

Mason, F. Van Wyck. *Manila Galleon.* 1961. Novel about the circumnavigation of the globe by Commodore George Anson of the British navy during the War of Austrian Succession, 1740–1744. Rousing scenes of international colonial conflict.

Masur, Gerhard. *Simón Bolívar.* 2nd ed. 1969. The best, but incomplete, biography of the great Liberator.

Parry, J. H. *Trade and Dominion: The European Overseas Empires in the Eighteenth Century.* 1971. The standard account, stressing the European impact on the colonies.

*Peckham, Howard H. *The War for Independence: A Military History.* 1958. A brief survey which presents the problems of both sides.

*Available in paperback.

THE ERA OF THE FRENCH REVOLUTION (1789–1799)

The path leading to the scaffold was extremely rough and difficult to pass, the King [Louis XVI] was obliged to lean on my arm, and from the slowness with which he proceeded, I feared for a moment that his courage might fail; but what was my astonishment, when arrived at the last step, I felt that he suddenly let go my arm, and I saw him cross with a firm foot the breadth of the wood scaffold. . . . I heard him pronounce distinctly these memorable words "I die innocent of all the crimes laid to my charge; I pardon those who have occasioned my death; and I pray to God, that the blood you are now going to shed may never be visited on France."

He was proceeding, when a man on horseback, in the national uniform, waved his sword, and . . . the executioners . . . seizing with violence the most virtuous of Kings . . . dragged him under the axe of the guillotine, which with one stroke severed his head from his body. . . . The youngest of the guards, who seemed about eighteen, walked round the scaffold; he accompanied this monstrous ceremony with the most atrocious and indecent gestures. At first an awful silence prevailed; at length some cries of "Vive la Republique!" were heard. By degrees the voices multiplied, and in less than ten minutes this cry, a thousand times repeated, became the universal shout of the multitude, and every hat was in the air.

This gruesome scene, vividly depicted by a contemporary English observer, would have been unthinkable a century earlier when the reigning monarch, Louis XIV, was so powerful that he could claim to be the state. With his successor an astonishing reversal set in. The long reign of Louis XV was marked by immorality at court, political confusion and misrule, reckless squandering of money and military defeats. All of this tarnished the image of the French monarchy and bred popular discontent. The next king Louis XVI (1774–1792) only made matters worse although the fault was not entirely his own. However inadequate he may have been, he was burdened from the outset with almost insoluble problems inherited from his predecessor and throughout his reign faced growing and converging

Assault and Fall of the Bastille. On July 14, 1789, a mob gathered outside the bastille seeking to obtain its arms. Prison guards panicked and fired into the crowd, killing nearly a hundred. In this painting a mutinous detachment of French soldiers, supported by a cannon, join the assault. Soon after, the commander of the fortress surrendered on condition that both he and his men be spared. Once inside, the frenzied crowd disregarded its pledge, butchered the commander and several other members of the garrison, and, placing their heads on pikes, paraded them through Paris. The fall of the bastille demonstrated that the king had lost control of the city.

pressures that even a man of far greater talent might have found overwhelming.

What began as a movement to limit royal absolutism mushroomed into a violent upheaval, shattering the old order and paving the way for widespread changes in Western society. The revolution passed through various stages, becoming more extreme and reaching the high tide of radicalism in 1793–1794 before a revulsion in public opinion led to the return of moderate rule. The revolution ended in November 1799 with the establishment of a military dictatorship. Ten years of revolutionary activity saw the overthrow of the monarchy, the end of feudalism and the proclamation of religious freedom, individual freedom and legal equality of all Frenchmen. The Revolution not only produced many lasting reforms in France, but also inspired similar movements in Europe in the nineteenth century.

FRANCE ON THE EVE OF THE REVOLUTION

At the accession of Louis XVI in 1774, France, although somewhat weakened by its defeat and loss of much of its empire in the Seven Years' War, was still the richest and most influential nation in Europe. Its varied climate, together with an extraordinary large area of good to excellent soil, permitted cultivation of a wide range of crops. Its commerce was expanding rapidly, thanks in part to ports on both the Atlantic and Mediterranean Seas, as well as on the Rhine River. Among the great powers, France enjoyed the highest standard of living with the possible exception of Great Britain which had a much smaller population. France, moreover, was envied and emulated throughout Europe. Its language was spoken by cultured Europeans and it led the way in art, literature, cooking, and fashion.

Slightly smaller in area than present day Texas, France had a population of about 25 million people in the late 1780s. Legally, French society was divided into three groups or orders. The First Estate was the clergy, the Second Estate the nobility, and the Third Estate everybody else. The category to which an individual belonged determined his legal rights and social status. The first two orders were privileged, (that is immune from certain taxes and laws), the third was not. By the eighteenth century these official classifications were obsolescent and no longer corresponded to the real distribution of wealth, influence or interest of the French people.

The First Estate, although numbering no more than 100,000 French clergy, owned about ten percent of the land in the nation. The church's income, derived from property, tithes, and fees was huge, estimated by some to be half of that of the government itself. The church was exempt from taxation but periodically voted a "free gift" as its contribution to the state treasury—the amount was always considerably less than direct taxes would have been. Besides its spiritual functions, the church performed many essential public services such as operating schools and hospitals and caring for the poor. On the whole, the clergy carried out its duties faithfully, particularly the lower clergy which was poorly paid and came formerly from the third estate. The high prelates, however, were vulnerable to criticism. The abbots, bishops, and archbishops shared the attitudes and way of life of the nobility into which they had been born. They kept a disproportionate share of church revenues to support their luxurious living style and too often fostered superstition and intolerance while impeding reforms and the dissemination of new ideas.

Alongside the clergy as a privileged order stood the Second Estate. The aristocracy comprised about 400,000 persons, including women and children, and had between a fifth and a quarter of the land. They did not form a cohesive group but were divided into ranks according to differences of wealth and social prestige. They ranged downward from the great aristocracy through the *noblesse de la robe* (nobility of the robe)—men who bought or inherited administrative or judicial offices which conferred noble status—to the impoverished *hobereaux* (little falcon), barely distinguishable from the simple farmers. All members of the French aristocracy, irrespective of the category to which they belonged, were entitled to special privileges, among them the right to wear a sword and exemption from the most burdensome of the direct taxes and from billeting troops. Since the death of Louis XIV the nobility had gradually recovered its political influence and power at the expense of the bourgeoisie. They now had a virtual monopoly of the best positions in the state, both civil and military, as well as in the church. Yet the aristocracy were not satisfied with their share of French power. During the last years of the old regime, as will be discussed, they made a concerted effort to end royal absolutism and to establish a constitutional monarchy under their control.

All those who were not clergymen or nobles fell within the Third Estate. The upper crust of the Third Estate were the bourgeoisie, a varied group that included merchants, manufacturers, shopkeepers, professional men, intellectuals, and skilled artisans. During the eighteenth century the bourgeoisie had made steady economic gains, in large measure due to the fivefold increase in French foreign trade. Some acquired huge fortunes and enjoyed tax exemptions. The more ambitious wealthy bourgeoisie sought to enter the ranks of the nobility.

The prosperity of the bourgeoisie was not shared by the petty craftsmen and unskilled laborers who were concentrated in a few centers, particularly Paris, Marseilles, and Lyons. A surplus of labor, together with high inflation, meant that wages did not keep pace with prices. During the half century before 1789 the cost of living increased by 62 percent while wages rose only 22 percent. As a result the purchasing power of the urban workers fell below subsistence level. The economic depression which gripped France in the late 1780s accentuated their suffering and fueled their resentment against the government.

Among the commoners the vast majority were peasants who lived and worked on the land. The peasants in France were better off than those elsewhere on the European continent. Serfdom had practically disappeared in France and many peasants owned their own land. The available evidence indicates that peasants owned between 30 and 40 percent of the land in France. Peasants who owned no land entered into leasing or sharecropping arrangements, or hired themselves out as day laborers on estates. Some landowning peasants were comfortably off, even prosperous. Most peasants, however, lived a very hard and marginal existence.

The combined burden of feudal obligations and state taxes weighed heavily on the peasantry. Proprietary peasants were required to give free service to the noblemen to whom their holding had once belonged, while those renting land had to make a cash payment or turn over a considerable portion of their crops to the lord. They also had to pay fees for use of the lord's mill, oven, wine press, and breeding stock. On top of this they had to shoulder a disproportionate share of the direct taxes levied by the state.

The economic conditions of the peasantry worsened during the last decades of the old regime. This was the result of poor harvests, a rise in prices, and the nobility's efforts to collect their dues more vigorously, revive old ones that had fallen into disuse, and increase the rent of their peasant lease holders and sharecroppers. With increased dues the customary discontent among the peasants reached fever pitch. Yet they remained essentially traditionalist in outlook. What they wanted was not a change in the system of government, but the opportunity to own land, or extend holdings, relief from taxation, and an end to vexatious manorial dues.

Theories on the Origins of the French Revolution

Few topics have generated as much discussion and controversy as the origins of the French Revolution. Often the explanations are both simplistic and contradictory. To some it was a legitimate uprising of the French people against an inefficiently centralized, corrupt and highly privileged system. But recent studies have shown that below the national level France was governed reasonably well. Others have held that Enlightenment thought corroded the old order by sapping faith in traditional values and institutions. This theory too has undergone scholarly revision. The ideas of the philosophes helped shape social programs once the royal system had broken down but they did not cause the revolution. The philosophes, besides distrusting the ignorant masses, never advocated the destruction of the monarchy or the social order.

Still another explanation stressed that the revolution was rooted in a class struggle. According to this Marxist view, the steadily prospering middle class, finding the avenues of upward mobility blocked by a resurgent aristocracy, fought to gain political control of the state and change social institutions for their own benefit. This neat and attractive thesis, once widely accepted by historians of the Revolution, has begun to crumble under the onslaught of new research. There does not appear to have been a deliberate attempt to thwart the social rise of ambitious bourgeoisie and in fact some recent works have suggested that entry into the nobility was more common after 1750 than before. The old nobility did consciously seek to monopolize political power in the second half of the eighteenth century, but this was aimed less at the bourgeoisie generally than at the newly ennobled men of great wealth. At any rate, their campaign was confined to the very highest posts in the bureaucracy and did not inhibit the recruitment of bourgeoisie candidates into the other levels of state service. Undoubtedly a certain number of non-noble civil servants felt frustrated but it is incorrect to say that the bourgeoisie as a whole conspired to tear down the system.

The latest scholarship also suggests that social divisions were not clearly defined in the pre-1789 era. Wealthy noblemen tended to have more in common with the upper bourgeoisie than with poor aristocrats. Bourgeoisie and aristocrats were all part of a single propertied elite and, contrary to Marxian theory, there was no significant difference in their value systems. Although tensions existed, there is little evidence of widespread hostility within the propertied elite. During the late 1780s most bourgeoisie supported the noble-led movement to establish a constitutional monarchy. It was not until quarrels broke out over the composition and voting procedures of the Estates General between September 1788 and June 1789 that the bourgeoisie began to show some consciousness of its own separate character and interests. Thus the bourgeoisie did not make the revolution; rather it was the revolution that made the bourgeoisie.

There is currently no general consensus on the deeper causes of the French Revolution. All that can be said is that it began as an effort to solve the financial crisis and as it unfolded drew upon undercurrents of unrest running through the ancient regime, the consequences of which substantially altered the whole fabric of France.

The Monarchy in Crisis

Louis XVI was nineteen years old when he succeeded his grandfather as king of France in 1774. Although a man of good moral character, personally frugal and well meaning, he lacked the qualities of statesmanship. His worst fault was his lack of self-confidence. The young king had a difficult time arriving at a decision, and when he finally issued an order, it was easy for someone with frequent access to his company, to persuade him to countermand it. Louis was further handicapped by his unpopular queen Marie Antoinette. The youngest daughter of Austrian Empress Maria Theresa, she was frivolous and extravagant and prone to interfering in the affairs of state.

What Louis wanted above all was to be loved by his subjects. His initial moves reflected his good intentions. He trimmed royal expenditures, appointed competent ministers and discussed ways to bring down bread prices. Showing less wisdom, Louis reversed his predecessor's policy by restoring the parlements and confirming their former prerogatives. The gesture was extremely popular for the masses viewed the high courts as a check on royal absolutism. What they failed to recognize was that the parlements, made up of judges who had purchased their office and who had noble status, were also an obstacle to social and economic reform.

Louis's most pressing concern in the pre-1789 period was to find some means to deal with the deepening financial crisis. What caused the government's financial plight was not the extravagance of the court but rather war costs and the upkeep of the army and navy. On the eve of the revolution, the debt stood at 4 billion livres, more than triple that of 1774. About half the increase resulted from France's participation in the American war for independence. The credit of the government fell so sharply in the 1780s that it was forced to pay interest rates of 20 percent on its loans—five times the normal rate. The interest payment on the national debt is estimated to have consumed half the total revenues.

Given the wealth of France, its debt was neither excessive nor disproportionate to those of other European powers. But the government was unable to carry the debt simply because expenditures greatly exceeded revenues. The government had only two options to overcome this dilemma. One was to repudiate the debt but to do so would destroy its credit. The other was to broaden the tax base to place a fair share of the burden on the privileged elements.

Louis, however, lacked the backbone to ram through a tax reform scheme over the objections of the aristocracy. His succession of controller-generals had no alternative but to extemporize and borrow money to cover the government's deficit. Then, in 1786, the bankers refused to make new advances. In despair, the king summoned an "assembly of notables," a handpicked body of leading aristocrats and churchmen, in the hope of winning its endorsement for a new tax plan. Convening at Versailles in 1787 the notables at first disbelieved the report of the crown's impending bankruptcy. When the existence of a huge deficit was verified they indicated they would contribute to the state treasury on condition the king agreed to give them greater control over the government. After several stormy sessions they were dismissed.

The pinch for money became so acute that Louis, with uncharacteristic firmness, decreed that a new land tax be levied on all landowners regardless of status. However the parlement of Paris declared the king's land tax illegal, asserting that any such measure required the consent of the nation through its duly chosen representatives—the Estates General. Reluctantly, Louis retreated and in July 1788 announced that the Estates-General would meet the following spring.

By the action of the parlement the aristocrats, the chief beneficiaries of the old regime, had brought the monarchy to its knees. In forcing the convocation of the Estates General they sought to safeguard their interests, preserve their social preeminence, and substitute their own rule for royal absolutism. Their triumph, however, was short-lived. The revolutionary wave they released assumed such proportions that in the end it destroyed the old regime and with it their order and their privileges.

The Convening of the Estates General

Until now the Third Estate, although resentful of the arrogance of the privileged orders, had enthusiastically and almost unanimously applauded their opposition to royal absolutism. This unity began to crumble after the issue of voting method in the Estates General was raised. The aristocracy wanted the three estates to follow the ancient custom of meeting separately and voting as a unit. The commoners quickly saw that under this system, with the nobility and clergy standing together, they would always be outvoted two to one. They insisted that the Third Estate should have as many deputies as the combined total of the other two and that voting should be by head, not by order. The confidence and boldness of the commoners was enhanced with the publication of Abbé Emmanuel Siéyès' pamphlet "What is the Third Estate?" which argued that since the Third Estate constituted the nation it should have a decisive voice in all political matters. After a period of indecision the King finally announced that the Third Estate was to have double representation but he failed to specify whether the three orders would sit together in a single assembly.

The election procedure was hurriedly worked out and early in 1789 voters met in the chief town of each district to make their selections. Both the First and Second Estates chose their representatives by direct vote. The deputies representing the Third Estate were for the most part commoners, although there were a few outsiders like Abbé Siéyès and comte de Mirabeau. All male members of the Third Estate who had reached the age of twenty-five and paid taxes were eligible to vote in a multi-stage selection process. This indirect method favored the educated elite with the result that most of the delegates came from the middle or upper middle class.

Each representative was required to bring with him a *cahier*, a list of grievances from his electors, to be presented to the king. These *cahiers*, many of which survive, show a surprising degree of unanimity on major points. As a rule, Frenchmen, while espousing loyalty to the crown, wanted to remove the iniquities in the tax and legal systems and desired a written constitution that would limit royal authority and ensure basic civil liberties. A few of the *cahiers* were written by women who objected to the restrictions imposed on their sex. They demanded public jobs, educational opportunities and, if married, changes in the marriage laws to give them greater control over their doweries and their children.

A striking aspect of the *cahiers* was the moderation of both the demands themselves and the tone in which they were made. There was no hint of an impending revolution. Nor were the difficulties of the period clearly reflected.

The election took place in the midst of widespread economic suffering. One problem was produced by the new commercial treaty between France and Great Britain which was put in force in May 1787. Freer trade with Great Britain boosted the exports of French grain and wine; it was undoubtedly a far sighted move for France's long run prosperity, but initially it was disastrous for certain French industries. Able to undercut any competitor, British manufacturers flooded French markets with their cotton, hardware and textile goods. Production in France slumped; a wave of bankruptcies occurred and unemployment reached staggering levels in the cities. In large parts of the country hail and drought had reduced the harvest. By the spring of 1789 grain prices had doubled. Since the lower classes spent as much as two thirds of their income on food during normal times, some idea may be gained of the seriousness of the situation. Riots swept across many provincial towns and cities with mobs attacking granaries and bakeries or forcing local authorities to lower prices for bread. The unrest spread to Paris in April 1789 when rumor of a wage reduction at the establishment of Reveillon, a wealthy wallpaper manufacturer, triggered severe disorders in which at least 50 of the rioters were killed or wounded. On top of all of this, the winter of 1788–1789 was unusually harsh and in Paris the municipal government provided bonfires to keep the poor from freezing to death.

THE NATIONAL ASSEMBLY

On May 5, 1789, a week after the Reveillon riots, the King formally opened the proceedings of the Estates General. The economic crisis and the resultant disturbances had increased the deputies' sense of urgency. The Third Estate, however, refused to take up any work until it was agreed that the three orders should meet in a single body and vote as individuals. This procedure would enable the Third Estate, with its double membership (600 as compared to 300 in each of the other two), reinforced by support of reform minded nobles and priests, to hold an assured majority. As was to be expected, the privileged groups reaffirmed the tradition of voting by order. The ensuing impasse widened the breach that had appeared several months before.

The king had again left the question unsettled at the first meeting of the Estates General. On the following days, he vacillated, careful not to offend anyone. The Third Estate broke the deadlock on June 17 by proclaiming itself the National Assembly and inviting the other orders to join it. On the morning of June 20, the deputies of the Third Estate, assembling for their daily debates, found their chamber locked. Unknown to them, the hall was being prepared for a royal sitting to be held two days later. Suspecting that the Estates General was about to be dissolved, the angry delegates moved to a nearby tennis court. Here, amid intense excitement and with upraised hands, they took an oath to remain in session until they had given France a constitution. The Tennis Court Oath, as it is known to history, marks the beginning of the French Revolution. It is an assertion that sovereign power resided in a new body that had no legal authority.

The king quickly lost control over the Estates General, failing to exert leadership or to present a program of reform. Under intense pressure from conservative advisers and from the queen's clique, Louis came down on the side of the privileged orders. At a royal session on June 23, the king annulled the resolution of June 17 and instructed the three estates to meet separately. The First and Second Estates went off to their meeting halls, but the Third Estate remained seated in defiance. When reminded of the

The Tennis Court Oath, June 20, 1789. A romanticized version by Jacques-Louis David, the most renowned artist of the day and an ardent republican. In the center of this painting, the members of the three estates join hands in a symbolic show of unity before a cheering National Assembly. Standing on the table with his right hand raised is Jean Bailly, president of the National Assembly. Below him Abbé Siéyès is seated quietly at the table. Mirabeau, with his hat in his left hand and wearing a black coat, is in the right foreground. Robespierre is standing between Mirabeau and Siéyès with both hands on his chest. Versailles.

king's wishes, Mirabeau rose to his feet and said in a thundering voice: "Go and tell those who sent you that we are here by the will of the people, and that we shall not leave except at the point of a bayonet." Troops were within call, but Louis hesitated to use them. Then a report that a Paris mob was being organized to march on Versailles shook his nerve. On June 27, Louis reversed his position and ordered the three estates to sit together and vote by head. The king's action implied recognition of the National Assembly's right to act as the highest sovereign power in the nation. But, as events would show, he could not bring himself to accept the new arrangement, because it meant the end of a regime he felt bound by honor to maintain.

Collapse of Absolutism and the End of Feudalism

Early in July, Louis, urged by the queen and reactionary courtiers, ordered the concentration of large numbers of troops in the vicinity of Versailles. The leaders of the National Assembly anticipated a royal *coup d'état.* Their suspicions were heightened on July 11 when the king dismissed his finance minister, Jacques Necker, whom they regarded as a champion of reform. In Paris, the populace, restless over increasing cost of food and terrified by the close proximity of royal regiments, went on a rampage, breaking into gunsmith shops and public buildings in search of arms. The three days of wild disorder culminated in the storming of the Bastille, a castlelike fortress supposedly filled with political prisoners. In fact it contained only seven prisoners, none of whom were altogether innocent.

Viewed as a symbol of oppression, the Bastille was razed to the ground. July 14, the date on which the Bastille fell, is a national holiday in France, celebrated as the birth of freedom and justice.

Frightened by the wanton destruction, a group of prominent bourgeoisie took control of the administration of Paris. They chose Jean Bailly as mayor and appointed the marquis de Lafayette, an honored figure since his participation in the American Revolution, to command the National Guard, which had been organized to police the city. The king, rather than undertake a siege of Paris, decided on appeasement. He recalled Necker and withdrew his troops from around Paris. On July 17 he visited Paris to show good will, indicating approval of the National Assembly and recognizing the new government of Paris. The crowds, suspicious at first, heartily cheered the king after he donned the new tricolor cockade, the revolutionary symbol—the colors of Paris, blue and red, combined with the white of the house of Bourbon. "From this moment," wrote the British ambassador in Paris, "we may consider France a free country, the King as a very limited monarch." Many of the leading court aristocrats, led by the king's younger brother, comte d'Artois, fled the country. It was the start of a great royalist emigration.

The disturbances in Paris coincided with a movement in the countryside known as the Great Fear. During the spring of 1789 there had been a number of local outbreaks among the peasantry sparked by the economic crisis. These disorders intensified in the latter part of July because of rumors that the aristocracy were employing brigands to burn crops,

pillage, a lation. could fin defense. The ginary, nourished the hatred of the nobility. w brigands did not appear, the peasa vented their anger by burning castles, confiscating land, destroying records of feudal obligations, and occasionally murdering nobles who offered resistance. Provincial authorities made little effort to contain the violence, which bordered on anarchy in many rural districts.

The reports of the rural insurrection spurred the National Assembly into immediate action. On the night of August 4, as the National Assembly was about to adjourn, a liberal nobleman, vicomte de Noailles, proposed the elimination of seignorial rights as a way to end the injustices of rural life. His suggestion was greeted with a thunderous applause. The nobility, realizing they were being asked to give up what they could no longer hold and assured of compensation, became as enthusiastic as the commoners. In a scene of great emotion, nobles vied with churchmen in renouncing traditional rights and immunities. The session, which lasted until dawn, produced historic changes. Serfdom, ecclesiastical tithes, and all forms of personal obligation were abolished. Hunting and fishing privileges were ended. Judicial and municipal offices could no longer be sold. The principle of equal taxation and civil equality was proclaimed. Finally, all citizens, regardless of birth, were eligible for any office, whether civil, military, or ecclesiastical. In one sweep the National Assembly had destroyed the feudal system.

This action opened the way for a

rance to emerge. Toward the
of August, the National Assem-
issued the "Declaration of the
ights of Man and Citizen," a document intended as a preface to the
impending constitution. The Declaration is of historic importance because it expresses clearly and suc-
cinctly the ideas that had become
central to eighteenth-century thought.
Suggested by the American and British Bill of Rights, the document was
permeated with the ideas of Locke,
Montesquieu and to some extent
Rousseau, and in effect summarized
the principles on which a new order
was to be built. It reflected the political and economic sentiments of the
middle class, affirming that sovereignty resided with the people; the
obligation of all citizens to pay taxes
proportionately to their incomes;
freedom of speech, press, and worship; and the right to own property
and to a speedy and fair trial. Posted
all over France the Declaration was
quickly translated into many languages and disseminated throughout
Europe and beyond.

The king gave no indication that
he would ratify either the sweeping
reforms of August 4 or the revolutionary principles of the Declaration.
His delay fed suspicion that he might
use force to undo the work of the
revolution. Social tensions were
heightened by the continued misery
of the people. Food was scarce, prices
exorbitant, and unemployment widespread. On October 5, an angry crowd
of women raided bakeshops in Paris
and then marched on the royal palace
at Versailles to petition for cheaper
bread. As the women trooped along,
it became clear that they also meant
to bring the king back to Paris, presumably to remove him from the grip
of evil counsellors. The king's promise of bread was not enough to dis-
perse the mob. Towards morning a
small group broke into the palace,
murdered several guards and narrowly
missed killing the queen. Lafayette,
who had arrived on the scene earlier
with detachments of National Guard,
drove out the invaders and restored
order. At the urging of Lafayette, the
king reluctantly agreed to go to Paris

with his family. In the afternoon of
October 6, the procession started for
Paris, the mob, with the royal carriage in its midst, shouting exult-
antly: "We have the baker, the baker's wife and the baker's boy. Now we
shall have bread." Arriving in Paris
at midnight the king and his family
were installed in the old Tuileries palace. A few days later the National
Assembly, or the National Constituent Assembly as it was now called
(because if was preparing a constitution), voted to follow the king.
Henceforth, both the king and the
Constituent Assembly would fall under the influence of the Paris mob,
which was readier than ever to resort
to violence to express its fears or
achieve its goals.

The Financial Crisis and the Civil Constitution of the Clergy

The Estates General had been summoned, it should be recalled, to find
a way to avert impending government
bankruptcy. During the summer of

The March of the Women to Versailles, October 1789. Driven by hunger, a crowd of
women marched 11 miles to Versailles and
compelled the king and his family to return
to Paris with them. Subsequently, women would
show similar resolution, participating in violent action and condoning terror, to achieve
the goals of the revolution.

1789, however, the financial crisis had become more acute. The old taxes had been abolished, but the new ones could not be collected. In desperation the Constituent Assembly confiscated church property in November 1789. The church owned about ten percent of the cultivated land of France and its total assets were valued at three billion livres, almost the equivalent of the national debt.

Against this property, the Constituent Assembly authorized the sale of treasury bills, or *assignats*. The *assignats* would bear interest at five percent and could only be redeemed by the purchase of former church lands. The *assignats* eventually depreciated to less than two percent of their face value, but in the meantime, when taxes were virtually uncollectable, they allowed the government to meet day-to-day expenses.

The Constituent Assembly, having deprived the church of its wealth and income, next reorganized the ecclesiastical system along lines more in accordance with the principles of the revolution. In February 1790 the Assembly dissolved most of the monasteries and forbade the taking of perpetual vows. This was followed by the enactment in July of the "Civil Constitution of the Clergy." Under the new law, the number of bishops was reduced from 135 to 83, that is, one for each of the new administrative divisions. All clergymen, bishops as well as priests, were to be paid by the state according to a fixed scale. Furthermore, they were required, like other public officials, to be elected by those they served. Thus the church became a department of the state, entirely removed from papal jurisdiction.

The pope, denied a role in administering the church and in ecclesiastical appointments in France, condemned the Civil Constitution. The Constituent Assembly responded by decreeing that all clergymen must take an oath to support the new arrangement. French churchmen found themselves impaled on the horns of a dilemma. If they took the loyalty oath, they would be excommunicated by the pope, and if they refused to do so, they would lose their posts and salaries and face the possibility of imprisonment. Only seven bishops and fewer than half the parish priests obeyed the state. The remainder, known as "nonjuring clergy," either went abroad and joined the growing numbers of émigrés (French royalists who had emigrated) or stayed in France and incited the faithful to resist the revolution.

The Civil Constitution was perhaps the most serious error of the Constituent Assembly. Few informed and pious Catholics would have disputed the need for reform. But imposing reforms without considering traditional procedures in the church alienated many who had previously supported the revolution.

The Constitution of 1791

The Assembly's primary task of drafting a constitution for the nation, begun in 1789, was completed by the spring of 1791. The constitution confirmed the transformation of France from an absolute to a limited monarchy. Although the king still controlled the army and navy and directed foreign policy, his authority over internal affairs was drastically reduced. He was allowed only a suspensive (temporary) veto over legislation. Any bill passed by three successive legislatures would become law even without royal assent.

Apart from legislative authority, the unicameral Legislative Assembly was to control both taxes and expenditures. This body consisted of 745 deputies elected for a term of two years. Despite the Declaration of the Rights of Man and Citizen, suffrage was extended only to "active citizens"— males over twenty-five who paid taxes equal to at least three days' wages. The rest, designated "passive citizens," were not allowed to vote. The political power of even "active citizens" was restricted. They could vote only for electors who actually chose the deputies. Property qualifications for electors and for deputies were so high they could be met by less than 50,000 persons. Still, although favoring the rich, the French political system was more democratic than that of any of its European neighbors, including Great Britain.

The Assembly also incorporated into the constitution many other reforms. In economic matters, it was inspired by the laissez-faire doctrine. Guilds and trade unions were suppressed, monopolies were ended, and custom duties and internal tariffs were lifted. Citizens were free to engage in the occupation of their choice.

The chaotic and illogical political units of the old regime were replaced by an orderly and uniform system. The country was divided into eighty-three departments of approximately equal size and each department was subdivided into districts, cantons and communes (see Map 56). Public officials were elected at every level of local government.

A thorough overhaul of the judicial system accompanied the restructuring of administrative divisions. The constitution swept away the old law

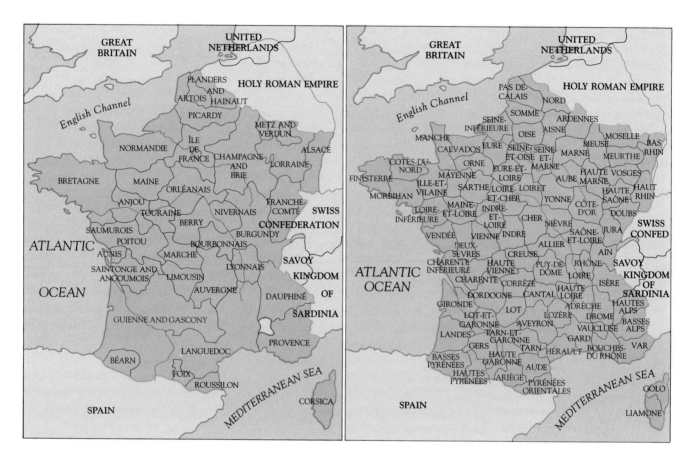

MAP 56

(Left) French Provinces and Regions before 1789; (Right) French Departments after 1789. Pre-revolutionary France was a complicated and illogical mosaic of provinces and regions with conflicting local administrations and varying degrees of self government. The National Assembly swept away the old internal divisions and reorganized the nation into 83 departments, each of which was named after its most striking geographic feature. The departments were roughly equal in size and were small enough so that no place would be more than a day's journey from the chief town.

courts, including the regional parlements, and established instead a rational system of lower and higher courts, all presided over by elected judges. It introduced the British and American concept of trial by jury for criminal cases. The penal code was humanized by eliminating torture and branding and by reducing the types of crime punishable by death. Historians have generally regarded the reorganization of the judiciary as among the Constituent Assembly's best work.

If the revolution brought significant advantages to ordinary French men it was less kind to women. Revolutionary feminists began with a burst of enthusiasm as they engaged in political action and took to sending delegations to the government. Their efforts, however, failed to change the status of women in public life. Their calls for the suffrage, equality in areas of public service, and access to a broad education were dismissed by revolutionary leaders who charged that their demands were unnatural because women belonged in the home. The only satisfaction that women found was in the piecemeal legislation between 1790 and 1794 that improved their private life. Inheritance laws were changed to guarantee the right of women to share equally with male heirs. Women reached majority at twenty-one (the same as men), could contract debts, and be witnesses in civil acts. Other laws treated both sexes equally in divorce suits and gave women a voice in the administration of their own property and in the rearing of their children. Most of these gains were short-lived. Napoleon's codes a decade later would cancel out practically all the advances the women had made.

The Rise of the Jacobins

Among the leading critics of the government were the political clubs, which became more and more revolutionary. In the early days of the Assembly, like minded delegates gathered in small informal groups for the purpose of discussing impending legislation. This practice led to the formation of political clubs. The most important of these organizations met in the monastery of Jacobin Friars, and its members were known as Jacobins. The ranks of the club swelled rapidly after nondeputies were admitted. The Jacobins exercised nationwide influence through their close-knit network of affiliate clubs, which may have numbered as many as 2000. Originally, the Jacobin club was moderate in its political orientation. But when radical elements gained control of its leadership, it became a center of revolutionary ideas and agitation.

The King's Flight Foiled

In June 1791, the king, unreconciled to the reforms forced upon him, secretly fled Paris with his family. His plan was to rally loyal supporters in the northeast and, together with such foreign help as could be mustered, return to his capital as master. Everything went so well initially that Louis, in his elation, neglected to maintain his disguise. He was recognized at Varennes, near the frontier, and sub-

sequently brought back to Paris under guard.

The king's attempt to flee and a note denouncing the revolution that he had left behind, made it clear he had joined the enemies of the new regime. The radical newspapers, led by *L'ami du peuple,* now began to clamor for the establishment of a republic. The middle-class-controlled Constituent Assembly suspended the king but shrank from proclaiming a republic, fearful that such action might deliver the government into the hands of the common people. Pretending that the king had been abducted from Paris, it reinstated him. Louis then formally accepted the constitution.

One of the last acts of the Constituent Assembly was to decree that none of its members could stand for election to the new legislature. This foolish law, made in a spirit of self-denial, assured that the Legislative Assembly would be composed of men with little political training. On September 30, 1791, the Constituent Assembly disbanded with the announcement that the revolution was over.

FAILURE OF THE MODERATE REGIME

The constitutional monarchy created by the Constitution of 1791 represented the bourgeoisie's desire to stabilize the revolution and block further changes. Launched with great expectations when the Legislative Assembly convened in October 1791, it lasted less than a year. The failure of the new system of government was principally due to three causes.

First was the king's unwillingness to accept the modest role which he had been assigned under the constitution. From the outset Louis, under constant pressure from the queen and her advisers, attempted to undermine the Legislative Assembly. Not only did he use his power of veto too often and too unwisely but he also made repeated secret appeals to his fellow monarchs to intervene on his behalf. By his obstructionism and duplicity, he played into the hands of the radicals.

Second was the disillusionment of the small shopkeepers, artisans and urban laborers, a disparate group collectively called *sans culottes* because they wore trousers in contrast to the breeches of the aristocracy. The chief beneficiaries of the reforms between 1789 and 1791 had been the bourgeoisie and the peasants. The bourgeoisie in effect had replaced the aristocracy as the ruling class. The peasants were no longer saddled with manorial obligations; many more owned property. But the *sans culottes,* despite their major role in making reforms possible, had gained little except theoretical rights and legal equality. They looked in vain for the government to control inflation, to provide bread and other necessities in adequate quantities and at prices they could afford. Frustrated, they became attracted to eloquent demagogues who were determined to see the revolution continue until it brought perfect democracy and complete equality.

The third reason for the demise of the constitutional monarchy was the outbreak of war against Austria and Prussia in April 1792. Wartime hysteria provoked violence and discord that moved the revolution from a moderate to a radical stage. The radicalization of the revolution led to the overthrow of the monarchy and the creation of a republic in what historians often refer to as the Second French Revolution.

The Revolution Goes to War

The events in France were of concern to the European monarchs who feared the spread of revolutionary ideas to their own lands. The outbreak and early progress of the revolution was applauded by the general public in Europe as a triumph of liberty over despotism. As the revolution became more radical, however, it prompted growing fears that it was undermining traditional society and civilization. All over Europe voices began to be raised against the developments in France. The most vocal were those of the émigrés or nobles who had fled France. Embittered by their experiences and eager to regain their old privileges, they plotted the overthrow of the new French regime. Leopold II of Austria was the first monarch to react to their appeals. He was, apart from his dislike of the revolution, concerned about the fate of his sister, Marie Antoinette, and he saw the possiblity of making territorial gains at the expense of France. On August 27, 1791, Leopold, in conjunction with Frederick William II of Prussia, issued the now famous Declaration of Pillnitz, hinting at the use of armed force if necessary to restore royal absolutism and order in France.

The declaration was seen in France as an insult and a threat. On April 20, 1792, the Legislative Assembly, hoping to unite the country behind the revolution, declared war on Austria. Louis supported the war, reasoning that an Austrian victory (which he

confidently expected) would enable him to regain lost authority.

The French army not only was woefully unprepared for war but also court circles had treacherously disclosed its campaign plans to the enemy. Predictably, French forces fared badly at the outset. The Austrians, joined by the Prussians soon after the start of hostilities, crossed the frontier and opened a drive toward Paris. With the country in imminent danger of falling completely in the hands of the invading armies, the Legislative Assembly called for volunteers from the provinces. One detachment from Marseilles brought along a marching song composed by Rouget de Lisle. This was the *Marseillaise*, a stirring summons to war against tyranny and now the country's national anthem.

The initial success of the monarchical armies weakened rather than strengthened the French monarchy. On July 25, 1792, the duke of Brunswick, commander of the joint armies of Austria and Prussia, published a proclamation threatening to level Paris if it resisted or if any harm came to the royal family. The Brunswick Manifesto, far from terrifying the Parisians into submission, aroused a more determined opposition. It confirmed suspicions that the king was in collusion with the enemy, thus strengthening the republicans. In the days that followed, Jacobin leaders worked diligently to organize a popular insurrection. The climax came on the night of August 9–10, when the mob ousted the municipal government of Paris and replaced it with a revolutionary commune. On the orders of the new commune officials, the crowds assaulted the Tuileries on the morning of August 10, compelling the king and his family to flee to the halls of the Leg-

islative Assembly for protection. To appease the excited mob, the Assembly suspended the king from office and called for a new constituent assembly to decide France's future.

The provisional executive council, set up to replace the king, was dominated by Georges Danton, the new minister of justice. A practical politician and one of the most eloquent Jacobin speakers, Danton saw that his first duty was to rally the country against the invaders. On September 1, a message reached Paris that the fortress of Verdun was about to fall. Popular journalists like Jean Paul Marat, editor of *L'ami du peuple*, warned that as soon as Brunswick neared the capital, imprisoned antirevolutionary suspects would be released from prison and attack the defenders from behind. Incensed crowds broke into jails, set up revolutionary tribunals, and summarily executed suspects found guilty. Between September 2 and September 7, as many as 1,500 prisoners were massacred. The orgy of violence was also carried into the provinces. The "September massacres" were a foretaste of things to come.

The National Convention and the End of the Monarchy

Elections for the constituent assembly, or as it was soon called, the National Convention, were held against a background of violence and hysteria. Most of the conservative elements were too frightened to vote or were turned away at the polls, with the result that the republicans won a sweeping victory. The National Convention began its deliberations on September 20, 1792, the same day on which French forces stopped the

Prussian advance at Valmy. Convinced that his army was not strong enough to reach Paris, the duke of Brunswick withdrew from French territory. The dramatic improvement in the nation's military fortunes meant that the National Convention was free to deal with other matters.

As a body, the National Convention was more radical than either of its predecessors. It contained no royalists, only different republican factions. The Girondists, so called because their leaders came from the region of Gironde, were now the most conservative elements in the convention. They represented the interests of the provincial propertied and commercial classes. They favored an end to revolutionary legislation, nongovernmental interference in the economy, and a decentralized system of government.

The Jacobins made up the radical wing. Aptly named the Montagnards (Mountain men) as they occupied the highest seats in the chamber, they came from the same class as the Girondists but differed from them in their social and political objectives. The Montagnards drew most of their support from Paris, and, mindful of working-class demands, insisted on universal male suffrage, state control of the economy, an all-powerful central government, and programs to help the poor. Their chief spokesmen were Danton, Marat, and Robespierre. The Montagnards had fewer deputies than the Girondists but they were better led and organized, more ruthless, and enjoyed the backing of the powerful Paris commune.

Between the two factions, the deputies of the Plain (because they sat on the lower seats in the assembly hall) constituted a majority in the convention. Although they were fervent nationalists and committed to the revolution, they lacked concrete principles. At first they sided with the Girondists, but fear of the unruly Paris mob drove them into the arms of the Montagnards.

In the early days of the convention, the various factions were in basic harmony. The deputies formally abolished the monarchy and declared France a republic. All parties agreed that the king was guilty of treason and that he could not be set free. The Girondists and Montagnards, however, were sharply divided on the king's fate. The Girondists, realizing that Louis's execution would have unfavorable repercussions abroad, wanted to hold him a prisoner and then banish him at the end of the war. The Montagnards demanded his death, convinced that the republic was in danger as long as he was alive. After a long debate, the king was condemned to death by a narrow majority. On January 21, 1793, Citizen Louis Capet, as Louis XVI was now called, was beheaded by the guillotine, the new official instrument of execution.

Louis XVI Mounting the Scaffold. This painting by C. Banazech is a reasonably accurate rendition of the scene. Security was heavy. Until the last moment it was feared that royalists would attempt to rescue the king and a double line of troops hedged the road between the prison and the Place de la Révolution where the scaffold had been erected. With the Abbé Edgeworth at his side, the king stood in cold, misty weather in a plain white waistcoat, gray breeches, and dark stockings. Moments earlier the executioners had tried to tie his hands behind his back but he had shaken them off. He went to his death with a courage he had failed to show while directing the affairs of state. Versailles.

ROBESPIERRE'S JUSTIFICATION FOR THE TERROR

What is the goal for which we strive? A peaceful enjoyment of liberty and equality, the rule of that eternal justice whose laws are engraved, not upon marble or stone, but in the hearts of all men . . .

We wish an order of things where all low and cruel passions are enchained by the laws, all beneficent and generous feelings aroused; . . .

In our country we wish to substitute morality for egotism, probity for honor, principles for conventions, duties for etiquette, the empire of reason for the tyranny of customs, contempt for vice for contempt for misfortune, pride for insolence, the love of honor for the love of money . . . that is to say, all the virtues and miracles of the Republic for all the vices and snobbishness of the monarchy. . . . That is our ambition: that is our aim.

What kind of government can realize these marvels? Only a democratic government. . . .

Now what is the fundamental principle of democratic, or popular government—that is to say, the essential mainspring upon which it depends and which makes it function? It is virtue: I mean public virtue . . . that virtue which is nothing else but love of fatherland and its laws. . . .

The splendor of the goal of the French Revolution is simultaneously the source of our strength and of our weakness: our strength, because it gives us an ascendancy of truth over falsehood, and of public rights over private interests; our weakness, because it rallies against us all vicious men, all those who in their hearts seek to despoil the people. . . . It is necessary to stifle the domestic and foreign enemies of the Republic or perish with them. Now in these circumstances, the first maxim of our politics ought to be to lead the people by means of reason and the enemies of the people by terror.

If the basis of popular government in time of peace is virtue, the basis of popular government in time of revolution is both virtue and terror: virtue without which terror is murderous, terror without which virtue is powerless. Terror is nothing else than swift, severe, indomitable justice; it flows, then, from virtue.[*]

A country lawyer from Arras, Robespierre was elected in 1789 to sit in the Estates General and subsequently represented a Paris constituency in the National Convention. His impatience with deliberative bodies convinced him that his ideal republic could be established only by state intervention. Opinions about Robespierre vary widely but in recent years there has been a tendency to view him less as a bloodthirsty dictator and more as a fanatical idealist whose zeal led him to adopt methods which he had previously condemned.

[*]Raymond Stearns, ed. *Pageant of Europe,* (New York: Harcourt, Brace and World, 1961), pp. 404–405.

The First Allied Coalition

After Valmy French armies drove the enemy back across the Rhine and invaded Belgium and Savoy. Flushed with victory, the Convention announced its intention to assist all people who desired to gain their liberty. This was tantamount to declaring war against every monarchical government in Europe. By the spring of 1793, Great Britain, The Netherlands, Spain, and Sardinia had joined Austria and Prussia in the first of five coalitions against France. Under the crushing weight of allied pressure, French revolutionary armies encountered reverses on every front.

Internal discontent compounded the difficulties facing the National Convention. The conservative, pious peasants of the Vendée region, already troubled by the Civil Constitution of the Clergy and the execution of the king, rose in rebellion when officials prepared to draft young men for military service. The continuing rise in prices, brought on by a scarcity of essentials, caused riots in Paris and in other cities.

The external threat and the internal disturbances created a struggle for power between the Girondists and the Montagnards. The issue came to a head on May 31, 1793, when a huge crowd of some 80,000, responding to the Montagnards' call for support, surrounded the Convention building and demanded the expulsion of the leading Girondists. After a feeble show of resistance, the Convention gave in to the pressure on June 2. Those not arrested went into hiding.

THE REIGN OF TERROR

With the expulsion of the Girondists the way was now open for the Montagnards to take control of the government. Their first move was to draft and push through the Convention a new democratic constitution which, among other things, abolished property qualifications as a requirement for the vote. The constitution was ratified by the people, but its operation was suspended until the conclusion of the war emergency. Instead the Convention increasingly abdicated power to a group of twelve deputies known as the Committee of Public Safety. From September 1793 until July 1794, the Committee exercised almost dictatorial authority and the Convention became a mere rubber stamp. The dominant member of the Committee was Maximilien Robespierre. A fervent disciple of Rousseau, Robespierre was determined to establish an ideal republic founded on justice, trust, equality and unselfish patriotism. To achieve his end, he was ready to employ any means, including coercion and capital punishment.

The problems facing the Committee were awesome. Rebellion had spread, fed in part by the expulsion of the Girondist deputies. Major provincial cities such as Toulon, Bordeaux, Marseilles, and Lyons were in revolt. In the Vendée the insurgents were holding their own against the government troops. Foreign armies had again invaded France. Drastic action was necessary to save the revolution and the republic.

France, those in authority believed, must present a united front, or, as Robespierre observed "a single will," before the nation's foreign enemies could be crushed. The policy adopted to achieve this single will was terrorism. A series of decrees, the most important of which was the Law of Suspects, rendered liable to arbitrary arrest any person suspected of being disloyal to the republic. At the disposal of the Committee of Public Safety was the Committee of General Security, a body supervising police activities, and the Revolutionary Tribunal, which suspended the usual legal procedure in the interest of speedy "justice." The policy of terror was not only confined to Paris but spread to the provinces where government agents were responsible for many barbarous practices. The Terror sought to destroy anyone, regardless of class origin, who appeared to threaten the republic. Among those who perished under the guillotine were Danton, Desmoulins and Hébert (revolutionary leaders at odds with Robespierre), Bailly, the former mayor of Paris, Marie Antoinette, and Charlotte Corday, a Girondist sympathizer, who had stabbed Marat to death. During

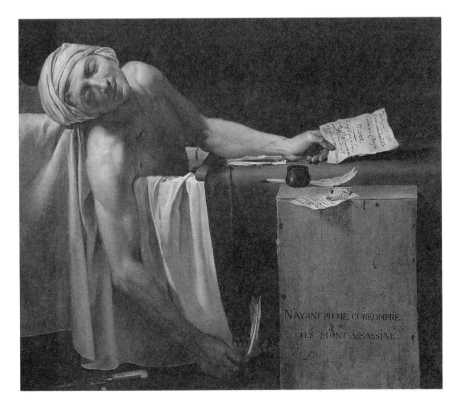

The Assassination of Marat. Detail. Founder of *L'ami du peuple,* a vituperative newspaper, Marat also served in the National Convention and as president of the Paris Jacobin Club. In July 1793, Charlotte Corday, a Girondist sympathizer, regarding Marat as an enemy of freedom and the cause of many of France's woes, went to his house and stabbed him while he was in his bath. In death Marat became one of the greatest of the revolutionary martyrs. Prints of this celebrated painting by David were sold everywhere in Paris. Royal Museum of Fine Arts, Brussels.

the Committee's ascendancy, it is estimated that between 35,000 and 40,000 people lost their lives.

Within the Committee, the defense of the republic was entrusted to Lazare Carnot, a professional soldier who was highly skillful both as an administrator and a strategist. In August 1793, a *levée en masse* was proclaimed, placing the entire human and material resources of the nation at the disposal of the government. All unmarried men from eighteen to twenty-five were drafted for combat service, and by the end of the year France's army stood at nearly 800,000. Under Carnot's supervision, the recruits were carefully trained, thoroughly disci-

plined, and infused with fighting zeal. He made a number of innovations such as improving the mechanism of supply in order to make his armies more mobile. Disregarding military seniority, he placed brilliant young generals at the head of the armies.

These changes swiftly turned the tide. By the end of 1793, the insurrection in the Vendée had been suppressed, Toulon recaptured, and the armies of the coalition hurled back to the frontiers. In the spring of 1794 French armies took the offensive and poured into neighboring nations.

While Robespierre and his associates were busy trying to keep the republic afloat, they also took mea-

sures to reshape French institutions and society. To keep the cost of living down, the government fixed wages and prices for essential commodities. Imprisonment for debt, slavery in the colonies, and the practice of primogeniture—the inheritance of property by the eldest son only—were all abolished. A new and uniform standard of weights and measures, the metric system, was established. It proved so convenient that most of the nations of the world eventually adopted it.

Inside and outside official circles anything that smacked of royalty and privilege was discarded. All titles were abolished and "citizen" and "citizen-

MAP 57

The French Republic and its Satellites in 1799. Between 1794 and 1799, the new French armies carried out a series of great campaigns. The French conquered almost all the neighboring countries up to the Rhine and the Alps which they soon declared to be their "natural frontiers." With the aid of native sympathizers, they set up a number of client states, beginning with the Batavian Republic (Dutch Netherlands) in 1795, and followed by the Helvetic Republic (Switzerland) in 1798 and four Italian republics—Ligurian Republic, Cisalpine Republic, Roman Republic, and Parthenopean Republic.

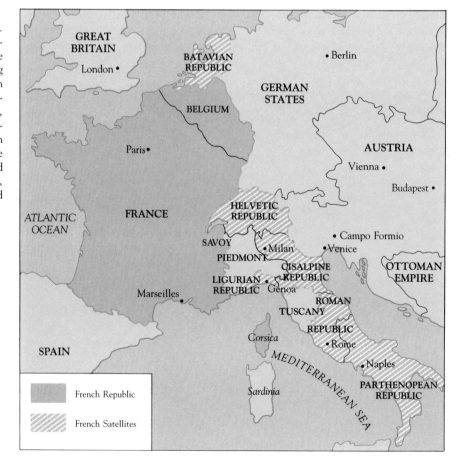

Execution of Robespierre and His Fellow Conspirators. In this engraving, Robespierre, with his lower jaw bandaged and being embraced by one of his followers, is inaccurately depicted as standing below the scaffold near the foot of the stairs. In fact Robespierre, his jaw shattered by a self-inflicted pistol shot at the time of his arrest, was in a semi-conscious state when he was driven by cart to the Place de la Révolution. On arrival, the executioners' assistants carried him down and laid him out prone until it was his turn to be executed. He kept his eyes shut and did not open them until he felt himself being carried up on to the scaffold where the bandage holding his jaw together was torn off. Strapped to the plank, he died screaming with pain.

ess" became the proper form of address. Women, imitating the fashion of ancient Rome, wore loose robes and allowed their hair to flow freely upon their shoulders. Even playing cards were not immune to social change. The design featuring kings, queens, and jacks was replaced by liberties, equalities, and fraternities, taken from the motto of the revolution.

Regarding the church as a counterrevolutionary and superstitious institution, the Committee launched a movement to de-Christianize France. Churches were converted into temples of reason where deists like Robespierre and his associates could worship the Supreme Being. A new calendar was introduced that eliminated Sundays and all church holidays and designated the birth of the republic, rather than the birth of Christ, as the beginning of Year I.

The twelve months of the year were all renamed and further divided into three weeks or decades of ten days, with the tenth day given to rest. National holidays to celebrate the revolution claimed the five or six days remaining at the end of the year. The new calendar was never popular, and it was unceremoniously shelved in 1806.

As the danger to the republic eased, little justification for terrorist rule remained, but Robespierre and his clique wanted to keep the terror going to retain power. Many in the National Convention began to fear that they would be the next victims. Their suspicions seemed to be confirmed when Robespierre appeared before them and indicated that a new purge was necessary to remove the unvirtuous men still in the government. The frightened deputies summoned enough courage to denounce him and

order his arrest. The *sans culottes* failed to rise in support of Robespierre because the execution of some of their leaders, particularly Hébert, had shaken their confidence in the Jacobins. On July 28 (9 Thermidor in the new revolutionary calendar) Robespierre was guillotined along with twenty-one of his followers.

THE THERMIDORIAN REACTION AND THE DIRECTORY

The fall of Robespierre ushered in the so-called Thermidorian Reaction, a period marked by a retreat from revolutionary excesses. The surviving Girondists surfaced and regained control of the National Convention, which in turn stripped the Committee of Public Safety of its absolute powers. They executed the chief ter-

CHRONOLOGY OF THE FRENCH REVOLUTION

1787	February	Meeting of the Assembly of Notables
1788		Parlement refuses to register tax edict
	August	Calling of the Estates-General
1789	May 5	Convening of the Estates General
	June 17	The Third Estate declares itself the National Assembly
	June 20	The National Assembly takes the Tennis Court Oath
	July 14	The storming of the bastille
	Late July	The Great Fear spreads in the countryside
	August 4	Abolition of feudal rights
	August 27	Declaration of the Rights of Man and of the Citizen
	October 5–6	March of the Parisian Women to Versailles
1790	July 12	Civil Constitution of the Clergy
1791	June 20–25	Flight of Royal family and arrest at Varennes
	August 27	The Declaration of Pillnitz
	October 1	The Legislative Assembly meets
1792	April 20	France Declares war against Austria
	August 10	Storming of the Tuileries
	September 2–7	The September Massacres
	September 20	The National Convention meets
	September 21	Abolition of the monarchy
	September 22	France proclaimed a republic
1793	January 21	Execution of Louis XVI
	Feb.–March	The European War spreads
	June 2	Sans Culottes purge Convention of Girondists
	September	Dictatorship of Committee of Public Safety
	October 10	Execution of Marie Antoinette
1794	July 28	Execution of Robespierre and the end of the Reign of Terror
1795	August 22	The Constitution of 1795 is adopted establishing the Directory
1796	May	Failure of the Babeuf Conspiracy
1797	September	Republican leaders purge legislative councils
1799	November 9	Napoleon overthrows the Directory

rorists and repealed much of the legislation adopted by the Committee. Thousands of political suspects were freed. The Paris Commune was dissolved and Jacobin clubs closed. Catholic churches reopened and numerous nonjuring priests returned from abroad.

The reaction against Jacobin ideals was reflected in the new constitution that the National Convention drew up in 1795 to replace the never-implemented constitution of 1793. Only property owners could vote for members of the legislature, assuring that control of the government would remain in the hands of the bourgeoisie. The legislature consisted of two chambers, the Council of 500 and the Council of Ancients with 250 members. Executive authority was vested in a directory of five members. These were chosen by the Council of Ancients from a list of nominees submitted by the Council of 500. On September 26, 1795, the National Convention dissolved itself, having finally completed its original purpose of writing a constitution.

The new republican regime, called the Directory after its executive committee, was unable to liquidate the war or deal effectively with the massive problems it had inherited. Social unrest grew, provoking challenges from both the right and the left. In Paris, radical malcontents found a leader in Francois Babeuf, self-styled "Gracchus," a journalist who advocated the abolition of private property and the introduction of a planned socialist economy. In the spring of 1796 Babeuf and his followers plotted an insurrection, but they were betrayed before their plans could be carried out. Babeuf was tried and executed and with his death the movement collapsed.

The threat from the right was more serious. Their earlier efforts to overthrow the government by force having failed, the royalists turned to the ballot box. In the spring of 1797, they won a substantial number of seats in both councils and even succeeded in capturing one of the directorships. The remaining directors, seeing the republic in danger of imminent collapse, organized a coup on September 4. With the aid of the army, they annulled most of the inconvenient election results and sent opposition leaders into exile.

The directors did not show the same dedication and ingenuity in solving the nation's ills as they did in clinging to power. As a group, they were divided, mediocre and corrupt. By 1799, military defeats, added to deepening economic difficulties, had thoroughly discredited the Directory. The public longed for a leader who could consolidate the nation after ten years of revolutionary upheaval. Such a figure, the popular military hero Napoleon Bonaparte, appeared on the scene. On November 9 (18 Brumaire), 1799, Bonaparte overthrew the Directory and proceeded to set up a military dictatorship.

SUMMARY

A unique combination of circumstances, not the least of which was the aristocracy's desire to maintain its privileges and extend its political power, prompted Louis XVI to call the Estates General for the first time in 175 years. But the aristocracy was unable to control the events that were set in motion and the initiative passed to the middle class. In a period of two years, from 1789 to 1791, the National Constituent Assembly transformed France into a limited monarchy, subordinated the church to the state, proclaimed the equality of all citizens, promoted the development of a free enterprise economy and improved the administration of justice. Indeed the work of the Assembly constitutes the most constructive phase of the revolution.

The revolution did not stop with the constitutional monarchy, owing to the king's obstructionism, the failure of the reformers to do enough for the city workers, and the war against Europe. The new Legislative Assembly, dominated by Jacobins, abolished the monarchy and executed the hapless Louis XVI. With France threatened by counterrevolutionaries and invading armies, the Jacobins imposed a reign of terror. Thousands of people from every walk of life were executed. The government of terror achieved its objective of saving France, but in the process brought about its own downfall.

There followed a reaction, an attempt to reestablish middle class rule without the excesses of the Terror. The new regime, the Directory, survived four years, during which it was burdened by war, a sagging economy and internal unrest. The Directory having lost all public support, the stage was set for a strong man who would impose order and consolidate the gains of the revolution.

The decade of the French Revolution is one of the greatest and most far reaching events in the history of modern civilization. It swept away the corrupt and despotic regime of the Bourbons and promoted the concept that sovereignty resided with the people; reconstructed society along the lines of Enlightenment thought; and accelerated the growth of the modern state. The revolution's impact outside of France was equally significant. Its fundamental principles of political liberty and social equality were universal in their appeal, spreading to the rest of Europe to Latin America, and eventually to the remaining world.

SELECTED SOURCES

Danton. Produced by Andrzej Wajda, this absorbing 1983 feature film is a savage condemnation of violent revolution, focusing on the conflict between Danton and Robespierre.

*Dickens, Charles. *A Tale of Two Cities.* Numerous editions. Colorful, sometimes moving novel based on the French Revolution. Skillfully captures the atmosphere of the revolution.

*Doyle, William. *Origins of the French Revolution.* 1980. The best synthesis of the recent literature on the subject. The author rejects the theory of a bourgeoisie revolution, arguing that this group and the aristocracy shared similar views and interests in the pre-1789 era.

*Hampson, Norman. *A Social History of the French Revolution.* 1964. A scholarly analysis dealing more with institutional rather than social developments.

Higgins, E. L., ed. *The French Revolution.* 1938. The story as related by contemporaries and eye-witnesses.

Jordan, David. *The King's Trial: Louis XVI vs. the Revolution.* 1979. A valuable study.

Jordan, David. *The Revolutionary Career*

493

of Maximilien Robespierre. 1985. A recent work suggesting that Robespierre experienced a spiritual revolution in 1788–1789 equal to the one that changed the face of France.

Kafker, Frank and Laux, James, eds. *The French Revolution: Conflicting Interpretations.* Revised 1983. Examines different appraisals of various aspects of the revolution.

*Lefebvre, Georges. *The Coming of the French Revolution.* 1957. A short analysis stressing the role of the nobility in precipitating the revolution.

*Levy, Darline G., Applewhite, Harriet B., Johnson, Marlene D., eds. and translators. *Women in Revolutionary Paris, 1789–1815.* 1981. A valuable collection of documents depicting the activities of women during the era.

Lyons, Martyn. *France Under the Directory.* 1975. Brief, clear and well-organized.

*Palmer, R. R. *Twelve Who Ruled.* 1941. Classic study of the Terror and the men who directed it. The author does not feel that Robespierre was as influential in shaping policy as has often been depicted.

*Roberts, J. M. *The French Revolution* 1978. A good treatment.

*Rudé, George. *The Crowd in the French Revolution.* 1959. Explores the composition and motives of the crowds that participated in the French Revolution.

*Sobul, Albert. *The French Revolution.* 1975. A contemporary Marxist perspective.

*Sutherland, D.M.G. *France, 1789–1815.* 1985. Excellent survey of the period with an up-to-date bibliography.

*Tilly, Charles. *The Vendée.* 1964. An analysis of the social and economic factors that led to the uprising in the Vendée.

*Available in paperback.

THE AGE OF NAPOLEON

Shortly before eight o'clock on the evening of July 23, 1815 the . . . English frigate H.M.S. Bellerophon sailed steadily before moderate breezes on an east-northeast course that would see her into Tor Bay early the next morning. She had made her landfall an hour earlier, raising the high land of Dartmoor off her larboard bow; and for some time now two men had been standing on the quarterdeck looking at the land. One, an angular six-footer wearing the uniform of a captain in the British navy, was Frederick Maitland, the Bellerophon's commanding officer. The other, reaching only to Maitland's shoulder and clad in a flannel dressing gown over which he had thrown a great-coat, was Napoleon Bonaparte. *

At Waterloo, a month earlier, Napoleon had seen his army shattered as it drove time and time again against the unyielding squares of British infantrymen. Broken by this defeat, he signed a second abdication, then surrendered to the captain of the man-of-war *Bellerophon,* asking to be allowed to spend his remaining days in England. As Napoleon stood on the deck of the British warship, one wonders what thoughts were passing through his mind. Was he concerned over the fate that awaited him? Did he reflect on his dramatic rise from obscure officer to emperor of the French? Did he reminisce about his spectacular accomplishments as a reformer when he stabilized and centralized France and made sweeping economic and legal changes and as a soldier when he conquered most of the European continent? Or was he reliving the critical moments at Waterloo and reproaching himself for failing to take certain steps that might have turned the tide of battle? One thing was certain. His life had been a romantic adventure.

CONTENTS

EARLY LIFE

Napoleon Bonaparte owed his rapid rise to good fortune and ability rather than to origin or wealth. He was born in August 1769 on the island of Corsica, which had become a French possession the previous year. Of Italian

Napoleon as First Consul. This portrait by Jean-Auguste Dominique Ingres depicts Napoleon as a liberal reformer, hard at work on affairs of state. While there are arguments about the extent of his enlightenment, it is clear that he was a dynamo of energy, able to work as many as eighteen hours a day without becoming exhausted. In this picture Napoleon, flattered by the First Consul's dress and with a slim figure, sensuous face, and hair trimmed in Roman style, presents an interesting contrast to the gaunt and rumpled appearance of the revolutionary general. Musee de Liege.

NAPOLEON ADDRESSES HIS TROOPS

Soldiers, you are naked, ill-fed; though the Government owes you much, it can give you nothing. Your patience, the courage you have shown amidst these rocks, are admirable; but they procure you no glory, no fame shines upon you. I want to lead you into the most fertile plains in the world. Rich provinces, great cities will lie in your power; you will find there honor, glory and riches. Soldiers of the Army of Italy, will you lack courage or steadfastness?*

Napoleon understood the importance of morale in warfare. A charismatic leader, he inspired his men by appealing to their vanity, honor, and love of France. The duke of Wellington, the British hero at Waterloo, once remarked that the presence of Napoleon on the battlefield was equivalent to a striking force of 40,000 men.

*Correlli Barnett, *Bonaparte* (New York: Hill and Wang, 1978) p. 41.

descent, he was the second son of an impoverished but well-connected family of lesser nobility. At the age of nine, he was sent to France to study to become an army officer. An average student, he showed a special aptitude in mathematics and history. In 1785, he received his commission as second lieutenant of artillery in the royal army. Napoleon selected the artillery corps, partly because it suited his mathematics skills and partly because it was less aristocratic than either the cavalry or the infantry. As he lacked a title or a powerful benefactor, it is unlikely that he would have risen to high command under the old regime. The Revolution, however, which induced many officers of noble birth to emigrate, threw open the gates of opportunity for professional soldiers who remained in France.

Bonaparte sympathized with the principles of the revolution and established close relations with the Jacobins. He first came to prominence in 1793 when he played a key role in the recapture of Toulon by Revolutionary forces. As a reward for his services he was promoted to brigadier general. The fall of Robespierre threatened to end Napoleon's career, but he regained favor in October 1795 when he delivered a "whiff of grapeshot" that saved the National Convention from attack by an angry mob. Early in 1796 he received command of the Army of Italy, the French army that was fighting the Sardinians and Austrians in northern Italy. Just before his departure, he married Josephine de Beauharnais, a widow six years his senior.

Bonaparte in his first field command showed himself a master in the art of war. His genius lay not in tactical or strategic innovation but in skillfully applying doctrines that he had been taught in school. From eighteenth-century French military reformers, he had learned such concepts as combining the firepower of a line of troops with the penetrating force of an advancing column, massing artillery to support the infantry at decisive moments, and dispersing forces widely in order to march swiftly and reuniting them quickly when it came time to fight. Napoleon also profited from the revolutionary *levée en masse* which gave him legions of well-disciplined and highly motivated soldiers. Seldom did he have to risk an engagement in which his forces were smaller than those of his opponent.

Napoleon departed from conventional battlefield tactics which stressed maneuver and fighting defensively from fixed positions. Instead, his strategy was based on bold, lightning attack. His aim was to concentrate a superior force against a weak segment of the enemy's line, opening gaps with artillery that would be penetrated, first by columns of infantry and then by waves of cavalry. Whereas the typical eighteenth century commander tried merely to force his opponent to retreat, Napoleon sought to annihilate the enemy.

Beyond tactical skill, other factors contributed to Napoleon's successes. His army lived off the land, freeing itself from dependence on slow-moving supply wagons. He shared the hardships and dangers with his men, gaining their admiration and respect. Finally, Napoleon surrounded himself with aides who owed their position to talent rather than seniority or influence.

The Italian campaign of 1796–1797 established Napoleon as a national hero in France. In a series of swift attacks, Napoleon routed the Sardinians and drove the Austrians from northern Italy. The effect of his victories was to complete the dissolution of the First Coalition by forcing Sardinia and Austria to follow the example of Spain, Prussia, and the Netherlands and accept peace terms highly favorable to the French Republic. Great Britain alone was left to carry on the war.

Back in France, Napoleon looked for fresh opportunities that would enhance his newly won popularity. He judged an invasion of Great Britain to be impractical as long as the Royal Navy reigned supreme on the seas. Instead, he obtained the Directory's permission to lead an expedition to Egypt, then a semiindependent province of Turkey. Bonaparte hoped to use Egypt as a base from which to destroy British commerce and naval predominance in the Mediterranean and to strike at Great Britain's colonial empire in India. Napoleon brought with him a number of experts to study the artistic and literary treasures of Egypt. Their most important discovery was the Rosetta stone which unlocked secrets of ancient Egyptian hieroglyphics. Militarily, the expedition accomplished little. Napoleon easily overran Egypt but on August 1, 1798, the celebrated British admiral Lord Nelson severed his link with the homeland by destroying the French fleet near the mouth of the Nile. A further year of campaigning in the Near East brought him no closer to his goal of undermining British power in the east.

News that the Directory was in deep trouble prompted Napoleon to abandon his army and return to France. While Bonaparte was in Egypt, the Directory had installed new republican governments in central and southern Italy as well as in the Netherlands and Switzerland. France's policy of expansion alarmed Austria and Russia and led them to join Britain to form the Second Coalition. With liberal sums of money supplied by the British prime minister, William Pitt, the continental partners were able to put large armies in the field. During 1799, they inflicted one defeat after another on the French and compelled them to evacuate Italy. Such was the military situation

when Napoleon landed in southern France on October 9, 1799. The public, knowing nothing about Napoleon's defeats, had read glowing accounts of his victories and gave him a rousing reception wherever he went. He quickly learned that the people were thoroughly disillusioned with the Directory and were eager for a change. Once in Paris, Napoleon, with the complicity of two directors, Roger Ducos and Abbé Siéyès, engaged in a plot to overthrow the Directory. The conspirators hoped to give their coup d'état the appearance of legality by persuading the two chambers to entrust them with the task of drafting a new constitution.

The coup d'état, set for 18 Brumaire (November 9), almost miscarried. On the pretext that the country was threatened by a Jacobin plot, Napoleon addressed each chamber in turn requesting permission to refashion the government. The Council of Ancients agreed to the proposed changes, but in the Council of 500, which contained many radical deputies, Napoleon was met with cries of "Down with the tyrant! Outlaw Him!" Fortunately for Napoleon his brother Lucien, who was president of the Council of 500, stepped in and saved the day. On his orders, the troops cleared the hall of hostile deputies. The remnant recognized Napoleon, Siéyès, and Ducos as provisional consuls and empowered them to revise the constitution. The Directory had ceased to exist.

THE CONSULATE

The Constitution of the Year VIII (1799), as drafted by Siéyès and revised by Napoleon, established a dic-

Napoleon as a Young General. A portrait of Napoleon when his star was on the rise following his victories over the Austrians. The shoulder length straggly locks, wrinkled uniform, and resolute expression all suggest Napoleon's dedication to the cause of Revolutionary France.

Napoleon attacked by hostile members in the Council of 500. In a romanticized painting by Francois Bouchot, Napoleon, the man of the hour, is shown standing his ground. Actually he lost his nerve when he encountered unexpected resistance and had to be rescued by the guards. Versailles.

tatorship under the guise of a democratic republic. It did not include a bill of rights or guaranteed freedoms of speech and press. As first consul, Bonaparte, aided by two other consuls, was made chief executive for ten years. He appointed key civilian and military personnel, directed foreign policy, and controlled legislation. He chose and directed the Council of State, a body that initiated all legislation. The three consuls appointed the Senate, which decided any constitutional questions in addition to selecting members of the bicameral legislature from a list of candidates chosen by popular voting. The two legislative bodies were the Tribunate, which could only discuss legislation, and the Legislative Body, which voted on the proposed laws without debating them. In a plebiscite which was not completed until February 1800, the voters, yearning for order and stability after a decade of revolutionary turmoil, voted overwhelmingly in favor of the constitution.

Napoleon the Man

Barely over five feet tall, dark, thin, and sallow, the new master of France did not cut an imposing figure. His physical appearance, however, belied his iron constitution. He required little sleep and possessed such energy that he could work eighteen hours at a stretch, day in and day out. Alert and extraordinarily intelligent, he easily grasped new ideas and facts which he filed away in his memory for later reference. He was an inspiring leader, able to captivate nearly everyone he met. He retained, even in defeat, the love and devotion of his troops, and eminent civilians could not help but admire his wide range of knowledge, rapid decisions, and quick grasp of complex problems.

Napoleon was convinced that as a man of destiny, he stood above all laws. "I am no ordinary man and the laws of propriety and morals are not applicable to me." Neither in his private nor public life did he show any concern for ordinary human beings. "I grew up upon the field of battle and a man such as I am cares little for the life of a million men." Unrestrained by religion, conventional morality, or aversion to bloodshed, he was prepared to employ any means to achieve his ends.

Napoleon was a man who placed his trust in reason, precision, and orderliness. He left as little as possible to chance. He once remarked that every project "must be carried out according to a system, because nothing succeeds by chance." As a realist, he understood that popularity was fleeting and that his reputation alone would not sustain him in power. If he failed to unite the different elements in France's fragmented society and resolve the major problems of the preceding decade, his popularity would fade and his regime would collapse.

Peace at Home and Abroad

Benefiting from the Revolution's work, Napoleon brought to completion the centralizing process begun by Richelieu and Mazarin and provided France with an honest and efficient government. He continued certain reforms of the revolution that were popular with the nation and that served his own purpose. On the other hand he reversed some of the revolutionary gains by suppressing all forms of free expression and by instituting a new absolutism. He believed political and social liberties would undermine good government and lead to anarchy. His regime had many of the characteristics of enlightened despotism, which had eluded France in the eighteenth century. Napoleon, however, had greater freedom of action than the Bourbon kings because he did not have to contend with an entrenched aristocracy.

If Napoleon hoped to make his regime stable, his most pressing need was to restore internal order and end the war with the other European nations. To accomplish the first task, Napoleon's troops wiped out most of the criminal bands that had plagued the countryside and suppressed for good the rebellion that had flared up intermittently since 1793 in the Vendée. The first consul also turned his attention to the war against the Second Coalition. His work was simplified when Tsar Paul I (1796–1801) of Russia, irritated by Great Britain's tedious blockading tactics, withdrew from the war. With lightning speed, Napoleon led his troops across the Alps and in June 1800 crushed the Austrian forces at Marengo in northern Italy. Later that year, another French army, commanded by General Moreau, defeated the Austrians at Hohenlinden in Bavaria. In February 1801, the Austrians signed the treaty of Lunéville, which extended French control over Italy and western Germany. Great Britain continued to fight alone, and in the summer of 1801 forced the remnant of the French armies in Egypt to surrender. Still, the British were war weary and, following protracted negotiations with Napoleon, concluded the Peace of Amiens in March 1802. Under the settlement, France retained most of its European conquests and recovered all the colonies that had been seized by Great Britain.

Domestic Reform

Peace gave Napoleon the opportunity to channel his boundless energy into domestic reform. To suggest that his government rested on a broad political base, Napoleon selected subordinates from different social backgrounds. He was unconcerned whether they were returned royalist émigrés or ex-Jacobins as long as they worked loyally for him and stopped quarreling with each other. His regime was composed of intelligent and conscientious administrators who approached problems with the rationality expected of men educated in the era of the Enlightenment.

Napoleon's authoritarian inclinations led him to direct the machinery of local government from Paris. In place of elected local officials, he substituted his own appointments: prefects in departments, subprefects in arrondissements, and mayors in communes, all responsible to him. This tightly centralized administration worked efficiently and expeditiously, but it afforded the people little direct voice in public affairs.

Napoleon remedied the state's financial plight, which had caused the downfall of the old regime and vexed

Napoleon scatters mob with a whiff of grape-shot

Napoleon's unsuccessful campaign in Egypt

Concordat between Napoleon and the Pope

Treaty of Amiens

Napoleonic Code

Napoleon's successful campaign in Italy

Napoleon establishes the Consulate

Napoleon becomes Emperor

the succeeding revolutionary governments. He established the Bank of France which, among other things, served to lend money to the state, freeing it from reliance on private financiers. Napoleon increased the state's revenues by reviving indirect taxes on consumer goods. He imposed strict economies on all branches of government and reduced corruption and embezzlement by supervising careful auditing of officials' receipts. These fiscal measures, together with the tribute extorted from the conquered populations, enabled him to keep the national budget in balance.

Another problem that Napoleon inherited was the conflict between the state and the Catholic church. Napoleon was personally nonreligious but, as a pragmatist, he clearly perceived the value of appeasing the large numbers of conscientious Catholics who had been alienated by the anticlerical legislation of the revolutionaries. Long and intricate negotiations with the Vatican finally resulted in the Concordat of 1801, which was to govern church-state relations in France until the beginning of the twentieth century. Catholicism was declared to be the faith of the majority of French people, a statement that fell short of restoring it as the official state religion. The pope agreed

to give up all claims to church property previously expropriated by the National Assembly and consented to confirm French bishops nominated by the first consul. The bishops were to appoint the lower clergy, subject to ratification by the state. Clergymen were obliged to take an oath of fidelity to the state, which would pay them a salary.

The following year Napoleon drew up a list of regulations known as the Organic Articles, and without consulting the pope, integrated them in the Concordat. The Articles, which further subordinated the church to the state, gave the government power to police the Catholic religion, including the right to exclude papal bulls from the country. Ardent republicans disliked even the amended version of the Concordat, but the great majority of French citizens welcomed the state's reconciliation with the Church of Rome.

The educational system, like the church, was exploited to strengthen Napoleon's regime. Napoleon was not concerned with bringing literacy to the masses but with grooming administrators and producing useful and patriotic citizens. In 1802, Napoleon ordered the establishment of secondary schools (lycées) in every major city as well as a number of schools of med-

icine, law, and design. A board of education in Paris, misleadingly termed the Imperial University, supervised all institutions of learning.

Napoleon retreated from the republican ideal of equality when in 1802 he founded the Legion of Honor, designed to reward military and civic achievement. All honorary distinctions and decorations had been abolished during the revolution, but shortly after Napoleon became first consul he is quoted as saying: "I don't think that the French love liberty and equality: the French are not at all changed by ten years of revolution. . . . They have one feeling—honor. We must nourish that feeling." Very highly regarded, the Legion of Honor remains even today the most cherished of national medallions.

The most celebrated of Napoleon's achievements was the codification of the laws. To the numerous legal systems of the old regime and the mass of royal decrees, the revolutionary governments had added thousands of laws. As a result gaps and contradictions alike existed in the body of the law. The National Convention had made efforts to reduce the laws of the land to a simple and uniform national code, but it remained for Napoleon to bring the work to completion. The task of codification was entrusted to a committee of legal experts, but Napoleon frequently presided over the sessions and took an active part in the discussions. The civil code, the first of five, went into effect in 1804. It was followed by the code of civil procedure, the code of commerce, the code of criminal procedure, and the penal code. The codes, known collectively as the Code Napoleon, had the high merit of being clear, comprehensive and nationwide in application.

The Code Napoleon incorporated many principles of the revolution: equality before the law, religious toleration, the right to choose one's profession, the sanctity of private property, and abolition of serfdom and primogeniture. But the code had its reactionary side, prohibiting trade unions, permitting the imprisonment of adolescent children by their fathers, denying illegitimate children rights accorded to those who were legitimate, and increasing the penalties for political crimes. Whatever its faults, the code was an enormous improvement over what had existed before. It remained the basis of French law after the overthrow of Napoleon, in addition to influencing modern legal developments in Belgium, the Netherlands, Italy, parts of Germany, and even distant Louisiana.

Napoleon's only serious failure during the period of the Consulate was his bid to restore the French colonial empire in the New World. In 1800, he coerced the weak Spanish government into returning to France the extensive territory of Louisiana west of the Mississippi. Bonaparte next planned to reconquer the rich sugar island of Santo Domingo, where the slaves had revolted and killed or expelled their French masters. For this

NAPOLEON'S SETTLEMENT WITH THE PAPACY

The Government of the French Republic recognizes that the Roman, Catholic and Apostolic religion is the religion of the great majority of French citizens.

His Holiness likewise recognizes that this same religion has derived and in this moment again expects the greatest benefit and grandeur from the establishment of the Catholic worship in France and from the personal profession of it which the Consuls of the Republic make.

In consequence, after this mutual recognition, as well for the benefit of religion as for the maintenance of internal tranquility, they have agreed as follows:

1. The Catholic, Apostolic and Roman religion shall be freely exercised in France: its worship shall be public, and in conformity with the police regulations which the government shall deem necessary for the public tranquility. . . .

"I swear and promise to God, upon the Holy Scriptures, to remain in obedience and fidelity to the Government established by the constitution of the French Republic. I also promise not to have any intercourse, nor to assist by any counsel, nor to support any league, either within or without, which is inimical to the public tranquility; and if, within my diocese or elsewhere, I learn that anything to the prejudice of the state is being contrived, I will make it known to the government."*

These provisions are part of the Concordat of 1801 which formed the basis of Napoleon's settlement with Pope Pius VII. Although the accord proved lasting, increasing friction developed between the two men, culminating in 1808 when a French army occupied Rome, imprisoned the pontiff, and annexed the Papal States to France. The pope countered by excommunicating Napoleon, an act that cost the French head of state considerable support among loyal Catholics. The Organic Articles, which were subsequently integrated into the Concordat, also brought public worship of Protestants under state regulation and assured them of religious freedom. In 1808 similar arrangements were made for the Jews.

*Frank M. Anderson, The Constitutions and Other Select Documents Illustrative of the History of France 1789–1901 (Minneapolis: H. W. Wilson, 1904), pp. 297–298.

purpose he sent an expedition of 33,000 men under the command of his brother-in-law, General Leclerc. After initial successes, vigorous black resistance and an epidemic of yellow fever forced Napoleon to abandon the island. The anticipation of renewed hostilities with Great Britain and the knowledge that Louisiana could not be held moved Napoleon to sell it to the United States in 1803.

Apart from the ill-starred overseas adventure Napoleon's policies as first consul were eminently successful. His numerous accomplishments won him wide support. To the middle class, he offered financial and administrative order, an economy relatively free of state interference and social mobility. To the peasants, he healed the long-standing schism with the Roman church and guaranteed an end to manorial dues and retention of lands they had already acquired. To the workers, he provided employment by creating a huge public works program and letting out contracts for military supplies. To the enlightened elements, he ensured religious toleration, freedom to choose one's profession, equality before the law, and greater educational opportunities. Only two groups were opposed to Napoleon's rule. One was an assortment of Jacobins who felt that Napoleon had betrayed the revolution; the other was a party of royalists who longed for a restoration of the old regime. Through the relentless efforts of Napoleon's secret police, both groups were silenced or driven underground.

If there was no serious discontent against Napoleon, it was not because his regime was without flaws. The vote was relatively meaningless, and such civil rights as freedom of speech, press, and assembly, which had been enjoyed during most of the revolution, were increasingly restricted. Women were held to have no role in society other than marriage. Primary education for girls was allowed to languish (although partly through restored religious orders, the rate of literacy among women did increase). Husbands controlled community property. A woman could not mortgage or sell even the property brought to the marriage by her dowry. Divorce was permitted, but the provisions were more restricted than those enunciated during the revolutionary period which included incompatibility. Napoleon's government recognized only mutual consent, adultery, beatings, and imprisonment as grounds for divorce, whereas desertion, which was frequent and left many women destitute, was not.

EMPEROR OF THE FRENCH

In 1802, Napoleon, taking advantage of his rising popularity, had himself appointed consul for life, a change approved in a national referendum. A new constitution, similar to the previous one, further strengthened his authority and empowered him to nominate his successor. Two years later, Napoleon seized on an unsuccessful attempt on his life to make himself emperor. He argued that if he were emperor, assassination would be meaningless, because his heir would preserve the system he created. Another constitution, again ratified by a plebiscite, proclaimed Napoleon hereditary emperor. On December 2, 1804, amid an imposing coronation ceremony in the medieval church of Notre Dame in Paris, Bonaparte assumed the title of Napoleon I, emperor of the French. The republic was dead.

The restoration of the monarchy was accompanied by changes in public life. The revolutionary calendar was replaced by the traditional one with its Sundays and religious holidays. The form of address "Citizen" and "Citizeness" gave way to "Monsieur" and "Madame." Napoleon revived court life with all of its trap-

Coronation of Napoleon and Josephine. This painting by David shows Josephine kneeling to be crowned empress by Napoleon. Moments earlier Napoleon, in defiance of tradition, had grasped the crown from the pope's hands and placed it on his own head. The pope accepted the indignity with resignation and paid the emperor back in kind when he withdrew while Napoleon read the constitutional oath. Louvre, Paris.

pings and formality. He established a new nobility based on merit and loyalty. In 1810, Napoleon resurrected an unpopular Bourbon device, the *lettre de cachet,* an administrative order bearing the royal seal. With these orders, French citizens could be imprisoned or exiled without a trial.

In 1809, Napoleon divorced Josephine because she had failed to bear him an heir. Soon afterward he married eighteen-year-old Marie Louise, daughter of Francis I (1792–1835) of Austria, linking his name with one of the oldest dynasties in Europe. In 1811, the new empress presented Napoleon with a son, given the title of king of Rome. The imperial succession appeared assured.

Mastery of Europe

While the Consulate had been characterized by peace and domestic reform, the empire brought continuous war. With the loyalty of the nation secured and with an enthusiastic and formidable army available, Napoleon sought to gratify his natural instincts for conquest and glory. Even before the establishment of the empire, France and Great Britain were again at war. During the one-year period of peace, Napoleon had annexed Piedmont in Italy, tightened his domination over Switzerland, attempted to revive France's colonial empire, and closed European markets to British goods. Napoleon's behavior persuaded the British that he was not serious about peaceful coexistence, and in May 1803 they declared war.

With the resumption of hostilities Napoleon concentrated more than 100,000 men and thousands of landing barges on the French coast at Boulogne for the purpose of invading

---

NAPOLEON CROWNS HIMSELF

The interior of the church of Notre Dame had been newly painted; galleries and pews magnificently adorned had been erected, and they were thronged with a prodigious concourse of spectators. . . .

It was a truly magnificent sight. The procession was opened by the already numerous body of courtiers; next came the Marshals of the Empire wearing their honors; then the dignitaries and high officers of the Crown; and lastly, the Emperor in a dress of state. At the moment of his entering the cathedral there was a simultaneous shout of *"Vive l'Empereur!"*

The procession passed along the middle of the nave, and arrived at the choir facing the high altar. The galleries round the choir were filled with the handsomest women whom the best company could produce, and most of whom rivaled in the luster of their beauty that of the jewels which they were covered.

His holiness went to meet the Emperor at a tribune [platform] which had been placed in the middle of the choir; there was another on one side for the Empress. After saying a short prayer there they returned, and seated themselves on the throne at the end of the church facing the choir; there they

heard mass, which was said by the Pope. . . . The Emperor and Empress, on reaching the choir, replaced themselves at their tribunes, where the Pope performed the ceremony.

He presented the crown to the Emperor, who received it, put it himself upon his head, took it off, placed it on that of the Empress, removed it again, and laid it on the cushion where it was at first. A smaller crown was immediately put upon the head of the Empress. . . . The Testament was presented to the Emperor, who took off his glove, and pronounced his oath, with his hand upon the sacred book. *

This lavish coronation ceremony took place in Notre Dame Cathedral in Paris, rather than at Rheims where the kings of France were crowned, because Napoleon wished to be regarded as the successor of Charlemagne, king of the Franks and emperor of the Romans. The invocation of Roman imperial pagentry and Carolingian associations was perhaps a portent that even at this early date Napoleon's ambitions extended beyond France, to include all of Europe.

*Louis De Bourrienne, *Memoirs of Napoleon Bonaparte,* vol. II (New York: C. Scribner's Sons, 1892), pp. 376–378 n.

England. He hoped to lure the British flotilla away from the Channel by sending Admiral Villeneuve and the French fleet to the West Indies. Then, having given the slip to Lord Nelson's ships, Villeneuve was to dash back and escort the invading force across the Channel. The plan miscarried. On October 21, 1805, Nelson, after brilliant maneuvering, destroyed Vil-

leneuve's fleet off Cape Trafalgar, Spain. The victory guaranteed Great Britain the supremacy of the seas and put a permanent end to French notions of a cross-channel invasion.

On land, however, Napoleon had his own way. By the time of Trafalgar, Austria, Russia, and Sweden had joined Great Britain to form the Third Coalition. Napoleon responded with a whirlwind campaign, sweeping into southern Germany where he defeated the Austrians at Ulm. Occupying Vienna he turned northward into Moravia and on December 2, 1805, the first anniversary of his coronation, he won his greatest victory at Austerlitz over the combined armies of Austria and Russia. While the remnant of the Russian army retreated into Poland, Austria signed a separate peace with France. By the treaty of Pressburg, the Austrian emperor Francis II ceded Venetia in Italy and holdings on the eastern shore of the Adriatic to France.

Napoleon used his newly won military dominance in southern Germany to establish the Confederation of the Rhine, a federal union consisting of Bavaria, Baden, Würtemberg, and thirteen lesser states. Napoleon was declared protector of the confederation, which was bound to France by an offensive and defensive alliance. The withdrawal of the sixteen German states from the Holy Roman Empire led Francis II to acknowledge the dissolution of that an-cient political entity after an existence of a thousand years. Henceforth he retained only the title of Francis I, emperor of Austria.

Provoked by Napoleon's high-handed methods in Germany, Prussia declared war on France on October 1, 1806. The Prussian army, led by the incompetent duke of Brunswick, had deteriorated badly since the days of Frederick the Great and was no match for Napoleon's seasoned veterans. Outmaneuvered and outgunned, the Prussian forces were humiliated at the twin battles of Jena and Auerstädt on October 14. Napoleon marched into Berlin two weeks later while the Prussian king, Frederick William III (1797–1840), fled to Königsberg in the east where he tried unsuccessfully to continue the struggle. The following year Napoleon imposed terms on Frederick William that left him little more than a French puppet. Prussia was compelled to reduce its army to 42,000 men and permit French troops to occupy its forts until a large war in-demnity was paid. Land west of the Elbe River was shorn from the rest of Prussia and added to several west German states, forming the Kingdom of Westphalia (which became part of the Confederation of the Rhine). Prussia had to give up all gains acquired though the partitions of Poland, out of which Napoleon created the Duchy of Warsaw. In all, Prussia lost half of its territory and population.

Driving headlong into east Prussia, the French emperor dealt with his only remaining undefeated continental opponent. After a bloody but inconclusive encounter with the Russians at Eylau, he won a decisive victory over them at Friedland in June 1807, inducing the young Tsar Alexander I (1801–25) to ask for an armistice. At Tilsit, the two emperors met on a raft moored in the middle of the Niemen River. Napoleon, anxious to convert Alexander into an ally, was charming and generous. The tsar formally recognized the changes that Napoleon had already made in central and western Europe, and in return was given

Napoleon at Eylau. The slaughter on the battlefield is vividly illustrated in this painting by Adolph Eugene Gabriel Roehn. Over 15,000 French soldiers, about one-third of Napoleon's army, lay dead or wounded in the snow. Chateau de Grosbois, Boissy-Saint-Léger, France.

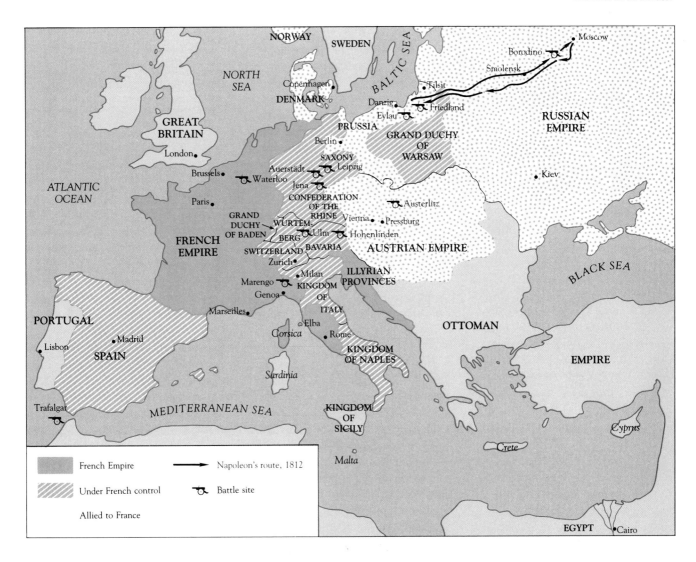

a dominant hand in eastern Europe. Napoleon did not exact an inch of Russian soil and asked only that Alexander pledge to cease trade with Britain and join the war against it. The Third Coalition had collapsed as had the previous two.

The Empire at Its Height

Tilsit marked the pinnacle of Napoleon's fortunes. The core of his Grand Empire was France, which was enlarged by the incorporation of Bel-

gium, the Netherlands, sections of German territory west of the Rhine and along the North Sea, parts of Italy, and the Illyrian provinces stretching along the Dalmatian coast of the Adriatic. Flanking the French Empire were nominally independent satellite states, ruled by Napoleon's relatives and friends. These included the kingdoms of Italy and Naples, Switzerland, Spain, the Confederation of the Rhine, and the Duchy of Warsaw. Finally came Prussia, Austria, and Russia, forced to become the

MAP 58

Napoleonic Europe, 1810. Napoleon in 1810 was at the height of his power, controlling an area that far exceeded the republican expansion of 1794–1799. The heart of Napoleon's domain was the French Empire which included, besides pre-1789 France, Belgium, the Netherlands, German territory to the Rhine and eastward to Hamburg, Italian lands down to Rome, Corsica, and the Illyrian Provinces. Surrounding the French Empire were layers of satellite states—the Confederation of the Rhine, the Grand Duchy of Warsaw, the Kingdom of Naples, Switzerland, and Spain. To the north and east were the allied states of Prussia, Austria, Russia, and Denmark.

507

allies of France through military defeat. The only European powers outside the Napoleonic orbit were Great Britain, Sweden, Portugal, and the Ottoman Empire.

Napoleon extended the principle and reforms of the revolution in all areas under his direct or indirect rule. He improved the administrative machinery by appointing capable officials. They introduced French legal codes, abolished class distinctions, freed peasants from serfdom and feudal dues, suppressed trade guilds, promoted public education, resisted church interference in secular matters and equalized tax burdens. Napoleon's purpose in implementing these reforms was based more on self-interest than on concern for the welfare of others. He understood that the preservation of his vast empire required efficient administration and the support of the conquered people.

In the annexed territories and satellite states, a considerable segment of the population, in particular the middle class who had chafed under restrictions imposed on them by divine right monarchies, initially welcomed the French as liberators. But the debit side of Napoleon's imperial rule brought political repression and financial exploitation. The French emperor ruthlessly persecuted all expressions of political independence, pilfered national treasures, and exacted recruits for his army and taxes for his war treasury. Before long, it became clear that his policies were intended above all to enhance his glory and that of France. Consequently the subject peoples came to view Napoleon as an oppressor and required only encouragement and assistance to actively resist his rule.

The Continental System

Since 1803 no strategy that Napoleon had been able to devise had succeeded against Great Britain. As long as the British remained in the war, they stood in the way, not only of his complete hegemony over Europe, but also of further conquests he aspired to in the Near East and India. Finding it impossible to strike directly at the British he decided to cut off their export trade with the continent, upon which they were heavily dependent. With the ruin of Great Britain's business community and the resultant mass unemployment, Napoleon was confident that its government would sue for peace or face bankruptcy and revolution.

Napoleon's policy of economic strangulation, called the Continental System, went into effect in 1806–1807. It forbade the entry of British goods into countries allied with or under the control of France. However, Napoleon lacked the navy to police the coasts and he could not gain the cooperation of the nations of Europe. The Continental System damaged but did not ruin Britain's economy. The British developed new markets in South America and in the eastern Mediterranean and their control of coastal waters enabled them to smuggle goods onto the continent. At the same time Napoleon's policy brought economic distress to the European countries that depended on the cheaper manufactured articles of Great Britain and on the British market for their own agricultural products. Continental trade stagnated, businesses closed, and unemployment rose. The economic hardships caused by the Continental System were in-

strumental in turning the European bourgeoisie, who generally had supported Napoleon's administrative and social reforms, against the overlordship of the French.

The Peninsular War

The first to defy the Continental System was Portugal, which refused to abandon its traditional alliance with Great Britain. Napoleon's response was immediate. His army poured into Portugal and on December 1, 1807, entered Lisbon without resistance. French troops remained in Spain to protect the lines of communication and supply and ignored official requests to withdraw. Their presence sparked popular riots. Napoleon, who was desperately in need of Spain's navy if he hoped to enforce the blockade against Great Britain, determined to overthrow the weak Spanish monarch, Charles IV (1788–1808), in favor of someone on whom he could rely. By threats and cajolery, he persuaded Charles to resign, whereupon he appointed his brother Joseph to the vacant throne.

Napoleon anticipated that his liberal reforms would move the Spaniards to rally around Joseph. That proved to be a fatal illusion. The presence of a foreign monarch, the exclusion of British goods, and the annulment of aristocratic and clerical privileges outraged Spaniards and hurt their pride. Spaniards of all classes united and rose in revolt, inspired by the same emotional patriotism that animated the French. Napoleon faced a new kind of warfare for which conventional tactics were useless. Guerrilla bands poisoned wells, ambushed small isolated units, raided convoys

Battle of Trafalgar

Decrees ordering continental blockade against Great Britain

Treaty of Tilsit between Napoleon and Tsar Alexander

Napoleon defeated at Leipzig

Napoleon returns and is defeated at Waterloo

Prussia defeated at battles of Jena and Auerstädt

Napoleon's invasion and retreat from Russia

Napoleon forced to abdicate; exiled to Elba

and outposts, and then disappeared into the mountains. Seeking to prolong Napoleon's agony, the British landed an army under Sir Arthur Wellesley (later the duke of Wellington), to aid the Spanish insurgents. The Peninsular War, which dragged on until 1814, drained Napoleon's treasury and tied down 400,000 French troops. "It was the Spanish ulcer," Napoleon subsequently said ruefully, "that ruined me."

The successes of the Spaniards against the French encouraged the Austrians to reenter the war in April 1809. Taking personal command, Napoleon marched swiftly into Austria and prevailed after a fiercely contested engagement at Wagram. The resulting treaty of Schönbrunn compelled Austria to give up 32,000 square miles and 3,500,000 people to France and its allies.

THE DECLINE AND FALL OF THE NAPOLEONIC EMPIRE

Although Napoleon was supreme in Europe between 1807 and 1812 and had only the war against England and the Iberian Peninsula to contend with, the forces of disintegration were already at work. The Continental System had aroused European resentment toward France. Moreover, the heroic struggle of the Spaniards and the tenacity with which the Austrians had fought served notice of the rising spirit of national pride and resistance in the subject states. Then too, Napoleon's army was not as powerful and dependable as it had once been. The great battles had thinned the ranks of his patriotic veterans and compelled him to rely on youthful, inexperienced French conscripts and foreign contingents of uncertain loyalty. Finally, the French emperor himself was not as alert as he had been earlier in his career. Overworked, overconfident, and in failing health—the symptoms of stomach cancer from which he is believed to have died had begun to appear—he was less thorough in planning his campaigns. Worse still, his growing ego and lust for conquests clouded his judgment, betraying him into unsound and dangerous schemes.

The Russian Debacle

Napoleon's disastrous campaign into Russia in 1812 marked a crucial turning point in his fortunes. Since Tilsit, a number of events had combined to produce a rupture between Tsar Alexander I and Napoleon. The Russian emperor had deplored the creation of the Duchy of Warsaw and became all the more irritated when it was enlarged after the Austrian war of 1809. He suspected that Napoleon planned to create a new Polish state that would eventually include his control of Polish territory. Alexander was further upset by Napoleon's marriage to Marie Louise, which seemed to indicate that his ally would be partial toward Austria, Russia's traditional enemy. Finally, the tsar resented Napoleon's annexation of the German state of Oldenburg where his uncle was the reigning duke.

Napoleon might conceivably have patched things up had the tsar not abandoned the Continental System. As an almost exclusively agricultural country, Russia had suffered extreme economic hardships when it was no longer able to exchange its surplus grain for British manufactured products. Alarmed by popular protests and agitation, Alexander permitted the gradual resumption of trade with Great Britain. Napoleon, rather than see his system collapse, decided to punish the tsar.

For the invasion, Napoleon concentrated an enormous army of

509

600,000 men, the largest yet assembled under a single command. Only about 40 percent of the troops were French, the rest unwilling conscripts from allied and subject states. In June 1812, Napoleon crossed the Niemen River and plunged into the immensity of Russia. Napoleon planned to force the Russians into a decisive battle and destroy them by sheer force of numbers. He carried with him only three weeks' supplies for, as in past campaigns, he counted on living off the countryside. From the beginning everything went wrong. Reluctant to face Napoleon in a single great battle, the Russians retreated steadily inland, destroying homes and burning crops as they withdrew. Under political pressure to protect Moscow, the Russian general Michael Kutusov made a stand at Borodino on September 7. Both sides lost heavily, but the French won out and a week later entered Moscow. Almost immediately, a fire, set intentionally or accidentally by the Russians, spread through the city, causing immense destruction. The lack of supplies and the impossibility of wintering in a ruined city left Napoleon with no alternative but to turn back.

The presence of a Russian army to the south compelled Napoleon to retire by the same route he had come, a route already stripped bare of supplies. The retreat, which began on October 22, turned into a nightmare. The Russians followed in the wake of the Grand Army and, while avoiding any major engagements, cut off stragglers and harassed the hungry troops in every possible way. To add to the hardships of the French, cold weather set in early and was unusually severe. Swollen streams and mountainous snowdrifts slowed down the line of march. Thousands of men dropped from exhaustion or froze to death; equipment, wagons, and even the sick and wounded were abandoned. In mid-December, about 50,000 ragged and half-starved men crossed the frontier into Germany. The rest, more than half a million, had deserted, perished, or fallen into Russian hands.

The War of Liberation

The inglorious end of the Russian campaign destroyed the myth that Napoleon was invincible. One nation after another joined Russia and Great Britain in the final coalition against the French. Napoleon raised a new army in France, but it was inexperienced and poorly equipped. Tired and worn out, the French emperor himself appears to have lost some of his genius for command. The main theater of war shifted to Germany. There Napoleon won several indecisive battles before he met the combined armies of his enemies at Leipzig, October 16–19, 1813, and suffered a crushing defeat. Leipzig marked the beginning of the end for Napoleon. His allies deserted him and his empire collapsed almost overnight.

Napoleon and his shattered army fell back across the Rhine, pursued by the forces of the coalition. During early 1814, Napoleon waged a brilliant defensive campaign with a meager force of untrained teenagers. The struggle was hopeless, however, and on March 31 the Allies triumphantly entered Paris. Disillusioned and facing mounting unrest at home, Napoleon abdicated and was banished to the tiny island of Elba off the coast of Italy. The victorious coalition restored the Bourbon dynasty to the French throne in the person of Louis XVIII, brother of the decapitated Louis XVI.

In 1815, Napoleon had his last brief interlude of glory known as the Hundred Days (March 20–June 29). During his nine months on Elba, he had yearned to regain his throne. Encouraged by reports that the French people were dissatisfied with Louis and that quarrels had broken out among the allies over the spoils, Napoleon slipped away from Elba and landed at Cannes, in southern France, on March 1, 1815. His name still evoked hero worship. Troops sent to capture him deserted to his standard and, as he approached Paris, Louis fled toward the Belgian frontier. Stunned by the news of Napoleon's return, the allied powers laid aside their differences and renewed their alliance. Napoleon quickly raised a new army and marched into Belgium where British and Prussian forces had collected. The French scored a minor success initially, but then were irretrievably defeated by the duke of Wellington at Waterloo on June 18, 1815. Napoleon abdicated a second time and chose to surrender to the British. He requested that he be allowed to stay in Great Britain, but to ensure the security of Europe the British shipped him off to the bleak island of St. Helena in the South Atlantic. There, under close supervision, he lived out a dreary existence until his death on May 5, 1821.

THE NAPOLEONIC LEGACY

Bearing in mind that it is not always possible to separate the French Revolution's impact from Napoleon's, we can nevertheless note a number of

instances in which his contributions were unique. By preserving and disseminating most of the principles of the French Revolution, Napoleon prevented the reestablishment of the old order in France and throughout much of Europe. Had he not come to power a restored Bourbon monarchy in 1800 or soon after might well have undone the achievements of the Revolution. Although falling short of its professed democratic ideals, Napoleon's regime guaranteed religious freedom, instituted efficient and evenhanded administration, and generally insisted on talent, rather than birth, as qualification for public office. In short he gave people, unaccustomed to such benefits, a taste of a new and better order. Some aspects of the Napoleonic system were so deeply rooted by 1815 that no restored monarch could have overturned them.

Napoleon taught succeeding gen-erations of authoritarian leaders the techniques of effective dictatorship. To stifle dissent and rally popular support, he relied on such devices as propaganda, the secret police, the plebiscite, foreign adventures, and state control of education and religion. Although Napoleon did not introduce most of these tools of authoritarianism, his contribution was to mold them into an effective instrument of state control.

In pursuing certain policies Napoleon unwittingly prepared the way for the unification of both Italy and Germany. By sounding the call for Italian freedom he awakened a spirit that survived his fall. In Germany his scheme amalgamating many of the small states influenced the settlement of 1815, which created 39 sovereign princes and cities in place of the more than 300 principalities.

Another lasting consequence of Napoleon's rule was the growth of na-

Napoleon at St. Helena. The engraving by Janet does not truly convey the bleak atmosphere of the island. Bored and disillusioned, the former emperor lost the will to live and grew extremely fat. He died on May 5, 1821, possibly from poison, as one recent study claims, but more likely from intestinal cancer which also claimed his father and two of his sisters. Bibliothèque Narmoltan.

tionalism, a major force in European life down to the present day. The establishment of an enlightened government and the glory attached to Napoleon's conquests created among French people a fierce sense of pride and devotion. Their aggressive acts in Europe, which expressed this feeling, provoked a nationalistic counterreaction in many of the areas occupied by French forces.

Napoleon's career has been the subject of endless debate. Determining the balance between good and harm done by Napoleon is difficult. He was in many ways a thorough reactionary and the cost of his wars in terms of death, destruction and human misery was incalculable. Throughout his career he remained convinced that the end justified the means. Yet his accomplishments in the sphere of domestic reform cannot be matched in any other comparable period in French history. His major legal and administrative reforms survived his fall and became part of the machinery of government and society, not only in France, but in many other European countries as well. Perhaps the best brief characterization of Napoleon is that of the eminent French historian Alexis de Tocqueville: "He was as great as a man can be without virtue."

SUMMARY

The emergence of Napoleon Bonaparte was due as much to the Directory, which gave him successive opportunities for glory, as to his military genius and personality. Not content with his lot as a successful general, Napoleon overthrew the Directory in a coup d'état in November 1799. The people trusted him to set matters right after the years of revolutionary experiment and disorder. Thus they gave overwhelming approval to his constitution which, although retaining the pretense of divided sovereignty, in effect established a dictatorship.

Napoleon provided honest and enlightened administration which for most of the French people more than compensated for the loss of political freedom. Under Bonaparte a concordat was negotiated with the papacy, laws were nationally codified, the educational system was reformed, taxes became more equitable, careers were open to talent, the debt was liquidated and the budget balanced, and business revived and expanded. The French showed their gratitude by overwhelming assent through plebiscites to make him consul for life in 1802 and emperor in 1804.

Napoleon came closer than any person to imposing a political unity on the European continent. Between 1805 and 1807, he cowed or defeated the European nations until Great Britain remained his sole adversary. To break Great Britain, Napoleon devised the Continental System, which aimed at cutting off British trade with the European continent. The British rode out the storm, however, by developing new markets and by smuggling goods to old customers on the continent.

Napoleon reached the high-tide of his career in 1807. Everywhere he went he replaced the feudal regimes with the same order that he had installed in France. The people who initially welcomed him as a liberator, however, soon came to realize that they had merely exchanged one absolute ruler for another. The Spaniards were the first to rebel after Napoleon installed his brother Joseph on the Spanish throne. With France's armies bogged down in Spain, the Russian tsar, wearied of the hardships caused by the Continental System, opened his ports to the British. Napoleon's invasion of Russia in 1812 ended in a catastrophe. The aura of Napoleonic invincibility had been shattered. The following year a powerful coalition defeated the French at Leipzig. His empire in a state of collapse, Napoleon withdrew to France where he was forced to abdicate. He was exiled to the island of Elba but within a year he was back in France. His last days of glory were brief, ending on the battlefield of Waterloo on June 18, 1815. If Waterloo closed the career of one of the most remarkable individuals of modern times, it also marked the beginning of a new kind of collaboration among the powers, made in an effort to establish a firm foundation for a lasting world peace.

SELECTED SOURCES

*Brun, G. *Europe and The French Imperium, 1799–1814* Rev. ed., 1957. A concise scholarly account of Napoleon's impact on Europe.

*Bergeron, Louis. *France Under Napoleon.* 1981. A judicious study of the regime and the men chosen by Napoleon to help him run it.

*Connelly, Owen. *Napoleon's Satellite Kingdoms.* 1965. A pioneer work focusing on the kingdoms of Naples, Italy, the Netherlands, Spain and Westphalia.

*De Caulaincourt A. *With Napoleon in Russia.* (various editions). Vivid memoirs by an aide-de-camp to Napoleon.

*Geyl, Peter. *Napoleon: For and Against.* 1949. A perceptive evaluation of the judgments made about Napoleon by French historians from 1815 to the mid 20th century.

*Herold, J. C. *The Age of Napoleon.* 1963. A well written popular history.

*Herold, J. C., ed. *The Mind of Napoleon,* 1961. A valuable selection from Napoleon's writings and conversations, arranged topically.

*Holtman, Robert. *The Napoleonic Revolution,* 1967. A straightforward assessment of Napoleon's accomplishments.

Lefebvre, Georges. *Napoleon,* 2 vols. 1969. Perhaps the most authoritative biography.

*Markham, Felix. *Napoleon,* 1964. A brief reliable biography.

Parker, Harold T. *Three Napoleonic Battles.* Rev. ed. 1983. Traces the decline of Napoleon's battlefield prowess through a study of three major battles.

Rothenberg, Gunther E. *The Art of Warfare in the Age of Napoleon.* 1978. Clear concise treatment of the warfare of the period and Napoleon as a military leader.

*Tolstoy, Leo. *War and Peace* (available abridged and complete in many editions). Classic novel about Napoleon's invasion of Russia.

Waterloo. Directed by Sergei Bondarchuk. This 1971 film with Rod Steiger as Napoleon and Christopher Plummer as Wellington, accurately depicts the events leading up to the climactic battle.

*Available in paperback.

THE AGE OF NATIONALISM AND IMPERIALISM

The nineteenth century was a period of paradox and change in western civilization. Between Waterloo in 1815 and the beginning of World War I in 1914, there were few major wars in the west, but a series of economic, social, and political changes kept the pot boiling in Europe, often spawning revolutions. The material wealth of the west multiplied, yet painful poverty beset the lower classes and intensified conflicts between social classes. Political freedom was extended to more Europeans and Americans than ever before, while imperialists enlarged their control of nonwestern peoples. Though some clung to old values and institutions, it was an age in which political, economic, social, cultural, and intellectual changes transformed the western world.

The emergence of modern methods of industrial production and modern sociopolitical ideologies influenced all other developments during the nineteenth century. The Industrial Revolution, beginning in the later eighteenth century in Great Britain, spread through much of Europe and the New World in the nineteenth, bringing with it a new emphasis on free competition and huge new industrial combinations. At the same time, liberalism, socialism, and modern nationalism challenged conservative allegiance to old ideals and institutions.

These two forces—industrial and ideological—engendered bitter clashes between conservative efforts to restore the old regime after 1815 and demands for reform or revolutionary change, culminating in the revolutions of 1848. The policies of conflicting nationalisms assumed special importance in the later nineteenth century, producing new great powers in Germany and Italy and undermining the multiethnic Habsburg and Ottoman empires. Social and political reforms brought the slow spread of civic rights, trade unionism, and socialism. Finally, the cultural and intellectual life of the century was highlighted by a conflict between romanticism in literature and the arts on the one hand and philosophical materialism and scientific progress on the other.

Between 1870 and 1914, relations among the western powers once again became more aggressive. The "new imperialism" brought almost all of Africa and most of Asia under some degree of western control. The diplomatic alliances and growing conflicts in the same period led to the outbreak in 1914 of the most devastating war Europe had ever seen. World War I was marked at its outset by tides of patriotic enthusiasm. It soon became apparent, however, that the weapons of war furnished by modern science and industry would make this conflict the most costly in human life that the world had yet seen. In the end, the peace settlement of 1919 was the creation, not of idealists who hoped that the war might be the one to end all wars, but of representatives of great powers who secured their nations' selfish interests at the expense of an equitable and lasting peace.

	1800	1810	1820	1830	1840	1850

Politics

Above line:
- 1815 Waterloo; Congress of Vienna
- 1832 British Great Reform Bill

Below line:
- 1804 Napoleon crowned emperor
- 1819 Metternich's *Carlsbad Decrees*
- 1848 Liberal/Nationalist revolutions throughout Europe

Economics & Society

Above line:
- Growth of free trade economies
- Industrialization of France and Germany

Below line:
- Population explosion begins
- Growth of U.S. abolitionist movement
- 1851 Crystal Palace Industrial Exhibition, London

Science & Technology

Above line:
- 1812 Georges Guvier begins study of fossils
- 1830 George Stephenson's *Rocket*
- 1822–84 Gregor Mendel; Genetics

Below line:
- 1807 Robert Fulton's steamship *The Clermont*
- 1827 First photographs taken
- 1837 Samuel Morse exhibits the telegraph
- 1859 Charles Darwin's *Origin of Species*

Religion & Thought

Above line:
- 1804–1872 Ludwig Feuerbach; Materialism
- Utopian Socialism

Below line:
- Georg Hegel (1770–1831)
- 1789–1857 Auguste Comte; Positivism
- 1806–1873 John Stuart Mill; Utilitarianism
- 1848 Karl Marx's *The Communist Manifesto*

Arts & Literature

Above line:
- 1808 Goethe's *Faust*
- 1819 Sir Walter Scott's *Ivanhoe*
- 1831 Victor Hugo's *The Hunchback of Notre Dame*
- Emergence of Realist Painting

Below line:
- Age of Romanticism begins
- 1770–1827 Ludwig von Beethoven
- 1797–1828 Franz Schubert
- 1809–49 Edgar Allen Poe
- 1855 Walt Whitman's *Leaves of Grass*

1860	1870	1880	1890	1900	1910	1920

1861
Proclamation of the Kingdom of Italy

1871
German Empire

1882–1907
Triple Alliance and Triple Entente

1914–18
World War I

1861–65
U.S. Civil War

1870–1920
The New Imperialism

1898–1902
Spanish-American War, Boer War, Philippine Insurrection

1919
Paris Peace Conference

1861
Czar Alexander I frees serfs

Growth of corporations and cartels

1870s–1920s
Women's suffrage movements

Carnegie and Rockefeller build multi-million dollar corporations

1865
Slavery abolished in the U.S.

Emergence of Labor Unions

"Jim Crow" laws spread in U.S. South

1860
First internal combustion engine

1822–95
Louis Pasteur

1856–1939
Sigmund Freud; Psychoanalysis

1879–1955
Albert Einstein; Theory of Relativity

1869
Dmitri Mendeleyev's periodic table of elements

1847–1931
Thomas Edison

1867–1934
Madame Curie; Radium

1805–72
Giuseppe Mazzini; Nationalism

1803–82
Ralph Waldo Emerson; Transcendentalism

1853–1899
Emergence of modern racism

1896–1917
Rise of Zionism in Europe

1844–1900
Freidrich Nietzsche; Irrationalism

1842–1910
William James; Pragmatism

1890–1915
Social Gospel spreads in U. S.

1866
Dostoievsky's *Crime and Punishment*

Emergence of Impressionist painting

1839–1906
Paul Cezanne

1869
Tolstoy's *War and Peace*

1840–1902
Emile Zola

THE RISE OF INDUSTRIAL SOCIETY
(1760–1900)

At the face the cutters had gone back to work. They often shortened their lunch time so they wouldn't stiffen, and their sandwiches, eaten in ravenous silence so far from the sun, seemed like lead in their stomachs. Stretched out on their sides, they hacked harder than ever, obsessed by the idea of filling as many carts as possible. . . . They no longer felt the water that was trickling over them and swelling their limbs, or the cramps caused by their awkward positions, or the suffocation of the darkness in which they faded like plants that have been put into a cellar. Yet as the day went on, the air became more and more unbreathable, heated by the lamps, by their own foul breaths, by the poisonous firedamp fumes. It seemed to cling to their eyes like cobwebs, and it would only be swept away by the night's ventilation. Meanwhile, at the bottom of their molehill, under the weight of the earth, with no breath left in their overheated lungs, they kept hacking away.

This description of men at work in a nineteenth-century coal mine is by Emile Zola, a French novelist famous for his on-the-spot research and realistic descriptions. Working men and women like these labored through exhausting days under brutal conditions in unthinking participation in one of the great events of human history—the Industrial Revolution. Their labors, as much as the ingenuity of inventors or the shrewd business sense of entrepreneurs, made the Industrial Revolution happen.

The importance of this great transformation of western society can scarcely be exaggerated. The technological changes brought by industrialization transformed the world and would alone justify calling the Industrial Revolution one of the great watersheds in world history. The achievements in applied science and engineering of the modern industrial state clearly dwarf all earlier accomplishments in these fields.

Economically, the industrialization of the west also produced awesome changes. Europe had experienced several important economic permutations in the centuries preceding the eighteenth. These included the commercial revolution of the late medieval period and the creation of a world market dominated by European overseas empires in the sixteenth century. The Industrial Revolution that began around 1760,

The Crystal Palace. This towering structure of steel and glass was the center of the first "world's fair" or industrial exposition, held in London in 1851. Built of prefabricated girders and plates, easily assembled and disassembled, the Crystal Palace symbolized both the remarkable advance of industrial technology and the leading role taken by Great Britain in the Industrial Revolution.

however, inaugurated the most astonishing economic expansion the world had ever seen, the west acquiring in a short time more material wealth than any earlier civilization had ever possessed.

The impact of industrialization went beyond technological and economic change to produce a whole new society. The Industrial Revolution further stimulated the population growth, which began to increase exponentially, and modern industrial cities, vastly larger than any earlier urban complexes, sprawled over the landscape. Historians believe industrialization significantly intensified the differences between social classes, especially during the earlier phases of industrial growth. Other problems, from the breakdown of the family to the alienation of many people from modern society, have been traced to the impact of the Industrial Revolution.

The following pages will tell the first part of this story. They will survey the birth of the modern industrial system in eighteenth-century Great Britain and its spread to continental Europe and to the Americas in the nineteenth. The chapter then discusses the rise of big business in the later 1800s and the appearance of many social problems. Later chapters carry the story down to the present.

THE INDUSTRIAL REVOLUTION

Historians agree that modern industrial society first took shape in Great Britain in the mid-eighteenth century. The nineteenth-century historian Arnold J. Toynbee described this change as a "revolution"—not a po-

litical upheaval but an "industrial revolution"—a label it has retained ever since.

The Industrial Revolution may be likened to an explosive chemical mixture. It was only when all the necessary components came together that industrial development became possible. The causal mix of the Industrial Revolution was a combination of natural resources and a growing labor force, increased economic demand and large accumulations of capital, continuing technological advances, and the rise of entrepreneurship in the west. These elements were concentrated more heavily in Great Britain than anywhere else in Europe in the eighteenth century.

Industrialization in Great Britain

The basic raw materials, iron for heavy machinery and coal as an essential energy source, were to be found in substantial quantities in the midlands and in the north of England. In Great Britain, furthermore, entrepreneurs found these minerals close together or near water for inexpensive transport. It was thus relatively easy for them to bring these basic resources together for industrial purposes, and then to ship the resulting manufactured goods to market.

The eighteenth-century agricultural revolution created the labor force necessary for industrial development. Progress in crop rotation, soil fertilization, and animal breeding made British agriculture perhaps the most productive in Europe, increasing the output of food and stimulating a rapid growth in population. More efficient agriculture also meant fewer farm laborers were needed, freeing more

British hands for industrial work. At the same time, landowners were enclosing village lands in the new farms, compelling many peasants to go to the city to look for work. Many would find jobs in the new factories.

The application of machine tools and technology to agriculture was most important in the first half of the nineteenth century since most people still made a living farming. Improvements not only increased production, but also unemployment. A. James Smith in 1823 developed a deep plowing process to drain otherwise marshy land. Later, sulky and gang plows mounted on wheels had levers that change the depth of the plowing, depending on the soil and the crop. Justus von Liebig discovered the chemicals essential to plant life, and in 1843 chemical fertilizer was being developed so that farmers were no longer totally dependent on decaying organic matter to restore soil fertility.

Harvesting grain was the most arduous seasonal farm labor. In 1834 Cyrus McCormick invented a reaper which in a few years was improved so that a bundle of the grain thus cut was bound into a sheaf. This eliminated cutting the grain with a sickle and tying the sheaves by hand. That same year John and Hiram Pitts invented a thresher which separated the grain from the straw and the chaff; this eliminated the process of spreading the grain on a platform and flailing it or driving animals around over it to achieve the same results. Ten years later a header was perfected which combined the cutting and threshing operations, although modern versions of the combine were not much in use before 1920.

Demand naturally increased with the population, stimulating a further

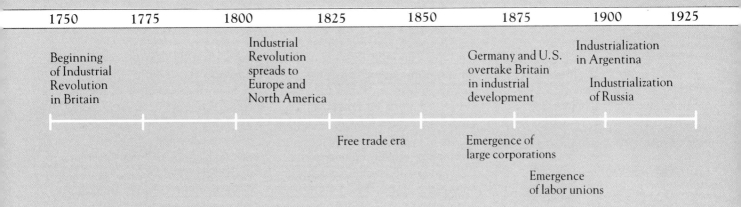

1750   1775   1800   1825   1850   1875   1900   1925

Beginning
of Industrial
Revolution
in Britain

Industrial
Revolution
spreads to
Europe and
North America

Germany and U.S.
overtake Britain
in industrial
development

Industrialization
in Argentina

Industrialization
of Russia

Free trade era

Emergence of
large corporations

Emergence
of labor unions

increase in industrial production. Demand was also created by increased prosperity; and Great Britain, with its large international trade and overseas empire, was perhaps the most prosperous country in Europe in the eighteenth century. Improvements in roads and canals further encouraged a profitable flow of goods, as did the absence of internal tolls and tariffs; after the union of England and Scotland, Great Britain was actually the largest free trade area in Europe.

Prosperity also fostered the growth of investment capital. Those who had made profits from commercial and colonial enterprises provided some of this money, investing in new ventures rather than plowing the money back into the old businesses. Great Britain's excellent banks, including Europe's strongest financial institution, the Bank of England, thus had large amounts of capital available for investment. Limited liability laws also helped by limiting any one investor's liability for a firm's debts to the amount of his own investment—again, an encouragement to invest.

Under these promising conditions technological advances came rapidly. Inventors and technicians typically developed new machines in attempts to solve recognized industrial problems, rather than through happy ac-

cidents or casual tinkering. Developments in one industry also furnished an expanded technological base from which entrepreneurs in other industries might borrow, thus contributing to further industrial growth. Another important factor was the weakening of the power of the guilds, opening the way to much more rapid innovation than the conservative craftsmen would have permitted.

Entrepreneurship, finally, was an essential catalyst for industrial expansion in Britain. The profits to be made attracted ambitious and ingenious men. The law of primogeniture, which turned entire landed estates over to the oldest son, and the relative lack of prejudice against being "in trade" sent well-educated, self-confident younger brothers into business.

As a catalyst, the entrepreneur brought all the other elements together in one industry after another. It was the entrepreneur who, by making a paying proposition out of the new technology, set the machinery of the industrial revolution in motion.

The New Industries
in Great Britain

New industries and new sources of energy went hand in hand in the later

1700s and the earlier 1800s. The steam engine, cotton textiles, and coal and iron are outstanding examples.

The steam engine was an essential source of power for industrial society in its earlier states. Steam had been used for the limited purpose of pumping water out of coal mines for generations before it found broader uses. In the 1760s, Scottish mechanic James Watt began to design steam-powered engines efficient enough for other industrial purposes. In partnership with the English entrepreneur Matthew Boulton, Watt produced engines that could do the work of up to twenty horses—the origin of the "horsepower" rating, which Watt was the first to apply. By the early nineteenth century, steam had replaced water power as the chief energy source of the booming Industrial Revolution.

The evolution of cotton textile manufacturing is an outstanding illustration of the dependence of industrialization on sources of power such as the steam engine. A growing demand for cotton cloth had already been created by imports from Asia. Parliament, however, had prohibited the importing of cotton textiles to protect English wool producers, typically peasants with spinning wheels and looms in their cottages. Eager entrepreneurs like the hard-driving,

521

ton thread and the weaving of these threads into cloth. The new machinery, too big and costly for cottage industry, had to be housed in large sheds —the first modern industrial factories. These new textile machines also rapidly outgrew human strength. They were therefore driven first by water power and then by the new steam engines.

The immense success of this new industrial system may be measured by the growth of the cotton industry in Britain. In 1770, British cotton manufacturing was minimal, her cotton experts negligible. By 1830, cotton cloth not only sold widely in Britain but also accounted for 45 percent of all that nation's foreign exports, much of it going to protected markets in the British colonies.

Two other industries that proved essential to the exploitation of new techniques in many areas of the economy were coal and iron production, both of which experienced major advances in the eighteenth century. England had burned off much of its forest cover by early modern times, and had begun to use coal instead of wood for home heating and for some industrial purposes even before 1700. In the eighteenth century, English coal miners developed a number of advanced techniques for extracting coal from greater depth. Particularly valuable was the use of steam power to pump water out of the deeper shafts.

Iron production also increased in this first century of the Industrial Revolution. Iron manufacturers learned to use coke (made from coal) instead of expensive charcoal (made from wood) for smelting higher grade iron. Ironmasters like John Wilkinson also learned to work iron more precisely and to apply it to many new purposes, from bridges to steam engine boilers.

From the beginning of the Industrial Revolution in Great Britain, the lives of the nation's working masses were transformed by the new forms of production. Workers no longer practiced skilled crafts in small shops or in their own cottages. Instead, they labored for long hours in large factories or in the mines. Women and children were also widely employed in factories, especially in the booming textile industry. Work there required less heavy labor and more alertness and dexterity. Women from poor families could thus add significantly to family income, and even small children could bring in a few shillings a week. The cost of their wages, however, was the suffering caused by long hours and need to work rapidly to keep up with the new machines.

THE SPREAD OF INDUSTRIALISM

Born in Great Britain in the eighteenth century, the Industrial Revolution spread to both continental Europe and the Americas in the nineteenth century. Entrepreneurs in other parts of the western world where the necessary resources, material and social, were most readily available first took up the new methods. These areas included such western European countries as France, Belgium, and the German states and, in North America, the growing United States. By the end of the century, industrialization had spread still farther, to southern and eastern Europe, to some

sometimes unscrupulous Richard Arkwright moved to satisfy the unmet demand. They imported raw cotton and began to produce cotton cloths in England.

As the market for cotton fabrics grew, technicians devised machinery to speed up both the spinning of cot-

Latin American countries, and to Japan.

For most of the nineteenth century, Great Britain maintained her industrial preeminence. But toward the end of the century, the unification of Germany and the increasing industrialization of the United States had made these nations serious rivals for global economic supremacy.

In the newer industrial nations, the basic elements for industrialization—resources and labor, demand and investment capital, technology and entrepreneurship—were not always combined as they had been in Britain. Capital was sometimes provided by government or by foreign loans rather than by local investors. The independent entrepreneur was sometimes replaced by government initiatives. One way or another, however, in the course of the nineteenth century, much of the western world was converted to new industrial societies.

The transportation and communication revolutions, meanwhile, continued throughout the nineteenth century in Europe and the Americas. Steam power contributed to the new ways of traveling and communicating among cities, nations, and continents. Transportation over land improved with hard-surfaced roads and growing networks of canals. But it was the steam locomotive that revolutionized passenger travel and freight haulage. George Stephenson's *Rocket* took to the rails in Britain in 1830, booming along at twelve miles an hour. Forty years later, in 1870, there were almost 900,000 miles of track in western Europe, and the United States had laid rails from the Atlantic to the Pacific.

Robert Fulton's American paddle-wheel steamboat, the *Clermont,* sailed on the Hudson River as early as 1807. But it was more than half a century before screw propellers and more efficient steam engines led to regular steamship voyages across the Atlantic, carrying freight as well as passengers. By the end of the century, iron and steel steamships with ten or twenty times the carrying capacity of the wooden sailing ships of earlier centuries regularly plowed the sea-lanes of the world.

The Industrial Revolution in Europe

The new methods of production and the new society they created spread from one European nation to another during the 1800s. Belgium, building on manufacturing traditions going back to medieval times and on large deposits of coal, became the continent's first industrialized nation. Belgian industrialists produced large quantities of iron and cotton textiles. Belgium also became the first continental country to have a complete

A Textile Mill in 1835. This engraving of a British cotton mill shows thread being spun by machinery in a large factory—a striking contrast with the traditional spinning wheel of earlier centuries. Note both men and women at work.

The Great Eastern. This early ocean-going steamship combined sails and steam power. Shown here in 1850 setting sail from Britain with the French Atlantic cable, the vessel illustrates nineteenth-century advances in both transportation and communication.

railroad network. France developed a base for industrialization during the decades around 1800, the period of the French Revolution and the rule of Napoleon. Standardized weights and measures, a national investment bank, an excellent system of roads, bridges, and canals, and the world's best engineering school—the Polytechnic in Paris—were all important ingredients. An innate French conservatism, that made small family firms the rule, did limit industrial expansion. Still, the French multiplied their production of coal, as well as textiles in Alsace, and of iron in Lorraine during the nineteenth century.

Germany's political division into three dozen separate small nations seriously hampered industrial growth for much of the nineteenth century. Industrial products often had to cross several tariff barriers to reach larger international markets through the port cities on the Baltic. This handicap was gradually overcome. The north German customs union or *Zollverein* established a "common market" for many of the German states in the first half of the century. The political unification of most of the German states under Prussian leadership in 1871 made the new German Empire a leading industrial nation as well. By 1900, Germany was overcoming Britain's long lead to emerge as Europe's most productive industrial power.

Industrial development also occurred in other parts of western Europe, including the Netherlands, the Scandinavian nations, Switzerland, and Austria. The industrial growth of northern Italy and of the dynamic little state of Piedmont in particular strengthened that region, which became the political center of a united Italy after 1860.

Government played a part in bringing the Industrial Revolution to many of these countries. Protective tariffs, subsidies, and large-scale capital investment by the state fostered industrial growth in Belgium, the German states, and elsewhere. But a number of factors limited or slowed the spread of industrialization in some parts of the European continent: in southern Europe, a lack of wealth and scarcity of iron and coal; in eastern Europe, relative poverty, technological backwardness, and the lack of a large, aggressive commercial middle class.

Nowhere were these problems more important than in Romanov Russia. This backward colossus of eastern Europe had never developed as large or dynamic a middle class as had western European nations. Lack of commercial wealth meant a lack of investment capital in private hands. The Russian government therefore attempted to take up the slack, following the pattern in Belgium and the German states. In the later nineteenth century, the tsarist regime began to negotiate foreign loans, especially from France, and to provide other support for such huge industrial ventures as the building of the Trans-Siberian Railway. By 1900, the giant of eastern Europe was at least beginning, slowly and painfully, to build a modern industrial society.

The Industrial Revolution in the Americas

In the American republics, which had evolved from European colonies in the New World, industrialization also began to spread in the nineteenth century. This was particularly true of the growing North American powerhouse, the United States, first in New England and, after the Civil War, across the nation.

The United States benefited from a number of advantages. Among these were the vast natural resources of the continent, including iron, coal, and oil, an increasingly important power source. The United States also had a multiplying population, reinforced by waves of immigrants from Europe and elsewhere. Industrial growth was further encouraged by investment capital, much of it initially supplied by Great Britain. As in Great Britain, government played a secondary role in American industrialization, though Congress did provide tariff protection for the American economy and land

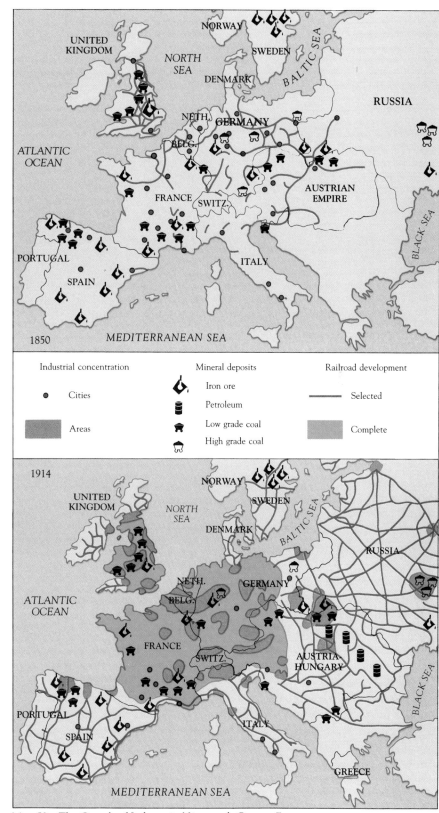

MAP 59 The Growth of Industry in Nineteenth Century Europe.

THE CRYSTAL PALACE INDUSTRIAL EXPOSITION: A DAZZLED VISITOR'S VIEW

This Palace tall,
This Cristial Hall,
Which Imperors might covet,
Stands in High [Hyde] Park
Like Noah's Ark,
A rainbow bent above it. . . .

There's Statues bright
Of marble white,
Of silver and of copper;
And some in zinc,
And some, I think
That isn't over proper

There's staym Ingynes
[steam Engines],
That stands in lines,
Enormous and amazing,
That squeal and snort
Like whales in sport,
Or elephants a-grazing. . . .

There's sacks of coals and fuels,
There's swords and guns,
And soap in tons,
And Ginger-bread and Jewels. . . .

So let us raise
Victoria's praise,
And Albert's proud condition,
That takes his ayes [ease]
As he surveys
This Cristial Exhibition. •

This comment on Britain's industrial exhibition of 1851 gives some sense of the dazzling variety of items on display at this early world's fair. British writer William Makepeace Thackeray has made his humble visitor properly respectful of the exposition's patrons, Queen Victoria and Prince Albert. The use of Irish dialect serves to heighten the feeling of the great gulf separating the lower classes from the high cultural and impressive material achievements of the age.

•W. M. Thackeray, "The Crystal Palace, 1851," in Geoffrey Grigson, *The Victorians* (London: Routledge & Kegan Paul, 1950), pp. 66, 68–70.

grants to railroads. In general, flamboyant and expansive entrepreneurs such as Andrew Carnegie, John D. Rockefeller, and Edward H. Harriman led America's industrial growth.

By the turn of the century, the United States was the world's largest producer of both industrial and agricultural products. Railways spanned the continent, and great industrial cities had spread from New England across the midwest. U.S. exports challenged European goods on the world market. Latin America in particular was coming under the economic influence of industrialized North America, but American goods were competitive as far away as China.

Some Latin American nations also developed industrially in the later nineteenth century. As in the north, a combination of natural resources with foreign capital—first from Britain, later from the United States—contributed significantly to the beginnings of industrial society in these nations. Nitrates in Chile, tin in Bolivia, and the discovery of oil in Mexico at the end of the century all drew foreign investors into these countries.

Argentinians built a boom on beef, wheat, and the processing of these and other agricultural products.

But industrialization did not proceed as rapidly in Latin America as it did in North America or in Europe. One reason was the widespread poverty of the southern continent and a consequent lack of domestic demand and domestic capital. Most Latin American nations therefore fell into a pattern of exporting raw materials and agricultural products to more developed nations in Europe and North America. Rather than developing strong industrial economies of their own, they imported manufactured goods from their industrialized trading partners.

New Industries in the Nineteenth Century

The new industrial system not only spread throughout the western world, but it developed in new directions during the nineteenth century. Whereas industrialists continued to mine coal and produce iron and textiles in increasing quantities throughout the century, entrepreneurs created a number of new industries, setting up steel and chemical manufacturing combines, producing hydroelectric power, and sponsoring amazing advances in transportation and communication.

Steel, a much stronger and more flexible construction material than iron, was created when technicians combined iron with carbon and such additives as tungsten or manganese. Technological breakthroughs in Great Britain and Germany made this process possible on a much larger scale in the later nineteenth century, and westerners were soon using steel for a wide variety of products, from sewing machines to trans-Atlantic steamers. By the end of the century, steel's potential for building construction was revealed in structures like the Eiffel Tower in Paris and, along with the new elevator technology, in the first skyscrapers in the United States.

The use of chemicals in industry also increased dramatically in the later 1800s. Chemists created artificial dyes for clothing and adapted alkalis for a range of products from textiles to soap, adding new industries. Chemical industrialists and technologists also developed photography and the manufacture of cheap paper for magazines and newspapers. Germany led the world in the manufacturing of industrial chemicals in the nineteenth century.

Inventors like Thomas Edison first harnessed electricity for industrial purposes in the later nineteenth century. Water and steam turbines made possible the generation of large quantities of electrical power. The new energy source was soon running trolley cars and lighting cities through the incandescent lamp. Even more striking was the introduction of vir-

tually instant communication by means of electricity. Samuel Morse tapped out the first telegraph message in history from Washington to nearby Baltimore in 1844. Undersea cables linked Great Britain with continental Europe in the 1850s, Europe with North America in the 1860s. Telegraph lines, like railway lines, soon bound the cities and nations of the western world.

Finally a number of other technological breakthroughs toward the end of the nineteenth century heralded some of the mass-produced manufactured products of the twentieth. The development of the combustion engine, for example, moved society toward the automobile age to come. New techniques of petroleum refining would make gasoline and diesel fuel available for cars and trucks. New metal alloys made possible a wide variety of tools and implements, as well as machine parts. Laboratory creation of rayon fabrics and chemical dyes revealed the possibility of clothing made of synthetic materials. The canning of food, perfected by the mid-nineteenth century, transformed the science of food preservation; refrigeration, invented in the second

half of the century, would revolutionize that science again in the twentieth century.

THE RISE OF BIG BUSINESS

The Industrial Revolution began in the government-regulated economy of mercantilism. Under the mercantilist system, royal bureaucrats and local guilds regulated wages, prices, and quality and set the terms of trade. Guilds determined how labor should be trained; governments decided which industries should be protected, which firms should get monopolies of major markets.

The Golden Age of Free Competition

Many of the entrepreneurs who guided the early stages of industrialization felt this government paternalism hindered rather than helped industrial growth. They agreed with Adam Smith, the eighteenth-century founder of modern economics, that free competition at home and free trade

The Age of Steam. This nineteenth-century picture shows the impact of steam power on several aspects of the modern industrial economy. Notice smoke rising from the factory stacks, steam from the locomotive, and the smokestacks on the canal boats.

abroad would lead to a great increase in the wealth of nations. These businessmen agitated for an end to mercantilist economic controls and in the early nineteenth century, they saw their efforts begin to pay off. The grip of the guilds—which had often become agents of government under mercantilism—was broken. Governments ceased to support the traditional monopolies, allowing freer competition in major markets. Great Britain led the way toward free trade by repealing a number of customs duties, climaxed by the repeal of the "corn laws" or protective tariffs on grain in the 1840s.

From the 1820s into the 1870s, free competition thus came to dominate much of the European economy. Older and newer power sources, old and new industries, and manufacturers of many products competed freely. In clothmaking, coal mining, and other industries, hundreds, even thousands, of small to medium-sized firms competed for business in a relatively unregulated market. Such free competition was widely believed to have many advantages. A competitive economy, it was urged, would eliminate inefficient producers. It would ensure the customer the best product at the lowest price. "Competition," business leaders commonly asserted, "is the life of trade and the law of progress."

The Coming of Industrial Combination

Difficulties arose with the new system as with the old. Competition could be brutal, the sort of fang-and-claw struggles that led to bankruptcies. Especially during the periodic business depressions of the nineteenth cen-

tury, many firms went under, their owners sometimes saddled with lifelong indebtedness. In time, some businessmen began to wonder if limited or controlled competition might better serve their own interests.

In fact some industries had little competition from the first. For instance, city governments often granted monopolies to public utilities and urban streetcar lines. National governments frequently capitalized and owned railroads in central and eastern Europe. Any producer who obtained a patent on a key part or process could enjoy a de facto monopoly in many parts of Europe.

In the last quarter of the nineteenth century, however, monopolies began to appear in other areas of the industrial economy. These new monopolies, and the control of the economy that resulted, were not the work of governments. They were established by businessmen themselves.

These new types of "industrial combination" were of two primary sorts: corporations and cartels. A corporation was the result of a merger of several smaller industrial firms into a single gigantic company. Aggressive entrepreneurs would buy out weaker rivals, strengthening their own position against other competitors, which might thus be absorbed in their turn. Such an industrial combination might include a number of firms in the same line of business, producing a "horizontal combination," such as the Nobel Dynamite Trust Company in Europe and Andrew Carnegie's U.S. Steel Corporation in the United States, which controlled manufacturers of the same product. Another form of industrial amalgamation was of companies in related businesses, often stages of the same process. The result

was called a "vertical combination." An impressive combine engineered by German industrialist Albert Krupp illustrates this pattern. Krupp began as a steelmaker, but bought up iron and coal mines and such user industries as railway manufacturers, shipyards, and the arms factories for which Krupp industries became famous.

Cartels, by contrast, involved no merging of companies, but were simply loose alliances based on "cartel agreements" between major manufacturers. Members of a cartel, for example, might agree to fix minimum prices. They might divide the market among themselves. They might set a maximum total output and then agree on quotas for each member. In these and similar ways, such agreements undercut free competition as effectively as monopolistic industrial combination did.

Attitudes toward cartels varied. In Great Britain and America, they were often considered illegal "conspiracies in restraint of trade." In Germany, they were legally enforceable agreements. Either way, giant corporations could virtually control the market for whatever they produced.

Cartels might be national or international in scope. The Rhenish-Westphalian Coal Syndicate brought 170 coal companies into common marketing arrangements that could virtually dictate the price of coal in western Germany. The shipping cartel that combined major British, German, French, Dutch, and Japanese shipping lines came close to setting steamship fares and shipping rates on the oceans of the world.

Such giant corporations and cartels, emerging after 1870, were the cornerstone of modern big business. Customers benefited from economies of production on a large scale, from standardization, long range planning, greater efficiency, and other advantages of sheer bigness. Small competing entrepreneurs, on the other hand, had little chance against these giants. Consumers' demands also seemed to have less effect on the market. Men in the boardrooms of big business, not the rough-and-tumble of the free marketplace, increasingly made decisions about quality, cost, and other crucial matters.

THE NEW INDUSTRIAL WORLD

The society that emerged under the impact of the Industrial Revolution exhibited both continuities with the past and important differences. Population growth, urbanization, and class conflicts, for instance, were not new; yet all three took new forms and increased in intensity or in sheer numbers during the eighteenth and nineteenth centuries.

The Population Explosion

The rapid population growth for the last few centuries is one of the most striking—and mysterious—features of modern history. Population statistics are not as dependable as historians would like for much of this period, and the causes of the phenomenon are much debated. But there is no doubt that the population of the western world grew at an unprecedented rate during the 1700s and 1800s.

Sample figures, where they are available, give a sense of this population explosion. The population of England, for instance, probably around

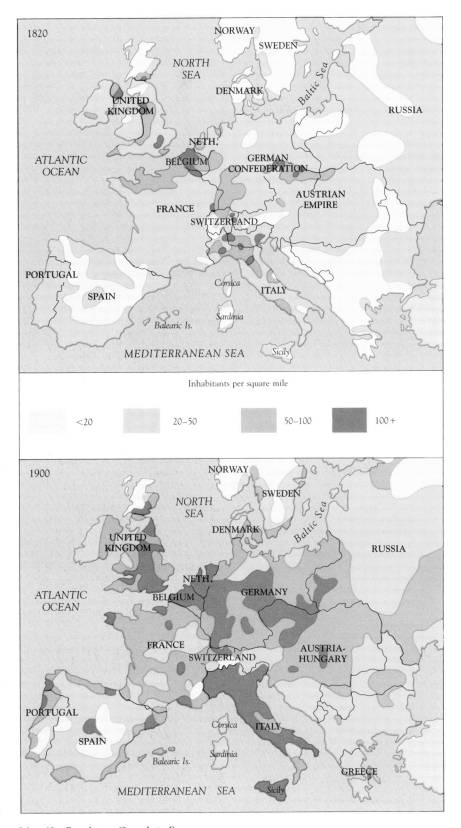

Inhabitants per square mile

| <20 | 20–50 | 50–100 | 100+ |

MAP 60   Population Growth in Europe.

529

COKETOWN

It was a town of red brick, or of brick that would have been red if the smoke and ashes had allowed it; but as matters stood it was a town of unnatural red and black like the painted face of a savage. It was a town of machinery and tall chimneys, out of which interminable serpents of smoke trailed themselves forever and ever, and never got uncoiled. It had a black canal in it, and a river that ran purple with ill-smelling dye, and vast piles of buildings full of windows where there was a rattling and a trembling all day long, and where the piston of the steam-engine worked monotonously up and down like the head of an elephant in a state of melancholy madness. It contained several large streets all very like one another, and many small streets still more like one another, inhabited by people equally like one another, who all went in and out at the same hours, with the same sound upon the same pavements, to do the same work, and to whom every day was the same as yesterday and tomorrow, and every year the counterpart of the last and the next.*

This description of "Coketown," an English industrial city, comes from Charles Dickens' novel of the Industrial Revolution, Hard Times. As early as the first half of the nineteenth century, this perceptive observer was able to see many of the problems of industrialization. This extract vividly depicts such modern urban problems as air and water pollution, the ugliness of early industrial cities, and the psychologically crushing monotony of labor controlled by the rhythm of the machines and the discipline of the factory whistle.

*Charles Dickens, Hard Times for These Times (New York: New American Library, 1961), pp. 30–31.

5 million in 1700, had almost doubled to 9 million by 1800, and had more than tripled again to 32 million by 1900. The population of Russia, the largest of the great powers, also tripled in the nineteenth century, from 36 million to 100 million people. New World populations grew even more rapidly. The population of the United States, less than 4 million in 1790, was pushing 100 million by the end of the nineteenth century.

Attempts to explain this sudden population surge have produced a wide variety of possible or probable causes. The Industrial Revolution, for example, created many new jobs, making it possible for young people to marry earlier and have more children. A combination of factors, including the agricultural revolution, and the introduction of such new crops as the potato, helped keep increasing numbers of these children alive longer. As modern medicine and sanitation developed, infectious diseases like smallpox and tuberculosis were less likely to be mass killers.

The consequences of the population explosion were varied. It has been suggested, for example, that the waves of violent ideologically based revolutions that swept over Europe between 1789 and 1848 are partly explainable by an increase in Europe's youthful population, since most re- volutionaries are young. There is certainly little doubt that the population increase gave the western world many more workers to mine the minerals, lay the rails, and labor in the factories of the industrial revolution.

Rise of the Industrial City

The city is as old as civilization. Urban living is in fact one of the defining features of civilized societies. The industrializing west, however, saw the emergence of a new form of urban complex: the modern industrial city. Rapid industrial development of a given area could turn a village into a town and a town into a city almost overnight. Workers flooded the cities seeking jobs in the new factories. Urban populations grew rapidly, since children could work alongside their parents in the mills and mines. Urban migration thus became a fundamental characteristic of industrial society.

The industrial cities of the nineteenth century were overcrowded and filthy. The water was polluted, the air thick with industrial smoke, and the factories scenes of many industrial accidents, whereas the slum tenements jammed whole families into a single room and provided a fertile breeding ground for disease. Industrial depressions threw many out of work, and crime was rampant.

By the end of the century, the work of reformers and the trickle-down of a modest prosperity began to alleviate some of these evils. The incomes and living standards of even the laboring masses inched upward. Housing improved in some cities, and working people could afford modest luxuries like meat, two sets of clothing, tobacco or a newspaper. Life expectancy among members of the lower class increased, slowly at first and then more rapidly.

Throughout the century, furthermore, the city remained, if not the most comfortable place to live, certainly the most exciting. In cities could be found shops, theatres, cafes, horsecars and then the electric tram, gas and then electric lights, and the telephone. All the charms of older cities and the wonders of the new age were concentrated in London and Paris, New York and Buenos Aires, the capitals of the new industrial civilization.

Classes and Masses in Europe

Like the city, social classes are as old as civilization. Such social divisions may be traditional castes, based on race, religion, lineage, or other accepted social differences. They may be fundamentally legal rankings, as the "estates" of early modern Europe

in large part were. In the new industrial society, however, class distinctions came to be based more and more solidly on one's place in the economic structure. Class conflict, furthermore, stood out particularly sharply in that time of social change and social tensions.

The old landed aristocracy, Europe's ruling class for so long, still retained much prestige and power. Almost everywhere, they held the top positions in traditional institutions like the army and the church. Nevertheless, the baron who could trace his ancestry back to the Norman Conquest had to make way for the "coal baron" whose proudest claim was that he was a "self-made man."

The most vigorous and aggressive class in the nineteenth century was the bourgeoisie, or middle class, whose leading elements were the bankers, wealthy merchants, and industrial

entrepreneurs who guided—and profited from—the Industrial Revolution, supported by a complex array of engineers, managers and clerks, shopkeepers, civil servants, journalists, lawyers, and politicians. Although men controlled the upper levels of middle-class society, women began to appear in increasing numbers in fields like teaching, nursing, clerical work, and writing. They also made their first breakthroughs into such traditionally male professions as medicine.

The leaders of the western bourgeoisie saw themselves as progressive, productive and deserving of their worldly success. The values they proclaimed—hard work, honesty, respectability, and so on—were in fact widespread. The middle class thus enjoyed a considerable amount of both wealth and respect in nineteenth-century Europe.

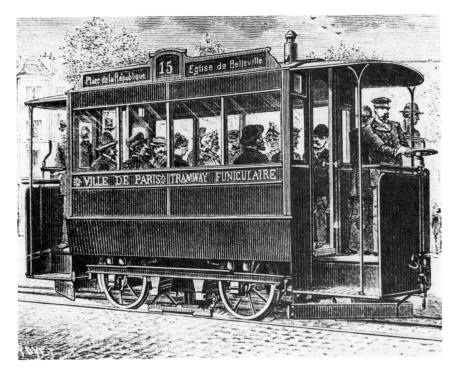

A Paris Streetcar, 1890. The latest thing in urban transit at the end of the nineteenth century, this French trolly car was operated by electricity. The appearance of such novelties as streetcars, telephones, gas and then electric lighting made cities exciting places to be as the Industrial Revolution advanced.

1750	1775	1800	1825	1850	1875	1900	1925

Watt's
steam
engine

Fulton's
steam boat

Stephenson's
steam
locomotive

Thomas Edison

Hargreave's
spinning
jenny

McCormick's
reaper

Atlantic
cable

Ford's
assembly
line

Morse
telegraph

Most Europeans, however, remained on the land in the nineteenth century, living as peasants in agricultural villages. Their conditions varied from the deep poverty of much of southern and eastern European peasantry to the relative prosperity of tenant farmers or freehold peasants in western Europe. All these country people tended to be socially conservative, loyal to regional customs and old social and religious authorities. They resented government exactions, including high taxes, and could be driven to revolt by hard times. Yet radicals who tried to convert peasants to revolutionary ideologies usually failed in the face of their fundamental conservatism.

The urban working class, finally, reached down to the very bottom of the social scale. Skilled artisans, even after the passing of the guilds, retained a sense of their rights and place in society. They were joined by a small group of relatively prosperous industrial foremen. But the increasing numbers of factory workers suffered under special handicaps. Often bewildered newcomers to the city, they were for generations helpless victims of slum crowding, harsh factory discipline, and exploitation by employers. Only in the later nineteenth century did some of these industrial

workers begin to win some of the advantages of the new industrial society, owing to a combination of increased productivity, the growth of labor unions, and the spread of democracy.

The condition of women and children in industrializing Europe attracted particular attention from reformers concerned with the impact of industrialization on the laboring masses. Women's traditional work included agricultural labor and domestic service, and children had always helped their parents. In the nineteenth century, however, women poured into the industrial work force, finding employment even in such heavy-labor industries as mining and metal work. Women and children were hired in largest numbers in the textile mills and the garment industry. Their condition eased somewhat as laws were slowly passed to limit their exploitation. But women were often excluded from highly skilled and better paying jobs and were seldom allowed to join early labor unions.

Throughout the nineteenth century, the impact of the Industrial Revolution tended to increase the differences and the conflicts between the classes. Industrial wealth enabled the middle class to take the leadership of society away from the aristocracy.

Lack of a share in that wealth reduced the relative status of peasant and urban workers. But industrialization greatly expanded the numbers of the urban work force, making them an important element in the history of the next century in Europe.

Classes and Masses in the Americas

The pattern of European society was in some respects repeated in the Americas as well; in other ways, the class divisions and problems of the masses of the people in the new nations across the Atlantic were significantly different. Notable differences also existed between the class structures of North and South America.

Latin America clung to the older European pattern of society throughout most of the nineteenth century. There, landed aristocrats remained very powerful masters of vast farms or ranches and owners of much of the mineral wealth of the southern continent. Landless peasants, including Indians, blacks, and *mestizos* (people of mixed ancestry) continued to be bound to the owners of the landed estates by peonage.

An urban middle class, however, had emerged in the cities of South America. This business bourgeoisie included many exporters of the agricultural products and raw materials of the great landowners. An urban working class was also recruited to build and operate seaports, railways, and similar facilities connected with export industries. These workers, often immigrants from Europe, began to organize unions and even to involve themselves in politics by the end of the nineteenth century.

In North America, the United States evolved along somewhat different lines. The landed gentry of the south and the cattle barons of the west never had the national preeminence enjoyed by the aristocracy in Europe or Latin America. There was an underclass of black slaves before the Civil War, most of them becom-

ing peons afterward. Immigrant farmers often suffered great hardship on the frontier. But the latter did not become the sort of tradition-bound peasantry found in the other two centers of western civilization.

The middle ranks of society thus became the ruling elite of the nation as the nineteenth century advanced. With the great industrial expansion of the post-Civil War period, U.S. business leaders acquired enormous wealth and considerable political power and social prestige as well. Although some condemned them as "robber barons" for their aggressive and often shady tactics, others hailed them as "captains of industry" for their resourcefulness and success. In the United States, even more than in Eu-

rope, the rags-to-riches image of the self-made entrepreneur won admiration and envy for the new industrial bourgeoisie.

America's industrial working class, like Europe's, suffered brutal hardships in the earlier stages of industrialization. As late as 1900, New York's Hell's Kitchen was as terrible a slum as London's East End. Labor Unions, however, had begun to organize in defense of their interests in the United States as they did in Europe. Farmers' organizations also grew more militant at the end of the century. Finally, as in Europe, the ballot box made working-class votes an important source of strength as the century turned.

SUMMARY

The Industrial Revolution was a crucial event in the history of the western world. This transformation of western technology had far-ranging economic as well as social consequences on both sides of the Atlantic.

The Industrial Revolution resulted from an explosive mixture of factors, including existing natural resources, an expanding labor force, growing economic demand, the accumulation of investment capital, technological ingenuity, and entrepreneurial leadership. This mix led to unprecedented industrial expansion, first in Britain, thereafter in continental Europe and the Americas. Steam power was harnessed to new forms of transportation, the railroads and steamships, and electrical energy to new means of communication, especially

the telegraph. The Industrial Revolution produced new industries and new sources of energy, including iron, coal, textiles, and the steam engine itself in the later 1700s and earlier 1800s, as well as steel, chemicals, and electrical power in the later 1800s. Leading industrial states besides Great Britain were Belgium, France, Germany, and the United States.

The Industrial Revolution transformed Europe's economic institutions. The new business leaders opposed government economic controls and succeeded in destroying the mercantile system. The unfettered free competition of the mid-nineteenth century, however, gave way after 1870 to a new form of control of the economy by the giant corporations and cartels that came to dominate the new industrial world.

Industrial society had several striking features. The population explosion multiplied the sheer number of western people. Urbanization drew an unprecedented proportion of them into the new industrial cities. Finally, the middle class became the dominant element in western society and the industrial masses a challenging new force in western life. In all these ways, industrialism influenced the development of the new society that emerged in Europe and the Americas during the later eighteenth and the nineteenth centuries. Another, very different, force that brought great changes to western society was the rise of new systems of ideas called ideologies, to which we turn in the next chapter.

SELECTED SOURCES

Ashton, T. S. *The Industrial Revolution, 1760–1830.* 1968. The English origins of the modern industrial system.

*Chevalier, Louis. *Laboring Classes and Dangerous Classes in Paris During the First Half of the Nineteenth Century.* 1981. Working-class misery and resentment in the early Industrial Revolution.

Cipolla, Carlo. *The Economic History of World Population.* 1962. Stimulating little book fitting the Industrial Revolution into the population history of mankind.

*Dickens, Charles. *Hard Times for These Times.* 1854. Novel about life in an English industrial city, with vivid characteristics of workers, entrepreneurs, and other social groups.

*Dreiser, Theodore. *The Titan.* 1914. Novel about a robber baron of America's Gilded Age.

Henderson, W. O. *The Industrialization of Europe, 1780–1914.* 1969. Compares British and continental patterns of industrial growth.

Korg, Jacob. ed. *London in Dickens' Day.* 1961. Brief contemporary glimpses of everyday life, from pubs to clubs, parks to prisons.

Landes, David S. *The Unbound Prometheus.* 1969. Survey of industrial development from the eighteenth to the twentieth centuries, especially good on technology.

The Molly Maguires. Film about a workers' rebellion in the Pennsylvania coal fields, with vivid images of life in the mines and company towns.

Porter, Glenn. *The Rise of Big Business, 1860–1910.* 1973. Good survey of big business in the United States.

*Available in paperback.

THE NEW IDEOLOGIES

Our faith in the purity and justice of our cause made us take the banner in our hands; the hope of freeing a great people from the tyranny of a thousand years led us to gird on our swords; relying on a powerful rising of brave men we marched forwards through the mountains . . . Many of us may languish on a foreign soil. Many of us may go home to everlasting freedom before our great task is accomplished. But when at last there are neither princes nor lords, when the generations succeed each other beneath the People's banner of liberty, equality and fraternity . . . then the sons of the people will be remembered who first declared war on the tyranny of the princes and led the way to the German Republic.

A common feature of the many revolutions and much of the social change of the last two centuries is the devotion of revolutionaries and reformers to some high ideal. The words above were written in 1848 to commemorate one of the many revolutions of that year, this one in the small German principality of Baden. But if the revolt was small, the ideals were not. The author invokes such potent nineteenth-century political ideas as justice, liberty, equality, brotherhood, and the sacred people. He admits that death or exile may be the short-term consequences of the revolt, but he is sure of the ultimate triumph of its principles. These revolutionaries of 1848, in short, were rebels with an ideological cause—as many have been over the past 200 years.

The adherents of social theories called ideologies aimed quite consciously at transforming western society and their long-term impact was considerable. The political history of the nineteenth century was probably influenced almost as much by the new ideas as the economic life was shaped by the Industrial Revolution.

The present chapter focuses on the surprising variety of theories about society that attracted substantial numbers of followers in the course of the last century. Many of these views still command belief in various parts of the western world today. The ideologies examined here include the older forms of conservatism and liberalism, which were widely accepted in the nineteenth century, as well as various nationalistic beliefs and two forms of socialism that date from that time.

Student Agitators, 1848. German student demonstrators prepare to move in this woodcut from the Revolutions of 1848. Note the banners, the school uniforms, and the disputatious gestures as the radicals argue over their next move—in this case, a demand for democratic reforms in the principality of Weimar. In the nineteenth century as in the twentieth, the appeal of ideologies has often been felt most powerfully by the young.

CONTENTS

537

Locke's
*Treatises
on Civil
Government*

Smith's
*Wealth
of Nations*

French Declaration
of Rights of Man

United States
Constitution

Marx's
*Communist
Manifesto*

Herder
preaches
cultural
nationalism

Burke's
*Reflections
on French
Revolution*

Wollstonecraft's
*Vindication of
Rights of Women*

Revolutions
of 1848

FOUNDATIONS OF NINETEENTH-CENTURY IDEOLOGIES

Central to the social thought of the later eighteenth and nineteenth centuries were new conceptions of humanity, society, and history. These views contrasted sharply with older views that had dominated European social thought for many centuries, and provided the basis for new ideologies about western society.

The Ideas of Humanity and Progress

One of these new views was belief in human goodness. Medieval Christian thinkers had believed that human beings, as children of Adam, were tainted by Adam's sin, an opinion shared by many leaders of the Reformation. The Enlightenment, however, had challenged this assumption, insisting that human nature was basically good. In addition, human beings were basically intelligent. Properly educated, ordinary people were quite capable of shaping their own destinies.

The nineteenth century carried this interpretation still further. Poets and philosophers as well as political ideo-

logues glorified humanity as even Renaissance humanists had never done. It is sometimes said, in fact, that the nineteenth century idealized the average human being to the point of creating a "religion of humanity." For many ideologues, workers, peasants, or simply the self-governing people embodied true nobility. It was to serve the people so conceived that ideologues of the nineteenth century formulated their theories and designed the new economic, social, and political institutions which began to emerge during this period.

The idea of progress was even more widespread than the religion of humanity. The scientific revolution had displaced old interpretations of natural phenomena with new knowledge. The *philosophes* of the Enlightenment pictured a world of the future based on rational principles rather than supernatural guidelines. The Industrial Revolution seemed to guarantee material progress for the western world. On this foundation of modern optimism rose the nineteenth-century ideal of social progress.

For ancient and medieval Europeans, society was a system of fixed, even divinely ordained, classes and rules. Social change could only mean a falling away from prescribed institutions and was therefore to be avoided

at all costs. In the nineteenth-century age of ideology, however, social change came to be looked on as a positive force, including social progress as well as material and intellectual advances. Each ideology had its own dream of a better world to come, but almost all worked zealously to bring about some form of progressive change. Belief in human goodness and in human progress thus underlay most of the social ideologies of the last century. Let us examine the unique nature of that century's social thought.

The Nature of Ideology

An ideology is a theory about human society. Unlike a social science, which seeks to describe and explain the way some aspect of society—government or the economy, for instance—actually works, ideologies are primarily concerned with the way society *ought* to be organized. Adherents of ideologies—ideologues—have historically often felt impelled to act on their beliefs, to attempt to change society from the way it is to the way they believe it ought to be.

Ideologies, then, serve as blueprints for the future. Such theories have often taken on many of the characteristics of secular religions. They have their prophets and their sacred scriptures in the writings of these thinkers. Ideologies do not offer objective judgments or theoretical understanding for its own sake. They frequently preach a militant faith involving a conflict between good and evil, as the particular ideology defines these terms. They generally feature a "chosen people," in whose interests the new society is to be designed. They have, finally, a secular version of paradise in the ideal society of the future that they propose to build. Temperamentally, at least, modern ideologues have been as much "true believers" as any religious crusader of earlier centuries.

NINETEENTH-CENTURY CONSERVATISM

One of the earlier modern ideologies to appear regarded itself as profoundly anti-ideological. This was nineteenth-century conservatism, which arose as a reaction against the French Revolution. Fearing this revolutionary onslaught on the old regime, particularly the specter of mob violence, from the 1790s on, these self-styled conservatives spoke up forcefully for the conservation or preservation of the traditional institutions and values that the Enlightenment and the French Revolution sought to destroy.

The Pillars of the Old Regime

Conservatives preached the virtues of three basic pillars of the old social order in particular: legitimate hereditary monarchy as a form of government, the established Christian churches in religion, and the predominance of the old landed aristocracy in society.

The monarchy, conservatives believed, was a divinely ordained institution, kings and queens were chosen by God to rule the peoples of Europe. Europe's royal dynasties—the Habsburgs, Hohenzollerns, Romanovs and the rest—had also stood the test of time. They had ruled for many generations, some for many centuries; and for conservatives, such historical roots conferred legitimacy. Monarchs furthermore often enjoyed the traditional loyalty of their people, so that monarchy seemed a guarantor of order and domestic peace.

The established state churches of Europe could be justified in many of these same ways. Roman Catholic, Greek Orthodox, and such older Protestant churches as Anglican and Lutheran all supported order, had historic roots, and of course claimed divine sanction. Conservatives were usually strong establishment Christians themselves and accused many of the new ideologues of atheism.

The traditional aristocratic ruling class of Europe was a third pillar of the old order in the eyes of conservatives. The roots of the landed nobility and gentry also went back to the medieval era, and they often enjoyed the traditional respect of the peasant masses of Europeans. Their higher level of education and the self-confidence and habit of command that went with their high status made them natural leaders of society.

Burke and Conservative Opposition to Change

Edmund Burke (1729–1797) was the English politician whose views best embodied this old-school conservative view. Fifteen years earlier, Burke had spoken up for the American Revolutionaries whom he believed were merely defending their traditional rights as freeborn Britons. By the 1790s, however, he was horrified at the excesses of the French Revolution, and at what he saw as its goals: the creation of a radically new society in defiance of established tradition. In his *Reflections* (1790) on that upheaval and in many speeches and other writings, he formulated a strong conservative argument against revolutionary change of any sort. These arguments would be central to the conservative view from his time on.

Burke believed, first, that little change in existing institutions and practices was necessary simply because of the superior nature of the present system. Long established social customs and institutions had demonstrated their value by their survival. Individuals had a duty to pass things of such proven value on to future generations. Even where a particular institution was not as useful as it might be, Burke objected to uprooting it because to do so might endanger the delicate and infinitely complex structure of society as a whole.

Other dangers suggested themselves as likely consequences of rapid or revolutionary social change. Rapid change, Burke believed, inevitably injured innocent people. Radical changes, furthermore, could only be imposed by force, so that revolution, paradoxically, might itself bring tyranny. Finally, political disorder led naturally to confusion in morals and values. Old ways were discredited before new ones won general acceptance, leaving many people adrift, unsure of right and wrong.

Such views strengthened conservatives in their resistance to the astonishing array of new ideologies they had to confront in the course of the nineteenth century.

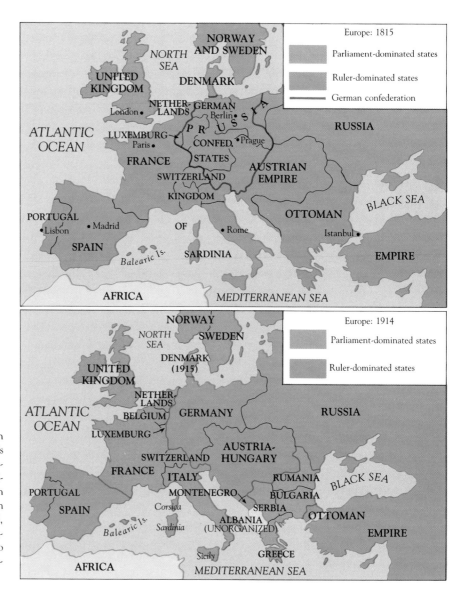

MAP 61
Liberal and Autocratic Regimes in Europe in 1815 and 1914. Liberalism, with its emphasis on an open society and representative government, made steady headway against authoritarianism during the nineteenth century. In general, liberal states were first established in western and then in southern Europe. By 1914, authoritarian regimes primarily under the control of the monarchy were largely confined to the Iberian peninsula and northeastern Europe.

NINETEENTH-CENTURY LIBERALISM

Nineteenth-century liberalism was the first of the new theories to emerge as a powerful challenger to conservatism and the institutions for which it stood. Like the other new views, liberalism was propagated and held primarily by educated middle-class people, but un-like the others it spoke specifically for the political and economic interests of the bourgeoisie itself.

Liberalism and the Bourgeoisie

By the nineteenth century, the middle class was the wealthiest group in a Europe where the wealth was increasingly concentrated in commerce, industry, and finance. But the middle class chafed at the remaining barriers to their economic progress and social and political advancement. Many businessmen saw regulation of the economy by governments and guilds as a handicap to further business growth. Despite their wealth, the bourgeoisie in 1800 remained largely excluded from political power in societies still dominated by monarchs and aristocrats. Middle-class Europeans also resented their lack of social prestige.

Liberal ideas often served as potent propaganda tools to help the middle class overcome these barriers during the nineteenth century. Liberal economic ideas supported the entrepreneurial challenge to mercantilist economic regulation. Liberal political theories justified middle-class claims to a share in the political leadership of Europe. The liberal ideology also glorified individual achievement, bestowing social prestige on middle-class citizens.

Some liberals, like Francois Guizot in France, openly asserted that the bourgeois citizenry were the best citizens of all. Unlike the aristocracy, the middle class was uniquely wide open to hard-working and talented recruits from the lower orders of society, who had simply to work their way up as many other self-made bourgeois citizens had. Also the fact that middle-class people had proved their mettle in business had larger political ramifications. Didn't such successful people have a right to a share of political power as well? Wouldn't the western world be better off entrusting its future to solid, responsible, yet aggressive and progressive business leaders?

In the long run, the liberal ideology would go beyond the special interests of one class. Liberal political ideas in particular would appeal to all classes and to supporters of other ideologies as well, and liberal political institutions would give more freedom to more people than ever before in its history.

Locke and Political Liberalism

Nineteenth-century liberal political theory grew out of the political ideas and struggles of the preceding two centuries. The liberal political tradition had first taken shape during England's seventeenth-century struggle for constitutional monarchy. It had developed further during the Enlightenment's intellectual challenge to the old regime, the American independence movement, and the French Revolution's root-and-branch assault on the old order. Liberal theorists referred enthusiastically to the British Bill of Rights, and French Declaration of the Rights of Man, and the American Declaration of Independence and Constitution.

Most important, liberals drew on the basic ideas of John Locke (1632–1704), the philosopher of the English revolution of the seventeenth century. All people, Locke had asserted, were born with certain natural and inalienable rights, the most important of which were liberty and equality. Special privileges like those traditionally granted the aristocracy and the church violated these rights. Nineteenth-century liberals elaborated these basic rights into a set of specific civil liberties: freedom of speech, freedom of the press, freedom of religion, equality of opportunity, and equality before the law. The contract theory of government was another Lockean view widely accepted by nineteenth-century liberals. According to this theory, people originally organized governments to protect their natural rights. All legitimate government is based on an agreement, a constitution or "social contract," in which the people voluntarily confide their natural rights to the protection of a particular government or set of laws.

For government to perform this function effectively, the constitution

Edmund Burke. This picture shows the prophet of modern conservative thought. Burke eloquently expressed the fear of the new ideologies felt by many traditionalists, both in his own time and throughout the following two centuries.

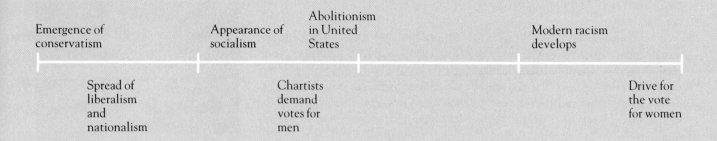

Emergence of
conservatism

Appearance of
socialism

Abolitionism
in United
States

Modern racism
develops

Spread of
liberalism
and
nationalism

Chartists
demand
votes for
men

Drive for
the vote
for women

must include several key political institutions. Among these were representative government, free elections, and a bill of rights. Representative government meant that the people would be ruled by a parliament composed of representatives of the people. Periodic free elections of these representatives would guarantee periodic evaluation of their stewardship by the people. A bill of rights, finally, would provide a clear statement of the one thing even a majority of the sovereign people could not take away: the civil liberties of the individual.

All this added up to the liberal political ideal: government by consent of the governed. Interpreted narrowly at the beginning of the century, this might mean little more than the rights of the bourgeoisie to vote and hold office. As the century advanced, however, liberals expanded their definition of "the governed" to include a much broader segment of society. By mid-century, campaigns were being mounted to extend the right to vote to all males. Calls for political rights for women had been raised by such pioneering feminists as Mary Wollstonecraft as early as the 1790s, although, demands for female equality were not widely taken up by such liberals as John Stuart Mill and activists

like Emmaline Pankhurst until the second half of the nineteenth century.

By the end of the century, civil rights for all and political participation for most of the population had become part of the liberal political creed. An expansive view of liberalism had brought much of the western world to the brink of a more democratic order.

Smith and Economic Liberalism

The economic ideas of the nineteenth-century liberals also drew on earlier thinkers, such as the Physiocrats of the French Enlightenment, especially their support of free trade. The great inspiration of nineteenth-century liberal economics, however, was Adam Smith (1723–1790), whose *Wealth of Nations* had appeared at the time of the American Revolution. Smith, it will be recalled, believed that the unregulated or free market was a function of natural laws.

From Smith the nineteenth century took over the law of economic supply and demand and applied it enthusiastically. Every aspect of the economy, liberals insisted, would be perfectly regulated if this natural law were allowed to operate freely. Public demand for a product would be bal-

anced by an appropriate level of supply as business hastened to satisfy this demand in order to profit from public willingness to pay for it. If prices were too high, competing firms would soon bid them down again. If wages were too low in some lines of work, no one would take these jobs until the wages went up—which they would have to do if the employers wanted to stay in business. Demand for sufficient products, lower prices, higher wages would in the long run guarantee these things would be supplied. The motive force was simply competition—individuals working in a spirit of enlightened self-interest. Thus guided by an "invisible hand," the free market would work for the benefit of all.

Economic liberals preached *laissez-faire*—and end to government regulation—with almost religious fervor. Free trade, free competition, and freedom of contract were articles of liberal faith. As noted in the last chapter, this doctrine produced a half-century of almost unfettered free competition in the middle of the nineteenth century. Even when monopolistic industrial combinations drastically limited real competition, old-fashioned economic liberals strongly opposed any *government* intervention in the economy.

Economic and political freedom were thus the fundamental principles of nineteenth-century liberalism. In the twentieth century, proponents of economic liberalism in particular would be the new conservatives, defending an economic status quo. In the 1800s, however, liberals were crusaders, as militant for social change as the supporters of socialism.

SOCIALISM EMERGES

Perhaps the most radical of all the new ideologies of the nineteenth century was socialism. This new doctrine, a product of the Industrial Revolution, could point to few proponents in earlier centuries. Its goal was to abolish a key feature of Europe's booming new industrial economy—private ownership of the productive machinery itself.

Socialism and the Industrial Working Class

If conservatism spoke for traditional institutions and liberalism for the bourgeoisie, nineteenth-century advocates of socialism found their most important constituency in the new working classes of an industrializing west. As with these other isms, socialism found its most articulate spokespersons among the educated people of middle-class origin. Although some socialists attempted to rally other groups than urban workers to their cause—peasants in overwhelmingly agricultural Russia, for example—their central concern was with the

factory hands, railway workers, miners and other laborers in the new and growing industrial sector of the economy.

The grievances of the industrial labor force were many and highly visible in the nineteenth century. Men, women, and children worked twelve-to sixteen-hour days in the mines and mills. Industrial accidents and occupational diseases were common in the unregulated workplace. Wages were low, lay-offs frequent, and unions illegal until the latter part of the century. Living conditions were appalling in the overcrowded slum tenements of industrial cities.

Europeans concerned with this disturbing situation—mass poverty in the richest society in history—offered a variety of answers to what was called the "social question." Religious groups and philanthropic organizations offered charity to the poor. Workers themselves struggled to organize labor unions and bargain collectively with their employers for better conditions. As the century advanced, liberal politicians and even some conservative ones began to legislate, hoping for workers' votes in return.

Socialism appeared as another and more radical solution to the problem of working-class poverty. It would take a variety of forms in the nineteenth and twentieth centuries. The emergence of two of these is discussed in the following pages: utopian socialism and Marxism.

Utopian Socialism

The earliest school of socialist thought was labeled "utopian" by a fellow socialist, Karl Marx, who was con-

vinced the utopian socialists were too naively idealistic to achieve anything in the real world. Utopian socialists believed the Industrial Revolution had drastically worsened the working and living conditions of the laboring class.

The London Poor. Famous illustrator Gustav Doré produced this vivid depiction of a corner in a London slum. The concern of socialists, liberals, and others for the plight of the lower classes seems understandable in the light of such conditions.

Many of them sought a solution in turning their backs on the Industrial Revolution.

These utopians advocated abandoning the new machinery, the factories, and the slums of the cities and returning to small-scale handicraft production in the healthy countryside. To make sure such small communities distributed the product of their labors fairly, utopians preached community ownership of housing units, workshops, and fields. The result would be self-sufficient, socialist communes.

The most influential utopian socialist was French thinker Charles Fourier (1772–1837). Fourier published detailed descriptions of such a commune, which he called a phal-lanstery. He envisioned a community of 1600 people. Everyone would own a share of the phallanstery and everyone would do a share of the work, each choosing the sort of work he or she preferred.

Utopian socialists saw no irreconcilable differences between the classes, appealing rather to the common humanity of the workers and bourgeois citizens who mingled at their meetings. Voluntary association, they believed, was the key to bringing the new society of socialist communes into existence.

A few such socialist communities were in fact established, both in Europe and in the United States. The U.S. in particular saw many short-lived Fourierist communities, as well as such famous examples as the British utopian Robert Owen's New Harmony in Indiana. Descendants of the utopian socialist ideal may be seen in such varied institutions as the Israeli *kibbutz* and the communes of the 1960s in the United States.

Marxism

The most important and enduring form of socialism to develop in the nineteenth century was Marxism.

Karl Marx (1818–1883) was a German philosophy student and journalist who lived most of his life in exile and poverty in London. There he helped establish socialist organizations, including the First International Workingmen's Association, an attempt to unite radical groups of all nations to fight for what Marx saw as the coming socialist revolution. More important, Marx wrote voluminously. He produced thick books like his highly theoretical study, *Capital* (the first volume published in 1867) and much more influential short tracts such as *The Communist Manifesto* (1848), which he wrote with his life-long friend and supporter, Friedrich Engels. No ideologue had more influence, particularly in the next century.

Marx viewed his predecessors, the utopian socialists, as naive in ex-

pecting the "social question" to be solved by voluntary communal association. He also thought it was foolish to abandon the immense productive capacity created by the Industrial Revolution. Economic determinism, class struggle, and what he believed was the coming world revolution were the identifying features of Marx's world view.

Living in a time of awesome economic changes, Marx came to believe that economic forces determined history. How people earned their living—how they related to the means of production—determined how they lived, what they believed, and what part they played in history. All other social expressions—politics, religion, and so on—were of no real importance. Only economic forces and factors, such as labor and capital investment, economic booms and depressions, shaped the course of human events. These economic forces and relationships were, Marx asserted, embodied historically in economic classes and in their relations to one another. Since economic forces were often in conflict, so too were classes. Class conflict ultimately was the most important factor shaping human history.

Marx saw the two key classes of his time as the capitalist investors who owned the new machines and factories and the industrial laborers, whom Marx called the proletariat. An inevitable conflict of interest between these two classes existed. The worker lived on his wages: The higher his pay the better off he was. The capitalist, however, depended on profits, and his profits would be higher the lower he could keep his wage bill. In this central conflict of interest be-

Karl Marx. The most influential of all socialist thinkers, Marx continues to influence the history of the twentieth century. This photograph, taken in his later years, shows him as he looked in the London suburb where he lived for much of his life as a political exile.

THE PROLETARIAT VERSUS THE BOURGEOISIE

The history of all past society has consisted in the development of class antagonisms . . . One fact is common to all past ages, *viz.*, the exploitation of one part of society by the other. . . .

The immediate aim of the Communists is . . . formation of the proletariat into a class, overthrow of bourgeois supremacy, [and] conquest of political power by the proletariat. . . .

The proletariat will use its political power to wrest . . . all capital from the bourgeoisie, to centralize all instruments of production in the hands of the state, *i.e.*, of the proletariat organized as the [new] ruling class. . . .

The proletarians have nothing to lose but their chains. They have a world to win.

Workingmen of all countries, unite!*

Karl Marx here outlines the class struggle of his day as he saw it and predicts the victory of the proletariat and the establishment of state socialism. The Communists mentioned here were one of many small socialist parties of the middle of the last century.

*Karl Marx and Friedrich Engels, *The Communist Manifesto*, ed. Samuel H. Beer (Arlington Heights, Ill.: AHM Publishing Company, 1955), pp. 23, 30–31, 46.

tween owners and laborers, the capitalists and the proletariat, Marx thought he detected the internal dynamic of his age.

Marxists believed this class struggle would lead finally to a revolt of the workers against the owners—a world revolution of historic proportions. Marx predicted the rich would continue to get richer, and the poor poorer, until the proletariat could endure it no longer and took to the streets. They would first overthrow the government, which Marxists saw as merely a tool of capitalist control, then move to the essential task of abolishing private capitalist ownership of the means of production. The workers themselves would thus be both the rulers of the new state and the owners of the factories, mines and farms of a socialized economy. Classes would disappear, the state would wither away, and a worker's paradise would replace the capitalist order.

Some of Marx's predictions, like those of Mill, Burke, and other ideologues, would turn out to be erroneous. The poor would get better off, not poorer, over the next century. Too, the predicted world revolution would not occur. In addition, Marxists would come to differ among themselves, contributing, to both the democratic welfare socialism of western Europe and the totalitarian communism of eastern Europe. Like the other ideologies discussed here, Marxism would play an important part in history although, offering only a partial view of human events.

NATIONALISM AND RACISM

Although the nation-states of Europe had appeared in the high middle ages and were well established by 1800, nationalism as we know it was in many ways a new phenomenon on the nineteenth-century scene. A sense of patriotic loyalty had evolved along with the nation-states, particularly in western Europe, but this feeling tended to reflect either simple enthusiasm for a popular ruler or hatred for enemies in time of war. Nationalism in the modern sense of the complex and intense identification with and allegiance to one's own nation is hard to find before 1800.

Nationalism and the Oppressed Nationalities

Over the next two centuries, modern nationalism emerged perhaps most intensely among the oppressed peoples of Europe. Established nations like Great Britain or France developed their share of national feeling, but nationalism became a particular passion among such stateless groups as the Germans, Italians, and many Slavic peoples. Some of these peoples lived under foreign rule, like the Slavic minorities in the Russian, Austrian, and Turkish empires. Some were divided groups, like the three dozen German-speaking states or the dozen separate nations of the Italian peninsula, both dominated by Austrian power. Longing for freedom and unity, these peoples with a common language and cultural heritage succeeded in carving out new nations for themselves during the century between the Battle of Waterloo in 1815 and the peace settlement following World War I in 1919.

A number of events combined to forge this passionate new faith in nationality. The French Revolution and the victories of Napoleon stirred patriotic feelings in France—and also among her defeated victims all across

Europe, from Spain to Russia. The leaders of the Europe-wide revolutions of 1848 and of the Italian and German wars of national unification between 1859 and 1871 became national heroes. Napoleon, France's greatest military leader, Giuseppe Garibaldi, the Italian guerrilla fighter, and Otto von Bismarck, Germany's "iron chancellor," were objects of patriotic idolatry.

Economic factors also played their part in stimulating national feeling. For example, railways and customs unions, promoted by hardheaded businessmen to expand their markets, helped create support for political union. The German customs union

MAP 62

National Minorities in Europe in the Nineteenth Century. Self-conscious ethnic nationalism flourished in nineteenth century Europe as never before. This map shows the distribution of language groups, the primary factor in determining ethnic nationality. Many European states included minority groups within their borders; these minorities, increasingly nationalistic, often demanded autonomy and sometimes independence.

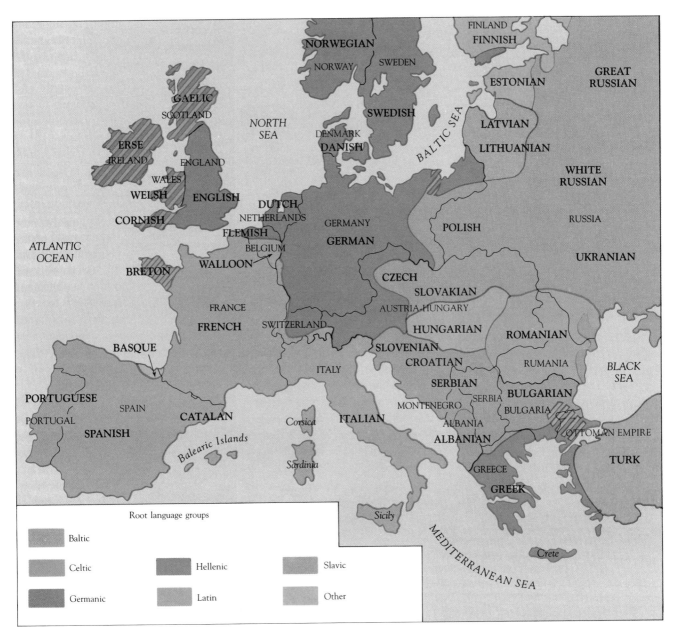

MANIFEST DESTINY

Texas is now ours. Her star and her stripe may already be said to have taken their place in the glorious blazon of our common nationality; and the sweep of our eagle's wing already includes within its circuit the wide extent of her fair and fertile land. She is no longer to us a mere geographical space—a certain combination of coast, plain, mountain, valley, forest and stream. She is no longer to us a mere country on the map. She comes within the dear and sacred designation of Our Country; no longer a *pays*, she is a part of *la patrie*; and that which is at once a sentiment and a virtue, Patriotism, already begins to thrill for her too within the national heart. . . .

Texas has been absorbed into the Union in the inevitable fulfillment of the general law which is rolling our population westward; the connection of which with that ratio of growth in population which is destined within a hundred years to swell our numbers to the enormous population of two hundred and fifty millions . . . is too evident to leave us in doubt of the manifest design of Providence in regard to the occupation of this continent. •

This vigorous expression of United States' nationalism was published in the United States Magazine and Democratic Review *at the time of the annexation of Texas in 1845. Many nineteenth century Americans thought they detected a national mission to occupy and rule the North American continent, a belief encouraged by the rapid growth in the size and population of the new nation.*

•John Louis O'Sullivan, "Manifest Destiny," in Hans Kohn, *Nationalism: Its Meaning and History* (Princeton, N.J.: Van Nostrand, 1955), pp. 141–142.

in particular laid the foundation for political unification of all the German states into the German Empire. The new railway networks helped many people get to know more of their homeland than their native villages. The peasant who sold his vegetables in the next country became as ardent a nationalist as the businessman who used the railroad to market his manufactured goods in the next country.

Nineteenth-Century Nationalisms and Nationalists

Ideologues played a central role in the rise of nationalism too. Purely cultural nationalists like the eighteenth-century thinker J. G. von Herder (1744–1803) urged the German-speaking peoples to discover their common cultural heritage. Herder believed that all Germans, and indeed all members of any national group, should be proud of their particular language, literature, ancient myths and habits of mind. More militant political nationalists like the Italian revolutionary Giuseppe Mazzini (1805–1872) insisted that national characteristics required a national state in which to find their fullest expression. In many places, students demonstrated, politicians organized, and mobs marched to the barricades to overthrow foreign rulers and establish new nations.

Many nineteenth-century nationalists believed in what the Germans called the "folk soul" or "folk spirit" of a spiritual essence possessed only by Germans or French people or some other national group. They believed this "soul" gave each people its distinctive national character, including such traits as "Anglo-Saxon virtues" like hard work and punctuality, the superior cultural sensitivity of the French, or American self-reliance.

Nationalists read their own history with particular eagerness, often finding in it a world mission. Thus Italians, who had given Europe leadership with the Roman Caesars and the Roman Catholic popes, would provide such leadership again. Britons had a mission to build a global empire. The United States had a "manifest destiny" to expand from the Atlantic to the Pacific and to be champions of freedom everywhere. Czechs in the Austrian Empire discovered in their past a history of struggle for freedom; Poles, most of them subjects of the Russian tsars, characterized their history as one of repeated foreign conquests and purifying martyrdom. Many pan-Slavic nationalists, by contrast, saw a great future for the far-flung Slavic peoples as a whole—led by the huge Russian Empire.

National feeling was often embodied in concrete symbols—for instance, banners like the French tricolor, the British union jack, or the American stars and stripes. Intense patriotic feeling might also be stimulated by the singing of national songs like "Brittania Rules the Waves,"

"America the Beautiful," or the powerful "Marseillaise."

Other symbolic evocations of nationhood were natural features infused with patriotic meaning. Germans personalized the Rhine River—the border with their national enemy France—as "Father Rhine." Many people saw something special in their "native soil"—the black earth of Mother Russia, for instance. Others detected unique qualities in the blood that flowed in their veins, an attitude embodied in such phrases as "red-blooded Americans" or "hot-blooded Latins."

Peasants Pause to Pray. French painter Jean-Francois Millet captured a popular sense of simple peasant piety in this painting, called *The Angelus*. Nationalists were particular admirers of the peasantry, whom they believed preserved the national spirit intact and uncorrupted by modern theories or foreign influences.

Nationalism, like liberalism and conservatism, found many passionate converts in the nineteenth century. Nationalism has in fact probably become the most powerful of all the ideologies over the past two hundred years.

The Development of Racism

The roots of racism may be ancient but racism as we know it is fundamentally a new ideology, in large part a spin-off from nineteenth-century nationalism.

The ancient Romans had strong class feelings but apparently little concern with racial differences. Medieval Europeans distinguished sharply between religious groups, but do not seem to have made much of a point of race. The explorers who built the first European overseas empires often felt superior to the alien peoples they encountered, and some of their accounts indicate an awareness of physical differences. More important to the explorers, though, were the differing customs of non-European peoples, who were condemned as living without law and without (religious) faith as Europeans understood these things.

Modern racism emerged from nationalism in the later nineteenth century, the offspring of an unlikely union between nationalistic belief in the mystical folk soul of a people and the new scientific discoveries in biology, in the age of Darwin. Racists concluded that the folk soul, or national character, was hereditary, "in the blood" or genes of such people.

It was a hazy concept at best. Thus one might speak of the German race (a national group), of the Latin races

(a language group), or of the Jewish race (a religious group). Since the later nineteenth century also saw a great wave of European imperial expansion overseas, racists also became negatively aware of larger racial groups. It was common to distinguish among white, black, yellow, and even brown and red races and to "prove" the superiority of the first and the degraded natures of the rest.

Social scientists today attribute differences in the character of various people to social and cultural influences rather than to folk souls or "blood," but racial differences were crucial for the popular racism of the later nineteenth and earlier twentieth centuries. In the later nineteenth century, the alleged superiority of the white race was used to justify European imperial conquest of the "lesser breeds." Within Europe, racism led to waves of anti-semitism, including the famous Dreyfus case in France, in which a Jewish officer in the French Army was framed for treason and condemned to the Devil's Island penal colony by a cabal of reactionary fellow officers.

SOCIAL THOUGHT IN THE AMERICAS

The new American republics continued to derive many of their ideas from Europe during the first century or so after independence. Inevitably, however, these new societies accepted, rejected, or modified European social ideas to suit their own conditions as well as develop original emphases in social thought.

Of the major European ideologies

discussed here, it seems fair to say that liberalism and nationalism made the largest number of converts in the Americas. Traditional conservative institutions, however, generated much support in Latin America, and socialist ideas reached both continents at the end of the nineteenth century.

Liberalism and Nationalism in the United States

The United States Constitution committed the new country to two of the central ideological concerns of the age of ideology: liberal government and national unity. Social thought—and social action—in the century that followed explored and developed these commitments in a New World setting.

Among the main currents of U.S. political debate during the nineteenth century, three expanded European liberal ideas in distinctive directions: Jacksonian democracy, abolitionism, and the cult of the self-made man.

In the 1830s, the presidency of Andrew Jackson (1767–1845) broadened the liberal political ideal to include the rough-hewn lower stratum of society. Andy Jackson's frontier supporters embodied a boisterous new image of "the governed" on whose consent liberal government must be based. Earlier than most western nations, then, the United States went beyond the respectable middle classes to include all adult white males in its concept of democracy, by extending the franchise.

The abolitionist movement of the 1840s and 1850s expanded that concept in another way, demanding Lockean liberty and equality for the

The Statue of Liberty in 1885. The familiar statue, a gift from France to the American people, is pictured here nearing completion in New York harbor. The statue was intended to symbolize a political ideal shared by the Third French Republic and the oldest of modern republics, the United States.

black slaves of the American South. Founding fathers like Thomas Jefferson had seen the paradox of a nation officially dedicated to freedom nevertheless including millions of slaves among its population. During the first generation after independence, the northern states had moved to abolish slavery within their borders, leaving slavery as the "peculiar institution" of the southern states. Abolitionist speakers developed fully the ideological contradiction of a nation that was, in Lincoln's words: "half slave and half free." Though black Americans would remain second-class citizens even after their emancipation in the Civil War, an ideological basis had been laid for their eventual acquisition of full political rights.

During the decades of rapid economic expansion after the Civil War, many Americans came to believe in freedom of opportunity with a new passion. The conviction that any hard-working boy could rise from "rags to riches," already popular among European liberal bourgeoisie, found many converts in the United States. The novels of Horatio Alger told this story over and over again, and many immigrants saw the mobile society of the United States as an opportunity to escape the stratified culture of Europe.

The federal Constitution had also committed the first thirteen states to national unity, although sharp divisions remained over the power of the federal government in relation to the rights of the individual states. Northern victory in the Civil War, seen by many northerners as a struggle to preserve the Union, reaffirmed that the United States would be "one nation, indivisible." It is not surprising, then, that in the late nineteenth century nationalism burned as brightly in the United States as it did anywhere else in the western world.

The United States had its victorious wars and its national heroes to identify with, from Washington and Jackson to the martyred Lincoln. Americans, despite regional differences, came to believe they shared distinctively American character traits, including self-confidence, a belief in the future, and commitment to social equality. Americans also thought they had a national mission, a "manifest destiny," to conquer the continent and to preach the virtues of democracy to the world. It was an American, Stephen Decatur, who epitomized the nationalist ideal in the famous phrase, "my country right or wrong!"

There was little room for old-fashioned conservatism in a country that did not have a monarchy, a hereditary peerage, or an established church. Socialism arrived with immigrant laborers during the harshest days of industrial exploitation of workers at the end of the century. Its future in a land of social mobility for most, however, would be as limited as that of conservatism.

The Isms in Latin America

The nations of Latin America, whose social characteristics more closely resembled Europe than those of the United States, were more open to the full range of European ideologies. In the southern half of the New World also, local circumstances and concerns to some degree modified European social views and added distinctly Latin American elements.

Monarchy was abolished everywhere except in Brazil after the wars of independence, but the Catholic church and the land-owning aristocracies remained as powerful in the new nations as in the old colonies. Conservative respect for church and aristocracy remained part of the system of social allegiances in Latin America throughout the century.

Since the Latin American countries were nominally republics, liberal political ideas also had an important place. In Latin America as in Europe, the leading liberals tended to be middle class advocates of material progress, the urban elite of port cities and national capitals. Liberal ideas also reached down the social scale, how-

ever, leading to the emancipation of black slaves in some Latin American countries considerably earlier than in the United States.

Post-Independence national unity was often resisted by regional rebellions in Central and South America. Struggles between back-country *caudillos* and nationalist politicians asserting the authority of big cities and central government led to many civil wars. The advocates of national unity, however, increasingly carried the day. Thus, Latin American countries also developed a strong sense of nationalism.

Latin Americans also developed a feeling of themselves *as* Latin Americans. They argued among themselves whether their civilization depended on Europe for its value or whether, as many intellectuals came to believe, their American Indian ancestors were also essential to their distinctive culture. National heroes like the liberator Simon Bolivar and awesome natural features like the Andes became nationalistic symbols. Like Germans, Italians, or Slavs, Latin Americans began to resent the influence of foreigners. The economic exploitation of Great Britain and later of the United States thus kindled nationalistic feelings as potent in Latin America as Austrian influence did among Germans or Italians.

Socialism reached Latin America with laborers from Europe at the end of the century, as it did the United States. But socialists in Latin America, working with the impoverished masses, would play a major part in political life and would become part of the basic political tradition there, as in Europe.

SUMMARY

An important part of the history of the nineteenth century was the emergence of social ideologies. Building on widespread belief in human perfectability, these theories of how society *ought* to be organized have found many followers in the western world over the past 200 years.

Nineteenth century conservatism, as urged by Edmund Burke, supported the established institutions inherited from earlier centuries: hereditary monarchy, state church, and landed aristocracy. Burkean conservatives proposed arguments against radical change that would be used by other conservatives in later generations.

Nineteenth-century liberalism built on the political ideas of John Locke and the economic theories of Adam Smith. Politically liberals believed in human rights and in government by consent of the governed. Economically, they opposed government regulation and espoused a free market subject only to the law of supply and demand. Initially, these views advanced the interests of the middle classes; later, political liberalism particularly gradually included many other groups.

Socialism was one solution to the problem of poverty among Europe's working classes. All socialists preached public ownership of the means of production to ensure a fairer distribution of the product. Utopian socialists advocated voluntary rural communes and small-scale production. Followers of Karl Marx insisted that class struggle would lead to a world revolution and the seizure of power by the proletariat.

Nationalism as we know it developed long after the nation-state, though it was especially strong among oppressed groups without countries of their own in the nineteenth century. Nationalists believed in national character, mission, and destiny. Some became racists late in the century, seeing heredity as a determiner of national character.

In the Americas, these ideologies had a varying success. Latin Americans found room for versions of conservatism, liberalism, nationalism and socialism. In North America, liberalism and nationalism flourished, committing the United States to such actions as the abolition of slavery and conquering a continent.

The impact of the new social ideologies was thus felt all across the western world in the nineteenth century. Nowhere, however, did ideological commitment play a larger part than in Europe during the earlier decades of that century.

SELECTED SOURCES

Burke, Edmund. *Selected Writings and Speeches*. ed. Peter J. Stanlis. 1963. Good collection, including a portion of his *Reflections on the Revolution in France*.

*Heilbroner, Robert L. *The Worldly Philosophers*. 1967. Highly readable presentation of the economic theories of nineteenth-century liberal thinkers.

*Kohn, Hans. *Prophets and Peoples: Studies in Nineteenth Century Nationalism*. 1946. Essays on leading German, French, Italian, and Russian nationalists, by a leading authority.

*Lichtheim, George. *Marxism: An Historical and Critical Study*. 1982. Excellent critique of nineteenth-century Marxism.

Manuel, Frank E. *The Prophets of Paris*. 1965. Stimulating account of the utopian socialists.

*Marx, Karl, and Friedrich Engels. *The Communist Manifesto*. 1971. Brief presentation of Marx's view of history.

*Schapiro, J. Salwyn. *Liberalism: Its Meaning and History*. 1985. A short summary of the liberal tradition, with brief extracts from leading liberals.

Schapiro, J. Salwyn. *Movements of Social Dissent in Modern Europe*. 1962. Overview of anarchism, syndicalism, Christian social dissent, and other nineteenth century ideological movements, with extracts.

Viereck, Peter. *Conservatism from John Adams to Churchill*. 1956. Brief survey, with excerpts from conservative thinkers on both sides of the Atlantic.

Ward, Barbara. *Nationalism and Ideology*. 1966. Puts modern nationalism in the broadest context of evolving human loyalties.

*Available in paperback.

RESTORATION AND REACTION
(1815–1833)

The Kings of Württemberg and Denmark arrived before any of the others . . . .
but the ceremony which by its pomp and splendor was evidently intended to
crown the series of wonders of the Congress was the solemn entry of Tsar
Alexander and the King of Prussia. . . .

From that moment Vienna assumed an aspect which was as bright as it was
animated. Numberless magnificent carriages traversed the city in all directions [the
imperial stables held fourteen hundred horses at the disposal of the royal guests]
. . . . The promenades and squares teemed with soldiers of all grades, dressed in
the varied uniforms of all the European armies. Added to these were the swarms
of the servants of the aristocracy in their gorgeous liveries . . . . When night
came, the theatres, the cafés, the public resorts were filled with animated crowds,
apparently bent on pleasure only. . . . In almost every big thoroughfare there was
the sound of musical instruments discoursing joyous tunes. Noise and bustle
everywhere . . . . Hence it is not surprising that the extraordinary expenses of the
fêtes of the Congress, during the . . . months of its duration, amounted to forty
millions of francs.

Doubtless, at no time of the world's history had more grave and complex
interests been discussed amidst so many fêtes. A kingdom was cut into bits or
enlarged at a ball; an indemnity was granted in the course of a dinner; a
constitution was planned during a hunt; now and again a cleverly placed word or
a happy and pertinent remark cemented a treaty. . . .[*]

In the autumn of 1814, a brilliant gathering of kings, princes, and
statesmen assembled in the animated capital of the Habsburg Empire to
draw up a peace settlement. As host to the treatymakers, the Austrian
government sponsored extravagant festivities, operas, and balls. For ten
months, rulers and diplomats, when not dining or dancing, worked to
remake the map of Europe. As a rule, they tried to restore conditions as
they had been before the French Revolution. They took precautions
against possible renewal of French aggression, returned legitimate monarchs
to their thrones, established a balance of power in Europe, and set up a
mechanism to crush revolutionary outbreaks at their source before they
could spread.

Liberty Leading the People. Detail. Liberty, represented by a composed and rational goddess,
holding the tricolor aloft, is seen uniting the workers and bourgeoisie to confront the forces of
political reaction. The intention of the artist, Eugène Delacroix, a founder of the romantic
school of painting, was to glorify the July Revolution in Paris in 1830 and to inspire future
generations of revolutionaries. The painting symbolizes the close relationship between the romantic movement in the arts and the movements of liberalism and nationalism from 1820 to
1850. Louvre Museum, Paris.

Metternich. The brilliant, strong-willed, and elegant Austrian foreign minister personified post-war reaction and so completely dominated European politics in the period 1814–1848 that it is sometimes known as the "Age of Metternich."

After 1815 most European regimes pursued conservative policies. Monarchies, supported by the aristocracy and clerical hierarchy, resisted bourgeoisie and workers' demands for constitutional government or national independence. The inevitable clash between the proponents of the old order and of change produced a rash of revolutions in Europe in the decade after 1820. The continental powers, in particular Austria, played a central role in preserving the status quo. By maintaining stability and suppressing dissent at home they were able to shore up less secure monarchical regimes elsewhere. The revolutions were stamped out nearly everywhere and in the few instances where they could not be averted, as in Belgium and Greece, they were steered in directions least harmful to the general public order.

THE CONGRESS OF VIENNA

After the first abdication of Napoleon in April 1814 the most pressing issue facing the victorious coalition was to set terms for France. As a successor to Napoleon, the allies restored the Bourbon monarchy in the person of Louis XVIII. The victors had the good sense to see that a punitive peace would handicap the new king's rule by associating him with defeat and humiliation. Under the provisions of the Treaty of Paris, concluded with Louis XVIII in May 1814, France not only avoided financial reparations but retained the boundaries of 1792, including various enclaves that had formerly been under foreign sovereignty. To deal with other questions, in particular those concerning the territories recently freed from the Napoleonic yoke, the powers agreed to hold an international conference at Vienna.

An imposing array of personalities met at Vienna from September 1814 to June 1815. Every European state except Turkey was represented. The commanding figure at the congress was Prince Klemens von Metternich (1773–1859), a highly gifted statesman wedded to conservative ideas. Foreign Minister of Austria since 1809, a post he held continuously until 1848, Metternich was determined to end the chaos of the past twenty-five years and inaugurate an era of peace and stability in Europe. To that end he sought to suppress liberal ideas and restore the balance of power so that no one country could dominate the European continent as Napoleon had. The interests of Great Britain were defended by its astute foreign secretary Viscount Castlereagh, whose main objective also was to reestablish the balance of power in Europe. Tsar Alexander I, who personally headed the Russian delegation, came to Vienna with a conviction that his country was entitled to territorial compensation, as did Prince Karl von Hardenberg, the principle spokesman for the Prussian King Frederick William III. Charles Maurice de Talleyrand, representing defeated France, was not expected to have a voice in shaping the decisions of the congress. The subtle and audacious Frenchman, however, exploited the disagreements among the victors and edged his way into their counsels.

With the possible exception of Alexander, all the principal statesmen at the congress shared Metternich's staunchly conservative outlook. The tsar was a religious mystic

METTERNICH'S CONFESSION OF "POLITICAL FAITH"

Presumption makes every man the guide of his own belief, the arbiter of laws according to which he is pleased to govern himself, or to allow some one else to govern him and his neighbors; it makes him, in short, the sole judge of his own faith, his own actions, and the principles according to which he guides them . . .

It is pricipally the middle classes of society which this moral gangrene has affected, and it is only among them that the real heads of the party are found.

For the great mass of the people it has no attraction and can have none. The labours to which this class—the real people—are obliged to devote themselves are too continuous and too positive to allow them to throw themselves into vague abstractions and ambitions. . . .

There is besides scarcely any epoch which does not offer a rallying cry to some particular faction. This cry, since 1815, has been *Constitution*. But do not let us deceive ourselves: this word, susceptible of great latitude of interpretation, would be but imperfectly understood if we supposed that the factions attached quite the same meaning to it under different *régimes* . . . . Everywhere it means change and trouble . . . .

The Governments, having lost their balance, are frightened, intimidated, and thrown into confusion by the cries of the intermediary class of society, which, placed between the Kings and their subjects, breaks the scepter of the monarch, and usurps the cry of the people . . . . The evil is plain . . . .

We are convinced that society can no longer be saved without strong and vigorous resolutions on the part of the Governments still free in their opinions and actions . . . . By this course the monarchs will fulfill the duties imposed upon them by Him who, by entrusting them with power, has charged them to watch over the maintenance of justice and the rights of all . . . .

The first principle to be followed by the monarchs . . . should be that of maintaining the stability of political institutions against the disorganized excitement which has taken possession of men's minds; the immutability of principles against the madness of their interpretation; and respect for laws actually in force against a desire for their destruction . . . .

The first and greatest concern for the immense majority of every nation is the stability of the laws and their uninterrupted action—never their change. . . .

Let them be just, but strong; beneficent, but strict.

Let them maintain religious prin-ciples in all their purity, and not allow the faith to be attacked and morality interpreted according to the *social contract* or the visions of foolish sectarians.

Let them suppress Secret Societies, that gangrene of society.

In short, let the great monarchs strengthen their union, and prove to the world that if it exists, it is beneficent, and ensures the political peace of Europe . . . that the principles which they profess are paternal and protective, menacing only the disturbers of public tranquility. *

Metternich's statement of his political principles, written in 1820 at the request of Tsar Alexander I, was designed to justify his policy and refute the ideas that had spawned the Revolution. His conservatism arose not only from conviction, but from a realization that any concessions to liberalism and nationalism would be fatal to Austria's position in Germany and Italy.

*Prince Richard Metternich, ed. *Memoirs of Prince Metternich*, (New York: Harper, 1881), Vol. 2, pp. 322–337.

whose contradictory tendencies baffled his contemporaries. Although an expansionist and autocratic ruler, he professed an enthusiasm for the ideas of the Enlightenment and the principles of the French Revolution. The conservatives either regarded him as a madman or suspected that he was employing liberalism as a cloak for Russian expansion.

The congress never met as a formal deliberative body, so the delegates of the lesser nations had little chance to influence the course of events. The main business of the Congress was carried out by the representatives of the great powers—Austria, Great Britain, Prussia, Russia, and later France—in secret conferences held amidst lavish balls, concerts, hunting parties, and festivals. The only time the congress met in full session was to ratify the arrangements made by the major states.

Congress of Vienna. The French portraitist Jean-Baptiste Isabey sketched each of the participants separately and then combined them into a single scene. Metternich is standing prominently on the left and pointing towards Castlereagh who is seated with his legs crossed in the center. Talleyrand, with his forearm resting on the table, is seated on the right. Louvre Museum, Paris.

In shaping the political destiny of Europe, the statesmen at Vienna were guided by five concepts: the containment of France, legitimacy, balance of power, war spoils, and compensation.

Regarding France, the generous settlement in May 1814 was undone when Napoleon suddenly returned from exile. Joyously welcomed by the French people, the Corsican again disrupted the peace of Europe during his "hundred days" of freedom. After Waterloo, more severe terms were imposed on France. Under the second Treaty of Paris of November 1815, France was pushed back to the frontiers of 1790, required to pay an indemnity of 700 million francs, and forced to maintain an army of occupation for a maximum period of five years. To serve as a barrier against any future French expansion, the allies erected a number of strong states around France's borders. The Dutch Republic, which had fallen to the French in 1795, was revived as the Kingdom of the Netherlands under the head of the House of Orange, King William I (1815–1840). To it was added Belgium, formerly the Austrian Netherlands. The Italian

Kingdom of Sardinia-Piedmont, hereafter referred to as Sardinia, was restored and enlarged by the incorporation of the Republic of Genoa. Prussia gained almost all of the left bank of the Rhine, and Austria became a major power in northern Italy.

The principle of legitimacy meant that legitimate monarchs (that is legal under the old regimes), displaced by the wars of the Revolution and Napoleon, should be reinstated on their thrones whenever practicable. Talleyrand had invented this concept to ensure the return of the Bourbons in France. Besides placing Louis XVIII on the French throne, the allied powers restored legitimate rulers in the Netherlands, Sardinia, Spain, Portugal, the two Sicilies, the papal possessions, and various German states. In general, however, the principle of legitimacy was ignored nearly as often as it was enforced.

One area where legitimacy was not extended was in Germany. Few wished to see the reestablishment of the Holy Roman Empire with its hundreds of petty states. Ardent German nationalists wanted Germany united into a single state under the Prussian king. But Metternich opposed such a plan,

regarding it as a threat to Austria's influence in Germany. The solution adopted was a compromise. The thirty-nine German states set up by Napoleon were joined in a loose confederation in which each member was left free to manage its own affairs.

The representatives of the major states at Vienna, led by Metternich and Castlereagh, were more consistent in applying the principle of the balance of power. An equilibrium of strength among the great powers was seen as the surest way to discourage aggression on the part of any one of them. The principle was also applied to the question of war spoils. Whenever one major state increased its holdings the others were entitled to equivalent gains, even if this necessitated violations of legitimacy.

The congress made every effort to distribute the spoils fairly among the victors or to compensate them for lost territory. Sweden received Norway from Denmark (an ally of Napoleon) in return for surrendering Finland to Russia. The British recovered Hanover and retained colonies and naval bases it had captured in the wars, notably Helgoland in the North Sea, Malta and the Ionian Islands in the

Mediterranean, Cape Colony in south Africa, and Ceylon in the Indian Ocean. For giving up Polish territory and the Austrian Netherlands, Austria was compensated with Lombardy and Venetia in northern Italy, as well as part of the Adriatic coast.

Thus far, agreement had not been difficult, but the disposal of Polish and Saxon territory threatened to disrupt the conference and embroil the great powers in another war. Alexander wanted Poland, partitioned among Russia, Prussia, and Austria in the eighteenth century, reconstituted into a single kingdom under his control. Prussia was prepared to surrender its share of Poland on condition it receive all of Saxony. Metternich, however, had no desire to see the penetration of Russian power into

central Europe or the growth of Prussian influence in the affairs of Germany. Castlereagh stood by Metternich, although he was more concerned with checking Russia's westward expansion. Talleyrand shrewdly used the rift between the victors to win a place for France in the deliberations. He arranged for a secret treaty in which France, Britain, and Austria pledged to go to war if necessary to restrain Russia and Prussia.

No sooner had news of the secret treaty leaked out than Russia and Prussia moderated their demands. Alexander I was permitted to take much of Poland, but Prussia and Austria retained some of their Polish districts. Frederick William III accepted about two-fifths of Saxony with the remainder being returned to the le-

MAP 63
Europe in 1815. The boundaries set by the Congress of Vienna were designed to prevent any one state from dominating Continental affairs. France was reduced to its pre-1792 borders. Great Britain, which had played a key role in overthrowing Napoleon, received only a few naval bases. The Netherlands was enlarged by the addition of Belgium, and Prussia gained the Rhineland and substantial sections of Saxony. Russia obtained Finland and a considerable part of Polish territories, but its advance into central Europe was blocked by the Congress. Austria received the Italian province of Lombardy and was awarded adjacent Venetia.

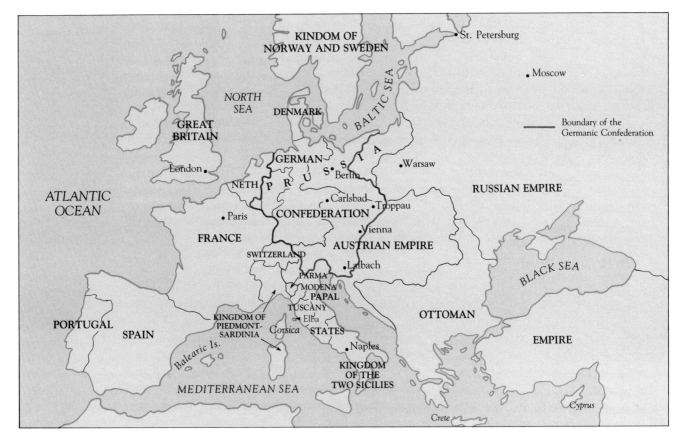

gitimate ruler in spite of his long fidelity to Napoleon. The acquisition of part of Saxony and Rhineland territory greatly enhanced Prussia's power and influence as a leading west European state. The new Prussia contained nearly one half of all the Germans living outside the Austrian Empire. The settlement of the Polish-Saxon question concluded the main work of the congress.

The victorious statesmen had grappled with enormously difficult problems and in a surprisingly short time resolved these in a reasonable way. That is not to say that everyone affected by their decision was pleased. The French Revolution and Napoleon had given wide currency throughout Europe to such ideas as equality under the law for all citizens, universal suffrage, and religious freedom, and, although the upheaval was over, these liberal concepts remained popular with both the intellectuals and the underprivileged. Simultaneously, a spirit of nationalism had grown in many of the lands subjugated by the French. After 1815, some people were determined to regain the liberal advantages they had lost at Vienna while others, living under alien governments, were equally determined to throw off the foreign yoke. In retrospect the most serious mistake of the peacemakers was to disregard the democratic and nationalist sentiments that had emerged with such vigor in the preceding quarter century. By doing so they opened the door to popular unrest and revolution, which they worked so hard to circumvent. That they failed to recognize and provide for these forces should not seem strange. They would have been more than human if they had yielded to forces they considered dangerous or anticipated future problems.

Until recently, it was customary to denounce the Vienna settlement as a conspiracy of reactionary monarchs to stamp out liberalism, nationalism, and social justice. But in view of the colossal errors of the peacemakers after the twentieth century world wars, historians today are generally impressed with the achievements of those of 1815. The distribution of power devised by the Congress gave Europe a long period of relative stability in international affairs. No conflict of any consequence occurred in Europe until the outbreak of the Crimean War in 1854 and none involving all of the great powers until 1914.

REVOLUTION AND THE CONCERT OF EUROPE

A widespread feeling existed among the dominant powers that merely redrawing the map of Europe would not ensure permanent peace and that there was further need to formulate a code of international behavior. Tsar Alexander I was the first to seize the initiative. Under the influence of the pious Baroness von Krüdener, he came to believe that God had chosen him to lead society into a brighter and happier era. In September 1815, he invited his fellow sovereigns to join him in a "Holy Alliance" by which they would promise to abide by Christian principles in dealing with one another and with their subjects. No one except Alexander took the proposal seriously. Metternich, thinking it absurd to mix Christianity with politics, dismissed the Holy Alliance as "loud-sounding nothing," while Castlereagh, equally scornful, called it "a piece of sublime mysticism and nonsense." Nevertheless, to avoid offending Alexander, all the rulers of Europe signed the declaration save the prince regent of Great Britain (later George IV, 1820–1830) who replied, quite untruthfully, that the British constitution prohibited him from acting upon "abstract and speculative principles;" the pope who explained that he did not need instruction in his Christian duties; and the sultan of Turkey, who could hardly be expected to follow Christian teachings. The Holy Alliance had no practical function, being merely a statement of good intentions with no specific commitments or binding obligations.

Far more important as an instrument guaranteeing the peace settlement was the Quadruple Alliance, signed on November 20, 1815. In this document, Britain, Austria, Prussia, and Russia pledged to use force if necessary to safeguard the arrangements worked out at Vienna and to prevent the return of a Bonaparte to the French throne. The four major powers further agreed to consult with each other periodically on matters affecting Europe as a whole or whenever peace seemed threatened. Thus was born the so-called congress system, intended to regulate international relations. Whether this novel experiment would succeed depended on the continuing harmony of the wartime allies.

The first congress held under the new system convened in the historic city of Aix-la-Chapelle, in the Rhineland, in October 1818. The purpose was to complete the settlement with France, which had shown its good behavior under the restored Bourbon king, Louis XVIII. Besides authorizing a reduction in the indemnity and a withdrawal of occupation forces, the powers admitted France as an equal partner in the alliance which then became the Quintuple Alliance. Tsar Alexander used the occasion to circulate a memorandum in which he suggested that the member states guarantee to safeguard legitimate regimes everywhere. Britain's representative, Lord Castlereagh, flatly rejected the proposal. He maintained that his country was committed to prevent a revival of French aggression but would not obligate itself to act against unspecified contingencies. Metternich, who suspected Alexander's belated conversion to

absolutism, sided with Castlereagh. Before long, however, events would drive the Austrian foreign minister into the arms of Alexander.

In 1820–1821, Europe witnessed an outburst of revolutionary passion, motivated by a desire for liberal reforms. The first revolt occurred in Spain in January 1820 when army units, about to be sent overseas to reconquer the Latin American colonies, mutinied and marched on Madrid. Popular riots and demonstrations broke out in support of the army in Madrid, Barcelona, and other major urban centers. In a desperate attempt to appease his subjects Ferdinand VII (1814–1833) reinstated the

liberal constitution (issued by the Spanish Parliament in 1812 during the struggle against Napoleon), which he had revoked on his accession to the throne. The revolution in Spain proved contagious, spreading quickly to the Kingdom of the Two Sicilies, Portugal, and Sardinia.

The uprisings tested the solidarity of the Quintuple Alliance. At the first news of the Spanish disturbances, Alexander called for immediate intervention. Once again Castlereagh objected. The purpose of the alliance, he insisted, was to preserve the territorial settlement of 1815, not to meddle in the internal affairs of sovereign states. Metternich hesitated to

MAP 64
European Revolt, 1820–1831. In 1820–1821 and again in 1830–1831 liberal and national revolts against oppressive governments occurred in many European states. In most instances the great powers, with the exception of Great Britain, intervened to suppress what they considered were threats to European peace. Largely for selfish reasons, the European powers assisted the Greeks in their war for independence. Belgium managed to break away from Dutch rule only because Austria and Russia were embroiled elsewhere. France was alone among the major powers to have a successful revolution, replacing Charles X with the more liberal Louis Philippe.

561

				Greeks rise	
Congress of Vienna	Congress of Aix-la-Chapelle	Carlsbad Decrees	Revolutions in Spain and Italy	against Turkish rule	Monroe Doctrine
Quadruple Alliance formed			Congresses of Troppau and Laibach		

act until an insurrection in Naples forced Ferdinand I (1815–1825) to accept a constitution. Thereafter, Metternich became convinced that the tide of revolution must be checked before it engulfed all of Europe. At his urging, a congress of the great powers, which convened in the Silesian town of Troppau in October 1820, claimed the right to suppress domestic revolutions whenever they threatened the peace of Europe. Great Britain refused to endorse the new principle. This had no effect on the congress, which had reassembled at Laibach, farther south, when the wintry weather set in. Hence Austria, with its special interests in Italy, was authorized to crush the revolution in Naples. The Austrian army completed its assignment quickly, abolishing the constitution and restoring the absolute rule of Ferdinand I. On its way back, the army then helped to put down the revolt in the Kingdom of Sardinia.

The split between Great Britain and its continental allies was even more apparent at the next congress, held at Verona in northern Italy in October 1822 to deal with the insurrection in Spain. By then, Castlereagh was dead and his successor at the Foreign Office, George Canning, was unwilling even to pledge Great Britain's cooperation in maintaining stability on the continent. Canning was staunchly opposed to joint intervention on behalf of Ferdinand, but was unable to prevent a French expedition, which had the blessing of the congress, from crossing the Pyrenees and stamping out the reform movement in Spain in the summer of 1823. King Ferdinand followed his repudiation of the liberal constitution with a savage persecution of the revolutionary leaders.

The meeting at Verona in effect marked the end of Great Britain's association with the congress system. While the British refused to intervene in the domestic affairs of other states, Metternich and his continental partners believed that internal revolts called for immediate suppression, otherwise they were likely to lead, like the French Revolution, to international war. There could be no reconciliation between two so diametrically opposed views on the function of the alliance.

Although successful in Italy and Spain, the continental powers met their first defeat when they sought to reimpose the authority of Ferdinand over his rebellious subjects in Latin America. The independence movement in Latin America, begun as a reaction to Napoleon's presence in Spain and continued after the return of the reactionary Ferdinand, had triumphed nearly everywhere by the early 1820s. Since Ferdinand was in a hopelessly weak position, barely able to hold on to his own throne, Alexander and Metternich considered adopting common measures to win back the colonies for Spain. Great Britain, however, had developed a lucrative trade with the new Latin American states and was not anxious to see Spanish control restored. In 1823, Canning proposed that the United States and Great Britain issue a joint statement warning other European powers to keep out of the affairs of the western hemisphere. The leaders of the young republic, foreseeing the day when the United States might wish to invoke such a policy against Great Britain, decided instead to make a unilateral declaration. In a message to Congress in December 1823 President James Monroe included a statement that closed the Americas to further European colonization. The so-called Monroe Doctrine would have had little international significance had Canning not given it his immediate support. Great Britain's supremacy at sea ruled out any continental intervention in the New World. Thus the independence of Latin American was assured.

THE MONROE DOCTRINE

In the wars of the European powers, in matters relating to themselves, we have never taken any part, nor does it comport with our policy so to do. It is only when our rights are invaded, or seriously menaced, that we resent injuries or make preparation for our defense. With the movements in this hemisphere, we are, of necessity, more immediately connected, and by causes which must be obvious to all enlightened and impartial observers. The political system of the allied powers is essentially different, in this respect, from that of America. . . . We owe it, therefore, to candor, and to the amicable relations existing between the United States and those powers, to declare, that we should consider any attempt on their part to extend their system to any portion of this hemisphere, as dangerous to our peace and safety. With the existing colonies or dependencies of any European power, we have not interfered, and shall not interfere. But with the governments who have declared their independence, and maintained it, and whose independence we have, on great consideration, and on just principles, acknowledged, we could not view any interposition for the purpose of oppressing them, or controlling, in any other manner, their destiny, by an European power, in any other light than as the manifestation of an unfriendly disposition towards the United States. *

For the United States the statement was an important assertion of policy and marked the beginning of participation in affairs beyond its own shores. Left on its own, however, the youthful American Republic, which did not even possess a navy, would have been unable to enforce the new doctrine.

* Isidore Starr, Lewis Todd and Merle Curti, eds., *Living American Documents* (New York: Harcourt, Brace and World 1961) pp. 128–129.

An equally significant blow against legitimacy was struck by the Greeks in their bid for national independence. The Greek revolt, precipitated by the maladministration of Turkish officials and inspired by the ideals of the French Revolution, broke out in 1821 under the leadership of Alexander Ypsilanti. The struggle, which was marked by incredible savagery on both sides, posed a delicate problem for the statesmen of the great powers. They were all hostile to revolutions, but at the same time they felt the sultan of Turkey, being Muslim, was not in the category of a Christian prince. Alexander wanted to aid the Greeks, but Metternich dissuaded him from doing so. As far as the Austrian foreign minister was concerned, the Greeks were rebelling against their legitimate sovereign, and his solution was to let their revolt burn itself out "beyond the pale of civilization." By 1825, the Turks, with Egyptian help, were on the verge of crushing the uprising. This prospect inflamed European public opinion, which was pro-Greek for religious and cultural reasons. Encouraged by popular sentiment, Tsar Nicholas I (1825–1855), Alexander's successor, decided to intercede on behalf of the Greeks. He was joined by France and Great Britain, which was determined not to allow Russia a free hand in the Balkans. Over Metternich's protests, the three powers sent a squadron of warships to Greek waters in the summer of 1827. That autumn, the allied ships encountered a Turkish-Egyptian fleet in Navarino Bay and destroyed it. In the ensuing land campaign, the French cleared the Turks out of Greece, and a Russian army advanced almost to the gates of Constantinople. The Ottoman government had no alternative but to sue for peace. The Treaty of Adrianpole on September 14, 1829, among other things, recognized Greece as an independent kingdom. The successful revolt of the Greeks resulted in the first significant change in the map of Europe since the Congress of Vienna. Metternich's system had been breached.

METTERNICH AND THE SUPPRESSION OF DISCONTENT IN CENTRAL EUROPE

Metternich's fidelity to reactionary principles after 1815 stemmed more from practical considerations than from ideology. As a devoted servant of Emperor Francis I, he had done his best at the Congress of Vienna to reconstruct Europe as it had been prior to 1789. For Metternich, there could be no compromise with the forces of liberalism and nationalism. He knew the liberals wanted to eliminate the

563

Scenes from the Massacre at Chios. Delacroix depicts in characteristic style the contemporary revulsion in the West over the incident in which the Turks butchered 25,000 Greeks and enslaved some 45,000 after capturing the island of Chios in April 1822. This was in retaliation for an earlier atrocity at Tripolitsa where 12,000 Turks had been hanged, impaled, and roasted alive by their Greek captors. However, few Europeans were aware of what had happened at Tripolitsa. Louvre Museum, Paris.

traditional system of class distinction and absolute monarchy in favor of a new order based on social equality and constitutional government. Equally troublesome in his eyes was nationalist agitation. Therefore when the liberals and nationalists challenged the status quo in the Austrian Empire, Italy, and Germany, he adopted increasingly repressive measures against them.

Metternich's foremost concern was to preserve both the Habsburg Empire and the old established social order. Austria was (and still is) ethnically German, but the rest of the Habsburg domains were inhabited by Italians, Hungarians, Rumanians, and several Slavic nationalities, in particular Poles and Czechs. Lacking ethnic and linguistic unity, the provinces were held together mainly by allegiance to the crown. In the wake of the Napoleonic Wars, the various minority groups were stirred by nationalist sentiments, and they began to resent the emperor's rule. To have recognized the aspirations of those peoples would have meant the collapse of the Habsburg Empire. Metternich tried to check the growth of nationalism among the emperor's diverse subjects by planting spies everywhere, stationing troops in potentially troublesome areas, jailing agitators, and forbidding the importation of printed matter without special permission. Simultaneously he fostered a series of measures to guard against the rise of liberalism at home.

He enforced strict press censorship, strengthened the police, controlled university curricula, and prohibited students from forming societies. Metternich saw the Austrian Empire as a microcosm of Europe. What was good for Austria was good for Europe or, put another way, whatever threatened Europe threatened Austria. His attitude particularly affected political developments in Italy and Germany.

In Italy, Metternich had to combat the legacy left by Napoleon. The French leader had brought a measure of political unity, consolidating the fifteen states into three. He had provided enlightened administration and granted the people more liberty than they had ever known. Moreover he had urged an end to local rivalries, insisting that the salvation of Italy lay in national unification. The fall of Napoleon created political changes in Italy, but it did not extinguish the national spirit he had kindled.

The Congress of Vienna, however, left Austria more dominant than ever in Italy. The traditional states of Italy were reconstituted: Lombardy and Venetia were administered directly from Vienna; Austrian princes ruled in Tuscany, Parma, and Modena; and the remaining states were also under the thumb of the Habsburg government. Across Italy, conditions were restored, as far as possible, as they had been before 1789.

Notwithstanding the action of the Congress, popular desire for national unity grew, fed in large measure by hatred of Austria and dissatisfaction with the reactionary regimes in the Italian states. As in many other countries Italian liberals and patriots formed secret societies to organize resistance. The best known of these groups was the *carbonari* ("charcoal burners"), which was dedicated to overthrowing tyranny and foreign rule. In 1820–1821 and again in 1830–1831, the *carbonari* led revolts against local reactionary rulers. On both occasions, Austrian forces, from their base in Lombardy-Venetia, easily put down the uprisings. Held in check for the time being by stronger reactionary forces, the revolutionary spirit in Italy would reemerge in the 1840s.

As in Austria and Italy, Metternich's power was deeply felt in the German states. At the Congress of Vienna, Metternich had arranged for the reconstruction of the Germanies in such a way as to ensure Austria's ascendancy. He had blocked a proposal for a united Germany (from which Austria was certain to be excluded because most of her subjects were non-Germans) for fear that Austria would lose its dominance in central Europe. The solution finally adopted was to create the German confederation, a loose league embracing all the German speaking states, including Prussia and parts of Austria. Each state remained independent, the only restriction being that it could not enter into an alliance with a foreign power against any member of the confederation. The principal organ of the confederation, the Diet, which sat periodically in Frankfort under permanent Austrian chairmanship, had no authority. In practice, the confederation played no important role in German politics except when Metternich wished to use it for his own ends. During the immediate postwar period, Metternich helped to dissuade Frederick William III from granting the Prussian people the constitution they had been led to expect, and he coerced other German princes into revoking or limiting liberal reforms.

Within the German states, as elsewhere in central Europe, the French revolutionary era had evoked strong feelings of liberalism and nationalism. The progressive changes that had occurred in France led German liberals to believe that such reforms might serve Germany equally well. On the other hand, German patriots attributed Germany's defeat at the hands of Napoleon to the division of the country into small states. The creation of a strong national state, they felt, would prevent such misfortunes in the future. The Vienna settlements, as applied to Germany, disappointed both liberals and nationalists but did not doom their hopes.

The first real movement of protest against the status quo sprang up in the universities. Here students formed associations, known as *Burschenschaften*, whose aims were proclaimed in their slogan, "Honor, liberty, fatherland." In October 1817, the *Burschenschaften* for the University of Jena staged a giant festival to commemorate two great patriotic events, the fourth anniversary of the Battle of Leipzig and the tercentenary of Luther's ninety-five theses. During the rally some students, in a moment of exaltation, flung into a bonfire books by reactionary writers, a diplomat's wig, and a Prussian officer's corselet, to symbolize their contempt for political and military tyranny. The prank was harmless enough but it filled Metternich with anxiety.

In 1819, the murder of a reactionary playwright, August von Kotzebue, by a fanatical student gave Metternich an opportunity to strike. In the summer of that year, Metternich persuaded the representatives of the

The Assassination of August von Kotzebue. In this contemporary engraving the dramatist August Kotzebue, who was reputed to be a Russian spy, struggles in vain to free himself from the grip of a disturbed theological student named Karl Sand. Young Germans hated Kotzebue because he mocked the student movement and because they believed that his reports had induced Tsar Alexander to abandon liberalism. Bibliothèque Nationale, Paris.

major German states, assembled in Carlsbad at his request, to draw up a set of harsh measures which were later adopted by the Diet of the confederation. The so-called Carlsbad Decrees outlawed student associations, tightened censorship laws, restricted academic freedom, and prohibited the granting of any constitution "inconsistent with the monarchical principle." Vigorously enforced by agents and police, the Carlsbad Decrees effectively contained liberal and nationalist opinion in Germany for many years.

AUTOCRACY IN RUSSIA

When Alexander I inherited the throne in 1801, he seemed determined to win a place in history as a philosopher-king. Schooled in the ideals of the Enlightenment, Alexander talked freely about the rights of man and the obligations of a monarch to his subjects. At the outset, he formed a committee of liberal advisers and pushed through a number of mi-

nor reforms that seemed to herald the coming of a new age. But on substantive matters he did nothing, abandoning his early interest in constitutional reform and in abolishing serfdom.

Alexander became increasingly reactionary in the last decade of his reign. As he grew older, he turned to religious mysticism, and he came to regard the Enlightenment and the French Revolution as a gigantic attack on Christianity. Metternich undoubtedly assisted in the tsar's conversion to extreme conservatism. He never lost an opportunity to point out that liberal ideas would incite disorder and violence, that the only way of preserving Christian peace and charity was for Russia to join Austria in rooting out the evils of liberalism. By 1820, Alexander had become as fervent as Metternich in urging the suppression of liberal movements in Europe. The tsar's changed attitude was also felt inside Russia. His main adviser was General Alexis Arakcheev, a harsh disciplinarian who encouraged him to break all contact with progressive circles. Together they fol-

lowed a rigidly conservative policy, curtailing what little freedom existed in the press and universities and punishing political dissenters. Indeed, Alexander showed, on an increasing scale, the same kind of arbitrariness he had condemned as a young monarch.

The death of Alexander in December 1825 sparked the first and only liberal uprising in Russia in the nineteenth century. One result of the domestic repression under Alexander had been the growth of secret societies that agitated for reforms, including the establishment of a constitution. The leaders of these societies were liberal intellectuals and army officers, many of whom had been affected by the spirit of the French Revolution during their campaigns in western Europe. An uprising had been in preparation for several years when Alexander died suddenly. Since Alexander had no children, the crown normally would have passed to his brother Constantine. But in 1822, Constantine had renounced his right of succession in favor of his younger brother Nicholas, who, oddly enough, was not informed of this development. Thus for three weeks, the question of succession was left in confusion as each of the brothers protested that the other should be tsar. During the brief period of uncertainty, the leaders of one of the army's secret societies organized a mutiny among the troops quartered in St. Petersburg. The plotters had acted precipitously, without adequate preparations or clear objectives. Taking immediate charge, Nicholas encountered little difficulty in smashing the rebellion. The mutinous officers were apprehended, five of them were hanged and the others were condemned to forced labor or exiled to Siberia.

The Decembrist Revolution, as it is called, had the effect of strengthening Nicholas I's inborn authoritarianism. To forestall any further attempts to change the status quo, he set up a police state in Russia that was even more repressive than Metternich's, on which it was modeled. For thirty years, Nicholas stood as a symbol of extreme autocracy, waging a relentless battle against all reformist activity at home and offering Russian troops to European nations endangered by revolution.

THE BOURBON RESTORATION IN FRANCE

After Waterloo, Louis XVIII returned to the throne he had abandoned so abruptly when Napoleon reappeared from exile in 1814. Fat, crippled by gout, and nearly sixty years old, the king had sufficient political judgment to realize that the achievements of the past quarter century could not be

wholly undone. To heal the wounds of the Revolution he pursued a policy of compromise, steering between the ultra royalists on one hand, and the liberals and radical reformers on the other.

On assuming the throne, Louis granted his subjects a charter, or constitution, that made France the most liberal monarchy in Europe. The charter, which was to remain in force until February 1848, safeguarded basic liberties and set up a two-chamber legislature on the British model. However, deputies were required to be forty years old or over and pay direct taxes of at least 1000 francs—a considerable sum. To vote in elections, individuals had to be at least thirty years old and pay taxes equivalent to no less than 300 francs. What this meant was that the electorate was limited only to about 100,000 men out of a population of 29,000,000. While the charter did not allow democratic participation in government, it did involve a higher proportion of the population in politics than was the case in the countries farther to the east.

The king's moderate spirit was reflected in other ways as well. He preserved the best of Napoleon's accomplishments, such as the judicial system, the system of state education, the civil service, the Concordat with the pope, and the Bank of France. Furthermore, he did not seek wholesale punishment of revolutionary leaders or allow confiscated estates, which had since passed into other hands, to be returned to their former owners.

The king's most difficult task was to restrain the ultraroyalists, known as the ultras. These diehard aristocrats, many of whom were returned *émigrés*, were determined to regain

Nicholas I. This lithograph after a painting by F. Krüger captures the autocratic bearing of the handsome and dignified emperor. As grand duke commanding a brigade of guards, Nicholas had placed more value on drill and discipline than on initiative. As emperor he left no doubt that his ideal was a disciplined state in which all subjects recognized that their first duty was to obey authority.

both the privileges and the property they had lost during the Revolution. After they gained control of the lower house (the Chamber of Deputies) they wreaked vengeance on former revolutionaries and Bonapartists. At the insistence of the allies, who feared a national uprising, Louis dissolved the Chamber and held new elections. A moderate majority was returned and during the next four years the administration relaxed censorship of the press, paid off the war indemnity (which ended allied occupation), and generally put French finances in good order. But in February 1820, the duke of Berry, the king's nephew, was assassinated by a Bonapartist fanatic, and in the emotional wave that followed, the ultras swept back into control of the Chamber. Ultra pressure compelled the government to clamp controls on the press, revise electoral laws to benefit the old aristocracy, strengthen the church's role in education, and send French troops to Spain in 1823.

The drift toward reaction quickened appreciably when Louis XVIII died and he was succeeded by his brother, who reigned as Charles X (1824–30). Father of the recently murdered duke of Berry and for many years the acknowledged leader of the ultras, Charles made no secret of his intention to reestablish royal absolutism. His elaborate coronation ceremony in the cathedral at Rheims recalled the splendor of the ancient regime. Then, with the assistance of the ultras, he set out to achieve his purpose.

One of the administration's first acts was to indemnify the émigrés for the loss of their property during the revolution. To finance the measure, the royal government reduced the rate of

interest on the national debt from 5 to 4 percent. Actually the bill gave the beneficiaries substantially less than they had hoped for and, while it victimized state bondholders, it did assure safe title to those who had purchased national lands. At a rather low cost the land question was at last settled. But the debate surrounding the bill, in both parliament and the press, had been bitterly partisan and many Frenchmen saw the indemnity as an insult, a fine to punish the nation for the events of 1789. This incident was followed by the king's unsuccessful attempt to restore primogeniture—whereby the eldest son, or next male heir, of a deceased, inherited the entire estate—to check the fragmentation of aristocratic estates. Dedicated to the prerevolutionary alliance between "throne and altar," Charles further extended the church's influence over education and made sacrilege a crime punishable by long imprisonment or even death. The king's dogged pursuit of policies designed to benefit only the nobility and the church infuriated the bourgeoisie, the very people whose cooperation was vital to the survival of his regime.

THE REVOLUTIONS OF 1830

Charles failed to take seriously enough the growing signs of popular discontent in France. In March 1830, the Chamber of Deputies passed a vote of no confidence in the government. Charles dissolved the Chamber but the outcome of the new elections only strengthened the opposition. Refusing to accept the verdict of the voters,

Charles decided to abolish the constitutional charter and rule as an absolute monarch. In a series of ordinances issued on July 26, 1830, he imposed tight restrictions on newspapers, dissolved the new Chamber before it assembled, amended the electoral law so as to disenfranchise most of the middle class, and called for another election.

Under bourgeoisie leadership, the Parisians staged an armed insurrection. During the "three glorious days" (July 27–29) they threw up barricades in the narrow streets and drove the royal forces out of the city. On August 2, Charles abdicated and left hurriedly for Great Britain. The more extreme elements among the insurrectionists wanted to abolish the monarchy but the moderates prevailed and the crown was entrusted to Louis Philippe, the Duke of Orleans and a descendant of a younger brother of Louis XIV.

The year 1830 saw revolution spread like brushfire across Europe. By throwing off the Bourbon yoke, the French had repudiated the principle of legitimacy laid down at the Congress of Vienna. News of the uprising in France triggered similar explosions in Italy, Belgium, and Poland. As previously noted the Italian revolts, organized by the *carbonari*, quickly succumbed to superior Austrian force. The Belgian-Dutch union, created as a matter of international convenience, had proved most unhappy. The Belgians were Catholic and spoke Flemish or French, whereas the Dutch were militant Calvinists. Furthermore, the Belgians resented the harsh rule of William I, who imposed on them Dutch laws, officials, and language. In the face of the king's refusal to make changes, the Belgians

Charles X
succeeds
Louis XVIII

Death of
Tsar
Alexander II

Charles X
of France is
overthrown;
Belgium throws
off Dutch rule

Decembrist
Revolution

Treaty of
Adrianople

Italian and
Polish revolts
unsuccessful

Alliance
between
Austria,
Prussia,
and Russia

declared their independence and set up a constitutional monarchy. Unable to suppress the revolt, William appealed to the conservative alliance for help. But the Concert of Europe did not act, largely because the Russian tsar was busy pacifying the Poles and Austria was tied down by revolutions in Italy. The upshot was that the Dutch king had no choice but to recognize the independence of Belgium. The Poles were less fortunate in their struggle against their Russian overlord. They fought heroically, but they were no match for the much larger Russian army, and by 1831 their resistance had been effectively broken.

Jarred in the 1820s and cracked in 1830, the Metternich system continued to operate but with reduced effectiveness. France, like England, became committed to a more moderate foreign policy. On the other hand, Austria, Prussia, and Russia were firmly resolved to prevent any more breaches in the Vienna settlement. In 1833, they formally pledged to render joint assistance to any sovereign threatened by revolution. Little did they realize that the forces of nationalism and democracy were too powerful to be repressed for any length of time.

SUMMARY

After the downfall of Napoleon, representatives of the victorious nations assembled at Vienna in 1814–1815 to draw up a peace settlement. The intention of the peacemakers was to return to the prerevolutionary Europe of 1789, that is, to undo the work of the French Revolution whenever possible and to revive the power and glamour of the monarchical regimes. Guided by Metternich, the Congress of Vienna imposed lenient terms on France, restored legitimate monarchs in many European states, and reestablished the balance of power. Although not free of flaws, the Vienna settlement spared Europe the ordeal of international conflict for a century.

To preserve the territorial settlement and the balance of power, Austria, Great Britain, Prussia, and Russia formed the Quadruple Alliance. In 1818, France was admitted to the compact after paying its indemnity. The spirit of unity among the major nations ended in the early 1820s when revolutions broke out again. While Great Britain disapproved of intervention in the domestic affairs of other states, the remaining powers, led by Metternich, wanted the alliance to stamp out any subversive movement that threatened the status quo.

Metternich loathed the liberal and nationalist ideals released by the French Revolution. He regarded any attempt at reform as opening the floodgates to radicalism and revolution. His fear of nationalism was no less. Composed of many ethnic groups, the Austrian empire was particularly vulnerable to nationalistic unrest. Tradition, Metternich believed, was the cement that held together the disparate parts of the Empire. Thus he did his utmost to discourage and repress liberal and nationalist movements in the Habsburg realm and wherever else he could bring his influence to bear. Although he succeeded in driving these revolutionary forces underground, he was unable to destroy them.

Russia followed the pattern of

Austria. On assuming the throne, Alexander I had visions of converting Russia into a progressive state with a well-regulated monarchy. During the early years of his rule, he ordered a number of minor reforms but refused to face squarely the central issues of serfdom and autocracy. As he grew older, he turned to religious mysticism and eventually abandoned the enlightened idealism of his young manhood. By 1820, he had joined Metternich in devising and encouraging repressive measures against liberal movements in Europe.

In France, the Bourbons were restored to power after the defeat of Napoleon. Louis XVIII steered a moderate course, recognizing that the French people would not tolerate a return to the pre-1789 order. But his successor, Charles X, was an uncompromising reactionary who tried to revive the glamour and practices of the old regime. His actions, culminating with the issuance of the July ordinances, alienated the bourgeoisie and led to his downfall.

The revolution in France in 1830 inspired other uprisings in Europe. Belgium proclaimed its independence from the Netherlands and established a liberal government. Austria and Russia were tied down elsewhere and could not come to the assistance of the Dutch king. Nationalism triumphed in Belgium, in contrast to the outcome of the revolutions in Italy and Poland where the insurgents lacked the military strength to achieve their objectives. Two generalizations can be made about the revolutions of 1830. First, they succeeded only in the countries where the insurgents represented a large segment of the population. Second, they sharpened the differences between the monarchies of the west and the autocratic regimes of central and eastern Europe. The revolutions that ousted the Bourbons in France and created a separate Belgium state were not reversed by the conservative powers. There were now three representative governments in the west. But the movement toward political democracy, which had been advanced by violence in France and Belgium, was achieved with much less bloodshed in Great Britain.

SELECTED SOURCES

*Artz, F. B. *Reaction and Revolution, 1814–1832.* 1934. A broad and detailed survey from the liberal viewpoint.

Bartlett, Christopher J. *Castlereagh.* 1967. Good biography of the often misunderstood British foreign secretary.

Bertier de Sauvigny, G. de. *The Bourbon Restoration.* 1967. A scholarly appraisal of French politics between 1814–1830 by a historian sympathetic to the Bourbon government.

Droz, J. *Europe Between Revolutions, 1815–1848.* 1968. A valuable survey of the period.

Hugo, Victor. *Les Miserables.* Available in many editions. A classic novel that graphically describes injustice and poverty in Paris in the 1820s and 1830s. It was effectively brought to the screen in 1935 with stunning performances by Frederick March and Charles Laughton.

*Kissinger, H. A. *A World Restored.* 1964. A careful analysis of the efforts of Metternich, Castlereagh, and other notable statesmen to stabilize European politics, 1812–1822.

*May, A. J. *The Age of Metternich, 1814–1848.* 1933. Brief introduction to the period.

*Nicolson, Harold. *The Congress of Vienna.* 1946. Well written and balanced view of the process of peacemaking.

Palmer, Alan. *Metternich.* 1972. Lively biography, focusing more on Metternich's private life than on his diplomacy.

Pinkney, David. *The French Revolution of 1830.* 1972. An important study which reinterprets the nature of the July revolution.

*Schwartz, H. F. ed. *Metternich, the Coachman of Europe: Statesman or Evil Genius.* 1962. Excellent cross-section of opinions on the man.

*Taylor, A. J. P. *The Habsburg Monarchy, 1809–1918.* 1948. A concise and well-organized account, emphasizing the effects of nationalism on diplomacy and politics.

Troyat, Henri. *Alexander of Russia.* 1982. A popular biography.

*Available in paperback.

REFORM AND REVOLUTION

The paving stones seemed to leap from the ground and to form themselves into bulwarks . . . manned by citizens, artists, laborers, professional men—hastily armed with all sorts of weapons, from rifles and shotguns down to pikes, axes, and hammers. There was no preparation, no plan, no system, in the uprising; everybody seemed to follow a common instinct . . . Behind the barricades women were busy bringing food and drink for the fighters and caring for the wounded.

Carl Schurz, a young German who subsequently emigrated to the United States, describes here a tumultuous scene in Berlin in March 1848, one of a number of uprisings that erupted almost simultaneously in Europe. These uprisings reflected discontent with political systems that based their authority on a coalition of monarchy, landed gentry, church, and the upper middle class. For decades the conservative regimes in Europe had remained inflexible, disregarding such changes in society as the growing power of the capitalists, the social abuses brought about by industrialization, the increase in the number of urban workers, and the emergence of a vocal intelligentsia imbued with new ideas—liberalism, nationalism, and socialism. The periodic revolutionary outbreaks in the 1820s and early 1830s should have served notice to the European leaders that their regimes were out of step with the times but the signs of unrest went unheeded, except in a few countries. Consequently, beneath the surface of European life gathered forces that eventually came to a head in 1848. The revolutions began with much promise but all ended in defeat. This chapter discusses the social and political reform programs in Great Britain, Russia, and France, and then examines the causes that produced the uprisings of 1848, traces the various movements, and accounts for their failure.

CONTENTS

The Fortunes of Liberalism. This engraving appeared in *Bell's Weekly Messenger* in the issue of April 15, 1832, to trumpet the passage of the Great Reform Bill. A sober-looking King William IV is in the center, surrounded by the victorious Whig cabinet and its leader, Lord Grey. Below, the Tories are seen fleeing from the raging British lion.

REFORM IN GREAT BRITAIN

Great Britain experienced no revolution or armed uprising in the post Napoleonic period. For a generation, the British had not only waged a desperate struggle against France but also developed their industries and maintained their political and social institutions. In 1815, Great Britain commanded greater power and higher respect than any other state in the western world. It was seen as the model nation, enjoying the benefits of progressive laws, social stability, the highest standard of living in Europe, and a time-tested parliamentary system. Comparing conditions on the continent, the average Briton had good reason to be proud of his country.

Yet there existed in Great Britain problems that were serious enough to cause sober-minded Englishmen to view the future with anxiety rather than complacency. The king, George III (1760–1820), had been declared legally insane in 1811. His eldest son, who became regent and later George IV, was a dissolute and irresponsible man, intensely hated by his subjects. Parliament, where the real power lay, was far from democratic. The House of Lords was made up of Anglican higher clergy and the hereditary aristocracy. The House of Commons consisted of landed gentry, rich merchants, and wealthy financiers. Property qualifications restricted the vote to about 5 percent of the adult male population. To make matters worse, there had never been a systematic redistribution of seats, so that many of the new industrial

cities such as Birmingham and Manchester were unrepresented while some country villages, which had been almost depopulated, continued to send members to the House of Commons. The two great political parties in Britain, the conservative Tories and the slightly more liberal Whigs, did not differ much on matters of principle, for both were controlled by the aristocracy. The common folk and the rising middle class were thoroughly dissatisfied with an arrangement that deprived them of a voice in government.

The years immediately following 1815 witnessed a bitter struggle between the masses clamoring for political and economic reform and a government determined to resist any change whatsoever. At the close of the Napoleonic Wars, the cancellation of defense contracts and the simultaneous demobilization of some 400,000 soldiers caused severe unemployment. The industrial crisis was aggravated by the enactment of a new Corn Law, which almost totally excluded cheaper foreign grain. Even those who did have work could barely exist because of the high price of home grown grain. A widespread feeling of disillusionment and frustration coalesced to produce social unrest that at times exploded into violence. Both the ruling Tories (in power almost continuously since 1783) and the Whigs attributed popular agitation not to poverty and hardship but to the evil influence of Jacobin ideas. Their remedy for the discontent was repression. In December 1816, a riot broke out in Spa Fields, London, and several months later the prince regent was attacked in his carriage. These incidents encouraged the govern-

ment to suspend the right of habeas corpus and prohibit all large public meetings. Still, demonstrations continued, with radical reformers calling above all, for changes in the parliamentary system. On August 16, 1819, a large crowd assembled in St. Peter's Field, Manchester, to listen to a radical orator named Henry Hunt. Attempting to arrest the speaker, the militia charged into the crowd, trampling on hundreds and killing eleven. The event was popularly dubbed the "Peterloo Massacre," in contemptuous comparison to the great victory at Waterloo. The government, terrified that the country was on the verge of a revolution, hastily drafted legislation, that, among other things, restricted public meetings, outlawed "seditious and blasphemous" literature, and authorized the search of private houses for arms.

The government was further convinced that these measures were amply justified when it unearthed the so-called Cato Street Conspiracy in February 1820. A group of extreme radicals, led by Arthur Thistlewood, plotted to murder the entire cabinet at a dinner and set up a revolutionary government. Betrayed by a spy, the conspirators were arrested in a loft in Cato Street, London. Five of them were hanged. The immediate result of the frustrated assassination plot was to provide new support for the government's repressive policies.

In the 1820s, the atmosphere in Great Britain improved dramatically. An upturn in the business cycle and better harvests eased public unrest. The Tory prime minister, Lord Liverpool, reshuffled his cabinet, bringing in a number of younger men more in tune with the times. The new faces in the cabinet included George Canning at the Foreign Office, William Huskisson at the Board of Trade, and Robert Peel at the Home Office. Canning broke with the Concert of Europe and sided with independence movements in Latin America and Greece. Huskisson moved in the direction of free trade by removing commercial restrictions and reducing import tariffs. Peel liberalized the criminal and penal statutes and created a modern police force for London. Furthermore, the government repealed the legislation prohibiting labor unions and removed restrictions against dissenting Protestants and Roman Catholics, allowing them the same rights as Anglicans to sit in Parliament or hold other public office.

On one issue the Tory party would not budge—altering the system of representation in the House of Commons. Whig leaders were almost as hostile to democratic ideals as the Tories. They too believed the masses were unfit to take a responsible part in politics. But they were willing to make concessions for practical ends. By advocating moderate reforms, they hoped to forestall violent mass pressure for further innovations and gain the votes of the newly enfranchised industrial bourgeoisie. The Whigs got their opportunity in the summer of 1830 when King George IV died and was succeeded by his brother William IV (1830–1837). According to custom, the change of monarchs required a new general election. Waging a vigorous campaign in favor of electoral reforms, the Whigs won a narrow majority at the polls. A new Whig ministry headed by Earl Grey came to power.

From 1830 to 1832, the Whigs struggled to push a reform bill through Parliament. The measure was blocked several times by the conservative House of Lords. Earl Grey then obtained a reluctant pledge from King William that if necessary he would nominate enough new peers to assure passage of the bill in the House of Lords. Confronted by this threat, the Lords yielded and in June 1832 the measure became law. The Great Reform Act, as it was enthusiastically called, redistributed seats in the Commons, increased the representation of the new industrial areas at the expense of the depopulated counties, and extended the suffrage to many of the lesser bourgeoisie and leaseholders, as well as to all householders paying the equivalent of £10 a year rent. The number of voters thereby increased by almost 50 percent, from approximately 450,000 to 650,000 persons. The newly enfranchised did not include the great majority of agricultural laborers and industrial workers in the cities. Since the law did not provide for a secret ballot, voters in the smaller districts remained subject to the old electoral methods of bribery, influence, and intimidation.

Although the Great Reform Act was not as democratic as many of its radical supporters would have liked, it represented a turning point in British constitutional history. It established the supremacy of the House of Commons over the House of Lords and elevated the industrial bourgeoisie to the level of the landed aristocracy and divided control of the government between them. Equally important, it created a favorable climate for the orderly achievement of further reforms. Finally, parliamentary re-

form led to a gradual realignment of political parties. The aristocratic Whigs merged with the industrial bourgeoisie, progressive Tories, and intellectual radicals to become the Liberal party. The majority of Tories, together with a few old Whigs and bourgeois elements, formed the Conservative party.

Both parties, showing increasing sensitivity to popular opinion, supported a series of reforms in the 1830s and 1840s. In 1833, Parliament abolished slavery in the British Empire, and in the Factory Act of that year reduced and regulated child labor in the textile industry. A new Poor Law in 1834 ended relief to able-bodied indigents and compelled them to earn their keep in workhouses where they were made to live in primitive and degrading conditions. Unemployment was to be treated as a crime and made so undesirable that individuals would exert every effort to avoid public support. The measure offended humanitarians and was hated by the poor but the general public favored it as a means to reduce taxes and compel the able-bodied to find jobs. The Municipal Corporations Act of 1835 replaced the self perpetuating local bodies with corporations elected by all taxpaying residents. The crowning achievement of this period was the repeal of the Corn Laws in 1846, which greatly reduced the price of bread. As the Corn Laws were the principal redoubt of the protectionists, their repeal meant that the remaining tariffs and other restraints on trade fell in quick succession, so that by 1852 Great Britain was virtually a free-trade country. To be sure, inequalities remained in British society but the means existed by which social

Peterloo
Massacre

Tsar
Nicholas I
imposes
reactionary
repressive regime

Louis
Philippe

Russia's
laws
codified

Repeal of
the Corn
Laws

Whigs
end
Tory
rule

Great
Reform
Bill

changes could be achieved without violence.

CHANGING RUSSIA

Russia entered the nineteenth century lagging far behind western Europe in political, social, and economic development. There were no institutions for popular input in the government: the tsar's will was law. His decrees were enforced by a huge bureaucracy that was corrupt and inefficient. The industrialization of Russia had not yet begun, and the overwhelming majority of the population was engaged in agriculture. The people living on land were divided into two classes, the nobility and the peasantry. The former continued to enjoy its traditional privileges, unlike the aristocracy of western Europe which had seen much of its power eroded. In control of nearly all the land, the Russian nobility was also exempt from military service and from taxation. The great mass of the tsar's subjects, perhaps as much as 95 percent, were peasants and of these most were still serfs bound to the land and without any civil rights. Tsar Alexander I had recognized the need for change but his projected reforms, with

few exceptions, never went beyond the verbal stage.

In contrast to Alexander's ambivalence, the next tsar, Nicholas I, harbored no doubts about the correctness of royal absolutism. Trained as a soldier, he ran the country as though it was an army, expecting his subjects to obey his every command without question. The Decembrist Revolution remained fixed in his mind and thereafter he bent his efforts to forestall any further attempt to change the status quo. To prevent the spread of liberal ideas, the press was censored, schools and universities were supervised, decrees prohibited travel abroad and the entry of subversive literature, and a newly created secret police organization called the Third Section was empowered to arrest and deport suspects without legal process. Nicholas tried to shape public attitudes by establishing an official philosophy. The Russian people were taught to put faith in orthodoxy, autocracy, and nationality—the traditional Orthodox religion, the rule of the tsar, and policies consistent with Russia's unique character.

Although Nicholas would not touch the basic autocratic institutions, he favored innovation and improvements. Under the direction of Mi-

chael Speransky, a brilliant administrator, the Russian laws were codified for the first time in almost 200 years. In 1838, Russia's first railroad was built, a fifteen mile line between St. Petersburg and the tsar's summer palace at Tsarskoe Selo. Nicholas personally disapproved of serfdom but took no steps to abolish it. He did not wish to throw the economy of the country into chaos or incur the wrath of the nobility, the mainstay of his autocratic regime. Nevertheless he ended certain extreme abuses connected with serfdom such as selling members of a single family to different buyers.

Like his predecessor, Nicholas pursued an active and repressive foreign policy. He defeated Persia in 1828 and the following year intervened in the Greek War of Independence. He adopted punitive measures against the Poles after their unsuccessful revolution in 1830–1831, ending what was left of Poland's autonomy and undertaking a campaign to stamp out Polish national sentiment. A champion of the Metternich system, the tsar sent 200,000 troops to assist Austria in suppressing a revolt in Hungary in 1849. For the next five years, Nicholas was almost certainly the most powerful man in Europe.

The Charge of the Light Brigade. Because of a badly drafted and wrongly interpreted order, a brigade of British Light Cavalry was sent to make an open charge against Russian artillery. Of the 673 men who took part in the twenty minute charge, 247 were killed or wounded.

Nicholas's ambition to make Russia the dominant power in the Near East led him to provoke hostilities with Turkey. Britain and France, determined to preserve the balance of power in the eastern Mediterranean, declared war on Russia in 1854. Sardinia, for reasons of its own, joined the Turkish side in 1855. The struggle was confined mainly to the Crimean peninsula where the allies became bogged down in a long, costly siege of the great naval base at Sevastopol. The Crimean War is best remembered for the charge of the Light Brigade at Balaclava and the heroic work of a nurse named Florence Nightingale in organizing field hospitals for cholera-stricken British troops. Both sides conducted military operations with gross ineptitude. The death of Nicholas in the spring of 1855 spared him the agony of witnessing the fall of Sevastopol in September. His son and successor, Alexander II (1855–1881), hastened to conclude an armistice at the start of 1856 when Austria threatened to join the allies. At the Peace of Paris, Russia pledged not to maintain a fleet in the Black Sea or interfere in the affairs of the Ottoman Empire.

Defeat in the Crimean War and acceptance of a humiliating peace discredited the autocratic system enforced by Nicholas I. The war itself showed that the state was corrupt, militarily weak, and economically backward. The feeling became widespread, penetrating even into high bureaucratic circles in St. Petersburg, that Russia had to modernize if it hoped to keep up with other European states. Although Alexander was no liberal, the spreading discontent in the land compelled him to undertake major reforms.

The greatest evil under the old system, most Russians agreed, was serfdom. It was morally reprehensible, contributed greatly to the retention of primitive and wateful methods of farming, and troubled the authorities with nightmares of a mass uprising. Talk of emancipating the peasants had originated in the eighteenth century. Both Alexander I and Nicholas I supported such a policy in theory, but

Florence Nightingale. Born into a wealthy family, she won imperishable fame for her work in tending to the sick and wounded in the Crimea and for provoking sweeping reforms in army medical care and public health nursing.

577

neither had the courage to act. After the Crimean War Alexander II realized the issue could no longer be delayed.

Against much opposition from the landed nobility, Alexander issued an emancipation edict in March 1861. Implemented in stages, the measure freed the serfs and provided them with a certain amount of land which the government had purchased from the aristocracy. The peasants were required to repay the state for their allotments through annual installments (called redemption payments) over a period of forty-nine years. For administrative and fiscal reasons the land was given to the *mir*, or village commune, and not directly to the individual peasant. The *mir* distributed the land, supervised farming operations, and collected payments due to the state. Since the village as a whole was responsible for the redemption payments, no one was allowed to move elsewhere without the permission of the *mir*.

The emancipation edict created hardships for both the nobility and the newly freed serfs. In general, the aristocrats, deprived of their free supply of enforced labor, lacked the initiative, knowledge, and capital to farm their own lands profitably. Many went bankrupt or sold their estates. The peasants, for their part, received inadequate land allotments or were burdened with heavy redemption payments. In many cases, they were condemned to bare subsistence or worse in recurrent famine years. Besides, while they were liberated from the jurisdiction of the nobility, they remained bound to the soil and to village regulations. Although freeing the serfs was the most important humanitarian reform in nineteenth cen-

tury Russia, it produced widespread poverty and universal complaint.

The abolition of the landlord's traditional authority over the peasantry made it necessary to reorganize local government and the judicial system. In 1864, the tsar established elective provincial and district assemblies, or *zemstvos*, on which the nobility, the middle class, and the peasants were represented. These assemblies had charge of such local matters as primary education, public health, the maintenance of roads and bridges, and the encouragement of industry and new agricultural methods. Although handicapped by insufficient funding, they helped significantly to raise the material and cultural level of the country, as well as to provide public-minded citizens with some experience of representative institutions.

In the same year that the *zemstvo* law was passed, Alexander introduced sweeping changes in the archaic and corrupt Russian judicial system. A sequence of lower and higher courts was created. To limit outside influences, judges received state salaries and were appointed for life. All classes were equal before the law. Trials were made public and the defendant had the right to be represented by a lawyer of his own choosing. Trial by jury, based on the western model, was established for serious cases.

While his enthusiasm lasted, Alexander pushed through other noteworthy reforms. He relaxed press censorship, allowed Russians to travel abroad freely, showed greater toleration toward the Jews and other minorities, and altered military service so that all able-bodied males, regardless of status, were drafted into the army. The effect of Alexander's re-

forms was to bring Russia's institutions and practices closer in line with those of the western European nations.

The far reaching innovations introduced by the government encouraged demands for greater liberalization. Alexander was eager to conciliate his subjects but not at the expense of weakening his autocratic power. Once he saw that his critics would be satisfied with nothing less than a parliamentary government he grew resentful and turned his back on reform. Consequently, a wave of unrest spread across the country and discontented elements began to engage in underground activities. These ranged from moderates expressing a desire for a constitution to anarchists who espoused a philosophy of violence taught by Michael Bakunin. One group of extremists, known as the People's Will, had as its goal the assassination of the tsar. After a number of narrow escapes, Alexander decided to call a consultative assembly in March 1881 to consider new reforms. On the day he signed the measure he was killed by a terrorist bomb. The assassination of Alexander ended the era of reform in Russia.

THE BOURGEOIS MONARCHY IN FRANCE

The July revolution of 1830 was followed by the establishment of a constitutional monarchy that was somewhat more liberal than the discredited regime of Charles X and dominated by the bourgeoisie. Before the crown was offered to Louis Philippe, the liberals in Parliament had revised the

Liberal–Nationalist Revolutions throughout Europe

Failure of the Chartist movement in Great Britain

Emancipation Edict

Assassination of Tsar Alexander II

Fall of Louis Philippe

Austria suppresses revolt in Hungary

Crimean War

charter in such a way as to ensure their ascendancy. They abolished hereditary membership in the Chamber of Peers, did away with Catholicism as the state religion, and decreed that the king could not abrogate constitutional guarantees. By lowering property qualifications, the suffrage was enlarged from about 100,000 to 200,000. Nevertheless, only about 3 percent of the adult male population qualified to vote for the Chamber of Deputies. The chief beneficiaries of the new system were the upper middle class—bankers, merchants, and industrialists.

Louis Philippe was a very different monarch from either of his predecessors. He carefully avoided pomp and ceremony and dressed and behaved like a typical prosperous bourgeois. His hard work and instinct for thrift appealed to the masses. Often he could be seen walking the streets of Paris with an umbrella under his arm. Along the way he would stop to shake hands and converse with the common folk. Although his posters proclaimed him the citizen-king, in reality Louis Philippe distrusted the masses and believed that democracy would lead to anarchy.

The monarchy of Louis Philippe made a conscious effort to promote the interests of the bourgeoisie and

to win its sympathy. The government pursued a cautious foreign policy, reversing France's customary authoritative stand in the affairs of Europe. At home it suppressed trade unions, protected the small farmer, and encouraged the growth of industry and the construction of railroads. A wave of prosperity spread over the country.

Notwithstanding his good intentions and respect for the constitution, and the nation's healthy economy, Louis Philippe was unable to win broad popular support. Nationalistic elements disapproved of his pacifist foreign policy and longed for a revival of Napoleonic heroics. The old aristocracy, which had retired from public life, remained faithful to the memory of the Bourbons. Intellectuals and republicans denounced the government for its refusal to broaden the franchise and enact sweeping reforms. More ominous perhaps was the condition of the urban workers who had not shared in the national prosperity. The majority were caught up in the hardships that usually accompanied the first stage of industrialization. They toiled up to fifteen hours a day for meager wages and lived in damp, dirty city tenements or hovels. They were less interested in politics than in protecting their jobs and securing better wages and the right to

organize trade unions. The regime of Louis Philippe paid scant attention to their demands. In eighteen years, it took only two steps to improve the welfare of the industrial class: a measure in 1833 to increase the number of primary schools, and a poorly enforced law in 1841 designed to limit child labor in factories to eight hours. The frustration of the depressed workers expressed itself in a series of strikes and violent demonstrations in the early 1830s. Troops were used to crush each disturbance. By ignoring the social and economic conditions that had produced the unrest, however, the government invited further turmoil.

1848: THE YEAR OF REVOLUTIONS

In 1848 a fresh outburst of revolutionary activity broke over Europe. Among the major powers, only Great Britain and Russia escaped the revolutionary storm, although the former came close to experiencing its fury. The causes of the upheavals varied from place to place, but certain elements were common to most of them. Nationalism was an important factor in the uprisings. It not only inspired the Germans and Italians to make a bid for national unity but also provoked the subject peoples of the Habsburg Empire to seek political independence. Liberalism was another potent force in 1848. The goals of the various liberal groups differed from one area to another. In states controlled by absolute monarchies such as Prussia and Austria, liberals demanded more representative government and abolition of remaining feudal practices. In western Europe, where constitutional government had already been achieved, liberals wanted political power extended to all classes. A general economic crisis heightened the tensions caused by nationalist and liberal movements. The years 1846 and 1847 were marked by crop failures and industrial layoffs. High unemployment and rising prices produced widespread misery. The resultant economic hardships intensified popular discontent with the existing regimes. The upheaval in France in February 1848 set off a chain reaction of revolutionary events in Europe.

The Fall of Louis Philippe

Opposition to the July Monarchy, stifled in the 1830s, revived after 1840 when François Guizot replaced the relatively popular Adolphe Thiers as prime minister. A prominent historian before entering the political arena, Guizot was convinced that only the wealthy middle class possessed the competence to deal with public affairs and the right to vote should therefore be limited to the affluent. To those who cried for an extension of the franchise Guizot's standard reply was "Enrichissez-vous" ("Get rich"). Apart from enjoying the close confidence of the king, he maintained himself in office for eight years (1840–1848) by encouraging business expansion, shamelessly manipulating elections, and by offering jobs and bribes in exchange for support in the Chamber of Deputies. Guizot became the focal point of much of the growing discontent.

A severe economic crisis in 1846–1847 increased working class distress and led to a protest campaign that culminated in the overthrow of Louis Philippe. In the summer of 1847, opposition groups united to stage a series of political dinners throughout France calling for electoral reform and an end to corruption in the government. Annoyed by this agitation, the authorities banned a banquet scheduled for February 22, 1848, in the radical quarter of Paris. On the appointed day, mobs of excited people filled the streets of the capital and sporadic fighting broke out. On February 23, Louis Philippe dismissed Guizot, but that evening a unit of soldiers, guarding Guizot's residence, rashly fired on a crowd of unruly demonstrators, killing and wounding fifty-two persons. The incident set Paris ablaze. With the rebels in control of the city, Louis Philippe abdicated and followed Guizot into exile in England. For the second time in a generation, constitutional monarchy had failed in France.

The Second French Republic

After the downfall of Louis Philippe, political power passed to a provisional government that immediately proclaimed France a republic and or-

Victory to the People. A lithograph by Janet Lange shows the Paris mob invading and ransacking the Throne Room in the Tuileries Palace, February 24, 1848, after the departure of Louis Philippe.

dered the election of a Constituent Assembly to write a new constitution. The government was dominated by moderate elements but included several socialists led by Louis Blanc. A journalist and historian by profession, Blanc wanted the state to guarantee the right of employment and to organize social workshops that the workers themselves would own and operate. The capitalist moderates abhorred Blanc's socialist blueprint but as a measure to calm the passions of the city's poor agreed to set up national workshops. Placed under the supervision of an unsympathetic minister, the workshops functioned as relief projects and not as Blanc had intended. Concentrated in Paris, the workshops enrolled more than 100,000 idle men from the city and the provinces. Although some recruits worked on municipal improvements, most received wages for doing nothing. The impression drawn by the country at large was that the experiment was a costly failure, meant to support an indolent Paris mob.

The growing friction between moderates and radicals led to a bloody conflict. In May 1848, eight million Frenchmen went to the polls to elect a Constituent Assembly. Frightened by the specter of socialism, the aristocracy, bourgeoisie, and peasants (who still made up the bulk of the population) united to choose a Constituent Assembly that was much more conservative than the provisional government. One of the first acts of the Assembly was to dissolve the workshops, viewed as a waste of funds and as a breeding ground of working-class radicalism. The workers and their radical supporters resisted. With the cry of "Bread or Lead," they took to the streets, determined to set up a

true socialist republic in the palace of the existing system. The struggle had the character of a class conflict which accentuated its ferocity. After four days (June 23–June 26) of the most savage street fighting Paris had known, the insurgents were crushed by troops under General Louis Cavaignac. The government followed up its victory with a program of severe repression. Thousands of rebels were executed or deported to penal colonies overseas. All socialist clubs and newspapers were shut down, and Louis Blanc, threatened with prosecution, fled to England.

By November, the Constituent Assembly had completed the constitution for the Second French Republic. Fear of working-class radicalism was evident in the new document. The Assembly declared property inviolable and scrapped the "right to work" clause that had been written in the first draft of the constitution. At the same time, it acknowledged individual rights such as free speech, freedom of the press, and security from arbitrary arrest. It vested strong executive power in a president and provided for a single legislative body, both to be elected by universal suffrage. France emerged from the revolutionary storm as a middle class rather than a worker's republic.

National Resurgence in Italy

After the last failure of the *carbonari* revolts in 1830–1831 three new schools of national thought arose to direct the Italian independence movement known as the *Risorgimento,* meaning resurgence or reawakening. Giuseppe Mazzini, a revolutionary writer and founder of Young Italy, advocated a democratic cen-

tralized republic. Another movement was the Neo-Guelf, which took its name from that of the medieval papal party. Led by the liberal priest Vincenzo Gioberti, the Neo-Guelfs looked to the pope to head a federation of Italian states, each with its own ruler and constitution. Finally, a faction centered around Marquis Massimo d'Azeglio maintained that the solution for a united Italy was a liberal monarchy headed by the king of Sardinia. Each of those schemes was put to the test during the revolution of 1848.

The revolutionary process was already under way in Italy when Louis Philippe's reign came to a sudden end. The revolutionaries struck initially in the Kingdom of the Two Sicilies in January 1848 and compelled King Ferdinand II (1830–1859) to grant a liberal constitution. Within six weeks, Leopold of Tuscany (1824–1860), Charles Albert of Sardinia (1831–1849), and Pope Pius IX (1846–1878) had yielded to similar pressures. Then the revolution spilled over into Lombardy and Venetia, the Habsburg provinces in the north.

The insurrection in Austria, described in the next section, had encouraged nationalists in Lombardy and Venetia to unfurl the standard of revolt. The inhabitants of Milan threw up barricades in the streets and in five days (March 18–22) of furious fighting drove out the Austrians. The citizens of Venice likewise expelled the Austrians and on March 22 proclaimed a Venetian Republic. On that same day, Charles Albert of Sardinia, responding to popular demands, declared war on Austria. As the surge of nationalist fervor swept across the peninsula, contingents of soldiers from all over Italy, including the Papal

581

MAZZINI ON THE ORIGIN AND PURPOSE OF "YOUNG ITALY"

After deep study both of the history and the intimate social constitution of our country, I was led to prefix Unity and the Republic as the aim of the proposed association. . . . I may, however, state that I was not influenced by any mere political conception . . . of elevating the condition of the single people whom I saw thus dismembered, degraded, and oppressed; the parent thought of my every design was a presentiment that regenerated Italy was destined to arise the *initiatrix* of a new life, and a new and powerful Unity to all the nations of Europe. . . . I saw regenerate Italy becoming at one bound the missionary of a religion of progress and fraternity, far grander and vaster than she gave to humanity in the past.

The worship of [ancient] Rome was a part of my being. The great Unity, the One Life of the world, had twice been elaborated within her walls. Other peoples—their brief mission fulfilled—disappeared forever. To none save her had it been given twice to guide and direct the world. . . . Why should not a new Rome, the Rome of

the Italian people—portents of whose coming I deemed I saw—arise to create a third and still vaster Unity; to . . . utter, not to individuals but to peoples, the great word Association— to make known to free men and equals their mission here below?. . .*

Imprisoned as a carbonist in 1830 Giuseppe Mazzini (1805–1872) became disillusioned with the movement, which was handicapped by want of good leaders and the lack of clear-cut principles. While in prison, he conceived of the idea of a new society whose goal would be to incite anti-Austrian and antiabsolutist uprisings and help to create a united Italian republic. Despite his personal magnetism and courage, his efforts at insurrection failed dismally and he proved equally inept as a politician. He fled Italy after the short-lived Roman Republic of 1849 and the realization of his main aim was achieved by other leaders. Nevertheless it would be difficult to overestimate the importance of his role in forging Italian unity.

*Life and Writings of Joseph Mazzini (London: Smith and Company, 1891), Vol. I, pp. 34–38.

were again in control of Lombardy.

The faltering revolutionary movement enjoyed a brief resurgence before collapsing altogether. An uprising in Rome forced Pope Pius to flee, and in February 1849 a republic was organized with Mazzini as the dominant authority. The following month, Charles Albert renewed the war with Austria and invaded Lombardy. Defeated at the Battle of Novara, he abdicated the throne in favor of his eldest son, who became Victor Emmanuel II (1849–1878). From the Two Sicilies where he had sought refuge, the pope appealed to Catholic Europe for help. The newly elected president of the Second French Republic, Louis Napoleon, eager to ingratiate himself with his Catholic subjects, responded immediately. A French expeditionary force overwhelmed the rebels and restored the Papal States to the rule of Pope Pius. Finally, in August 1849, the Austrians put an end to the Venetian Republic after a prolonged siege and bombardment of Venice. Austrian dominance over the peninsula was once more asserted, and the old political order reestablished.

Turmoil in the Habsburg Empire

The semi-feudal Austrian Empire was ripe for revolution in 1848. Its corrupt and cumbersome government, headed by the feeble-minded Ferdinand I (1835–1848), had long ignored the signs of discontent from almost every quarter of the empire. The peasants, who made up the bulk of the population, remained shackled by feudal burdens. The growing middle class wanted a voice in the government and an end to economic controls. Urban laborers suffered from

States and the Two Sicilies, joined Sardinia. Italy, it seemed, was about to be freed from the Austrian yoke.

This hope was quickly extinguished. At the end of April 1848, the pope, who could ill afford to support a war against a leading Catholic power, announced his neutrality. His action cut the ground from beneath those who had looked to him to lead the struggle for Italian liberation. In

May, the king of the Two Sicilies, having routed the revolutionaries and scrapped his constitution, also withdrew his contingents from the war. The Sardinians failed to follow up initial successes and allowed the Austrians to recover their balance and strengthen their forces. On July 24 Austrian forces under General Joseph Radetzky crushed Charles Albert's army at Custozza and within ten days

Location of revolt
Boundary of the German Confederation

KINGDOM OF NORWAY AND SWEDEN

NORTH SEA

BALTIC SEA

DENMARK

RUSSIAN EMPIRE

SCHLESWIG HOLSTEIN

GREAT BRITAIN

HANOVER

NETHERLANDS

Berlin

P R U S S I A

ATLANTIC OCEAN

BELGIUM

HESSE

Dresden

Frankfort

Prague

Cracow

Paris

Baden

Stuttgart

Munich

Vienna

Budapest

FRANCE

SWITZERLAND

AUSTRIAN EMPIRE

Milan

Venice

PARMA

MODENA

Florence

OTTOMAN EMPIRE

PORTUGAL

SPAIN

KINGDOM OF SARDINIA

Corsica

Rome

Sardinia

KINGDOM OF THE TWO SICILIES

GREECE

MEDITERRANEAN SEA

Palermo

Sicily

MAP 65
Principal Centers of the Revolution, 1848–1849. In 1848 revolutions broke out all over Europe, sparing only Great Britain and Russia among the great powers. The uprisings failed, not only because of the strength of the conservatives, but because hostile national minorities fell out with each other and antagonisms developed between the anti-capitalist urban workers and the bourgeoisie. The reactionary regimes quickly recovered their poise and extinguished the flickering flames of liberty and nationalism in the insurgent countries.

economic depression and appalling working conditions. On top of demands for reform, the various ethnic groups throughout the Habsburg realm yearned for a measure of autonomy. Nationalism, the greatest threat to the empire, ran strongest among the Italians of Lombardy and Venetia, the Czechs of Bohemia, and the Magyars of Hungary.

The events in France in February 1848 sparked disturbances across the Habsburg domains, beginning in Vienna. On March 13, a mob of workers and students rioted in the streets of the capital and clashed with soldiers guarding the imperial palace. That same day Metternich, under pressure from the royal family, re-

signed and sought haven in Great Britain. Confused and intimidated by the revolutionaries, Ferdinand promised to grant freedom of speech and to summon a Constituent Assembly. However, Ferdinand reneged on his promise to convoke an Assembly and instead decreed a constitution on April 25. In the face of renewed disorders, the royal family fled to Innsbruck, leaving Vienna in the hands of a revolutionary council. In July, a Constituent Assembly met in Vienna. One of its first acts was to liberate the peasants from their remaining servile obligations.

The revolution spread beyond the capital to other parts of the Habsburg Empire. As we have seen, the inhab-

itants of Lombardy and Venetia drove out the Austrian garrisons and proclaimed their independence. In mid-March, the Hungarian Diet, under the leadership of Louis Kossuth, enacted the March Laws which made Hungary practically autonomous, tied to Austria only through a common sovereign. These laws also abolished serfdom, ended the special privileges of the nobility and church, and guaranteed freedom of religion and of the press. Ironically, the Magyars did not extend the same rights to the Croats and other minorities within the borders of Hungary. The beleaguered Ferdinand reluctantly assented to Hungarian demands for autonomy and several days later granted substan-

583

A Revealing Portrait. In this contemporary Dutch caricature, Pope Pius IX removes the mask of his savior and reveals his true face. Once reputed to be a liberal, the Pope followed a reactionary policy when he resumed power in 1849.

tially the same status to Bohemia. Many of the other subject nationalities also were calling for independence or extensive reforms. Unable to respond to these extraordinary challenges, the Habsburg government seemed on the verge of dissolution.

The tide began to turn in June 1848 when imperial armies crushed the Czechs in Bohemia. A pan-Slavic Congress, which met at Prague early in June, demanded that the Habsburg Empire be converted into "a federation of nations all enjoying equal rights." Nationalistic passions set off serious disturbances, in the course of which the wife of Prince Windischgrätz, commander of the Austrian garrison of Prague, was fatally wounded by a stray bullet. Enraged, Windischgrätz bombarded Prague, forced its surrender, and reestablished the authority of the emperor.

The next step taken to counter the revolution was in Vienna itself. Here a new and more radical uprising had occurred in October forcing Ferdinand, recently back from Innsbruck, to flee again. The violence of the radicals alienated the middle class and the mass of peasantry, who, having achieved their main goal, desired a restoration of order. Windischgrätz, returning from Bohemia, broke into the city and executed the radical leaders. In November 1848, Prince Felix von Schwarzenberg, brother-in-law of Windischgrätz, was appointed chief minister of the Habsburg government. Single-minded and ultra-conservative, Schwarzenberg persuaded the inept Ferdinand to abdicate in favor of the latter's eighteen-year-old nephew, Francis Joseph (1848–1916). Then Schwarzenberg withdrew the concessions made to Hungary, declaring that the new emperor was not bound by the acts of his predecessor.

By the early spring of 1849 only Hungary continued to hold out against the Austrian government. Infuriated by Schwarzenberg's treachery, the Magyars declared Hungary a republic, wholly divorced from the Habsburg house. The Austrian government, exploiting the animosities of ethnic minorities against the Magyars, were joined by an army of south Slavs when its forces invaded Hungary. The Magyars under Louis Kossuth fought with extraordinary courage and drove back the invaders. The new emperor Francis Joseph appealed to Russia for assistance. Tsar Nicholas I complied, fearing the revolutionary virus might spread to Russian Poland unless it was checked. In the summer of 1849, the combined might of Austria and Russia overwhelmed the rebels. Kossuth fled to Turkey, eventually taking refuge in the United States.

A False Dawn in Germany

News of the expulsion of Louis Philippe caused wild excitement in

Germany, where the chances of a successful revolution seemed most favorable. Germany did not suffer from either ethnic disunity or the presence of a foreign power on its soil, but the unhealthy economic situation aggravated discontent. Industrial workers labored twelve to fourteen hours under brutalizing conditions; artisans, facing severe competition from the new factories, saw their incomes fall and their opportunities for employment decrease; and the peasants faced crop failures, debt, and onerous obligations to the aristocracy. In many areas of Germany, the poor in towns and countrysides supported the liberal and nationalist aims of German intellectuals and businessmen.

In the petty German states, changes occurred peaceably, with few instances of violence. The princes hastened to make liberal concessions, relieved that their subjects did not demand republican government. During March and April 1848, the rulers of Baden, Würtemberg, Bavaria, Saxony, Hanover, and other states, called to their side moderate liberals whom they would formerly have ignored or persecuted, established jury systems, relaxed press censorship, and granted constitutional charters.

In Prussia, however, concessions came only after violent street fighting. As tensions mounted in Berlin owing to King Frederick William IV's (1840–1861) unwillingness to accept the demands of liberal reformers, scuffles broke out between troops and demonstrators. On March 18, 1848, during one such incident, a shot was fired and the troops responded with a volley into the crowd. Barricades went up and for two days bloody fighting raged in the streets. Sickened by the bloodshed, Frederick William withdrew his troops from the city and made peace with the insurgents. He accepted a ministry dominated by his most vocal critics and promised to summon an assembly to draw up a constitution.

With the apparent triumph of liberalism in Prussia and in other German states, attention shifted to Frankfurt where a National Assembly convened to debate the future of a united Germany. No government had dared to oppose the nationalists' call for a National Assembly, which had the sanction of the Diet of the German Confederation. The delegates, chosen on the basis of universal suffrage, came predominantly from the educated middle class. Although moderate and sensible, they showed their political inexperience by arguing endlessly over abstract issues. They found it particularly hard to decide on the most crucial question of all, whether the non-German-speaking portions of the Habsburg Empire should be included in the projected German state. Ultimately, the Austrians themselves broke the deadlock by refusing to consider any union

Revolutionary Fighters Resisting Royal Forces, Berlin, March 18–19, 1848. During the street disorders, barricades were constructed from anything that could be found—nearby trees, furniture, pavement stones, barrels and fruit stalls. Most of the insurgents were artisans, but merchants and students also participated in the fighting. When the Berliners emerged victorious they forced King Frederick William to go through a grotesque ceremony of saluting the corpses of slain revolutionaries. Recalling the incident in later life, Frederick William remarked, "We all crawled on our bellies."

FREDERICK WILLIAM TO THE PEOPLE OF PRUSSIA

Taking as a pretense the interests of Germany, the enemies of the fatherland have raised the standard of revolt, first in neighboring Saxony, then in several districts of south Germany. To my deep chagrin, even in parts of our own land some have permitted themselves to be seduced into following this standard and attempting, in open rebellion against the legal government, to overturn the order to things established by both divine and human sanction. In so serious and dangerous a crisis I am moved publicly to address a word to my people.

I was not able to return a favorable reply to the offer of a crown on the part of the German National Assembly [the Frankfurt Assembly], because the Assembly has not the right, without the consent of the German governments, to bestow the crown which they tendered me, and moreover, because they offered the crown upon condition that I would accept a constitution which could not be reconciled with the rights and safety of the German states.

I have exhausted every means to reach an understanding with the German National Assembly. . . . Now the Assembly has broken with Prussia. The majority of its members are no longer those men upon whom Germany

looked with pride and confidence. The greater part of the deputies voluntarily left the Assembly when they saw that it was on the road to ruin, and yesterday I ordered all the Prussian deputies who had not already withdrawn to be recalled. The other governments will do the same.

A party now dominates the Assembly which is in league with the terrorists. While they urge the unity of Germany as a pretense, they are really fighting the battle of godlessness, perjury, and robbery, and kindling a war against monarchy; but if monarchy were overthrown, it would carry with it the blessings of law, liberty, and property. . . .*

There is no doubt that Frederick William would have welcomed the crown of a united Germany if it had been offered freely by his equals, the sovereign German princes. In this address to the nation on May 15, 1849, explaining his reasons for rejecting the crown offered by the Frankfurt Assembly, he made no effort to conceal his disgust with the liberal ideology of the Assembly and with the circumstances that led to its convocation in the first place.

*James Harvey Robinson, ed., *Readings in European History* (Boston: Ginn, 1906), pp. 571–72.

that excluded their non-German possessions. In March 1849 the Frankfurt Assembly adopted a federal charter calling for a constitutional monarchy with a parliament elected by universal male suffrage. The crown of a united Germany was offered to Frederick William of Prussia, but he declined to accept it from a popular assembly. He had no wish to incite Austria to war or, as a believer in authoritarianism, to become head of a democratic Germany. With no other candidate in sight, most of the delegates of the Frankfurt Assembly dispersed in disillusionment.

Before the Frankfurt Assembly disbanded the situation in Germany had changed drastically. The unity of purpose that had made the March revolutions successful broke down. Fear and ill feelings arose among the different classes and nationalities which the reactionary rulers were able to exploit and thus nullify the gains of the revolution. Emboldened by the success of the Austrian government in suppressing the disorders in Vienna, Frederick William struck back in the autumn of 1848. He replaced his liberal ministry with an ultraconservative one and at the same time brought back his troops to Berlin. Finding that his actions had scarcely caused a murmur, he then dissolved the Constituent Assembly and drafted his own constitution, under which most of the political power would remain in the hands of the king. Once in firm control of Berlin, Frederick William sent troops to crush revolutionaries in other German states. The constitutions and reforms granted in 1848 were either revoked or abridged. Many who had participated in the struggle for democratic principles fled to neighboring countries. As was the case in Italy, the revolution in Germany ended with a major defeat for the cause of political freedom and national unity.

Revival of Chartism in Great Britain

Great Britain avoided revolution in 1848 but faced a serious challenge from the radical Chartist movement. This workers' organization grew out of discontent with the Reform Act of 1832. Favoring further political democratization, the group adopted a People's Charter in 1838. The six-point charter called for universal male suffrage, annual parliaments, the secret ballot, equal electoral districts (that is, districts with approximately the same number of inhabitants), abolition of property qualifications for parliamentary candidates, and salaries for members of Parliament. The Chartists promoted their cause by widely disseminating their demands and by holding huge rallies. In 1839 and again in 1842, the House of Commons easily defeated motions to consider the charter. Strikes, riots, and other popular disturbances followed the rejection of the charter, and on each occasion the authorities took stern repressive measures. Thereafter, Chartism lost some of its impetus as its leaders split into two groups, one favoring militant action and the other peaceful means. But in 1848, news of the February uprisings in France encouraged a last ditch effort to invigorate the movement. In April Chartist leaders organized a massive demonstration to present to Parliament a petition embodying their original demands and supposedly bearing six million signatures. The British government, backed by 70,000 constables, forbade the procession but allowed a small party to take the petition to Parliament. On examination, the petition was found to contain about four million forged signatures, including those of Queen Victoria

(1837–1901) and the duke of Wellington. After this fiasco the movement disappeared from the British scene. Chartism failed because of the following reasons: the disunity of its leaders; an upswing in the economy after 1848; trade unionism, which diverted the attention of many workers from parliamentary reform; and perhaps most important of all, the strength of the opposition. Although Chartist demands were considered radical in their day, all but one—annual parliaments—were subsequently enacted into law.

An Assessment of the Revolutions of 1848

Inspired by noble aims, the revolutionary movements of 1848 began with great promise only to end in defeat and disappointment. The revolutionaries gained the upper hand in the opening stages because the European leaders were reluctant to use their superior force. The reactionary governments, however, regained their courage and moved quickly to subdue the uprisings. Another element explaining the failure of the revolutions was the disintegration of the alliance between middle-class liberals and urban workers. The middle class favored reforms that would give them a fair share of political control but were unsym-

pathetic to the workers' demands for social and economic change. Frightened by the excesses of the mob, they abandoned the revolution and in some cases joined the old order in suppressing the workers. The inexperience of popular leaders further undermined the revolution. Through improper planning or bickering, they lost valuable time that the forces of reaction used to prepare a counterstroke. Finally, ethnic rivalries ensured the defeat of nationalist movements in central Europe. In general, the various groups seeking political concessions hated one another more than they hated the absolutist governments that lorded over them.

Although the revolutions ended in failure, they left their mark on Europe. France adopted universal male suffrage. Serfdom was abolished permanently in the Austrian Empire. In Sardinia, Victor Emmanuel kept the liberal constitution his father had granted in 1848. Parliaments were established in all the German states, even if most of them were not democratic. Nevertheless, these gains were slight in comparison to the effort made. After 1848, many middle-class reformers became convinced that violence was not an effective way to reshape society, placing their faith in the British example of gradualism and peaceful change.

SUMMARY

In the wake of the Napoleonic Wars, Great Britain experienced an economic depression that produced social unrest. Frightened by the specter of French revolutionary Jacobinism,

the Tory government responded with stern measures. In the 1820s, as the depression and unrest eased, the government yielded slightly to the pressure for reform. But the Tories would

not budge on the central issue of broadening popular participation in the government. This attitude was instrumental in their defeat in 1830. The new Whig ministry, overcoming several setbacks, succeeded in forcing a Reform bill through Parliament in 1832. The Reform bill was followed by a wave of legislation that helped to transform every aspect of British life.

Practically impervious to western penetration, Russia pursued its own peculiar course during the first half of the nineteenth century. Beginning with Alexander I, the tsars saw the need to modernize their backward nation. Minor changes were initiated during the reign of Nicholas I, a man detested for his heavy-handed repression. Russia's defeat in the Crimean War encouraged his successor, Alexander II, to introduce thoroughgoing reforms. His reign witnessed the emancipation of the serfs, the reorganization of the judicial system along western lines, and the establishment of limited and regional self-government. Before he was assassinated in 1881, he had prepared Russia to take a place among the modern nations of Europe.

During the reign of Louis Philippe, France became the first major country on the continent to move toward democracy. But the process fell short of completion. The king catered to the landed interests, alienating large numbers of his subjects, particularly the distressed industrial workers. The climax came on February 22, 1848, when a street demonstration turned into a revolution. Louis Philippe abdicated, and a provisional government of republicans and socialists took control of the state. In April, a majority of moderate and conservative republicans was elected to the Constituent Assembly, which disbanded the workshops set up by the provisional government. The desperate and poverty-striken proletarians resorted to arms, but they were crushed after four days of savage fighting. The Constituent Assembly then completed a moderate constitution for the Second French Republic.

The February revolution in France had immediate repercussions through-out Europe, encouraging liberals to fight for constitutions and, in areas under foreign domination, for national independence. In the early stages, it appeared as though the aspirations of liberals and nationalists would be achieved. Amid great popular enthusiasm and high hopes, fearful rulers in Italy and Germany readily granted concessions. Furious revolts in Hungary, Bohemia, and the Italian provinces for a time threatened the existence of the Habsburg Empire. The reactionary regimes recovered from the first shock of revolution, however, and moved decisively to smash the revolutions. The insurgents fought heroically but they were no match for regular armies. The failures of the revolutions of 1848 temporarily discredited liberalism and socialism. Nationalism survived and flourished but would take a form far different from the romantic idealism of the pre-1848 period.

SELECTED SOURCES

*Briggs, Asa. *The Age of Improvement.* 1959. A moderate and gracefully written survey of political and social history in Great Britain in the first half of the nineteenth century.

*Dickens, Charles. *Great Expectations* and *Oliver Twist.* Both novels available in many editions. The former is an attack on class distinctions in British society, and the latter paints a vivid picture of the degradation and poverty that accompanied the advent of industriali-zation in early nineteenth-century London. Both novels were produced as motion pictures by David Lean in 1946 and 1948, respectively.

*Duveau, Georges. *1848: The Making of a Revolution.* 1967. Perhaps the best account of the two revolutions in France in 1848.

Lincoln, W. B. *Nicholas I: Emperor and Autocrat of all the Russians.* 1978. A major study of the often reviled tsar.

*Hamerow, T. S. *Restoration, Revolution,* *Reaction: Economics and Politics in Germany, 1815–1871.* 1958. A scholarly account showing how the transformation of the economy, from agrarian to industrial, affected political events.

Howarth, T. E. B. *Citizen King.* 1961. Readable biography of Louis Philippe.

*Langer, W. L. *Political and Social Upheaval, 1832–1852.* 1969. A broad treatment, rich in detail and interpretation.

Mosse, W. E. *Alexander II and the Mod-

ernization of Russia. 1958. Discusses the reforms of the tsar liberator and the beginnings of the revolutionary movement in Russia.

•Namier, L. B. *1848: The Revolutions of the Intellectuals.* Rev. ed. 1964. An influential essay, especially critical of the German nationalists.

Postgate, R. *The Story of a Year: 1848.* 1975. A lively and well-illustrated account as seen from England.

•Robertson, Priscilla. *The Revolutions of 1848.* 1952. An entertaining and thematic treatment, covering the whole range of revolutionary disturbances.

•Rudé, George. *The Crowd in History, 1730–1848.* 1981. Analyzes the make-up of those who participated in the revolutions and what their aims were.

•Stearns, Peter. *1848: The Revolutionary Tide in Europe.* 1974. A sound general study.

•Available in paperback.

THE POLITICS OF NATIONALISM

Standing erect, his gaze firmly fixed on those who were awaiting him, the image of venerable nobility the aged monarch [William I] ascended the dais where he would be crowned, ... There he stood on the very place once occupied by Louis XIV's chair of state, dressed in the uniform of his First Regiment of Foot Guards, adorned with the ribbon of the Order of the Black Eagle as well as a number of other orders, ...

The Crown Prince energetically commanded, "Remove your helmets to pray!", whereupon Rogge, the court chaplain, recited the liturgy according to Prussian military usage, followed by a performance of a soldier's choir. . . .

Then Bismarck, his face pale, wearing tall riding-boots so that he looked like a giant, bowed deeply before the approaching Emperor. On his shoulders he wore the epaulettes of a lieutenant-general, for he had just been promoted to that rank. In his left hand he held his massive helmet, in his right hand the coronation charter, which he read. . . . Then I heard the Grand Duke von Baden shout in a loud voice, "His Majesty Emperor Wilhelm the Victorious, long may he live!" Three times a thundering "Long live the Emperor!" issued from innumerable throats . . . ; flags fell, sabers were drawn from their sheaths, helmets were waved in the air. Again and again the soldiers roared "Hurrah's," almost drowning out the three regimental bands playing "Hail to thee in the victor's wreath!" as loud as they could.

This scene of the creation of the German Empire, described by Bismarck's chief of secret service, represents the culmination of the German people's drive for unification, one aspect of the nationalism sweeping Europe in the middle of the nineteenth century. Taking place in the Hall of Mirrors in Versailles on January 18, 1871, the event symbolized both the final unification of the German states into one nation and the replacement of France by Germany as the most powerful state on the continent of Europe. Nationalism, which had failed to realize its goals in the revolutions of 1848, was thereafter led by shrewd and calculating men who respected power and knew how to use it. Typical was Count Camilio di Cavour, who united most of the Italian Peninsula into a nation-state through diplomacy and war. By the same tactics, Otto von Bismarck forged the many German states into a single political unit under Prussian leadership.

Garibaldi Landing in Marsala, Sicily, 1860. The intrepid Garibaldi with a small army of 1000 volunteers captured Sicily and Naples, opening the way for the unification of most of Italy under the single rule of Victor Emmanuel II. The grey trousers, red shirt, silk neckerchief, and heavy sword made up the romantic costume which he habitually wore and by which he became known across Europe.

In France, already united, Napoleon III's regime displayed a different pattern of nationalism in its attempt to consolidate loyalty to the state. His policies demonstrated how the programs developed under authoritarian institutions could appeal to a broad spectrum of interests at home and promote imperialistic adventures abroad.

Nationalism also showed its destructive face in this period. Napoleon's regime was eventually smashed by discord at home and by the greater nationalistic power of Prussia. In the multicultural Austrian and Ottoman empires, ethnic nationalism steadily dissolved loyalties to the traditional state. Amid heightening international tensions and war, some ethnic groups won their independence, while the others continued to demand their freedom.

FRANCE, 1848–1870

France's experiment with a republic was short-lived in the wake of the political revolution of 1848. Elected president of the republic in 1848, Louis Napoleon Bonaparte seized power in an almost bloodless coup and in 1852 made himself emperor of the French with the title of Napoleon III. The French people quickly supported the rule of Napoleon III (1852–1870), which brought prosperity and order at home, imperialist glory abroad, and prestige throughout Europe. When Napoleon's regime weakened under his mistakes and finally collapsed in the Franco-Prussian War, the French returned to republican government.

From Republic to Empire

After the workers' uprising was suppressed in June 1848, the Constituent Assembly drafted a constitution for the Second French Republic. Although it contained provisions against radical political activity, the constitution was more democratic than any other in Europe, guaranteeing freedom of speech and of the press, the right of assembly, and protection from arbitrary arrest. The constitution provided for a single-chamber legislative assembly and a president, both to be elected by universal male suffrage. To guard against a potential usurper, or "man on horseback," the president was forbidden to seek immediate reelection after his four-year term of office.

In the presidential elections held in December 1848, Louis Napoleon Bonaparte won an overwhelming majority, polling twice as many votes as the three other candidates combined. Nephew of the first emperor of France, Louis Napoleon had grown up in exile, mainly in Germany and England. In 1836 and 1840, as the Bonapartist pretender, he made two farcical attempts to seize the throne from Louis Philippe. Imprisoned in 1840, he escaped in 1846 to Great Britain, remaining there until the summer of 1848 when the situation in France was safe enough to permit him to return. He owed his landslide election victory to his name which to millions of Frenchmen meant order and national glory.

Louis Napoleon may have been sincere when he took the oath of office to uphold the constitution, but he violated that promise before his term had expired. Shrewd and opportunistic, Napoleon used his presidential office to win over important segments of the population. He earned the gratitude of the Catholics by sending troops to restore Pope Pius IX to power in Rome in 1849 and promoting the Falloux law, which increased the church's control over education. By restricting the activities of the radicals, preserving private property, and encouraging business enterprise, he endeared himself to the landowning peasants and bourgeoisie. Nor did he overlook the army, bestowing honors, staging banquets for officers, and distributing much-cherished foods like champagne and sausage to the men in the ranks.

Despite the constitution of 1848, the "man on horseback" now appeared. In 1851, when the Legislative Assembly turned down his request to extend his term of office from four to ten years, he prepared a military coup d'état. On December 2, 1851, the anniversary of Napoleon I's coronation and of his victory at Austerlitz, the French president dissolved the Assembly and proclaimed a temporary dictatorship. Scattered resistance among workers in Paris and in some of the larger towns was quickly overcome, and a plebiscite on December 20 ratified Louis Napoleon's action and authorized him to revise the constitution.

Put into effect in January 1852, the new constitution made the President a virtual dictator, although the government retained the name of republic. This pretense ended on December 2, 1852, when Louis Napoleon, with the sanction of another plebiscite, proclaimed himself hereditary emperor. Assuming Napoleon's son, now dead, would have been Napoleon II, Louis chose the title Napoleon III and the Second Empire was born. Most Frenchmen did not lament the demise of the republic, preferring the security of a benevolent despot to the uncertainties of self-government.

The Second French Empire: The Authoritarian Period

Napoleon III modeled his new imperial regime and its constitutional forms after that of his illustrious uncle. Although the structure of government retained the outward forms of a parliamentary system, the chief of state had almost unlimited authority, controlling the army, foreign affairs, legislation, and finance. The Legislative Assembly, which was elected by universal male suffrage, lacked the power to amend or initiate bills. It could only vote on what the emperor proposed. Elections were rigged to ensure the return of government-sponsored candidates.

Napoleon's rule until 1860 is customarily called the "authoritarian empire." The government kept strict control over the press, forbade the formation of labor unions, and stifled political dissent. No evidence exists that the country at large resented the loss of civil liberties. Napoleon gave Frenchmen what they wanted most, namely, order, prosperity, and glory abroad. His regime was popular with the peasants, still the largest group, the church, and the middle-class property owners. Financiers, industrialists, and professionals occupied the highest political posts and profited most from his favors. Furthermore, the government increased its base of support among the tradition-

ally republican urban workers and even among the aristocracy, who generally regarded Napoleon as an upstart.

The decade of the 1850s in France saw an unparalleled expansion of the economy, brought about at least in part by the government's policies. With a good understanding of practical economics, Napoleon sought to create conditions that would foster economic growth. The state founded banking investment corporations, such as the Crédit Mobilier, which lent large sums of money for business projects. Railroad mileage increased five-fold, steamship lines were founded for overseas trade, and canals built to facilitate commercial traffic. An economic liberal, Napoleon struck at protectionism, lowering tariffs and encouraging a trend towards free trade throughout western Europe. Some French industries suffered and some workers were displaced by outside competiton, but overall foreign commerce expanded by more than 5 percent annually. New business firms multiplied rapidly, particularly after 1863 when a law made investments less risky by limiting the liability of stockholders to the value of their stock. The Second Empire was a hey-day for the entrepreneurial bourgeoisie, many of whom amassed great fortunes and lived in luxury.

While catering to the middle-class, Napoleon also did what he could to better the lot of the urban workers. He built new housing and founded hospitals, societies for the relief of the poor, centers to distribute free medicine, and homes for the aged. The government provided work by inaugurating a costly public works program. The most elaborate of these was the rebuilding of large sections of

Paris under the direction of Baron Georges Haussmann. He ordered slums cleared, constructed a sewage system, erected hundreds of new buildings, and remodeled old ones. He replaced the narrow and crooked alleys that had aided two revolutions with broad streets like the Champs d'Elysée. These avenues were not only beautiful but also too wide for revolutionaries to successfully maintain barricades in the face of artillery and cavalry. Open vistas were dotted with parks, gardens, and historical landmarks. Paris was transformed into the most glamorous city in Europe.

The reconstruction of the capital was but one aspect of the emperor's effort to enhance the image and prestige of France. His court recalled the splendor of the First Empire. His beautiful wife, Eugénie, promoted the arts and as a leader of fashion, made Paris the international center for high society. The Paris exhibition of 1855 proclaimed to the world French achievements under Napoleon III.

Although a pacifist at heart, Napoleon embarked on an aggressive foreign policy, seeking to restore France to its dominant role in European politics. In the Crimean War, he joined Great Britain and Turkey to frustrate Russia's expansionist aims in the Mediterranean. The choice of Paris for the peace conference, was another triumph for Napoleon, who emerged as the arbiter of Europe. Napoleon's interest in national movements also led him to support the liberation of northern Italy from Austria.

During this period, France rapidly expanded its colonial empire. The French completed the conquest of Algeria and began to penetrate west Africa. They expanded their area of

Paris under the Second Empire. Typical of the spectacular face lifting of the city was the Boulevard des Italiens with its broad street lined with trees, sidewalks, and elegant buildings of uniform height. Within the new Paris a kind of generalized social segregation emerged. Haussmann's remodelling project destroyed large areas of mixed housing and replaced them with new apartment buildings far too expensive for the workers. The center of Paris became largely bourgeoisie with the proletariat crowded into their own new suburbs—the "red belt" as it was later called.

control in Indo-China and annexed Tahiti, New Caledonia, and other Pacific islands. By 1860, Napoleon's prestige at home and abroad stood at an all-time high.

The Second French Empire: The Liberal Period

During the 1860s, Napoleon's hold over the French began to crumble. The first signs of trouble came in foreign affairs, where he stumbled from one blunder to another. First, he

became embroiled in an unrealistic scheme to control Mexico as a step in reestablishing a French empire in the western hemisphere. Dispatching nearly 40,000 troops to enforce French overlordship, he had a Habsburg prince, Maximilian, proclaimed emperor of Mexico. The U.S. government, caught in the Civil War, could do no more than protest vigorously in the name of the Monroe Doctrine. When the Civil War ended, the United States threatened to use its formidable battle-trained forces to ex-

1848		1856		1864
Second French Republic established	Louis Napoleon dissolves the Republic and proclaims himself emperor		Austro–Sardinian War	Kingdom of Italy formed	Danish War
Louis Napoleon elected president of the Republic	Cavour appointed prime minister of Sardinia			Bismarck appointed minister–president in Prussia	

pel the French. That prospect, coupled with the cost of maintaining the French garrison in the face of rising Mexican resistance and the menacing turn of events in central Europe, induced Napoleon to withdraw, abandoning Maximilian. Mexican nationalists led by Benito Juarez captured Maximilian and executed him.

Napoleon also fared poorly in Europe. During the Austro-Prussian dispute, as will be seen, Napoleon used poor judgment and was repeatedly outmaneuvered by the wily Otto von Bismarck. Napoleon not only failed to secure territorial compensation for remaining neutral but contributed to the rapid growth of Prussia.

Beginning in 1860, Napoleon compromised his autocratic rule by a series of political concessions that ushered in the "liberal empire." He may have been a sincere liberal who wanted to establish order before developing a constitutional system, but it is more probable that his reforms were in part a response to growing criticism, particularly of his failures in foreign policy. The government relaxed press censorship, legalized strikes, and gave workers a limited right to unionize. A political opposition was permitted to function, the Legislative Assembly gained control of the budget and increased authority over legislation, and the cabinet was made responsible to the Legislative Assembly. The Second Empire appeared to be moving in the direction of a constitutional monarchy similar to that of Great Britain.

The liberalization of Napoleon III's government led to his downfall. His reforms alienated some of the emperor's old supporters without satisfying his critics. Despite a plebiscite in May 1870 endorsing the constitutional changes, the Second Empire rested on a shaky foundation. As a means to ensure the imperial succession, Napoleon took a nationalist stand in a dispute with Prussia. The resulting Franco-Prussian War shattered the Second Empire at a single stroke. On September 2, 1870, the emperor and his army, caught in a trap, were forced to surrender at Sedan, in northeastern France. News of the debacle was the signal for republican elements in Paris to sweep away the discredited regime of Napoleon III and to proclaim a republic. Released by the Prussians, Napoleon joined his family in Great Britain, where he died in 1873.

The Second Empire, for all its faults, did much for France's internal development and set a powerful example in shaping the course of the modern national state. Napoleon III demonstrated to nationalist leaders in other lands, such as Cavour and Bismarck, how to obtain popular support for official policies by emphasizing material progress over political freedom and consolidating national unity and state power through war.

THE UNIFICATION OF ITALY

Before 1848, Italy was a patchwork of petty states, or, as Metternich contemptuously called it, "a geographical expression." The revolution of 1848–1849 gave three main national movements an opportunity to unite Italy, but they failed, leaving Austria more firmly entrenched than ever in the peninsula. After this experience, two nationalist groups were discredited: Mazzini's Young Italy, which had been unable to arouse popular support, and the Catholic liberals who found themselves leaderless when the pope, embittered by the radicalism of Mazzini and his followers, turned ultraconservative. Italian nationalists now looked to the Kingdom of Sardinia to lead the drive for unity. When other Italian states were reverting to reac-

Count Cavour. Few people would have guessed from Cavour's appearance that he was a calculating and devious diplomat. With his benign expression, stocky figure, metal rimmed glasses, and ill-fitting clothes, he looked more like a clerk or shopkeeper than a statesman.

tionary and corrupt rule after 1848, Sardinia's young king, Victor Emmanuel II, retained the liberal constitution granted by his father.

Cavour: Architect of Italian Unity

Using Sardinia as its base, a new campaign for unification began to crystallize under the leadership of Count Camilio di Cavour (1810–1861), one of the most gifted statesmen of the nineteenth century. A wealthy aristocrat with the outlook of a progressive bourgeois, Cavour was not a liberal idealist or romantic dreamer like those who had participated in the revolutions of 1848. A practitioner of tough-minded statecraft, Cavour's great strength was his ability to view things coolly and objectively and to acquire the prerequisites for success before committing himself to a course of action. He did not have an exact blueprint to unite Italy. His immediate aim was to expel Austria from Italy, absorb Lombardy and Venetia, and trust that other annexations might follow later. Cavour recognized that Sardinia, with its five million citizens, was no match for Austria. He had no faith in Mazzini's concept of a spontaneous popular uprising, and was convinced that unification could only be achieved with the help of a foreign power. From 1852 until his death in 1861, with two brief interruptions, he was the virtual ruler of Sardinia, dominating both the monarch and parliament.

As a preliminary step toward his goal, Cavour sought to make Sardinia a model state that other Italians would envy. He subordinated the church to the state, reorganized government finances, and strengthened the army.

With great energy, he tackled the task of developing the economy. He negotiated commercial treaties, removed internal duties, built railroads (which also had strategic value), encouraged new industries, improved agricultural methods, and welcomed foreign capital and expertise. All this, in a brief period, made Sardinia the most dynamic economy in Italy. Cavour became much admired in Italy and throughout western Europe.

Cavour and Napoleon III

Cavour entered into the larger European scene when, to enlist the friendship of Great Britain and France, he sent a small contingent to fight alongside their armies in the Crimean War. Cavour soon saw that his best chance to unify Italy lay with Napoleon III, who was of Italian ancestry and had been a *carboneri* and taken part in the revolts of 1830–1831. Napoleon gave Cavour a sympathetic hearing, but he was reluctant to act because the clerical party in France was certain to oppose any movement that might endanger the pope's temporal rule.

At length the two statesmen reached an understanding. In January 1858, a fanatical Italian nationalist narrowly missed assassinating the emperor and his wife, convincing Napoleon that his life would not be safe unless he actively supported the cause of Italian unity. Napoleon met Cavour and agreed that France would help Sardinia annex Lombardy and Venetia if Austria were made to appear to be the aggressor. In return, Sardinia would cede to France the French-speaking provinces of Nice and Savoy.

Skillfully pursuing a policy of provocation, Cavour incited Austria to declare war against Sardinia in April 1859. Austria's timid conduct of operations allowed the French time to arrive on the scene. As a result, the Austrians were defeated in two bloody battles in June, and driven out of Lombardy.

Suddenly, Napoleon deserted his ally and on July 11, 1859, concluded an armistice with the Austrian emperor, Francis Joseph. The French emperor, who had personally led his troops in battle, was sickened by the carnage, but the more compelling reason for his reversal was his suspicion that he had underestimated the strength of Italian nationalism and that a strong Italian state, on the French border was not in the best interest of France. He was also concerned over the growing unrest among French Catholics and feared that Prussia might be tempted to aid Austria. Austria kept Venetia but ceded Lombardy to France, which then turned it over to Sardinia. Victor Emmanuel accepted the terms, overruling Cavour who wanted Sardinia to continue the war until all northern Italy was liberated. In protest, Cavour resigned his premiership.

The vitality of Sardinia's leadership inflamed Italian nationalism. In the fall of 1859, popular uprisings in north central Italy expelled the governing authorities in Parma, Modena, Tuscany, and Romanga (the northern part of the Papal States). Plebiscites followed in these areas, confirming popular desire for a merger with Sardinia. Napoleon was not enthusiastic about the prospect of so great an expansion of Sardinian territory, but Cavour, now back in office, gained the French emperor's approval by finally surrendering Nice and Savoy. Cavour had no immediate plans to continue the unification process, preferring instead to rest and consolidate Sardinia's new gains.

MAP 66
The Unification of Italy, 1859–1870. With the help of France, Sardinia acquired Lombardy in a war against Austria in 1859. Shortly after, revolutionaries seized power in Modena, Tuscany, Parma, and Romagna and voted to join with Sardinia. The nationalist movement spread south and in 1861 culminated in the creation of a new Italian state that included all but Venetia and Rome. Italy received Venetia as a reward for being Prussia's ally in the Seven Weeks War, and took possession of Rome in 1870 when France withdrew its garrison.

TWO REDSHIRTS' VIEWS OF GARIBALDI

I shall never forget that day when I first saw him on his beautiful white horse. He reminded us of . . . our Savior . . . everyone said the same. I could not resist him. I went after him; thousands did likewise. He only had to show himself. We all worshiped him. We could not help it.*

Born with the instincts of a soldier, Garibaldi took real pleasure in risky and venturesome enterprises. He liked to feel free to act on his own, just as he liked to feel he could rely on blind obedience, simply because he was so supremely confident in his own good luck and his skill in planning and execution. He did not often ask advice, and disliked being given it unasked. He loved liberty and it was what he fought for; yet to meet a real emergency he advocated giving dictatorial powers to a single individual . . . . One thing which did a great deal of harm to Giuseppe Garibaldi was his habit of thinking all men honest, and his assumption that everyone was as selfless and devoted to their country as he was. . . . He liked people to speak only when they had something to say, and yet . . . Woe to those who made him repeat an order or who failed to carry it out precisely. Even his glance had to be obeyed! Yet we all looked on him more as a father than as a soldier or dictator. Merely to see him smile conveyed an idea of how good, how patient and modest, how full of compassion and genuine affection he was to those who were fond of him.**

A charismatic leader, as these descriptions illustrate, Garibaldi had learned the skills of a revolutionary fighter during the thirteen years he spent in South America. He returned to Italy in 1848 and took an active part in the short-lived Roman Republic. Driven into exile, he made his way to New York, where he accumulated a small fortune that enabled him to buy the island of Caprera off Corsica and build a home. Garibaldi reemerged in 1859, convinced that the destiny of Italy was linked to the House of Savoy. Thus, in the interest of Italian unity he sacrificed his republican principles and served under Cavour, a man he distrusted and disliked.

*An unidentified artist, cited in Christopher Hibbert, Garibaldi and His Enemies (Boston: Little Brown, 1966), p. 45.

**Giuseppe Bandi, quoted in Denis Mack Smith, ed., Garibaldi (Englewood Cliffs: Prentice-Hall, 1969), pp. 134–135.

few weeks he was master of the island. Next he crossed over to the mainland and advanced almost unopposed on Naples. Deserted by many of his men, Francis fled, and Garibaldi entered Naples amidst the joyful acclaim of the populace.

The impetuous Garibaldi planned to follow up his swift success with a march on Rome, news that upset the Sardinian authorities. Garibaldi's action was bound to lead to French intervention, since Napoleon III had stationed a garrison in Rome to protect the pope. To forestall this danger, a Sardinian force, under Victor Emmanuel, hastened south to intercept Garibaldi. On the way, the Sardinians, with the tacit consent of Napoleon, seized all the remaining papal territory except Rome and a tiny area around it. When confronted by Victor Emmanuel and his army, Garibaldi yielded gracefully and went back to his farm on Caprera.

Italy was now virtually united. Before the close of the year, the Two Sicilies and the remaining papal provinces of Umbria and the Marches, voted overwhelmingly for union with Sardinia. On March 17, 1861, the Kingdom of Italy was proclaimed with Victor Emmanuel as king. Cavour died on June 6, 1861, at the age of fifty-two, worn out by his strenuous labors.

The political heirs of Cavour cleverly exploited international complications to complete the new Italian state. In 1866, Italy allied itself with Prussia against Austria and attempted to seize Venetia. Although the Italians were defeated, the Prussians won decisively and compelled Austria to cede Venetia as part of the settlement. Four years later, in the midst of the Franco-Prussian War, Napoleon III withdrew his troops from

The Kingdom of Italy

At this point, Giuseppe Garibaldi (1807–1882), entered the picture. A native of Nice, Garibaldi, like many Italian nationalists, was enraged by the cession of Sardinian territory to France. Collecting an army, he proposed to take Nice and hold it against the French. Cavour, however, persuaded him to divert his expedition to Sicily, where a revolution had broken out against the reactionary policy of the new Bourbon ruler of the Kingdom of the Two Sicilies, Francis II (1859–1860). Garibaldi landed in Sicily in May 1860 with 1,000 untrained "redshirt" volunteers. Gathering men as he campaigned, he overcame resistance quickly and within a

Rome. On September 20, 1870, Italian troops took possession of Rome, except for the Vatican and its environs. By plebiscite, the Romans voted to join Italy, and the following year Rome became the capital of Italy. After twelve years of intermittent warfare and an even longer period of complex political maneuvering, the fragmented Italian states had been consolidated into a united, sovereign nation.

THE UNIFICATION OF GERMANY

Unification in Italy was paralleled by consolidation in Germany. After the failure of the Frankfurt Assembly in 1849 the mood of the German liberal nationalists changed from philosophical speculation to cynical realism. Stirred by the events in Italy during 1859–1861, they pursued the cause of German unity with renewed vigor.

Prussia after 1850

Prussia, unwittingly, had already taken a major step towards the unification of Germany with the formation of the German Customs Union, or *Zollverein*, to reduce and regularize tariffs among the states. By 1852, all the German states except Austria had become members of the *Zollverein*, which stimulated economic activity and strengthened middle-class sentiment for national unity. A vast railroad network linked the regions, facilitating the movement of goods (and armed forces) and helping to break down parochial interests. More important, as it turned out, the *Zollverein* paved the way for the political

unification of Germany under Prussia's leadership.

Prussia's position was strengthened by a host of other assets. Its industrial development was phenomenal, changing the predominantly agricultural character of the kingdom. Banks were founded, factories were built, new roads and rail lines transected the country, and small towns grew into thriving commercial centers. All this economic progress was in sharp contrast to conditions in other German states, particularly in Austria, where industrialization had barely begun and communications were backward. Prussia, moreover, had a well-established system of free public schools.

Still, the absence of an enlightened and effective ruler made it unlikely that Prussia would soon extend its hegemony over Germany. At home, Frederick William IV followed a reactionary policy in which he muzzled the press, forbade public meetings, and jailed political opponents. In foreign affairs, Prussia played second fiddle to Austria. When Frederick William invited the north German states in 1850 to form a federal union under his presidency, Austria, backed by Russia, threatened war. Frederick William yielded and agreed to reestablish the old Austrian-dominated German Confederation.

The prospect that Prussia would make a significant contribution to the cause of national unification seemed even more remote during the troubled early reign of William I (1861–1888), Frederick William's successor. William was already sixty-four when he became king and was, if anything, more conservative than his brother. A professional soldier, he was convinced that Prussia's future role in

Germany and Europe depended on its military strength. He supervised a plan to modernize and enlarge the Prussian army, but it was blocked when the lower house of parliament refused to vote the necessary taxes. Apart from not wanting to pay the increased taxes, the liberals, who now dominated that body, feared an all-powerful army. If they could win this test, they hoped to make the monarchy subservient to the legislature, as it was in Great Britain. After two years of deadlock, William was on the verge of abdicating the throne when in 1862 he appointed Otto von Bismarck to lead the fight against parliament.

Bismarck and the State

The man called on to serve as minister-president (equivalent to chancellor or prime minister) of the cabinet was forty-seven years old and a member of the Prussian Junker, landowning aristocracy. Bismarck had previously held various diplomatic posts, including ambassadorships to Russia and France. These assignments gave him valuable political experience and firsthand knowledge of the leaders and conditions in Europe. His loyalty to the king and to Prussia was complete. The idea of forming a new German state came to him only gradually, developing out of his concern for Prussia's power and security. Tough, autocratic, crafty, and master of diplomatic intrigue, he seldom allowed ethical considerations to influence his judgment. In Bismarck's first speech before parliament, he stated bluntly how state business would be conducted: "The great questions of the day are not to be decided by speeches and majority resolutions—therein lay the mistake of 1848 and

Otto von Bismarck. The architect of German unity and one of the most formidable personalities of the nineteenth century, Bismarck was a political genius who was to dominate German and even European politics for three decades. A realist concerned with the application of power, devoid of all scruples or sentiment, he believed that his foremost duty as a statesman was the pursuit of the reasoned interest of the state.

1849—but by blood and iron." As the consummate practitioner of *Realpolitik,* "the politics of reality," Bismarck came to be called the "Iron Chancellor."

When parliament continued to resist the proposed taxes, Bismarck ordered them collected anyway. This was an unconstitutional move, but the Prussian people, habitually deferential to the king and army, paid the taxes without protest. By successfully defying parliament, Bismarck severely undermined constitutionalism and liberalism and ensured that the monarchy would dominate the nation's political life.

War with Denmark and Austria

In 1864, Bismarck saw an opportunity to acquire territory when the Schleswig-Holstein question resurfaced. The two duchies, lying just south of Denmark and populated by a mixture of Germans and Danes, had long been administered by the Danish crown. Holstein was inhabited predominantly by Germans and belonged to the German Confederation. In November 1863, the new Danish king, Christian IX (1863–1906), announced the union of Schleswig with Denmark, causing an

uproar among German nationalists. Preempting action by the confederation, Bismarck persuaded Austria to join Prussia in a war against Denmark. Quickly overpowered, the Danes were compelled to relinquish Schleswig and Holstein. The victors agreed to jointly administer the duchies, Holstein to be occupied by Austria and Schleswig by Prussia.

Austria's turn was next. Bismarck had long concluded that Prussia's advancement required the expulsion of Austria from German affairs. His first step was to isolate Austria diplomatically. He supported Russia's suppression of the Polish rebellion in 1863 and thus gained the tsar's friendship. Hinting at possible French acquisitions of territory in the Rhineland, he obtained Napoleon III's promise of neutrality in the event of an Austro-Prussian conflict. Bismarck completed his diplomatic maneuvers in 1866, when he formed an alliance with Italy against Austria. Italy was to receive Venetia in return for active assistance.

Bismarck had now set the stage to defeat Austria and remove its influence in German affairs. In the summer of 1866, Bismarck goaded Austria into declaring war by expressing disapproval of Austria's administration of Holstein and ordering Prussian troops into the duchy. With a population twice that of Prussia and with the support of most of the German states, Austria was expected to win. However, Austria was unprepared for war and further handicapped by having to fight on two widely separated fronts. By contrast,

MAP 67

The Unification of Germany, 1864–1871. Prussia, under Bismarck's leadership, brought about the unification of Germany in three stages. In 1864 Prussia and Austria defeated Denmark over the Schleswig-Holstein issue. Prussia then crushed Austria in a short war in 1866 and the next year set up the North German Confederation which was headed by its king. Following Prussia's victory over France, the south German states joined the North German Confederation which, together with the provinces of Alsace and Lorraine, completed the formation of the German Empire.

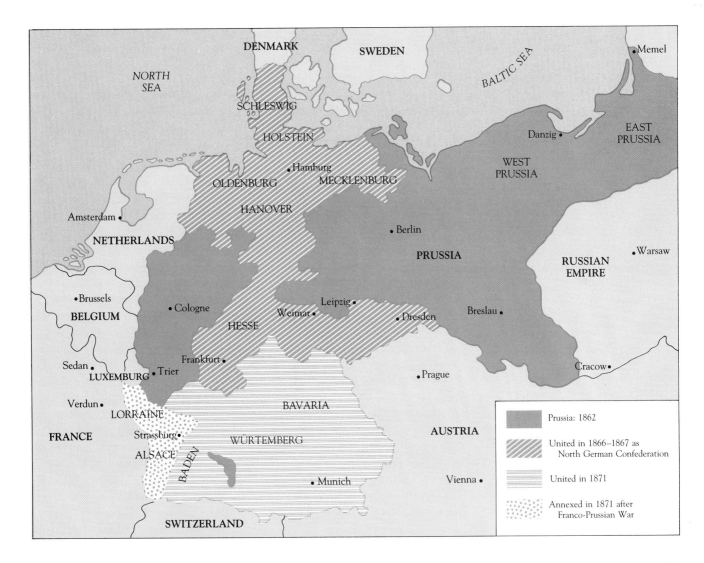

Legend:
- Prussia: 1862
- United in 1866–1867 as North German Confederation
- United in 1871
- Annexed in 1871 after Franco-Prussian War

THE EMS DISPATCH, JULY 1870

The Original Message

[William I's Telegram:] M. Benedetti [the French ambassador] intercepted me on the Promenade in order to demand of me most insistently that I should authorize him to telegraph immediately to Paris that I should obligate myself for all future time never again to give my approval to the candidacy of the Hohenzollerns should it be renewed. I refused to agree to this, the last time somewhat severely, informing him that one dare not and cannot assume such obligations. . . .

[Heinrich Abeken's relay to Bismarck:] His Majesty himself, . . . decided not to receive the French envoy again but to inform him through an adjunct that His Majesty had now received from the Prince confirmation of the news which Benedetti had already received from Paris, and that he had nothing further to say to the Ambassador. His Majesty leaves it to the judgment of Your Excellency whether or not to communicate at once the new demand by Benedetti and its rejection to our ambassadors and to the press.

Bismarck's Edited Version

After the reports of the renunciation by the hereditary Prince of Ho-

henzollern had been officially transmitted by the Royal Government of Spain to the Imperial Government of France, the French Ambassador presented to His Majesty the King at Ems the demand to authorize him to telegraph to Paris that His Majesty the King would obligate himself for all future time never again to give his approval to the candidacy of the Hohenzollerns should it be renewed.

His Majesty the King thereupon refused to receive the French envoy again and informed him through an adjunct that His Majesty has nothing further to say to the Ambassador.*

The edited version of the telegram was released for publication in France on July 14, Bastille Day. The resulting commentary on it by sensational newspapers so inflamed popular passions that it created an atmosphere in which compromise and reason became impossible. Napoleon III was hesitant about declaring war but second thoughts were swept away by nationalist hysteria and his own belligerent cabinet.

*Louis L. Snyder, *Documents of German History*, (New Brunswick, N.J.: Rutgers University Press, 1958), pp. 215–216.

the newly reformed Prussian army was in a high state of efficiency. It was led by General Helmuth von Moltke, a master strategist, and equipped with breech-loading rifles called needle guns, which fired six times as fast as the old muzzle-loading type used by the Austrians.

The conflict, popularly called the Seven Weeks War, was brief. With astonishing speed, the Prussian army broke the resistance of the German states before they had time to join hands with the Austrians. Then, using the railroads, Prussian columns converged on the main concentration of Austrian troops in Bohemia. At Sadowa on July 3, 1866, the Prussians won a decisive victory and Austria sued for peace.

Bismarck wisely offered Austria lenient terms. He had gotten what he wanted—the exclusion of the Habsburgs from German affairs—and he saw no reason to make Austria a permanent foe. Austria had to pay a small indemnity, consent to the dissolution of the German Confederation, and recognize Prussia's territorial gains in the north. In a separate settlement, Austria gave up Venetia.

The North German Confederation

The Seven Weeks War also changed the configuration of Germany. Together with Schleswig and Holstein, Prussia annexed Hanover, Nassau, Hesse-Cassel, and the free city of Frankfurt. These acquisitions closed the gap between Prussia's eastern and western provinces and raised its population by nearly 5 million to a total of 24 million. To replace the defunct German Confederation, Bismarck set up the North German Confederation, embracing all the German states north of the river Main. The twenty-two component states retained autonomy in domestic matters, but conduct of foreign policy and control of the military forces were in the hands of the president of the confederation, the king of Prussia. The four states south of the river Main—Bavaria, Würtemberg, Baden, and Hesse-Darmstadt—were free to organize as they chose. They were Catholic and had no desire to form a union with Prussia. Bismarck was content to bide his time until they were ready to come in on their own. He did, however, negotiate defensive alliances with all four states, obligating them to join Prussia if it were attacked.

In four years in office, Bismarck

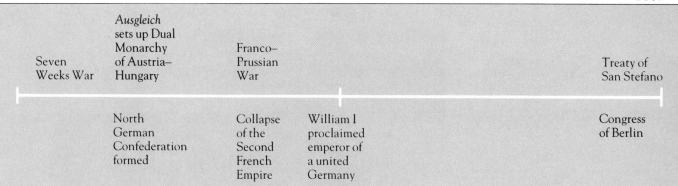

used pride in Prussian nationalist accomplishment to overwhelm liberalism and arrest the development of parliamentary government. The liberals, who had savagely condemned Bismarck for his authoritarian ways, with a few exceptions turned into submissive admirers. In August 1866, Bismarck asked and received from the legislature retroactive assent for his unconstitutional measures of the previous years.

The Franco-Prussian War and the Establishment of the German Empire

With Austria out of the way, Bismarck turned his attention to France. Bismarck was convinced that only a conflict with France would ignite the nationalistic feelings of the south German states and induce them to join the Prussian-dominated North German Confederation. All that remained was to get France to declare war so that Prussia would not appear to be the aggressor. There was never any doubt in Bismarck's mind that when war came, Prussia would emerge victorious.

Bismarck was aided in his designs by the situation in France. The spectacular expansion of Prussian power had filled Napoleon III and his countrymen with alarm. Napoleon believed that an Austro-Prussian war would be a long drawn-out affair that would leave both sides exhausted. France would then step forward as mediator and claim territory on its northwestern frontier. Napoleon, like most other Europeans, was shocked by Austria's sudden defeat. Napoleon's critics blamed his government for failing either to prevent it or to exact some kind of territorial compensation such as France had received during the unification of Italy. Coming on the heels of the Mexican fiasco, the diplomatic reverse in Germany impelled Napoleon to do something dramatic, preferably at the expense of Prussia, if his regime were to survive.

Napoleon's opportunity to retrieve his prestige and save his dynasty came in the summer of 1870 when Leopold of Hohenzollern, a distant relative of William I, accepted the throne of Spain. Horrified at the prospect of a Hohenzollern monarchy on its southern border, France protested vehemently. William, against Bismarck's advice, persuaded Leopold to withdraw his acceptance. Napoleon, not content with his diplomatic victory, made further demands. The French ambassador was sent to Ems, a spa in western Germany, to seek assurances from William that Leopold's candidacy would not be renewed in the future. The Prussian king firmly but politely refused to give any such commitment, after which he forwarded an account of the interview to Bismarck in Berlin. Bismarck saw an opportunity, as he described it, to "wave a red flag" before "a Gallic bull." He edited the Ems dispatch to make it appear as if the French ambassador and the Prussian king had insulted each other and leaked it to the press. Indignation flared up in both nations but it was the French government that decided upon war in July 1870.

In the ensuing Franco-Prussian War, France, diplomatically isolated by Bismarck, fought alone. By showing proof of Napoleon's designs on the Rhineland and alluding to the defensive alliance, Bismarck brought in the south German states on Prussia's side. The French army, although reputed to be the best in the world, was in fact poorly organized and led by officers wedded to antiquated concepts. On the other hand, Prussia's forces were superbly trained and equipped, and its general staff, its skills sharpened by the Danish and Austrian experiences, had been planning this war for nearly three years.

Effective French resistance collapsed in a matter of weeks. Von

Napoleon III and Bismarck after the battle of Sedan. His army beaten, Napoleon clung to the hope that his personal intervention with the Prussian King would mitigate the surrender terms. On his way to Prussian headquarters Napoleon encountered Bismarck who had been forewarned of his coming. The two men greeted one another politely, then walked over to a wayside cottage and sat on chairs by the door. Bismarck steered the talk into political channels for he was determined not to allow the French Emperor to see William I until the terms of capitulation had been signed.

Moltke's forces poured into France and bottled up one large French army in the fortress of Metz. In attempting to relieve Metz, an army personally led by Napoleon III was encircled at Sedan and hammered by artillery fire until it capitulated on September 2. In October the French army at Metz surrendered. Major fighting was over, although Paris held out until January 28, 1871.

Unlike Austria, defeated France was severely punished by the Prussians. By the terms of the Treaty of Frankfurt, France had to pay an indemnity of 5 billion francs and cede to Germany Alsace and part of Lorraine. The defeat and the treaty terms instilled in the French a burning hatred and a desire for revenge.

On January 18, 1871, ten days before Paris fell, William I was proclaimed emperor of Germany at Versailles. The new German empire included the North German Confederation, the four southern states, Alsace, and part of Lorraine. In less than eight years, Bismarck had forged German unity by outwitting rivals, exploiting rapidly changing events in Europe, and engaging in three brief wars. As a reward for his service, he was appointed the first imperial chancellor, a post he held for the next nineteen years.

ETHNIC NATIONALISM IN CENTRAL AND SOUTHEASTERN EUROPE

In Austria-Hungary, loyalty to the dynasty and to the Catholic church were unifying forces that created feelings of common interest among the various ethnic groups of the Habsburg realm. Nationalist leaders wanted to gain a greater voice for their people within the empire, not to destroy it. The situation was different in the Ottoman Empire, where the majority of the inhabitants in the Balkans were European in speech and Christian in religion. Inspired by western ideas of freedom and secularism resulting from increased contact with western Europe and responding to continued Turkish oppression and corruption, various Christian groups resorted to arms in a bid for independence.

The Creation of the Dual Monarchy of Austria-Hungary

The revolutions of 1848–1849 had shown grave dissatisfaction among Austria's subject nationalities with a form of government that failed to recognize their historic rights or make allowances for their cultural differences. The best way to avoid disruptions in the future would probably have been to create a federal system that would have granted the principal ethnic groups local autonomy. The young Habsburg monarch, Francis Joseph, however, although honest and hardworking, was a staunch autocrat. Instead of working with the non-German areas of the empire, Francis Joseph and his leading officials adopted a policy of absolutism and centralization in an attempt to transform the Habsburg realm into a true nation-state. They abolished the provincial diets and placed local administration in the hands of officials sent out from Vienna. They also inaugurated an intense program of Germanization,

making German the only official language and the chief language of instruction in higher education.

The new imperial scheme provoked sharp nationalist resentment, most of all among the Magyars (Hungarians), the largest non-German group. Their attitude contributed significantly to Austria's defeat during the Austro-Sardinian War of 1859, when their discontent reached such alarming proportions that the Austrian government was afraid to withdraw its troops from Hungary for use in battle.

In an attempt to placate the disaffected non-Germans, Francis Joseph established a new, partially decentralized constitutional system with provincial diets and a *Reichsrat*, (imperial diet). In the eyes of the non-German majority, the new constitution had serious flaws. It left the emperor with supreme authority, assured German domination of the *Reichsrat* and limited the power of the provincial diets. From the beginning, the Magyars refused to send delegates to the *Reichsrat* and insisted on concessions that would make them virtually independent.

With Austria's embarrassing defeat by the Prussians in 1866, however, Francis Joseph, now dependent on the good will of the Magyars, approved the *Ausgleich* (Compromise) in 1867, which recognized the Magyars as equal partners within the empire. The *Ausgleich* transformed the Habsburg kingdom into the Dual Monarchy of Austria and Hungary. The two parts of the empire had a common sovereign, the head of the House of Habsburg, and common ministers of foreign affairs, defense and finance. Otherwise, Austria and Hungary were autonomous, each with

its own constitution, parliament, and official language.

The new settlement met the wishes of the Magyars but offered few concessions to the other subject nationalities, who, taken together, made up a majority in each state of the Dual Monarchy. For the next half century, ethnic nationalist conflicts would dominate the internal politics of Austria-Hungary.

Tumult in the Balkans

The growing ethnic nationalism that weakened the Habsburg monarchy during the nineteenth century tore the Ottoman Empire apart. Comprised of many nationalities, religions, and traditions, the sprawling Ottoman state was a theocratic absolutism, ruled by a sultan. The once powerful empire had begun to crumble in the eighteenth century because of internal conflicts, corruption, and inefficiency. By the beginning of the nineteenth century this process of decay was so advanced that the empire's complete dissolution appeared imminent. Like greedy relatives waiting for the death of a wealthy uncle, each of the great powers stood ready to claim a good share of the Ottoman estate.

Had the great powers cooperated as did the interested parties that carved up Poland in the eighteenth century, the Ottoman Empire would have ceased to exist. Russia, eager to acquire a warm water port and access to the Mediterranean, was prepared to hasten the death of "the Sick Man of Europe." Other powers, however, feared a Russian advance in the Balkans. Austria was concerned that Russia would create a great Slavic state that would eventually absorb the Slavs

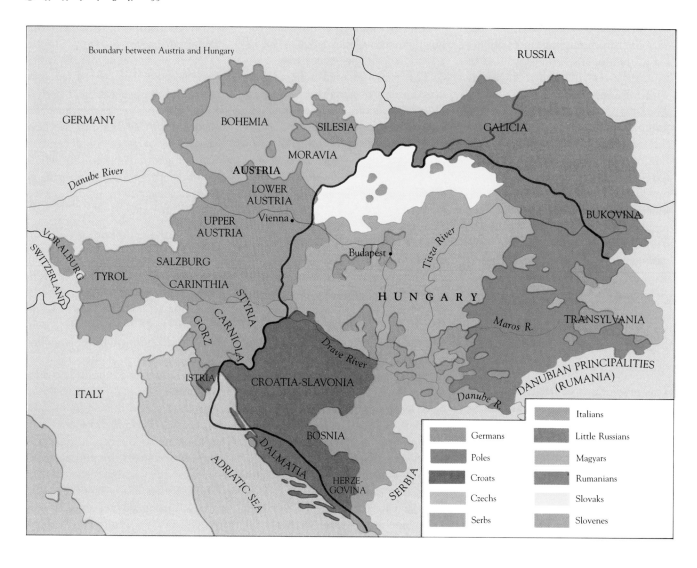

MAP 68

The Dual Monarchy in 1867. Austria and Hungary were on an equal footing and the division was fairly even with respect to territory and population. Austria included the Slovenes, Czechs, Poles, Ruthenians, and some Italians; Hungary, the Slovaks, Croats, Serbs, and Rumanians. The main flaw in the Compromise of 1867 was that it did nothing to solve the nationalities question. It had the long run effect of converting the desire of the subject nationalities for autonomy within the empire into a desire for independence from the empire.

of the Habsburg realm. Great Britain believed that a Russian warm water port would threaten British maritime interests in the Mediterranean. Similarly, France had no wish to see Russia expand southward. Thus rivalry among the European powers helped to extend the life of the Ottoman Empire.

Although the powers were partially successful in preventing the dismemberment of Turkey from without, they had little effect on the

disruptions inside the empire. During the nineteenth century, the subject peoples in the Balkans, most of whom were Christians, became increasingly restive and sought to gain their freedom. By the 1860s, the sultan's government had been compelled to acknowledge the independence of Greece and to grant internal autonomy to Serbia and Rumania. In 1875, the inhabitants of Bosnia and Herzegovina attempted to assert their independence, and within a few months the revolt had spread to Bulgaria. The sultan's armies suppressed these uprisings with massacres.

Turkish atrocities in Bulgaria gave the Russians an excuse to intervene in the Balkans in 1877 to protect the Christian minorities. The Turks put up a stubborn fight, holding the Russians at bay at the fortress of Plevna in Bulgaria for almost six months. At length, the Russians broke through and advanced to within a day's march of Istanbul. At this point, worried that other powers would intervene on behalf of Turkey, the tsar hastily concluded the Treaty of San Stefano with the sultan. The agreement recognized the creation of a large autonomous Bulgarian state under Russian protection and complete independence for Serbia, Rumania, and Montenegro. The European powers, however, were alarmed at the prospect of Russia assuming jurisdiction over so large a portion of the Balkans and insisted on an international conference to reconsider the treaty of San Stefano.

The Congress of Berlin in 1878 was the most distinguished gathering of European statesmen since the Vienna Congress of 1814–1815. The Treaty of Berlin confirmed the independence of Serbia, Rumania, and Montenegro. The Bulgaria that Russia had designed was reduced by two-thirds and deprived of access to the Aegean Sea. Austria received the right to administer the Turkish provinces of Bosnia and Herzegovina. Russia gained little besides Bessarabia, which

The Congress of Berlin, 1878. The painting is by Anton von Werner, a contemporary artist. Seated on the left is Prince Gorchakov, the Russian foreign minister, clasping the arm of Disraeli, the British prime minister. Bismarck, the chairman and host of the conference, is in the center foreground with Count Andrassy, the Austro-Hungarian foreign minister, on his right and Count Shuvalov, the Russian ambassador to Berlin, on his left. In the right rear, with the bald head, is Lord Salisbury, British foreign secretary, flanked by the Turkish emissaries.

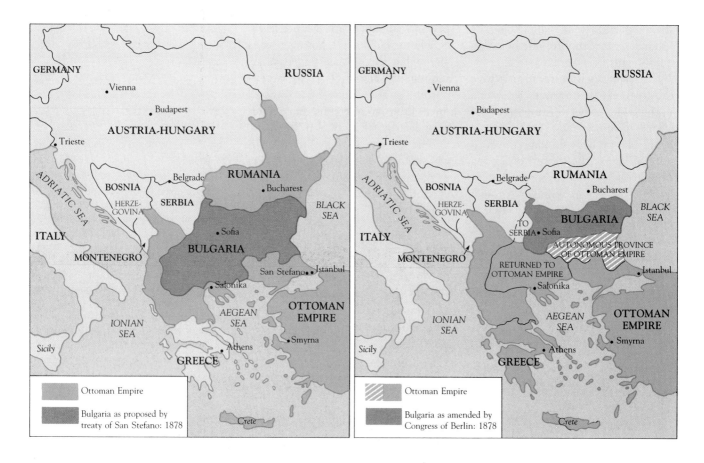

MAP 69

Southeast Europe in 1878, before and after the Congress of Berlin. The main feature of the Treaty of San Stefano was the creation of a large Bulgarian state that would stretch from Macedonia to Salonika and which would be occupied by Russian troops for two years. The treaty was unacceptable to the western powers, in particular Great Britain, since it threatened to make Russian influence paramount in the Mediterranean. The Congress of Berlin revised the treaty, dividing Bulgaria into three zones with varying degrees of autonomy, all nominally within the Ottoman Empire: the principality of Bulgaria, administered by a Christian governor but under the suzerainty of the sultan; East Rumelia which was to remain under the "direct authority" of the sultan; and Macedonia which was returned to the Ottoman government.

it had lost in 1856, and several districts in the Caucasus. In a separate agreement, the Ottoman Empire ceded Cyprus to Great Britain in return for a pledge of aid if it were attacked.

The Treaty of Berlin avoided another Crimean War, but it left many continuing problems for later statesmen to deal with. Few of the participants and beneficiaries were satisfied. Russia had been deprived of the fruits of its victory. The Ottoman Empire had lost most of its territory in Europe, and what remained was in a precarious, exposed condition, a constant temptation for covetous neighbors. The freed Balkan states were angry because they had received less territory than they claimed. Finally, the treaty failed to safeguard the rights of Christian minorities still under Turkish rule. In the years that followed, the entire Balkan region was to remain a hotbed of militant nationalism, seething with intrigues, rivalries, and disorders.

SUMMARY

As president of the Second French Republic, Louis Napoleon quickly revived the empire, proclaiming himself Napoleon III. During the first half of Napoleon's rule, the nation was relatively content. Napoleon's government subsidized economic expansion and won military glory, compensating for the absence of political freedom. After 1860, however, Napoleon encountered diplomatic reverses and the mood of the country changed ominously. To pacify growing domestic unrest, Napoleon gradually transformed his empire into a constitutional monarchy. Just when he appeared secure he blundered into a war with Prussia. The surrender of French forces at Sedan triggered an internal insurrection that deposed him and restored republican government.

Count Cavour, the liberal prime minister of Sardinia, recognized that Italian unity could not be achieved without foreign assistance. He won the support of Napoleon III in a successful war against Austria, and as a result Sardinia acquired all the north Italian states except Venetia. In 1860 Garibaldi and his small band seized control of Sicily and southern Italy. Garibaldi turned over his conquests to Sardinia and in March 1861 the Kingdom of Italy was announced. The process of unification was completed when Italy acquired Venetia in 1866 and Rome four years later.

During the 1850s German unification seemed far away, but the situation changed quickly after the Prussian king, William I, appointed Otto von Bismarck as minister-president in 1862. A master of power politics, Bismarck instigated three wars in six years. Each was carefully planned and successfully concluded and each brought Prussia closer to its goal. The first against Denmark enabled Prussia to share with Austria the administration of Schleswig and Holstein. A dispute over Schleswig and Holstein led to a brief, successful conflict with Austria in 1866. With Austria expelled from German affairs, Bismarck formed the North German Confederation. After Bismarck goaded Napoleon III into declaring war, the superior Prussian army quickly triumphed. At the moment of victory, the German states federated into the German Empire, now enlarged by the provinces of Alsace and Lorraine acquired from defeated France.

Whereas nationalism promoted the unity of Italy and Germany it was pulling apart the Austrian and Ottoman empires along ethnic lines. Prussia's military victory in the Seven Weeks War compelled the dominant German minority in Austria to take into partnership the restless Magyars of Hungary. The *Ausgleich*, however, failed to provide for the interests of the other ethnic groups that formed a majority in the empire. The suppressed minorities of the Ottoman Empire became nationally conscious during the nineteenth century, and over the years one group after another emerged as an independent nation. As the various ethnic groups sought to fulfill their nationalist aspirations, the Balkan political scene would be dangerously inflamed by the rivalry of the great powers.

SELECTED SOURCES

*Crankshaw, Edward. *Bismarck*. 1981. A lively account, rather critical of the Iron Chancellor.

Gooch, Brison D. *The Second Empire: the Reign of Napoleon III*. 1969. A well-informed study.

*Howard, Michael. *The Franco-Prussian War*. 1967. A fascinating and meticulously researched study by a leading British military historian.

Kann, Robert A. *The Multinational Empire*. 2 vols. 1950. Highlights the searing force of nationalism in the Habsburg Empire.

*Lampedusa, Giuseppe de. *The Leopard*. Various editions. A historical novel set in Sicily at the time of Garibaldi's landing in 1860, focusing on the changes being experienced by an aristocratic family; also a 1963 film by Lucino Visconti.

Miller, William. *The Ottoman Empire and Its Successors*. 1948. A standard work.

*Pflanze, Otto. *Bismarck and the Development of Germany*. Vol I. 1963. A valuable work covering the period from 1815 to 1871.

Ridley, Jasper G. *Garibaldi*. 1974. A judicious and balanced biography of the colorful Italian patriot.

Smith, Denis Mack. *The Making of Italy, 1796–1870*. 1968. A scholarly overview of the Italian problem in the nineteenth century.

Smith, Denis Mack. *Victor Emmanuel, Cavour and the Risorgimento*. 1971. A valuable analysis of the relationship of the two figures and their contributions.

Smith, William H. C. *Napoleon III*. 1973. Discusses the contradictory features of the man.

*Stavrianos, Leften S. *The Balkans, 1815–1914*. 1962. Good survey of the troubled area.

*Zola, Emile. *Germinal*. Various editions. A novel dealing with the plight of coal miners during the Second Empire.

*Available in paperback.

DOMESTIC REFORM AND SOCIAL STRIFE BEFORE WORLD WAR I

. . . from my balcony, I could see a large crowd moving. . . . [including] many intellectuals, women, and children. Before ten minutes were over shots resounded in the direction of Troitzky Bridge. One bullet whizzed past me, another one killed the porter of the Alexander Lyceum. The next thing I saw was a number of wounded being carried away from the scene in cabs, and then a crowd running in disorder with crying women here and there. . . . There was no one present to speak to the workmen and make an attempt to bring them to reason. I do not know whether the same thing happened everywhere, but on the Troitzky Bridge the troops fired rashly and without rhyme or reason. There were hundreds of casualties in killed and wounded, among them many innocent people. . . . the workmen were completely alienated from the Czar and his government.

The above spectacle, described by Count Serge Witte on "Bloody Sunday," January 22, 1905, was the Russian government's answer to petitions for reforms by its downtrodden workers. European industrialization had rapidly produced an urban working class that was poorly paid and wretchedly housed. Since factory owners were reluctant to raise wages and improve working conditions, workers gradually organized themselves in various ways to face the entrenched power of capital. The result was an emerging class struggle in industrializing nations late in the nineteenth century.

In many nations, labor agitation was intertwined with political and social change. The years from 1830 to 1870 in European political life had seen the rise of liberal, constitutional governments dominated by the bourgeoisie. From 1871 to 1914, particularly in western Europe, governments moved toward universal suffrage, partly from the desire to placate the increasingly restless urban workers. The period after 1871 also witnessed the introduction of social welfare legislation. Both for humanitarian reasons and to deflect the growing interest of the workers in socialism, governments assumed responsibility for the social and economic

CONTENTS

Ulster Anti-Home Rule Demonstration. The leader of the Ulster forces in Parliament, Sir Edward Carson, center, is being cheered upon his arrival at a rally against Home Rule. A ruthless and brilliant politician, single-minded in his hatred of home rule, Carson was ready to challenge the constitutional authority of the British Liberal government. To carry out his goal he had the sympathy and financial backing of the Conservative party as well as a private army of 100,000 men in Ulster.

611

problems arising from industrialization. In so doing they laid the foundations for the modern welfare state.

This chapter deals primarily with domestic affairs, first discussing the labor movement and its attraction to socialism, which came to play an increasingly important role in the political life of Europe and the United States. It then examines how Europe faced the challenges of political and social change, proceeding from nations that established the most successful liberal governments to those in which authoritarian elements still predominated as of 1914.

THE RISE OF TRADE UNIONS AND SOCIALISM

By the latter half of the nineteenth century, the Industrial Revolution was well established across Europe and in the United States. With it had come labor exploitation. Factory workers received low wages for toiling long hours in dismal, unsanitary and unsafe factories. Their work was dull and impersonal. No job security existed; during cycles of economic depression, workers would frequently find themselves unemployed and reduced to even greater misery. They did not suffer passively, however. By the middle and later nineteenth century, larger and larger numbers of workers were taking action to improve their lives.

Labor Organizes

One way the working class tried to better its lot was by forming labor unions and participating in collective bargaining. Early labor unions were weak, localized, and usually short lived being opposed by the employers and prohibited by law. Unions did not achieve legal recognition in Great Britain until 1871, in France until 1884, and in Germany until 1890. In the United States, they remained in constitutional limbo until 1935. For a generation after 1850, the labor movement was organized by craft—skilled workers in the same trade. The craft unions aimed modestly at improving the wages and working conditions of their own members by peaceful negotiations and resorted to strikes only in desperation.

In the 1870s and 1880s a new type of labor organization came into existence, the industrial union, which was not limited to members of a single craft or to those with highly technical skills, but included all the workers, including the unskilled, in any given industry. The industrial unions engaged in strikes, boycotts, and violence against strikebreakers, and some were closely associated with radical ideologies. In the pre-World War I decades, many large strikes took place throughout Europe and the United States as unions sought, sometimes successfully, to redress grievances and improve wages for their members. Once workers found that unions could obtain real and immediate gains through collective bargaining, they flocked to them in great numbers. Between 1910 and 1913, trade union membership rose from 2 million to 4 million in Great Britain, from 850,000 to 3 million in Germany, and from 250,000 to 1 million in France. In the United States, membership reached 2,700,000 by 1913.

As unions grew stronger, they gained political influence. By 1900, all the major nations, with the exception of Russia, contained broadly based, if not always democratic, electoral systems. Workers used their access to the ballot to pressure governments to recognize their right to strike and to deal with the social consequences of industrialization. Through their political power, they managed to generate a number of reforms for the working class.

Socialism, Syndicalism, Anarchism

Many workers, not satisfied with merely improving working conditions, became converts to Marxian socialism and its call for public ownership of the means of production. Marxian socialists agreed on what was wrong with capitalism but they differed on the proper methods of realizing their ideal society. Marx, presuming the exclusion of the worker from politics, believed the change to socialism would be preceded by violent revolution. By the end of the nineteenth century, however, many socialist revisionists, led by the German Eduard Bernstein, had abandoned revolutionary ideology. They pointed out that, contrary to Marx's prediction, the living standard of the workers was steadily improving and the bourgeois state was gaining in strength as it became more democratic. Instead of trying to overthrow the state, socialists ought to cooperate with capitalist political parties to draw the state in the direction of socialism.

By 1914, reformist, democratic socialism had become the predominant form of Marxism. It achieved its greatest success in Germany, where the Social Democrats, revisionists in practice if not in theory, became the largest party by 1914. Jean Jaurès, by far the most popular French socialist leader, insisted that Marxism was sufficiently elastic to be adapted to democratic, parliamentary conditions. In England, where Marxism was weak, the Fabian Society, made up of intellectual radicals, and the Labor party were committed to a peaceful, gradual, and democratic move to socialism. In the United States, Eugene Debs, the Socialist party candidate in the 1912 presidential election, received nearly 1 million votes out of 15 million votes cast.

One hostile reaction to the growing socialist emphasis upon moderation was the rise of syndicalism (from *syndicat* the French word for trade unions). The goal of the syndicalists was to make the trade unions the most powerful institution in society, replacing the state as the owner and operator of the means of production. In their view, strikes and violence were the best weapons to end bourgeois dominance. With the notable exception of France, syndicalism had the most appeal in European nations where industrialization was still a novelty and unions were weak, as in Italy, Spain, and Russia. In the United States, the syndicalist Industrial Workers of the World, or "Wobblies," were a formidable disruptive force in western mines and lumber camps.

The industrial workers' efforts to improve their lot was not exclusively national. From the beginning, Marx had sought to develop a sense of international class solidarity among the proletariat. He believed all workers were comrades with interests that transcended the limits of national loyalties. In 1864, to promote his cause, he helped to form the International Workingmen's Association, known as the First International. Weakened by savage quarrels between anarchists led by Bakunin and the majority commanded by Marx, the First International broke apart in 1873. Delegates of various socialist parties, meeting in Paris in 1889, formed the Second International. In 1900, at its annual congress, all member parties agreed that no socialist should hold a cabinet post in a bourgeois government, but each national socialist party still reserved the right to determine its own policies. The Second International foundered in 1914 over the role of socialist parties in a capitalist war. In the end, most workers chose loyalty to the nation over loyalty to class.

By the early twentieth century, the efforts of the industrial workers to improve their situation, often made in conjunction with enlightened leaders from the middle and upper classes, had borne some fruit. Between 1870 and 1900, the purchasing power of the worker rose by about 50 percent in the industrialized nations. The improvement was due to trade union activity, government intervention in the economy, greater productivity brought on by mechanization, and the gradual fall in prices of food and other necessities.

Before 1914, the major European industrial nations, but not the United States, had also put into place many elements of what has come to be called the welfare state. Welfare state programs included old age pensions, workmen's compensation for on-the-job illness or injury, unemployment compensation, maximum hour and minimum wage legislation, and laws mandating safe working conditions,

Early Demonstration of Socialist Groups in London. Although Marx spent thirty years in London he made no attempt to create an organized following in his adopted country. In 1881 H. M Hyndman, a professed Marxist, founded the Social Democratic Federation but he failed to command a large following. Far different and more effective was the Fabian society, a small group of intellectuals including George Bernard Shaw, H. G. Wells, and Sidney and Beatrice Webb. Its members were not revolutionaries but gradualists, believing that the socialist state would come when the proletariat was sufficently educated to vote it into power. The Fabians encouraged the political activity of the trade unions and cooperated with them in founding the Labor Party.

First International founded

End of Victorian Compromise in British politics

French Constituent Assembly elected

Kulturkampf

Second British Reform Bill

Revolutionary Paris Commune

French Constitution

Third British Reform Bill

among other benefits. Nevertheless, the working class as a whole continued to struggle for security and many of its members continued to be alienated by a system that consigned them to a life of hardship and poverty. In the sections that follow, the labor situation is examined nationally, along with another major theme of the period, the growth of political enfranchisement.

GREAT BRITAIN AFTER 1850

Thanks to an evolving constitutional system, Great Britain had avoided the kind of revolutionary upheaval that periodically afflicted the continent. During the reign of Queen Victoria, the monarchy was brought into harmony with the trend towards political democracy. Victoria revealed a strict regard for the constitutional process and adjusted herself, as no British monarch had done before, to playing a limited role in the country's political life. Her dignity, intelligence, stern moral rectitude, fervent patriotism, capacity for work, and proper family life, all mirrored middle class conventions and values. As a result, she recaptured for the crown the re-

spect and admiration her predecessors had frittered away.

In the middle of the nineteenth century Great Britain was still a virtual oligarchy. In the aftermath of the First Reform Bill of 1832, only one adult male in eight could vote for members of the House of Commons, and Parliament remained essentially an undemocratic body. From 1832 until 1867 the landed gentry and the upper middle-class worked together to control the government while adopting paternalistic policies toward the poorer classes, a situation sometimes called the Victorian Compromise. As a consequence, the policies of the two national political parties, now called Liberals and Conservatives, became blurred, almost indistinguishable.

The Gladstone-Disraeli Era

The death of Lord Palmerston, the symbol of the Victorian Compromise, and the appearance of two remarkably astute party leaders opened a new reform chapter in British politics. The son of a rich Liverpool merchant, William Gladstone (1809–1898) was mindful of commercial interests, although he began his career as a Conservative before gradually shifting his allegiance to the Liberal party, which

he led to victory for the first time in 1868. A deeply religious man, he was a zealous reformer, believing God had chosen him to carry out His divine will. Gladstone's rival and counterpart, Benjamin Disraeli (1804–1881) was a Christian of Jewish descent. Although without the advantages of birth and social position, he was exceedingly ambitious, imaginative, and cultured, as well as a gifted speaker and writer. By sheer hard work and audacity, he climbed to the upper ranks of the Conservative party and became the chief spokesman for the landed aristocracy. For a generation, Gladstone and Disraeli alternated in the office of prime minister, and their personal rivalry stimulated reform.

The growth of the nation's working classes led to renewed agitation for the extension of the franchise in the early 1860s. In 1866, a combination of Liberals and Conservatives defeated a moderate bill that would have added about 400,000 persons to the voting lists, sparking angry demonstrations in the industrial cities. Disraeli, convinced that reform could no longer be delayed, wanted the Conservatives to enjoy the credit and win the allegiance of the underprivileged. His government presented an even more radical bill which passed with Liberal support. The Second Reform Bill of 1867 lowered the tax and rental qualifications for voting, thus enfranchising many skilled urban workers and doubling the electorate from one million to two million. It was a significant reform, notwithstanding that some groups still had no voice in their government.

The extension of the franchise brought in its wake a series of overdue domestic reforms as both parties sought to gain adherents among the new voters. In 1870, Parliament established a framework for a national system of education. The reform of the army began the same year: short-term enlistments were permitted, flogging was abolished, and the purchase of commissions eliminated. Parliament also introduced the secret ballot, legalized labor unions, and improved public health facilities. Beginning the welfare state, it introduced compensation for injured employees and set minimum standards of sanitation in the mines and factories.

During Gladstone's second ministry (1880–1885), the franchise was again broadened. The Third Reform Bill of 1884 added some two million agricultural laborers and artisans to the voting rolls. Now four out of five males had the right to vote.

The New Liberals Consolidate the Welfare State

The period of social reform was temporarily interrupted during the decade of Conservative rule (1895–1905), but the Liberals returned to power in 1905 in a landslide, committed to a bold program of social change. Gladstone's heirs were more sensitive to the needs of the common people, hoping to integrate them into the national community. The so-called New

Liberals believed in using the power of the state to aid the underprivileged groups, and continued to build up the welfare state. Led first by Henry Campbell-Bannerman and after 1908 by Herbert Asquith and supported by the newly elected members of the Labor Party, the Liberal party attacked the evils of the industrial system with zeal. The Workers Compensation Act, which initially had a narrow application, was extended to include all industries in 1906. The Liberals provided free meals to undernourished school children and enacted the Old Age Pension Act, which granted state pensions to indigent persons over seventy. The Trade Board Act in 1909 set up a commission to regulate wages and protect employees from undue exploitation in factories.

The crowning achievement of the period was the adoption of a compulsory insurance plan. The National Insurance Act of 1911 created a fund, the premiums being shared by the workers, employers, and government, to assure an ailing person of hospital and medical care as well as a small weekly income. Although termed socialistic and denounced as irresponsible by critics, these and other measures helped significantly to improve the condition of the many workers who lived on the edge of starvation.

The social programs, combined with heavy expenditures on naval construction, forced the government to find additional sources of revenue. In 1909, the chancellor of the exchequer, David Lloyd George, drafted a budget that shifted the tax burden to the wealthy classes. Its most controversial provision was a heavy tax on unearned income, such as investments, inheritance, and increases in

the value of land. The House of Lords, which was dominated by Conservatives, vetoed the budget bill, defying the House of Common's traditional control of taxation.

The Liberals responded by putting an end to the veto power of the upper chamber. The House of Commons enacted the Parliament Bill, stipulating that the Lords could not block legislation of which they disapproved, only delay it until it had cleared the lower house in three successive sessions. Before the bill was introduced into the House of Lords in mid-1911, Asquith announced that the king had promised, if necessary, to create enough new peers to ensure its passage. The House of Lords passed the bill grudgingly. The Parliament Act was another step toward democratic government, for it gave to the elected representatives of the people final decision in legislative matters.

Another issue confronting the Liberal government was how to deal with the suffragette movement, which had begun a sensational campaign to gain voting rights for women. To emphasize the seriousness of their commitment, the suffragettes chained themselves to lampposts, started fires in mailboxes, smashed department store windows, and even destroyed art objects in the British Museum. It was not until after World War I that Parliament enacted complete universal suffrage. Women owed their victory less to their militant tactics than to their active role in the war effort. In 1918 the franchise was extended to all males over twenty-one and all women over thirty. Ten years later, British women received the vote on the same terms as the men.

A new militancy appeared as well in the trade unions in the pre-1914

Suffragettes Escorted by Police in 1914 after a Demonstration outside Buckingham Palace. When arrested and put in jail many suffragettes would go on hunger-strikes. The government, anxious not to have them die in jail, adopted so-called "cat and mouse" tactics. They kept them in jail until they were exhausted whereupon they were released. After they recovered they were arrested again.

period. Between 1910 and 1913, workers, angry because their wages had not kept up with costs, generated a wave of unrest which included strikes and violence.

Worst of all, in Ireland, Catholics and Protestants were on the verge of civil war. For some fifty years, the Irish problem had plagued successive British governments. Ireland was Catholic except for six northern counties known as Ulster, where a large colony of Protestants from Scotland lived. Treated as conquered people, the Irish Catholics had never made willing subjects. Gladstone tried to remedy Irish grievances by giving Ireland home rule through its own parliament, with London retaining control of foreign policy. In 1886 and again in 1893, he brought forth Home Rule Bills, but both were rejected. For nearly two decades the Irish issue

remained dormant. Then during the budget fight in 1911, Irish nationalists in Parliament supported the Liberals and in return received a pledge that a Home Rule Bill for Ireland would be passed.

A new Home Rule Bill cleared Parliament in 1914. No provisions had been made for the Protestant minority in Ulster who were about to be submerged in an autonomous Ireland. Supported by the Conservative leaders and by much of British public opinion, the Ulstermen began to organize a force of armed volunteers, determined to resist home rule. Irish nationalists in the south recruited their own army to counter the Ulstermen. The onset of World War I compelled the Liberal government to postpone the application of home rule until after general peace was restored.

For all its social and political prog-

ress, Great Britain was beset by increasing domestic strife in the years immediately before World War I. Traditional respect for authority and due process of parliamentary law appeared to be breaking down. Indeed, the nation's mood was so militant that internal conflicts might have broken out had the war not begun in 1914.

FRANCE AFTER 1870

Parliamentary democracy was achieved in France in a far more dramatic fashion than in Great Britain. Born in the midst of war and civil strife, the Third Republic survived a continuing series of crises in the decades between 1870 and 1914.

The Birth of the Third Republic

The Third Republic was created more by default than by design. Revolutionaries in Paris had replaced the deposed regime of Napoleon III with a provisional government of National Defense. The leaders of the new regime struggled valiantly to turn the tide of war, but the situation was beyond hope and on January 28, 1871, Paris capitulated. Bismarck made it clear that he would discuss peace terms only with a constitutionally elected government. Accordingly Frenchmen went to the polls to elect a National Constituent Assembly. Since the republicans wanted to continue the futile and unpopular war, the majority of people voted for conservative candidates, electing 400 monarchists and only 200 avowed republicans. The first official action of the Assembly was to accept Germany's peace terms.

MRS. EMMELINE PANKHURST'S ADDRESS TO SUFFRAGETTES ON OCTOBER 17, 1912

The only recklessness the Suffragettes have ever shown has been about their own lives and not about the lives of others. It has never been, and it never will be, the policy of the women's Social and Political Union recklessly to endanger human life. We leave that to the enemy. We leave that to the men in their warfare. It is not the method of women. No, even from the point of view of policy, militancy affecting the security of human life would be out of place. There is something that Governments care far more for than human life, and that is the security of property and so it is through property that we shall strike the enemy.

Be militant each in your own way. Those of you who can express your militancy by going to the House of Commons and refusing to leave without satisfaction, as we did in the early days—do so. Those of you who can express militancy by facing party mobs at Cabinet Ministers' meetings when you remind them of their falseness to principle—do so. Those of you who can express your militancy by joining us in our anti-Government by-election policy—do so. Those of you who can break windows—break them. Those of you who can still further attack the secret idol of property, so as to make the Government realize that property is as greatly endangered by woman suffrage as it was by the Chartists of old— do so. And my last word is to the Government: I incite this meeting to rebellion.*

The agitation for the enfranchisement of women entered a militant phase when Mrs. Emmeline Pankhurst founded the Women's Social and Political Union in 1903. The tactics of the members, initially confined to heckling politicians at meetings, became progressively more strident with Mrs. Pankhurst's call. It is doubtful if their conduct, which both amused and angered the British public, advanced their cause. As it was such legislation had to wait until after the war. A similar campaign in the United States brought the vote to women in 1920.

*Quoted in Antonia Raeburn, *The Militant Suffragettes* (London: Michael Joseph, 1973), p. 183.

In March, the Assembly moved to Versailles, but before it could create a permanent government for the nation, it became involved in a bitter civil war. To the population of Paris, largely republican in sentiment, the peace settlement was an act of betrayal. They resented, moreover, the monarchists' domination of the National Assembly and the latter's decision to transfer the capital to Versailles, once the symbol of Bourbon absolutism. Declaring their independence from the rest of France, they set up their own city government, or Commune. The Commune was dominated by small property holders and was not socialistic, or indeed very radical. Talks having broken down, the National Assembly decided to subdue the city by force. The fighting was extremely brutal and went on for

Hostages Executed by the Paris Commune. In this illustration the Communards, in reprisal for the summary execution of several of their leaders, are about to shoot sixty-two hostages whom they had seized. Those put to death included the archbishop of Paris and a number of priests.

two months. In a final act of desperation, the Communards set fire to numerous public buildings and executed hostages, including the archbishop of Paris. Attacking troops shot on sight anyone with a weapon, and at the end executed thousands of prisoners. More than 20,000 Communards were killed and thousands more were subsequently deported to the penal colony of New Caledonia in the South Pacific. The propaganda spread by the French government, which linked the events in Paris to a conspiracy directed by the International Workingmen's Association, created intense opposition in many countries to socialism and to other forms of labor organization. In France itself, the civil war retarded the development of trade unions and an effective socialist party, as well as bequeathing a legacy of hatred that widened the gulf between the propertied classes and the workers.

Despite the monarchist majority in the National Assembly, France did not become a monarchy. The monarchists were divided between the Orleanists, supporters of the count of Paris, grandson of Louis Philippe, and the Legitimists, supporters of the count of Chambord, grandson of Charles X. The resulting stalemate led the National Assembly to pass a series of laws known collectively as the constitution of 1875. Nominally republican, the constitution could, with slight modification, operate under a monarchy. In this way France became a republic, although it was not until 1879 that republicans gained complete control over the legislative and executive branches of government.

The French republican government resembled the British system, although far less stable. It was made up of a two chamber legislature with the Senate elected indirectly and the Chamber of Deputies elected directly by universal male suffrage. The two houses sitting together elected the president, who was essentially a figurehead. The real power lay with the prime minister and his cabinet, themselves accountable to a majority in the legislature. But unlike the British two-party system, the French had a large number of loosely organized factions. Since no one group commanded a majority in the Chamber, ministries necessarily represented coalitions working temporarily together and subject to collapse the instant one or more of the parties withdrew. In the period preceding World War I, France had no fewer than fifty cabinets. The frequent changes of government made it impossible to frame long-range plans.

Challenges to the Third Republic

If the republic was established, it was not out of danger. Monarchists, embittered by their own inability to agree on a king, remained hostile. It was difficult for French Catholics to be enthusiastic about a regime that sought to restrict the influence of the church by banning religious instruction in the state school system, curtailing the activities of religious orders, and legalizing divorce. Nationalists, with burning dreams of revenge against Germany, denounced as cowardly the pacific European foreign policy of the Third Republic, although its colonial policy was relatively aggressive. Political factionalism and scandals left many sober-minded Frenchmen defrauded of their hopes. Finally, left-wing malcontents felt the republic was insufficiently democratic.

All these disparate elements joined together in the late 1880s and put their trust in a new man of destiny, General Georges Boulanger (1837–1891). Boulanger owed his rise, not to outstanding ability, but to his dashing appearance and charm, and to a shrewd public relations campaign. He reached the height of his popularity in 1889 when he gained a resounding victory in a parliamentary by-election in Paris. Conditions were ripe for a coup d'état, but Boulanger wanted to gain power by legal means. In desperation, the government circulated rumors of his imminent arrest for conspiring against the state. At this point, Boulanger lost his nerve and fled to Brussels, where he committed suicide on the grave of his mistress in 1891.

After Boulanger came a far more serious crisis, one that embittered and divided French opinion for years and nearly shattered the republic. In the fall of 1894, Captain Alfred Dreyfus, a Jewish officer on the French general staff, was convicted by a military court of having delivered secret documents to a foreign power, presumably Germany. As punishment, he was condemned to life imprisonment on Devil's Island, a notorious penal settlement off French Guiana, South America. It subsequently developed that Dreyfus had been convicted on forged evidence and that the real culprit was a certain Major Ferdinand Esterhazy. But the army tried to hush matters up, evidently to protect its prestige in a time of international tension. That proved impossible once the issue broke into public print. It assumed national

proportions with newspapers ranging themselves on one side or the other. Emile Zola whipped up republican opinion with his blistering attack on the army in his famous letter, *J'Accuse*. The resulting uproar sometimes took the form of open clashes in the streets. As a rule the defenders of Dreyfus were republicans whereas those in the opposite camp were anti-republicans—monarchists, clericists, army officers—and anti-Semites. In a new trial in 1899 the judges excluded evidence in Dreyfus's favor and again found him guilty, but the president of France pardoned him ten days later. In 1906, he was completely exonerated and reinstated in the army with the rank of major.

In the aftermath of the Dreyfus affair, the aroused republicans, strengthened by the elections of 1902, showed their enemies no quarter. The army was purged of officers known for their strong royalist or clerical leanings. The length of military service was reduced from five to two years and the army's disciplinary code was liberalized, changes that were intended to prevent the subversion of the values of French youth by reactionary officers.

Simultaneously, the government struck at the church. A series of laws provided for the expulsion of all religious orders save those specially authorized by parliament and excluded all religious orders from teaching in either private or public schools. The most drastic anticlerical legislation was the repeal of the Concordat of 1801, in which the state renounced both its right to make church appointments and its obligation to pay the clergy's salaries. The Catholic church in France was reduced to a private, self-supporting organization.

Meanwhile, France moved slowly toward the welfare state. The heavy indemnity paid to Germany and the loss of the valuable industrial region of Alsace-Lorraine had severely retarded the nation's economic growth in the late nineteenth century. French industry tended to be small in scale and lagged behind that of Great Britain, Germany, and the United States. France's working class was smaller, and therefore less influential, than its British and German counterparts.

Successive French republican governments were slow to come to grips with the social and economic problem of the industrial age. During the generation after 1870, they legalized trade unions, permitted workers to strike, fixed the minimum working age for children at thirteen, and introduced social and accident insurance. However, the ruling class drew the line at the advanced social legislation the workers called for. In 1905, various labor and socialist groups combined to form the United Socialist Party. By 1910, the Socialists had become a major party, having elected 105 of their members to the Chamber of Deputies. Between 1905 and 1910, the Socialists skillfully used their strength to help pass such social measures as old age pensions and regulations governing working hours and conditions.

An important segment of French workers embraced the doctrines of revolutionary syndicalism forcefully expounded by Georges Sorel. Scorning the parliamentary process, they preferred direct action in the form of sabotage and strikes as a means to undermine the capitalistic order. Their most ambitious effort was the staging of a major railway strike in 1910. Prime Minister Aristide Briand reacted swiftly, proclaiming a national emergency and calling in military aid. Reservist strikers were ordered, as soldiers, to run the trains or face a court martial. Syndicalist solidarity melted away and the strike collapsed.

During the years from 1910 to 1914, France was more stable than it had been at any time since 1871. Most Socialists had become revisionists and committed to the Republic. Although class divisions persisted, a new nationalism was emerging, bred by the growing threat from Germany. The Republic was achieving unity in time to meet its greatest challenge.

ITALY AFTER 1871

After unification Italy's aspirations for great power status were inhibited by its poverty and serious internal problems. The majority of Italians were illiterate. The nation had to import key industrial raw materials such as coal and iron, which severely limited the size of its industrial establishment. Italy remained predominantly agricultural, with most of its peasants struggling to eke out a marginal existence from the poor soil and primitive farming methods. The wealth of Italy, moreover, was unevenly divided, which accentuated regional differences. In the industrialized regions in the north, the people enjoyed a standard of living approaching that of France. In the south, the illiterate peasants lived in grinding poverty under feudal institutions. Many Italians, especially from the south, emigrated to the western hemisphere and Australia.

A major problem in Italian politics was the conflict between church and state, which divided Italian public opinion and complicated relations with certain Catholic nations. In 1871, the Italian government offered to give Pope Pius IX an annuity and to make the Vatican a sovereign state in return for recognition. The pope, however, refused all offers of compromise. Regarding himself as the "prisoner in the Vatican," he forbade Catholics to hold political office or to vote in elections. The church partially relaxed its ban in 1904, but it did not come to terms with the Italian government until 1929.

Italy's ineffective parliamentary system was another source of weakness. Like Great Britain, Italy was a constitutional monarchy; the king was essentially a figurehead, and power resided in a cabinet responsible to the lower house. The nineteenth-century franchise was sharply restricted by property qualifications, but these were gradually lifted, and by 1912 adult males age thirty and over could vote. But unlike Great Britain no strong political parties developed, and Italian politics were as unstable as that of France. Governing was conducted by precarious coalitions and sustained by open corruption. This was the process known as *trasformismo*, which meant using any conceivable means to transform the opposition into a pliable body of adherents. Such a state of affairs not only discredited representative government but also let pressing social and economic problems go unresolved.

The corruption and paralysis of the Italian government contributed to popular dissatisfaction. The restlessness of the impoverished workers in particular spurred the government of Giovanni Giolitti, the man who dominated Italian politics between 1903 and 1915, to enact basic reforms. Parliament legalized labor unions and encouraged collective bargaining, introduced laws regulating factory conditions, and nationalized the insurance companies and the railroads.

Despite these reforms, many Italians became attracted to the violent programs of anarchism and syndicalism on the left and supernationalism on the right. Strikes, riots, and other forms of lawlessness became endemic. In the spring of 1914, the government was forced to call out the army to suppress the wave of violence that accompanied strikes in a number of northern industrial cities. Numerically inferior but no less sinister was an extreme rightist group that counted among its leading spokesman the poet Gabriele d'Annunzio. It exalted the state, preached the glory of battle, and favored subordinating the concept of liberty to that of obedience. Calling for action to end the existing regime, which it considered dull and mediocre, it wanted Italy in the hands of a new elite, men who were versed in the ways of power. Thus both the anarchists and supernationalists were prepared to use violence to attain their ends. By 1914, their exhilarating rhetoric had made a great impact on the young people. The future looked bleak for Italy's fragile democracy.

GERMANY AFTER 1871

Founded in 1871, the German Empire was already the strongest nation on the continent and every year added to its strength. Its people were educated, disciplined, and hardworking. The German army was the finest in the world. Its unparalleled economic and industrial growth had transformed it into a wealthy nation, matching Great Britain and the fast-rising United States.

The New German State

Unlike the nations in western Europe, Germany failed to develop a liberal parliamentary government. The constitution of 1871, stressing unity rather than representative government, established a tight federal union of twenty-five states under Prussia's leadership. Supreme executive authority was lodged in the emperor, who exercised it over the armed forces, foreign affairs, and the general enactment of laws. The upper house of the legislature, the *Bundesrat*, consisted of appointed delegates representing the various states. The members of the lower house, the *Reichstag*, were elected by universal male suffrage. The Prussian-dominated *Bundesrat* was the principal legislative organ, whereas the *Reichstag* was essentially consultative, with little power to enforce its will. Unlike Great Britain or France, the chancellor did not serve at the pleasure of the parliament but was appointed by the emperor and responsible only to him. As long as he enjoyed the emperor's confidence, as was the case with Bismarck, he could rule the nation with almost dictatorial authority.

The German constitution had been shaped by Bismarck to coincide with his autocratic philosophy and to fit his own personality. Given that Germany had been born in an atmosphere of war and was still beset by sharp social, religious, and regional differences, Bismarck saw in a strong, centralized monarchy the best guarantee of national unity. He understood that effective government could not be conducted without the participation of political parties, but he viewed them as mere interest groups to be called on for support. He would not tolerate any opposition to monarchical policy, regarding it as an act of disloyalty.

Politics Under Bismarck

Bismarck showed far greater talent in foreign affairs than in handling domestic problems. As a diplomat, he worked patiently and skillfully to consolidate Germany's position in Europe and to maintain the status quo. He was less surefooted at home, especially when he attacked German Catholics and socialists, two groups he believed had extranational loyalties transcending their allegiance to the German state.

Throughout the 1870s Bismarck engaged in the so-called *Kulturkampf* (struggle for civilization), a campaign designed to destroy the influence of the Catholic church in Germany. In 1870, Pope Pius IX promulgated the doctrine of papal infallibility, giving Bismarck his opportunity. Bismarck chose to interpret the doctrine as a challenge by the church to state authority, thus serving as pretext for his persecution of Catholics. Between 1872 and 1875, he issued a series of laws that expelled the Jesuits from the country, prohibited religious orders from taking part in educational work, placed clerical education under state supervision, and made civil marriages obligatory. To resist Bismarck, a Catholic or Center party emerged as a strong force, precisely the reverse of what he had intended. Shortly after, the Iron Chancellor belatedly recognized the folly of alienating the empire's Catholics. Not only were they too powerful to break but they were also potentially a strong bulwark of conservatism against the rising tide of socialism and radicalism, in Bismarck's eyes the more dangerous opponents. With the accession of the moderate Pope Leo XIII (1878–1903) in 1878, Bismarck gradually abandoned his campaign. By 1887, most of the obnoxious legislation had been repealed.

Bismarck's efforts to suppress socialism were equally unsuccessful. The growth of socialism, which accompanied the development of German industry, alarmed Bismarck, whose memory of the Paris Commune was still fresh. Equating socialism with anarchy, he viewed it as a threat to the stability and unity of the empire. The Social Democratic party in Germany was revisionist, however, not revolutionary. Supported by both trade unions and intellectuals, its goal was the peaceful achievement of socialist measures within the constitutional framework.

In 1878, two attempts upon the life of William I, neither of which actually originated with the socialists, provided Bismarck with an excuse to steer an antisocialist law through the Reichstag. Socialist meetings and publications were banned. The Socialist Democratic party was outlawed and many of its leaders were imprisoned or sought refuge abroad.

Ironically, Bismarck's preoccupation with the socialists brought the welfare state to conservative Germany earlier than to more liberal nations. Realizing that wretched working conditions were the major source of socialist strength, Bismarck sponsored a paternalistic social reform program designed to undercut the So-

William I with Bismarck. In this illustration, Bismarck, who for so long had things his own way, appears to be lecturing rather than reporting to the Emperor. When William II ascended the throne in 1888, he longed to make his own mark in the world and had no wish to be kept on leading strings by the old chancellor. The two men soon began to clash, and following a series of disputes over domestic and foreign policies, the new kaiser forced Bismarck to resign in March 1890.

cial Democrats. The parliament enacted a sickness insurance bill in 1883, an accident insurance bill in the following year, and in 1889 a pension plan for the aged and permanently disabled.

But neither Bismarck's repressive tactics nor his enlightened social legislation succeeded in weaning the workers from socialism. In 1890, the new Emperor William II (1888–1918), abruptly dismissed Bismarck and allowed the antisocialist legislation to lapse. The Social Democrats surfaced and in 1912 won a resounding victory, securing a plurality with one-third of the votes.

The electoral gains made in 1912 by the Social Democrats, the chief critics of the government, reflected popular discontent with the emperor's personal rule, particularly his for-

eign policy. Demands became more insistent for a new constitution that would restrict the prerogatives of the crown and make the chancellor responsible to the *Reichstag.* The outbreak of World War I put a temporary end to the rising movement for constitutional reform.

AUSTRIA-HUNGARY AFTER 1867

In the Dual Monarchy, social and political reforms made some headway in Austria despite an atmosphere of continuing crises spawned by ethnic nationalism. Industry flourished in certain areas of Austria, resulting in a large urban proletariat class that vied with agrarian interests in shaping na-

tional policy. Hungary, on the other hand, remained overwhelmingly agricultural, with nearly half the land belonging to a relatively few wealthy families. A generation after the abolition of serfdom in 1848, no more than one peasant in four owned the land he worked. Within the empire, political radicalism was kept in check by repressive laws and benevolent welfare state legislation.

The overriding problem in the Dual Monarchy was the conflict among its many subject nationalities. In Austria the dominant Germans were outnumbered two to one. The Poles were well treated, and alone among the various nationalities seemed contented. The Italian-speaking districts of Trent, Trieste, and Istria longed to unite with Italy. Slovene nationalists wished to join with Croats and

Serbs to recreate a south Slavic state. The largest ethnic group, the Czechs of Bohemia, culturally advanced and technically skilled, were the most vocal and dissatisfied of all the subject nationalities. Determined to be placed on the same footing as the Magyars, they agitated for a triple rather than a dual monarchy. To placate them, Emperor Francis Joseph offered autonomy in 1871, but the Magyars vetoed the proposal, fearing it would stir up similar demands from the Slavs in Hungary. Despite this setback, the Austrian government continued to make efforts to satisfy the wishes of its non-German groups. It opened up the civil service, allowed minorities more control over local affairs, and permitted use of their respective languages in schools and administrative offices.

When the Austrian government extended its reform program to politics, however, disorder ensued. In 1907, Austria introduced universal male suffrage, which gave the non-Germans a majority in the *Reichsrat*. Heated debates frequently degenerated into fistfights and unruly demonstrations that made it impossible for the legislature to carry on business. For years at a stretch, the emperor had to resort to his emergency powers and rule by decree. Political democracy, it seemed, was incapable of functioning in a nation of such diverse and divided peoples.

The Magyars of Hungary made no pretense at conciliating their Slovak, Rumanian, Serb, and Croat minorities, seeking instead to assimilate them. Although the Magyars made up less than half of Hungary's population, they occupied almost all the seats in parliament. They persistently refused to extend the suffrage. Property qualifications were so high and

the electoral laws so complicated that only 25 percent of the males could vote. The Magyars forced the use of their own language in schools and in all state services. Local autonomy in the non-Magyar provinces was restricted or abolished. The subject nationalities in Hungary were even more restless than those in Austria. The Croats and Serbs in particular clamored for union with independent Serbia and turned increasingly to their conationals outside the empire for support.

The ramshackle Austro-Hungarian Empire was held together by the loyalty of the army, the support of the Catholic church, and the masses' deep-seated veneration for Emperor Francis Joseph. It was like an old rotten ship, able to sail in calm seas but unlikely to survive a violent storm.

RUSSIA AFTER 1881

Social and political reform made little headway in Russia before World War I. The domain of the Romanovs was the most autocratic state in Europe, and throughout the nineteenth century remained untroubled by parliaments, political parties, and mass movements. Alexander II had made a conscientious effort to modify the Russian system, but after his assassination in 1881, no further reforms were enacted for a generation.

Political Reaction and Economic Progress

The new tsar, Alexander III (1881–1894), was determined to avenge his father's death and to revive the repressive regime of Nicholas I, with its motto of "autocracy, orthodoxy, and

Francis Joseph I. This striking portrait of Francis Joseph in later life shows him to be alert, genial, humble, and strong-willed, and conceals the weariness and sadness he must have felt at the time. Apart from the difficulties in holding the Dual Monarchy together, he was beset by inordinate personal tragedies—his brother, Maximilian, was executed in Mexico in 1867, his only son, Rudolph, committed suicide in 1889, his wife was shot in 1897, and his heir, Francis Ferdinand, was assassinated in 1914.

nationalism." He broke up radical organizations or drove them underground. He reduced the power of the *zemstvos*, censored publications, denied the right of assembly, and tightly regulated such education as existed.

Konstantine Pobedonostsev, procurator of the Holy Synod (director of the Russian Orthodox Church) and the tsar's most influential adviser, carried out a rigorous policy of Russification to bring the national minorities into the national fold. The Russian government, for example, deprived the Finns of their autonomous constitution and compelled them to adopt the Russian language as the medium of instruction in schools and colleges. Pobedonostsev used coercive, often brutal, methods, to convert the subject peoples to Russian Orthodoxy. The Jews suffered horribly from periodic state-encouraged *pogroms* (mob attacks on persons and property), and tens of thousands sought asylum in the United States and elsewhere.

Although politically and socially repressive, Alexander III was also interested in bringing Russia into the industrial age. The man most closely associated with Russia's industrial expansion was Count Serge Witte, minister of finance from 1892 to 1903. He promoted the development of the railway system, including the enormous Trans-Siberian Railway that linked European Russia with the Pacific. He encouraged industry through subsidies, protective tariffs, and guaranteed dividends. By placing Russia on the gold standard, Witte attracted much foreign capital, especially from France. Between 1885 and 1900 the index of industrial production tripled: Russia ranked fourth among the world's iron producers and second in the production of petroleum. Nevertheless, in terms of overall industrial output, Russia was greatly inferior to any of the advanced powers.

Growing Discontent

Rapid industrialization brought extreme hardships for the working class in Russia, as it had in western Europe half a century earlier. Hours of employment were long, wages low, and working conditions miserable. The workers had no medium to voice their discontent, since labor unions were not permitted. The government did try to improve matters, such as reducing the hours of labor for children, but did not provide the bureaucracy of inspectors necessary to enforce these laws on the factory owners.

Besides the workers, Russian society included two other dissatisfied groups, the peasants and middle-class liberals. The peasants were burdened with heavy redemption payments and excessive taxes. Because their plots of land were small and farming techniques crude, their yield was low and many still had to work on the large estates of the nobles simply to exist at a marginal level. Moreover, progressive middle-class elements, alienated by the years of harsh repression in the 1880s and 1890s, began to call for change to constitutional government.

Political parties emerged as an inevitable consequence of growing antigovernment sentiment. In 1903, businessmen and professionals combined with enlightened aristocrats to form the Constitutional Democratic or Cadet party, which favored peaceful reform and a constitutional monarchy. The Social Revolutionaries had many more followers and were much more radical, promising a free farm to each peasant family after the monarchy had been destroyed and the landed estates taken from the nobility.

As it would turn out, the most important new political group was the Social Democratic Party. Inspired by the teachings of George Plekhanov (1857–1918), Russian Marxists organized the party in 1898, appealing to the tiny but rapidly growing industrial proletariat. Five years later, the Social Democrats split into two factions. The *Mensheviki* (minority) wanted a broad, democratic party. They believed that after the overthrow of the imperial regime, a period of transition would ensue, during which cooperation with the bourgeois parties would be necessary before socialism could be implemented. The *Bolsheviki* (majority) preferred a small, tightly knit party under authoritarian leadership. Directed by Vladimir Ulianov (1870–1924), whose underground alias was Lenin, they insisted on an immediate dictatorship of the proletariat without collaboration between socialists and liberal bourgeoisie.

The opposition groups made little headway in Russia before World War I. As protest was not permitted, all political parties operated in clandestine fashion, which reduced their effectiveness. Many political leaders were in jail, in Siberian concentration camps, or, like Lenin, in exile.

The Revolution of 1905 and Its Aftermath

A mass upheaval in 1905 compelled Tsar Nicholas II (1894–1917) to grant political concessions. Much of the unrest stemmed from the nation's fal-

1887	1896	1905	1914
Second International formed	Dreyfus case	Social Democrats divide into moderate *Mensheviki* and radical *Bolsheviki*	Massacre of Bloody Sunday in Russia	Parliament Bill curtails power of House of Lords
Bismarck forced to resign			Separation of Church and State in France	Home Rule Bill clears Parliament

tering economy and its debacle in the Russo-Japanese War. On January 22, 1905, Father George Gapon led a huge but orderly crowd of workers to the Winter Palace in St. Petersburg to petition the tsar for reforms. For no apparent reason, imperial troops opened fire on the demonstrators, killing hundreds and wounding many more. The massacre triggered mutinies in the armed forces, peasant attacks against landlords, and strikes in many parts of the nation, culminating in a general strike that paralyzed the national economy.

Nicholas II reluctantly yielded under the tremendous pressure of events, issuing a manifesto in October 1905 in which he promised to grant a constitution and guarantee individual freedoms. He further promised to restrict the prerogatives of the crown and to extend lawmaking power to a Duma or parliament elected by a moderately liberal franchise. The October Manifesto gave the appearance, if not the substance, of converting autocratic Russia into a constitutional monarchy, and it divided the opposition. The middle-class ceased its agitation, but the workers rejected the concessions as insufficient and tried to carry on by themselves. The government crushed the labor disturbances and restored order at the end of 1905.

The government, having regained its footing, withdrew most of the promises it had made. During the next two years, Nicholas promulgated a series of edicts that reinstated his autocratic powers and reduced the Duma from a legislative to a consultative body. To ensure its cooperation in the future, the tsar revised the electoral system to guarantee the domination of the landed gentry. Peter Stolypin, a conservative with little sympathy for parliamentary government, controlled the administration.

Stolypin's policy combined repression with reform. He was ruthless in hunting down terrorists and breaking up revolutionary cells. At the same time, he was sufficiently enlightened to realize that the tsar's regime would not survive unless basic structural reforms were made to reduce internal discontent. Under his leadership, laws were enacted legalizing labor unions, reducing the work day in most cases to no more than ten hours, and establishing sickness and accident insurance. The central feature of his program was aimed at improving the lot of the peasants. Beginning in 1906, a series of laws allowed the peasants to leave the *mir* (commune) and to own their land, canceled their remaining redemption payments, and set up land banks to assist those who wanted to extend their holdings. Stolypin believed that a prosperous and independent class of peasant proprietors would become a conservative bulwark of the regime. In 1911, a terrorist assassinated Stolypin. His objectives might have been realized if fate had only given Russia time. The land reform process was slow and complicated, and only a small percentage of Russian peasants had become independent farmers when World War I broke out. Pursued to their conclusion the land changes might have headed off the revolution that toppled the tsar's regime in 1917.

SUMMARY

The major political and social issue in the years 1870–1914 was how to integrate the growing mass of urban workers into the national community. The urban proletariat, suffering from economic exploitation, actively

625

began attempts to improve wages, hours, and working conditions through labor unions and collective bargaining. When the middle and upper classes, anxious to placate unrest, extended the franchise, the workers used the vote as another weapon to further their cause. They particularly supported moderate socialist parties that were dedicated to bringing in public ownership of the means of production by peaceful, constitutional means. A minority of workers embraced the radical doctrines of revolutionary Marxism, syndicalism, and anarchism. The capitalist leaders of national governments tried to head off socialism by enacting significant measures to promote the welfare of the masses.

Western European parliamentary states such as Great Britain, France, and Italy saw a steady shift of the political spectrum to the left. In Great Britain the Liberals and Conservatives brought in universal male suffrage in the late nineteenth century and after 1905 the New Liberals ushered in state socialism. Major problems remained, however, particularly the threat of violence over Irish home rule. The Third Republic in France, weathering a series of crises in the last years of the nineteenth century, provided a system of government that was democratic but far less stable than that of Great Britain. French social legislation was a modest beginning. Italy remained a poor and struggling country, further weakened by a conflict between church and state and a faulty parliamentary system. The practice of bribing the opposition was a serious obstacle to the growth of Italian democracy.

In Germany, Austria-Hungary, and Russia, special circumstances retarded or overwhelmed the spread of democracy, although in the first two instances the welfare state made headway. In Germany, concern for keeping the newly united nation cohesive led to a constitution under which autocratic elements predominated and to the conservative leadership of Bismarck. To ward off socialism, Bismarck brought the welfare state to Germany, but nevertheless in 1912 the Social Democrats achieved a plurality in the *Reichstag*. In Austria-Hungary, restless ethnic minorities dominated political life. The Austrian government made concessions to the proletariat by providing benevolent legislation that regulated working conditions. At the same time, it tried, albeit unsuccessfully, to appease its subject nationalities. Hungary pursued a policy aimed at eradicating rather than appeasing opposition. Russia, rapidly expanding its industrial base, remained a repressive autocracy, making only token concessions to the workers and others demanding a parliamentary form of government. As a result, opposition parties, including the revolutionary Marxist Bolsheviks, sprang up. By 1914, most major western nations had committed themselves to the welfare state, a trend that would continue down through the twentieth century. Democracy had become entrenched in western Europe and the United States, but it had difficulty in becoming established elsewhere, a situation that would persist after World War I.

SELECTED SOURCES

*Clayton, Roberts, and Roberts, David. *A History of England, 1688 to the Present.* 1985. Well written with up-to-date interpretation on controversial issues.

*Craig, Gordon. *Germany, 1866–1945.* 1980. An excellent survey, stressing political developments.

*Crankshaw, Edward. *Shadow of the Winter Palace.* 1978. A good overview of Russian history during the century before the revolution of 1917.

Cross, Colin. *The Liberals in Power, 1905–1914.* 1963. Discusses the social legislation that laid the foundation of the welfare state in Great Britain.

I Accuse. Jose Ferrer's portrayal of Alfred Dreyfus is outstanding in this poignant 1958 motion picture that he also directed.

*Lindemann, Albert S. *A History of European Socialism.* 1983. Particularly good on comparison of socialist and syndicalist movements.

*May, Arthur J. *The Habsburg Monarchy, 1867–1914.* 1951. A brief and valuable survey.

*Mayer, Arno J. *The Persistence of the Old Regime in Europe to the Great War.* 1981. A controversial work arguing that the landed gentry remained a vital force in public life before World War I.

Smith, Denis Mack. *Italy: A Modern History.* 1969. Deals with the period after 1861 and stresses Italy's failure both to develop viable liberal institutions and solve its economic problems.

•Taylor, A. J. P. *Bismarck.* 1967. An engaging account of the man and statesman who dominated European politics in the second half of the nineteenth century.

Thompson, David. *Democracy in France Since 1870.* 1964. Surveys the problems of parliamentary government.

•Turgenev, Ivan. *Fathers and Sons.* (Various editions.) A novel probing the generational conflict in the context of social and political upheavals in late nineteenth century Russia.

•Available in paperback.

NINETEENTH-CENTURY CULTURE

After the fear of revolution had died down, the Victorians became liberal and tolerant to a very remarkable degree. When Gilbert and Sullivan made fun of the Army and Navy, nobody objected except Queen Victoria.

Marx and Kropotkin, who would nowadays be of interest to Scotland Yard, were unmolested. Although many men thought Darwin wicked, no one thought of making a law against evolution such as was enacted in Tennessee. The Metaphysical Society, which consisted of a small collection of eminent men, debated in correct Parliamentary style the question of the existence of God. A member who had not been present enquired anxiously of one who had: "Well, is there a God?" To which the answer was: "Yes, we had a very good majority."

British philosopher Bertrand Russell thus analyzed the nineteenth-century mind for a BBC program half a century later. Russell, born in Queen Victoria's reign, was himself a rebel and an iconoclast. His views are a good place to begin a survey of the varied and self-contradictory culture that existed in the century between Waterloo and World War I.

At first glance, the intellectual and artistic trends of the last century may even seem to run counter to its political and economic history. Europeans in the nineteenth century were increasingly prosperous, free of major wars, and rulers of global empires. Yet such important cultural movements as romanticism and materialism, such towering intellects as Darwin and Freud seemed to challenge many of the most cherished beliefs and values of this immensely successful society. Far from celebrating western achievements, artists and thinkers appeared ro reject the culture and convictions on which those accomplishments were based.

From another point of view, however, these intellectual and artistic rebellions may be seen as a sign of strength. Here was a society powerful and self-confident enough to tolerate—even though sometimes grudgingly—the heretical ideas of some of its most gifted citizens. As Bertrand Russell points out, the greatest nineteenth-century thinkers were allowed to speak their minds in spite of their unpopularity—and enriched the culture thereby.

This chapter looks at some of the main currents of the cultural life of the last century. These include the romantic revolt in the arts, science and the

CONTENTS

Gare St. Lazare, Paris, by Claude Monet. Detail. Impressionist painters like Monet found as much challenge in the new urban industrial world of steam and power as in the quiet countryside. Their real subject—the play of light on matter—also had a scientific feel in the later nineteenth century. Fogg Museum of Art, Harvard University.

Romantic Movement

Goethe

Beethoven   Scott   Hugo
             Byron   Poe
                          Turner
                            Chopin

challenge of materialism, and the disturbing ideas of the Darwinists, the Freudians, and others who sought the origins and essence of humanity in some novel and unpopular directions. The chapter also includes a look at the emerging culture of the new American nations.

THE ROMANTIC REVOLT

The romantic movement was not primarily a wave of enthusiasm for romantic love, though that was part of the program. Romanticism was a far-reaching world view, particularly important in the arts, which gained currency in the late eighteenth and the first half of the nineteenth century. Romanticism had broader implications, however, not only offering new ways of writing, painting, and composing music, but also challenging the basic attitudes of Europeans toward society and themselves. This chapter begins with a survey of romantic literary and artistic trends. It then turns to the larger romantic challenge to the rational self-image of the nineteenth century, emphasizing throughout the rebellious spirit of the romantic movement.

The Romantic Movement in Literature

In the late 1700s, some European writers began to rebel against the rigid rules for writing laid down by seventeenth-century classicism and eighteenth-century neoclassicism. The new school refused to be limited to "serious" subjects like philosophy, Greek and Roman history and mythology, or the life of the aristocracy. Its practitioners did not want to make use only of classical forms and styles. They felt an urge to express their emotional responses in literature, rather than offering only rational analysis, balanced judgments, or sardonic wit. These new writers, most of whom were young, became known as *romantics,* a name derived from the medieval tale of adventure, love, and often magic and fantasy.

The forms of literature romantic writers espoused reflected their opposition to classical formality. Romantic poets, for example, favored short lyric poems over long epics or philosophical poems. Many rejected the old-fashioned "poetic" language prescribed by classicists, insisting on words used by real people, especially humble country people rather than educated city folk. They refused to be

limited to the verse forms of their classical models and invented their own forms of poetry or drama instead.

Exotic settings predominated in romantic writing. Sometimes these were faraway places, like north Africa, the Near East, or even the forests of the New World. In other times, romantic fiction and poetry was set in colorful past periods of history, like the medieval era or the Renaissance. The success of Victor Hugo's *Hunchback of Notre Dame* (1831) and Sir Walter Scott's *Ivanhoe* (1819) illustrate this enthusiasm for medieval times.

The heroes of romantic poetry, plays, and prose fiction tended to be rebels and outcasts or at least unconventional in their behavior. Great lovers, wanderers in the world, bearers of dark secrets, romantic heroes were often seen as supreme egoists, glorifying the individual at the expense of society. A number of the romantic writers were themselves rebels, socially and even politically. George Gordon, Lord Byron, one of the most admired of romantic poets, was a thoroughly romantic character, living a scandalous life, engaging in radical politics, dying while still young in the Greek War of Independence from Turkey.

The romantics thus demanded not only freedom to innovate in literature but the chance to express their inmost emotional feelings as well. Strong feelings stood at the center of the romantic world view. Among the romantic emotional responses that were turned to literary effect were love, joy in nature, and awe in the presence of the supernatural. Personal love in particular dominated romantic poetry, plays, and fiction, and the love poem became a primary romantic form. Romantics admired not the cynical wit of the Enlightenment but passion that sprang straight from the heart.

Love of nature was also an important romantic theme. Poets like William Wordsworth felt an almost mystical closeness to trees, fields, streams, mountains, and oceans. Like Rousseau—who is often seen as a precursor of the movement—romantic writers preferred the natural world to the artificial sophistication of cities, the simple peasant cottage to the cultivated salon, seeing in these the deepest wellsprings of pure feeling.

The supernatural, dismissed as superstition by their enlightened predecessors, also found an important place in the romantic view of life. Johan Wolfgang von Goethe, Germany's greatest writer, brought the Devil himself on stage in his *Faust* (1808). Mary Shelley's *Frankenstein* (1818) was written at this time, and the original "Gothic" novels were full of haunted castles and other horrors.

The Romantic Movement in Painting and Music

The romantic determination to let the imagination have free reign, unfettered by rules, revealed itself also in

---

WHEN I WAS YOUNG

(1)

All thoughts, all passions, all delights,
Whatever stirs the mortal frame,
All are but ministers of Love,
And feed his sacred flame.

Oft in my waking dreams do I
Live o'er again that happy hour,
When midway on the mount I lay,
Beside the ruin'd tower.

The moonshine, stealing o'er the scene,
Had blended with the lights of eve;
And she was there, my hope, my joy,
My own dear Genevieve! . . . .

(2)

Verse, a breeze 'mid blossoms straying,
Where Hope hung feeding, like a bee—
Both were mine! Life went a-maying
With Nature, Hope, and Poesy,
When I was young!*

These extracts from poems by the English romantic poet Samuel Taylor Coleridge develop a number of typical romantic images. The first poem is dedicated to the "sacred flame" of romantic love. The second begins with "verse" or "poesy" (poetry)—one of the arts in which romanticism was strongest. Both conjure up romantic natural scenes: a moonlit mountain with ruined tower, a breeze-blown flower. Youth, also a major romantic enthusiasm, is implied in the first and emphasized in the second extract. Such phrases as "Nature, Hope, and Poesy" almost sum up the emotional creed of the romantics.

*Samuel Taylor Coleridge, "Love" and "Youth and Age" in Arthur Quiller-Couch, ed., *The Oxford Book of English Verse* (Oxford: Clarendon Press, 1953), pp. 670, 673.

---

painting and music. In both these arts, romantic emotionality, excitement, and color are vividly present. Romantic painters also rejected the rules for the arts formulated by the classical tradition. They used richer colors and deeper shadows than did neoclassical artists. Their composition aimed for violent motion instead of balance. They also liked to paint nature and exotic locales removed in space and time. John Constable's idyllic pictures of the English countryside were much admired. The French romantic Eugene Delacroix was famous for dramatic subjects set in the medieval period or the Near East, such as his *Entrance of the Crusaders into Jerusalem.* J.M.W. Turner, the English painter of seascapes, produced dazzling swirls of color, in sunsets and

storms at sea as the romantic imagination conceived them.

As musical composers, romantics turned away from the rules of composition developed over the past two centuries, preferring to let strong feeling and free-flowing musical imagination give their work its conviction. In pursuit of feeling, they expanded the orchestra, adding wind and percussion instruments to the predominantly stringed instruments of earlier times. French composer and conductor Hector Berlioz, who wrote both symphonies and operas, combined orchestra, solo voices, and choral singing in his treatments of such romantic subjects as *Romeo and Juliet* and *The Damnation of Faust.*

The music of the romantic period was thus intensely emotional. Mel-

Buttermere Lake, by J. M. W. Turner. The romantic feeling for nature is effectively captured in this oil painting by the famous British artist. The works of man are dwarfed here by the beauty of water, mountains, and sky, and by the rainbow arching over the scene. Tate Gallery, London.

ody flourished, and the song, like the lyric poem, presented a short, intense expression of powerful feeling. Franz Schubert's songs are still considered among the most beautiful ever written. Romantic composers also turned to peasant folk songs for inspiration, again expressing their admiration for the simple, unsophisticated reactions of country people.

The romantic ego, reflected in dashing writers like Byron, is also sometimes realized in the heroic sym-phonies of Ludwig von Beethoven, as well as in the brilliantly melodic piano compositions of Frederic Chopin. Chopin, a Pole who worked in Paris, also became a celebrated romantic personality. Virtuoso soloists and famous conductors were hailed as archetypal artistic geniuses, and music began to be looked upon as the highest of the arts in the course of the nineteenth century. Italian concert violinist and composer Niccolo Paganini, for instance, played so brilliantly that his audiences sometimes burst into tears, yet lived so colorful a life that some said he had bought his talent by selling his soul to the Devil!

Romanticism as a Cultural Revolt

The romantics, personally unconventional and artistically rebellious, were sometimes political radicals as well. Besides Byron, the poets Shelley and Wordsworth and other romantic writers had strong liberal sympathies. In France, Victor Hugo wrote at the time of the Revolution of 1830 that "romanticism is liberalism in literature."

Even more important, the romantic movement signified a deeper cultural revolt with long-range consequences. For the romantics were early explorers of cultural alienation and nonrationalism, both of which would haunt the modern world throughout the nineteenth and twentieth centuries.

Cultural alienation is the feeling of being a stranger in one's own culture, not at home in the time and place in which one is born. Romantic artists—and many of their readers—felt out of place in the new industrial society of nineteenth-century Europe. Smoky cities, materialistic entrepreneurs, the worship of science and the machine, all had little appeal to these lovers of forests and flowery fields.

Romanticism expressed this sense of cultural alienation by its passion for peasants and the countryside, for exotic far-off places, or for the colorful medieval past. This feeling of alienation also underlies the charac-

ter of the romantic hero, the bandit, revolutionary, or outcast wanderer estranged from his own society. Romantic characters such as the hero of Goethe's *Sorrows of Young Werther* (1776), who died for love, were also alienated from society in a way that went beyond their personal problems. Like Werther, some of these rebellious souls chose death as the ultimate escape from a world that seemed crass and unfeeling.

At the deepest level, finally, the rebellion was a revolt against reason itself and as such the birth of modern nonrationalism. By nonrationalism we mean not irrational or silly behavior, but the deliberate rejection of the rational faculties as the fundamental or highest human quality. Romantics rejected the classical tradition in large part because it was too intellectual, too ordered. They had no use for science, preferring to be entranced by the beauty of nature rather than analyzing it. The primacy of the emotions had superseded the glorification of reason.

This romantic absorption in the emotions led to a wide-ranging exploration of the nonrational aspects of the human psyche, especially with all the dimensions of love. (The very word *romantic* has come to mean "concerned with love.") Romantics also glorified sorrow, a passion for beauty, and the egoistic force of will they detected in a hero like Napoleon. As we noted, their feelings for nature approached the mystical, and some were stirred by intense religious feelings or by other powerful responses to the supernatural. Romantics even probed their own dreams in poems like Coleridge's "Kubla Khan," searching for deep truths in the mys-

teries of nonwaking life. The emotions, romantics believed, could give insights unobtainable by mere logic. Aristotle's assertion that "man is the rational animal" was answered by Wordsworth's romantic declaration that "our meddling intellect misshapes the beauteous form of things: we murder to dissect."

MATERIALISM AND POSITIVISM

As romanticism began to fade about the middle of the nineteenth century, materialism, a new world view, took its place. The nineteenth-century materialist view had its roots not in the arts, like romanticism, but in the physical sciences. It offered a new way of interpreting the world, often called positivism. In addition, the materialist world view was increasingly influential in the arts of the later 1800s, including the movements of realism and naturalism in fiction.

If romanticism was inspired by the emotions, materialism concerned itself with hard realities. Romanticism dreamed of idealized love, faraway places, and mysteries reason could not fathom. Materialism explored the ultimate nature of the world in laboratory test tubes or on microscope slides. Its heroes were not romantic wanderers, but the real people in the noisy, dirty streets of nineteenth-century cities. Positivism explained this material world purely in terms of objective observations. This view, materialists insisted, was only common sense. Moonlit towers and medieval knights had no place in the real world. In the latter part of the

Pasteur in His Laboratory. This picture reflects some of the intense scientific curiosity of the French biologist. Notice also the nineteenth-century laboratory equipment on which Pasteur depended.

nineteenth century, many Europeans came to agree.

A New Age of Scientific Achievement

A large number of scientific discoveries contributed significantly to knowledge of the physical universe in the course of the nineteenth century. These discoveries both deepened understanding of the material world and added to the prestige of the physical sciences and of the scientific approach to understanding the world.

Some of these discoveries expanded human knowledge of the nature of matter itself. Thus, for instance, an early nineteenth-century schoolmaster named John Dalton formulated a more modern version of the ancient Greek atomic theory, already revived in a crude form by early modern scientists. By the end of the century, the atomic composition of the material elements had been tabulated in Dmitri Mendeleyev's atomic table.

Meanwhile, other scientists explored the structure of matter above and below the atomic level. The molecular theory explained the three states of matter—solid, liquid, and gas—in terms of clumps of atoms called molecules in rapid motion. Soon after 1900, subatomic physics began to penetrate the miniature solar systems of protons, electrons, and neutrons, of which atoms themselves were believed to be composed.

Science in the nineteenth century even began to provide explanations for perhaps the most mysterious of physical phenomena: life itself. The cell theory of living tissue was confirmed in the early 1800s when cells—which had been found in plants as

early as the 1600s—were discovered in animal tissues as well. All cells, it developed, were made of the same chemical compounds. The properties of these compounds could be studied just as the characteristics of any other chunk of matter could be analyzed. Life itself, it seemed, had a purely material basis.

The germ theory of the causation of disease also took shape during this century. Louis Pasteur and others discovered that tiny organisms, which they called germs, were the cause of many diseases. Medicine was thus put on a truly scientific—and materialistic—basis, as medical scientists devoted themselves to concocting substances that would kill germs to cure disease.

The theories of more controversial scientists like Darwin and Freud, as we shall see, aroused bitter debate. But even these controversial investigators added to the prestige and interest of the sciences for later nineteenth-century people.

Materialism

The resurgence of the sciences in the nineteenth century produced new isms, including materialism and positivism. The materialistic world view built on the most recent wave of scientific discoveries and on the revived prestige of the scientific study of the material world. This nineteenth-century materialism did not mean love of material possessions, a definition often assigned to the term today. Rather, it was the philosophical belief in matter, to the virtual exclusion of spiritual things.

To some extent, this rejection of the ancient western belief in a spiritual world beyond this material realm came from the sciences themselves. Nineteenth-century geological studies, for instance, discovered that the Earth had not been created by divine decree a few thousand years ago, as Bible chronology seemed to indicate. Rather, the globe had taken many millions of years of slow development to reach its present state. Darwinian evolution raised an even greater furor by insisting that the human race itself had not been created as it is today, but had developed from other forms of life.

The most militant and thoroughgoing materialists, however, were not scientists but philosophers who saw larger implications in the continuing success of scientific investigations. It was they who asserted most strongly the materialist world view; that matter and matter alone exists.

In this sweeping materialist philosophy, the entire cosmos was composed of tiny particles of matter operating entirely on mechanical principles, the "laws of nature." Such a cosmos had no place for spirit. There was, said German materialist Ludwig Feuerbach, no God in heaven, no immortal soul in humans. Religion was an illusion. God was made in man's image, to serve human psychological needs for spiritual support in times of trouble. Other materialists said God was merely the sum total of all the scientific laws—"the supreme law of the universe." Such a God had none of the personal attributes of the Judeo-Christian God, and certainly no special concern for humanity or for individual human beings. As for the soul, it was no more than an individual personality and would cease to exist when the individual human organism did.

Positivism

The label *positivism* is a broad one, sometimes used to include most of the materialistic ideas just discussed. The primary concern of the positivist, however, is how people *understand,* how they can know the truth about the world. It is a theory of knowledge, rather than a theory about reality— though it began by accepting the materialist view of the nature of things.

The founder of modern positivism was the French thinker August Comte, who is also commonly known as the founder of modern sociology. Comte's "positive philosophy" defined three stages in our attempts to understand the world in which we live: theological, metaphysical, and positive. Early humanity, Comte said, made sense out of the world by inventing spiritual beings called gods, spirits, and so on, human-like supernatural creatures who were in charge of nature. The metaphysical or philosophical stage in our understanding was reached when gods were replaced by principles—philosophical abstractions—governing nature, like the *entelechy* or purposive force in nature proposed by Aristotle. Finally, modern empirical science had enabled us to draw "positive" conclusions about the world from the observation of the material world itself. For Comte and his successors, the last-named way alone was the road to truth.

Positivists believed that scientific methods should be applied in all disciplines. Personal prejudices and beliefs must be set aside in the rigorous pursuit of objective truth. Some positivists, like the English historian Henry Thomas Buckle, demanded that social scientists follow the physical sciences in their heavy dependence on mathematical analysis. By count-

ing and calculating, historians and others could escape conclusions based on vague impressions and arrive instead at objective data.

Positivism often produced rather dry and unsatisfying conclusions, leaving out of consideration both the emotion central to the romantics and the spiritual concerns of many Christians. For positivists, feelings like love and appreciation of artistic or natural beauty were merely subjective illusions. As for religion, Christ was at best a wise teacher and perhaps no more than a myth, like Apollo or Zeus. For much of the second half of the nineteenth century, materialism and positivism had the enthusiastic support of many advanced thinkers.

Realism, Impressionism, and the Novel

Realistic and impressionistic painters and many nineteenth-century novelists related in a variety of ways to the current fascination with the material world. So-called realist painters appeared on the scene in Paris around 1850. Reacting vigorously against romantic "prettifying" of the natural world, realists insisted on painting life as it really was. Gustave Courbet, for instance, painted a peasant funeral in meticulous detail, from the bored priest and expectant gravedigger to the country people gossiping throughout the service in the background. He "didn't paint angels" because, he said, he "never saw one."

The impressionist painters who emerged in France in the 1870s dedicated themselves with scientific zeal to "seeing things" by painting the components of perception. Their goal was to recreate the impact of light and color on the human eye—paint-

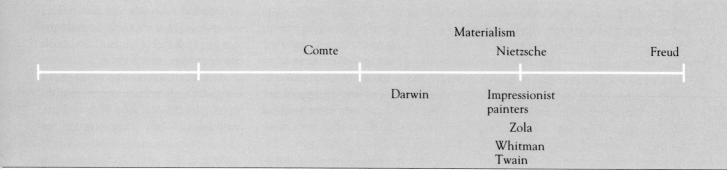

1800   1825   1850   1875   1900

Materialism

Comte   Nietzsche   Freud

Darwin   Impressionist
             painters
             Zola
             Whitman
             Twain

ing an "impression" of reality rather than the thing itself. Their investigations of light led the impressionists to break up subtle shades of color into basic primary colors and set these pigments side by side on the canvas, allowing the eye of the observer to do the mixing. The result was a rough, unfinished-looking picture if you stood close to it, but a brilliant effect of color and light if you viewed it from the proper distance. Impressionists such as Claude Monet found in the shifting reflections of light off water—lily pools, the Seine River—an ideal subject for their experiments in the impact of light on the human optic nerve.

The novel was clearly influenced by nineteenty-century trends in science and society. The modern novel had from its eighteenth-century beginnings been much concerned with everyday life as it was lived by Europe's middle-class—its readers. Nineteenth-century novels in fact bring the society of that period to life in a way no history book can. Jane Austen depicted the country life of Great Britain's gentry in intimate detail. Charles Dickens's larger-than-life characters played out their dramas against the background of industrializing England, including the gritty society of London. Honoré de Balzac,

in his immense series of novels called *The Human Comedy,* similarly depicted all classes of society in France. One cannot read Count Leo Tolstoy's huge *War and Peace* (1869) or Fyodor Dostoyevski's haunting *Crime and Punishment* (1866) without learning an immense amount about the aristocracy and the urban lower classes of nineteenth-century Russia.

In the later 1800s, writers calling themselves "realists" and "naturalists" carried this concern with often ugly realities of life to an extreme. The famous French naturalist Emile Zola produced a series of novels about all levels of French society in the last third of the century, including volumes about such grim subjects as alcoholism, prostitution, and the tragic impact of a miners' strike on the workers. Zola observed his subjects as closely as any scientist, taking detailed notes on everything from high finance to the food markets of Paris. He examined his characters with pitiless objectivity and even claimed for his fictions the status of scientific studies of genetic variation over several generations in the members of a single family.

Few people admire Monet's pictures or read Zola's novels purely for their scientific interest. But that interest was there nonetheless, as in-

spiring to these later nineteenth-century artists as love and nature had been to the romantics of the first half of the century.

EXPLORING
HUMAN ORIGINS AND
THE NONRATIONAL MIND

Romanticism and materialism had both shaken and challenged the beliefs and values of nineteenth-century Europeans. Another intellectual current of the later decades of the century had an even more disturbing effect. This was the exploration of the origins of humankind and the nonrational aspects of human character, both linking us more with our animal ancestors than with our highest intellectual achievements.

Romantic concern with emotional responses and materialist interest in baser human impulses had pointed toward this new emphasis on the nonrational. Among the more prominent thinkers whose views were applied to the new science of behavior that evolved were Charles Darwin the English biologist and Sigmund Freud the Austrian psychoanalyst. The German philosopher Friedrich Nietzsche, in contrast, engaged in a radical critique of conventional, "rational" society while asserting the superiority of the nonrational.

Though the romantics had pioneered in asserting the importance of the emotional faculties, the nonrationalism of the later nineteenth century drew heavily on the materialism of the decades after 1850. The result, particularly in the work of Freud, was to give claims for the centrality of the nonrational in human character a scientific validity it had not had before. This nonrationalist image of human nature, based on romanticism, materialism, or a combination of the two, would survive to become one of the main themes of twentieth-century culture as well.

Darwinism and Social Darwinism

No nineteenth-century theory aroused more controversy than Darwinian evolution. Yet even while opponents decried Darwin's conclusions, many other thinkers seized upon evolution as a tool for social analysis. In this way, so-called "social Darwinism" became almost as important in nineteenth-century thought as biological evolution itself.

Charles Darwin (1809–1882) was an English naturalist who studied biology in a practical yet thoughtful way all his life. The problem he set out to solve was how to account for the infinite variety of species of living things, a phenomenon that impressed him particularly during a round-the-world scientific expedition he joined in his youth. After long years of studying fossils, animal breeding, hybrid plants, and other aspects of his problem, Darwin published his ex-

---

CUTTING UP FROGS

And there, walking through the garden and stepping over the flower beds, came Bazarov. His linen coat and trousers were spattered with mud; slimy swamp weeds clung to the crown of his old cap; in his right hand he held a small sack, and in the sack, something was wiggling. . . .

"What do you have there, leeches?" Pavel asked.

"No, frogs."

"Do you eat them or breed them?"

. . .

"I'm going to split the frog open to see what's going on inside of him; since you and I are no different from frogs, except that we walk on our hind legs, I'll find out what's happening inside of us too."

"What good will that do you?"

"Then I won't make a mistake if you fall sick and I have to cure you."

. . .

"You're . . . interested in physics?" Pavel asked . . .

"Physics, yes; and natural science in general. . . . A passable chemist is twenty times as useful as any kind of poet" . . .

"So," said Pavel, barely raising his eyebrows as though he were falling asleep. "You, therefore, don't acknowledge art?"

"Art is just a means of making money, as sure as hemorrhoids exist," Bazarov exclaimed with a contemptuous smile.*

In this exchange from Ivan Turgenev's Fathers and Sons, *a novel of generational conflict in mid-nineteenth-century Russia, a hardboiled young materialist challenges everything his romantic elders hold dear. Bazarov, a medical researcher, casually asserts the superiority of science over art, of practical knowledge over poetry. His tone is that of the second half of the century, with its harsh realism, its conviction that cutting up frogs is useful, while love of art is "just a means of making money."*

*Ivan Turgenev, Fathers and Sons, trans. Barbara Makanowitzky (New York: Bantam Books, 1959), pp. 16, 21, 23.

---

planation in *The Origin of Species* (1859), a book as important in the history of science as Newton's *Principles of Natural Philosophy* two hundred years earlier.

Darwin declared that all species, including humans, were the product of a long biological development, or evolution. This process involved two crucial factors: variation and competition for survival.

All individual members of a given species, Darwin said, differed from one another, and these variations were hereditary—that is, they could be passed to their offspring. In this world,

there were never enough food, mates, shelter, and other necessities of life for all the creatures born into it. The result was an intense struggle for existence, a competition in which those individuals who had characteristics, or variations, that were best fitted for the particular environment survived. These survivors then passed on their particular characteristics to succeeding generations. In time, unsuitable variations would disappear and a new species, better adapted to its environment, would take shape through this "survival of the fittest."

In an ice-age climate, for instance,

mammoths with particularly heavy coats of fur would be likely to survive and reproduce, until only the wooly mammoth remained. The fastest gazelles would escape the tiger, until speed became a primary characteristic of the species. The human race itself, Darwin declared, was the product of such an evolutionary process. Our ancestry could be traced back to creatures something like modern apes, who were in fact our evolutionary cousins.

Social Darwinists took up this theory and applied it to contemporary human institutions and practices. Fang-and-claw competition among businessmen and the dominant position of the middle class in society could both be justified in terms of survival of the fittest. The new wave of imperial conquest upon which Europeans embarked in the 1870s was defended as an example of the triumph of the superior—more fit—white race. Even war could be seen as a healthy form of competition that would lead to the survival of the fittest form of society.

Opposition to Darwinism, however, was as vocal as support for it. The Darwinian theory of a struggle for survival, of "nature red in tooth and claw," had little in common with the Enlightenment vision of nature as a system of harmonious natural laws. Darwin's view also contrasted strikingly with the romantic emphasis on the beauty and divinity of nature. Further, the Christian morality of the age was affronted by the efforts of social Darwinists to justify such activities as war and unbridled competition as socially healthy for the species despite the pain inflicted on the individual.

Most disturbing to nineteenth-century sensibilities, however, was the Darwinian assumption that human beings were only very clever animals, relatives of gorillas and chimpanzees. The very existence of the Christian soul seemed to be denied by evolution, human reason dethroned from its central place by science itself. However far we had evolved, we were still merely animals, our nature animal nature at its core.

Freud and the Unconscious

Sigmund Freud (1856–1939) was an Austrian physician who began his career as a specialist in nervous disorders in Vienna at the end of the nineteenth century. His patients included a number of people who seemed to have symptoms for which no clear physical causes could be determined. In treating these ailments, Freud worked out the basic principles of developmental psychology, the core of the twentieth-century discipline of psychoanalysis.

Freud made the revolutionary claim that the dominant element in the human psyche was neither reason nor any other conscious faculty, but the unconscious mind. The mind, like an iceberg, existed mostly below the surface of consciousness, and it was the unconscious mind that determined conscious behavior. Decisions, in short, were not made on the basis of rational or moral considerations, nor by conscious acts of will at all, but by unconscious drives and instincts.

Probing the unconscious through analysis of dreams, Freud came to the even more disturbing conclusion that the central unconscious drive, what he called "libido," was the sex instinct, though he later came to think of it as a more generalized, all-encompassing desire. Human behavior, he believed, was the result of the interaction of libidinal energies with the external social forces that attempted to tame and direct our instincts. The repression and control of basic drives, while necessary for life in civilized society, could also cause deep psychological problems like those he treated in turn-of-the-century Vienna.

Freud, like Darwin, stirred up violent opposition. Once more, morality, spirituality, and reason were denied their central place in human nature. Primacy this time was assigned directly to nonrational drives and instincts closer to the impulses of barnyard animals than to the mental processes of educated nineteenth-century people.

Nietzsche and Nonrationalism

The German philosopher Friedrich Nietzsche (1844–1900) launched an open and violent intellectual assault on the highest—and in his view most misguided—spiritual and moral beliefs of his day. In strange books with provocative titles like *Antichrist* (1895), *Beyond Good and Evil* (1886), and *Thus Spake Zarathustra* (1885), Nietzsche attacked everything the nineteenth century valued and exalted "the will to power," an instinct that lay beyond the reach of most people. When he went hopelessly insane in 1889, he had few followers. By the turn of the century, however, he was a cult hero for growing numbers of students, artists, and intellectuals.

Nietzsche's condemnation of his age was sweeping. Intriguing statesmen, greedy businessmen, hypocritical preachers, dishonest liberals, and bloodthirsty generals were all exposed to jeering contempt. Worse even than their leaders were the masses of Europeans. The common people—meaning ordinary people of all social classes—were for Nietzsche cowards and conformists, a "herd animal." The essence of what he called their "slave morality" was a desire for revenge on the few truly exceptional people among them.

The only hope for humankind, Nietzsche believed, lay in the irrational will to power of the outstanding few, so far superior to run-of-the-mill humanity as to deserve the label "supermen." The will to power, as Nietzsche defined it, was a drive for self-transcending freedom, a longing to be more than human, which had no fixed goal. Power over the self, power over the future—the Nietzschean will was as nonrational an ideal as the century produced.

Others joined in the rediscovery of the nonrational, especially in the 1890s. The French philosopher Henri Bergson preached the *elan vital*, a milder instinct than Nietzsche's, an urge toward freedom, wholeness, intuitive understanding, and vitality that went beyond reason and social usefulness. The French socialist Georges Sorel, in his *Reflections on Violence* (1908), insisted that not reason but instinctive acceptance of a great social myth leading to such violent direct action as a general strike could bring change to Europe. Artists and

FACTS WHICH CANNOT BE DISPUTED?

(1)

The main conclusion arrived at in this work, and now held by many naturalists who are well competent to form a sound judgment, is that man is descended from some less highly organized form. The grounds upon which this conclusion rests will never be shaken, for the close similarity between man and the lower animals, in embryonic development, as well as in innumerable points of structure and constitution . . . are facts which cannot be disputed. [*]

(2)

Mr. Darwin . . . declares that he applies his scheme . . . of natural selection to man himself, as well as to the animals around him. Now, we must say at once that such a notion is absolutely incompatible not only with . . . the word of God . . . but . . . with the whole . . . moral and spiritual condition of man. . . . Man's derived supremacy over the earth . . . man's gift of reason; man's free will and responsibility; man's fall and man's redemption; the incarnation of the Eternal Son; the indwelling of the Eternal Spirit—all are equally and utterly irreconcilable with the degrading notion of the brute origin of him who was created in the image of God. . . . [**]

Charles Darwin, in the first extract, claimed the scientific evidence of embryology and anatomy supported his view that human beings had evolved from "some less highly organized form" of life. Bishop Samuel Wilberforce, a leading opponent of Darwinian evolution, responded by pointing in horror to the "moral and spiritual" implications of evolution. Darwin's "facts which cannot be disputed" convinced the large majority of biologists, yet are still debated today, mostly because of the religious and moral implications that so disturbed Wilberforce.

[*]Charles Darwin, *The Descent of Man*, in *Darwin*, ed. Philip Appleman (New York: W. W. Norton, 1979), p. 196.
[**]Samuel Wilberforce, review of *The Origin of Species*, in Basil Duke Henning, Archibald S. Ford, and Barbara L. Mathias, *Crises in English History 1066–1945* (New York: Henry Holt, 1957), p. 451.

scholars alike sought to explore the intuitive, the instinctual, the deep, nonrational drives they believed truly governed human behavior.

Scientists like Darwin and Freud spoke from the scientific materialism of the second half of the century. Artists and thinkers like Nietzsche and Bergson expressed the revival of concern with the emotional and even spiritual side of human nature that came with the end of the century.

Both groups, however, reflected a growing western fascination with the nonrational core of human character.

EMERGENCE OF AMERICAN CULTURE

The cultural life of the new American nations followed its own course in the

Friedrich Nietzsche. One of the most reviled and admired thinkers of the nineteenth century, Nietzsche is shown in a pensive mood in this photograph. An iconoclast always, he became a cult figure after his death in 1900.

nineteenth century, although it continued to be heavily influenced by the cultural currents of Europe. Major differences continued between the Latin republics of the south and the United States, the major power of North America. Latin American culture was still closer to that of continental Europe, though Latin Americans increasingly sought to define their own identity as a New World fusion of cultures. The United States, although influenced by British culture in particular, produced some highly individualistic artists and some distinctively American schools of thought.

Art and Thought in the United States

The culture of the United States partly reflected that of Europe throughout the nineteenth century. Both romanticism and literary realism, for instance, had their devotees across the Atlantic. The American poet and short-story writer Edgar Allen Poe displayed the romantic's fascination with the emotions and especially with the supernatural. Herman Melville's novels of the south seas took romantically-inclined readers to primitive places far from the counting houses of Boston or New York.

American realists in the later years of the century seldom matched Zola's naturalistic passion for the brutal side of life. Nevertheless, writers like Hamlin Garland depicted the life of midwestern pioneers and farmers with an uncompromising realism that included the loneliness, drabness, and hard work as well as the strength of spirit sometimes found there. At the turn of the century, such realistic novelists as Theodore Dreiser and Stephen Crane brought a touch of European harshness to their portrayal of human cruelty and the grim underside of American society. The muckraking social novels of Frank Norris, which exposed the seamier side of American business and politics, were directly influenced by the work of Zola.

Nineteenth-century American painters were mostly trained or influenced by European artists. Winslow Homer's seascapes have a strongly romantic feeling for nature. The American impressionist Mary Cassatt moved permanently to Paris. Distinctively American subjects did tempt some United States' artists, however, including the romantic painters of the Hudson River school and George Catlin, who painted American Indians.

The United States in its first century also produced some isms of its own. The transcendentalist movement of the pre-Civil War period displayed a distinctively American confidence in the divine essence of each individual. Such transcendentalists as Ralph Waldo Emerson preached freedom and self-reliance as typically American virtues. During the Gilded Age of American industrial growth after the Civil War, William James expounded another characteristically American philosophy: pragmatism. James defined the truth of an idea in terms of its practical usefulness. Truth, he said, is what works—an idea that just suited the bustling, not overly idealistic, United States of his time.

Some of the United States' most famous writers were striking individuals. Mark Twain's humorous narratives of life in the pre-Civil War south and on the western frontier had no parallel in Europe. Henry James' novels examined another distinctly American subject: the conflict between relatively simple and straightforward Americans and sophisticated, worldly Europeans. Poets Walt Whitman and Emily Dickinson also had no obvious counterparts elsewhere. Whitman's passionate *Leaves of Grass* (1855) hymned the potential greatness of a whole people. Dickinson's short, exquisitely crafted lyrics explored her own soul and the spiritual dimensions of simple things.

Latin American Culture

In South as in North America, new cultures were emerging as the nineteenth century drew to a close. Although Latin American scholars and writers drew heavily on European cultural sources, they used these to help them achieve their own cultural and intellectual independence from the Old World. Latin American men of letters also frequently combined literature with political affairs or even armed struggle. José Martí, for example, Cuba's most honored writer, was a poet who died fighting in Cuba's rebellion against Spain in the 1890s.

Romanticism had a longer and deeper influence on Latin American literature than it did in North America, but it was a romanticism adapted to Latin America's cultural needs. South American writers appear to have had little enthusiasm for the towering romantic ego or for the supernaturalism of the Gothic romance. They did seize on the romantic glorification of freedom, the primacy of emotion,

and in some cases the superiority of the primitive. Glorifying the wide, free life, for instance, the Argentine poet José Hernandez praised the freedom-loving gaucho, the cowboy of the pampas. Mexican poets honored the memory of the ancient Aztecs, and Brazilians celebrated their Indian ancestors. Paralleling Victor Hugo, Argentina's Domingo Sarmiento defined romanticism as "a true literary insurrection."

Realism, naturalism, and positivism also made their appearance in Latin America in the last decades of the century. A positivist school of historians writing in Mexico, Argentina, Brazil, and Chile documented the worst abuses of the old Spanish colonial regime, from the conquistadors to the Inquisition. Realistic and naturalistic novelists exposed the materialistic inhumanity of the Industrial Revolution in those nations. Chilean realist Alberto Blest Gana, influenced by Balzac, depicted a money-grubbing society in novels like *Arithmetic in Love* (1860). The Brazilian writer Euclides da Cunha's *Rebellion in the Backlands* (1902) mingled realistic and romantic influences in a powerful evocation of primitive Brazilian backwoodsmen in revolt against an oppressive government.

An underlying concern of much of this writing was the desire to explore and establish a genuinely Latin American culture, distinct from that of Europe. By condemning their European ancestors and glorifying their Amerindian ones, by evoking such clearly South American phenomena as the gaucho of the pampas, these writers strove to achieve a sense of their own cultural uniqueness.

Emily Dickinson. The American poet is depicted here as a young woman. Despite a narrowly circumscribed life in the small town of Amherst, Massachusetts, Dickinson revealed a creative genius that could encompass the broadest of human concerns.

SUMMARY

The culture of the nineteenth century was complex and often challenging to the conventional beliefs and values of the age. Romanticism, in the first half of the century, materialism, in the second half, and an exploration of nonrationalism at the end of the century dominated the life of the European mind. In the Americas, these and other themes emerged in the cultures of the new nations.

Romanticism in literature, painting, and music asserted the superiority of the emotions over reason and exalted nature, underdeveloped cultures, far-away places, and colorful periods of the past. Romantic artists also rejected the formal rules for the arts required by the classical tradition, insisting instead on the free play of the imagination. As a cultural revolt, romanticism expressed a growing sense of alienation from the vulgarities of nineteenth-century industrial civilization and stressed once more the emotional response over intellectual analysis.

Materialism drew from the continued progress of the physical sciences the conclusion that only the material world existed. Dismissing religion as an illusion, this world view insisted on positivistic knowledge, derived exclusively from empirical observation. Realists attempted to describe this material world in paint or prose. Impressionists tried to paint light as the eye sees it, naturalists like Zola to describe human beings as mere biological organisms, without spiritual or moral dimensions.

Nonrationalism explored the animal origins and instinctive drives beneath human reason. Darwinian evolution stressed the struggle for existence, Freudian psychoanalysis found the sex drive at the heart of life, and Nietzsche glorified the will to power.

The cultural history of the Americas reflected both European influences and New World concerns. The growing United States produced some writers influenced by romanticism and realism, but also gave birth to such distinctive schools of thought as transcendentalism and to such unique talents as Mark Twain and Emily Dickinson, Walt Whitman and Henry James.

Latin American culture in the nineteenth century stuck closer to European models, from romanticism to naturalism and positivism. But Latin American writers used these forms and ideas to define the uniqueness of their culture, lauding freedom and their Indian heritage and condemning their Spanish colonial past and the industrializing present.

The western peoples were proud of their cultural accomplishments in the nineteenth century, as they were of their increasing wealth and power. In the later nineteenth century, this sense of cultural superiority was heightened by the dramatic expansion of western empires, the topic of the following chapter.

SELECTED SOURCES

Bloom, Harold, and Lionel Trilling, ed. *Romantic Prose and Poetry.* 1973. Anthology of the literature.

Clark, Kenneth. *The Romantic Rebellion: Romantic Versus Classic Art.* 1973. Well-written, well-illustrated essays on leading artists by a leading art historian.

*Crane, Stephen. *Maggie: A Girl of the Streets.* 1978. The seamy underside of American society at the end of the nineteenth century, by a leading American realist.

*Dumas, Alexandre. *The Count of Monte Cristo.* 1982. Novel by a leading romantic writer, packed with romantic themes, from love and adventure to a hero with a dark secret and a feud with the powers of society.

*Eiseley, Loren. *Darwin's Century: Evolution and the Men Who Discovered It.* 1958. Thoughtful and readable account of the early evolutionists.

*Freud, Sigmund. *On Dreams.* 1963. An essay by the founder of psychoanalysis on dream interpretation as a gateway to the unconscious mind.

*Schenk, H. G. *The Mind of the European Romantics.* 1979. One-volume survey of this complex subject.

*Shattuck, Roger. *The Banquet Years.* 1968. Vigorous and colorful profile of Paris culture in the bohemian end-of-the-century years.

Smith, H. N. *Democracy and the American Novel.* 1978. A discussion of U.S. fiction during this period.

*Stern, J. P. *Friedrich Nietzsche.* 1978. Brief discussion of this strange prophet of nonrationalism.

*Available in paperback.

THE NEW IMPERIALISM

At midday on Tuesday, June 22, 1897, Queen Victoria of England, Defender of the Faith, Empress of India, ruler of the British Dominions beyond the Seas, arrived at St. Paul's Cathedral to thank God for the existence of the greatest Empire ever known.

The representatives of an imperial caste awaited her there. Bishops of the Church of England fluttered hymnal sheets and remembered half a century of Christian effort—the suppression of slavery, the conversion of heathen tribes, mission stations from Niger to Labrador. Generals and admirals blazed with medals and remembered half a century of satisfactory campaigning. . . . There were scholars in the gowns of Oxford and Cambridge, the twin powerhouses of British ideology. There were poets, musicians, and propagandists, whose transcendental theme of the day was the splendor of imperial Britain.

. . . Behind these marshals, soldiers from every part of the Queen's Empire honored the royal presence. The Chinese from Hong Kong wore wide coolie hats. The Zaptiehs, Turkish military policemen from Cyprus, wore fezzes. The Jamaicans wore white gaiters and gold-embroidered jackets. There were Dyaks from Borneo, and Sikhs from India, and Canadian Hussars, and Sierra Leone gunners, and Australian cavalrymen, and British Guiana police, and Maltese, and South Africans, and a troop of jangling Bengal Lancers. . . . [these soldiers represented] nearly 400 million subjects living in all five continents, honoring a thousand religions, speaking a thousand languages—people of every race, culture, stage of development.

This scene of imperial splendor depicts one point in the Diamond Jubilee, a ceremony marking the sixtieth year of the reign of Queen Victoria. The Jubilee also celebrated the glory and majesty of the British Empire, the world's greatest imperialist dynamo at the height of western power around the globe. In the latter part of the nineteenth century, a complex of motives set the most powerful states of Europe, along with the United States and Japan, into a spasm of imperialistic conquest. This period of aggression has been called the New Imperialism, to distinguish it from the earlier era of 400 years of overseas conquest, sometimes called the Old Imperialism. Much of the process was accident and incident rather than

The Beginning of the Modern Imperialist Era. In this somewhat primitive painting French troops are seen assaulting Algiers in 1830. Their success opened the way for the French to eventually take control of northwest Africa and in general inaugurated the European conquest of Africa and other parts of the world.

645

grand design, but by 1914 the imperialist states had beaten off indigenous resistance and rebellion and taken direct control over much of Asia, Africa, and the Pacific. Meanwhile, the United States and Great Britain had established indirect control over much of Latin America. Although the powers engaged in vigorous competition and confrontation, no wars broke out among imperialist nations. The accumulated tension stemming from the imperialist rivalries, however, contributed significantly to the Great War of 1914.

CHARACTERISTICS OF THE NEW IMPERIALISM

The imperialism of the late nineteenth century both resembled and differed from the imperialism of earlier centuries. The motives were roughly the same, but the roster of imperialist powers had greatly changed, including for the first time a nonwestern nation. For the conquered peoples, however, the new imperialism meant the same as the old—some form of subjugation.

Old Motives Made New

Four major motivations can be found for the New Imperialism. All of them—economic, strategic, cultural, and nationalistic—had been present in the Old Imperialism but now took a more virulent form in the New.

As in the Old Imperialism, the New Imperialism was impelled in large part by economic interests, but those that reflected the needs of a new day. The

Old Imperialism was primarily concerned with acquiring consumer goods. Nineteenth-century western powers were still interested in consumer goods, but now they also sought abundant supplies of coal, iron ore, copper, other industrial ores, and (later) rubber and petroleum.

Manufacturers were also interested in finding mass markets abroad. Domestic markets in industrial nations were rapidly becoming saturated, and sales outside were needed. Ideally, these areas should be heavily populated, such as Nigeria, India, or China, and there should be no competition from other western manufacturing nations, so that the highest possible prices could be charged.

Nations in the late nineteenth century also seized certain areas for strategic reasons, especially to provide naval bases to protect the sealanes between the important colonies and the conquering nation. The Hawaiian Islands and Aden are prime examples of such strategic locations. The imperial powers also took Reunion, Midway, and many other islands to obtain food, fuel, and water for vessels and for telegraph relays. Imperialist nations often seized and fortified otherwise unprofitable interior areas in Africa and Asia as buffer zones to shield valuable areas from real or potential enemies.

Another major motive was cultural imperialism, whereby western nations pressed their ideas and values on other cultures by persuasion or force. The New Imperialism was often self-conscious and doctrinaire in imposing its culture on the nonwestern world. Westerners were proud of what they perceived to be the great economic, scientific, technological, social, and religious progress of their

civilization, and this attitude was reflected in their imperialist policies. Two influential doctrines helped to transform this pride into justification for conquest. A new outbreak of racist thought extolled the superiority of the white race, and Social Darwinists proclaimed that nature had ordained that some human groups would flourish and that the less fit would perish.

As in the Old Imperialism, spreading the Christian religion was a major aspect of cultural imperialism. Previously, the Roman Catholic church had taken a far more active and successful role in securing converts than the Protestant sects, but this situation changed significantly during the course of the nineteenth century. The aggressive efforts of the French government to spread Catholicism in Africa, Asia, and Polynesia were often matched in missionary vigor by Protestant church organizations, such as the Anglican church's Society for the Propagation of the Gospel.

In effect, most westerners were sure that imperialistic conquests conformed to the laws of God and nature. As the west saw it, the conquered groups would benefit by being under the tutelage of a superior culture and given an opportunity to discard their backward ways. As members of an inferior race, however, these peoples, in the eyes of most westerners, could never be expected to grasp the essence of western civilization and would only ape its outward forms.

Finally, the nationalism that was surging across the western world in the late nineteenth century found expression in part in colonial rivalries among the major powers. Bismarck at first believed that colonies caused more trouble with other major states than they were worth, but he changed

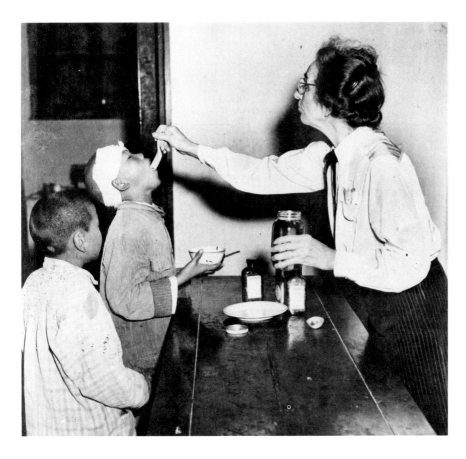

A Benign Aspect of Imperialism. In addition to conquest and spoilation, imperialism often brought with it life-saving advances in medicine and sanitation. Here an American missionary in China dispenses cod-liver oil and vitamins. Women played a significant role in cultural imperialism, serving as missionaries, nurses, and teachers.

his mind. Possessing a colonial empire was one of the hallmarks of national prestige. Rising powers such as Germany and Italy became convinced that they, too, should acquire colonies and challenge the established colonial powers.

Quite often, imperialist powers seized areas without known economic or strategic value simply to forestall national enemies. Competing states even claimed coral atolls, desert sands, and icy wastes. By 1914, imperialist nations controlled directly or indirectly most of the globe.

The Impact of Technology

New technology provided the means to gratify imperialist desires. The military might of the west during the Old Imperialism had been formidable, but the firepower of nineteenth century western armies and navies was overwhelming; any area in the world could be conquered by rifled artillery and machine guns and any subsequent rebellions suppressed. Imperialist nations could now profitably penetrate deep into Africa and Asia, because railroads and river steamers could bring valuable commodities out to the coast and carry manufactured goods inland. From modern harbors in the colonies, the new iron ocean-going ships, powered by steam-driven screw propellers, carried larger cargoes to their destination faster and more safely than the old sailing ships. Engineers built and constructed canals that cut to less

than half the journey from India to Great Britain or from New York to San Francisco.

A New Mix of Participants

The cast of imperialist nations changed greatly by the late nineteenth century. Three of the great colonial powers of the earlier era, Portugal, Spain, and the Netherlands, lacked the economic and military resources to compete with the powerful industrial states and took no significant role in the new era. Spain actually lost ground, losing her remaining Caribbean and Pacific possessions to the United States. By 1900 Portugal and Spain controlled only a few fragments in the

Atlantic, Africa, and (the Portuguese) in Asia. The Dutch were fully occupied in holding on to their rich domains in the East Indies and to a few Caribbean possessions. Of the original imperial powers, only Great Britain, France, and Russia participated vigorously in the new scramble. In terms of overseas empires, Great Britain had a large initial advantage over the French. The British already controlled colonies across most of the globe, and their vainglorious saying, "The sun never sets on the British Empire" already came close to the truth. The French, although a powerful continental state, had no more extensive colonial holdings than the Spanish or Portuguese.

The three traditional imperial powers were joined by several rising powers that held no overseas possessions. The entrepreneurs of Belgium and of the new nations of Italy and Germany were looking overseas for raw materials and markets, and their governments also became involved in these ventures. Also, for the first time, two nations outside of Europe, the United States and Japan, were ready to challenge European power.

Although colonial competition was fierce and many blustering confrontations took place, no wars broke out among the competing powers. Disputes were usually settled over whiskey and wine at international conferences or in foreign office drawing rooms, as diplomats drew arbitrary lines across rough charts of Africa and Asia, allotting this area to one imperialist power and that to another. Often in the process African and Asian groups were divided and put into different colonies or rival peoples thrown together into one colony. Although disputes over colonies did not cause

any wars directly, colonial confrontations contributed to the onset of World War I. Ironically, the European powers weakened themselves so much during the conflict that after the war their control over conquered peoples began to decline.

THE CONQUEST OF AFRICA

In the most spectacular example of the New Imperialism at work, European nations gobbled up nearly all of the continent of Africa in just thirty-five years. Ironically, Africa, the first continent touched by the Old Imperialism, had subsequently been virtually ignored by Europeans, who were preoccupied by the greater riches of Asia and the Americas. Except for the southern tip of Africa Europeans were only present in small slave-trading enclaves on the coast. By the nineteenth century, the interior of Africa was still largely unknown to Europeans, who called it the Dark Continent.

The good fortune of being ignored by Europeans finally ran out. Early in the century, the French and British made some advances, and mid-nineteenth century European explorers such as Henry Stanley whetted the appetite of Europeans by bringing back news of precious metals, valuable consumer goods, and industrial raw materials. In 1879, when the Belgians moved into the Congo River basin (eventually acquiring control of an area seventy-five times larger than Belgium), almost all of Africa was still independent of Europe. The scramble for colonies soon picked up momentum, and by 1914 nearly all of the continent was in European hands. To

minimize the chances that war would break out among the competing nations, European nations met at an international conference at Berlin in 1884–1885. There they agreed that the first nation to effectively occupy an area and notify other nations would be confirmed in possession.

Although they fought back, for the most part the technologically unsophisticated Africans had no chance to successfully resist. The Zulus in southern Africa and the followers of the Mahdi, the Muslim religious leader in the Sudan, initially defeated British armies but eventually succumbed. Nor did Africans tamely endure European controls. By 1915 twenty-seven major revolts, affecting most of the colonies, had taken place. The Berbers in the Sahara were never completely conquered, as the history of the French Foreign Legion attested. Still, by 1914, the continent was firmly in the possession of the European imperial powers. Only two small nations, Ethiopia, which defeated an Italian invading force at Adowa in 1896, and Liberia, founded by former slaves from the United States, survived as nominally independent states.

The French and British in Africa

Beginning in 1830, France moved into Algeria and established secure control over the coast there after thirty years of bitter fighting with the Muslims. The French government encouraged French settlers, *colons*, to come to the area, where they dispossessed Muslim landholders and thus monopolized the lucrative production of dates, figs, grapes, and citrus fruits. From their base in Algeria, plus those established on the Atlantic coast in

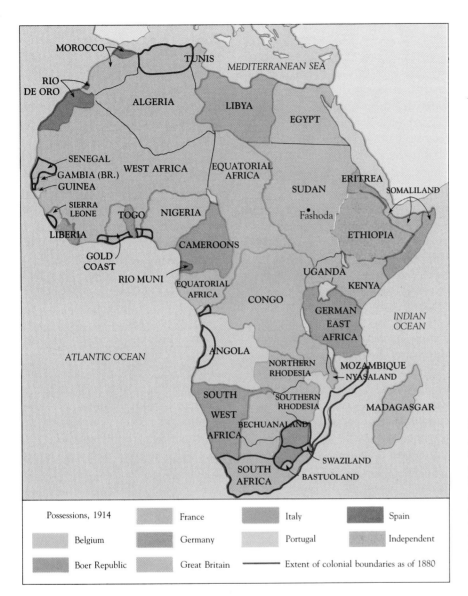

MAP 70
Africa in 1914. After a single generation of intense expansion, nearly all of the African continent was in the grip of European powers by the outbreak of World War I. Great Britain and France dominated Africa, holding great contiguous blocks supplemented by other scattered possessions. Portugal, the oldest colonial power, had consolidated its string of trading posts into three colonies, while the late arriving Germans and Italians had to settle for scattered holdings.

Senegal and elsewhere, the French moved into the interior of western Africa. By the 1890s, the French controlled about 40 percent of Africa and 26 million people, most of their holdings comprising a vast block extending from the shores of the Mediterranean to the banks of the Congo River. Still, the French had even bigger plans: They hoped to move eastward across the northern half of Africa to link up with their foothold on the Red Sea.

Great Britain's strategy evolved slowly, first centering around Egypt and then becoming continental. The Suez Canal, connecting the Red Sea and the Mediterranean, opened in 1869. It was built by an international corporation dominated by the French, but the British, interested in obtaining the shortest trade route to India,

acquired control of the company in 1875. To protect this vital link, the British took over de facto control of Egypt (although it technically remained a province of the Ottoman Empire) and later created a large naval base at Alexandria. In the 1880s, the British moved southward up the Nile Valley to help the Egyptians take possession of the Sudan, a process delayed for more than a decade by Mus-

649

lim resistance led by the Mahdi. By 1898 the British held the Sudan, Uganda, and also Kenya, where a few British would later settle. British possession of these areas blocked the French from extending their control eastward to the Red Sea, and in 1899 a French military expedition into the Sudan came face to face with British forces at Fashoda, on the White Nile. Ultra-nationalist "yellow" press in the two nations whipped up belligerent hysteria, and war seemed imminent, but the French, beset with internal divisions and unprepared to take on the British navy, backed down.

Meanwhile, the British were advancing northward out of southern Africa. In 1806, the British had seized the area at the Cape of Good Hope from the Dutch, coming into control of about 15,000 Boers (farmers), or Afrikaners. The Boers resented British controls, however, and during the 1830s and the 1840s began a mass migration, the Great Trek (journey), out of British jurisdiction into rela-

tively open areas inland. In the 1850s, they created two independent nations, the Transvaal and the Orange Free State. British settlers filled in the coastal areas vacated by the Boers. Later in the century, the British headed north around the Boer republics, led by the "Empire Builder" Cecil Rhodes. By the 1890s, Rhodes had suppressed local black resistance in the temperate plateau north of the Boer republics, which had once been the African state of Great Zimbabwe. A few British settled there, naming the area Rhodesia.

While Rhodes was spreading British power northward, Great Britain went to war with the Boer republics. Gold had been discovered in the Transvaal, and a gold rush followed, with many non-Dutch swarming into the area. The Boers discriminated against these outsiders, including British subjects, and a series of incidents fomented by both sides led to the Boer War (1899–1902), in which the British conquered the republics.

During the course of the fighting the outmatched Boers resorted to hit-and-run guerrilla tactics, farmers by day becoming *kommando* fighters by night. The British retaliated by putting families from an entire district into internment camps to cut off civilian support for the guerrillas. This and other brutal tactics brought down severe criticism on the British, but other colonial nations resorted to similar measures. In 1910, the British federated the two former Boer republics with two English colonies into the Union of South Africa, a self-governing and ultimately Afrikaner-controlled dominion of the British Empire.

The British also controlled a series of colonies along the coast of western Africa. The most notable was Nigeria, a heavily populated area useful for marketing goods; later, it proved to have large petroleum deposits. Altogether, the British controlled 43 percent of Africa and 66 million people. Still, the heart of British impe-

Guerrilla Warfare. Here Boer *kommandos* look over the terrain during their war with the British in southern Africa. Their unconventional methods of fighting, such as not wearing uniforms, attacking from ambush, and blending in with the civilians, provoked harsh countermeasures, including shooting Boers after they surrendered and placing whole populations in internment camps. Guerrilla warfare became a major mode of combat after World War II, especially in struggles for independence and in movements of social revolution.

Europeans begin to carve up Africa

British complete conquest of Burma

French complete conquest of Indochina

Japan defeats China

Spanish–American War

Last of European defeats of China

Rhodesia organized by Cecil Rhodes

Ethiopians victorious at Adowa

rialism lay in eastern Africa, where some Britons envisioned filling in the remaining gap between Uganda/Kenya and Rhodesia, enabling them to control a continuous bloc of territory "from Cape to Cairo." However, the Germans stood in the way.

New Imperialist Powers Appear

At the same time that Great Britain and France, the established colonial powers, were scooping up huge domains in Africa, the two new nations of Germany and Italy were also elbowing into the race, although under the disadvantage of finding most of Africa preempted by other nations. The Germans occupied four areas on the coast of Africa, one of which, Southwest Africa, was rich in diamonds. Italy, a nation much feebler than the three states already discussed, had to settle for barren leftovers. The Italians took over much of the land of the Somalis on the Horn of Africa in the east, and seized Libya in 1912 from the moribund Ottoman Empire. However, the French faced them down over Tunisia, the part of Africa closest to Italy. Most humiliating of all, the poorly armed Ethiopians, the only Christian state in Africa, repelled Italian efforts to conquer them.

The Impact of Imperialism on Africa

Although many African colonies were not worth the cost of administration and protection, many of them did become profitable. Out of the continent poured such consumer goods as diamonds, gold, ivory, animal skins, sugar, coffee, chocolate, figs, dates, grapes, citrus fruits, and peanuts. After World War I the west exploited Africa for industrial raw materials such as uranium, bauxite, iron ore, copper, tin, rubber, petroleum, and cotton. The 120 million Africans were also a huge market for the cheap massproduced products of European industry.

The impact of colonial rule varied widely across the African continent. Many Africans seldom saw whites or felt much effect from white rule. In contrast, those unfortunate Africans who lived in areas designated for economic development often lost their lands and were worked to death for little or no pay in the mines and on the plantations of their white masters. At the same time Europeans saved many lives by suppressing tribal warfare and Arab slave raids and by instituting public health measures.

The attitude of racial and ethnic superiority held by the European white

conquerors strongly influenced colonial policy. The British kept their distance from peoples whom they considered innate inferiors who could never be assimilated. As a consequence, they kept local government in the hands of compliant village chiefs, and on the whole let their subjects practice their own culture as long as the general rules of government were obeyed and peace was maintained. Local practices which grossly offended British sensibilities, however, such as infanticide, were suppressed. Africans were allowed to function in the colonial government and army, but it was presumed they could never be the equal of a Briton.

Officially, French colonial policy was not racist. Africans were invited to partake of the glories of French culture and to think of themselves as French. On the other hand the French were the ultimate cultural imperialists, dismissing with contempt the idea that Africans, particularly Muslims, might have a culture equal to that of the west. They created a centralized colonial administration and pursued a vigorous assimilation policy intended to eventually eradicate African cultures and incorporate all colonials into the French way of life. In practice many French colonial officials and the colons in particular

651

treated Africans with racist contempt.

As was true of the Old Imperialism, at all stages colonialism depended on the technique of "divide and conquer." Most of Africa was not settled by whites, and in general European governments did not have the military and bureaucratic personnel to conquer, hold, and govern their huge colonies. Therefore, one local group was given favored treatment in return for helping the whites defeat and control other groups, often traditional enemies. Favored groups such as the Bagandas in Uganda and the Senegalese in French West Africa were taken into the colonial army and police forces, given a basic western education, and awarded lesser positions in the colonial bureaucracy.

The impress of the institutional and ideological aspects of western culture also varied widely across Africa. The purely technological aspects of western civilization, from railroads to medical clinics to the machine gun, were respected by virtually all Africans. Other aspects of Western culture made less headway. The Muslims of the northern third of Africa, as always, rejected western values and institutions and doggedly resisted the attempts of the French to assimilate them culturally. On the other hand, the values and institutions of the west made a significant impact in non-Islamic Africa, often destroying or altering local cultures. Many Africans came to prefer some or all aspects of western education, law, bureaucratic and military organization, political processes, and forms of government. Owing to intense missionary efforts by both Protestants and Catholics, many Africans in the southern two-thirds of the continent embraced

Christianity. Some even came to prefer the west's concepts of social and family relationships and its languages, calendar, and dress. Many Africans took up western culture to live as well as possible in a world they could not change, but a few Africans learned the ways of the west to be able to use them someday to drive out the colonial masters. Whether or not Africa regained its independence, western civilization had made an indelible impact.

EUROPEAN IMPERIALISM IN ASIA

Compared with the sudden swoop on Africa, European imperialism in Asia was rather an acceleration of a process that had been going on for four centuries. Asian principalities and empires over the first three centuries had generally been able to hold the Europeans at bay. By the eighteenth century, however, western military superiority was so overwhelming that the princes of India and Indonesia were being subjugated. By the nineteenth century, the great Chinese Empire itself, already weakened internally, was crumbling under foreign attacks.

India: The Heart of the British Empire

By 1850, the British East India Company had virtually completed the conquest of the Indian subcontinent and was in control of about 250 million people. In 1857, British control was challenged when Company sepoys rebelled over religious issues. Rebellion then spread for economic

and political reasons, and took fourteen months of heavy fighting to suppress. British control was not again seriously threatened until Mohandas Gandhi's civil disobedience campaigns in the 1930s. The British government took control of the area from the company in 1858, ruling 60 percent of the subcontinent directly and the rest indirectly through the great princes of India. India became the centerpiece of the British Empire, symbolized in the coronation of Queen Victoria as Empress of India in 1876.

India was a gold mine for the British. British and Indian-owned plantations produced rice, jute, cotton, and tea. Some modern textile and steel mills were built, as well as an extensive railroad network. India was perhaps more important to Great Britain for imports than for exports. Hundreds of millions of Indians bought British manufactured products, even if only the cheapest and shoddiest. In addition, taxes and government monopolies imposed on the Indian masses aggregated enormous sums of money.

As in Africa, hundreds of thousands of British controlled hundreds of millions of Indians, not only through military force, but also through the technique of divide and conquer. India was a geographic expression rather than a unified culture, containing a kaleidoscope of ethnic groups, languages, and religions, all accompanied by historic animosities. It was easy for the British to get Indians of one background to help them subdue and control Indians of another. Nepalese Gurkha troops were always reliable, and many Bengalis and Sikhs, as well as millions of other Indian individuals, aided British rule and received preferment in return.

India had a major impact on Great

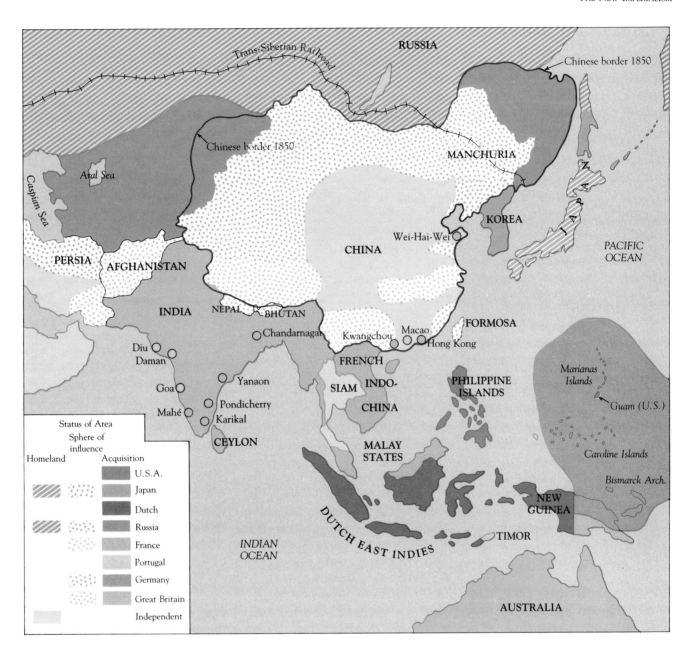

Map 71

Asia in 1914. Much of Asia was now controlled by imperialist powers. Most of Southern Asia had become colonial possessions of European nations and the United States. Independent states such as Persia and China were fast coming under the control of foreign nations. Japan, the new imperialist power in Asia, had annexed Formosa and Korea and also dominated large areas of China.

Britain. Affairs in India affected the lives and livelihoods of millions of Britons who never saw the subcontinent. Hundreds of thousands of Britons were in India, serving in the military or government, conducting business matters, or visiting, and some spent the rest of their lives there.

Britons of even modest income lived well in India and were able to retire comfortably back home in Great Britain.

Life in the Raj, as the British called India, had much the same racist and cultural dynamics as in British Africa. Most Britons looked down on Indi-

A Symbol of Imperial Power and Glory. India was the "jewel of the Empire," Great Britain's most valuable imperial possession, a source of immense wealth and great pride. The British monarch was also the monarch of India, and twentieth century British kings went to India to be so crowned. In this scene at the 1911 *durbar* (court), King George V and Queen Mary, newly crowned King Emperor and Empress of India, receive the homage of the Indian princes.

ans, even maharajahs, as inferiors who were capable only of learning the outer forms of western culture, but who could never really be western. Most Britons were also contemptuous of India's ancient civilization. They generally ignored its philosophical, religious, and artistic insights and concentrated instead on what they perceived as social abuses, especially the subjugated status of women. They eliminated the thuggees (who killed and robbed as a religious act), banned suttee (the burning alive of widows), and tried to eliminate the practice of child brides.

For the Indians, as for Africans, British occupation had an ambiguous impact. The masses of Indians had lived an impoverished and illiterate life toiling for the benefit of the elite before the British came; now they toiled for two sets of masters. As India became more involved in the world

market economy, the landlords planted less food and more cash crops. At the same time, the British were cutting the death rate by improving sanitation and other public health measures. As a result the population rapidly expanded while the per capita food supply fell, causing periodic famines.

Western civilization had a distinct impact on India. Western technology was accepted by the great majority. A few, such as Gandhi, believed that production in the home, such as spinning cotton, would be a better way to raise the economic and psychological threshold of the downtrodden. To adjust to a British-run world some Indians learned English, picked up a rudimentary western education, and copied British dress and social customs.

A few Indians of the elite, some of them attending British universi-

ties, studied British concepts of civil liberties, politics, law, and government. They became convinced that Great Britain should live by its own principles of liberty and free India. An independent India should adopt aspects of western education, law, and representative government and meld those with the traditional cultures of India. To bring about independence, nationalists formed the Indian National Congress in 1885. The Congress, at first a mere debating society, moved after 1905 to mass demonstrations, boycotts, and sporadic terrorism against the British.

Western social and religious institutions made little headway in India. Ever since the Portuguese had arrived in 1498, Christian missionaries had been active on the subcontinent, but by the twentieth century, less than 2 percent of the overall population was Christian. A few elite western-educated Hindus had become convinced that some regressive social aspects of Hinduism should be reformed, but otherwise retained their faith. The Muslims and Sikhs and the great majority of the Hindu population were unmoved by Christian evangelism. In the practice of most social and familiar customs, life went on for the great majority of Indians as if the Europeans had never come.

Protecting India: Imperialist Confrontations in Asia

British imperial policy revolved around protecting India. To secure the trade routes between the subcontinent and Great Britain, the British by the mid-nineteenth century had seized many islands in the Atlantic and Indian oceans and the Mediterranean Sea, and had taken control of Egypt and South Africa. India was not yet secure, however, because the British perceived the imperialist expansion of the French in southeast Asia and the Russians in central Asia to be new threats that would have to be thwarted.

In 1840 the French began their penetration into southeast Asia by annexing Cochin China. Thereafter, they steadily expanded their area of control, taking over Cambodia, Laos, and the rest of Vietnam. They came for the rubber, tin, petroleum, and rice of the area, to spread Catholicism and French culture, and for nationalist glory. To create a buffer zone between India and the French and also to exploit the resources of the area, the British took over Burma and expanded from Singapore onto the Malay Peninsula. Although tension was at times high, neither nation

wanted war, and therefore both nations allowed Siam to retain a precarious independence as a convenient buffer zone between the two spheres of influence.

Although Great Britain avoided war to the east of India, to the west it found itself embroiled in a dangerous confrontation with tsarist Russia. The Russians had moved steadily southeastward through central Asia during the nineteenth century, conquering the historic Muslim khanates there and approaching India from the northwest. The Russians were next interested in taking control of Afghanistan and Persia, which in the eyes of the British would mean a direct overland threat to India. Furthermore, control of Persia would allow the Russians to construct a naval base on the Indian Ocean that would give them an opportunity to disrupt the vital trade route between Great Britain and India. The British made it quite clear to the Russians that any attempt to take direct control of Persia and Afghanistan would mean war, but the Russians refused to back down. About 1900 the first war fostered by the New Imperialism appeared to be imminent. A belligerent music hall song expressed the mood in Great Britain:

> We don't want to fight,
> But by Jingo! if we do
> We've got the ships,
> We've got the men
> And got the money, too!

Events elsewhere averted a Russian-British conflict. Imperialist conflicts provoked the Japanese to attack and defeat the Russians in 1905, weakening the Russians and cooling their imperialist ardor. Both Great Britain

and Russia increasingly feared rapidly rising, aggressive Germany. Encouraged by the French, the British and the Russians hammered out a rapprochement in 1907. For the vague understanding that Great Britain would not attack Russia if Russia should become involved in war with Germany, the tsarist government gave way in Asia. The Russians limited themselves to a sphere of influence in northern Persia, while acknowledging British dominance in Afghanistan and southeastern Persia. The "Jewel of the Empire" was safe.

The Transformation of Australasia and the Pacific

British imperialism in Australia and New Zealand paralleled the pattern in British North America. Europeans had conquered the native populations by the end of the nineteenth century and had taken over most of the land for a white domain. Australia subsequently prohibited Asian immigration. Eastern Australia and much of New Zealand were temperate areas much like the British Isles and attracted many settlers from there. They came originally for sheep ranching and farming, but quickly developed a balanced economy, including substantial manufacturing.

Finding two attractive replicas "Down Under," and remembering its North American experience, the British government collected the six Australian colonies into the self-governing Commonwealth of Australia in 1901 and set up the equivalent for New Zealand in 1907. Labor governments brought in the welfare state in both nations. Women had the vote there by the 1890s.

The New Imperialism was as active

1898	1902	1906	1910	1914

Boer War

Open Door in China

Russo–Japanese War

Japan completes annexation of Korea

Panama Canal opens

Fashoda Crisis

Boxer Rebellion

Roosevelt Corollary

Moroccan Crisis

in the Pacific as it was in other parts of the world. The economic value of the area was slight, and most of the islands had little strategic value, although the imperialists' fevered imaginations readily supplied some. A scramble ensued like the one in Africa, occasionally becoming quite heated. In 1898 the inhabitants of Samoa watched a British, a German, and a U.S. naval squadron threaten one another in the strategically remote harbor of Pago Pago. A typhoon devastated the squadrons and calmed matters down momentarily, but the island grab went roaring on. By 1914 nearly all of the thousands of islands and coral atolls in the Pacific Ocean sported the flag of one of the imperialist nations.

The European Onslaught on the Manchu Empire

During the course of the nineteenth century, imperialist nations began to take over China, the one great prize that had hitherto escaped them. For thousands of years, the autocratic Chinese Empire had been one of the world's most advanced and powerful civilizations, dominating east Asia economically, militarily, and culturally. The Chinese saw themselves the "Central Kingdom" around which the

rest of the world revolved and considered all others, including westerners, to be tributary barbarians. Whereas western traders sought tea, silk, porcelain and many other commodities, there was little that the Chinese wanted in return except payments in gold, silver, and furs. Trade with the west was a profitable but minor aspect of the Chinese economy, and the Manchu dynasty, as the Ming dynasty before it, permitted westerners to trade only in the Canton area of south China.

By the nineteenth century, several major factors led to the undoing of the Manchu dynasty. Westerners in the era of the Industrial Revolution began to see China not only as a supplier of consumer goods but also as a source of coal, iron ore, and other industrial raw materials. Above all, China, like India, represented a huge market where hundreds of millions of people would buy European manufactured products. In addition, the Chinese, unused to borrowing from other cultures, had done little to industrialize or build up modern armed forces. Each major European nation by the nineteenth century now had the military strength to defeat the Chinese. Furthermore, the Manchu dynasty was weakened by a series of rebellions. European nations were now

ready to attack the huge but flabby empire to force it to agree to advantageous trade; the prospect also existed of later carving up China like Africa and the rest of Asia.

In a series of wars beginning in 1839 and ending in 1885, the Chinese Empire was left prostrate at the feet of the victorious British, French, German, and Russian "barbarians." After the first war, the British forced the Chinese government to commence diplomatic relations, to admit opium grown in India, and to open more ports to trade. Other nations forced the Chinese to do the same. The Chinese had to surrender areas in central Asia and along the northeast Pacific coast to Russia. The British took over Tibet as a protectorate as did the Russians in Manchuria. The four powers seized six coastal ports as colonies, the largest being Great Britain's Hong Kong.

Loss of territory on the fringes of the empire was secondary compared with two disastrous patterns the west now imposed on the Chinese: monopoly zones and extraterritoriality. By the end of the century, Great Britain, France, Germany, and Russia had secured monopoly zones, or spheres of influence, in populous and economically valuable eastern China. In each zone a European nation had the exclusive right to secure the raw materials and commodities and to enjoy a monopoly on selling goods to the people of the area. European gunboats patrolling the coasts and rivers of China secured these zones against both European competitors and interference by the Chinese government. Actually, although some tension existed, the imperialist powers essentially let one another alone; there was plenty of China to go around. Latecomers, however, would be faced with forcing—perhaps fighting—their way in. China was saved from direct dismemberment by fear among the western powers that any attempt to directly conquer a portion of China would mean war.

For the Chinese, the injury of monopoly zones was greatly intensified by the insult of extraterritoriality. Although earlier eras of western civilization, most recently the eighteenth century, had regarded Chinese civilization with respect, that attitude had faded by the heyday of the New Imperialism. Westerners now looked on the technological backwardness, widespread poverty and illiteracy, and even the impressive high culture of China with contempt. One poet spoke for most westerners when he wrote, "Better fifty years of Europe than a cycle of Cathay." Western missionaries flocked into China to convert the "heathen Chinese," although to little effect.

In a demonstration of their power and as an expression of their contempt for Chinese justice, western powers added to their treaties clauses stipulating that the Chinese government should have no jurisdiction over western citizens. Westerners would live in a European quarter in the treaty ports under their own laws. Those accused of criminal acts outside the quarter would be tried in the quarter by western judges.

The "unequal treaties," as the Chinese called them, were extremely humiliating to the inheritors of a proud civilization. Antiwestern sentiment came to a head in 1900, when the Boxers, who hated westerners and westernized Chinese, took control of Peking. Supported by the ruling Dowager Empress Tz'u Hsi, who also hated foreigners, the Boxers besieged the foreign legation section of the city until an international relief expedition drove them off. China was subsequently forced to pay an indemnity. The indemnity and the unequal treaties convinced many Chinese that the

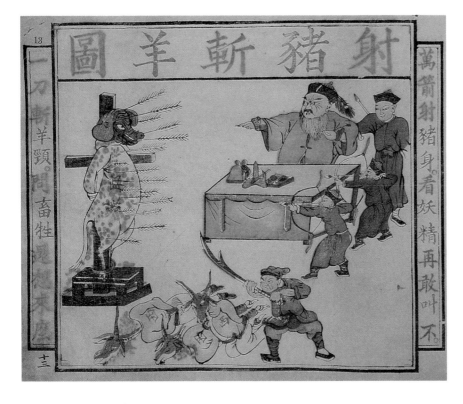

Hostility to Imperialism. This 1891 woodcut depicts Chinese resentment at the intrusion of the "foreign devils" in general and the penetration of Christianity in particular. A Mandarin official orders Christ, depicted as a pig, to be executed with arrows, and the Chinese Christians, shown as sheep, to be beheaded. Such hatred of western imperialism was found all over the world.

THE WHITE MAN'S BURDEN

1899

The United States and the Philippine Islands

Take up the White Man's burden—
    Send forth the best ye breed—
Go bind your sons to exile
    To serve your captives' need;
To wait in heavy harness
    On fluttered folk and wild—
Your new-caught, sullen peoples,
    Half devil and half child.

. . . .

Take up the White Man's burden—
    The savage wars of peace—
Fill full the mouth of Famine
    And bid the sickness cease;
And when your goal is nearest
    The end for others sought,
Watch Sloth and heathen Folly
    Bring all your hope to nought.

. . . .

Take up the White Man's burden—
    And reap his old reward:

The blame of those ye better,
    The hate of those ye guard—
The cry of hosts ye humour
    (Ah slowly!) toward the light:—
"Why brought ye us from bondage,
    "Our loved Egyptian night?"

Take up the White Man's burden—
    Ye dare not stoop to less—
Nor call too loud on Freedom
To cloak your weariness;
    By all ye cry or whisper,
By all ye leave or do,
    The silent, sullen peoples
Shall weigh your Gods and you.

Take up the White Man's burden—
    Have done with childish days—
The lightly proffered laurel,
    The easy, ungrudged praise.
Comes now, to search your manhood
    Through all the thankless years,
Cold-edged with dear-bought wisdom,
    The judgment of your peers!*

Although somewhat patronizing here, Rudyard Kipling, the chief poet of imperialism, like many Europeans at the turn of the century, had come to see the United States as a major western power. A number of influential Britons were now stressing common Anglo-Saxon bonds across the Atlantic, replacing the enmity between the two nations stemming from earlier times. In this poem, from the title on, Kipling expresses the prevailing western/white attitude of superiority towards nonwestern/nonwhite peoples.

*Rudyard Kipling, *Rudyard Kipling's Verse: Definitive Edition* (New York: Doubleday, Doran, 1940), pp. 321–322.

Manchu dynasty had to be replaced by a government strong enough to drive out the "foreign devils."

THE RISE OF THE UNITED STATES

After more than four hundred years of expanding over the rest of the globe, European nations faced competition from outside Europe in the late nineteenth and early twentieth centuries. One new competitor was the western nation of the United States of America and the other was the partly westernized nation of Japan. Although it was not evident at the time, European preeminence around the globe was in fact about to decline, both inside western civilization and around the world.

The United States Becomes an Imperialist Power

By the end of the nineteenth century the United States had arrived on the threshold of great power status. Its population, the world's fourth largest, was the most literate and longest-lived in the world. The standard of living of Americans equaled that of the major powers of western Europe. It provided the basis for a stable republic characterized by—for white males—representative government and constitutionally protected individual rights and liberties. The United States was virtually self-sufficient in food and in industrial raw materials, and it led the world in agricultural exports, iron ore and coal output, iron and steel production, and in railroad mileage. Its manufacturing output had increased so markedly that it was rapidly catching up to the leading European imperial powers in the value of manufactured products sold abroad. Like other rapidly industrializing nations, the United States increasingly looked overseas for raw materials, consumer products, and markets. The

United States possessed only a small army because of the protection furnished by two oceans and the tradition inherited from Great Britain that standing armies were a threat to republican government. However, because it protected a growing overseas commerce, the U.S. navy had increased in size until by 1914 it was the third largest naval force.

Although the United States in the late nineteenth century possessed the needs and the means to become a major imperial power, it had not summoned the will. Advocates of the traditional U.S. policy of supporting self-determination for colonial peoples controlled national policy. In 1898–1899, however, war and other circumstances dropped a number of territories into the lap of the United States. By 1900 expansionists armed with the standard economic, strategic, cultural, and nationalistic arguments for imperialism had won the day. In any case, Americans had already compiled a record of imperialism in North America, expanding with a sense of "Manifest Destiny" at the expense of the British, Spanish, Mexicans, and the Amerindians.

The Caribbean Becomes a U.S. Lake

As an imperialist power, the United States was primarily interested in dominating the western hemisphere. This outlook represented a new expression of overseas imperialism: The target was not nonwestern areas but weaker western states. In particular, the United States intended to pursue three goals: to prevent European states from threatening it from the Caribbean, to obtain a canal across Central America, and to dominate trade with Latin America and Canada. The United States was in a powerful position to achieve these goals. No other independent nation in the hemisphere was strong enough to successfully oppose it, and most European states were too immersed in Asia and Africa and in European affairs to exert sufficient power across the Atlantic.

In five years, 1898–1903, led by presidents William McKinley and the staunch imperialist Theodore "Teddy" Roosevelt, the United States attained its objective of controlling the Caribbean. In a "splendid little war" brought on by tensions over Cuba, the United States totally defeated Spain and forced it to surrender Cuba and Puerto Rico, its two last possessions in the New World. The United States kept Puerto Rico as a possession and built naval installations there. It allowed Cuba to gain nominal independence but made that nation an economic and political protectorate. The United States leased strategic Guantánamo Bay in perpetuity for development as a naval base. With its new bases, the United States was now in a dominating naval position in the Caribbean, and this fact was

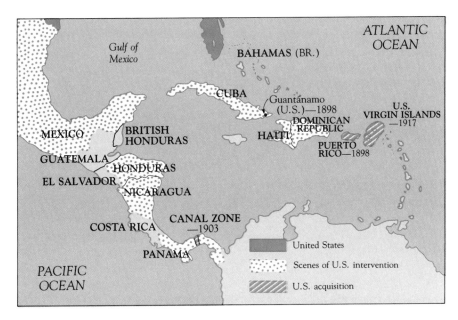

MAP 72
U.S. Imperialism in the Caribbean to 1934. The United States secured firm control of the Caribbean region during the early twentieth century. Through acquiring bases in Cuba and Puerto Rico and controlling the Panama Canal, the United States succeeded in strategically dominating the region. It enforced its supremacy by intervening in or occupying for varying periods most Latin American nations in the area. Some, such as Nicaragua, were taken over several times.

ratified by the 1901 Hay-Pauncefote Agreement. Great Britain, distracted by the Boer War, agreed to withdraw its naval forces from the Caribbean, in return for a U.S. pledge that the British would have unencumbered rights to use a future canal across Central America.

In 1903 the United States completed its major strategic goals. It supported a separatist movement in the Columbian province of Panama, and the new nation became a U.S. protectorate. Panama promptly granted the United States the right to complete a canal begun and abandoned by a French company and to control in perpetuity a thirteen-mile territorial strip, the Canal Zone, on both sides of it. The new Panama Canal, opened to international traffic in 1914,

was an impressive multilock project cut through mountains. Meanwhile, U.S. medical authorities eliminated the scourge of yellow fever throughout much of the Caribbean, a major public health breakthrough. For the United States, the Caribbean was becoming *mare nostrum,* "our sea."

The United States was not completely secure in the Caribbean, however. When a combined European fleet led by Germany bombarded Venezuela in 1902 for violating its treaty and loan obligations, the United States jumped into action. Fearing that after intervention European nations would establish themselves in Latin America and become a threat to U.S. interests, the United States announced an expansion of its 1823 Monroe Doctrine. The new Roosevelt Cor-

ollary stated that if Latin American nations exhibited "chronic wrongdoing" the United States would exercise international police power and intervene in that nation, reordering its finances and restoring order. European nations would thus have no legitimate reason to intervene in the Caribbean. The Roosevelt Corollary was successful; European nations sent no more expeditions to the Caribbean, and the United States was left in military control of the area.

In the long run the Roosevelt Corollary brought problems as well as opportunities. Up to 1934, the United States sent armed forces one or more times to six nations in the Caribbean, occupying three of them for more than a decade. This "Yankee Imperialism" created increasing hostility to the Co-

Technological Imperialism. The Panama Canal, here shown under construction, was the engineering marvel of the early twentieth century. Cut through a mountain range and operated by means of a system of hydraulic locks, it was a much greater technological feat than the Suez Canal, which was essentially a ditch through flat terrain. The Panama Canal was the realization of centuries of hope of those in international commerce for a direct connection between the Atlantic and the Pacific, avoiding the distance, time, and danger of the passage around Cape Horn.

lossus of the North among Latin American nations during the twentieth century.

The United States restricted its military intervention to the Caribbean, but its economic penetration proceeded throughout Latin America. European nations, particularly Great Britain, were well ahead of the United States in investment, but aggressive Dollar Diplomacy steadily increased the U.S. share. U.S. businessmen made extensive capital investments in Latin American petroleum, copper, coffee, fruit, rubber, tin, sugar, and other products. By 1913, the United States had taken the lead in exports to Latin America.

With many valuable investments and markets in Latin America, U.S. citizens were interested in Latin American nations that could both guarantee law and order and offer economic incentives, and were not choosy about the form of government that provided them. This meant that the United States and U.S. business firms often worked with dictators such as Porfirio Díaz in Mexico, and as a consequence became a partner to the exploitation of the masses. In a later day many Latin American reformers and revolutionaries would look upon the United States and its citizens as their enemies.

The United States and Canada

Americans were also interested in expansion north of the border. Ever since the War for Independence many Americans had wished to bring Canada into the Union. The British government, learning from experience, countered by uniting several colonies and the possessions of the Hudson's Bay Company between 1867 and 1871

into a federation called the Dominion of Canada, allowing it to control its internal affairs. Early in the twentieth century, Canada gained control over its external affairs. This was the first instance of devolution, the process in which an imperial power peacefully surrendered its hold over a former colony. In the meantime, Americans shifted their interests in Canada to economic penetration. By 1914, almost one quarter of U.S. foreign investments were in Canada, although the British still dominated trade there by a wide margin.

U.S. Imperialism in Asia

The United States had been interested in the China trade from early in its history, and had built the fastest sailing ships in the nineteenth century, the China Clippers, to make the long voyage to China as efficient as possible. By 1900, through a variety of circumstances, the United States had assumed a major role in the Pacific, with possessions extending from Alaska to Samoa. Its main accomplishment, however, was to accumulate a string of island stepping-stones leading from the west coast of the United States through the Hawaiian Islands (annexed in 1898) to the Philippines on the threshold of China. Like the Cubans, the Filipinos had been fighting a guerrilla war for independence from Spain at the time the United States took the Philippines in the Spanish-American War. The United States, for a mixture of strategic, economic, and racist reasons, refused to allow the Filipinos independence and held the Philippines as a possession, President McKinley informing the public that God supported the move. The Filipinos in

1899 revolted and began a protracted guerrilla war that dwarfed the war with Spain in forces, expense, and casualties before the insurgents were finally defeated. During the struggle, Americans resorted to the same anti-guerrilla tactics of internment camps and slaughter of civilians that they had condemned elsewhere. Meanwhile, the United States created naval bases at Pearl Harbor in Hawaii and at Subic Bay in the Philippines.

With a base established in the heart of east Asia, the United States pursued its goals of obtaining a share of Chinese raw materials and marketing its manufactured products in China. Although the United States had major ambitions in east Asia, its strategic and military position was the weakest of the imperial powers. Unlike the Caribbean, which was adjacent and contained no formidable rivals, the United States found it difficult to apply significant power six thousand miles away in east Asia in the teeth of established imperial powers. In these circumstances, the United States was fortunate, through its traditional diplomatic policy of taking advantage of European quarrels, to attain part of its goals. In 1899 and 1900 Secretary of State John Hay announced that the European monopoly powers had agreed to an "Open Door," allowing all nations to trade freely in China. Actually, the European powers had not uniformly assented to Hay's proposition, but fear of adding the United States to their list of enemies kept European powers from disavowing the principle.

As the Open Door gained acceptance, U.S. businessmen, engineers, and missionaries became increasingly active in China, and U.S. gunboats cruised the major rivers of China

Imperialism in Asia. U.S. troops engaged in suppressing the insurrection in the Philippines are shown after storming a village defended by lightly-armed Filipinos. The insurgents had originally been fighting for their independence against the Spanish; when they found that the United States was going to hold the Philippines rather than grant independence, they also fought the Americans, but were eventually defeated.

to protect them. Unequal treaties imposed on hapless China allowed Americans to enjoy the same extraterritorial immunity from Chinese justice as did the Europeans. In contradiction to its Open Door policy, the United States tried to establish monopoly zones in Korea, Manchuria, and Fukien, but was warned off all three by the Japanese.

THE RISE OF JAPAN

The emergence of Japan as a world power was more disturbing to the European sense of economic, military, and cultural superiority than the rise of the United States. In one generation, Japan performed one of the most remarkable feats in modern history. An isolated and technologically backward eastern state, by adopting western technology and some aspects of western social organization, trans-

formed itself into one of the world's major imperialist powers, expanding in east Asia at the expense of both the European powers and the United States.

Confronted in the 1850s by U.S. naval power and forced to sign unequal treaties, the Japanese leaders quickly saw that they would go the way of the rest of Asia unless they built up an industrialized base and modern military power. Unlike the Chinese, who had scorned outside ideas and practices, Japanese cultural dynamics permitted borrowing and adapting from other societies. Previously Japan had incorporated many aspects of Chinese culture; it now took the best from the west. Missions went to Europe and the United States to study western industrial and military technology, education, bureaucracy, and government. By the end of the nineteenth century Japan had built a powerful industry, a modern transportation network, and a large mer-

chant marine. The Japanese eliminated illiteracy and provided a broad technological and vocational education to undergird their industrialization. Japan also constructed a large fleet of modern warships and organized a large, well-equipped and efficient army. Japan, no longer having to fear for its safety, forced outside powers to give up the unequal treaties.

Despite its impressive accomplishments, Japan suffered from many severe problems. The Japanese people were subjected to a grinding discipline of long hours, low pay, heavy taxes, and a standard of living well below the more affluent nations of the west. The structure of the Japanese government was an unstable amalgamation, with western-style political parties and a parliament coexisting uneasily with the role of the emperor and the power and respect accorded to military men.

It was the economic problems of

Japan, however, that had the greatest historical impact. Like Great Britain, Japan had become dependent on importing foodstuffs from abroad and therefore vulnerable to rival states cutting off such supplies. The demands of Japanese factories forced Japan to look abroad for coal and iron ore as well. In addition, as in the west, Japan's growing industrial output forced the Japanese to seek overseas areas where it could sell its goods.

By the turn of the century, Japan's economic problems were severe enough to impel the Japanese government to plan to take over at least a portion of East Asia, which held all the food, raw materials, and markets the Japanese needed. In command of formidable military forces close to home, facing an impotent China and western powers operating far from their homeland, the Japanese were in a good position to expand.

The Japanese warmed up for their confrontation with the western powers by attacking their Asian neighbors. They defeated China in 1895 and annexed the strategic island of Formosa (Taiwan). At the same time, they began to enter Korea, both to control Korea's supply of iron ore and coal and to counter Russian penetration. In 1900, Japan joined an international expedition sent to Peking to put down the Boxer Rebellion.

By 1905, the Japanese were ready for Russia. In addition to their presence in Korea, the Russians held control of the iron ore and coal of Manchuria and had constructed two naval bases threatening Japan. Japan launched a surprise attack in 1905, seizing the Port Arthur naval base and driving the Russian army out of Korea and southern Manchuria. Meanwhile, the Japanese navy sent the Russian Baltic fleet to the bottom of the sea when it arrived off Japan. The Battle of Tsushima Straits astonished western observers, but more important, Japan's defeat of a major western power electrified the nonwest and gained it great respect. With Russia defeated and Japan exhausted, both sides agreed to end the war. Japan gained full control of Korea and southern Manchuria. Now admired and feared in Asia and respected in the west, the Japanese were ready to expand further.

Meanwhile, many educated Chinese were coming to the same conclusion the Japanese had come to a generation earlier: China would have to develop western technology, bureaucracy, government, and military techniques if the "foreign devils" were ever to be driven out. More and more individuals from the Chinese elite went to the west and to Japan to study, and some of them began to work toward bringing down the Manchu dynasty, now widely regarded as incapable of organizing the Chinese people to expel the foreigners.

In 1911, the dynasty collapsed, and a republic was proclaimed, under the leadership of U.S.-educated Sun Yatsen and his Nationalist party. Sun's program called for the development of modern nationalist consciousness among the Chinese, a representative government to mobilize the national

The Rise of a New Power in Asia. A western cartoon published shortly before the 1905 war shows Japan challenging the Russian bear. Japan is pictured in traditional garb, but the kimono decorations of artillery and ships indicate that the west is aware of Japanese modernization. The cartoon suggests, however, that the bear has the advantage.

will, a socialist program to most quickly modernize Chinese industry, and land reform to bolster agricultural output.

Most of the traditional family, social, and cultural values of China were to remain intact. In effect Sun, like many Asians and Africans, hoped to emulate the Japanese: Westernize enough to drive out the West.

SUMMARY

From the middle of the nineteenth century until 1914, in the era known as the New Imperialism, major European nations, soon followed by the United States and Japan, began to take control of much of the overseas world. These powers were impelled by the demands for raw materials and markets brought on by the Industrial Revolution and by a variety of strategic, cultural, and nationalistic motives.

Beginning about 1880, European imperialist nations overran Africa in one generation. France absorbed most of western Africa, Great Britain took over much of Eastern Africa from Egypt to the Cape of Good Hope, and other European powers conquered most of the rest. Although Africans resisted conquest and often revolted against European controls, European military superiority was too great. The

British, French, Germans, and Italians had a series of confrontations with each other, but no wars developed. Great Britain, however, did have a war with the Dutch Afrikaners.

In Asia, Great Britain was chiefly concerned with exploiting India and protecting it from both the French to the east and the Russians to the north and west. Meanwhile, European powers defeated the Chinese Empire, dividing it into zones where the victors monopolized raw materials and markets.

During this period, the United States, already a major economic power, became a leading imperialist power. Beginning in 1898, it took military and economic control of the Caribbean and penetrated the economies of South America and Canada. The United States also acquired a string of possessions across the Pa-

cific, chiefly Hawaii and the Philippines. From these possessions, the United States elbowed into the China trade.

Japan also became an imperialist power in this period, adopting a number of western characteristics, including the West's industrial economy and modern military establishment. Now a major power, Japan expanded in east Asia, finally defeating Russia in the process. Japan looked to expand further in Asia, a design that would in particular lead later in the twentieth century to conflict with the United States. In the short run, imperialist conflicts contributed significantly to the outbreak of World War I. Meanwhile some among the subjugated peoples searched for ways to regain their independence from their colonial masters.

SELECTED SOURCES

*Achebe, Chinua. *Things Fall Apart.* 1978. A fictionalized account of the ambiguous effects of European contact on tribal society in Nigeria.

Elegant, Robert. *Mandarin.* 1983. A novel depicting the interplay of traditional and western culture in late nineteenth century China.

Griswold, A. Whitney. *The Far Eastern Policy of the United States.* 1968. A well-written overview of U.S. imperialism in the Philippines and China.

*Morgan, C. Wayne. *America's Road to Empire.* 1968. A description of the motives and course of action of the early stages of U.S. imperialism.

*Oliver, Roland, and Anthony Atmore. *Africa since 1800.* 1981. A standard account of Africa before and during imperialism.

*Robinson, Ronald, and John Gallagher, with Alice Denny. *Africa and the Victorians.* 1961. A controversial discussion of the motives and the process of imperialism.

*Robinson, Donald. *The Raj.* 1981. An overview of the nature of British rule in India. Also a BBC television production.

Story, Richard. *Japan and the Decline of the West in Asia.* 1979. A concise survey of the expansion of Japan from 1894 to 1943.

*Available in paperback.

THE PATH TO WORLD WAR I
(1871–1914)

The fleet is launched, and in building . . . Its spirit is the same as that which inspired Prussian officers at Hohenfriedberg, Königgrätz, and Sedan; and with every German warship that leaves the docks another guarantee of peace on earth is launched upon the waters . . . The duty of our German youth . . . is to hold fast to the conviction that our Lord God would never have so striven for our German Fatherland if He had not meant great things for us. We are the salt of the earth, but we must make ourselves worthy so to be . . . Then only shall it be written of the German people as you may read upon the helmets of my First Regiment of Guards: "Semper talis!" [Ever true!] Then . . . we shall stand, our hand upon our sword-knot, and our shield upright before us on the soil, and say: "Tamen! [Nevertheless!] Come what will!"

These remarks by Emperor William II of Germany typify the narrow, bellicose nationalism that pervaded Europe in the late nineteenth century. Fanned by a sensational popular press and irresponsible, rabble-rousing politicians, national loyalties reached an emotional level that was kin to hysteria. Europeans came to believe in the moral, material, and military supremacy of their own nation and in the inferiority of other peoples. Inflated patriotism nourished the furious scramble to acquire overseas empires, supported the universal demand for ever-stronger fighting establishments, and contributed to the rise of an alliance system that divided Europe into two hostile groups of powers. Altogether, these elements created an atmosphere that was dangerously receptive to war.

CONTENTS

THE UNDERLYING CAUSES OF THE WAR

No one country desired or deliberately provoked the war that rocked the world in August 1914. The origins of the conflict cannot be explained solely on the basis of the events that immediately preceded it. Fundamen-

William II. The German emperor is usually pictured as the prototype of the warlord—overbearing, arrogant, and brutal. Indeed he took immense pleasure in appearing in the military dress of his regiment, complete with decorations, sword, and spiked helmet. Believing that his power came from God, he talked to his ministers and to his people like an officer speaks to his soldiers, lecturing or giving them orders.

667

tally the First World War was the product of destructive forces spawned during the preceding decades. Among the deeper causes of the war one must include nationalism, the arms race and militarism, imperialism, and the alliance system. These elements were inevitably interrelated but for purposes of simplicity and analysis each will be treated separately.

Nationalism

Nationalism, which had roots in the era of the French Revolution, had assumed particularly dangerous forms by the start of the twentieth century. In some instances, it encouraged subject nationalities to seek independence or to join their fellow nationals in neighboring states. In others, it led nations to regard certain areas outside their borders as rightfully theirs on the ground they were inhabited by fellow nationals. In still others, it caused states to claim military and cultural superiority that entitled them to exercise dominance over a desired portion of Europe. The most prominent manifestations of nationalism were in Austria-Hungary, Serbia, Russia, Germany, France, and Italy.

The divisive effect of ethnic nationalism was particularly evident in the Habsburg realm. The creation of the Dual Monarchy of Austria-Hungary in 1867 had kept the Slavs of the Habsburg Empire subordinate to the German Austrians and to the Magyars of Hungary. By the turn of the century, Slavic nationalist groups, having concluded that their people would never acquire equal status, intensified efforts to topple the Austro-Hungarian Empire. Such an event would have permitted some Slavic elements like the Czechs to form independent states of their own and others, like the Rumanians and the Serbians, to join the national states of their kinsmen across the border.

Freed from Ottoman rule in 1878, Serbia had dreams of a greater Serbia that would include fellow Slavs in the southern part of Austria-Hungary and in two nominally Ottoman provinces, Bosnia and Herzegovina. After 1903, when Peter I (1903–1921) came to the throne, Serbian nationalists launched a program of agitation and subversion to provoke discontent among their fellow Slavs and to draw them away from the Habsburg Empire.

Serbia's activities were encouraged and sometimes abetted by the Pan-Slavists in Russia. This group of nationalists believed that it was the duty of Russia, as the most powerful Slavic state, to protect other Slavic states and to free Slavic minorities from the yoke of foreign bondage. More ardent exponents of Pan-Slavism dreamed of bringing all the Slavs of eastern Europe under Russia's control.

The German counterpart to Pan-Slavism was the Pan-German League, founded in 1895 to spread the doctrine of the superiority of the German race and culture. Pan-Germans envisaged one great German state, uniting all the Teutonic peoples of central Europe, and the creation of a vast overseas empire. The League helped to coordinate the activities of other nationalist societies and developed powerful connections and support in government, industrial, and journalistic circles within Germany.

France and Italy represented a different form of nationalism. French national pride smarted under the humiliating defeat of 1870–1871, which had diminished France's stature as a great power. Ardent nationalists desired a war against Germany to avenge the defeat at Sedan and to recover Alsace and Lorraine. This *revanchist* (revenge) sentiment gained wide support in France in the 1880s and was kept alive by the jingoistic element of the French press. Similarly, Italians wished to annex *Italia Irredenta*—territory chiefly inside Austria-Hungary that was substantially inhabited by ethnic Italians. As in France, patriots clamored for the return of the "lost provinces," although these areas had never been under the jurisdiction of the modern Italian state.

Nationalism penetrated the mind and emotions of Europeans and influenced other forces that contributed to the coming of war. It supported the drive for overseas empires and provided the impulse for ever-stronger fighting services to ensure national safety. In the opinion of many observers, rampant nationalism was the single greatest cause of World War I.

Imperialism

In carving up the colonial world, western nations acted in fierce competition. Although the European imperialist powers did not go to war with one another over colonial matters, bitter rivalries in Africa and Asia brought European nations close to war, and Russia was defeated by Japan as a result of clashing imperialist interests in Asia. Great Britain made enemies of all the major imperial powers. In particular, it had major confrontations with France in North Africa and with Russia in Central Asia. Italy, disunited until after mid-century, made a late start in the colonial race and clashed with France over North

Africa. Like Italy, Germany achieved unification late. Bismarck discouraged the acquisition of overseas territories lest it lead to a confrontation with Great Britain, the world's foremost colonial power. After the accession of William II in 1888, however, Germany launched an aggressive campaign in search for undeveloped lands. Germany's belated entry into the race meant that the most desirable areas had already been preempted. Thus each time Berlin sought to exert control or influence over a certain portion of the globe, it was apt to clash with another imperialistic power. On several occasions, Germany's assertive and irresponsible behavior threatened to plunge Europe into the maelstrom of war. The result was that Germany, although gaining little in the way of colonies, reaped much ill will, not only among the European nations, but also with the United States and Japan.

The Arms Race and Militarism

The atmosphere of suspicion and fear after 1870 gave rise to a bitter and costly armaments race. In the name of national security, western states vied with one another in strengthening their armies and navies. Huge sums were spent on military equipment and ships, and all the major powers, except Great Britain and the United States, adopted conscription. German and Austrian military spending doubled between 1910 and 1914, and the expenditures of other European nations increased markedly. By 1914, Germany and France each had about 800,000 men in uniform with millions of trained reservists.

Alarmed by the growth of German sea power, Great Britain in 1906 launched a new class of battleships, the *Dreadnought*, superior to any warship then in existence. Germany commenced soon after to build them

too, forcing the British to spend huge sums to keep its navy as large as the next two fleets combined. Meanwhile, the United States, a fast-rising imperialist and economic power, was building a "Great White Fleet" that would be the third largest in the world, behind Great Britain and Germany, by 1914. Such contests not only drained national reserves but also increased hostile feelings and distrust between nations.

As the Europeans embarked upon an unrestricted arms race they also embraced militarism, a spirit that exalts military virtues and ideals. The German general Frederick von Bernhardi, reflecting the influence of Charles Darwin, wrote: "If it were not for war we should probably find that inferior races would overcome healthy, youthful ones by their wealth and numbers." For the French philosopher Ernest Renan, warfare was "the sting which prevents a country from

A Symbol of the Arms Race. The appearance of the British *Dreadnought* in 1906 rendered all of its predecessors obsolete. The battleship could run on oil as well as coal but more important, it was heavily armored and possessed ten twelve-inch guns. In action it could stay out of range of the lesser guns of the older ships and enjoy a tremendous advantage in hitting power. The *Dreadnought* heightened Anglo-German naval rivalry. Since each nation was starting from near equality as far as *Dreadnought* construction was concerned, neither wished to be left behind. National Maritime Museum, Greenwich.

going to sleep." In Italy, Gabriele d'Annunzio glorified war as the noblest form of human expression. The German historian Heinrich von Treitschke justified military conflict as the best method of solving a nation's problems. Under the influence of such powerful advocates of militarism, President Theodore Roosevelt and Kaiser William II agreed on the stimulating effect of war, the former saying, "No triumph of peace is quite as great as the sublime triumphs of war." Thus before 1914, the general public had been conditioned to view war as a glorious adventure and as essential to progress.

The growing mood of militarism heightened military influence in shaping official policy. Political leaders consulted army and naval officers more frequently and listened more thoughtfully to their advice. On occasion, strong military personalities superseded the civilian authorities in certain areas of policy. This was especially evident during the final crisis in the summer of 1914 when military considerations handicapped the search for a peaceful settlement. The vital issue was over mobilization, a process that normally required several weeks to complete. The nation that first achieved battle-readiness enjoyed a decided advantage because it could fight according to its own war plans rather than having to improvise in response to an attack. No country therefore could allow a potential enemy a significant head start in mobilizing its forces. In ordering mobilization, as they had been urged to do by their generals, political leaders thought they could still avoid war. But mobilization was tantamount to war. Once an army was prepared for war, it followed that it would com-

mence operations at once to gain the benefit of the strategic initiative. Conversely, seeing a rival state mobilizing would provoke a nation to mobilize faster and strike first.

The conviction that an arms race would inevitably lead to war stirred many individuals to organize peace societies and to call for disarmament and the arbitration of international disputes. In 1899 and 1907, delegates of twenty-six and forty-four nations, respectively, met at international peace conferences at The Hague in the Netherlands. They set up the Hague Tribunal, to which quarreling parties might refer their disputes if they wished. Paradoxically, the conferees also produced rules for the proper conduct of war.

Prominent individuals also supported the peace movement. The American steel tycoon Andrew Carnegie created the Carnegie Endowment for International Peace. Alfred Nobel, who had invented dynamite, established the Nobel Peace Prize and other prizes for the betterment of the human condition. These efforts, however, proved to be too weak to slow the march of militarism.

Alliances

Despite their growing military establishments, many nations felt the need for additional security and looked around for allies. They hoped that alliances would provide the additional margin of superiority that would deter aggression; the alliances that formed in the late nineteenth century were intended to prevent war, not provoke it. But belonging to a military alliance carried risks that were not sufficiently weighed at the time. Depending on the terms of the alli-

ance and the circumstances of the moment, an alliance sharply increased the chances that a local conflict would spread into a general war.

BISMARCKIAN DIPLOMACY, 1871–1890

The new alliance system in Europe was originally built around Germany by Bismarck and at first helped maintain peace. The unification of Germany, coming on the heels of Prussia's decisive victory over France, opened a new era in European diplomacy. The new German state possessed a large and growing population, enormous industrial capacity, abundant natural resources, and the finest army in Europe. The emergence of this powerful and dynamic state upset the balance of power created by the Congress of Vienna. For the first time since Napoleonic France, a nation was strong enough to dominate the European continent. Bismarck understood the general distrust Prussia's victories had aroused among the established states. Germany, he insisted after 1871, was a contented power and wanted no further territorial gains. His principal task, as he saw it, was to forestall a war that might undo his achievement. For the next two decades, he labored as skillfully to prevent war as he had once sought it.

The cornerstone of Bismarck's foreign policy was to keep France weak and isolated diplomatically. The Iron Chancellor was haunted by fears that France would strike at the first favorable opportunity to avenge the humiliation of 1870–1871 and regain

the provinces of Alsace and Lorraine. There was little chance that the French alone would make such an attempt. What worried Bismarck was a French forged coalition against Germany. The most effective way of depriving France of allies was to bind all of its potential friends to Germany. To that end Bismarck engineered a major alliance in 1873, composed of Germany, Austria-Hungary, and Russia. Known as the League of Three Emperors, it committed the signatories to maintain friendly neutrality in the event one of them was at war with a fourth power. It was valid for three years and could be renewed.

In the ensuing years, Bismarck faced great difficulty in trying to keep the growing enmity between Austria and Russia from breaking into the open. For many years Russia's expansionist policy in the Balkans had been opposed by Great Britain. After 1877 Austria, sometimes encouraged by Great Britain and Germany, vigorously pursued an expansionist policy of its own in the Balkans. This angered Russia, which had long regarded the area as within its sphere of influence.

The first serious crisis in the League of Three Emperors appeared at the Congress of Berlin in 1878 which resolved the dispute arising from

A "Threatening" Situation. This cartoon suggesting how the alliance systems would work was illustrated in the Brooklyn *Eagle* in 1913. Serbia, having captured a port on the Adriatic, is threatened by Austria. Russia promptly comes to the aid of Serbia whereupon Germany rushes to Austria's protection and threatens Russia, and so on down the line.

the Russo-Turkish war. Bismarck, referring to himself as an "honest broker," played a major role in determining the terms of the final settlement. Russia, victorious over the Turks, appeared to gain less than Austria, which had not even participated in the war. Russian leaders felt cheated and directed their anger at Bismarck, who they held had favored Austria's interests.

When the League was not renewed in 1878, Bismarck was compelled to find an alternative. In 1879, he negotiated a secret agreement with the Habsburg government. The resulting Dual Alliance obligated either country to come to the aid of the other if attacked by Russia. Germany and Austria secured a new partner, Italy, in 1882. Humiliated and outraged by France's occupation of Tunisia in 1881, the Italians sought to strengthen their diplomatic position by seeking ties with the Dual Alliance, despite their hostility to Austria over the issue of *Italia Irredenta*. The treaty signed among the three powers established the Triple Alliance which endured until the First World War.

Despite the setback at the Congress of Berlin, Bismarck managed to reestablish and maintain friendly ties with the Russian government. Although the Iron Chancellor chose Austria as a close ally in preference to Russia, he was eager to keep the tsar from moving into the French camp. In 1881, he revived the League of Three Emperors, but six years later it was allowed to lapse when a new flare-up in the Balkans disrupted the uneasy collaboration between Austria and Russia. To repair the damage Bismarck, in 1887, concluded a separate agreement with Russia called the Reinsurance Treaty. By its terms, both

empires promised to remain neutral if either became involved in a war with another power. However, the partners would not be bound in case Germany attacked France or Russia attacked Austria.

After nearly two decades of diplomatic maneuvering Bismarck had achieved his goal of isolating France. He had an alliance with Austria and Italy, a formal understanding with Russia, and friendly relations with the remaining major power, Great Britain, which pursued its traditional policy of noninterference in continental affairs. But German hegemony in Europe was only temporary. The major flaw in Bismarck's policy was that it was too intricate to succeed in the long run. Indeed, even if Bismarck had remained in power, it is questionable whether he could have kept his own system from breaking down.

THE SHIFTING BALANCE, 1890–1907

After 1890, alliances worked in the direction of war rather than peace. The young Kaiser William II dismissed Bismarck in March 1890 and proceeded to change the direction of Germany's foreign policy. An ambitious man, eager to assert himself in world affairs, William did not wish to remain under Bismarck's shadow. A deformed left arm undoubtedly contributed to his insecurity, which he tried to disguise by swagger and tough talk. Neither he, nor the men he appointed to head the government, possessed Bismarck's insight and tact. After 1890, Germany's foreign policy, lacking guidelines, was frequently inconsistent and belligerent.

The first act of the new German leadership was to repudiate one of the basic features of Bismarck's diplomatic system—close ties with Russia. Leo von Caprivi, chancellor from 1890 to 1894, was hostile to the Reinsurance Treaty, preferring a formal agreement with Great Britain, which was then in continual conflict with Russia. On his advice, strengthened by that of influential members of the German Foreign Office, William allowed the Reinsurance Treaty to lapse. Given the tsar's known dislike of republican institutions, German leaders were confident he would never agree to an association with France. But they underestimated the compelling force of national self interest.

By refusing to renew the Reinsurance Treaty, the German government paved the way for a Russo-French rapprochement. The French were delighted by the unexpected turn of events, and seeing the opportunity to hem in Germany on two sides, began to court the Russians. Faced by an obvious hardening of the German-Austrian alliance and in need of French capital to finance railroad construction and other industrial enterprises, the tsar's government responded cautiously but favorably to the overtures from Paris. The new friendship was confirmed in 1894 by a defensive pact directed against the Triple Alliance.

The new alignment of powers caused apprehension in Great Britain, which faced the unenviable possibility of a continental alliance against it. In the last decade of the century, the island kingdom did not have a single friend on the continent. It was involved in bitter colonial rivalries with France, Russia, and Germany. The storm of abuse that fell on Great

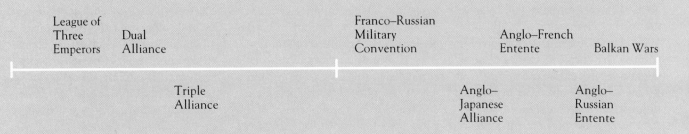

1871	1892	1913

League of Three Emperors Dual Alliance

Triple Alliance

Franco–Russian Military Convention

Anglo–French Entente

Balkan Wars

Anglo–Japanese Alliance

Anglo–Russian Entente

Britain during the Boer War (1899–1902) brought home to the British the degree of their international unpopularity. The British government realized that its army, which had such difficulty in subduing 50,000 Boer farmers, would stand little chance against a coalition of European opponents. The desirability of acquiring allies became increasingly apparent.

British statesmen preferred to try for an agreement with Germany, a logical step in view of Great Britain's traditional rivalry with France and Russia. The Germans feared that such an alliance might drag them into a war with France or Russia or both. Instead the German government insisted that Great Britain join the Triple Alliance. London declined to do so. British misgivings increased as William II embarked on an aggressive "world policy," abandoning Bismarck's strategy of confining German interests to Europe. The central issue that caused the negotiations to break down was Germany's decision in 1900 to initiate a huge shipbuilding program designed to challenge Great Britain's supremacy of the seas within twenty years. For Great Britain, dependent on the import of food and raw materials, it was imperative that the Royal Navy be able to protect

British shipping. By gaining control of the seas, a hostile power could interfere with British overseas trade or even blockade the island itself. To prevent this the British struggled to maintain their naval supremacy, but German pride would not yield to such superiority. As the German navy grew and as the kaiser's policies appeared more threatening, London turned elsewhere to establish friendly relations.

In 1902, Great Britain departed from its old policy of isolation, and entered into a defensive alliance with Japan. The agreement provided for mutual aid in the event that either partner was attacked by two or more powers. The purpose was originally to check Russian advances in the Far East, but as Germany increasingly became the center of fear and hostility, both signatories came to look upon the treaty as an opportunity to check German expansion into the Pacific and east Asia. Under conditions of war or threat of war in Europe, the treaty would enable the British to leave their interests in Asia protected by Japan and to concentrate their fleet in Europe to face the growing German navy.

Great Britain underwent an even greater shift in foreign policy in 1904

when it drew closer to France, hitherto its most serious rival. In 1903, the new British monarch, Edward VII (1901–1910), journeyed to Paris where he was welcomed with great popular enthusiasm, and several months later the French president paid a return visit to London. The friendly feelings thus engendered produced diplomatic conversations, culminating in the *Entente Cordiale*, a French term meaning "friendly understanding." Both nations resolved all outstanding colonial disputes. In particular Great Britain recognized France's paramount interests in Morocco and in return received a free hand in Egypt. The *Entente Cordiale* was not a military alliance, and it is unlikely that it would have assumed the character of one had Germany behaved with more restraint.

The *Entente Cordiale* was barely concluded when the German government tried to test it by provoking a crisis over Morocco. In the spring of 1905, Kaiser William visited Tangier where he announced German support of Moroccan independence. The French denounced the speech, but when the situation became threatening, agreed to Germany's demand that the future of Morocco be determined by an international conference. Prince Bernhard von Bülow, Germany's chancellor from 1900 to 1909, hoped to destroy the *Entente Cordiale* by showing France that it could not rely on Great Britain. Von Bülow was disappointed in his expectations. At the conference, held in Algeciras at the southern tip of Spain in 1906, all the major powers except Austria voted to give France a dominant voice in the internal affairs of Morocco. Germany's diplomatic blunder strengthened the Entente by producing talks between British and French military and naval authorities for possible cooperation in case of war. Once Britain became closely associated with the French, it was only a matter of time before expediency dictated a settlement of differences with France's continental ally, Russia.

With Paris' encouragement, Great Britain and Russia came to an understanding in 1907. Previously, the two powers had been bitter enemies, with a long history of rivalry in many regions of the world. However, Russia's defeat at the hands of Japan in 1904–1905 changed the picture. The British now had less to fear from the tsarist empire. The Russians, for their part, saw a rapprochement with Britain as the key factor in reestablishing their position in Europe. The Anglo-Russian convention was similar to the *Entente Cordiale* arranged three years earlier. No formal treaty of alliance was signed but the British and Russian governments settled conflicting claims in central Asia and laid the foundation for wider collaboration. The agreement completed the three-way power bloc of Britain, France, and Russia, soon to be known as the Triple Entente. Because Great Britain refused to make military commitments to the French and the Rus-

sians, the Triple Entente could not be classified as a military alliance. Nevertheless it evolved in that direction as Britain inescapably became entangled in the aspirations and quarrels of its political associates.

Thanks to the incompetence of the kaiser and his ministers, Germany's diplomatic position had slipped dramatically since 1890. France had emerged from isolation with close ties to Russia and Great Britain, two of the leading powers in Europe. Italy at best was an uncertain ally. The Italians and French were interested in ensuring each other's neutrality in the event of a future Italian seizure of Tripoli and French takeover of Morocco. In 1902, the two nations sealed a pact by committing themselves to remain neutral in case either party became involved in a war with a third power, an agreement that contravened Italy's promises to Germany in the Triple Alliance. Germany had only one staunch ally, Austria, and such were the conditions in that troubled empire that it was more likely to need help than to provide it.

CONFLICTS AND COMPROMISES, 1907–1914

By 1907, the great European powers had grouped themselves into two blocs, the Triple Alliance and the Triple Entente. Between 1907 and 1914, the European scene was marred by a series of crises, each of which seemed highly threatening at the time. Although in every instance solutions were found and major warfare avoided, these crises tended to solidify the re-

spective alliance systems and to widen the gulf separating the two camps.

In October 1908 Austria proclaimed the annexation of Bosnia and Herzegovina. The Congress of Berlin of 1878 had placed the provinces under Austrian administration, although they nominally remained a part of the Ottoman Empire. The arrangement satisfied Vienna until a revolution in the Ottoman Empire in 1908 brought in a group of modernizing reformers called "Young Turks." Austria feared that if the Ottoman government became stronger, it would demand a return of the occupied territory. The Habsburgs were also anxious to counter the advances of the greater Serbia movement. Nationalists in Serbia longed to create an enlarged state in the Balkans that would include their Slavic kinsmen in Bosnia and Herzegovina. Austria's high-handed move infuriated the Serbs, who turned to Russia for help. Germany, resentful that it had not been warned in advance of Austria's plans, nevertheless gave its ally unqualified support. The Russians had not sufficiently recovered from their defeat in 1904–1905 to wage war against the combined might of Germany and Austria. Yielding to a German ultimatum, they acknowledged Austria's new acquisitions. The crisis humiliated both Russia and Serbia and created additional tensions in the Balkans.

The next major incident occurred in 1911 when Germany again challenged France's presence in Morocco. Since 1906 the French had been nibbling away at Morroco's integrity. In the summer of 1911, a French army marched into the interior to occupy Fez, the capital, where anti-European disturbances had broken out. The Germans, interpreting the move as a

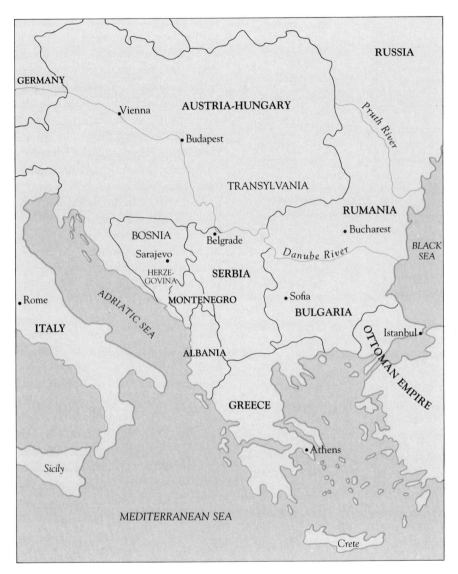

MAP 73

The Balkans in 1914. Although the Congress of Berlin in 1878 had recognized the independence of Rumania, Serbia, and Montenegro, and Bulgaria as an autonomous principality within the Ottoman Empire, the Balkan peninsula remained a politically unstable area. The territorial ambitions of the independent states, new and old, together with their hatred of the Ottoman Empire, led to successive conflicts culminating in the Balkan Wars of 1912–1913. Overlying the clashing interests of the smaller states in the Balkans were those of Russia and Austria-Hungary. As the lines were sharply drawn and uneasiness in informed circles mounted, the German ambassador in Paris gloomily observed that "peace is at the mercy of an accident."

step toward complete control of Morocco, countered by sending the gunboat *Panther* to the coastal city of Agadir, allegedly to protect German nationals in the region. Germany's real purpose was to extort territorial concessions from France but this was unknown to the British, who believed that Berlin meant to convert Agadir into a naval base on the Atlantic. As at Algeciras, the British lined up solidly behind the French. Just when war seemed imminent, a compromise was worked out. Germany received a slice of the French Congo in return for recognizing French rights to Morocco. The effect of the second Moroccan crisis was to increase Great Britain's fear and distrust of Germany. It drove Great Britain closer to France and turned the *Entente Cordiale* into an active military alliance.

Taking advantage of the Ottoman Empire's struggle with the Italians over Tripoli, the Balkan nations of Greece, Bulgaria, Montenegro, and Serbia joined forces to fight Turkey in 1912 to acquire its remaining possessions in Europe. The Balkan allies won a

A TERRORIST GROUP: THE PAN-SERBIAN BLACK HAND SOCIETY

Article 1. This organization has been created with the object of realizing the national ideal: the union of all the Serbs. All Serbs . . . and all who are sincerely devoted to this cause, may become members.

Article 2. This organization prefers terrorist action to intellectual propaganda and for this reason must be kept absolutely secret from persons who do not belong to it.

Article 3. This organization bears the name "Union or Death."

Article 4. To accomplish its task, the organization:

1. Brings influence to bear on Government circles . . . and on the whole social life of the Kingdom of Serbia. . . .

2. Organizes revolutionary action in all territories inhabited by Serbs.

3. Outside the frontiers of Serbia uses every means available to fight the adversaries of this idea.

4. Maintains amicable relations with all . . . who entertain feelings of friendship towards Serbia. . . .

5. Lends help and support in every way possible to all peoples and all organizations struggling for their national liberation and for their union.

Article 25. Members of the organization are not known to each other personally. It is only the members of the Central Committee who are known to one another. *

In the aftermath of the Bosnia-Herzegovina crisis the Serbian foreign minister established a patriotic society (National Defense Association) that undertook cultural activities to foster Serbian national spirit and encouraged military training in anticipation of an eventual clash with Austria. Regarding the NDA as insufficiently aggressive several of its members founded a secret organization known as Union or Death, but commonly called the Black Hand. With members among army officers and civilians of all classes, this terrorist group was headed by Colonel Dragutin Dimitrijevic, later to become chief of Serbian military intelligence.

*"Statutes of Black Hand Society" (1911), in W. Henry Cooke and Edith P. Stickney, eds., *Readings in European International Relations Since 1879* (London: Harper & Brothers, 1931), p. 309.

---

succession of victories and were on the verge of overrunning Istanbul itself when the great powers intervened to prevent a total collapse of the Ottoman Empire. At the peace conference, the Ottoman Empire was stripped of all its territory in Europe except Istanbul and its environs. The real difficulty was in arbitrating the claims of the victors. In a secret arrangement made before the war, Serbia had been promised an outlet to the Adriatic through Albania. But now Austria, fearful of an increase in Serbia's power, objected, and at its insistence, Albania was established as an independent state.

The second Balkan war erupted less than a month after the first one ended. Deprived of a section of Albania, Serbia, supported by Greece, demanded part of Bulgaria's share of Macedonia by way of compensation. After bitter recriminations Bulgaria attacked its former allies. Turkey and Rumania in turn entered the conflict on the side of Serbia and Greece. Beset on all sides, the Bulgarians quickly came to terms. Turkey regained Adrianople, and Serbia, Greece, and Rumania also made gains at the expense of Bulgaria. Not content with its recent acquisitions, Serbia invaded Albania but withdrew upon receiving an ultimatum from Austria.

The warfare in the Balkans in 1912 and 1913 exacerbated national rivalries in that troubled region. Bulgaria and Turkey, embittered over the loss of territory, waited for a favorable opportunity to strike back. As for the victorious states, none were entirely satisfied with their gains and at least one, Serbia, nursed a major grievance. Twice since 1908, Serbia had been frustrated by the Habsburg government—once when the Austrians annexed Bosnia–Herzegovina and again in 1913 when they blocked Serbia's access to the Adriatic. To the Serbs, the Habsburg monarchy was an evil monster that prevented their nation from becoming great and powerful. "The first round is won," the Serbian prime minister was quoted as saying at the conclusion of the second Balkan war. "Now we must prepare the second against Austria."

HOW WAR CAME, JUNE–AUGUST 1914

The recurring crises and the fears these events had created did not induce the European powers to exercise greater caution but rather increased their determination to avoid past failures. By 1914, national rivalries, sharpened by

Francis Ferdinand and His Wife Being Greeted by a Local Official on Arriving in Sarajevo. As the royal automobile proceeded along the main boulevard toward the city hall one of the would-be assassins hurled a bomb which missed its mark but wounded several bystanders. At the city hall the scheduled program was altered to permit the archduke to visit wounded officers in the hospital. On the way there a second conspirator suddenly jumped on the running board of the car and shot both the archduke and his consort.

the feverish armaments race, had brought tensions in Europe to the breaking point. Only an incident was needed to set off the explosion.

Sarajevo and Its Aftermath

The war was triggered on June 28, 1914, when the Archduke Francis Ferdinand, heir to the Austrian throne, and his wife were shot to death as their motorcade drove through the streets of Sarajevo, capital of Bosnia. The assassin, Gavrilo Princip, was a Bosnian student of Serbian nationality. He belonged to a secret Serbian terrorist society, the Black Hand, which had as its ultimate aim the union of all southern Slavs under Serbian rule. The archduke became a victim of the Black Hand because it was widely believed that on his accession he intended to place the Slavs on the same autonomous footing as the Germans and Magyars within the Habsburg realm. If such a policy had been carried out, the south Slavs in the Austrian Empire might have lost their enthusiasm for union with Serbia. The murder plot had been hatched in the

Police Seizing Princip Moments after He Shot the Royal Couple. Princip, who was under twenty when he broke the law, was not subject to the death penalty. Sentenced to the maximum of twenty years at hard labor he died in prison of tuberculosis on April 28, 1918. Visitors to Sarajevo today can view the monument erected to honor Princip whose deed led indirectly to the formation of a large Serbian state.

THE AUSTRIAN ULTIMATUM TO SERBIA (JULY 23, 1914)

The history of the past few years, and particularly the painful events of the 28th of June, have proved the existence of a subversive movement in Serbia, whose object it is to separate certain portions of its territory from the Austro-Hungarian Monarchy. This movement, which came into being under the very eyes of the Serbian Government, subsequently found expression outside of the territory of the Kingdom in acts of terrorism, in a number of attempts at assassination, and in murders. . . . The Royal Serbian Government has done nothing to suppress this movement.

It is clear from the statements and confessions of the criminal authors of the assassination of the 28th of June, that the murder at Sarajevo was conceived at Belgrade, that the murderers received the weapons and the bombs with which they were equipped from Serbian officers and officials . . . and finally, that the dispatch of the criminals and of their weapons to Bosnia was arranged and effected under the conduct of Serbian frontier authorities.*

There followed ten demands, the most important of which were that all patriotic societies engaged in anti-Austrian activity be dissolved, that all anti-Austrian teachers and books be eliminated from the public schools, that public officials implicated in anti-Austrian propaganda be dismissed, and that Serbia accept the collaboration of Austrian officials in the eradication of anti-Austrian propaganda in Serbia and in the investigation of the assassination. In reply Serbia accepted all the demands except the ones referring to the participation of Austrian officials in the suppression of anti-Austrian propaganda and in the proceedings against those implicated in the crime.

*Max Montgelas and Walter Schücking, eds., Outbreak of the World War: German Documents Collected by Karl Kautsky (New York: Oxford University Press, 1924) pp. 603–606.

Serbian capital, Belgrade, and was the brainchild of Colonel Dragutin Dimitrijevic, chief of intelligence of the Serbian army and a leading figure in the Black Hand. There is no evidence that the Serbian government played a direct role in the conspiracy. Nevertheless, several members of the cabinet, among them the prime minister, were aware of the planned assassination and took no effective steps to prevent it.

Key Austrian officials, led by Count Leopold von Berchtold, the foreign minister, decided to use the assassination as a pretext to punish Serbia, which for many years had fanned political unrest among the Slavic population of the Habsburg Empire. Before taking any action, Austria obtained unconditional assurances of support from the kaiser. On July 23, Vienna, fortified by Germany's "blank check," delivered an ultimatum to Serbia (that had not been shown to the kaiser), couched in terms calculated to make its rejection certain.

The Serbians were unexpectedly conciliatory, accepting all but two of the demands and offering to submit the entire matter to the Hague Tribunal. "A brilliant diplomatic triumph; no excuse for war," exclaimed Kaiser William when he learned of Serbia's submission. Austria, however, deemed the reply unsatisfactory and on July 28 declared war on Serbia. Austria's haste was due to its desire to crush Serbia before other countries could be drawn into the dispute. Belatedly, the Germans tried to restrain the Austrians by urging only the occupation of Belgrade in northern Serbia.

Russia's response to Vienna's action destroyed all hopes of localizing the conflict. The Russians realized they could not leave Serbia in the lurch again if they wanted to retain any influence in the Balkans. Russia, because of its vast size, poor railroad system, and inefficient bureaucracy, required considerably more time than Germany or Austria to complete its military preparations. Buoyed by promises that it could count on French aid, the tsar's government ordered mobilization on July 29. Several hours later, Tsar Nicholas II modified the order to partial mobilization after he received a personal note from his cousin William begging him to help preserve the peace. The next day, the Russian general staff warned that once partial mobilization was under way, a sudden change to general mobilization would be slow and difficult to organize. Reluctantly, the tsar reissued the order for general mobilization.

The Germans perceived the order for general mobilization as equivalent to a declaration of war. The full deployment of the Russian army would have ruined the strategic plans that General Alfred von Schlieffen had devised in 1905 to prepare for the contingency of a two-front war. Prepared in the aftermath of the Franco-Russian alliance, the plan called for a holding action against the slow-moving Russians while the main German forces invaded France through Belgium. With France beaten, the Germans could turn their full power against the Russians. In this way, von Schlieffen had hoped to avoid a prolonged war on two fronts. Military considerations therefore explain why the Germans were deeply alarmed at the news of Russia's general mobilization order. On July 31, Berlin sent the tsar's government an ultimatum demanding immediate cessation of military preparations and asked France what course it would take in the event of a Russo-German war. The Russians did not bother to reply, prompting Germany to declare war on August 1. France answered on August 1 that it would consult its own interests and immediately began to mobilize. Two days later, Germany declared war on France.

The German assault on France began with an invasion of Belgium on August 3, a move that brought Great Britain into the conflict. Until this time, London, beyond promising that the Royal Navy would protect the French coast and shipping against German attack, had refused to give any definite pledges of military aid. The British Cabinet hesitated to act because much anti-war and isolationist sentiment still existed in the country and in Parliament. London's indecisive attitude led the German leaders to conclude that Great Britain would stay out of the conflict. However, the British cabinet decided to declare war when it received news that Germany had violated Belgian neutrality, to which all the great powers had been formally pledged since 1839. Apart from the factor of honor, it had traditionally been British policy to prevent any major continental state from dominating the Netherlands and Belgium, lying directly across the Channel. Thus at noon on August 4, the British government gave the Germans twelve hours to withdraw from Belgian soil. No reply was received and at midnight on August 4 Great Britain found itself at war with Germany. "The lamps are going out all over Europe," said Sir Edward Grey, the British foreign minister, as he gazed reflectively from the windows of his office at the city gaslights being put out in the London dawn; "we shall not see them lit again in our lifetime."

The two conflicting groups came to be generally called the Allies and the Central Powers. Initially, the Allies consisted of Great Britain and the British Empire, France, Russia, Serbia, and Belgium. Germany and Austria-Hungary made up the Central powers. Italy had deserted its partners on August 3, claiming its obligations to the Triple Alliance did not include supporting a war of aggression.

From the beginning of the conflict, both camps scrambled to acquire new recruits. Late in August 1914, Japan joined the Allies, partly because of its pact with Great Britain but mostly because it wanted to attack Germany's possessions in the Far East. Turkey, afraid of a victorious Russia, entered the war in November 1914 on Germany's side. Italy remained on the sidelines during the early months, weighing competing territorial offers, until finally throwing its lot with the Allies in May 1915.

"The Lamps Are Going Out All Over Europe." These words, uttered by Sir Edward Grey, the British foreign secretary, on the eve of the war, were featured in a cartoon in the *Chicago Daily News* and would become the epitaph of nineteenth century Europe and the Victorian and Edwardian eras.

CHRONOLOGY OF EVENTS LEADING UP TO WORLD WAR I (June 28–August 4, 1914)

June 28	Archduke Francis Ferdinand is assassinated
July 5	Austria receives a "blank-check" from Germany
July 23	Austria delivers an ultimatum to Serbia
July 28	Austria declares war on Serbia
July 29	Russia mobilizes
July 31	Germany demands that Russia demobilize
August 1	Germany declares war on Russia
August 3	Germany declares war on France
August 4	German troops invade Belgium
August 4	Great Britain declares war on Germany

In the fall of 1915, Bulgaria ranged itself alongside of the Central Powers. The following year Portugal and Rumania joined the Allies, as did the United States, Greece, and about half of Latin America in 1917. In all thirty nations were drawn into the conflict, and of these most fought against the Central Powers.

The Question of War Guilt

Few questions have been debated at greater length or with more passion than the responsibility for World War I. During the war and for many years afterward, scholars and laymen alike in Allied countries believed that Germany, by pursuing a policy of aggression, bore the predominant responsibility for the outbreak of the conflict. In time, as new evidence unfolded, it became apparent that the problem was more complex than originally perceived. Currently, most historians agree that it is impossible to blame the global conflict on any one country or policy. Clearly during the decades prior to 1914, each European power had added to the mounting tensions by strengthening its armed forces and extending its alliances.

Moreover, all the original participating nations must in some measure accept responsibility for the immediate cause of the war. The incident that brought on the final crisis was a crime planned by Serbians with the knowledge of the Belgrade authorities. Austria's determination to crush Serbia in a quick local war was both short-sighted and dangerous. Germany did try to restrain Austria, but only after it had foolishly given its ally a "blank check." Although the order to mobilize may have appeared justifiable to Russian leaders, it was the decisive factor in widening the conflict. France, instead of working to bring about a compromise, encouraged the Russians to stand firm. Had the British publicly announced their support for France, had they been more explicit in their intention to fight for Belgium, it is conceivable that Germany would not have launched an attack in the west. There is no doubt that all the nations involved committed serious mistakes of judgment during the critical weeks. Although historians may differ about the relative guilt of the powers, clearly no nation bears the main responsibility for the war and none are completely free from blame.

SUMMARY

After 1871 Bismarck organized an involved system of alliances designed to maintain Germany's new hegemony in Europe and to isolate a revengeful France. In 1873, he formed the League of Three Emperors, composed of Germany, Austria-Hungary, and Russia. This combination proved unworkable owing to the incompatibility of Austrian and Russian interests and ambitions. Bismarck replaced Russia with Italy to establish the Triple Alliance, and at the same time kept the tsar's government tied to Germany by the secret Reinsurance Treaty. Bismarck's diplomatic moves ensured the continuance of a general peace and left France cut off from potential allies.

The system that Bismarck painstakingly constructed over two decades was quickly dismantled by Kaiser William II, who ascended the throne in 1888. William dismissed the old chancellor in 1890 and personally assumed control of Germany's foreign policy. Among the kaiser's first acts was to abandon the Reinsurance Treaty, a move that drove Russia into the arms of France. No less damaging was the kaiser's adoption of policies that led to the estrangement of Great Britain. Great Britain responded by developing closer relations with France. In 1907 the Triple Entente was formed after Great Britain and Russia settled their colonial differences.

In the pre-1914 years, nationalism, the arms race, and imperialist rivalries, contributed to the acute state of international tension. Crises erupted periodically, threatening to bring the interlocking alliances into war but each time the diplomats maneuvered their way out of the trap and calm was restored.

None of the participating powers wanted a general war, but it was equally true that none did all they could to prevent the conflict. Without a long-range policy to maintain the peace it was inevitable that improvised efforts to smooth over disputes would ultimately fail with a resulting clash of arms. The assassination of the Archduke Ferdinand by a Serb nationalist on June 28, 1914, provided the spark for the war. Austria, taking for granted the complicity of the Serbian government, decided once and for all to settle accounts with its troublesome neighbor. When war broke out between Austria and Serbia, the system of alliances and the exigencies of military planning and mobilization schedules dragged Europe into the maelstrom.

SELECTED SOURCES

Albertini, Luigi. *The Origins of the War of 1914.* 3 Vols, 1952–1957. Generally considered to be the best and most objective among the major works on the diplomatic origins of the war.

Balfour, Michael. *The Kaiser and His Times.* 1972. An excellent biography of William II.

Dedijer, Vladimir. *The Road to Sarajevo.* 1966. The definitive study of the events leading up to the assassination. The author, who had access to Serbian and Bosnian sources, defends the idealism of the conspirators.

*Fay, Sidney. *The Origins of the World War.* 2 vols. 1928. The first and most influential of the revisionist accounts, by an American scholar.

*Fischer, Fritz. *Germany's Aims in the First World War.* 1967. A highly controversial study, emphasizing Germany's role in bringing on the war.

*Koch, Hannsjoachim W. ed. *The Origins of the First World War.* 1972. A collection of essays with different interpretations on the causes of World War I.

*Lafore, Laurence. *The Long Fuse: An Interpretation of the Origins of World War I.* 1965. A short, well written account stressing Austrian-Serbian tensions.

*Mann, Thomas. *The Magic Mountain.* Various editions. A novel depicting the malaise in European society during the period leading up to World War I.

*Remak, Joachim. *The Origin of World War I.* 1967. A brief, balanced introduction to the subject.

Schmitt, Bernadotte E. *The Coming of the War 1914.* 2 vols. 1930. Scholarly treatment critical of Germany's role.

Schmitt, Bernadotte E. *Triple Alliance and Triple Entente.* 1934. Brief, lucid account of the formation of the pre-war alliances.

*Taylor, A.J.P. *Struggle For Mastery in Europe, 1848–1914.* 1971. Witty, clever account of the power politics of the period.

Thomson, George M. *Twelve Days.* 1964. Thorough and engaging study of the twelve days preceding the outbreak of the war.

*Tuchman, Barbara. *The Proud Tower.* 1966. An absorbing panorama of Europe before the war.

World War I: CBS Film series—Part I, *Doomed Dynasties of Europe;* Part 2, *Assassination at Sarajevo: Pretext for War.* Approximately 16 minutes each. Black and White.

*Available in paperback.

WORLD WAR I

No one would believe that in this howling waste there could still be men; but steel helmets now appear on all sides out of the trench, and fifty yards from us a machine-gun is already in position and barking.

The wire-entanglements are torn to pieces. Yet they offer some obstacle. We see the storm-troops coming. Our artillery opens fire. Machine-guns rattle, rifles crack. The charge works its way across. Haie and Kropp begin with the hand-grenades. They throw as fast as they can, others pass them, the handles with the strings already pulled. Haie throws seventy-five yards, Kropp sixty, it has been measured, the distance is important. The enemy as they run cannot do much before they are within forty yards.

We recognize the distorted faces, the smooth helmets: they are French. They have already suffered heavily when they reach the remnants of the barbed-wire entanglements. A whole line had gone down before our machine guns; then we have a lot of stoppages and they come nearer.

As this harrowing scene indicates, World War I differed radically from previous conflicts. It was not only unprecedented in geographic scope and in the size of the armies engaged, but modern technology had also unveiled new and terrible weapons—tanks, airplanes, submarines, flame throwers, poison gas, and machine guns—that took an enormous toll in human lives. The machine gun, which gave the defender a decided advantage over the attacker, dominated the war on land. In the three and a half years of trench warfare thousands of local attacks, such as the one described above by the fictional German soldier in E. M. Remarque's *All Quiet on the Western Front*, shifted the line a little here and there but no decisive break-through occurred until the final weeks of the war in 1918.

The struggle developed into a grim war of attrition, extending beyond the battlefields to the factories, banks, laboratories, and farms. Warfare became total, calling upon the entire human and material resources of a nation.

The Assault. This detail from a painting by H. de Groux skillfully captures the fiery determination of the French soldier in combat. Putting their faith in the offensive in all circumstances, French generals squandered lives on a reckless scale in a futile attempt to eject the Germans from France. Whatever may be said about the folly of the French High Command, there was never any doubt about the heroism and dogged resolution of the rank and file or of the officers who led them into battle. France suffered the highest rate of casualties in proportion to total available manpower. During the first sixteen months of combat the number of men killed alone was nearly two thirds of a million—a figure without precedent in history.

THE BELLIGERENTS

As the war broke out, each side had certain advantages. Germany overshadowed its allies, furnishing plans and on occasion supplying commanding officers for their armies; this gave the Central Powers much closer unity of command than the Allies displayed. The Allies did not achieve unity of planning until the closing months of the war. Possessing excellent leadership, discipline, and equipment, the German army was the best in the world. Germany also had a good stock of ammunition, ample supplies of coal and iron, and the most extensive industrial complex in Europe. The Central Powers further enjoyed interior lines of communication that enabled them to transfer their forces rapidly from one front to another. By contrast, the Allies were widely separated; Russia was virtually cut off from its partners in the west.

The Allies had on their side larger land forces, greater economic resources, and naval predominance. Between 1914 and 1918 the Allies mustered 40 million men, including contingents from the British colonies, French Africa, and Latin America, against 21 million for their opponents. That preponderance is somewhat misleading, however; the Russian army, which numbered 12 million men, was poorly trained and equipped and for the most part badly led. Despite Germany's powerful industrial machine, the Allies as a group possessed an overwhelming advantage in material resources. The Allies also commanded the seas, enabling them to mount a blockade that would prevent the Central Powers from importing war supplies while assuring Allied control of the resources of neutral countries overseas. If the struggle should turn into a long-term test of strength, time clearly worked to the advantage of the Allies.

MAP 74
Europe in 1914.

A Visit to the Front. The Kaiser, arriving by train to inspect German troops, is shown here speaking with General von Fabeck. Seen between them is General von Falkenhayn who, after the battle of the Marne, had succeeded von Moltke as supreme commander of the German army. Falkenhayn was himself replaced in August 1916 by the team of Hindenburg and Ludendorff who had won imperishable fame on the Russian front.

1914: THE MILITARY DEADLOCK

In the last half century, European conflicts had been brief, concluded by a few decisive battles. On that basis, and ignoring the war of attrition that had characterized the civil war in the United States, both the Allies and the Central Powers had prepared plans for another short offensive war. France's Plan XVII called for a headlong advance into Lorraine. On the other hand, Germany's Schlieffen Plan presumed that the cumbersome Russian military machine could be contained by relatively weak forces while the bulk of Germany's army strove for an early knockout of France. A quick victory in the west was to be achieved by a holding operation on the left in Alsace-Lorraine, coupled with a strong right wing that would wheel through Belgium and northern France, capture Paris, and then crush the French armies in a pincer grip. Once the French were beaten, the Germans could concentrate their full power in the east and dispose of the Russians at their leisure.

Neither strategy succeeded. The French encountered unexpected resistance in Lorraine and their attack soon collapsed. The Germans came within forty miles of Paris, but the Allied forces rallied and launched a counteroffensive along the Marne River. After four days of furious fighting (September 6–9) the Germans retreated to prepared positions on the Aisne. The German armies had outrun their supplies, stretched their endurance too far, and failed to maintain close touch with general headquarters. More important perhaps, the German chief of staff, Helmuth von Moltke (nephew and namesake of the brilliant nineteenth-century strate-

Joffre and French. General Joffre, the French Commander-in-Chief, is chatting with his British counterpart Sir John French while his deputy, General Douglas Haig, looks on. Towards the end of 1915, French was recalled to England and replaced by Haig. A year later, Joffre suffered a similar fate when he was retired to a decorative post with the rank of Marshal of France. His place in the French High Command was taken by General Nivelle whose gigantic offensive, launched on April 16, 1917, met one of the bloodiest repulses of the war and precipitated a mutiny in the French Army. Relieved of his command, Nivelle was replaced by General Pétain on May 15, 1917.

gist), had reduced the striking power of his right wing to send reinforcements to the eastern front, where the Russians were showing unexpected aggressiveness. The defeat at the Marne irreparably dislocated the Schlieffen Plan and forced Germany into a protracted two-front war.

In the next few months, each side tried to outflank the other but only succeeded in extending the line to the English Channel. Before the close of 1914, the war of movement had settled into a war of position. The armies faced each other in a continuous line that snaked more than 500 miles from Switzerland to the sea. In spite of numerous attacks and counterattacks, sometimes involving hundreds of thousands of men, the battlefront remained virtually unchanged for three years.

The war on the long eastern front where the Russians faced both the Austrians and the Germans was relatively fluid with considerable gain and loss of territory. But there were extended periods of stalemates when the opposing armies dug long lines of trenches and glared menacingly at each another.

In mid August 1914 two Russian armies invaded East Prussia, one from the east and the other from the south. In alarm von Moltke recalled General Paul von Hindenburg from retirement and appointed the brilliant Erich Ludendorff as Hindenburg's chief of staff. Recognizing the wide gap between the two Russian armies, the new team laid plans to fight them one at a time. At Tannenberg (August 25–31) and a week later at the Masurian Lakes (September 6–15), the Germans dealt the Russians crushing blows and sent them reeling out of East Prussia. Meanwhile, however, the Russians swept through the Habsburg province of Galicia and threatened to break across the Carpathian Mountains into the Hungarian plain. To take pressure off the Austrians, Hindenburg invaded Poland, but the Russians brought him to a standstill short of Warsaw. By the end of 1914, the two sides were locked in a stalemate much like that in France.

MAP 75

The Western Front, 1914–1918. The Germans achieved their deepest penetration in the opening weeks of the war when they came within sight of Paris before being pushed back beyond the Marne River. Thereafter the front stabilized as both sides constructed a vast network of trenches that stretched from the Alps to the North Sea. For over three years, little land changed hands in spite of the frightful loss of life entailed by trench warfare. With Russia out of the war the Germans launched a massive offensive which, although successful at first, was ultimately stopped just short of Paris. Aided by the newly arrived American reinforcements the Allies counterattacked, steadily rolling back the Germans who finally accepted armistice terms in November 1918.

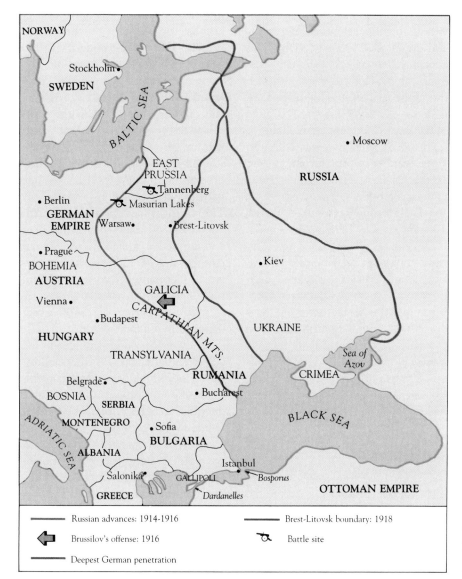

MAP 76
The Eastern Front, 1914–1918. After some success in East Prussia, the Russians suffered shattering defeats at Tannenberg and the Masurian Lakes and were forced to withdraw from German territory. In 1916 the Brusilov offensive failed after a promising start and from then on the Russian position deteriorated. Racked by two revolutions in 1917, which further undermined Russia's war effort, and with German troops advancing deep into the Ukraine, the new Bolshevik government agreed to accept German peace terms. The Germans acquired sizeable annexations even though they had to evacuate the territory east of the line drawn by the Treaty of Brest-Litovsk.

THE WAR AT SEA AND IN THE COLONIES

From the first hours of war, Allied naval superiority was used to good effect. Despite occasional German victories at sea, such as Admiral Count Maximilian von Spee's squadron sinking two British cruisers off the coast of Chile, the Allied navies had captured, sunk, or driven into port all enemy merchant ships and surface raiders by the spring of 1915. The main German fleet remained at its home base until May 1916, when it emerged to fight the British navy. The resulting Battle of Jutland (May 31–June 1, 1916) ended indecisively, and the German fleet returned to port. Strategically, the battle was a major Allied victory: the British remained in control of the seas and the Germans made no further attempt to challenge them.

With virtually no shipping of their own, the Germans had to rely on neutral ships for their imports, and this in turn led the Allies to impose an economic blockade of Germany. Under international law, only war supplies and certain specified raw materials were regarded as contraband. The British ignored the legal distinction between contraband and non-contraband goods and claimed the right to confiscate all products that might conceivably help the German war effort. Great Britain's high-handedness on the seas brought angry protests from neutral countries, in particular from the United States, and for a while relations between Washington and London were strained. But meanwhile, the Allied blockade slowly strangled Germany by virtually cutting off its importation of war materials and food. Malnutrition became so widespread by the end of 1918 that it played an important part in Germany's decision to surrender.

Pressed by the Allied blockade, Germany used a new weapon, the submarine, for a counterblockade. Great Britain was far from being self-sufficient, particularly in food, and depended heavily on extensive shipping for survival. In February 1915 the German authorities proclaimed the waters around Great Britain a "war zone" in which they would sink on sight both Allied and neutral ships. This policy was highly successful at first, and merchant ships were sunk almost daily. On May 7, 1915, the British liner *Lusitania,* which, as the Germans apparently knew, carried cases of munitions for the Allies, was torpedoed off the coast of Ireland. About 1,200 people died, more than 100 of them Americans. The western world was appalled by the immensity of the disaster and President Wilson of the United States sent three vigorously worded notes of protest to Berlin. On September 1 the German government, after much legalistic quibbling, informed Washington that henceforth liners would not be sunk

without warning and without providing for the safety of passengers and crews. But German submarines continued to attack merchant vessels at an accelerated pace, although they failed to shut off Allied commerce.

Since the Germans were unable to send aid to their overseas colonies, these were easy prey for the Allies. In the Far East, Japan occupied several undefended German islands in the Pacific, and with token British assistance took Tsingtao in China. New Zealand seized Samoa and Australia took over New Guinea. In Africa, South Africa conquered German Southwest Africa, whereas Togoland and the Cameroons fell to a combined Anglo-French force. In German East Africa, Paul Lettow-Vorbeck maintained German resistance in the interior until the end of the war, although most of the colony had fallen.

THE HOME FRONT

World War I was the first total war, with the civilian population almost as fully mobilized as the soldiers. As the conflict dragged on, with no end in sight, both democratic and autocratic governments increasingly controlled broad facets of their nation's economic and social life.

In all the belligerent countries, the public had greeted the onset of hostilities with enthusiasm and demonstrations of patriotism. Each side believed in the righteousness of its cause, and few anticipated the horrors that would accompany modern war. In many towns and cities, crowds con-

ditioned by years of nationalistic propaganda surged through the streets singing, cheering, waving flags, and showering gifts and flowers on the troops departing for the front. Political parties, even those bitterly critical of the government in the past, rallied to the national cause. In Great Britain, the Conservative party abstained from criticizing the reigning Liberals and in May 1915 became partners in a coalition government. The political factions in the French Chamber laid aside their differences and formed a *Union Sacrée.* In an emotional scene, the parliamentarians in Germany agreed to a political truce and then heard the kaiser say, "I recognize parties no more. I recognize only Germans!"

Every major country engaged in the war eventually had to introduce drastic economic planning and controls to ensure the proper and equitable distribution of resources. The areas of common concern were munitions, food, and manpower. The British government centralized the manufacture of munitions, introduced military conscription, promoted the employment of women in factories to free men for the armed services, and placed restrictions on labor union activity. In France, the authorities rationed consumer goods, allocated men between the factories and the battlefront, and supervised the construction of new industries around Paris to replace those lost in areas under German occupation. After the United States entered the war, technocrats like Bernard Baruch presided over national economic controls unprecedented in U.S. history.

Germany, under greater pressure to conserve war materials, managed its economy efficiently. Under the di-

Women at Work in a Munitions Plant. In view of the horrendous loss of life in battle, it became necessary to draft hitherto exempt workers whose jobs in the war factories and mines were regarded as essential to war production. To remedy the labor shortage at home, women were recruited to take over many of the jobs to which they had previously been denied access. Women accepted not only white-collar and light factory work, but also heavy labor positions such as in steel mills, road and railroad construction, and open-face mines.

rection of Walter Rathenau, an industrial executive, the government set up a War Raw Materials Department that allocated raw materials on a priority basis, developed new production techniques, and created many substitute commodities such as artificial nitrates, cellulose clothing, bark coffee, and turnip bread. At the same time, the government dealt with the acute labor shortage. It forcibly imported workers from the occupied territories and mobilized every male in the nation between sixteen and sixty, decreeing that those not in active military service take jobs in factories, in offices, or on farms. In the last two years of the war, however, no amount of ingenuity could solve Germany's shortages of food and manpower.

In addition to conserving resources, all warring governments sought to win over neutral countries and maintain high morale among their own civilians through the use of propaganda and censorship. The Allies won the propaganda war in the neutral world, often by distorting or falsifying events to whip up hostility against Germany. They accused the Germans not only of having started the war but also of frightful atrocities, particularly in Belgium, where the Germans had in fact executed innocent civilians to terrorize the rest of the population into submission and destroyed the precious library of the University of Louvain. But the Germans had not, as the Allies maintained, impaled children on bayonets or tied living priests by their feet to serve as clappers for bells.

Propaganda played an equally important role at home. As the unprec-edented slaughter on the battlefield showed no sign of letting up, the early euphoria gradually changed to despair and a yearning for peace. Leaders on both sides had to sustain the nation's will to go on fighting. Newspapers, artists, advertisers, movie makers, and academicians deluged the public with a constant stream of propaganda, inciting them to hate the enemy and to believe their sacrifice would lead to a better world. Civilians were exhorted to work overtime, buy bonds, plant gardens, and donate money and property to help the war effort. Lawmakers subjected newspapers to rigorous censorship, placed restrictions on civil liberties, and punished by prison sentences or death persons who disseminated information to the enemy, spread defeatism among the population, or made unpatriotic speeches.

GERMANY IMPOSES BREAD RATIONING (MAY 16, 1918)

The development of the grain importation from the Ukraine unfortunately does not permit our bread-provisioning for the last months of the harvest year to be based upon this uncertain and not clearly determined source. Therefore, in order to be certain, we are chiefly dependent for the rest of the year upon the German domestic stocks. The small stores available for the distribution require a cutting down of consumption. Accordingly the governing board of the Reich Grain Department has in its session of the 11th instant, with the approval of the directorate, decided the following to become operative from June 16 of this year:

● The daily flour ration for those justified to receive provisioning will be reduced from 200 to 160 grams.

● The hitherto prevailing bonuses for heavy and heaviest workers remain. The ration to be used by the self-provider, which has already been reduced since April 1, does not undergo a new change.

● The re-establishment of the old rations will take place as soon as sufficient imports from the Ukraine are in the hands of the Reich Grain Department; at latest, however, when early threshing of the domestic crop of 1918 has filled the stores of the Reich Grain Department.

● It is impossible this year to give compensation in meat for the flour reduction as was the case last year. After the great reduction of our hog stocks the present meat ration exerts such a considerable inroad upon our cattle reserves that a further claim would most seriously endanger the milk and fat provisioning.

● A compensation will be granted by an increased ration of sugar; the distribution of victuals during the weeks of smaller bread rations will be increased.

Germany produced only about eighty percent of its food supply before the war, and food production declined still further after 1914 because of shortages of farm workers, horses, and nitrogen for fertilizers. With the above announcement the War Food Department reduced the daily allotment of flour, a mainstay of the German diet. This was one of the many privations endured by the German people throughout the war. Before the fighting ended in 1918, 750,000 Germans had died of hunger.

*Ralph H. Lutz, *Fall of the German Empire, 1914–1918*, Vol. 2 (Stanford: Stanford University Press, 1969), pp. 196–97.

THE STALEMATE ON LAND, 1915–1917

By 1915, the troops in the west had fortified themselves in a vast network of trenches that became more elaborate as time went on. The troops in the front line trenches constructed underground shelters, deployed machine guns and mortars, and set up dense barbed-wire entanglements. Behind the front trenches were one or more support lines, and further back heavy artillery. Between the opposing armies was a desolate stretch of territory called "no man's land."

The generals on both sides were baffled by the stalemated military situation. Trained in the nineteenth century and not grasping the effects of twentieth-century weapons on tactics and strategy, they could think of no other way of overcoming the deadlock except by frontal attacks. If enough men and guns were concentrated in a given area, the commanders were convinced, sooner or later they would break through the enemy's line and into open country. The attacks were preceded by a prolonged artillery bombardment intended to cut lanes through the wire, smash the front line trench system, and leave the surviving defenders in a state of shock or hysteria. When the barrage lifted, the attacking troops with fixed bayonets would go "over the top" in waves and advance across no man's land.

All too often, the attacking troops discovered the barrage had not done what was expected, with the result that the defenders were able to get back into position, set up their machine guns, and mow down the advancing infantry. Despite frightful losses, gains were always negligible, sometimes measured in yards. In 1915, the French army mounted a series of attacks against the German line, but did not gain more than three miles in any one place, suffering 1,430,000 casualties. In 1916, the Germans lost 336,000 men in a vain effort to capture the French fortress of Verdun. That same year, the British, assisted by the French, launched a great drive on the Somme salient and lost more than 600,000 men without any appreciable gains. In April 1917, an enormous French offensive in Lorraine was an unmitigated disaster, with losses of nearly 200,000 troops. The morale of the French army cracked, and a wave of mutinies spread through division after division. The French command eventually got the mutinies in hand by improving front line conditions and arranging for better food and more frequent leave periods. It should have been apparent that human courage alone could not overcome artillery, barbed wire, and machine guns, but rather than reevaluate the conditions under which the new war was being fought, the military continued to apply old concepts or merely improvised tactics for local battlefield situations.

Early in 1915, the British and the French made a major effort to outflank the western front by attacking Turkey. An Allied victory here would have had the added advantage of opening communications with Russia. The operation, however, was badly mismanaged. An Anglo-French fleet,

attempting to force its way through the Dardanelles, was checked by mines and by fire from Turkish forts. A landing on the Gallipoli Peninsula followed, but it met such fierce Turkish resistance that Allied troops had to be withdrawn after great losses of men and material.

The Allied failure at Gallipoli induced Bulgaria to come in with the Central Powers in 1915. In the autumn the Serbian army, which had twice repulsed the invading Austrians, was overwhelmed by Bulgarian and Austro-German forces; the remnant of the Serbian army was evacuated to the island of Corfu.

A new front was added in May 1915 when Italy entered the conflict on the side of the Allies. Negotiated the previous month, the secret Treaty of London promised Italy, as compensation for its intervention, stretches of Austro-Hungarian territory plus further acquisitions at the expense of

the Ottoman Empire. It proved to be a dubious bargain for the Allies. For two years Italy engaged in a dozen bloody but indecisive battles in an effort to break through Austrian defenses along the Isonzo River. In October 1917, the Austrians, with German help, broke through at Caporetto, sending the Italians in a disorderly rout. French and British reinforcements were hastily rushed across the Alps, enabling the Italians to hold the line along the Piave River. The Italian front remained relatively quiet until the last weeks of the war.

When the Germans proved unable to eliminate France they turned their offensive power against Russia. In May 1915, Austro-German forces mounted a new offensive that inflicted staggering losses on the Russians and compelled them to abandon Galicia and most of Poland. Commitments elsewhere prevented the Germans and Austrians from launching a decisive

Trench Warfare on the Western Front. For nearly four years the two great armies were cramped in a double line of trenches from which futile attacks to dislodge each other were repeatedly launched. Life for the common soldier alternated between boredom and the extreme unpleasantness of rat-infested trenches, the occasional horrifying experience of battle, inclement weather, sniper fire, and loss of comrades. Trench warfare left terrible psychological as well as physical scars on many of those who survived.

Sinking of
Lusitania

Battle of the
Marne

Dardanelles
Campaign

Failure of
Brusilov
offensive

Battle of
Jutland

Battles of
Tannenberg
and the
Masurian
Lakes

Italy
enters
the war

Battles of
Verdun and
the Somme

drive to knock Russia out of the war. In June 1916, the Russians, displaying amazing recuperative powers, staged a counteroffensive under General Alexis Brusilov that opened a wide gap in the Austrian lines. The Germans, with troops brought up from the western front, rushed into the gap and brought the Russian advance to a halt. The Russian army, which had lost another million men during Brusilov's drive, sank into a state of apathy from which it never recovered. Discontent and unrest were greatly accelerated among the Russian civilians by recurring military defeats, food shortages, and the inefficiency and corruption of the government. In March 1917, a spontaneous outbreak of riots assumed such menacing proportions that the tsar was forced to abdicate. The provisional government that succeeded the tsar failed to reckon with the war weariness of the masses and chose to continue the struggle. In November 1917, the Bolsheviks, pledged to peace, overthrew the provisional government and promptly signed an armistice with Germany. The collapse of the eastern front meant that Germany would be able to throw its full weight against the western Allies.

BREAKING THE STALEMATE, 1917–1918

In January 1917, the Germans announced their intention of sinking all ships, belligerent or neutral, that entered the war zone around the British Isles. The Allied blockade had created such alarming food shortages within the Central Powers that the German high command considered defeat inevitable if the war lasted much longer. They concluded that the only chance of breaking the British blockade was to resume unrestricted submarine warfare and knock Great Britain out of the war. The Germans calculated that by sinking 600,000 tons of shipping a month, they could starve the British into submission within six months. Unrestricted submarine warfare was likely to bring the United States into the conflict, but they saw the risk as worth taking. German leaders were confident that since the United States was unprepared for war, it could not mobilize its resources quickly enough to make a difference.

Germany lost its gamble, although in the early months of 1917 the submarine campaign met and even ex-

ceeded the expectations of its sponsors. The submarines sank 570,000 tons of shipping in February and again in March, and, as the days grew longer, sent another 875,000 tons to the bottom in April. With food reserves reduced at one point to a mere six weeks, Great Britain faced the grim prospect of starvation. Gradually, however, the British adopted countermeasures in the form of depth charges, mines, aerial reconnaissance, hydroplane detectors, and the convoy system, where destroyers escorted groups of merchant ships. These steps proved effective enough, along with naval support from the United States, to assure Great Britain's survival.

The Intervention of the United States

Unrestricted submarine warfare not only failed to bring the British to their knees but also, as anticipated, caused the United States to join the Allies. Although the overwhelming majority of Americans wished to remain at peace at the beginning of the war, few heeded President Wilson's call to be impartial in thought as well as in deed. Despite the Allied blockade, the American people were bound to

Great Britain by cultural ties and harbored a sentimental enthusiasm for France that dated back to the days of Lafayette. Germany, on the other hand, was seen as ruthless and unprincipled, sentiments reinforced by a shrewd and extensive British propaganda campaign. The United States also had a significant financial and industrial stake in the war effort of Great Britain and France. Since Germany was cut off by the British blockade, most U.S. commerce was with the western Allies. The Allies needed enormous amounts of war material from the United States, and as a consequence the value of U.S. trade soared. Millions of laborers and farmers as well as a few wealthy industrialists and munition makers thus had a stake in Allied victory.

Despite their pro-Allies sympathy, most Americans in early 1917 still wished to stay out of the war, but Germany's resumption of unrestricted submarine warfare soon pushed them into it. For two and a half years, President Wilson had sought to keep the United States neutral, while mediating among the belligerents. In 1917 he made one last effort to end the war, by asking the participants to state the terms on which they would agree to stop fighting. Wilson followed with a speech before the U.S. Senate on January 22, 1917, in which he called for a "peace without victory," but the appeal came too late to have any positive effect. The Germans had already decided to unleash their submarines against all vessels bound for Allied ports.

On learning of Germany's intentions, Wilson promptly broke off diplomatic relations. He still hoped to keep the United States out of war but

subsequent events forced his hand. In January 1917, the German foreign secretary, Arthur Zimmermann, instructed his minister in Mexico City to seek a military alliance with the Mexican government. If the United States entered the war, Germany would help Mexico recover the territories it had lost to its northern neighbor in 1848. The British intelligence service intercepted the message, decoded it, and handed it to the U.S. government. Published on March 1, 1917, the Zimmermann telegram further inflamed anti-German sentiment in the country. This revelation was followed by the sinking of several American ships. Public opinion now moved sharply in favor of war. President Wilson, realizing no great power could submit to its merchant ships being destroyed day after day, decided the United States must fight back. At his urging, Congress declared war on Germany on April 6, 1917.

If the United States entered the war late, its contribution to the Allied cause was vital, perhaps decisive. U.S. intervention gave the war-weary Allies an immense psychological lift, for it came at the height of Germany's submarine campaign and when Russian resistance had all but collapsed. Although it would take a year before its troops reached the front in any significant numbers, the United States supplied the Allies with immediate and important financial, material, and naval aid.

The Final Phase

At the beginning of 1918, Ludendorff, who now directed Germany's military operations, was confronted

with the necessity of forcing a decision in the west before American strength could be brought to bear. He transferred troops from the eastern front to reinforce those in the west for a massive blow designed to bring Great Britain and France to terms. On March 21, 1918, the Germans began a series of assaults that made deep penetrations into Allied territory, and by the end of May the Germans had reached Chateau Thierry on the Marne, only forty miles from Paris. General Ferdinand Foch, recently appointed supreme commander of the Allied forces, called on U.S. troops under General John "Black Jack" Pershing for help. On May 31, two U.S. Army divisions and a brigade of marines supported the French and helped to blunt the German thrust. In July, when the Germans made their last great effort to break through to Paris, 85,000 Americans were in the lines that withstood their assault. Throughout the summer of 1918, American troops poured into Europe at a rate of 200,000 a month and restored offensive power to the shaken and badly depleted Allied armies, eventually taking over a section of the front. Germany, on the other hand, could not replace the million casualties it had sustained in the spring and summer attacks. It had to rely on the very young and the very old, with the result that the combat value of its divisions in France declined sharply.

In July, Foch began a series of counterattacks that steadily drove the Germans from their main positions into open country. Under relentless pounding the morale of the German army collapsed. On August 8, termed by Ludendorff "the black day of the

LUDENDORFF CALLS FOR AN ARMISTICE (AUGUST 13, 1918)

On the 13th there was a discussion between the Chancellor, the Field-Marshal [von Hindenburg], Secretary of State von Hintze, and myself, in the Field-Marshal's room at the Hotel Britannique. I reviewed the military situation, the condition of the army, and the position of our allies, and explained that it was no longer possible by an offensive to force the enemy to sue for peace. Defense alone could hardly achieve this object, and so the termination of the war would have to be brought about by diplomacy. At the moment our line on the Western front was holding, though, in view of the element of uncertainty which the insubordination of some of the troops had introduced into our calculations, circumstances might necessitate a withdrawal of the front. I sincerely hoped, however, that the army in France would stand fast. The state of affairs on the Western front was naturally bound to make an unfavorable impression on our allies. In this connection, the morale of our army and people became a matter of even greater importance than before. I laid special emphasis on this. . . . I . . . emphasized the necessity for speeches by our ministers calculated to make an impression abroad,

and the importance of even now inaugurating a propaganda department for educating public opinion.

The Field-Marshal said nothing about the state of feeling at home; he took a more optimistic view of the military situation than I did. Secretary of State von Hintze drew, from what he had heard, the logical conclusion that peace negotiations were essential, and that we should have to bring ourselves to take up a very conciliatory attitude.*

It was Ludendorff, not the Chancellor (Prince Max von Baden) or the kaiser, that first raised the idea of approaching Wilson for peace talks. In late October 1918 he changed his mind, urging a continuation of the fighting rather than acceptance of Allied terms. As a result he was dismissed by the kaiser. In the post war period Ludendorff helped spread the legend that the German army had not been beaten in the field but had been "stabbed in the back" by sinister forces at home.

*Erich von Ludendorff, *Ludendorff's Own Story* Vol. 2, (New York: Harper and Brothers, 1920), pp. 334–35.

German army," the British for the first time successfully employed masses of tanks to break through the trench system, smashing the German lines east of Amiens. With Allied armies sweeping forward in every sector, Ludendorff told the kaiser that the war was lost. Although the army had not yet been driven back into Germany,

Ludendorff urged the government to make peace before Germany was completely defeated in the field.

While Germany entered into negotiations to achieve a cease-fire, its allies dropped out of the war one by one. A combined army of French, British, Greeks, and Serbians drove up the Balkan Peninsula from Salo-

nika, Greece, and forced Bulgaria to conclude an armistice on September 30. Turkey, with British and Arab forces in control of its Middle East holdings, followed suit a month later. Austria-Hungary, its ethnic minorities in open revolt and its armies disintegrating, sued for peace on November 3.

Mounting internal convulsions increased the pressures on Germany to seek peace. Led to believe as late as September 1918 that victory was certain, the German people who had endured great hardships and privations, were shocked when they discovered the truth. Their disillusionment and disgust led to a loss of faith in the government. On November 3, 1918, German sailors at Kiel mutinied and ran up the red flag. The revolt quickly spread, and many German cities were rocked by widespread rioting. Under pressure from the military leaders, the kaiser abdicated on November 9 and fled across the border into the Netherlands. Two days later, a German commission accepted armistice terms. At 11 A.M. on November 11, 1918 the First World War came to an end.

The effects of the four-year conflict on western civilization were devastating. At least ten million people, soldiers and civilians, were killed, with twice that number wounded, many of them maimed. The cost of the war was incalculable, not only dissipating the national wealth of the belligerents but also leaving them deeply in debt. The First World War swept away the autocratic monarchies of Germany, Austria-Hungary, and Russia, and destroyed much of the old order throughout Europe. It also created immense dislocations in Europe's political, social, and economic structures. The resulting tensions and resentments led to the emergence of the totalitarian state. The war also heralded the beginning of the end of European primacy in world affairs.

THE PARIS PEACE CONFERENCE

In January 1919, delegates of the victorious nations gathered in Paris to decide the fate of Germany and its associates. The Central Powers were not represented, nor was Russia, which had dropped out of the war and was currently under Bolshevik control. As in most major peace conferences, the delegations of the lesser states were only consulted in cases involving their direct interests. The leaders of the great powers, the "Big Four," composed of President Wilson of the United States, and prime ministers Georges Clemenceau of France, David Lloyd George of Great Britain, and Vittorio Orlando of Italy, played the main role in drawing up the terms for the defeated powers.

Allied Goals

The Allied leaders were anxious to lay the foundations of a lasting peace, but they differed on the means to achieve it. Only Wilson made no financial or territorial claims on the defeated nations. His vision of a just and enduring peace was embodied in his Fourteen Points (see box), proclaimed in a speech to the Senate in January 1918. However, he could not sell his program to the European leaders. He had dignity and idealism but he lacked both physical stamina and experience as a diplomat, and he was further handicapped by the victory of the rival Republican party in the congressional elections of November 1918.

The war aims of the other allies, best expressed by Clemenceau, clashed with some of the principal points in Wilson's program. Nicknamed "The Tiger," Clemenceau was a cynical, hard-nosed politician, contemptuous of idealism and Wilson's Fourteen Points. "Mr. Wilson bores me with his Fourteen Points," growled the Ti-

ger, "Why God Almighty has only ten." His main object was to cripple Germany and destroy its capacity to wage war so that it would never again menace France. Lloyd George, in keeping with Great Britain's traditional foreign policy, wanted to prevent any one power from dominating Europe. Thus he was not eager to see France become too powerful or Germany too weak. On the other hand, he was committed to a hard line having pledged during his reelection campaign in December 1918 to punish the kaiser and extort heavy reparations from Germany. Among the Big Four, Vittorio Orlando played the least constructive role. He came to the conference with the single-minded purpose of claiming the territories Italy had been promised in the secret treaty of 1915, and hoped to get more besides.

The Versailles Treaty

Formal peace negotiations, which lasted from January to May 1919, were marked by tension and acrimony.

The Big Four at Versailles. The big four take time out from their heavy schedule to pose for photographers. From left to right: Vittorio Orlando, David Lloyd George, Georges Clemenceau, and Woodrow Wilson.

WILSON'S FOURTEEN POINTS

1. Open covenants of peace, openly arrived at.

2. Absolute freedom of navigation upon the seas . . . alike in peace and in war . . . .

3. The removal, as far as possible, of all economic barriers.

4. Adequate guarantees given and taken that national armaments will be reduced to the lowest point consistent with domestic safety.

5. A free, open-minded, and absolutely impartial adjustment of all colonial claims.

6. The evacuation of all Russian territory and such a settlement . . . as will secure [for Russia] . . . an unhampered and unembarrassed opportunity for the independent determination of her own political development and national policy.

7. Belgium . . . must be evacuated and restored.

8. All French territory should be freed and the invaded portions restored, and the wrong done to France in the matter . . . of Alsace-Lorraine . . . should be righted.

9. A readjustment of the frontiers of Italy should be effected along clearly recognizable lines of nationality.

10. The peoples of Austria-Hungary . . . should be accorded the freest opportunity of autonomous development.

11. Rumania, Serbia, and Montenegro should be evacuated; occupied territories restored; Serbia accorded free access to the sea.

12. The Turkish portion of the present Ottoman Empire should be assured a secure sovereignty, but the other nationalities which are now under Turkish rule . . . [should have] autonomous development.

13. An independent Polish state . . . should include the territories inhabited by indisputably Polish populations . . . [and should] be assured a free and secure access to the sea.

14. A general association of nations must be formed under specific covenants for the purpose of affording mutual guarantees of political independence and territorial integrity to great and small states alike.*

Wilson's hopes for a peace settlement, based on his Fourteen Points, were dashed by the intrusion of Old World power politics and national egotism. The peace treaties repudiated most of Wilson's program. Self-determination was not always observed, the victors did not disarm, the Allies intervened in Russia, economic barriers remained, colonial adjustments ignored the interests of the local populations and so on. In fact, all but five of Wilson's Fourteen Points were ignored.

*Congressional Record, LVI, 1918, Part I, 680–81.

Wilson frequently found himself at odds with his colleagues. Their most serious difference was over the future of the Rhineland, German territory west of the Rhine and a strip thirty miles wide on the east of it. For security reasons Clemenceau wanted to turn the area into a buffer zone under permanent French control, but he finally agreed to a compromise on receiving an Anglo-American pledge of assistance in case Germany again attacked France. This agreement, however, was killed by the U.S. Senate.

Another crisis arose from Italy's demand of Fiume and the surrounding Adriatic lands, territories that had not been promised to Italy in the Treaty of London. Wilson, backed by Clemenceau and Lloyd George, not only rejected Orlando's claim to Fiume but also refused to grant Italy the Dalmatian coast that it had been promised in the secret treaty. He wanted to include these areas in the new state of Yugoslavia as essential outlets to the sea. The dispute reached a climax when Orlando withdrew from the conference in a huff, leaving the issue unresolved. In 1920, Italy and Yugoslavia signed the Treaty of Rapallo, which gave Italy the province of Istria and established Fiume as a free city, but confirmed Yugoslavia's control of the Dalmatian coast. Italian embarrassment and hostility at what they considered humiliation and betrayal at the conference was one factor that subsequently led to the Fascist dictatorship of Benito Mussolini.

Since no man emerged as the dominant figure in Paris, agreement on the remaining issues was possible only by reconciling the opposing viewpoints. It did not take long for Clemenceau and Lloyd George to realize that Wilson's most cherished goal was a League of Nations and they did not hesitate to use their support for it as a bargaining lever to wring concessions from him. Wilson gave ground on a number of important issues, including exacting huge reparations from Germany and allowing the victorious nations to seize the colonies of the Central Powers. The American president knew that he was compromising the idealism of his Fourteen Points, but he led himself to believe that the League of Nations, once in operation, would correct any flaws in the treaty.

The completed Treaty of Versailles was harsh. In the first place, it deprived Germany of about one-tenth of its prewar territory and population. In the west, France reacquired Alsace and Lorraine, and Belgium and Denmark received small strips of territory. The Saar Valley was placed under international control for fifteen years, after which a plebescite would determine whether it would be ceded to France or returned to Germany. The Rhineland was to be demilitarized and occupied by the Allies for fifteen years. In the east, Poland obtained a major block of territory, including a corridor to the sea, which separated East Prussia from the rest of Germany. Danzig, lying at the mouth of the Vistula River, became a free city under the supervision of the League of Nations. Certain districts with a large Polish population in East Prussia and Upper Silesia were to be polled to determine if they wished to join Poland.

Germany was also to surrender its overseas possessions. They were awarded to the League of Nations, which in turn assigned them to various Allied powers for administration until they would be ready for independence. The Allies in fact treated them as new colonies to add to their imperial collection. France, Great Britain, South Africa, and Belgium divided Germany's colonies in Africa. Japan received German holdings and concessions in China as well as the Pacific islands north of the equator; the German possessions in the Pacific south of that line went to Australia and New Zealand. The Japanese had wanted a free hand in China as well, but they were blocked by Wilson and left the conference dissatisfied.

The treaty contained stringent disarmament provisions. The victors re-

MAP 77
Europe after 1919. The post World War I settlements radically altered the map of Europe. Germany had to return Alsace-Lorraine to France while Bulgaria lost its coastline to Greece. Italy acquired South Tyrol, Trieste, and Istria. The greatest changes occurred in east Europe where seven new, fully sovereign states were created. The Habsburg Empire was broken up and the independence of Czechoslovakia, Poland, and Yugoslavia was recognized. On the Baltic the subject nationalities of the Russian Empire, namely the Finns, Estonians, Latvians, and Lithuanians, also gained their independence.

697

duced the German army to 100,000 men and prohibited heavy artillery, tanks, and airplanes. They deprived the German navy of submarines and limited it to six small battleships totaling 50,000 tons. Universal conscription was abolished.

The Allies had stipulated before the armistice was signed that Germany pay for war damages. A reparations commission was appointed to fix the precise amount to be paid by Germany. In 1921, the commission set the reparations bill at $33 billion. In the meantime, Germany was required to pay $5 billion in gold and in kind to the Allies.

To justify their reparations claims, the Allies wrote a war guilt clause into the treaty, placing the entire responsibility of the war on Germany and its allies. The Germans bitterly resented the charge. It is true that German leaders had behaved irresponsibly for many years before 1914, as well as during the critical weeks before the outbreak of the war, but they did not willfully plan the subjugation of Europe. No less humiliating, in the eyes of many Germans, was the demand that the former kaiser be tried as a war criminal by an international court. But the Dutch refused the Allied request for his extradition and the trial never took place.

When the treaty was presented on May 7, 1919, to the German delegates summoned to Paris, they were shocked at the severity of the terms. In the negotiations that led to the armistice, the German government had been told that the future peace would be based on the Fourteen Points, with two reservations: first, that the British would not immediately lift their blockade of Germany; and second,

that Germany was to compensate the civilian population of the Allied countries for damage done "by land, by sea, and from the air." The Germans, however, were not informed of the additional treaty provisions, which Wilson had reluctantly approved. When they saw the results of the conference, the Germans charged, with justification, that the Allies had acted in bad faith. But the Allied statesmen refused to relent except for slight modifications, and warned the Germans that they must accept the treaty or face a renewal of the war. On June 28, 1919, the fifth anniversary of the murder of Archduke Francis Ferdinand, the treaty was signed in the Hall of Mirrors at Versailles. German humiliation and resentment over the Versailles Treaty directly contributed to the establishment of the Nazi dictatorship of Adolph Hitler.

The treaty also incorporated the covenant (charter) of the League of Nations. The main objectives of the league were to "guarantee international cooperation and to achieve international peace and security." Members had to promise not to resort to war but to seek arbitration if regular diplomatic methods proved unsuccessful in resolving disputes. Failure to abide by the rules could result in the league imposing economic sanctions or taking military action against aggressor nations.

The Settlements with Germany's Allies

The Versailles pact was followed in 1919 and 1920 by treaties with the other defeated nations. Named after the suburbs of Paris in which they were signed, they were closely modeled after the Versailles Treaty; all

included provisions for reparations and the reduction of armed forces.

The Treaty of St. Germain with Austria formalized the dissolution of the Habsburg Empire. Austria was obliged to recognize the independence of Czechoslovakia, Poland, Yugoslavia, and Hungary. It was to cede to Italy Trieste and also the South Tyrol/Trentino, which contained 250,000 Austrian Germans. Austria emerged as a small republic with a quarter of the area and a fifth of the population of its prewar portion of the Dual Monarchy. Furthermore, it was forbidden to unite with Germany.

Hungary, now separated from Austria, received equally harsh treatment. Under the Treaty of Trianon it lost large blocks of territory to Czechoslovakia, Yugoslavia, and Rumania. The once-proud Magyar kingdom was stripped of three-quarters of its territory and two-thirds of its population.

Bulgaria also paid the penalty for siding with the losers. By the Treaty of Neuilly, it was forced to cede small bits of territory to Rumania and Yugoslavia and eastern Thrace to Greece, a loss that left it without an outlet to the Aegean Sea. As a result, more than one million Bulgarians were placed under foreign rule.

In the Treaty of Sèvres, Turkey was compelled to surrender lands inhabited by non-Turks. Armenia momentarily became independent, and states of the Arabian Peninsula achieved permanent independence. Greece acquired nearly all of Turkish territory in Europe as well as some islands in the Aegean. France received a League of Nations mandate over Syria, whereas Great Britain secured mandates over Palestine and Iraq.

Zimmermann telegram	Muntiny in French Army	Russia signs armistice with Germany	Germany signs armistice with the Allies	Versailles conference opens
	U.S. enters the war		Failure of Ludendorff offensive	Versailles Treaty

Evaluation of the Peace Settlement

Few peace treaties in recent memory have provoked sharper criticism or produced more controversy than those hammered out in Paris in 1919 and 1920. The treaties were denounced by the defeated nations, and critics in the west charged that they were punitive, in flagrant violation of the Fourteen Points, and certain to breed future wars. John Maynard Keynes (1883–1946), a brilliant British economist, was most influential in shaping public reaction in both Great Britain and the United States. In his book *The Economic Consequences of the Peace* (1919), he termed the Versailled Treaty a ruinous, "Carthaginian" peace that was immoral and unworkable. He argued that, in spite of the incalculable war damage, the reparations imposed were beyond Germany's capacity to pay and would be fatal to its economy, which in turn would lead to the economic ruin of Europe.

In the post-World War II period, scholars have taken a more tolerant view of the work of the peacemakers of 1919. Such defenders of the peace conference insist that Germany, unlike Carthage, was not destroyed. Left politically united, with its industrial strength relatively intact, Germany recovered quickly and enjoyed a high level of prosperity in the late 1920s before the Depression struck. They claim that Hitler's rise to power was due less to the Versailles Treaty than to its nonenforcement. They observe, using as an example Brest-Litovsk (the treaty by which Germany had imposed crippling conditions on Russia) that if Germany had won the war, it would almost certainly have imposed harsher terms than the Allies did. They also call attention to Germany's war aims, which called for, among other things, the annexation of parts of France and Poland and the creation of a number of satellite states.

Critics of the treaties sometimes tend to overlook or minimize the haste engendered by the need to legitimize new nations, the conflicts over means and ends, and the postwar hatreds under which the peacemakers labored. As Colonel Edward House, Wilson's confidant, put it, "Looking at the Conference in retrospect there is much to approve and much to regret. It is easy to say what should have been done but more difficult to have found a way of doing it."

SUMMARY

In August 1914, the belligerents went into battle confident that the conflict would be over in a few months. The French attack broke down completely while the Germans almost reached Paris before they were halted. Allied efforts to evict the Germans from France proved unsuccessful, and consequently both sides dug in for a long period of trench warfare. In the east, a stalemate developed as the Germans smashed two invading Russian armies but lacked the reserves to follow up their victories. Over the next two years neither the acquisition of new allies nor the establishment of new theaters of action materially affected the struggle. In the meantime,

699

the governments of the belligerent nations took steps to subordinate every aspect of public and private life to the demands of the conflict.

Although unable to prevail on land, the Allies succeeded during the first year of the war in attaining naval supremacy, at least on the ocean's surface. Great Britain drove enemy warships and merchantmen from the seas, enforcing a strict blockade to prevent Germany and its allies from importing war supplies from abroad. Germany responded by waging a submarine campaign to destroy British shipping. Angry reaction in the United States compelled the German government to modify its policy, but in January 1917, the Germans, suffering unbearable hardships as a result of the British blockade, resumed unrestricted submarine warfare. This brought the United States, with its immense human and material resources, into the conflict, more than compensating for the loss of Russia, which had dropped out of the war because of major domestic upheavals.

In the spring of 1918, the Germans made a desperate bid to overwhelm the Anglo-French armies in France before the Americans could turn the tide of war, but they failed because of exhaustion and the timely arrival of American troops. Thereafter, the Allies took the offensive and slowly drove the Germans out of most of France. Finally, Germany, its armies everywhere in retreat, faced with a social revolution, and deserted by its allies, agreed to an armistice which went into effect on November 11, 1918.

At the Paris Peace Conference the victors imposed severe peace terms on the defeated Central Powers. The treaties contained some of Wilson's idealism, but mostly reflected Clemenceau's cynical realism. Whether or not the vanquished nations were treated unjustly has been a matter of debate. Nevertheless it is true that the post-war settlements, far from preserving the peace, fostered resentments, particularly in Germany and Italy, and contributed to the depression of the 1930s and to the outbreak of World War II.

SELECTED SOURCES

Ashworth, Tony. *Trench Warfare, 1914–1918.* (1980). A vivid picture of the life and strain on the men in the trenches.

Birdsall, Paul. *Versailles Twenty Years After.* (1941). A balanced reassessment of the conference and its long-term effects.

Cobb, Humphrey. *Paths of Glory.* 1935. A fictional account of the French army, extremely critical of the high command.

*Falls, Cyril. *The Great War, 1914–1918.* 1959. Clear, concise account by a leading military expert.

*Fussell, Paul. *The Great War and Modern Memory.* 1975. A deeply engaging book about the British experience on the western front and some of the literary means by which it has been remembered and mythologized.

*Horne, Alastair. *The Price of Glory.* 1963. The story of the carnage at Verdun.

*James, Robert Rhodes. *Gallipoli* (1965). The best one-volume study of that ill-fated expedition.

*Lederer, Ivo J., ed. *The Versailles Settlement: Was it Foredoomed to Failure?* 1960. Collection of essays representing various points of view.

Mantoux, Etienne. *The Carthaginian Peace, or The Economic Consequences of Mr. Keynes.* 1946. The author, a French economist, refutes Keynes's contention that the Versailles Treaty was too harsh on Germany.

Mayer, Arno J. *The Politics and Diplomacy of Peacemaking.* 1968. A left-wing view arguing that the decisions of the peacemakers of 1919 were influenced by fear of Bolshevism and to a lesser extent by domestic radicalism.

Mee, Charles L., *The End of Order: Versailles, 1919.* 1980. A useful account, critical of Wilson.

*Remarque, Erich Maria. *All Quiet on the Western Front.* 1928. The classic pacifist novel in which the author, drawing on his own experiences, graphically depicts the horrors endured by the ordinary soldier.

*Tuchman, Barbara. *The Guns of August.* 1962. Well-written and lively account of the plans and opening battles of the war.

Williams, John. *The Other Battleground—The Home Fronts—Britain, France and Germany.* 1972. A readable study of the impact of war on civil and domestic life.

Zeman, Z.A.B. *The Gentlemen Negotiators.* 1971. Study of diplomacy during the war.

*Available in paperback.

THE CONTEMPORARY ERA

The twentieth century has been a turbulent age of violent conflicts and startling new directions. Global war, cold and hot, has afflicted the contemporary era. Despite this, material progress has reached even the lower classes of western society. Amazing progress in the sciences and sometimes baffling new trends in thought and art have further complicated the story of western civilization in this century.

Economic problems, totalitarianism, and World War II dominated the period 1918–1945. During the 1920s, the west survived the disillusionment generated by the first great war of the century and entered a period of fleeting and uncertain prosperity. The west continued to hold many people in colonial bondage, although its grip was weakening. The 1930s brought the terrible economic collapse of the Great Depression. While established democracies weathered this catastrophe, Germany, Italy, the Soviet Union, and other nations produced rigidly centralized totali-

tarian governments. Between 1939 and 1945, World War II destroyed most of these totalitarian states at a heavy cost in lives and material ruin to all the nations involved.

Main trends in the second half of the twentieth century include the Cold War and the collapse of Europe's overseas empires, as well as a long period of prosperity punctuated by economic difficulties. Two armed camps, the United States and the Soviet Union, have faced off in highly propagandized political, economic, technological, and military contest. The wave of liberation movements that spawned the new, "third world" countries of the later twentieth century has also triggered disturbing clashes of interest and outlook between the economically developed west and disadvantaged nonwestern nations. Within the west, such crises as the major recession of the late 1970s and early 1980s have marred a period of generally unparalleled affluence. Europe flourished in this era, an era that saw it lose its colonial empires and become a puppet in the international cold war. Its economy recovered and attained worldwide impact, and the vestiges of autocracy in western Europe were

swept away by strong forces of democracy.

Continuing trends of the century, finally, include some staggering technological, intellectual, and artistic achievements. The Industrial Revolution has borne fruit in an amazing new world of electronic and atomic marvels, including such popular inventions as the automobile and the television set and such epochal triumphs as the harnessing of atomic energy and the exploration of outer space. Modern thought has altered nineteenth-century ideologies in formulating updated versions of conservatism, liberalism, socialism, and nationalism and in constructing such uncomforting philosophies as existentialism. Modernism in the arts has meant exploration of challenging themes and experimentation with dazzling new forms in literature, painting, sculpture, architecture, and music. Such widely popular arts as the motion picture and jazz and rock music have been among the results.

	1900	1910	1920	1930

Politics

1922
Mussolini's
"March on
Rome"

1914–18
World War I

1933
Hitler
becomes
Chancellor
of Germany

1910–20
Mexican
Revolution

1917
Russian
Revolution

Joseph
Stalin
gains
power
in U.S.S.R.

Economics & Society

1908
Henry Ford
develops the
assembly
line

1926
British
General
Strike

1929
Stock Market
Crash; Great
Depression

Soviet
five-year
plans

1856–1915
Frederick
Taylor;
Efficiency
Studies

1883–1946
John
Maynard
Keynes

Roosevelt's
"New Deal"

Science & Technology

1936
BBC establishes
the first
television
service

1849–1936
Ivan Pavlov

1879–1959
Albert Einstein

1903
Wright
brothers
invent the
airplane

1867–1934
Madame Curie

1928
Alexander
Fleming
discovers
penicillin

Religion & Thought

Split between
"modernist" and
"fundamentalist"
Christians

1929
Lateran
treaties

1859–1952
John Dewey

Age of
Secularism,
Relativism,
Pragmatism

1919
Karl
Barth's
*Epistle to
the Romans*

1927
Martin
Heidegger's
Being and Time

1901–78
Margaret
Mead

Arts & Literature

1913
Igor
Stravinski's
*The Rite
of Spring*

1929
Maria Remarque's
*All Quiet
on the
Western Front*

1939
John Steinbeck's
*The Grapes
of Wrath*

Jazz
develops
in the
U.S.

1922
T.S. Eliot's
The Wasteland

1869–1959
Frank Lloyd Wright

1940	1950	1960	1970	1980

1945
World War II
ends; founding
of United
Nations

Asian and
Middle Eastern
states gain
independence

African
nations
gain
independence

1939
Hitler
invades
Poland;
WW II begins

The
Cold War
in Europe

1961–62
Berlin Wall;
Cuban
Missile
Crisis

1948–1980s
Arab-Israeli
conflicts

1957
Founding
of the
Common
Market

1968
Worldwide
student
unrest

World
population
reaches
4½ billion

The
Holocaust

Institution
of *apartheid*
in South
Africa

Martin Luther
King leads
U.S. civil
rights
movement

Oil
shortage
triggers
worldwide
recession

1970
First
complete
gene
synthesis

1945
Development
of the
atomic bomb

1962
Structure
of DNA
determined

Microchip
revolution

1942
First
automatic
computer
developed in U.S.

1957
First
man-made
satellite

1969
First
man on
the moon

1977
First
space
shuttle

1944
Jean-Paul
Sartre's
No Exit

1908–86
Simone
de Beauvoir

1962–65
Second
Vatican
Council

1889–1951
Ludwig
Wittgenstein

b. 1908
Claude
Levi-Strauss

Development
of Liberation
Theology in
Latin
America

1944
Samuel
Beckett's
*Waiting for
Godot*

1961
Joseph
Heller's
Catch-22

1945–82
Five Nobel
prizes for
Latin American
literature

1912–1956
Jackson
Pollock

Gwendolyn
Brooks'
poetry and
novels

1962–70
The Beatles

ECONOMIC AND SOCIAL TRENDS OF THE TWENTIETH CENTURY

One cannot foretell the surprises or disappointments the future has in store. . . . There may be tragic struggles, grim grapplings of race with race and class with class [like] the Great War. . . .

Yet, clumsily or smoothly, the world, it seems, progresses and will progress. . . . Gathered together at last under the leadership of man, the student-teacher of the universe, unified, disciplined, armed with the secret powers of the atom, and with knowledge as yet beyond dreaming, Life, forever young and eager, will presently stand upon earth as upon a footstool and stretch out its realm amidst the stars.

H. G. Wells (1866–1946), famous for his imaginative and prophetic science fiction, thus ended his immensely popular nonfiction book, *The Outline of History.* Writing in 1920, when atomic energy and space flight were still science fiction notions, Wells seems to have had some glimpse of their real potential. In the aftermath of World War I, he foresaw the possibility of other "tragic struggles" ahead, although he could not, of course, imagine the events of World War II or the cold war. Finally, it is notable that though he was writing in the grim and disillusioned years after the Great War, when many intellectuals lost faith in western civilization, Wells still believed in progress. He expected the twentieth century to move ahead with the help of "knowledge as yet beyond dreaming" to a brighter tomorrow.

Despite such catastrophes as World Wars I and II, the Great Depression, and the cold war, the western world, as Wells predicted, has enjoyed outstanding material progress in the present century. The economy has had its ups and downs, but the overall economic trend for developed western nations has risen to a level of affluence unmatched in history. The technological advances of this century are also unparalleled, giving western people a productive capacity unequaled in quantity, intricacy, or quality.

The Champs Elysées, Paris. The surge of traffic on this main boulevard reveals the continuing vitality of the European economy and of western society. This photo, taken from the Arche de Triomphe, shows the rush of both vehicular and pedestrian traffic that could be found in many great cities of the western world.

As a society, westerners have benefited impressively from the new wealth and the new technology, achieving unprecedented levels of health, education, and material welfare.

This chapter surveys the economic and social trends in the west from the beginning of the century to the 1980s. It also looks at discoveries of the scientists and accomplishments of the engineers who have guided the development of our material culture.

TECHNOLOGICAL TRENDS

Underlying the fluctuations in economic history and the new forms of economic organization of the west in this century has been the accelerating advance of western technology. Ingenious men and women have multiplied inventions so rapidly that such nineteenth-century wonders as the steam locomotive or the telegraph have come to seem quaint and old-fashioned. In basic heavy industry, in the production of consumer goods for the millions, and in the marvels of modern high technology, the twentieth century has surpassed all earlier periods.

Heavy Industry and Agriculture

Heavy industry—sometimes called "smokestack industry"—provided the solid foundation for industrial growth over most of the twentieth century, as it had during the nineteenth. There were changes, however. Even before 1900, iron and coal were giving way to steel and petroleum as the essential materials of industrialization. Steamships and railroads continued to be the most important means of transportation through the first half of the new century, but from World War II on, automobiles, trucks, and airplanes increasingly replaced them. Road builders used asphalt and concrete to build permanent road surfaces, revolutionizing land transportation.

Influential breakthroughs in manufacturing included the assembly line, automation, and the use of efficiency studies to increase productivity. The assembly line was a method of arranging the machines used for each stage of a manufacturing process along a conveyor belt that carried the item being constructed from one group of workers and machines to the next. Henry Ford (1863–1947) used assembly lines to great advantage in his automobile factories. This process has been carried still farther by the recent introduction of automation. Computer electronics has made it possible to put entire manufacturing facilities into the hands of robot machinery, all but eliminating the industrial worker. Finally, efficiency studies, pioneered by Frederick Taylor early in the century, detected wasted time and motion in the plant or office, showing where improvements could be made. All of these developments speeded up the processes of industrial production, making goods less expensive to manufacture and bringing them within the buying capabilities of larger numbers of western people.

Americans and Russians have become the global leaders in heavy industry. The United States led in the production of oil, steel, and other heavy industrial products for more than half the century. Cities like Pittsburgh and Detroit became internationally known for their steel mills and automobile factories, and forests of oil derricks put Texas on the industrial map. The Soviet Union's rapid progress in heavy industry perhaps occurred because such large-scale projects proved particularly adaptable to the centralized planning that is the core of the Soviet system. Hydroelectric dams and industrial complexes like Magnetogorsk, Russia's "steel city," sprang up in impressive numbers in the 1930s. Today, the Soviet Union is ahead of the United States in heavy industrial production, and Japan is not far behind the two leaders. Twentieth-century builders everywhere have used such modern materials as structural steel, poured concrete, and plate glass, combined with the electric elevator, to fill western cities with skyscrapers.

The mechanization of agriculture, also begun earlier, proceeded rapidly in the century of the tractor and a variety of specialized harvesting equipment. Agricultural technicians promoted the widespread application of chemical fertilizers and insecticides, and agricultural scientists developed new and inexpensive varieties of seeds that produce hardier and more abundant crops. The so-called green revolution that resulted has enormously increased agricultural productivity.

Consumer Goods

Food and clothing, household implements, and recreational devices are all consumer goods. So greatly has technology transformed the realm of consumer goods that today's young people might have some difficulty even recognizing such commonplace equipment of a century ago as washboards or buggywhips.

Two new groups of materials for the manufacture of consumer goods were introduced over the middle decades of this century: plastics and synthetic fibers. Useful objects of all sorts are made of the artificial materials called plastics, and a broad range of clothing is woven of synthetics or of a mix of synthetic and natural fibers. These artificial "raw materials" have furnished manufacturers of consumer goods with predictable levels of durability, toughness, resistance to heat, and other conditions they need to meet the demands of increasingly selective consumers. In affluent western Europe and the United States, the new consumer technology has produced a culture of waste. Cheap discardable items such as tin, glass, paper, and plastic containers have created a "throw-away" economy.

All the common household appliances in use today became widely available for the first time in the present century. The gas oven was invented in the 1870s and the electric oven in the 1890s, though the latter did not come into wide use until after World War I. Electric washing machines, vacuum cleaners, and refrigerators became common only in this century and electric dishwashers after World War II. Telephones were invented as early as 1876, but were not widely available until after 1900. Although canned goods were common as early as 1850, frozen foods were a post-World War II phenomenon.

The automobile, a costly consumer item, was made economically available to the masses through Henry Ford's assembly-line manufacturing techniques in 1908. In 1913, a million cars were on American roads; in 1970, more than 100 million. Goods

A Ford Model T. Mass-produced automobiles like this famous Ford car gave middle-class Americans a new freedom of movement in the 1920s. These women have paused in their touring to draw water from a well, perhaps to replenish the auto's radiator.

707

An Automatic Factory

Imagine, if you will, a factory as clean, spacious, and continuously operated as a hydroelectric plant. The production floor is barren of men. Only a few engineers, technicians, and operators walk about on a balcony above, before a great wall of master control panels, inserting and checking records, watching and adjusting batteries of control instruments. All else is automatic. Raw materials flow in by conveyor, move through automatic inspection units, fabricating machines, sub-assembly and assembly lines, all controlled from the master plans, and arrive at the automatic packaging machines as finished products—radios, refrigerators, tractors, fountain pens, carburetors, helicopters, or what you will.

This factory of tomorrow will be as different from the present manufacturing establishment as a hydroelectric plant is different from an old steam-power installation fed by a line of boiler tenders and men digging coal. *

The dazzling technological progress of the twentieth-century west has moved steadily toward fulfilling this mid-century prophecy. The Canadian authors of this article accurately predicted the sort of automated assembly line now coming into increasingly widespread use in Japan, the United States, and Europe.

*E. W. Leaver and J. J. Brown, "Machines Without Men," in Leonard Engel, ed., New Worlds of Modern Science (New York: Dell Publishing Co., 1956), pp. 365–366.

were delivered by trucks over networks of highways in Europe and the United States. Entrepreneurs increasingly laid out business districts and residential areas on the assumption that shoppers and homeowners would own automobiles.

In the affluent west, luxury recreational or entertainment items came to be considered virtual necessities. Motion picture theaters spread to countless towns and cities from the 1920s on. Millions of families brought radios into their homes during the first half of the century and television in the second half. Whole industries, like that devoted to musical records and tapes, have grown up to satisfy the demands of western consumers for entertainment.

The United States has undoubt-

edly been the leader in mass production of consumer goods in the twentieth century, although today Japan is pressing hard upon it in everything from automobiles to electronics. Western European countries have maintained standards of technological quality and craftsmanship that continue to earn them a high place in the international marketplace.

High Technology

The technological achievements of the twentieth century far transcend those of any other age. Individual inventions, small in themselves—like the vacuum tube or the microchip— have had remarkable consequences in many fields. In the second half of the century particularly, technology

has turned the science fiction of earlier times into hard science with amazing rapidity.

Medical science, which made impressive advances in the nineteenth century, has made even more spectacular progress in the twentieth. Building on such earlier discoveries as anesthetics, antiseptics, and the germ or microbe theory of the causation of disease, scientists have carried both surgical and chemical medicine to unprecedented levels. Researchers discovered vaccines for diseases ranging from such killers as yellow fever, tuberculosis, diphtheria, and polio to measles. The discovery of vitamins and the growth of scientific understanding of human nutritional requirements provided a basis for fighting rickets, beriberi, and similar diseases. German doctors in the 1930s developed sulfa drugs, and British scientists in the 1940s chemically isolated penicillin, both killing the microorganisms that cause disease.

Medical surgery has also made astonishing advances. Medical pioneers first used X-rays to look at the insides of living human bodies in the 1890s, and today radiation treatment for various forms of cancer is common. Surgeons have also learned to transplant tissues and whole organs from one human being to another. Medical scientists have developed mechanical support systems for failing lungs, livers, and hearts and, on a still experimental basis, implanted artificial hearts in human beings.

An even broader area of technological advance has been the post-World War II "computer revolution." Scientists have developed computers that can operate much more rapidly than the human brain and can record and instantly retrieve immense quantities of information. Thanks to progress in miniaturization, computers also have come in increasingly small packages and are applied to an expanding variety of tasks, from recording airline reservations to guiding artificial satellites and intercontinental ballistic missiles in their orbits. Today, the Japanese and others have "robotized" entire factories with computers.

The latest technology has been increasingly applied to military weaponry. Even a short list of the technical innovations in warfare shows what a difference technology makes when human beings see it as a matter of life and death. The military technicians of World War I for the first time used machine guns and submarines in large number and introduced the flame thrower, poison gas, and tanks, among other innovative devices. Designers in World War II developed more efficient submarines, tanks, and machine guns, and added such weapons as amphibian landing craft, and incendiary and "blockbuster" bombs. During World War II also, atomic scientists in the United States learned to use subatomic particles moving at accelerated speeds to split other atoms, producing the atomic bomb that leveled Hiroshima. After the Second World War, scientists expanded the arsenals of the great powers to include napalm, rockets, military helicopters, jet bombers, laser weapons, and intercontinental missiles. Early in the cold war arms race between the United States and the Soviet Union, physicists unlocked the secret of atomic fusion, creating the immensely more powerful hydrogen bomb.

The entire age of flight is encapsuled in the twentieth century. Leonardo da Vinci speculated on flying machines as early as the sixteenth century, and human beings had risen above the Earth in balloons in the eighteenth century. But it was not until 1903 that the Wright brothers, Orville and Wilbur, built and flew a propeller-driven heavier-than-air craft for the first time. Aviators in small airplanes conducted reconnaissance missions and dogfights in World War I and carried the mails between the wars. In World War II, the multiengine bombing plane came into its own, and after the war military and commercial airlines moved rapidly to more powerful, faster jet propulsion.

Human beings also began to ex-

The Concorde Takes Off. The supersonic passenger jet, built by an Anglo-French consortium, is the fastest in the world. As such, it constitutes a vivid symbol of the rapidity of both technological growth and the pace of modern living.

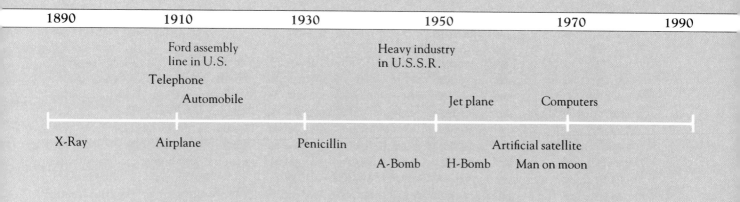

| 1890 | 1910 | 1930 | 1950 | 1970 | 1990 |

Ford assembly line in U.S.

Telephone

Automobile

Heavy industry in U.S.S.R.

Jet plane

Computers

X-Ray

Airplane

Penicillin

Artificial satellite

A-Bomb   H-Bomb   Man on moon

plore the space beyond Earth's atmosphere during the twentieth century. In 1957, the Soviet Union put the first artificial satellite, Sputnik, into orbit around the Earth, and in 1961 a Russian, Yuri Gagarin, circled the Earth in such an orbital space vehicle. In 1969, an American, Neil Armstrong, became the first human to set foot on the surface of the Moon. In the 1980s, American spacecraft landed on Mars, and Voyager II photographed planets and their moons as far out from the Sun as Uranus. Today, research work in orbit and deep-space probes is common. The entire age of flight, from the Wright brothers to the moons of Uranus, has taken place within a single human lifetime.

The capabilities of twentieth-century technology are remarkable, but real dangers exist in the accelerating pace of technological change. Modern industry has provided immense quantities of material goods, but it has also polluted the air and water and created "acid rain" that has defoliated large areas of forest. Automobiles have put a whole society on wheels, yet auto accidents also injure millions and kill tens of thousands every year, and autos contribute heavily to health-harming pollution. High technology has produced dazzling accomplishments like the first

human being on the Moon—and disasters like the explosion of the U.S. shuttlecraft *Challenger* in 1986, which killed all seven astronauts on board.

Atomic power perfectly illustrates the promise and the menace of high technology. Atomic weapons, stockpiled in huge quantities in both eastern and western Europe, have created a balance of power that some claim has helped prevent wars between the developed nations for more than four decades after World War II. Yet those same atomic stockpiles threaten global annihilation if such a conflict should occur.

One of the most influential breakthroughs in twentieth-century technology has been the development of peaceful uses for nuclear energy. Scientists have released the energy from the nucleus of the atom in forms that are used to produce electricity for industrial and home use. Today, substantial proportions of the electricity consumed in industrial societies is produced by nuclear energy. But even the peaceful use of the atom to generate power has seemed a dubious blessing to some. For although atomic power plants provide cheap energy, the problem of accidental damage to reactors and the consequent spread of radiation is considerable. The devastating explosions that took place at

a Soviet nuclear power plant at Chernobyl in 1986 raised radiation levels in many parts of Europe, cost dozens of lives, and threatened the lives of thousands of lives, and threatened the lives of thousands.

ECONOMIC ORGANIZATION

The rate of economic development of the western world has varied from region to region during the twentieth century. North America is better off economically than South America, western Europe than eastern Europe. Westernized Japan has pushed its way into the forefront of the rich nations. Despite this variation, however, the overall economic picture has been one of upward surges and downward slides. World War I produced an economic boom that generally lasted through the 1920s. Then, in the 1930s, the Great Depression settled across the western world. The 1940s and, ironically, World War II saw another great upward surge in production and affluence for the United States. After the war, this prosperity spread to the former Allies and defeated nations and continued through the 1950s and 1960s. In the earlier 1970s, a disastrous rise in the price of petroleum, a basic source of industrial power, triggered another major economic downturn. Usually called a recession rather than a depression, this decline has continued into the present decade. Today, a recovery appears to be taking shape, partly owing to a sharp decline in the price of petroleum.

The Shifting Nature of Work

The typical industrial enterprise of the nineteenth century was owned and operated by the same person, an entrepreneur. This early architect of industrial growth invested his own or borrowed capital in his business venture, bought the raw materials he needed, and paid his work force. The latter, the laborers in the new factories, were hardworking men and women who spent long hours tending the new machines that lined the factory sheds. This pattern was challenged in the twentieth century as the nature of work itself changed.

A fundamental shift occurred with the "managerial revolution." Today, major enterprises are rarely run by their owners. Capitalist ownership of big companies is spread among many investors. These stockholders, however, vote only on such major decisions as mergers or a plunge into a new line of business. Professional managers or executives, trained in business schools and moving from one firm to another, control daily operation and long-range planning.

The work force has also changed. As the century advanced, entrepreneurs installed sophisticated machinery, replacing more and more factory workers. A growing percentage of the labor force came to work in offices at white collar jobs, rather than reporting to the gates of manufacturing plants. Jobs in government

and in the front offices of the factories began to outnumber jobs on the assembly lines. Automated agriculture and factories meant that the supply of laborers outstripped the supply of jobs—a problem still unsolved.

The trend toward service industry employment, which includes a wide range of occupations, from hotel or restaurant work to jobs in hospitals, schools, and public service, has marked another major occupational shift for the industrialized west. Although they use the new industrial technology, from microwave ovens to X-ray machines in their work, these service workers do not manufacture anything.

The Changing Role of Women

By 1900, women were already integrated into many phases of the industrial economy and into the economic life of the west in general. In the nineteenth century, women had been incorporated into the labor force in such major industries as textiles and garment manufacturing. They had also established their claims to such respectable professions as teaching and nursing. Throughout the present century, women have entered the work force in increasing numbers in these and other occupations, while also pressing harder for more places at the top, in the most respected professions and at managerial levels in the business world.

A variety of factors have combined to expand women's role in the economy. The two world wars drew women in large numbers into heavy industry, replacing men drafted into the armies in essential war work. Technological advances have also played a part:

HOW CAN YOU TAKE PRIDE IN YOUR WORK?

I'm a dying breed. A laborer. Strictly muscle work . . . pick it up, put it down, pick it up, put it down. We handle between forty and fifty thousand pounds of steel a day. (Laughs) I know this is hard to believe—from four hundred pounds to three- and four-pound pieces. It's dying.

You can't take pride anymore. You remember when a guy could point to a house he built, how many logs he stacked. He built it and he was proud of it. I don't really think I could be proud if a contractor built a home for me. I would be tempted to get in there and kick the carpenter in the ass (laughs), and take the saw away from him. 'Cause I would have to be part of it, you know.

It's hard to take pride in a bridge you're never gonna cross, in a door you're never gonna open. You're mass-producing things and you never see the end result of it.*

Despite the immense material progress of the past two centuries, some have lamented the loss of the artisan's joy in a job well done that came with the triumph of the machine. Here a Chicago steelworker expresses this feeling that modern mass production and the consumer society, oriented toward buying things rather than making them, have deprived many of pride in their work.

*Mike Lefevre, in Studs Terkel, Working (New York: Avon Books, 1972), pp. 1–2.

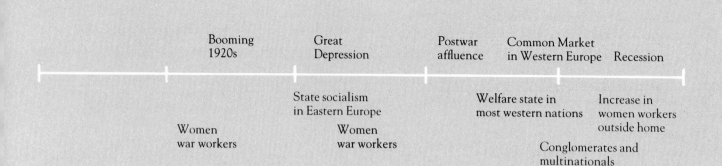

| 1890 | 1910 | 1930 | 1950 | 1970 | 1990 |

Booming
1920s

Great
Depression

Postwar
affluence

Common Market
in Western Europe   Recession

State socialism
in Eastern Europe

Welfare state in
most western nations

Increase in
women workers
outside home

Women
war workers

Women
war workers

Conglomerates and
multinationals

Labor-saving devices have freed women from onerous housework, and modern contraceptive techniques have allowed them to plan and limit family size to make more time for work outside the home. Finally, ideology has been an important factor. Liberals and feminists in the west and communists in the east have joined in supporting women's demands for equal treatment in the workplace.

Today, one-third of the workers in western Europe and the United States and almost half the Soviet work force are women. Women are entering prestige professions like law and medicine in increasing numbers: One-quarter of British doctors and more than half of all Russian physicians are women. Women have been accepted more slowly in top management positions in the business world, however. Women also continue to be paid less than men. Nevertheless, a trend toward fuller and more equal participation by women in the economic life of the industrialized west has been established.

Changes in Corporate Organization

Despite efforts to restrain the growth of big business, immense organizations have dominated ever larger sec-
tions of western economic life. Huge corporations and international cartels, developed during the preceding century, remain important. Some novel forms of large-scale economic organization such as conglomerates, franchising, and multinational corporations have also emerged, however, and today loom large on the business scene.

The popularity of the conglomerate has reflected the increasing complexity of big business. A conglomerate does not bring together production stages in a single process, like an old-fashioned vertical combination, nor does it unite competitors in the same line of business, as horizontal combinations do. Instead, the conglomerate brings producers in a broad spectrum of different fields under a single corporate umbrella. A conglomerate might thus buy up firms manufacturing soap flakes, books, and pharmaceuticals, and then perhaps add television stations or vacation resorts to the mix. Such firms sacrifice the expertise that goes with specialization. But they can achieve economic balance and the freedom to move into profitable areas of investment wherever they might be found.

The trend toward franchising has perhaps been particularly strong in service industries, an increasingly im-
portant sector of the economy. The procedure is to lease the right to use a trademark or a format, to sell a product, or to share in a central pool of information beyond the reach of a local operator. Such businesses as hotel or fast-food chains, automobile dealerships, or service stations are often franchise operations. Limited capital, local knowledge of business conditions, and individual energy are thus brought together with central organization, economies of scale, and other advantages of bigness.

The multinational corporation, finally, while not new, has played a particularly large part in post-World War II business life. Multinational corporations are not loose agreements among major firms in several countries, like international cartels. They are, rather, immensely large corporations that own and operate subsidiary firms or factories in a number of nations. Developed western countries have frequently built factories in less developed nations, where labor is cheaper. By stabilizing such a subsidiary, a multinational can also avoid tariff barriers, since the goods are produced inside any such system of protective tariffs. Thus U.S. factories have been opened in considerable numbers in both Europe and Latin America since World War II. More recently,

Japanese manufacturers have begun to set up factories and produce goods in the United States.

The Changing Role of the State

Government played an important part in the economic life of the west in earlier centuries, both stimulating and regulating business enterprise. Mercantilistic royal officials sold monopolies, established protective tariffs, or signed trade treaties intended to strengthen the national economy. During the nineteenth century, national governments in Europe built railroads and capitalized other ventures too costly for a small middle-class to finance.

In the twentieth century, the economic role of government has continued to be important. In western Europe, North America, Japan, and most of Latin America, private capital still owns most businesses, and private business people make most operating decisions. In the 1920s and 1930s, however, the government of Soviet Russia took over almost all of that nation's economic institutions. Other east European communist nations nationalized many industries in the 1940s and 1950s, when they became client states of the Soviet Union. Western Europe, recovering from World War II, invested public capital to rebuild industry. Many third-world nations, low on private capital, also established government-run industries, marketing boards, and other devices for government support and operation of struggling new economies in the 1950s and 1960s. Most capitalist nations, in fact, have developed some nationalized industries in the twentieth century, from national airlines and television networks to

---

AN AGE OF AFFLUENCE

Throughout our national experience, the most varied types of observers have agreed in emphasizing America's bounty. Explorers [in earlier centuries] marveled at wealth previously undiscovered; travelers . . . contrasted the riches of America with the scarcity of the lands from which they came; millions of inhabitants of the Old World . . . responded as immigrants to the lure of the land of plenty, the land of promise, where they could "dwell like kings in fairyland."

In every aspect of economic welfare the national differentials between the United States and other countries [were] immense. . . .

[Economic] data . . . show that the United States [at midcentury], with 7 percent of the world's population [had] 42 percent of the world's income. . . .

In 1949 reliable computations showed that the average American consumed 3,186 calories daily . . . unquestionably the highest nutritional standard in the world. The compilation of statistics might be extended endlessly. *

This massive American economic preeminence around 1950 was due to a number of factors. Long-range causes certainly included a wealth of natural resources, a skilled population, and the rapid progress of technology. The United States also benefited from the economic recovery during World War II and the great destruction that conflict brought to other industrial nations.

*David M. Potter, *People of Plenty* (Chicago: University of Chicago Press, 1954), pp. 80–81, 83.

---

government-operated banks or steel mills, and retained older public services such as highways, mail delivery, telegraph, telephone, and railroads.

A key feature of twentieth-century government involvement in economic life has been central planning. In communist nations like Soviet Russia, an elaborate bureaucratic structure plans and allocates goals and resources for all parts of the economy. In such western European nations as France or in Japan, government boards now investigate the international market, encourage research in potentially profitable areas, and generally help private capitalists to do well in the world. At the international level, post World War II groups like western Europe's Coal and Steel Com-

munity have helped businesses in member nations to plan and regulate the production of these vital commodities.

Private enterprise, in its older or newer forms, is a major component of long-term economic growth in much of the western world. But government continues to play a role in the economies of western nations. Defining the relative parts to be played by private capital on the one hand and the state on the other has been an important task of the evolving economic organization of the twentieth-century west. Government regulation in the public interest has steadily increased during the century, and laws regulating the working conditions of labor, the purity of food and drugs, the practices of stock markets or banks, land usage, and water and air pollution are now common.

SOCIAL DEVELOPMENTS

The material lives of ordinary human beings during the twentieth century have improved in many ways other than through technological advances. These social developments include a number of changes in the size and distribution of population, medicine and health care, education, and general welfare.

Population Trends

Population growth has continued at an accelerated pace. World population numbered more than 1.5 billion at the beginning of the century; more than a third were citizens of western countries, including some 400 million Europeans, 80 million North Americans, and more than 60 million Latin Americans. By the 1980s, because of technological advances and improved health care, world population shot up to 4.5 billion. Of this total, more than a third still live in the west, despite rapid population growth in nonwestern regions. Among

Skyscrapers of Sao Paolo. Brazil's second largest city and one of the largest in Latin America, Sao Paolo's skyline reflects the explosive growth of modern urban society everywhere. Though beset by many of the urban problems of the twentieth century, the city continues to draw population from the small towns and backwoods of Brazil.

western populations, those of the two western superpowers, the United States and the Soviet Union, are both near 250 million today. The major European powers outside the U.S.S.R.—Britain, France, West Germany, and Italy—have more than 50 million inhabitants each. The largest Latin American populations are those of Brazil, more than 135 million, and Mexico, almost 80 million.

Most world nations have seen the population explosion as a problem rather than a blessing. In the majority of western states, however, population has been growing at a relatively modest rate, slightly more than one-half of 1 percent a year. In Europe, indeed, many nations have achieved zero population growth, births almost exactly balanced by deaths. The problem has been more serious in Latin America, where the growth rate is comparable to that in Asia and Africa—between 2.5 and 3 percent a year. This rate of growth in the three less-developed continents threatens to swamp the world with some 7 billion people by the end of the century.

Besides sheer growth, another continuing feature of twentieth-century population history has been the trend toward urbanization. In Russia, a nation of peasants in 1900, 50 percent of the people lived in cities in the 1970s; in Great Britain, the figure was 80 percent. Most of this growth in urban population came from rural migration, which brought peasant farmers to Paris, campesinos (country folk) into Sao Paolo, and black Americans from the rural south to Detroit.

Rapid urbanization was swiftly followed by problems of sanitation, health care, education, crime, and especially housing, as slums around the city centers sprang up. Since World War II, some western governments have built public housing projects or "new towns" to house the less affluent. With population growth, small towns have been transformed into new cities throughout Europe and the United States, and the American-style suburb has provided pleasant living areas for middle- and upper-class citizens who work in the cities. In eastern Europe, the Russian government has built new industrial-housing complexes in the Urals and beyond.

Welfare

The lives of almost all western peoples have been materially affected by the growth of what has come to be called the welfare state during the present century. The goal of welfare legislation has been to provide basic goods and servies to ensure a level of physical well-being below which no citizen of the modern industrial state should be allowed to fall—a goal beyond the economic and technological capacities of the preindustrial world. The welfare state appeared in the late nineteenth century and spread all across the industrialized west during the twentieth century. Bismarck's social legislation in the 1880s and laws passed by the British Liberal party around the turn of the century were major early steps toward the welfare state. In the 1930s, totalitarian leaders promised many forms of social services, and the onset of the Great Depression led democratic governments in Europe and the Americas to offer relief for the unemployed and other forms of "social security." It was only after World War II, however, that communism in eastern Europe and welfare capitalism in western Europe and North America brought basic care to most western people.

The developed welfare state has provided old age pensions, relief for unemployed workers, and public health care for the sick. Related programs have offered low-cost public housing, cheap or free food for those in need, child care for working parents, special services for the elderly and handicapped, and much else. The goal of cradle-to-the-grave security has by no means been completely achieved, however.

The growth of the welfare state has always had its critics. Some believe too much security dulls initiative and makes people less likely to work hard to support themselves or to get ahead. Others claim that especially during economic downswings like that of the 1970s, even wealthy nations simply cannot afford the full range of welfare benefits.

Medicine and Health Care

Many western populations are today healthier and longer lived than any people in history, thanks partly to major improvements in medicine and health care. In addition to clinics and hospitals, better plumbing, improved sanitary conditions, and public health programs have contributed to better health and longer life, especially in the United States and Europe.

The health of citizens of western nations has also been improved by social programs that have provided inexpensive or free health care. After World War II, the British Health Care Act set up a comprehensive program of socialized medicine. In the United States, private health insurance plans and health maintenance organiza-

Alexander Fleming, Discoverer of Penicillin. The British scientist is shown surrounded with the still relatively modest apparatus in use as recently as the 1920s and 1930s. Scientists in other lands also contributed to the development of this wonder drug.

tions have furnished somewhat similar services, whereas federal programs like Medicare and Medicaid partly subsidize health care for the aged.

None of these approaches to public health have been free of flaws. Government-run health services are challenged for inefficiency, whereas private health insurance companies do not include all citizens or cover all medical problems. Above all, the poorer nations of Latin America and southern Europe are simply unable to offer as much care as their people need. The health statistics for Latin America are closer to those for Africa and Asia than to the figures for North America or Europe. Still, today western people as a whole are freer of disease, in better physical condition, and likely to live twenty years longer than their great grandparents in 1900.

Education

In a technologically sophisticated age, peoples around the world have rec-ognized the importance of education as a preparation for modern life in the twentieth century. In all parts of the west, governments have offered more years of formal education and specialized training, although there have been differences of emphasis and in the amount of education available.

By the end of the nineteenth century, most European nations provided free grammar school education, and two-thirds of the American states had some form of public grade school education. Today, virtually all North American and European children attend grammar school, as do most Latin Americans. In addition, four-fifths of North Americans, two-thirds of Europeans, and one-third of Latin Americans go on to secondary school. Policies on advanced education, however, vary significantly. In the United States, almost half the population has access to some sort of higher education. European nations accomplish in their secondary schools what is normally completed in the United States in the first two years of college. As this requires European students to pass rigorous examinations before going on to college, the numbers doing so have been limited to less than one-fifth of their young people. In Latin America, finally, lack of financial and educational resources has held the figure down to 5 percent.

A striking feature of the expansion of education in the west has been its spread across segments of society traditionally excluded from much schooling. Public education means education available to the poor as well as to the rich. The relaxation of ancient sexist taboos has given women access to learning at the highest levels in Europe and North America—and to the careers that are open to those with advanced training.

Theories and disputes about the goals of education have been common in the twentieth century. In the developed western countries, theorists have urged education as a means of producing good citizens or for self-development. Communist governments promote education for building socialism, whereas relatively under-developed Latin American countries agree with the rest of the third world that technological advancement is a major goal of higher education. Ordinary people see education as a means of getting ahead in society, as a gateway to better jobs or higher status. Most western peoples value education, and more of it has been available in the twentieth century than ever before.

SUMMARY

Despite fluctuations, the material lives of the western peoples have improved greatly during the present century. In spite of cycles of prosperity and depression, economic organization has grown more intricate and technology more ingenious, producing in much of the west a society that is better housed, healthier, and better educated and cared for than ever before.

Basic technological trends of the twentieth century have included mammoth heavy industrial projects, exploiting steel and concrete, petroleum, and hydroelectric and nuclear power to produce cities of skyscrapers and industrial complexes that have dwarfed those of the preceding century. Consumer goods, as often made of plastics and synthetics as of natural resources, have included a dazzling array of household goods, new means of transportation and communication, and a unique variety of recreation for all. From the frontiers of high technology, meanwhile, have come a steady stream of new mechanical marvels, from airplanes and submarines to nuclear weapons, computers, and spacecraft.

On the basis of this technological development, big business has evolved in new directions. The managerial revolution and the rise of service industries and white-collar work has modified the "smokestack" industrial image of the preceding century. Capitalism has generated such flexible structures as conglomerates and franchising and has linked the globe ever more tightly in a web of multinational corporations. The role of the state in the economy has also grown, imposing government ownership and central planning in communist countries and some government regulation and support for private business in capitalist ones.

An explosive increase in population and the rapid growth of cities have been outstanding social developments of the century. Medicine has become more scientific and health care more widely accessible. Social legislation has offered many of the basic material requirements to a large proportion of western populations. Education also spread to meet the needs of the modern technological age.

In this changing society, finally, western people have begun to understand the world in which they live in very different ways. The thought of the twentieth century is dealt with in the next chapter, and the art of the age in the chapter that follows.

SELECTED SOURCES

*Allen, Frederick Lewis. *Only Yesterday.* 1931. Vivid and concrete social history of the United States in the 1920s.

Barnet, R. J. *Global Reach: The Power of the Multinational Corporations.* 1974. Account of this important twentieth-century trend in industrial organization.

*Bell, Daniel. *The Coming of Post-Industrial Society.* 1976. Social impact of technology in the late twentieth century, described by a famous sociologist.

Childs, M. *Sweden: The Middle Way.* 1961. The welfare state and democratic socialism.

*Galbraith, J. K. *The Affluent Society.* 1962. Witty and critical analysis of the western economic scene after World War II, by a well-known liberal economist.

Kindleberger, Charles. *The World in Depression, 1929–1939.* 1975. Good overall account.

Laqueur, Walter. *The Rebirth of Europe.* 1970. European revival after the Second World War.

*Pike, Frederick. *Spanish America, 1900–1970.* 1973. Surveys the century in the Spanish-speaking countries of Latin America.

*Sullerot, E. *Women, Society, and Change.* 1971. Women and social change in Europe in the later twentieth century.

2001. Stanley Kubrick's epic film of the future exploration of the universe.

*Available in paperback.

TWENTIETH-CENTURY THOUGHT

Much of modern thought relates to the theme of the destruction of cultural unity, and the main dramas of thought [are] centered on this theme . . . one that goes far to account for a large number of cultural phenomena: the malaise of students, for example; the violence of revolutionaries, the hysterias of popular culture, the resort to drugs, even the inability to think clearly—amid a welter of "information"—about foreign and domestic policies of all sorts. This is an age of specialization, of intellectual fragmentation.

A recent intellectual historian has thus described the complexity and the conflict that have characterized the intellectual life of the twentieth century. This divided quality of the modern mind has been reflected in many aspects of our times, from revolutionary politics to social malaise and moral disagreements.

The fragmentation of the western mind in this century has affected many people who are not scientists, philosophers, religious thinkers, or ideologues. Overwhelmed by masses of information and free access to rival theories, western people have argued, agitated, and fought one another over ideas as seldom before in their history. For many, this inability to develop a unified world view, a new intellectual synthesis, has constituted a major failure; for others, however, it is a positive reflection of the sheer wealth and variety of ideas in the twentieth century.

SCIENTIFIC ADVANCES

The scientific achievements of the past century have been enormous. In less than a hundred years, scientists have split the atom and probed the depths of the human psyche, outlined the evolution of the universe, and learned many of the secrets of life itself. Like the age of Isaac Newton, the century of Albert Einstein has seen impressive advances in our understanding of the world we live in. The section that follows surveys this new knowledge in the fields of physics, astronomy, biology, and psychology.

Jean-Paul Sartre and Simone de Beauvoir. Two of the twentieth-century's leading intellectuals are here shown in Paris, which to many Europeans remained the intellectual capital of the world in the twentieth century. Sartre and de Beauvoir were close companions until his death in 1980.

Physics:
From Relativity to
the Search for
the Unified Field

Physicists in the twentieth century have uncovered many mysteries—and begun at least to formulate some answers. Among the mysteries have been light, radiation, and the relativity of all physical phenomena.

Even before the turn of the century, scientific experiments raised seemingly unanswerable questions about the nature of light. Light behaved sometimes as though it were composed of waves, sometimes as though it were quanta (a series of separate pulses of energy). Science, it seemed, could not explain the "real" nature of light at all, but only describe its sometimes self-contradictory behavior. Similar challenges to common sense resulted from exploration of the phenomenon of radiation. In her experiments with radium, Marie Curie (1867–1934) discovered that this rare element lost weight as it gave off radiant energy. Mass, it appeared, was being converted into energy, thus breaking down the traditional scientific distinction between the material and the immaterial.

The theory of relativity proposed by Albert Einstein (1879–1955) challenged scientific common sense even further. Einstein insisted that all physical phenomena were not absolute, independent entities, but were relative to one another. The basic nature of anything, he asserted, is fundamentally determined by its relationships to other things. He defined space and time, not as separate entities, but as parts of a four-dimensional "space-time continuum." This space-time, he said, has the three traditional spatial dimensions—length, breadth, and depth—and a "fourth dimension," time.

It was a bewildering new world for

Marie Curie. The famous French scientist is shown in her laboratory with her scientist husband, Pierre. Popular interest in the progress of science continued strong in the twentieth century, as this newspaper picture indicates.

laypersons and scientists alike. Physicists formulated broad conclusions about the relationships of matter that offered guidance through the labyrinth of the physical world. They discovered, for example, that the "indivisible" atom is really composed of still smaller particles, including bits of positively and negatively charged energy called protons and electrons. The electrons were initially seen as revolving around a nucleus of heavier protons, so that the new-model atom looked rather like a miniature solar system—except that the orbiting particles were not lumps of matter like planets, but sparks of pure energy in motion. Subsequent research multiplied the kinds of particles and offered a much more complex image of their motions. Thus a new explanation of the nature of matter was formulated—which made the billiard-ball atoms of the seventeenth century and the crude philosophical materialism of the nineteenth look very simplistic indeed.

The Newtonian vision of a single law of gravity has also been upset by twentieth-century scientists. Einstein suggested that gravity is not a force of attraction linking any two objects but a field of forces through which objects move. This gravitational field affects the motions, not only of material things, but of such manifestations of pure energy as light itself. Even more striking, perhaps, the work of Curie and others on radiation made it clear that gravity was not the only fundamental force affecting the behavior of the universe. Three basic forces have in fact been distinguished in this century: gravity, the "strong force" holding the atomic nucleus together, and the "electroweak force" revealed in such phenomena as electromagnetism and radioactivity. The formulation of a "unified field" theory that would reduce these three governing forces to a single underlying principle has been the great goal of twentieth-century physics.

Astronomy: From the Big Bang to the End of the World

Twentieth-century astronomers have greatly expanded our detailed knowledge of the universe as a whole. In the process, they inspired the development of new instruments for probing the farthest reaches of space. They also constructed some startling and still debated theories about the history of the universe, from its beginning to its probable end.

New tools for astronomical observation have included bigger and better telescopes to gather in the light of stars farther away than any ever seen before. Spectroscopes have made possible the analysis of light to determine the elements that produced it—and thus the composition of the most distant stars. Radio astronomy has studied other forms of radiation from the universe. In the past several decades, space probes have taken human beings to the Moon to gather raw materials for study, transported cameras to other planets to collect photographic data, and put a telescope into orbit to extend the reach of our instruments still further into space.

With such sophisticated instrumentation, astronomers have been able to map the reaches of space and to analyze the flaming interiors of stars. They have discovered that the cosmos is composed of immense collections of millions of stars called galaxies. They have proposed such intriguing possibilities as the existence of "black holes" in space—burned-out stars with gravitational fields so strong that nothing, not even light, can escape from them. They have studied in detail such nearby phenomena as comets and meteors, believing it possible that other planetary systems might be swinging around other stars in the depths of space.

New cosmological theories about the history of the universe as a whole have also emerged, seeking to explain the origins and predict the probable fate of the cosmos. The "big bang" theory, widely held today, asserts that the universe is not stable or fixed, but is expanding constantly in size. Perhaps 15 billion years ago, according to this thesis, all the matter and energy in the universe was condensed into a single, unimaginably dense "cosmic fireball." This ball then exploded, producing the big bang with which the universe as we know it was born. The history of the cosmos since has been the story of the expansion and cooling of the fragments of matter and energy thus unleashed.

Where it will all end has remained more controversial. Some scientists believe that the expanding universe will gradually run out of energy, cooling and spreading until all the stars are burnt out and the cosmos itself left dead and cold. Others see this expansion ending as gravity slowly reins in the scattering fragments from the primal explosion and pulls it all back together again. Still others suggest that the coming contraction of the universe will not end the story, but will be followed by another big bang and another expansion and contraction—that ours is a "pulsating" universe, cyclically reborn again and

And so, as I promised at the start, we have followed the quest of mankind out toward the endlessly receding horizon. We began with man's narrow vision of a patch of flat earth and have paused now at the point where man pictures a universe 26,000,000,000 light-years in diameter pulsating at a vast period of 82,000,000,000 years.

Nor need we feel that we have now plumbed the universe to the utmost. Astronomy has been advancing at an ever-accelerating pace for four centuries now, and there are no signs, as yet, of any leveling off. More has been learned about the universe in the last quarter century than in all man's history before; what, then, may lie ahead in the next quarter century?*

Science writer Isaac Asimov thus summed up the progress of scientific knowledge in the field of astronomy in the middle 1960s. As his concluding question suggested, that progress continued unabated over "the next quarter century." Between the 1960s and the 1980s, human beings have landed on the moon, put robot spacecraft on the surface of Mars, and sent other probes to photograph the rings of Saturn, the moons of Jupiter, and other astronomical phenomena.

*Isaac Asimov, The Universe from Flat Earth to Quasar (New York: Avon Books, 1966), p. 302.

again. Despite all the new cosmologies, some have continued to hold the traditional Judeo-Christian concept that God invented the world in seven days.

Biology: The Evolution of Evolution

Charles Darwin's nineteenth-century theory of biological evolution through natural selection and adaptation remains central to twentieth-century biology. Biologists, however, have introduced modifications into the basic evolutionary theory. In addition, whole new subjects of investigation have arisen in such areas as genetics and ecology.

Although challenges to Darwinism have been raised, particularly by religious supporters of the theory of a single divine creation, most biologists continue to accept the theory of slowly evolving species of plants and animals over hundreds of generations. Scientific understanding of the mechanics of evolution has, however, changed. Some biologists, for example, have come to believe that evolution is not a process of small changes adding up to large transformations over long periods, but rather consists of relatively rapid major change interspersed with long, static periods of little change in any given species. The fundamental concept of evolutionary change by natural selection of favored characteristics remains at the heart of modern biology.

Botanists and zoologists, especially those seeking to increase and improve the world's food supply, have accelerated the "natural selection" process. Perhaps the best-known example of this is hybrid corn, which now produces more than twice the yield in a shorter growing season than was possible fifty years ago.

Major new directions of biological discovery in the twentieth century have focused on the genetic base of all life and on the ecological interaction of many species in a system of related life forms. At the microscopic level, biologists discovered an acid called DNA that proved to control the chromosomes that compose the nucleus of the living cell. These DNA molecules, twisted around each other in a complicated "double helix" pattern, program living tissue to develop and reproduce itself through cell division—that is, to perform all the basic processes of life. At a different level of organization of life, ecologists have studied the way in which species of animals and plants interact with each other and with other aspects of their common environment. Through their discoveries of the interrelatedness of all living matter, ecologists have reminded people that what they do to their common environment affects the lives and even the survival of other species than their own.

Anthropology: Prehistory, and Cultural Relativism

The sciences of anthropology and psychology emerged in the later nineteenth century and developed rapidly in the twentieth. These new fields of study concerned themselves with the physical and mental characteristics of human beings, especially with their behavior, as individuals and in groups. We examine these two new human

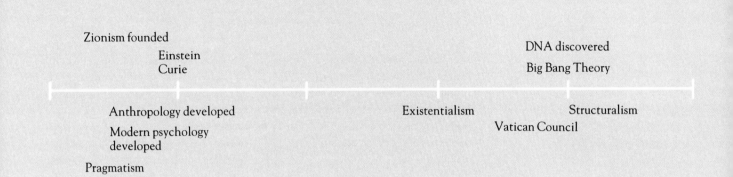

sciences in this and the following section.

The science of anthropology grew up in the wake of Charles Darwin's discoveries about human biology. Physical anthropologists studied the biological differences among the racial subdivisions of the human species. Cultural anthropologists investigated the beliefs and ways of life of peoples who lived in older and simpler forms of society, like those that had flourished before the growth of cities and nations.

Some anthropologists worked with archaeologists and biologists to learn about humankind's prehistoric ancestors. As early as the 1850s, these scientists began to piece together bits of bone and crude stone tools to assemble the story of early human life on earth. The work of investigators like the Leakey family—Louis, Mary and most recently their son Richard—accumulated much evidence on the nature and development of prehistoric humanity. Such discoveries led to the recognition that the human race and its precursors went back many thousands and even millions of years.

Many disputes arose over human prehistory. In the early days some scientists refused to accept the claims for the great age of bones, insisting they must be the remains of deformed modern humans. They rejected prehistory as they had Darwinism, because the new field implied the evolutionary development of the human race. Although many disagreements about early forms of human or prehuman life remain, the immensely long reach of human prehistory into the past is generally accepted today.

Anthropologists who studied preurban cultures that survive today often went to live for a time with isolated, technologically primitive peoples to understand them better and to learn about cultural evolution. One of the best-known twentieth century anthropologists, Margaret Mead (1901–1978), became famous for her observations of how young people grow up in South Pacific island societies. Some anthropologists have also applied their theories to western people as well, as Mead did when she wrote about the gap between younger and older generations in the contemporary United States.

This anthropological approach has sought to judge each society or culture by its own standards, rather than by any single, universal set of standards or norms. Anthropology has thus contributed to an attitude of cultural relativism, which has become widespread in the twentieth-century west. Western standards of right and wrong, the cultural relativist has asserted, are valid only for our own society and time. Other cultures and peoples might have different standards that would work as well in their society as ours do in our culture.

Psychology: Freudianism and Behaviorism

Both Sigmund Freud (1856–1939), the founder of modern analytic psychology, and Ivan Pavlov (1849–1936), the pioneer of the rival behaviorist school of psychology, formulated some of their key insights before the turn of the century. Both behaviorism and Freudianism and its offshoots, however, have achieved their full flowering in the twentieth century.

Freud, the most influential single investigator of the human psyche, had explained that all human attitudes and actions are rooted in the unconscious mind. The basic human drive, he believed, is libido, originally conceived as the sexual instinct, later as the source of a broader range of human desires. In the twentieth century, Freud further developed and applied his ideas of unconscious instincts shaping thoughts and behavior. After World War I, he began to see not one but two basic human impulses, a life-

Sigmund Freud. This drawing of the founder of psychoanalysis is by the modernist artist Ben Shahn. The picture reflects the feeling many had that Freud saw deeply into what had traditionally been considered the darker side of human character.

affirming urge related to the libido and a "death instinct" that could drive the human race to destroy itself in holocausts like the First World War. Freud also applied his theories to the largest aspects of the human past, explaining religion and civilization itself as products of psychological needs and conflicts.

Several disciples of Freud's broke with the master and developed their own psychological theories, examining human behavior in terms of other unconscious instincts than those Freud had proposed. Alfred Adler, for instance, saw an aggressive urge to superiority as the central human motive and explained many psychological problems as the result of "inferiority complexes." Carl Jung developed such basic psychological types as "introvert" and "extrovert" and found deep psychological meaning in the symbols of the great world religions. Others applied Freudian doctrines in areas Freud himself had not explored, as, for example, the psychoanalysis of children, pioneered by Melanie Klein.

The chief rival of Freudianism in the twentieth century has been the behaviorist school founded by the Russian physiologist Ivan Pavlov (1849–1936). Pavlov and his successors, including the American psychologist B. F. Skinner (b. 1904) explored their subject, not in a clinic or psychiatrist's office, but in laboratories. Their primary conclusion has been that human actions, like those of other animals, are caused by "conditioned reflexes." According to this theory, behavior that earns rewards —from nature, from society, from authority figures or laboratory experimenters—tends to be repeated to earn further rewards. In contrast, behavior that is met by punishment tends not to be repeated and soon disappears. Child rearing, commercial advertising, and government propaganda all in their various ways depend on such conditioning to manipulate human behavior.

For behavioral psychologists then, human free will is a delusion. For behaviorists, human conduct was shaped, not by unconscious instincts, but by the conditioning impact of the external environment.

PHILOSOPHIC AND RELIGIOUS TRENDS

The most influential currents of western philosophy during the twentieth century have also focused on the material world, on how best to understand it and on how to get along in it. Professional philosophers in our time have given comparatively little attention to absolute truths or mystical revelations. Instead, such attitudes as secularism, relativism, and pragmatism and more formal schools of thought such as existentialism and structuralism have dominated the philosophy of this century.

Secularism, Relativism, and Pragmatism

The secular attitudes of later nineteenth-century materialism have spread still more widely in western countries in the twentieth century. Many Europeans and Americans have come to believe that whereas science has discovered verifiable truths about this material world, religious convictions about the spiritual world are matters of opinion rather than of fact.

The real world, for the twentieth-century secular mind, is the world of matter known to the senses and studied by scientists.

Modern institutions have reflected this prevailing secularism. Totalitarian countries typically discourage religion, in part seeing in it a rival to the prevailing ideology. Most western democracies, however, have also institutionalized the separation of church and state, rejecting any established or state-supported church and providing public rather than religious education.

Accompanying secularism has been a rise in cultural and moral relativism over the past 100 years. According to the twentieth-century relativist, a particular belief or practice should not be judged right or proper in absolute terms, but only in terms of its own culture. Behavior considered immoral in one society might be quite moral according to the standards of another culture. In the same way, a statement might be "true" for one person, but not for another, whose opinions happen to be different.

This relativistic view has been encouraged by such varied twentieth-century trends as cultural anthropology and Einsteinian physics. As noted earlier, anthropologists have increasingly tended to describe preurban peoples in their own terms, instead of judging their conduct by the standards of western societies. Einstein's claim that even space and time are relative seemed to legitimize a similar attitude toward many other things, including religion and morality.

The philosophy of pragmatism encouraged a more active, positive attitude toward this world without certainties. Twentieth-century pragmatist John Dewey (1859–1952) fol-lowed his nineteenth-century predecessor William James in insisting on judging ideas by their social usefulness. Dewey's instrumentalism saw ideas as tools, means to an end, valid if and to the extent that they worked in society.

This pragmatic, can-do attitude, originally associated with optimistic Americans, has become common in many parts of the western world. For many, dedication to getting the job done—whatever the job might be—has replaced devotion to higher principles, whether religious or ideological. To some, it seems a shallow viewpoint that puts a premium on material success. To others, it is an attitude uniquely suited to modern technological society.

Existentialism, Structuralism, and Analytic Philosophy

Two major philosophic systems have also taken shape in the course of the twentieth century: existentialism and structuralism. Each can be seen as an extension of the attitudes just described—existentialism as a reaction to the materialistic or secular world view, structuralism as a radical extension of the prevailing relativism of this century. Neither philosophy is as optimistic as the pragmatic "can do" attitude, though both are more sophisticated systems of ideas.

Existentialists trace the roots of their world view to nineteenth-century thinkers such as Nietzsche, who proclaimed the "death of God" in a materialistic age. Leading twentieth-century existentialists include the German philosopher Martin Heidegger (1889–1976) and the French writer Jean-Paul Sartre (1905–1980). Such abstract tomes as Heidegger's *Being and Time* and disturbing fictions like Sartre's play *No Exit* and his novel *Nausea* express the existential mood of the middle decades of the century, particularly after World War II.

Sartre defines existentialism with the pithy phrase "existence precedes essence." By this, he seems to mean that material existence is the fundamental reality, and that essences, external thoughts, or spiritual beings are only myths intended to explain the harsh realities of life. For existentialists, the harshest thing about human existence is its sheer meaninglessness. Some existentialists have been exhilarated by the total freedom this situation gives them to make up meanings, to impose value on a valueless world. More often, however, suffering and despair have been the existentialist responses to an absurd universe. A world without spiritual presences or higher purposes has seemed totally pointless, filling them with a deep malaise that they described as *Angst*—anxiety or anguish. For a generation that had survived the horrors of the Great Depression and the second global war of the century only to see the world plunged into the cold war, absurdity and anguish seemed fitting responses to the age.

Structuralists, more recently influential, tend to be anthropologists or students of language and literature, rather than philosophers or writers. Structuralists agree with existentialists on the meaninglessness of the universe, but they focus their attention on the efforts of individuals or societies to impose meaning and order on the cosmos through language. In their concern with the process of how words "structure" the universe in people's minds, they frequently seem to be saying that no material reality

EXISTENTIAL FREEDOM

But, on the other hand, most of the resisters [to the Nazi occupation], though beaten, burned, blinded, and broken, did not speak. They broke the circle of evil and reaffirmed the human—for themselves, for us, and for their very torturers. They did it without witnesses, without help, without hope, often even without faith. For them it was not a matter of believing in man but of wanting to. Everything conspired to discourage them: so many indications everywhere about them, those faces bent over them, that misery within them. Everything concurred in making them believe that they were only insects, that man is the impossible dream of spies and squealers, and that they would awaken as vermin like everybody else.

They had only to decide . . . whether there would be anything more than the animal [in the world]. They remained silent [under torture] and man was born of their silence. We knew [in the resistance] that every moment of the day, in the four corners of Paris, man was a hundred times destroyed and reaffirmed. *

French existentialist Sartre, who worked in the underground during World War II, here describes the existential courage and freedom of his fellow resisters in the hands of the Nazis. Such people, he believed, recognized that only their lives and deeds could give value to a miserable world. By refusing to betray their comrades, their free and courageous decisions gave meaning to a meaningless universe.

*Jean-Paul Sartre, "What Is Literature?" in H. J. Blackham, ed., *Six Existentialist Thinkers* (New York: Harper and Row, 1959), p. 158.

exists beyond these subjective mental structures.

Structuralists like the Swiss linguist Ferdinand de Saussure (1857–1913) believe the structure of a language reveals the way in which a given people organize their world intellectually. French structural anthropologist Claude Lévi-Strauss (b. 1908) sees repeating patterns in myths as a system of structures by which a people define not only their world but also themselves as a people. The strong implication of these doctrines is that no one can get beyond such subjective patterns of understanding. These various ways of imagining the world are reality.

The twentieth-century emphasis on science and materialism is also reflected in the development of conceptual or linguistic analysis in Great Britain and the United States. Led by such thinkers as Bertrand Russell (1872–1970) and Ludwig Wittgenstein (1889–1951), early analytic philosophers believed we could best discover the structure of the world by reducing, or analyzing, our complex thoughts or statements into their simplest parts. At their simplest, thought and language patterns exactly reflect the structure of the world.

Analytic philosophers have often claimed that the simplest parts of our thoughts and statements about the world are sense perceptions. Some, for example, logical positivists, have gone so far as to say that statements in science have meaning, but those in ethics or religion, which deal with concepts not easily shown to be sense related, do not.

More recent analytic philosophers have shied away from the radical conclusions drawn by some of their predecessors, abandoning the idea that the key to the structure of the world lies only in sense perception and emphasizing instead the variety of our modes of thought and the complexity of meaning that the languages we use exhibit.

Christianity and Judaism in the Twentieth Century

Despite the inroads made by twentieth-century philosophies in traditional Christian beliefs, Christianity has remained a powerful element in the twentieth-century west. Christian thinkers themselves, however, who have also faced a complex world of social change and intellectual challenge, responded in a variety of ways.

Modernism and fundamentalism have been two conflicting currents of twentieth-century Christian thought. Modernism, originating in Europe, has adopted the methods of modern science and historical scholarship to refute scientific and historical objections to traditional Christian doctrines. For example, modernists successfully rebuffed nineteenth-century materialists who questioned the existence of the historical Jesus. On the other hand, Christian modernism has tended to advance purely symbolic interpretations of biblical statements that could not be reconciled with modern secular scholarship. Thus for instance, when geologists insisted that the Earth had taken billions of years rather than seven days to reach its present condition, modernists were willing to read the biblical "days" as symbolic language for geological ages.

Christian fundamentalism, stronger in the Americas than in Europe, has

| 1890 | 1910 | 1930 | 1950 | 1970 | 1990 |

Nationalism powerful in Europe

Stalinist communism in U.S.S.R.

Internationalism in Europe

Reagan conservatism

Women's Suffrage Movement

Keynesian economics

British welfare state

Civil rights in U.S.

New feminism

reacted to similar secular challenges by digging in its heels and insisting on the literal truth of the Bible. Like the modernists, some fundamentalists have adopted the tools of their opponents; the creationist opposition to Darwinism, for example, has tried to refute evolution more by reading the fossil record differently than by piling up scriptural citations. More important for many fundamentalists, however, has been the reassertion of Christian moral standards as they understand them, in opposition to moral relativism, sexual liberation, and other new ethical trends.

Another important stream of twentieth-century Christianity was the stress many Christians put on the contemporary social relevance of religion. Some late nineteenth- and twentieth-century Christians have believed that religion furnishes the best guide to solving many modern social problems, from poverty to political oppression. Sometimes these solutions have taken a basically conservative form. Europe's Christian Democratic political parties have covered a broad political spectrum, whereas the Moral Majority movement in the United States has taken a strongly conservative stand on social issues.

Other attempts to find Christian solutions to society's problems have been more liberal. At the turn of the century, for instance, the Protestant social gospel movement in the United States promoted legislation to regulate wages and hours, along with other social welfare measures. In the 1970s and 1980s, Catholic liberation theology in Latin America has sought to help poverty-stricken peasants by sponsoring farmers' cooperatives or defending the rights of Indians.

The most important single religious event among Christians in the twentieth century was the Second Vatican Council, 1963–1965. This meeting of bishops of the Roman Catholic Church, embracing over half of the world's Christians, prescribed a far-reaching "renewal of the Church." For instance, the Council changed the language of worship from Latin to the daily languages of the people. Furthermore, Catholics other than clergy gained a larger role in planning and administering church activities. The Council taught that true Christians are found outside the Catholic Church, encouraging Catholics for the first time to cooperate with the "separated brethren" in Protestant and Orthodox churches. These and other decrees marked a great turning point in Catholic life, releasing new energy and stirring new controversy.

Judaism, a religious tradition older than Christianity, has also evolved in recent times. Some Jews in the twentieth century have stuck determinedly to the beliefs and religious practices of their ancestors, whereas others have been more willing to reinterpret past traditions in the light of contemporary experience. Orthodox Judaism, the most traditional form, prescribes rigorous adherence to the teachings of the Bible and the Talmud. Reform Judaism, by contrast, asserts this ancient faith must be reinterpreted in terms relevant and meaningful to the modern age. Still other Jews take up positions midway between these two views.

The special concerns of Jews in the twentieth century have been Zionism and the problem of assimilation. Zionism was a form of Jewish nationalism that emerged in the later nineteenth century. Combining a desire to reclaim their ancient homeland with modern notions of nationalism and socialism, European Zionists began purchasing land in Palestine and migrating there. Well established in the 1920s, the movement was accelerated by Nazi actions to exterminate European Jews. In 1948, supported by most Western nations and opposed by Arab nations, Zionists established the modern state of Israel.

Jewish concern over assimilation reflected the other side of the coin—the place of Judaism in predominantly Christian western societies. Despite outbreaks of anti-Semitism and the ensuing Holocaust during World War II, most Jews feel at home in western nations and have adapted, like Christians, to an increasingly secular society. For some, this process of assimilation into the majority culture seems to threaten the long-term survival of Judaism as a faith and a historic tradition.

SOCIAL THOUGHT

Twentieth-century theories about society have drawn heavily on the ideologies of the nineteenth century. We can discuss the social thought of this century in large part under the same headings—conservatism, liberalism, socialism, nationalism, and feminism—that served for that earlier period. But twentieth-century versions have been more than continuations of those earlier isms. All the major western ideologies have undergone significant transformations in our times.

Some of these changes are purely intellectual in their origins, others primarily matters of shifts in political appeal. Disputes over intellectual points have led to splits in some major ideologies, to changes of emphasis in others, and sometimes even to unexpected recombinations of ideas and ideological alliances. Some twentieth-century ideologues have sought support from different social groups besides their nineteenth-century constituencies, including the new nations of Asia and Africa. The following section outlines some of these important changes in the major ideologies inherited from the nineteenth

Conservative Triumph in Britain. British Prime Minister Margaret Thatcher waves the flag, celebrating the victory of her Conservative Party in the 1983 elections. Britain was one of the first western nations to move to the right during the resurgence of conservatism in the 1980s.

century and modified to suit the conditions of the twentieth.

Conservatism and Liberalism

Conservatism, dedicated to preserving traditional institutions and eternal principles, might seem particularly unresponsive to change. In fact, however, conservatives of the later nineteenth and twentieth centuries significantly modified their ideas. Although retaining much of fundamental traditionalism, modern conservatives took up the defense of new institutions and absorbed some of the ideas of more liberal ideologies.

Conservatives in the present century have preserved the fundamental conservative determination to defend the best of the ancient political principles and time-tested institutions. Thus religious principles have remained central to their thinking, and they have worked to defend the established Christian churches against secularism or outright atheism. More broadly, conservatives have continued to oppose any rapid or radical change in society, arguing that revolutionary change has always been likely to do more harm than good.

A crucial shift brought a new set of institutions and ideas to the core of more recent conservative thought. Twentieth-century conservatives gradually ceased to champion the old monarchies, state churches, and hereditary aristocracies of Burke's day. Instead, they became more and more dedicated to the preservation of the free enterprise capitalist economic system and to the economic principles of Adam Smith—the heart of liberal economic thought in the preceding century. Modern conservatives soon became the most vigorous

defenders of private enterprise against socialism, insisting that the law of supply and demand and free trade, unfettered by government regulation, are the surest guarantees of prosperity.

Conservatism also began to come to terms with the liberal political ideology before the nineteenth century was over. Western European and North American conservatives particularly became staunch upholders of political democracy, of civil rights, and of government by consent of the governed. Conservatives, albeit reluctantly, have also accepted many features of the welfare state, although recently pressing for the dismantling of some social programs and a return of others to private enterprise. The central conservative impulse has thus remained the same, but the focus is in some ways strikingly different.

Liberalism in the twentieth century has also retained some of the original liberal creed, abandoned some older liberal emphases, and added new notions borrowed from other modern ideologies. In general, twentieth-century liberals have retained their political convictions but moved away from their earlier support for free-market economic theories toward an accommodation with modern socialism.

By 1900, liberal doctrine had evolved far toward the conviction that government should be by and for all the people, not merely those with a substantial stake in society. The trend toward full male suffrage was nearing its climax at the end of the 1800s, and women received the right to vote in a number of western nations during the opening decades of the new century. Concern for the political rights of the ruled led to such major breakthroughs as the American civil rights movement of the 1960s, when the

civil disobedience campaign of Martin Luther King (1929–1968) helped win civil liberties for blacks in the United States.

Liberals, however, have tended to abandon older liberal economic views, leaving belief in the free market and laissez-faire to conservatives. Such twentieth-century liberal economists as John Maynard Keynes (1883–1946) felt that government intervention in the economy is essential in times of crisis like the Great Depression of the 1930s. Other liberals insisted that the natural rights doctrine inherited from John Locke should be expanded beyond political, legal, and religious freedom to include such new rights as decent housing, health care, unemployment relief, and retirement benefits. Modern liberals have thus collaborated with socialists in constructing the twentieth-century welfare state. Whereas members of the British Labor party who built the welfare state in that country were socialists, the New Deal Democrats who did some of the same in the United States were ideological liberals, committed to the belief that social and economic rights are as important as political ones.

Socialism and Communism

Socialism moved in two directions in the later nineteenth and the twentieth centuries. As we have seen, western European socialists evolved toward social democracy, the socialism of the democratic welfare state. In eastern Europe, however, the Russian Marxists moved in the opposite direction, toward the totalitarian rigors of communism.

Under a repressive tsarist government, Russian socialists saw no

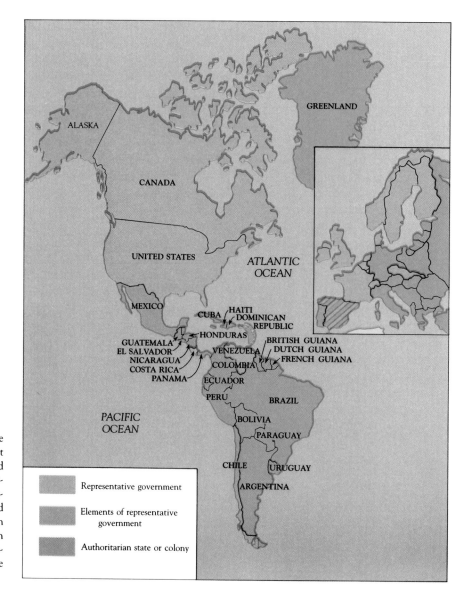

MAP 78
Liberal and Authoritarian Regimes in the Americas in 1936. In the depths of the Great Depression of the 1930s, the western world experienced a resurgence of authoritarian government on both sides of the Atlantic. Europe's overseas empires were traditionally ruled autocratically, and new totalitarian regimes in Europe and personalist dictatorships in Latin America had also appeared. Liberal institutions survived only in parts of Western Europe and in North America.

other way to achieve their ends except through revolution. Their leader, Lenin, developed a version of Marxism that preserved much of Karl Marx's original theory. For Lenin, the only way to public ownership of the means of production was through violent action. Lenin explained the failure of Marx's predicted world revolution to

materialize by western capitalists' using Europe's empires overseas as a source of wealth to bribe their domestic working classes with economic concessions at home. Only violent revolution, Lenin believed, could defeat this alliance of capitalism and imperialism.

As the twentieth century advanced, the political differences between the two socialist camps widened. Western social democratic parties believed in democracy, whereas Leninist communist parties did not. In most western democracies, however, both socialist and communist parties, plus other Marxist organizations, sought voter support.

Nationalism and Internationalism

Nationalism has probably been the ism with the most widespread appeal in the twentieth century. Particularly in the first half of the century, nationalism was widespread all across the western world. After World War II, passionate loyalty to the individual nation-states declined somewhat in Europe, though it remained strong in the Americas and spread to many of the new nations that emerged with the collapse of the European overseas empires.

Allegiance to the nation clearly outweighed all other loyalties in the minds of Europeans during the two world wars. It was also a key feature of the totalitarian ideologies of Nazi Germany, fascist Italy, and militaristic Japan between the wars. Since 1945, however, a spirit of internationalism has been more common among many European peoples. International organizations like the Common Market, holiday travel across national frontiers, memories of past wars, and fears of future ones have

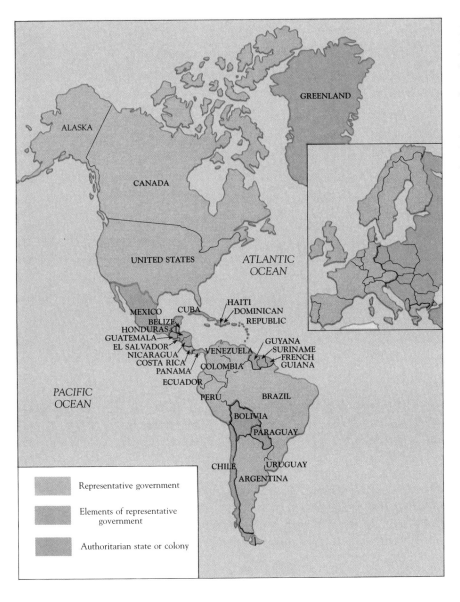

MAP 79
Liberal and Authoritarian Regimes in the Americas in 1986. As the twentieth century drew towards a close, liberal regimes predominated in North and South America and western Europe. Authoritarian governments were to be found primarily in the communist nations of Europe and the Americas and in a few surviving dictatorships in Latin America. The prospects for stability for the new republican governments in Latin America was unclear.

731

PREACHING SOCIALISM

For about twelve years . . . I sermonized on socialism at least three times a fortnight average. I preached whenever and wherever I was asked. It was first come first served with me: whether it was for a street corner, a public-house parlor, a market place, the economic section of the British Association . . . a cellar or a drawing room. My audiences varied from tens to thousands . . .

[A Socialist] must be keen enough to make him actually prefer spending two or three nights a week in speaking and debating to going to the theater, or dancing or drinking or even sweethearting . . . It is at such lecturing and debating work, and on squalid little committees and ridiculous little delegations to conferences of the three tailors of Tooley Street, with perhaps a deputation to the mayor thrown in once in a blue moon, that the ordinary Fabian workman or clerk must qualify

for his future seat on the town council, the school board, or perhaps the Cabinet.

British playwright George Bernard Shaw, who was also an active socialist, here describes the work of the Fabian Society, a social-democratic organization that became the ideological core of the British Labor party. Organized in the 1880s, the Fabians took their name from the Roman general Fabius, whose slow-but-sure campaign defeated Hannibal. After more than half a century of constitutional political crusading like that which Shaw describes, the Fabian-dominated Labor Party finally swept to power in the election of 1945 and began to build the welfare state in Great Britain.

*George Bernard Shaw, "The Fabian Society: What It Has Done and How It Has Done It," in Anne Freemantle, ed., *This Little Band of Prophets* (New York: New American Library, 1960), pp. 35–37.

encouraged Europeans to identify less with their separate nations and more with Europe as a whole.

In the Americas, national feeling has remained of paramount importance. North American involvement in the two world wars and United States leadership in the cold war fostered strong national loyalty. Nationalism in Latin America has been encouraged by resentment of United States intervention in the affairs of the southern republics. But even in the Americas there have been signs that regional identity might be replacing nationalistic loyalties. Few wars between Latin American nations have occurred in the twentieth century, and the boundaries between

the United States and its neighbors to the north and south are ungarrisoned.

With the disintegration of the western empires after World War II, western-style nationalism flamed up in many former colonies. Political leaders of third world nations in the twentieth century, like spokespersons for oppressed European nationalities in the nineteenth, have endeavored to kindle patriotic loyalties in the hearts of their countrymen. Allegiance to new African nations and to ancient Asian states newly freed from European control has become a powerful force in the third world. Arising as a form of antiimperialism, these new nationalisms have been the cement that holds recently liberated

peoples together. Such nationalism has also stimulated conflicts between third world countries, as it had earlier between the nations of the west.

Feminism

During the twentieth century, thinking about the nature and condition of the female half of the human race has passed through a number of stages. In each, exploration of feminist themes has been closely related to the current concerns and life-styles of western women. The result has been an evolving body of theory concerned with the importance—or unimportance—of sexual differences in modern society.

Through the first two decades of the century, the political drive for women's suffrage continued to be the focus of feminist activity. But even militant crusaders for women's political rights tended to accept a traditional view of woman's basic nature. This view asserted the virtue and nobility of female character, stressed the importance of the family as woman's natural sphere, and claimed that once given the vote, women would exert a morally cleansing influence on political life.

Between the two world wars, women turned from political crusading to personal emancipation. Serious feminist thought languished, but some women demanded and got an unprecedented degree of social and sexual freedom. The pleasure-seeking "flapper" of the 1920s and the career woman of the 1930s seemed to embody new female ideals and a broader definition of what it could mean to be a woman.

Following World War II, feminist thought was reborn in the writing of such insightful students of the female condition as Betty Friedan (b. 1921), Germaine Greer (b. 1939), and Simone de Beauvoir (1908–1986). Friedan's widely read *The Feminine Mystique* (1963) averred that the traditional female commitments to other people—as wives and mothers—did not in fact provide adequate fulfillment for women, that even the most affluent suburban home was little more than a gilded cage. De Beauvoir, one of France's leading intellectuals, explored the subject even more broadly in *The Second Sex* (1949), which examined the subordination of women in history and myth as well as in modern ideologies and contemporary social practice.

Recently, two schools of feminism have emerged. One view stresses the similarities between the sexes, declaring that all apparent differences beyond purely physical ones are the result of differing patterns of child rearing and of the different roles assigned to men and women by society.

Suffrage Fighters on the March. Women marched for basic rights, above all for the right to vote, on both sides of the Atlantic in the earlier twentieth century. Votes-for-women activists are shown in this photograph parading down Fifth Avenue, New York City, in 1915.

A second line of feminist thought states that women possess innately female characteristics, including a larger capacity for nurturing, caring and dealing with people generally than do men. Those who have taken this latter view, however, emphasize the application of these talents to larger spheres of human activity than the family, suggesting that female political leaders might be less likely to embark on aggressive wars or that women might make excellent business managers because of their knack for human relations.

THE FRAGMENTED MIND OF THE TWENTIETH CENTURY

An often discussed aspect of twentieth century thought is its fragmented nature. To many students of the intellectual history of this century, recent western thought seems to lack coherent direction. Twentieth-century western people have accumulated vast quantities of knowledge and an impressive inventory of intricate theories. But the best minds of the century have tended to be so narrowly specialized in their knowledge that they can scarcely communicate that knowledge, to each other or to the public at large. In addition, the variety of theories generated no longer seems to add up to any single point

of view. What is lacking, many feel, is a broad synthesis, a drawing together of our new knowledge and our diverse opinions into a distinctively twentieth-century western point of view. As the century draws toward its end, however, such a synthesis does not seem likely.

An Age of Specialization

The west in the twentieth century has acquired enormous amounts of knowledge. As the decades pass, raw data piles up in records repositories, on paper and film, on tapes and microchips. Collections of statistical data alone furnish mountains of information unparalleled in the past. Scientists, social scientists, journalists, and others fill libraries with detailed accounts of the world. When it comes to the collection and narrating of facts, this century is clearly unmatched.

But in many ways, the resulting flood of knowledge has been more overwhelming than enlightening. No one is able to master so much information. The twentieth century therefore has become an age of specialization, a century of experts. Specialization does provide a means of mastering the masses of facts, each person becoming an authority on his or her narrow area of expertise. It also has led to the drastic compartmentalization of knowledge. Experts in, say, nuclear physics, urban sociology, marine engineering, or medieval history

speak in private languages and deal with matters comprehensible only to other specialists.

The twentieth-century mind has thus become fragmented at the most basic factual level. Western people are so thoroughly specialized that very little of their knowledge is common to them all.

Theories in Conflict

Twentieth-century westerners are even more drastically divided by many, sometimes violent, conflicts of basic theories and points of view. Disputes between older and newer approaches—between traditional religion and modern science, for instance—have been especially divisive. Clashes between the major modern ideologies have also been common—between rival nationalisms, for example, or between democracy and totalitarianism. The high degree of freedom of expression in large parts of the western world, furthermore, has encouraged sometimes angry debate over a wide range of issues, from political or economic policies to moral or religious matters.

These vigorous theoretical disagreements make the fragmentation of the western mind even more disturbing. Not only are twentieth-century people increasingly unable to communicate facts across boundaries of specialist expertise, they bitterly disagree over what those facts mean.

SUMMARY

The intellectual life of the twentieth century is a complex, often contradictory, frequently brilliant chapter

in the long story of the evolving western mind. In science, in philosophy and religion, and in social thought,

western thinkers have drawn on the ideas of the past and moved in new directions to produce both major contributions to knowledge and bitter conflicts of opinion.

In the physical sciences, a veritable second scientific revolution has occurred. Physicists in the age of Einstein and Curie have diagrammed the atom, redefined matter in terms of energy, and produced theories about the relativity of time and space. Astronomers have explored the universe with amazing new instruments and offered theoretical accounts of the beginning and end of the cosmos. Biologists have elaborated the theory of evolution and probed the nature of life itself. Anthropologists and archaeologists have traced human origins into the prehistoric past, and the conflicting psychological theories of the Freudians and the behaviorists have explained the human mind in terms of instincts and conditioning.

Philosophy and religion have continued the trends of the nineteenth century in these fields. Secularism, relativism, and pragmatism have further undermined the faith of many in absolute truths and spiritual realities. Existentialists and structuralists have refined these iconoclastic tendencies in disturbing systems of philosophy. Christian thought has responded to these challenges in various ways, adopting the methods of modern scholarship or reasserting religious fundamentals, offering relevant stands on social issues or urging Christianity's ancient message of personal salvation. Judaism has also been divided in its response, Orthodox thought standing firmly for tradition, Reform Judaism adapting to new views.

The ideologies of the nineteenth century have continued to shape twentieth century social thought, but have also changed with the times. Conservatives have adopted some of the views of earlier liberals, whereas liberals have come to terms with socialism. Socialists split into the rival camps of social democracy and Leninist totalitarianism. Nationalism inspired some forms of totalitarianism also, but remained strong in democratic nations and in the new countries of the third world, though it has recently given ground to a new internationalism.

A distinguishing feature of the thought of the age is its divided and fragmented character. Specialization and disputed viewpoints disturb some, though others see a rich pluralism in such a diversity of views. This tendency toward division and conflict has been particularly marked in the artistic and cultural life of the century, to which we now turn.

SELECTED SOURCES

*Barrett, William. *Irrational Man: A Study of Existential Philosophy.* 1958. Good overview, from nineteenth century origins to Sartre.

*Coates, William H., and Hayden V. White. *The Ordeal of Liberal Humanism.* 1970. Survey of western intellectual thought in the nineteenth and twentieth centuries, with emphasis on challenges to a liberal western mainstream.

*Crossman, Richard, ed. *The God That Failed.* 1950. Ideological commitment and disillusionment on the left in the 1930s.

Feuer, Lewis S. *Einstein and the Generations of Science.* 1974. The crucial beginnings of the second scientific revolution and the men who made it happen.

*Kuhn, Thomas. *The Structure of Scientific Revolutions.* 1962. Much-discussed analysis of the scientific mind and the ways in which it restructures our world view.

*Labedz, Leopold, ed. *Revisionism: Essays on the History of Marxist Ideas.* 1962. Many varieties of socialist thought in this century.

*Niebuhr, Reinhold. *The Nature and Destiny of Man.* 2 vols. 1964. A monumental Christian perspective on western history, shaped by the twentieth-century experience.

*Sartre, Jean-Paul. *No Exit and Other Plays.* 1955. The existential world view presented in dramatic form.

Snyder, Louis. *The New Nationalism.* 1968. The spread of nationalism to the third world.

*Stromberg, Roland N. *After Everything.* 1975. Stimulating, brief survey of cultural trends in the second half of the century.

*Available in paperback.

TWENTIETH-CENTURY CULTURE

In poetry, physics, practical life there is nothing . . . that is any longer moored to a certainty, nothing that is forbidden, nothing that cannot be stood on its head and glorified. . . .

Nothing which lasts is of value . . . That which changes perpetually lives perpetually. . . .

There is a reevaluation going on in the art of the world today. There is a healthy mockery, a healthy anarchic spirit abroad. . . .

No art is perfect until you have smashed it.

These defiant words, written in 1912, were those of Benjamin de Casseres, a man who, although not himself an artist, clearly sensed the mood of challenge and change that was to grip the arts throughout the twentieth century. The "reevaluation going on in the art of the world today" was a cultural rebellion that would make the modern arts virtually synonymous with cultural revolution.

The culture of the twentieth century represents the most decided break with the culture of the past since the Renaissance. As in that earlier period, new art forms, new styles, new goals in the arts have once more appeared on all sides. Whether modernism, as the new culture was commonly called, represented a new beginning or the end of an age—or neither—remains unclear. But one thing is undeniable: Twentieth-century culture is one of the most exciting periods in the artistic history of the western world.

The present chapter begins its survey of this complicated subject with the factors that shaped the culture of the new age, and continues with discussions of modern art, modern literature, and the flowering of popular culture in the twentieth century.

CONTENTS

Pablo Picasso's *Woman in Black Hat.* This Cubist painting typically reduces the subject to its basic shapes and planes. The picture was done in the 1920s, when the Spanish painter's Cubist technique was well developed. Toledo Museum of Art.

737

THE ROOTS OF TWENTIETH-CENTURY CULTURE

The origins of this startling break with the traditional culture of the past are complex. Cultural currents, historical and social developments, and even technological advances all contributed to the modernist revolution in the arts.

Cultural, Historical, and Social Influences

Among the cultural and intellectual influences on twentieth-century culture have been nineteenth-century romanticism and materialism, a variety of nonwestern cultures ranging from Africa to Japan, and the fragmented mind of the twentieth century west itself. Each of these factors has enriched the arts of this century in its own way.

From romanticism, modern artists inherited an emphasis on the value of the emotions over that of the rational mind. In this tradition, twentiety-century writers and artists have glorified love, sex, suffering, and violence and delved deep into such emotional experiences as dreams, drugs, and madness. Like their romantic predecessors, these most recent western artists have often felt powerfully alienated from western society itself.

Nineteenth-century materialism and its offshoots were particularly influential for twentieth-century writing. Like such earlier naturalistic writers as Emile Zola, many more recent authors have been fascinated by the grimy underside of modern life, vividly depicting criminal, immoral, and hypocritical behavior in their works. Sigmund Freud taught a number of twentieth-century writers and artists to seek truth in the depths of the unconscious mind.

Other cultures have also had an impact on western culture in this century. Imperial expansion continued to bring western people into closer contact with the artistic traditions of other peoples. Some western artists especially profited from these cultural discoveries. Such major non-European achievements as Polynesian art, Persian miniature painting, Japanese prints, and African wood sculpture all stimulated western art and artists in the decades around 1900.

The radical fragmentation of twentieth-century thought, particularly the tendency toward narrow specialization and ideological conflict, also left its mark on the arts. The result has been a divided century in the arts, a period that has produced more conflicting schools and movements in literature and art than any earlier period.

Some of the broader historical trends of this century have influenced its artistic life. The great global wars of the twentieth century, for example, have become the subjects of major works of literature and art. Divisive wars like the Vietnam war have stimulated antiwar books, films, and other artistic critiques. Revolutions and civil wars like those in Russia, Mexico, and Spain have generated substantial art and literature, much of it inspired by the ideologies that inflamed these cataclysms. The Great Depression of the 1930s, the youth revolt of the 1960s, and other social upheavals in the western world have been both subjects for and influences on artists and writers.

Of the social trends of the period that have had an impact on its culture, perhaps the most important has been the emergence of a much larger, better educated, and more prosperous audience for the arts. First during the 1920s and again during the decades after World War II, economic growth, public education, and the relatively wide distribution of both have made culture accessible to millions of people. This huge new audience has supported both a sizable high culture establishment—from art museums to opera—and a much larger, increasingly sophisticated popular culture, particularly for films and music. In the popular arts especially, affluent twentieth-century youth have developed an elaborate culture all their own.

Technological Influences

The unmatched technological achievements of the twentieth century have affected culture as they have every other aspect of the century's life. Technology has not only turned established arts in new directions but also spawned whole new art forms and magnified the struggle of people to find individual purpose in life. From popular culture to the fine arts, the cultural life of the age has felt the impact of one new mechanical marvel after another.

In architecture, for instance, new building materials like structural steel and poured concrete liberated the architect's imagination from the restrictions of pillars, arches, flying buttresses, and other engineering requirements of earlier building and al-

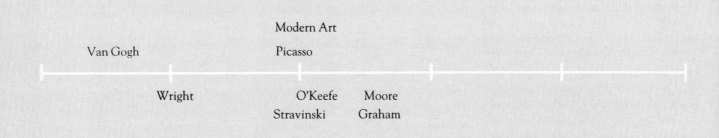

Modern Art

Picasso

Van Gogh

Wright   O'Keefe   Moore

Stravinski   Graham

lowed the soaring skyscrapers and complexes that have completely altered the urban landscape.

A later twentieth-century development that has had a profound effect on another ancient art form is the application of electronic technology to music. The results include simple amplification of voices and instruments, the distortion and mixing of these sounds, and even the production of new musical sounds without either voices or instruments. Electronics has affected the musical scene from the most popular to the most esoteric forms, and made today's sounds distinct from the music of any other age.

A series of technological innovations created a totally new art form, the art of the film. Motion picture technology, which had produced little more than arcade attractions by 1900, advanced through silent and sound films, from black and white to color, from narrower to wider screens. It also developed a vast repertoire of special effects techniques, until there seemed to be no imaginative construct that could not be graphically depicted in moving pictures. Producers, directors, screen actors, and a range of other talented people have taken advantage of these technical possibilities, producing films that have riveted movie audiences around the world.

The size of the audience for both high and popular culture has also multiplied manyfold by unprecedented advances in the ability to reproduce and disseminate artistic creations to millions of people. Improvements in techniques of color reproduction have made great painting available in high-quality books, slides, and other forms. The evolving technology of sound reproduction, from cylinder to disk to tape and finally to laser disks, with its ever higher fidelity, has put symphony orchestras and rock groups in any living room. Radio in the first half of the century and television in the second half have brought drama and music at all levels to the masses. Since the invention of printing in the Renaissance, there has been no such quantum jump in the availability of culture.

MODERNISM AND THE ARTS

The most striking characteristic of modern art is the bewildering variety of new "schools" or styles that have appeared in this century. Even a partial list of such movements in the visual and dramatic arts and in literature since the 1880s indicates this variety. Such a list would include post-impressionism, symbolism, aestheticism, the decadents, art nouveau ("new art"), expressionism, futurism, cubism, functionalism (in architecture), modern dance, dadaism, surrealism, absurdism (in theater), abstract expressionism, pop art, op art, earth art, the new realism (in painting), postmodernism (in literature), and many, many others. The slow shift from medieval to Renaissance art or from classical to romantic styles thus gave way to a torrent of change in the arts of the twentieth century.

The Arts in Revolt Against Tradition

Three common features seem to link these new schools. Almost all of them have vigorously rejected the western artistic tradition of their predecessors. Almost all have sought to blaze new trails, to achieve something new at all costs. Almost all have concentrated heavily on the formal elements of their art—on style rather than content. Each of these characteristics is explored here as a defining feature

739

THE NEW ARTIST

The new painter creates a world. . . . The new artist protests: he no longer paints (i.e., reproduces symbolically and illusionistically), but creates directly, in stone, in wood, in iron and tin, rocks and locomotive organisms that can be turned in every direction by the limpid winds of his momentary sensation. Every pictorial or plastic work is useless. . . . Order = disorder; ego = non-ego; affirmation = negation; all are supreme radiations of an absolute art. Absolute in the purity of cosmic and ordered chaos, eternal in the globule second without duration, without respiration, without light, without control. . . .

Art is a private matter; the artist does it for himself; any work of art that can be understood is the product of a journalist. *

A dada manifesto, quoted here, spoke for one of the most colorful art movements of the twentieth century. Dadaism, founded during World War I, was a deliberately negative movement, rejecting all traditional styles and offering only chaos in their place. Sponsoring programs of noise music, writing nonsense verse, painting in a trance, and purchasing "ready-made" sculpture at the local hardware store, the dadaists defied all earlier definitions of the nature of art.

* "The Dada Manifesto," in Malcolm Cowley, Exile's Return: A Literary Odyssey of the 1920s (New York: Viking Press, 1951), p. 149.

of modern art, giving some unity to otherwise disparate movements.

Many of these schools of art produced militant manifestos denouncing the "old masters" or the traditional styles. Others simply demonstrated their rejection by ignoring all the models and maxims left them by the past. Thus modern painters tended to ignore the realistic figure drawing and convincingly three-dimensional perspective that had made western art look "lifelike" ever since the Renaissance. Modern architects no longer built public buildings with Greek or Roman façades or churches in medieval Gothic style. Modern composers broke with the traditional harmonies that had been evolving in the west for hundreds of years.

Modern artists have seen themselves as pioneers blazing new trails. Their manifestos often proclaimed originality as the highest artistic value. Each artist's goal was an artistic style that looked like no one else's. The result of this quest for novelty, coupled with the rejection of formal training by some artists, was art that seemed strange and even crude—painting that looked as though a child had done it, music that sounded like cacaphony to most listeners.

This apparent crudeness, however, reflects also the third key feature of modernism: an overpowering concern with the formal elements of style rather than content. Modernist painters have been much more interested in arranging colors, lines, or shapes on canvas than with accurately depicting a person, place, or thing. Modernist sculptors or architects balanced masses and volumes, composers deployed notes and chords, modern dancers explored the potential of gesture and motion. The particular subject or theme of the work might inspire the arrangement of these stylistic elements, but it was always the elements themselves that primarily concerned the modernist.

Painting

Twentieth-century painters have broken drastically with the Renaissance tradition in their art. Some retained at least a roughly representational style, though their passion for originality and for the exploration of the formal elements carried them far from Renaissance lifelikeness. Others abandoned representative art altogether, producing instead purely abstract patterns of lines, shapes, colors, or textures.

Postimpressionists such as Paul Gauguin (1848–1903) and Vincent van Gogh (1853–1890) painted recognizable pictures of peasants or South Sea islanders, sunflowers or fields of wheat. In the work of Van Gogh, however, anatomical accuracy or proper perspective gave way to vibrant compositions of dazzling yellows, searing greens, blues, and golds. Georgia O'Keeffe (1887–1986), who helped forge an American school of modernism early in the century, generalized her landscapes or closeup paintings of flowers into aesthetically compelling curves, whorls, or blocky masses. Pablo Picasso (1881–1973), most famous of all twentieth-century painters, changed his style every few years over most of his ninety-year lifetime, but never abandoned representation entirely. Picasso's most famous style, cubism, divided real objects, as in his naked Ladies of Avignon or the spritely Three Musicians, into fragmentary shapes, curvilinear or rectangular, which he then recombined.

The somewhat later trend to pure abstraction is illustrated by Piet Mondrian's (1872–1944) famous compositions of brightly colored strips and frequently rectangular shapes, extremely decorative but clearly intended to look like nothing at all. Jackson Pollock (1912–1956), one of the giants of the New York school after World War II, became perhaps the best-known abstract expressionist painter. He created huge canvases crisscrossed endlessly by meandering lines of paint, forming intriguing, sometimes quite dramatic, but obviously nonrepresentational patterns.

It was a long way from Leonardo da Vinci's realistically depicted human beings to Jackson Pollock's winding curls and squiggles of line. Yet both were great innovators, and both were, in their differing ways, masters of the formal elements of painting.

Sculpture and Architecture

Twentieth-century sculpture and architecture broke as decisively with western traditions as painting did. Architects and sculptors also went back to basic elements, to masses and space, volumes, shapes, and textures. The result in each case was a free-form, three-dimensional construction that was more likely to be influenced by African wood carvings, the properties of structural steel, or the whimsical imagination of the artist than by the art of the Renaissance or ancient Greece.

The monumental reclining figures sculpted by Henry Moore (1898–1986) reveal identifiable heads, arms, and legs in their heaving curvilinear masses, but it was the masses themselves that mattered to Moore. Constantine Brancusi's *Bird in Space* looks very like a vertical feather, but it was the sweeping, upward-reaching lines of the polished bronze that gave the sculpture its effect.

Jackson Pollock at Work. Pollock frequently laid his large canvases on the floor in order to cover them more easily with his sweeping patterns of line and color. This picture was taken at his Long Island, New York studio in the 1950s.

741

Other modernist sculptors, like abstract painters, abandoned the representational element altogether. The widely popular mobiles of Alexander Calder (1898–1976) are collections of pieces of metal strung on wires and hung from the ceiling, so delicately balanced that they move at a breath. In contrast to the light, airy quality of Calder's work are the solid assemblages of David Smith (1900–1965), a dedicated worker in steel who built his nonrepresentational constructions in a machine shop. The controversial "earth artist" Christo hung a curtain across the Grand Canyon and ran a fence across a California county to achieve striking effects of shape and texture on the land.

Architecture also produced major breaks with older styles and striking use of new techniques. The motto of architect Louis Sullivan, "form follows function," marked the turning point for architectural modernism around 1900. Henceforth, the purpose, or function, of a building, the environment in which it was located, and the remarkable possibilities of modern construction methods and materials would guide modern builders.

Sullivan's even better-known disciple, Frank Lloyd Wright (1869–1959), thus integrated the reinforced concrete of houses like Falling Water into the rock, trees, and small waterfall around it—yet gave the building a breathtaking drama by suspending its cantilevered masses over empty space. R. Buckminster Fuller (1892–1985) gave the world the geodesic dome as a basic building form. Architects of the "international style" used curves as often as traditional right-angles in plans for homes, office buildings, and other structures. Le

Corbusier's startling church of Notre Dame du Haut, for instance, came out all curves and contours in poured concrete. Wright's famous Guggenheim Museum in New York was built as a single ascending-spiral display corridor around an open central space. Skyscrapers that looked like towers of glass, airline terminals that suggested wings in flight, opera houses like tilted seasheels over the water—twentieth-century architecture has never ceased to amaze and often to delight.

Music and Dance

Music and the dance have also achieved some impressive modernist breakthroughs. Composers, musicians, and dancers, who deal almost exclusively with formal elements, have experimented freely with new sounds and movements, resulting in forms of art that could have come in no other century but this.

Modern music and dance deliberately sought to sever their connections with the western musical heritage. This evolving body of art had begun with polyphonic singing and a few stringed and keyboard instruments in early modern times and had built the mighty symphony orchestra, the opera, and the ballet over the intervening centuries. Musical Paris in the 1910s and 1920s was therefore shocked by such unconventional productions as *Rite of Spring* of Igor Stravinski (1882–1971). This modern masterpiece was produced by Sergei Diaghilev's ballet company and choreographed by the flamboyant dancer Vaslav Nijinsky. Primitive sacrificial rites, exotic settings, weird tones, deliberate discords, and jarring rhythms combined to cause a near riot at its opening night in 1913. Another in-

fluential effort to take music in new directions made use of all twelve tones in the octave instead of only the eight whole notes. Arnold Schonberg (1874–1951) and Anton Webern (1883–1945) were early twelve-tone composers.

Modern dance moved in some astonishing new directions outside the framework of the traditional ballet. As early as the turn of the century, the dazzling Isadora Duncan challenged the formal ballet style of her time with movements of total spontaneity. Improvising every performance, Duncan claimed only natural forces like wind and sea as her teachers. During the middle decades of the century, Martha Graham (b. 1893) established a more lasting tradition of modern dance with her freewheeling dance company. Graham combined technical innovations like tightening and release of muscles with passionate self-expression. Graham often retold old myths from modern, frequently female perspectives, as in *Night Journey*, her reworking of the Oedipus story from Jocasta's point of view.

Modern music in the late twentieth century has sometimes eschewed musical instruments and human voices altogether. Today, composers use tapes of natural, nonmusical sounds or computer-guided synthesizers to generate purely electronic, artificial tones. "Computer music" tends to be highly rational, even mathematical in its organizing of sounds. Innovators like John Cage (b. 1912), by contrast, have aimed for complete spontaneity and even pure random chance in their arrangement of sound patterns. Cage has presented concerts in which half a dozen harpsichords played different compositions at the same time!

Martha Graham Dancing. One of the pioneers of modern dance, Graham is shown here dancing in *Acrobats of God* in 1961. Graham was able to communicate ideas and emotions through gesture, movement, and pose. Something of the exhausting physical demands made by the dance is revealed in this photograph, taken during Graham's later performing years.

MODERNISM IN LITERATURE

If the other arts vigorously rejected the traditions of the past, twentieth-century literature has violently challenged the society of the present day. Even more startling in some ways than the clash of the artistic isms has been the thunder of the modern writer at war with his own world.

Literature in Conflict with Society

The sense of alienation, common among other artists as well, has been most directly expressed in contemporary poetry, drama, and prose fiction. The roots of this hostility to society go back to the alienation of nineteenth-century romantic artists from the bourgeois society of their day. Modern writers have also believed, as the romantics had, that art is a high calling. Writers are special people, endowed with honesty and insight denied to the mass of men and women.

Other sources of the twentieth-century writer's sense of separation from his time are to be found in the age itself. Writers have often been deeply disturbed by the wars and revolutions and the economic ups and downs that have characterized this century. They have frequently been influenced also by the ideologies and intellectual currents of the time, from Marxism and Freudianism to the broader relativism and secularism of many of their contemporaries. To all these, they have reacted articulately and sometimes passionately, embracing some currents of opinion, vigorously challenging others.

The following sections analyze these literary reactions. The first surveys some of the prime targets of this literary critique. The second looks at the writer's own artistic goals. The third section considers the experi-

743

The Alienated Poet

[James Joyce] is at once alienated and indestructible, he is an exile from his own country and an exile even from himself, yet he survives the annihilating fury of history. In the unpredictable and fearful future that awaits civilization, the poet must be prepared to be alienated. . . . He must dedicate himself to poetry, although no one else seems likely to read what he writes; and he must be indestructible as a poet until he is destroyed as a human being. In the modern world, poetry is alienated; it will remain indestructible as long as the faith and love of each poet in his vocation survives.*

Delmore Schwartz, the poet who thus summed up the writer's vocation and isolation, himself died neglected and poor. His alienation was similar to that of the famous novelist James Joyce, author of Ulysses *and other experimental works, whose writing was repeatedly criticized, censored, and banned.*

*Delmore Schwartz, "The Vocation of the Poet in the Modern World," in Reginald Gibbons, ed. *The Poet's Work: 20 Masters of Twentieth Century Poetry on . . . Their Art* (Boston: Houghton Mifflin, 1979), p. 91.

mental and innovative techniques that have distinguished much of twentieth-century literature.

Rejection of the Modern World

Modern writers have attacked the society in which they lived for a number of vices. These include materialism and greed, shallowness, moral rigidity and hypocrisy, militarism and imperialism, lack of integrity and spiritual emptiness. The objects of their strictures have been business, the professions, high society, and the prosperous middle classes—in short all the "best people"—whereas the poor and the ignorant have been praised as people uncorrupted by the system. As the century progressed, some authors expressed approval of people who violated the traditional taboos against sexual promiscuity and addiction to alcohol and other drugs. Some saw even criminality and insanity as admirable traits. It became almost a commonplace of twentieth-century literature that since society is hopelessly depraved, only its victims, outcasts, and enemies are worthy.

Each major event of the century has furnished material for probing literary analysis. Antiwar literature, for example, is voluminous. Erich Maria Remarque's *All Quiet on the Western Front* tells the brutal truth about World War I as it was experienced by a dwindling platoon of German soldiers, whereas Joseph Heller's *Catch-22* offers a satirical vision of World War II. The most widely acclaimed novel of the Russian Revolution is Boris Pasternak's *Dr. Zhivago*, a story of love in a society disintegrating under the buffetings of that historic cataclysm. The poetry of Anna Akhmatova depicts the sufferings of the Russian people from World War I through the Stalinist persecutions and World War II in vivid images and moving verse. John Steinbeck follows the drifting victims of the Great Depression westward to California in *The Grapes of Wrath*. Totalitarianism also found its subtle or savage literary critics, including Arthur Koestler in his study of an idealistic communist crushed by Stalinism, *Darkness at Noon*, and Günter Grass in his phantasmagoric vision of Nazism and its aftermath, *The Tin Drum*.

Other failings of the age have also come in for critical treatment at the hands of the century's writers. Scott Fitzgerald revealed the hollowness at the heart of the glamorous jazz age in *The Great Gatsby*, and Ernest Hemingway did the same for the lost generation in Europe in *The Sun Also Rises*. D. H. Lawrence's *Lady Chatterley's Lover* and John Osborne's play *Look Back in Anger* both condemned the class society in Britain, from different perspectives. Marcel Proust's multivolumed *Remembrance of Things Past* exposed the decadence of French society at the beginning of the century. Such authors as Gabriel García Márquez more recently have done the same for Latin American culture in the late twentieth century in books like *Autumn of the Patriarch*.

A sense of the spiritual emptiness of the age, finally, pervades much of its literature. T. S. Eliot, the American poet who lived most of his life in England, is perhaps the most famous spokesperson for this view. In poems like *The Hollow Men* and *The Waste Land*, he depicts the twentieth century as a time without spiritual values, an age of unhappy people going nowhere. As described in literature, at least, it is indeed a century singularly low on high ideals or noble purposes.

The Triumph of Experimentalism

Some of the most celebrated modern fiction, drama, and poetry is extremely experimental in style. Like other artists, many writers have con-

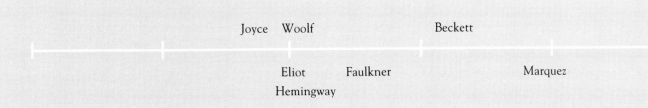

Joyce   Woolf   Beckett

Eliot   Faulkner   Marquez

Hemingway

centrated more on technique than on subject matter or message. As in the other arts, the result of this experimentation with literary forms has been to further cut the writer off from his or her audience and from the age.

Modernist poetry, for example, abandoned the fixed poetic meters and rhyme schemes, as well as the sentimentalism of much nineteenth-century verse. The new poets have taken as their subject matter the unhappiness or anguish of modern life, using free verse and depending more on imaginative images than on clarity or even grammar. Eliot's *Waste Land,* for example, presents its ideas in memorable word pictures; its specific line of argument, however, could only be understood by most readers with the help of footnotes.

Modernist drama has turned away from the realistic plays of the preceding century. Twentieth-century playwrights offer highly experimental works, sometimes eliminating sets and costumes, plot lines, and even believable characters. The resulting plays sometimes illustrate strong ideological beliefs, as in the work of Berthold Brecht. They may bring to life the deeper anxieties of the century, as Samuel Beckett has done in plays like *Waiting for Godot.* Audiences, however, have sometimes found it hard to tell what Beckett's oddly costumed characters, who are waiting for somebody named Godot—who might or might not be God—are talking about most of the time.

Twentieth-century fiction has also turned its back on such traditional conventions of earlier novels and stories as setting, clearly defined characters, and coherent story line. Virginia Woolf (1882–1941), for instance, developed a "stream of consciousness" style in which the entire story is told as it appears to the characters themselves, rather than telling readers what is "really" happening. Latin American "magic realist" writers such as Gabriel García Márquez (b. 1928) combine believable events with dreamlike or purely fantastic sequences, giving the reader an odd sense of being trapped in a highly realistic fairy tale. The climactic work of perhaps the most famous of all the modernists, James Joyce (1882–1941), carried these experimental tendencies to their extreme. His *Finnegan's Wake* was written in a private language largely invented by Joyce himself and takes place entirely in the dreaming mind of the book's hero—who was sound asleep the whole time.

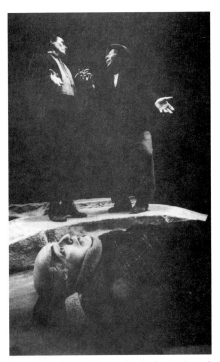

Samuel Beckett's *Waiting for Godot.* Didi and Gogo, the two tramps who are "waiting for Godot" throughout Beckett's play, engage in one of their endless, aimless arguments, while another member of the cast gives up entirely. Beckett, one of the leading "absurdist" playwrights of the years after World War II, had no obvious message for his audiences except the futility of life. Nevertheless, the combination of music-hall wit, slapstick clowning, and a suggestion of depths of meaning made the Irish dramatist's plays exciting theater.

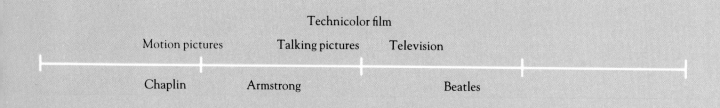

Self-Expression and Deliberate Obscurity

Both subjects and styles have thus come between modern writers and their readers. Perhaps an even more central element in the conflict between literature and society, however, has been the writers' declining interest in communicating with readers at all.

Many twentieth-century writers see the point of literature, as of the other arts, not in communication but in self-expression. What matters is not communicating with a popular or even a highly educated audience, but is expressing the artist's life experiences or view of the world in whatever words or images best embody them. Such writers have sometimes employed shocking images of brutality, sexuality, or madness. Obscure allusions, concepts borrowed from alien cultures, foreign languages, and even references to events in the writer's own life that readers could not possibly know of have been commonly used to express the author's point of view.

As a consequence, some of the best twentieth-century literature is deliberately obscure and difficult to understand. Writers like Joyce and Eliot simply cannot be grasped without lengthy scholarly commentaries and footnotes. Vivid images and broad themes, like the malaise of the age, might come across powerfully to concerned readers. The quality of mind and the literary skill of such writers is unquestioned. Yet they are cut off from much of the reading public by their commitment to self-expression before all else and by their willingness to be deliberately obscure to accomplish this end.

POPULAR CULTURE

While many of the most talented artists and writers have gone their own way in the twentieth century, the public at large has moved in other directions. This century has produced perhaps the most vigorous and sophisticated popular culture in western history.

The Rise of the Mass Media

The rise of media of communication that could reach large groups of people probably began with the invention of printing with movable type in the fifteenth century. It was only in the nineteenth century, however, that further advances in printing presses and paper manufacture combined with the growth of public education to produce a truly mass readership. The novels of Charles Dickens, Alexander Dumas, and many other popular writers were serialized in mass circulation newspapers and magazines before being printed in books.

The twentieth century has seen another and even greater leap forward in the expansion of the mass media. High-speed presses, more years of compulsory education, cheap paperback books, and the spread of public libraries further expanded the market for popular fiction. In addition, the invention and mass production of the electronic media and the motion picture created a whole new potential for mass culture. Sound recording and radio, film and television, brought music, drama, and much more to whole populations on a scale never before imagined.

Other, broader trends also helped shape the emerging mass media. Less rigorous moral constraints, the greater prominence accorded to youth and youthful tastes, and the openness of western society to new ideas and minority viewpoints have influenced popular culture. The following sections survey particularly the growth

746

The Rolling Stones. Lead singer Mick Jagger and guitarrist Keith Richards rock and roll on a U.S. tour in the 1970s. Second in international acclaim only to the Beatles, the Stones epitomized the irreverent, raunchy spirit that made British rock groups particularly popular with the young.

of popular music and the evolution of film and television as outstanding manifestations of the mass culture of the twentieth century.

Popular Music

The history of popular music in this century clearly illustrates the extent to which the historic center of the western world has shifted from Europe to the United States. Some of the most successful performers, notably leading rock groups of recent decades, did come from Europe. Some of the most popular rhythms, including dance music like the tango, the samba, and the rhumba between the wars and the more recent reggae, originated in Latin America or the Caribbean. Nevertheless, such internationally acclaimed popular forms as jazz and rock first took shape in the United States and bear the unmistakable stamp of that nation's experience, particularly black experience.

Black American musicians invented jazz in New Orleans around the turn of the century. Drawing on a rich musical heritage reaching back to West Africa and including the spirituals sung in black American churches, jazz musicians improvised a brassy, syncopated style. In the 1920s and 1930s, jazz giants like Louis Armstrong and Duke Ellington took the new music north and into the mainstream of white culture to give the "Jazz Age" its name. Europeans were also soon dancing to "le jazz hot" and cheering black performers like Josephine Baker. Following World War II, jazz evolved in a number of directions, producing some of the most complex popular music of the century.

Rock and roll, however, has been the predominant form of popular music around the world during the second half of the century. Rock also drew heavily on black American rhythms, as well as on the country and folk music of the rural South.

The black composer and singer Chuck Berry was a shaping influence on the new form, but Elvis Presley emerged in the middle 1950s as the first rock superstar. Such British groups as the Beatles and the Rolling Stones made the new style the favorite of young people around the world in the 1960s.

Depending on a strong beat, the electric guitar, electronic amplification, and dazzling staging and lighting, rock musicians have sold out their concerts and circulated millions of copies of their songs on records and tapes. Their performances are emotional experiences for their young fans. Though their lyrics are sometimes attacked, particularly for sexual explicitness, some rock performers are skilled musicians, and rock lyrics often deal with the experience of growing up in terms their young audiences can readily understand. They also have often addressed political controversies of the day. The lyrics of Bob Dylan, for example, served as social protest for the youth of the 1960s and 1970s.

THE DREAM MACHINE

The movie is not only a supreme expression of mechanism, but paradoxically it offers as product the most magical of consumer commodities, namely dreams. It is, therefore, not accidental that the movie has excelled as a medium that offers poor people roles of riches and power beyond the dreams of avarice. . . .

The Hollywood tycoons were not wrong in acting on the assumption that movies gave the American immigrant a means of self-fulfillment without any delay. The strategy . . . meant that . . . the American way of life was [soon] exported to the entire world in [film] cans. The world eagerly lined up to buy canned dreams. The film not only accompanied the first great consumer age, but was also incentive, advertisement, and, in itself, a major commodity.[*]

Marshall McLuhan, the famed "media expert" of the 1960s, thus defined the wide appeal of the film medium. From its beginning, the movies created a fantasy world of "canned dreams" into which anyone could escape for the price of admission. This most successful of the century's popular arts also became the ideal commercial product, offering audiences escape from the harshest realities into the world of the imagination.

[*]Marshall McLuhan, *Understanding Media: The Extensions of Man* (New York: McGraw-Hill, 1965), p. 291.

Film and Television

The twentieth century's greatest contribution to western culture, however, may well be the motion picture. A fundamentally popular art form, film has also produced some unquestioned masterpieces of high culture. Both as a theatrical form and as adapted for the home television screen, moving pictures seem to be the most universally appealing of modern arts. Like popular music, both "the movies" and "TV" are in large part an American contribution to western popular arts.

The distinctive feature of the film arts is that they are pictorial in form, depending on the impact of images on the human eye for their primary effect. Most of the basic devices for enhancing this impact were developed during the era of silent film, during the first decades of the century. Directors and cameramen early learned the value of the closeup to point attention, the dramatic effects of camera angle, the use of location shooting for authenticity, and much more. Sound and color added to the vividness of the medium, as did the increasing attention to accurate settings and astonishing special effects. Actors also recognized the need for a more low-keyed, natural style when they had to project, not to the last row of the balcony, but only as far as the camera lens and the microphone. The result has been a dramatic medium of almost unparalleled excitement, intimacy, and power.

Television, flourishing after 1950, added its own unique possibilities. These perhaps have more to do with storytelling and character development than with the techniques of filming. From radio, television inherited the program format, in which the same central characters had new adventures every week. Television itself has evolved the more flexible miniseries form, in which one story, often derived from a successful novel, is told in installments adding up to many hours in length. Both these approaches allow the more complex portrayal of character and the more elaborate development of stories.

Film produced its own array of artistic genius from the very beginning. Director D. W. Griffith invented many basic techniques of filmmaking around the First World War. Charlie Chaplin brought artistic sensitivity to his portrayal of "the little tramp" victimized by the modern world between the world wars. Gifted filmmakers like Luis Buñuel, Federico Fellini, and Ingmar Bergman experimented with modernist film techniques after World War II. Actors like Lawrence Olivier gave some of their greatest performances in motion pictures.

The motion picture, however, has also produced a long series of stars whose immense popularity has been rooted, not in innovative techniques of brilliant performances, but in personal qualities with a broader appeal. Stars such as John Wayne or Marlene Dietrich had a personal strength, warmth, or glamour with which audiences around the globe could identify easily on the screen. Technical virtuosity also has a broad popular appeal, transporting viewers out of their humdrum daily lives into mansions and penthouses, steaming jungles or distant wars, a glamorized past or fantastic future worlds. Torrid love scenes, wild automobile chases, and violence of all sorts have become parts of the imaginary lives of millions thanks to the movies.

The Americanization of popular culture throughout the west and around the globe is a notable feature of the postwar world. Many twentieth-century social commentators have noted the widespread influence of American jazz and rock music, films and television programs on both Europe and Japan. Families in Bogotá, Tokyo, and Rome watch avidly as the television soap opera *Dynasty* unfolds.

SUMMARY

The culture of the twentieth century has been characterized by rapid change, conflict, and an endless barrage of novelty. In some ways, the audience for the fine arts narrowed to the few who were willing or able to keep up with the latest fashions. In other ways, owing to the wealth and technical ingenuity of the century, the arts have become accessible to a greatly larger audience than ever before.

A medley of influences has shaped twentieth-century culture. These include a nineteenth-century cultural legacy ranging from romanticism to Freudianism. Another important influence has been the history and society of this century, with its wars and revolutions and its increasingly literate and affluent population. Technological developments have also produced new materials and media of communication with unparalleled artistic potential.

"Modernism," as much of the high art of the age has been dubbed, took the form of a bubbling brew of new schools in all the arts. These artistic movements rejected past traditions and explored the possibilities of the formal elements that had always been the basic tools of the artist's trade. Painting and sculpture sometimes retained the representational form in a crude way, but moved toward pure abstraction. Architecture exploited steel, concrete, and glass to produce unprecedented free-form buildings, and music broke up its tonal and rhythmic patterns and moved beyond voices and instruments to purely electronic music.

Modernism in literature meant not only the rejection of past tradition but of present-day society also. Twentieth-century writers have exposed the faults of modern attitudes and institutions and offered vivid fictional critiques of the major events and trends of the times. Many modern writers also joined the other arts in experimenting with formal elements, employing new images and language to express their artistic visions.

The popular arts have also changed rapidly over the century. Popular music includes such vigorous new styles as jazz and rock, which spread throughout the western world and beyond. So did the even more novel forms of film and television, revealing the vast potential of moving pictures to delight mass audiences everywhere.

SELECTED SOURCES

Arnason, H. S. *History of Modern Art.* 1977. Excellent illustrations and clear discussion.

The Beatles. *The Sergeant Pepper's Lonely Hearts Club Band.* The artistry of rock music, in one of the most famous albums of a classic group.

*Borges, Jorge Luis. *Labyrinths.* 1977. Intriguing short fictions by the dean of Latin American modernists.

*Eliot, T. S. *The Waste Land and Other Poems.* 1955. Pivotal poems in the broodingly critical modernist mode.

*Esslin, Martin. *The Theater of the Absurd.* 1961. Clear introduction to the leading experimental playwrights of the mid-twentieth century.

Gone with the Wind. 1939. One of the most popular films ever made, exploiting the medium's capacity for both spectacle and character development.

*Joyce, James. *Portrait of the Artist as a Young Man.* 1964. Not as experimental as his later fiction, but a vivid picture of the writer alienated from his world.

*McLuhan, Marshall. *Understanding Media.* 1965. Pithy commentary on the mass media and their impact on audiences.

*Pasternak, Boris. *Dr. Zhivago.* 1981. Moving novel of the Russian Revolution as seen by a Russian poet who lived through it.

*Woolf, Virginia. *To the Lighthouse.* 1964. Major novel by a leading modernist.

*Available in paperback.

DICTATORSHIP CHALLENGES DEMOCRACY (1917–1939)

Liberalism only flourished for half a century. It was born in 1830 . . . and the highest point of its success was the [revolutionary] year 1848, when even [Pope] Pius IX was a liberal. . . . The sea of liberalism, after having accumulated an infinity of Gordian knots, tried to untie them in the slaughter of the First World War—and never has any religion demanded of its votaries such a monstrous sacrifice. . . . Now, today, the liberal faith must shut the doors of its deserted temples, deserted because the peoples of the world realize that its worship . . . will lead . . . to certain ruin. In addition, let it be pointed out that all the political hopes of the present day are anti-liberal.

During the two decades between the peace treaty that ended World War I in 1919 and the outbreak of World War II in 1939, the western world faced a number of new challenges. Western people had to come to terms with new technology, with rapid social change, and with the greatest depression in modern history. No challenge was greater, however, than that posed by the rise of antiliberal political creeds and systems. The most frightening among these was the new form of dictatorship called totalitarianism.

The "funeral oration" for liberalism quoted above was pronounced by Benito Mussolini, the dictator of Fascist Italy. During the 1920s and 1930s, people even in the liberal democracies wondered if he might not be right. For during the thirties especially, authoritarian regimes of several kinds rose to power in a number of European and American nations. Before that decade was over, a powerful alliance of such states, including Germany, Italy and Japan, would challenge liberal nations like Great Britain, France, and later the United States to an ultimate test of strength on the field of battle.

This chapter begins with the Russian Revolution of 1917 and its immediate consequences. It then turns to the problems of the democracies between the wars. Finally, it traces the rise of Nazism, fascism, communism, and other forms of authoritarian government in various parts of the western world between 1919 and 1939.

CONTENTS

A Nazi Rally. Ready to march, German soldiers stood at attention to hear Hitler speak at a Nuremberg rally in the later 1930s. Such rallies gave concrete embodiment to such Nazi principles as strength, discipline, and absolute obedience to the Leader, Adolf Hitler.

THE RUSSIAN REVOLUTION AND ITS CONSEQUENCES

The Russian Revolution of 1917, like the earlier revolutions in France and British North America, was rooted in serious social problems. Also like the other revolutions, the revolt in Russia was the work of a dedicated band of revolutionaries—the Bolshevik party led by Lenin (1870–1924), born Vladimir Ilyich Ulyanov.

The Bolshevik Revolution

Russia at the beginning of World War I was the most politically authoritarian and economically backward of the great powers. The Romanov dynasty of Nicholas II (1894–1917) still regarded itself as a divine-right monarchy. The tsarist regime ruled with the help of a large bureaucracy, an army that could be used against rebellious subjects as well as against foreign enemies, and a secret police that had made Siberia notorious as the site of Russian penal col-onies. The new legislature, the Duma, had little real power. Russia's economy remained relatively undeveloped despite efforts by recent tsars to modernize the nation. The peasant majority, in spite of the liberation of the serfs, was still poverty stricken, ignorant, and comparatively unproductive. The new technology of the western world had only begun to make an impact on Russian industry. With the largest territory and population of any European nation, Russia's potential was very great, yet it was in some ways a feeble giant in 1900.

When World War I broke out in 1914, the 1905 pattern of defeat and popular unrest was repeated. This time, however, Russia suffered a much worse defeat in war, and a particularly vigorous revolutionary group was on the scene—Lenin's Bolsheviks. Rejecting the contemporary trend of western European socialism toward democracy and reformism, the Bolsheviks insisted that only Marxist revolution could bring significant change to so autocratic and backward a society as tsarist Russia.

Their chance came in 1917. Three years of war had shattered the home front as well as Russia's armies. Enormous casualties, shortages of food, fuel, and housing, government inefficiency and corruption, and rumors of treason in high places finally turned the Russian people against Nicholas II. Under pressure from street rioters, liberal politicians in the Duma, and some of his own generals, the tsar abdicated in February 1917. The provisional government, headed by Alexander Kerensky, faced the same insurmountable problems as the tsarist regime had in coping with war.

Kerensky's refusal to withdraw from the conflict set the stage for Lenin's radical Bolsheviks to seize power. In the spring of 1917, following the fall of the tsar, Lenin and some of his lieutenants, including Leon Trotsky, returned from exile to plan for taking over the government and setting up a rural organization of Soviets—councils of workers, soldiers, and peasants. Meanwhile, after a final disastrous military failure in the summer, Russian soldiers began to mutiny,

Lenin Speaks. V. I. Lenin, speaking in a somewhat more lowkeyed style than many authoritarian leaders, addresses a rally in Moscow in 1917. In later years, Communists, like other totalitarian parties, organized large-scale parades and public spectacles as expressions of the solidarity and loyalty of the party.

workers to strike, and masses of city dwellers to demonstrate in the streets once more. Worker's councils (Soviets) took over a number of cities. Lenin and his followers organized brigades of workers and sympathetic servicemen—especially sailors—to move against the provisional government.

The Bolshevik revolution itself was relatively easily accomplished. Bolshevik units seized the headquarters of the Kerensky government in the Winter Palace in St. Petersburg in an almost bloodless coup. Several weeks later, the walled Kremlin in Moscow fell to them after a pitched battle. Lenin was thus installed as ruler of Russia after only a few weeks of fighting in a handful of cities. But the real work of the Bolsheviks was only beginning.

The Russian Civil War

Not seizing power but holding onto it became the biggest accomplishment of Lenin and his fellow revolutionaries. The new government had many enemies, both at home and abroad. Between 1917 and 1921, however, the Bolsheviks not only successfully resisted all efforts to overthrow them but also began to consolidate their power.

The Bolsheviks—renamed the Communist party in 1918—moved quickly to get out of the war and to mobilize against their many opponents. They made peace with the Germans unilaterally, surrendering huge territories in the Treaty of Brest-Litovsk in February 1918, to end the relentless pressure of the German armies. This move outraged the Allies, but it did get the Bolsheviks out of the war that had destroyed Nicholas II and Kerensky. At home, mean-

---

RED GUARDS

Down in front of the Soviet palace an auto-truck was going to the front. Half a dozen Red Guards, some sailors, and a soldier or two, under command of a huge workman, clambered in and shouted to me to come along. Red Guards issued from headquarters, each of them staggering under an arm-load of . . . grubit—which, they say, is ten times as strong, and five times as sensitive as dynamite; these they threw into the truck. A three-inch cannon was loaded and then tied onto the tail of the truck with bits of . . . wire.

We started away with a shout, at top speed of course; the heavy truck swaying from side to side. The cannon leaped from one wheel to the other, the grubit bombs went rolling back and forth over our feet, fetching up against the sides of the car with a crash. . . .

Occasionally a patrol tried to stop us. Soldiers ran out into the road before us, shouted "Stoi!" and threw up their guns.

We paid no attention. "The devil take you!" cried the Red Guards. "We don't stop for anybody! We're Red Guards!" and we thundered imperiously on.[*]

John Reed, who wrote this vivid description of Bolshevik workers heading for the front, was an American journalist in Russia at the time of the Russian Revolution. Reed's uncritical radical sympathies and the fact that he did not speak Russian led to many errors in his famous book, Ten Days That Shook the World. His enthusiasm and his skill as a writer, however, did capture much of the flavor of the exciting early days of the revolution.

[*]John Reed, Ten Days That Shook the World (New York: Random House, 1960), pp. 308–309.

---

while, the Communists divided up large estates among the peasants, announced the nationalization of the means of production, and attempted to mobilize the workers into labor armies to support the new war effort required by the outbreak of civil war.

During this period also, Lenin moved to strengthen the party's hold on the shattered nation. He organized the beginning of a Communist bureaucracy to replace that of the Romanovs. His right-hand man, Leon Trotsky (1879–1940), put together the Red Army, well organized, trained, and disciplined. To deal with sometimes violent internal opposition, the Communists established their own secret police, then called the Cheka, later called by many other names. Under pressure, the new Russian government thus turned to levers of control very like those used by the tsarist regime: bureaucrats, soldiers, and secret police.

The domestic enemies of the Communists included rival revolutionary parties, national minorities, and tsarist military units. The Social Revolutionary peasant party, for example, outnumbered the Bolsheviks at the constitutional convention that the Bolsheviks called soon after their seizure of power. Lenin responded to this challenge by dissolving the convention. When the peasant revolution-

MAP 80

The Russian Revolution and Civil War. After they had seized power in major Russian cities, the Bolsheviks had a long struggle to win control of the rest of the nation. From 1917 to 1921 the area controlled by the Reds was surrounded by anti-Bolshevik White armies and other opponents of the new regime, including the western allies. During this time also, minority nationalities in Finland, Poland, the Baltic states, and elsewhere rebelled successfully, although the Baltic States and eastern Poland were regained by the Soviet Union during World War II.

aries attempted to assassinate Lenin, the Bolsheviks turned the Cheka against them, arresting and executing many of these rivals for revolutionary power and sending them, as the Bolsheviks said "into the dustbin of history."

Minority nationalities within the Russian Empire, conquered by the tsars, took advantage of the turmoil to rebel against the new government in Moscow. Poland and the Baltic states of Finland, Estonia, Latvia, and Lithuania were all successful in securing their independence. Rebellions in the Caucasus and in Russian central Asia, on the other hand, were crushed. Tsarist armies, including

Cossack troops, also rebelled and briefly held most of the country. Even after the execution of the last of the Romanovs and his family by provincial Bolshevik authorities, these "White Russian" forces stayed in the field. The Red Army, however, defeated the last of the Whites by the early 1920s.

Besides these domestic enemies, the Bolsheviks faced attacks from beyond their frontiers. British, French, and American troops, for example, landed at several Russian ports in 1918 to prevent supplies intended for tsarist armies before the revolution from falling into German hands. These Allied units, however, were soon pro-

viding material support for counter-revolutionary Russian forces, sometimes coming into combat with the Reds. Meanwhile, Russia's old imperial rival Japan invaded from the east, and newly independent Poland invaded from the west. An army of Czech prisoners of war, freed on condition they leave the country, briefly controlled stretches of the Trans-Siberian Railway. But by 1922, the Red Army had cleared the Russian mainland of all these enemies too.

The Russian Civil War, coming on the heels of the most destructive international war to date, was a terrible experience for the newly created Soviet Union. Reds and Whites launched rival reigns of terror, executing supporters of their opponents in mass lots. Physical destruction, hunger, and suffering were widespread. The Communist leaders also acquired at this time a fear of "capitalist encirclement" that continues to have a potent effect on Russia's relations with the west. Most important, perhaps, it was under the pressures of the Civil War that the Communist system of authoritarian rule was first forged and imposed on Russia, now called the Union of Soviet Socialist Republics, or in its shortened form, the Soviet Union.

Bolshevism Fails Elsewhere

As Marxists, Lenin and his colleagues believed in the inevitability of a worldwide workers' revolution against capitalism. As revolutionaries, many of them felt impelled to work actively to encourage such revolts. Attacked from all sides during the Civil War, furthermore, some of them feared the Communist regime in Russia could not survive for long without the support of successful Marxist revolutions elsewhere. In the years after 1917, therefore, the Bolsheviks attempted to export revolution, particularly to central and eastern European nations.

In 1919, the Russian Communist leaders set up an international organization called the Communist International, or Comintern. The purpose of the Comintern was to spread revolutionary Marxist-Leninist ideas and to channel material aid and advice to struggling Communist revolutionaries in other nations.

Inspired by the example of the successful revolution in Russia and sometimes helped by the Communist International, revolutionary groups engaged in uprisings in Germany, Hungary, and elsewhere. The most famous left-wing rebellion in Germany after World War I was that of the Spartacists, who briefly occupied Berlin itself early in 1919. The German Army, however, crushed the Spartacist revolt and summarily executed its leaders. In Hungary, in 1919, a communist government organized by Bela Kun, an admirer of the Bolsheviks, was suppressed in its turn by the military. Russian Communist agents further encouraged street actions in the Baltic states and offered advice on organization and tactics to revolutionaries in China, on their far eastern frontier. But as the 1920s advanced, these insurrections also came to nothing. It became apparent that the world revolution was not imminent after all.

The Comintern continued to be an instrument of Soviet foreign policy throughout the interwar period. Through the International, Russian Communist leaders encouraged radicals and liberal sympathizers in other nations to support policies favorable to the "workers' motherland"—the Soviet Union.

Perhaps the most important result of these efforts to build support for communist revolution elsewhere, however, was to stimulate anticommunist feeling in other parts of the world. A number of western European workers' organizations rejected the appeals of the Communist International. The long feud between democratic western European socialists and totalitarian Russian communists may be traced back to resistance of many European and American Marxists to the Soviet-controlled Third International. Fear of communism also strengthened the appeal of right-wing agitators and dictators. Both Mussolini in Italy and Hitler in Germany, for instance, played very successfully on popular fears of communist revolution created by the abortive attempts at revolution of the years immediately after World War I.

THE DEMOCRACIES BETWEEN THE WARS

During the two decades between World War I and World War II, the western democracies underwent trying times. The moral malaise and underlying social problems of the 1920s were succeeded by the economic breakdown of the Great Depression in the 1930s. Under these pressures and strains, the leading democratic societies bent but did not break.

Recovery and New Beginnings

In some ways, the west seemed to be thriving during the decade after the Great War. Politically, liberal republics were established in some European nations that had been run by autocratic monarchs before the war. Germany, in particular, under the Weimar Constitution promulgated in 1919 after the overthrow of Kaiser William II, had one of the most democratic governments in the world. Such established democracies as Great Britain and the United States strengthened democratic institutions by granting women the right to vote after the war.

Economically, most of the 1920s looked like a time of booming prosperity. There was a brief depression

Bolshevik
Revolution   Comintern organized   Stalin in
power

First
Five
Year
Plan

Russian Civil War   Mussolini
in power

Wall
Street
crash

immediately after the armistice and a wave of inflation in the early twenties that badly hurt Europe's middle classes. From about 1923 on, however, prosperity seemed to return. The United States, clearly the world's richest nation, doubled its industrial production over the decade, and the value of stocks and bonds skyrocketed on the Wall Street stock exchange. Great Britain's standard of living began to rise again, and the French economy stabilized, though it did not improve rapidly, during the 1920s.

Perhaps most visibly, the social customs of the "roaring twenties," as the press sometimes called the decade, were markedly more liberal. Young women in particular rejected the protected life-styles of the prewar years. Short skirts and bobbed hair were symbols of the greater freedom of women to hold jobs, live independently, and assert their general social and moral emancipation. The automobile liberated "flaming youth" of both sexes to seek entertainment away from home, and drinking, smoking, and recreational sex became more open and, in some segments of society, even respectable. The Ford car also made the Sunday drive and the long-distance vacation favored leisure-time activities of middle-class families, particularly in the United States.

The Tensions and Disillusionment of the Twenties

Underlying these positive trends, however, were real tensions in western society. Political democracy was often accompanied by political instability. In multiparty states like France and Germany, the party alliances needed to govern were so fragile that governments frequently fell from power after only a few months. In other great powers, such as Italy and Russia, authoritarian governments were already installed in the 1920s.

Beneath the surface prosperity of the decade, important segments of western society were still mired in poverty. Farmers and miners in the United States and elsewhere were badly hurt by the postwar decline in demand for their products. Much of Great Britain's industry was out of date. French industry was too conservative in outlook for rapid growth and hindered by labor shortages, wartime destruction, and postwar inflation. Germany suffered from the heavy reparations demanded by the Versailles Treaty and from the occupation of the Ruhr, its industrial heartland, by the French in the early 1920s. In addition Germans had undertaxed themselves to pay for World War I,

contributing to their serious inflation in the postwar period.

Each nation also had its special problems. The United States, under a series of conservative administrations, experienced a "red scare," during which Marxists and other radicals were harassed, arrested, and, if aliens, deported. A prewar trend toward racism and hostility to all who were not native-born Americans resulted in new immigration laws that cut off the flow of Asian and southeast European immigrants. The nation also saw a wave of anti-Semitism and a resurgence of the Ku Klux Klan, whose violence was directed primarily against blacks.

In Europe, Great Britain struggled with her perennial Irish problem. Following the Easter Rebellion of 1916 and a renewal of Irish terrorism and British repression after the war, London agreed to an autonomous Irish Free State that included most of the island. The British, however, retained direct control of Northern Ireland, with its substantial Scotch-Irish Protestant population. The divided Ireland that resulted satisfied no one.

The continental powers also had their difficulties. France, fearful of the revival of German power across the Rhine, pressed the Weimar Republic to make reparations payments and occupied the Ruhr to force compliance. This move, however, brought on the great German inflation of 1923, further undermining Germany's capacity to keep up its payments to its former enemies. The French also began to construct a presumably impregnable defensive line across its eastern frontier, the Maginot Line—which the German armies would simply circle around (through Belgium) when World War II finally came. Weimar Germany itself was under sometimes intense pressure from the communists on the left and the Nazis and other antidemocratic parties on the right.

The democracies were swept by a current of deep social anxiety and disillusionment during the decade after World War I, a mood that would both weaken them and encourage the rise of totalitarian states in the next decade. The war left many survivors bitter about the immense human costs and apparently useless slaughter. Some intellectuals felt the catastrophe reflected a profound weakness in the western societies that had made and fought the war. Some European veterans, by contrast, seemed to remember the days of authoritarian commanders and comradeship in the trenches so fondly that they once again put on uniforms—this time in the paramilitary forces of rising totalitarian leaders and war veterans like Hitler and Mussolini.

Each nation, again, had its own particular disillusionments and anxieties. In the United States, the failure of Woodrow Wilson's last crusade for the League of Nations and the accompanying collapse of progressivism made people indifferent about reform in general. In Germany, the Versailles peace and the problems of the Weimar regime bred a sense of na-

tional humiliation and a belief in many quarters that republican government meant weak government. In Great Britain, the victory of the Bolsheviks in Russia and their alleged support for a great general strike by British workers in 1926 intensified class antagonisms to the highest pitch of the century. Altogether, the western world was in considerable social and moral disarray when, at the end of the decade, it blundered into the Great Depression.

The Great Depression

The roots of the terrible depression of the 1930s lay in the fundamental economic weaknesses of the 1920s. Because western societies were tied economically to colonial and other nonwestern societies, furthermore, the Great Depression was a world depression. This second major catastrophe of the century, finally, helped to bring on the rise of totalitarianism and World War II.

Among the basic causes of the depression were overproduction, international debt, arising mostly from wartime expenses, and a mass of shaky investment in stocks and bonds. The west had geared up for a level of industrial and agricultural production during World War I that could not be sustained during peacetime. Wages were generally low, which meant that, despite the spread of installment-plan buying, the general population lacked purchasing power. Only middle-class purchase of such large consumer items as automobiles, especially in the United States, supported production during the 1920s. When middle-class consumer demand weakened at the end of the decade, there was little to maintain the unstable prosperity. To

protect domestic production and employment, the major powers engaged in a protective tariff war, which helped reduce international trade by 1930 to one-fourth that of prewar levels.

The tangle of international debts—reparations Germany owed the victorious Allies, war debts the Allies owed the United States—also contributed to the onset of the Depression. Only U.S. loans and U.S. investment in Germany kept this cycle of payments moving at all, and even U.S. support eventually proved insufficient. International economic collapse seemed imminent as all parties proved unable to meet their financial obligations.

Much of the capital to support both continued production and foreign loans turned out to be little more than shaky IOUs. Because stock markets in those days were virtually unregulated, speculators were able to buy stocks mainly on credit, sometimes building up debts far beyond their actual ability to pay. When the value of their stocks went down, such investors went bankrupt in large numbers. The resulting wave of bankruptcies caused stock values to decline still further, precipitating the Great Depression.

The collapse began with the Wall Street crash of October 1929, when a panic on the stock market revealed its fundamental weakness. Soon bankrupt industrialists were closing their factories and putting their employees out of work. These unemployed could not afford to purchase goods, causing other factories to go under in turn. The economies of colonies and other nonwestern lands collapsed also. These areas sold agricultural products, raw materials, and other basic commodities to the more developed nations;

as their best customers could no longer buy from them, these regions also slid into decline.

The Great Depression shook the governments of the western nations. Some nations, such as the United States, responded creatively within the framework of their democratic institutions to the crisis. Others, such as Germany, turned to totalitarian solutions. Many, like Great Britain and France, muddled through, preserving democracy but accomplishing little to conquer the Depression.

The impact of the economic collapse may be indicated by a few rough figures. By 1932, production in France was down by 28 percent, in the United States by 30 percent, in Germany by close to 50 percent. A quarter of all American workers were unemployed; in Germany, the figure was approximately 40 percent. Governments, inevitably, were blamed for the disaster. The German chancellor Hein-

rich Bruning was dubbed "the Chancellor of Hunger." In the United States, the shantytowns that filled up with jobless people were popularly known as "Hoovervilles," after President Herbert Hoover.

The United States, however, began to fight back under the administration of Democratic president Franklin Roosevelt, who took office in 1933. Roosevelt was an upstate New York aristocrat who had a humor and compassion that appealed to the common citizen; crippled by polio, his courage was contagious. With the help of his politically concerned and active wife, Eleanor, and a team of reforming advisers dubbed the "brain trust," FDR immediately launched his New Deal.

The New Deal was a series of innovative, often piecemeal, reforms intended to pull the country out of the Depression. Although the Depression persisted until World War II,

these efforts heartened the country and alleviated some of the suffering. New laws and new government bureaus provided relief payments for the hungry, low-cost mortgages, public works jobs for some of the unemployed, and assistance for farmers. The New Dealers also gave support to unions, a job program for unemployed youth, and loans to business, coupled with some regulation of business and finance to correct the abuses that had triggered the collapse. Most important, the New Deal began to build a welfare state in the United States, providing modest federal unemployment compensation, a beginning at old-age pensions, regulation of wages, hours, and conditions of labor, and other benefits, many of them already legislated in Europe.

Great Britain, France, and other western democracies did not respond as vigorously to the Depression. A series of basically conservative gov-

Franklin and Eleanor Roosevelt. FDR and his wife radiated confidence even in the depths of the Great Depression. Here they return from church on Easter Sunday, 1938.

ernments in Great Britain seemed to have little more to offer than the "dole," relief payments for unemployed workers and subsidies to farmers. A socialist premier, Léon Blum, tried to help French workers weather the economic decline by increasing wages and pensions and to stimulate economic revival, but his coalition government, like so many others, did not long survive.

Stronger measures were adopted by Europe's totalitarian governments and by autocratic regimes in Latin America and elsewhere. In some cases, as in Hitler's Germany, these authoritarian rulers were more successful in getting their economies moving again than were the democracies. But economic revival came at a high price.

THE EMERGENCE OF TOTALITARIANISM

Totalitarianism is a twentieth-century form of government. The word *totalitarian*, coined by Mussolini, is also used to describe a type of political party, a system of ideas, and the emotional commitment that built a new, antiliberal society.

The Nature of Totalitarianism

Totalitarian government aims at total control of society by rulers who exercise absolute authority over the politics, the economy, and the social and cultural lives—the hearts and minds—of their peoples. Totalitarianism depends on modern technology. The totalitarian leaders of the 1930s had the massive bureaucracy and the coercive technology to achieve these aims more effectively than any ab-

---

SIEG HEIL!

The sound of music comes nearer. Suddenly, at an order, every uniformed man springs to attention. Every arm in the crowd comes to the salute with the Hitler greeting. . . . The Leader comes forward to speak. . . .

"It is glorious to live in an age which confronts the men who live in it with heroic problems. Need and misery have overwhelmed our people. Germany finds itself without protection and without rights. Destiny sets us the grand task, to fight in these strained times, to fill with faith and truth the hearts of our crushed fellow countrymen, to give work to millions of unemployed, to build up a new society and to check its enemies with an iron fist. . . ."

The speech is over. As it has proceeded the voice has become higher, more staccato—hypnotizing as the rapid beat of drumsticks on the tom-

tom. The crowd is spellbound. As the speech concludes a storm of cheers and "heils" breaks out . . . Outside, in the warm streets, the night is gay with flags. The bon-fires light up the faces of young Storm-troopers.*

The emotional appeal of totalitarianism is well illustrated in this eyewitness account of the contagious enthusiasm kindled by a Nazi rally in 1933. These outdoor gatherings were held in sports stadiums, dramatically lit, and accompanied by singing, torchlight processions, and other emotionally stirring features. The uniformed party members, drawn up in military formations, greeted "the Leader" with rhythmic chants of Sieg Heil!—"Hail, victory!"

*Michael John, *Face of Revolution* (New York: Macmillan, 1936), pp. 38–40.

---

solute monarch or political despot of the past. They were also able to package their propaganda appeals in the new media—radio and motion pictures—giving them a powerful appeal.

Totalitarianism, however, has an additional feature: It builds on the totalitarian party. The Nazis in Germany, Fascists in Italy, and the Communists were all organized political parties before they were governments. They offered uniforms, rallies, careers for some and a sense of comradeship for all—irrespective of class background—which made many converts. Above all, totalitarian political parties offered a clear sense of purpose in the disillusioned and demoralized years between the wars.

Totalitarianism requires more than submission to government and membership in a party: It demands commitment to a totalitarian ideology. Communism, Nazism, and fascism were first of all systems of belief. Their basic ideas derived from the ideologies of the nineteenth century. Communism was built on the teachings of Karl Marx, whereas Nazism drew heavily on the racist nationalism of the later nineteenth century. Totalitarian ideologues modified and simplified these ideas into slogans and battle cries capable of inspiring masses of people to action. Like their nineteenth-century ideological precursors, the totalitarians aimed to change society. This they did with a vengeance in the 1930s.

Fascism in Italy

The first state with totalitarian aspirations was Fascist Italy, which began to take shape with Benito Mussolini's March on Rome in 1922. Mussolini, a prominent socialist before the war, changed his ideological commitment during that conflict. Resentful of the meager territorial gains Italy had made, he became a passionate nationalist. A charismatic figure, Mussolini was soon a leader of antisocialist fighting gangs called *Fasci di Combattimento*, or Fascists, who attacked labor unions, broke up socialist meetings, and otherwise expressed a common fear of left-wing revolution in the years after the Communist victory in Russia and communist uprisings elsewhere in Europe between 1918 and 1920.

The weak Italian constitutional monarchy was unable to deal with nationalist bitterness, fears of communism, and other postwar political and economic problems. In 1922, the Fascist "Blackshirts" announced a March on Rome to show their power, and King Victor Emmanuel III (1900–1946) avoided trouble by naming Mussolini the new premier.

With Mussolini the constitutional head of the government, the construction of the Fascist state began. Fascist Blackshirts continued to assault and even murder their foes in politics and the press. Mussolini meanwhile slowly reorganized the Italian political and economic systems. He eliminated freedom of speech and the free press, and in 1925, outlawed all rival political parties. In 1929, Mussolini attempted to end the long feud between the Italian government and the powerful Roman Catholic church by signing the Lateran Treaties with the pope, giving the pope sovereignty over Vatican City in Rome. In return for allowing the church continuing control over education in Italy, Mussolini won a free hand for the Fascists in dealing with other national institutions.

In the early 1930s, Il Duce—"The Leader"—began to restructure the country economically into what he called a "corporate state." Major industries were organized into two dozen "corporations," each run by committees of businessmen, union leaders, and Fascist party officials representing the government. In general, big business had a strong voice in these corporations, though the government purchased large chunks of major industries to help them through the Depression. In 1938, finally, the old Chamber of Deputies—Italy's elected legislature—was abolished and replaced by a Chamber of Fasces and Corporations.

During the 1920s and 1930s also, Il Duce surrounded himself with the militaristic pomp the world has come to expect of totalitarianism. The Fascist party drew heavily on the glories of the Roman Republic and Empire, such as its fasces symbol and its youth group, the Sons of the Wolf. Party members and such auxiliary groups as the Young Fascists often marched in review before him. Mussolini also enjoyed making ideological pronouncements like that quoted at the beginning of this chapter. More important, he embarked on an aggressively expansionist foreign policy.

Nazism in Germany

The most notorious and thorough-going right-wing totalitarian state was Nazi Germany, which took shape after the rise to power of Adolf Hitler in 1933. Hitler, Austrian by birth and a failed art student, had immigrated to Germany shortly before World War I. He served in the German army, was wounded and decorated, and returned from the front an ardent German nationalist. His skill as an orator won him leadership of the Nazi party, one of the right-wing street-fighting groups that threatened the stability of Weimar Germany. An attempted coup in Munich in 1923 netted him a short jail term, where he used the time to work on the book that turned out to be the master plan for achieving his vision of German world hegemony, *Mein Kampf (My Struggle)*. Plunging back into politics on his release, Hitler soon made the Nazis the largest political party in Germany.

Hitler made use of violent tactics already pioneered by Mussolini in Italy, organizing a uniformed paramilitary force of "Brownshirts" to terrorize his foes. He proved particularly expert at mobilizing support through mass rallies and the new mass media, radio and motion pictures. His passionate nationalism and his violent anticommunism made him a favorite with big business and the lower middle classes, with peasants and students. As the Great Depression paralyzed Germany's coalition government in the early 1930s, the Nazi party won additional seats in the Reichstag elections. Hoping to exploit Hitler's voter appeal for their own ends, a conservative faction persuaded aging President Hindenburg to appoint Hitler chancellor (prime minister) in 1933. The reverse, however, occurred: Hitler and the Nazis swept all opposition aside and became masters of the country.

The new leader moved rapidly to establish his control. He exploited an

Adolf Hitler and Benito Mussolini. The totalitarian rulers of Germany and Italy both enjoyed reviewing the troops. Militarism was a central feature of most of the authoritarian regimes of the interwar period.

attempt by a feebleminded Dutch communist to burn down the German Reichstag (legislature) to strengthen his hand. After calling for a new election, which increased the Nazi plurality in the Reichstag to 44 percent, he outlawed communist, socialist, and other left-wing parties. He also prevailed on other right-wing parties to disband and support the Nazi movement. He even purged the Nazis themselves of rivals and other elements he did not trust by turning his black-uniformed SS elite corps against them. Particular targets of this "blood purge" were the leaders of Hitler's own Brownshirts, whom he may have sacrificed to win the support of Germany's powerful army leaders, who feared the growing influence of this Nazi paramilitary force. Even totalitarian rulers had sometimes to make concessions to groups as powerful as the Roman Catholic church or the German army.

Hitler's power continued to grow. He ruled by an enabling act that gave him legislative decree powers during 1933, and he combined the office of chancellor and the president after Hindenburg died in 1934. Increasingly also, he called for personal commitment to him as Der Führer (The Leader) of the Nazi party and the German nation. With Nazis taking over both central and local government, Hitler rapidly became the absolute ruler of Germany.

As Mussolini did in Italy, Hitler put much of Germany's economy into the hands of big business. To put people back to work, the Führer also embarked on a massive public works program, including the first superhighways, or autobahns. In addition, he began to build a new, mechanized army in defiance of the Versailles Treaty. In return for this economic revival, German business was compelled to surrender its independence and German workers to give up their unions.

Hitler's ideological propaganda campaign to glorify himself, his party, and the German people was even more successful than Mussolini's. The Nazi party, the Hitler Youth, and other organizations channeled the energies of much of the population into party work. Paid vacations, sports shows, and other benefits kept the working masses happy, reminded them of their German roots in the countryside, and encouraged physical fitness for future service. The Nazi party encouraged German women to accept enthusiastically their traditional roles as housewives and mothers, but in the later 1930s the government also asked women to give a year of productive labor to the fatherland. Churches, schools, and other organizations were pressured to accept or teach Nazi doctrines.

Hitler was a passionate racist: Nazi propaganda celebrated the alleged racial superiority of Germany's "Aryan" stock and blamed the evils of capitalism, communism, the Versailles Treaty, modern art, and much else on the Jewish "race."

A feverish atmosphere of rallies and speeches, economic recovery, and increasing international aggressiveness filled the Hitler years. At the same time, Hitler's SS troops and his secret police, the Gestapo, spread a reign of terror among so-called undesirable elements of the population. They arrested, imprisoned, tortured, and executed many thousands of citizens of the "thousand-year reich," as Hitler called his new order. Caught in an accelerating Nazi terror, German Jews were first deprived of jobs, stripped of their civil rights, and forced to mark their persons and buildings with a Star of David. Later in the 1930s, they were attacked by mobs, murdered, sometimes compelled to emigrate, and finally imprisoned in concentration camps. After World War II began, they and millions of other European Jews would be executed as the Nazis attempted to carry out what they called the "final solution"—the extermination of the Jews.

Communism in Russia

In a sense, the oldest of totalitarian states was the Soviet Union, established when V. I. Lenin's Bolshevik revolutionaries—soon renamed Communists—seized power in Russia in 1917. Many historians, however, trace the emergence of genuine totalitarianism in the Soviet Union to the period of the rise of Joseph Stalin (1879–1953) to power in the late 1920s and to his transformation of the nation in the 1930s. For it was only then that the full array of economic centralization, police power, and glorification of the party and its leader took shape in the huge Communist country.

The Soviet Union did not move rapidly to full communism, despite Lenin's great power and dedication to transforming Russia along Marxist lines. Lenin had organized his Bolsheviks as a strongly centralized party, and after his success in 1917 his prestige was so great that his word was unquestioned. In the 1920s, however, Lenin began to back away from his earlier policies of "war communism" and from further imposition of centralized power or communist institutions on Russia. Believing the nation needed time to recover from its ordeal by war, revolution, and civil struggle, he tolerated privately owned peasant farms and small-scale private businesses, and even allowed a certain amount of cultural and intellectual freedom. Equal rights and educational opportunities were granted to women, and they were encouraged to enter the work force by the provision of public child care facilities. The Communists had, however, retained a monopoly of political power and had nationalized the "commanding heights" of the economy, including large-scale manufacturing, foreign trade, and banking. When Lenin died in 1924, then, the Soviet Union was something of a hybrid: an authoritarian state professing Marxist socialism but allowing a good deal of economic and some intellectual freedom.

Joseph Stalin succeeded Lenin as Communist party leader in the later 1920s and moved on to complete the communist revolution in the 1930s. Stalin's rise to power was the result of masterful and ruthless political maneuvering in the inner circles of the party. A skilled bureaucrat, or *apparatchik*, himself, he had the support of the party organization. His rivals, often ideologues and orators who had made larger contributions to the revolution than he had, apparently had much less understanding of the needs and ambitions of a party in power. By 1929, Trotsky and other opponents had been shunted aside and Stalin was being hailed as "the Lenin of today."

As early as 1928, Stalin began the massive socialization of the Russian economy. By putting Marxist policies into practice, he hoped that planning and central control would enable Russia to achieve a goal stated by Peter the Great two centuries earlier: to "catch up with the west" in economic power, in wealth, and technical sophistication. This was especially important to Stalin since Hitler and Mussolini, and many democratic leaders as well, were open enemies of the communist regime. An additional purpose was to strengthen the party's power over the nation and his own power in the party.

The method Stalin adopted was a series of Five-Year Plans to modernize industry, agriculture, and other elements of the economy and to increase production. Stalin believed he could bring about rapid economic growth through detailed central planning, allocating resources, and assigning production quotas to every economic sector, factory, farm, and worker.

The first three Five-Year Plans brought much turmoil and change. The results varied. In industry, the plans led to major gains, particularly in such heavy industrial projects as hydroelectric dams and tractor factories. In agriculture, almost all the small peasant farms were "collectivized"—reorganized as large sovkhozes (state-owned farms) or kolkhozes (farms collectively owned by farm workers). Agricultural production nose-dived under collectivization in

Russian Agricultural Workers in the 1930s. This "production meeting" in the open fields reflects Stalin's efforts to increase agricultural production through collectivization. Though pictures like this impressed outsiders, many Russian peasants bitterly opposed the collectivization campaign.

the early thirties and only slowly recovered. Agriculture, in fact, has remained a weak spot in the Soviet economy.

The overall political and social cost of this economic transformation was great. In Stalin's Russia, as in Hitler's Germany, millions died at the hands of the totalitarian rulers. Stalinist industrial discipline was a heavy burden on unskilled workers, many of them former peasants, who were rigorously punished for absenteeism, damaging the new machinery, or failing to fulfill their quotas. Even harsher was the treatment of the agricultural peasantry. Better-off peasants, called kulaks, were sent off to grim work camps in Siberia or in the Soviet Arctic, where many died at hard labor. Peasants who resisted collectivization or refused to provide their quotas of grain to feed the growing industrial cities were deprived of what grain they had

and left with no food for themselves. The struggle in the countryside, combined with bad weather, produced a series of terrible famines in the early 1930s, again causing many deaths.

The clearest manifestation of Soviet totalitarianism, however, was the appearance of a familiar pattern of police terror. Stalin believed he had enemies, both outside and inside the party, who were plotting against him and sabotaging his economic policies. He therefore sanctioned wave after wave of "purges"—arrests, public or secret trials, imprisonments, condemnations to labor camps, and summary executions. The victims were described as "class enemies"—Bolsheviks who betrayed their faith, German sympathizers, kulaks or industrial saboteurs, Trotskyites or capitalist agents—rather than "racial enemies" like the Jews in Germany. But their fate was essentially the same.

AUTHORITARIAN REGIMES

The totalitarian regimes were not the only antidemocratic governments to appear in western nations between the two world wars. In the 1920s and particularly during the 1930s, other authoritarian rulers rose to power in regions as far apart as eastern Europe, Latin America, and westernized Japan. This section surveys some of these governments, who gave further evidence of the antiliberal contention that the "historic tide" had turned against democracy.

Authoritarianism Elsewhere in Europe

A number of authoritarian governments appeared during the interwar decades, especially in the poor and

El Jefe and "Neodemocracy"

"Direct democracy?" Involuntarily, my mind went back to some experiences in the Dominican Republic a few years ago. There too, the Lider Maximo [Maximum Leader], who preferred being called El Jefe [The Chief], liked to visit his domain, see his subjects personally, and settle problems on the spot. To my dismay, I discovered that there was much to be said for his regime in purely physical terms, that the peasants worshiped him, that he could have won honest elections quite as overwhelmingly as his fixed election.

. . .

I [once] entered into a philosophical discussion with a leading official and asked whether El Jefe's unique system had a name. Gravely and courteously, he answered: "neodemocracy."

At bottom, all these "neo" and "direct" democracies rest on a simple proposition: that the Leader and his people are one and indivisible. Hence they need no representative institutions, no elections, no loyal or disloyal oppositions, no free or partially critical press, none of the rights and safeguards traditionally associated with democracy.*

Latin American "personalist" dictatorship is well illustrated by the rule of General Rafael Trujillo, who came to power in the Dominican Republic in 1930. Such rulers typically combined some economic modernization and a personal appeal to a favored group, such as peasants or urban workers, with immense wealth for themselves and brutal repression of any and all opposition. They also made the claim that Hitler and Mussolini made in Europe—that the Leader embodies in his own person the will of his people.

*Theodore Draper, Castro's Revolution: Myths and Realities (New York: Praeger, 1962). pp. 28–29.

technologically underdeveloped nations of eastern and southern Europe. Although lacking the ideological basis of totalitarian states, they did suppress civil liberties and some of them employed police brutality and terror. These were often nations dominated by traditional institutions like monarchies, established churches, or small, landholding elites. They were also lands frequently beset by the problems associated with early stages of industrialization or by ideologies like nationalism or socialism. In such an atmosphere of conflict between old institutions and new trends and ideas, autocratic government appealed to many people.

In eastern European nations, monarchs or military men often ruled. Kings governed autocratically for part of this period in Yugoslavia, Rumania, Bulgaria, and Greece. The dictatorships of Admiral Nikolaus Horthy in Hungary and of Marshal Joseph Pilsudski in Poland imposed military order, and the Baltic states also became dictatorships. Quasi-totalitarian parties also appeared in this part of Europe, such as the Iron Guard in Rumania or the Fatherland Front in Austria, where Kurt von Schuschnigg ruled in something of the spirit of his powerful German neighbor.

In Iberia, Spain and Portugal, like Italy, came under authoritarian regimes between the wars. Generals Primo de Rivera and Francisco Franco dominated Spanish affairs, the former ruling through the 1920s, Franco fighting his way to power in the bloody Spanish Civil War of the later 1930s. In Portugal, a military ruler, seeking a solution to the politically and economically chaotic conditions, appointed an economics professor named Antonio de Oliveira Salazar as prime minister in the early 1930s. Salazar made himself dictator of Portugal and ruled for the next three decades. In both of these Iberian countries, traditional elements such as the army, the Catholic church, and the landowners supported an authoritarian answer to social disorder and change, although some peasants and many urban workers resisted the imposition of autocracy.

Personalist Dictatorships in Latin America

Dictatorships also predominated in Latin America, particularly in the 1930s. The large majority of Latin American countries had been republics in form for more than a century by 1930, considerably longer than most eastern and southern European nations. But democratic forms had often cloaked autocratic realities in these states. As in Iberia, authoritarian power in Latin America had traditionally been based on the landlords, church, and armed forces, who dominated a backward and poverty-stricken peasant population. Since the later nineteenth century, however, urban export businessmen and their foreign customers, often British or American, had also demanded order in the interests of commercial devel-

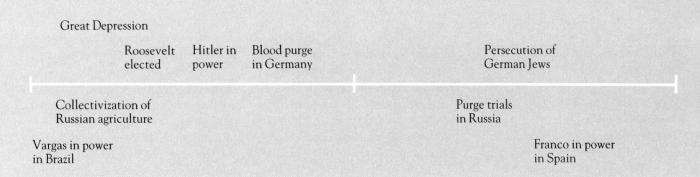

Great Depression

Roosevelt elected   Hitler in power   Blood purge in Germany   Persecution of German Jews

Collectivization of Russian agriculture   Purge trials in Russia

Vargas in power in Brazil   Franco in power in Spain

opment. Whether it was to preserve the traditional order or to encourage commercial growth, military rulers frequently provided the autocratic government required.

In the 1930s, "personalist" dictators flourished, especially in the larger and more developed Latin American nations. These rulers were sometimes popular with urban workers as well as with business leaders. This they managed by combining some welfare for the working classes with law and order and protective tariffs for business interests. Examples of such regimes include the Concordancia government in Argentina and the Vargas dictatorship in Brazil. Argentina's Concordancia was an alliance of military men, nationalists, and conservatives who seized control in 1930 and governed through the decade. They ruled by fixing elections and ruthlessly crushing politicians who opposed them. They also, however, helped Argentine industry to move out of small workshops and into sizable factories, a substantial economic advance. Brazil's Getúlio Vargas seized power in 1930 and dominated the politics of his country for the next quarter of a century. Vargas made opposition parties illegal, often ruled by decree, and sometimes mobilized the army to impose his will. At the same

time, he strengthened Brazilian industry and provided guaranteed employment, wages, and pensions for the urban working classes.

In Mexico, a unique balance between authoritarianism and the public welfare was achieved during the years between 1910 and 1940. The revolution that broke out in 1910 was long, confused, and bloody. The nation's dictator, Profirio Díaz, fled the country at the beginning of the struggle, leaving the field open to many rival factions and charismatic leaders. The exploits of rebels like Pancho Villa and Emiliano Zapata became legend in Mexico, but they did little to improve the lot of the population.

In 1917, however, an extremely liberal new constitution was promulgated for the nation. This document established democratic political institutions and gave government power to confiscate large estates, nationalize natural resources, set minimum wages and maximum hours of work, and otherwise regulate society. The new constitution also enabled the government to deprive the Catholic church in Mexico of much of its wealth, power, and influence over the masses.

A single party had emerged victorious in the revolution. This Party of the Mexican Revolution—later named the Party of the Revolutionary

Institutions (PRI)—still dominates Mexico's political life. The PRI tolerated no political opposition and selected each new president in private party conclaves before elections were even held. The party itself, however, included representatives of all the nation's major groups, peasants and workers as well as businessmen, the military, and other special interests. In general, mestizos replaced descendants of Europeans as the rulers of Mexico.

In accordance with the new constitution, furthermore, the PRI carried out many popular social reforms. These included the redistribution of large estates to small farmers, the nationalization of foreign-owned oil wells, and a general improvement in the condition of the country's Indian and mestizo population. President Lázaro Cárdenas in the 1930s enacted programs somewhat similar to those of the New Deal north of the border. But the southern nation remained impoverished despite these efforts at social change.

Militarism in Japan

Partially westernized Japan also became an authoritarian state in the 1930s, as it turned from civilian and business-oriented governments to

767

domination by a militantly nationalistic military officer caste. In the 1920s, business leaders and politicians had combined to expand Japan's markets overseas. Little of this new wealth, however, reached the peasantry outside the westernized cities. When the depression came in the 1930s, imposing still more hardship, many Japanese were willing to follow the lead of the military once more. These militarists charged liberal politicians and big business leaders with corruption and with abandoning Japan's ancient traditions in favor of immoral western ways. As fervid nationalists, they urged foreign conquests as Japan's national destiny. At home, secret societies of military officers attacked civilian politicians as Fascists and Nazis had in Europe— with assassinations and attempted coups. Abroad, they soon had the country embroiled in another long war with her huge but less-developed neighbor, China.

The Japanese militarists did not formally seize control, but military leaders and their allies predominated in a government over which young Emperor Hirohito presided. As the 1930s drew to a close, Japan signed agreements with totalitarian Germany and Italy, pointed at the Soviet Union and the United States. The resulting Axis alliance soon faced the western democracies in open battle.

SUMMARY

A central theme of western history between the world wars was the weakness of the western democracies and the rise of aggressive totalitarian states to challenge them. This drift toward military confrontation was particularly clear in the 1930s.

The Russian Revolution of 1917 cast a long shadow over the two interwar decades. Lenin and his Bolsheviks seized power relatively easily in a war-shattered nation, then clung to supremacy through the civil war that followed. Attempts to stimulate and encourage revolutions elsewhere, however, had no success. These attempts actually proved counterproductive, strengthening the hands of anticommunist totalitarians of the right during the 1920s and 1930s.

The 1920s were characterized by a fragile economic prosperity and increasing political freedom for the west. But western nations had deep-seated difficulties, including political instability, inflation, and some chronically depressed sectors of the economy. Also, many people were deeply disillusioned over the recent war, the society that had made it, and the Versailles peace that had ended it. The coming of the Great Depression in the thirties, which had its roots in the economic problems of the twenties, further weakened the major European democracies, Great Britain and France. In the United States, the economic downturn produced a strong leader in Franklin Roosevelt, whose New Deal legislation provided the foundations of the American welfare state.

During this period, totalitarian and other authoritarian regimes came to power in many western countries. The chief totalitarian states were Fascist Italy, Nazi Germany, and the Soviet Union under the Communists. In all of these nations, dictatorial government combined with one-party rule and ideological commitment to create brutal regimes that imprisoned or slaughtered millions of their fellow citizens. Less rigorous and bloody were the authoritarian governments of eastern and southern Europe and Latin America and the militarists who came to monopolize power in Japan.

SELECTED SOURCES

*Banner, Lois. *Women in Modern America.* 1974. "Woman's place" in the twentieth-century United States; brief and readable.

*Bullock, Allen. *Hitler: A Study in Tyranny.* 1971. Good account of the Hitler years as well as of the man.

*Burns, J. M. *Roosevelt: The Lion and the Fox.* 1970. A positive interpretation of Franklin Roosevelt's contribution.

Cabaret. 1972. A musical comedy and film that brilliantly highlights the moral disarray of the interwar years and the fanatical appeal of Nazism.

*Galbraith, J. K. *The Great Crash*. 1929. An account of the Wall Street stock market panic by a well-known economist.

*Koestler, Arthur. *Darkness at Noon*. 1941. Fictional attempt to explain Stalinist totalitarianism as it looked to an old Bolshevik in a Russian prison.

Maier, C. S. *Recasting Bourgeois Europe*. 1975. Comparative study of post-World War I recovery in France, Germany, and Italy.

Moorehead, Alan. *The Russian Revolution*. 1958. Extremely readable account of the events of 1917.

Triumph of the Will. 1936. Leni Riefenstahl's striking film of a Nazi rally.

*Ulam, A. B. *Stalin: The Man and His Era*. 1973. Scholarly and convincing treatment of the Russian leader.

*Available in paperback.

769

THE WORLD AGAIN AT WAR

For the first time, I could understand what my friends had meant when they said Hiroshima was destroyed. Nothing remained except a few buildings of reinforced concrete, . . . For acres and acres the city was like a desert except for scattered piles of brick and roof tile. I had to revise my meaning of the word destruction. . . . Devastation may be a better word. . . .

Towards evening, a light southerly wind blowing across the city wafted to us an odor suggestive of burning sardines. . . . sanitation teams were cremating the remains of people who had been killed. Looking out, I could discern numerous fires scattered about the city. . . . Towards Nigitsu was an especially large fire where the dead were being burned by hundreds. To suddenly realize that these fires were funeral pyres made me shudder, and I became a little nauseated.

Concrete buildings near the center of the city, still afire on the inside, made eerie silhouettes against the night sky. These glowing ruins and the blazing funeral pyres set me to wondering if Pompeii had not looked like this during its last days. But I think there were not so many dead in Pompeii as there were in Hiroshima.

Two days after the atomic bomb had fallen, Dr. Hachiya, like most of the rest of the world, did not yet understand the moment of historic magnitude entailed in the death of his city. The two bombs that ended the second world war of the twentieth century suggested that the next unlimited war could be the last event men and women would know.

No one had any idea when the trail of events leading to Hiroshima and Nagasaki began in the 1930s, that humanity would place itself in such a predicament. Hitler and Mussolini had committed a series of aggressive acts without having to fight, until the invasion of Poland finally brought on a general European war that no European nation really wanted. Japan's expansion in Asia, opposed by the United States, culminated in a surprise attack that had brought the war to Asia and the Pacific.

World War II, once begun, was waged with new weapons of such destructive magnitude, accompanied by episodes of such genocidal ferocity, that it became the most devastating occurrence in history. After the war, the hatred and suspicions the conflict engendered lay in uneasy juxtaposition with the technological power to destroy the Earth.

The Victorious Leaders. This photograph depicts the meeting of Winston Churchill, Franklin Roosevelt, and Joseph Stalin at Yalta in the Soviet Union, February 5–11, 1945. With Germany almost defeated, the three men and their aides spent most of their time discussing post-war concerns. There is still controversy over the effectiveness of the dying Roosevelt in maintaining U.S. interests. Imperial War Museum, London.

AGGRESSION IN THE 1930s

Looking back, it is easy to see the international events of the 1930s, an interplay of aggression and appeasement, as a slow buildup to World War II. To understand this pattern, it is important to examine these events against the background of the preceding fifteen years.

Satisfied and Unsatisfied Nations

World War I, coming after almost a century without any long wars in Europe, surprised and horrified Europeans. As a consequence, western leaders spent much of the following decade, 1918–1928, trying to ensure that such an international conflict would not happen again. The League of Nations, ratified as part of the Versailles Peace Treaty in 1919, was a sincere attempt to establish an international organization in which the powers could talk out their differences rather than fight over them.

Nations also completed other agreements designed to guarantee peace. In the area of disarmament, agreements signed at the Washington Naval Conference in 1921–1922 required the major naval powers to limit the total tonnage of their warships. The Locarno Treaties of 1925 resolved some ticklish international disputes, particularly between France and Germany. Finally, the Kellogg-Briand Pact of 1928, originated by the United States and France, and signed by more than sixty other countries, renounced the use of war "as an instrument of national policy."

The fact was, however, that these efforts to guarantee peace concealed basic disagreements that could lead to war. Many of them grew out of World War I itself, which had left some nations—particularly Great Britain, France, and the United States—basically satisfied with the outcome, but others bitterly unsatisfied. Germany, as an obvious example, strongly resented the "war guilt" clause, the heavy reparations imposed on it, its loss of colonies and territory, and the clauses forbidding it to have a significant military establishment. Italy, one of the victors, thought it had not gotten a large enough share of territory, especially in the nearby Balkans. Japan, which had also fought on the Allied side, believed its legitimate aspirations to power in China had been ignored in the peace treaty. The new Soviet Union, shunned because of its withdrawal from the war and its postwar talk of exporting communist revolution, sought international respect and feared the hostility of the capitalist nations.

In the 1930s these dissatisfied powers began to show their discontent in aggressive expansion. The satisfied nations, having nothing to gain from war, tried to maintain the peace at all costs. This, they found, could only be done by making repeated concessions to the other, increasingly aggressive, states. The result was the pattern of totalitarian aggression and democratic appeasement that marked the history of the thirties in international affairs.

Aggression on the Fringes of the West

The aggression by totalitarian and authoritarian forces began in areas of the world that were relatively unimportant to the west. These areas included Asia, where Japan attacked China early in the 1930s; Africa, where Italy invaded Ethiopia in the middle of the decade; and Spain, where authoritarian rebels fought a successful civil war against the liberal government in the later 1930s.

During the 1920s, the Japanese had increased their economic exploitation of both Korea and the neighboring northern Chinese area of Manchuria. This in turn brought Japan into conflict with General Chiang Kai-shek, leader of the Chinese Nationalist party, who had just seized power in China and was determined to resist Japanese penetration. Chiang's counterpressure then triggered a series of open aggressions by the Japanese military, the first authoritarian aggression of the decade.

The Japanese military acted in China without consulting Japan's elected civilian government, and indeed in opposition to the policies of that government. In 1931, Japanese officers occupied Manchuria and established a puppet government. The government in Tokyo resigned in disgrace, and the League of Nations issued a report condemning the action, but the Japanese remained masters of Manchuria.

In subsequent years, Japan expanded this control into other northern Chinese provinces. Then, in 1937, after another "incident" at the Marco Polo Bridge near Peking, the Japanese army invaded China proper. Over the next two years, Japan's modern fighting force easily overran the coastal regions of China, while Chiang Kai-shek's government retreated into the interior. Eastern China as a whole was ravaged by the Japanese invaders and by the Chinese themselves, who applied a "scorched earth" policy as they withdrew. Again, the world did nothing.

Mussolini's Fascist government preached a strident nationalism, including stirring reminders of the greatness of the ancient Roman Empire, which had once ringed the Mediterranean. In 1935, he launched an open invasion of Ethiopia, the only truly independent nation left in Africa. Ethiopia's emperor Haile Selassie made a moving appeal before the League of Nations on behalf of his country, but only a cutoff of petroleum sales to Italy could have stopped its modern war machine, and depression-ridden democracies such as Great Britain and France were unwilling to take this step. In 1936, after a brief and one-sided struggle, Italy's King Victor Emanuel was declared Emperor of Ethiopia.

The Spanish Civil War broke out in 1936 and ended in 1939, on the very eve of World War II. The Spanish conflict seemed to many western liberals a last chance to stop the aggressions of authoritarian and totalitarian regimes. Spain herself was a poor nation, traditionally conservative. In 1931, however, after a decade of military rule, liberal leaders managed to win power in Madrid. Over the next five years, supported by city workers, some peasants, socialists, and other ideologues, the government attempted a series of social, political, and economic reforms. In 1936, General Francisco Franco, representing much of the ousted power structure, including the Catholic church and the army, launched a revolution against the republican government. Liberals and totalitarian forces all over Europe took sides.

The governments of the democratic powers announced a hands-off policy in the civil war. Liberals, socialists, and others from a number of western countries formed brigades of volunteers to fight on the side of the republic, and the Soviet Union sent military advisers and aid. Much more help poured in for Franco, however; Mussolini sent tens of thousands of troops, while Hitler dispatched air support. The Condor Legion "terror bombed" Guernica and other towns with the intent of causing heavy civilian casualties, an ominous portent for future wars. By 1939, Franco had won, and the superior strength of totalitarianism in western civilization appeared to be established.

Nazi Aggression in Central Europe

While struggles on the fringes were still in progress, Adolf Hitler was on the march in the heart of Europe (see Map 81). After his rise to power in 1933, Hitler moved rapidly to restore Germany's strength and self-confidence. He began to rebuild Germany's armed forces in defiance of the provisions of the Treaty of Versailles. He announced a vigorous foreign policy, including a nationalistic insistence that the territories of German-speaking peoples of central Europe should be incorporated into his Third Reich (state), also called the Thousand-Year Reich. He also demanded "living space" for Germans, particularly in Slavic areas of eastern Europe, the traditional direction of German expansion since the medieval period.

Between 1936 and 1939, Hitler implemented his policies. His first move was to send the revived German army into the Rhineland in 1936.

This region had been established as a demilitarized buffer zone between Germany and France by the Versailles Treaty, but Hitler determined to reassert Germany's right to fortify its border regions. German military leaders worried that the French would send in troops to enforce the treaty, but Hitler guessed correctly that they would not. The German troops marched in unopposed, and the German high command did not challenge Hitler's judgment again.

Early in 1938, Hitler again violated the Versailles settlement by incorporating the German-speaking nation of Austria into his new empire. Austrian Nazis and many other Austrians supported this century-old notion of greater German unity, but Hitler depended primarily on bullying Austria's leaders and, once again, on sending in the troops. This second bloodless aggression substantially increased the size and population of the Thousand-Year Reich.

The most disturbing act of aggression and appeasement of the 1930s was Hitler's dismemberment of Czechoslovakia and the notorious Munich agreement of 1938. Within months of the absorption of Austria, Hitler turned his attention to the German-speaking minority in Czechoslovakia, which like Austria bordered on Germany. The German leader demanded the right to annex the Czech Sudetenland, where 3 million ethnic Germans lived. France and Russia had treaties requiring them to help the Czechs in the event of war, and Great Britain was also concerned. British Prime Minister Neville Chamberlain and other western leaders met with Hitler at Munich in September 1938, seeking a solution to the crisis; neither the Soviet Union

773

MAP 81

Central Europe, April 1939. This map depicts Germany after three years of consolidation and aggression under the leadership of Adolf Hitler. Italy, Poland, and Hungary also expanded. Although Hitler had to this point enlarged Germany without war, Great Britain and France had awakened to the futility of appeasement. Hitler's next aggressive move, directed against Poland, would meet with resistance and bring on World War II.

nor Czechoslovakia was invited. The solution they found, however, was yet another act of appeasement: They agreed that Hitler might annex the Sudetenland in return for guarantees of the freedom of the rest of Czechoslovakia. On his return from Munich, Chamberlain said that he had achieved "peace for our time." By March of the following year, Hitler and the authoritarian rulers of Poland

and Hungary had divided Czechoslovakia up entirely among them. One month later, Mussolini annexed tiny Albania, gaining some of the eastern Adriatic coast that had been denied Italy at the Versailles Peace Conference. The futility of appeasement was fast becoming apparent.

Hitler soon turned from Austria and Czechoslovakia to Poland. He took the port of Memel from Lithuania and

demanded the valuable German-speaking port city of Danzig, along with other concessions. British and French leaders, at last convinced that the German dictator was not to be trusted, announced that they would fight to defend the integrity of Poland. Hitler understandably doubted their resolve.

The Nazi leader, meanwhile, had been concluding a series of alliances with other totalitarian states. Agreements in 1936 and 1937 created the so-called Rome-Berlin-Tokyo Axis, publicly described as an alliance to restrain the further expansion of communism. In 1939, however, Hitler made his most startling diplomatic move—a nonaggression treaty with his communist archenemy, the Soviet Union. The Hitler-Stalin Pact of August 1939, declared that neither nation would attack the other and each would remain neutral if the other were menaced by a third party. This arrangement protected Hitler from a two-front war if the British and French should finally take up arms against Germany. A secret protocol also divided up all of eastern Europe into spheres of German and Russian influence, dividing Poland between the two spheres.

A week after the two most powerful totalitarian rulers signed this agreement, on September 1, 1939, Germany invaded Poland. Within days, Great Britain and France, abandoning appeasement at last, declared war on Germany. World War II had begun.

THE OPENING OF WORLD WAR II

World War II as it evolved became a truly global conflict compared with the Europe-centered struggle in World War I. The World War II combat-

The Nadir of Appeasement. At Munich, Germany, September 29–30, 1938 Neville Chamberlin (left) and Edouard Daladier (center left), hoping to avoid war in Europe, agreed to abandon France's ally Czechoslovakia. They gave Hitler (center), supported by Mussolini (center right), a free hand to absorb the Sudetenland, but he went on to seize the rest of Czechoslovakia, and in less than a year Europe was at war. For the remainder of the century, the term "Munich" has symbolized the futility of appeasing aggressors.

World War II in Europe and North Africa. In the first phase of the war, 1939–1942, Germany and Italy and their allies subjected most of Europe to their control, but failed to defeat Great Britain and the Soviet Union. In the second stage of the war, 1942–1945, powerful U.S. forces arrived in the west, and with the aid of the British, cleared the Mediterranean, then landed in France and pushed eastward into Germany. Meanwhile, the newly reconstituted, massive Soviet army drove westward through the Balkans, meeting the western allies in the center of Germany.

ants fought extensively on land in Europe, Africa, Asia, and the Pacific and conducted naval operations around the globe. In the course of the struggle, the new technology of destruction killed directly and indirectly more people than any war in history. Millions of civilians were killed, blurring the distinction between the home front and the battle front. When it was over, much of Europe and Asia had been destroyed.

Axis Advance in Europe

In Poland, the Germans demonstrated with spectacular success their new blitzkrieg (lightning warfare) tactics, combining tanks and air-

planes with infantry and artillery. German panzer (tank) columns, in conjunction with dive bombers and fighter aircraft, broke through the Polish lines. Pressing far into the rear, they disrupted Polish reinforcements and supplies, leaving isolated Polish units to be disposed of by the German infantry. At the same time, the German Luftwaffe (air force) terror bombed Warsaw and other cities, demoralizing the civilians. The campaign ended in three weeks. Meanwhile, the Soviet Union seized the eastern half of Poland (see Map 82).

Hitler now turned to his opponents in the west, which had been unable to help Poland. He offered peace if Great Britain and France

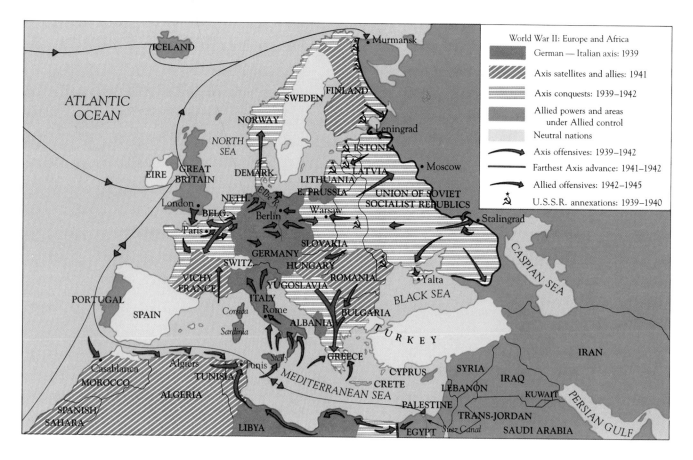

Blitzkrieg. German tanks race through open country to the English Channel in May 1940 after breaking through the French lines at Sedan. Panzer units such as these went on to cut off the British army, eventually forcing its evacuation to Great Britain. The tanks seen here are small and primitive compared to those developed later in the war, but the new technology and tactics they represented were devastating, particularly during the early part of the war.

would recognize his conquest of Poland; when they refused, he made plans to defeat them in 1940. Great Britain repeated its World War I performance, clearing German surface vessels from the oceans, setting up a blockade, and sending a small army to assist France. The French did not attack Germany as they had in World War I, but instead waited behind the supposedly impregnable Maginot line. In April 1940, in a prelude to the main assault on the west, the Germans occupied Denmark without resistance and conquered Norway in two weeks, gaining the Norwegian coast for air and submarine bases to attack British shipping.

In May, the Germans began their onslaught. They quickly conquered the Dutch and Belgians, whom they demoralized by terror bombing, and with blitzkrieg tactics smashed through French lines at Sedan. The panzers raced to the English Channel, cutting off the British army and some French troops from the main body of the French army. The British government evacuated most of the troops at Dunkirk, but had to abandon their supplies and heavy equipment. Faced with disaster, the new prime minister, Winston Churchill, called on the British people to rally. "We shall fight on the beaches, we shall fight on the landing grounds, we shall fight in the fields and in the streets, we shall fight in the hills; we shall never surrender." Meanwhile, the Germans drove across France, bypassing the Maginot line. With the French about to be defeated, Italy attacked France, an action Roosevelt called "a stab in the back."

On June 22, France surrendered and Hitler was master of continental western Europe. In the same railroad car on the same spot where the Allies had imposed armistice terms on the Germans in 1918, Hitler now dictated severe terms to the French. The Germans annexed Alsace-Lorraine and occupied northern and western France. They built bases on the coastline from which they could attack British shipping and launch an invasion of Great Britain. Unoccupied France, with its capital at Vichy, and most of the French colonial empire became allied to Germany. Not all the French capitulated, however; General Charles de Gaulle formed a government in exile and supported by small contingents from a few colonies that renounced Vichy authority, fought on at the side of the British.

With France defeated, Hitler turned his attention to the surviving enemy, Great Britain. He planned to use the Luftwaffe to destroy the British Royal Air Force (RAF), after which he could destroy the unprotected British fleet from the air. With the British fleet withdrawn or sunk, the superior German army would then be able to cross the Channel to conquer the British Isles. Through the latter half of 1940, in what came to be called the Battle of Britain, the RAF fought off the Germans. Frustrated, Hitler ordered the terror bombing of British cities, hoping to make the British population sue for peace, but this failed also. By the winter of 1940–1941, Hitler left the British to be slowly strangled by his submarine blockade. It was clear that even if Great Britain survived the blockade, it could not stop Hitler on the continent.

Axis-Soviet Confrontation in the East

While Hitler was overrunning western Europe, the Soviet Union hastened to create a buffer zone in anticipation of German attack. After occupying eastern Poland, in 1940 the Russians annexed Estonia, Latvia, Lithuania, and a Rumanian border province, all without a fight. A war with the Finns added some border sections of Finland and a site for a naval base. These Soviet advances drove most of the authoritarian governments in eastern Europe into alliance with Hitler.

In 1941, Hitler was ready to act on his vision of destroying the Soviet Union and turning eastern Europe into an area where Germanic families would be set up as a ruling class on lands worked by Slavic serfs. Mindful of Napoleon's disaster, he planned to attack in mid-May as soon as the Soviet Union's dirt roads had dried out from the winter thaw and to complete the conquest before cold weather arrived in October. To supplement German forces, he enlisted contingents from Italy, Hungary, and Rumania, while Finland fought a separate war against the Soviet Union.

Hitler had to delay his attack on the Soviet Union because of a series of disasters to the Italians, who were fast becoming a burden. Mussolini was losing his African possessions to the British, and the Italian fleet had been sunk. The Greeks had repelled an Italian invasion and were pushing into Albania, and Yugoslavia was about to join the British and Greeks. In April 1941, Hitler acted decisively. German forces and their Balkan allies quickly overran Yugoslavia and Greece. German panzer units under General Erwin Rommel arrived in Africa to bolster the Italians and to advance on the Suez Canal. The British government rushed Indian and ANZAC (Australian and New Zealand) troops to reinforce British forces in Egypt, the combined forces holding off Rommel. British forces went into the Middle East to control the petroleum fields; with the Russians, they took over de facto control of Iran.

Although the Balkan campaign had been successful, the time needed to accomplish it delayed Hitler's eastern attack until June 22, contributing greatly to his failure to defeat the Soviet Union in 1941. At first it appeared the Germans would win early and easily. German blitzkrieg tactics were again spectacularly successful: The Soviet air force was wiped out and entire Soviet armies were broken up and surrounded, with 4 million prisoners taken. However, the distances to be traversed and the amount of territory to be held were enormous, and by September the German offensive began to sag in the face of transportation and supply problems and the casualties caused by stiffening Soviet resistance. In December, Hitler had to halt for the winter still short of Leningrad and Moscow.

As Hitler's power grew, the leaders of the United States and eventually the public at large became increasingly concerned that unless halted, Nazism would conquer Europe and then cross the Atlantic. By 1940, the Roosevelt administration had successfully convinced a reluctant Congress and public that the nation needed to augment its economic and military strength. The armed forces were rapidly built up, undergirded by the nation's first peacetime conscription act. Meanwhile, U.S. industry boomed with war production, finally bringing the U.S. economy the rest of the way out of the Great Depression. In 1941 Congress enacted a multibillion dollar Lend-Lease program of military equipment for Great Britain and the Soviet Union. Merchant ships were armed, U.S. forces occupied Greenland and Iceland, and the navy began to escort convoys to British naval units waiting in the middle of the Atlantic. By the autumn of 1941, U.S. destroyers were in combat with German submarines, and the United States was rapidly approaching war with Germany.

Hell: Hitler's "New Order"

By the autumn of 1941, Hitler, as the master of Europe, was in a position to carry out his demonic vision of a "New Order" in Europe. He incorporated parts of Poland, Czechoslovakia, Yugoslavia, and France into the so-called Greater German Nation, which he envisioned as the homeland of the superior Aryans, the master race. He stripped the conquered areas of industry, raw materials, and food, causing widespread hunger, and ordered Germany's allies to supply products on terms favorable to Germany. He directed the authorities in the occupied areas and the allied states to deport "undesirables," eventually numbering 9 million, to Germany to be used as slave labor to replace German workers in military service.

1931	1933	1936	1938	1940

Japan annexes Manchuria

Hitler annexes the Rhineland

Japan attacks China

Germany annexes Austria and the Sudetenland

Germany invades Poland

Hitler comes to power

Italy conquers Ethiopia

Spanish Civil War

As a focal point of the New Order, Hitler intended to exterminate the Jews and Gypsies of Europe. In the east, special execution teams rounded up and shot them, along with resistance fighters and Communist party members; a major massacre of Jews took place at Babi Yar in the Ukraine.

After 1941, nearly every area under Hitler's control sent their Jews to special extermination camps where men, women, and children were systematically gassed. Approximately 6 million Jews, about 75 percent of the European Jewish population, were put to death. Eight million in the slave labor camps perished from overwork, malnutrition, disease, and abuse. Many other Europeans outside the death and labor camps died or were disabled from the same causes.

Confrontation Between Japan and the United States

While Germany was conquering Europe, Japan also continued to expand (see Map 83). By 1940, Japanese forces had secured eastern China's coal and iron ore supplies, as well as its seaports and major industrial centers. Although

the war with Chiang Kai-shek still dragged on, the Japanese also planned to push southward to secure a supply of the vital resources of southeast Asia, held mostly by western powers weakened or defeated by Japan's ally Germany.

During 1940 and 1941, the Japanese rapidly penetrated southeast Asia. Japan forced the British to close the Burma Road to China and pressured the Vichy government to allow Japanese occupation of northern Indochina, cutting off the supply routes to China. Japan signed the Tripartite Pact with Germany and Italy, each agreeing to aid the other if any one of them was attacked. Their hand thus strengthened, the Japanese moved into southern Indochina in 1941 and appeared to be ready to attack the western colonies in southeast Asia.

As the Japanese moved south, the United States rapidly emerged as their major opponent. Fearing a loss of its trade in a Japanese-dominated Asia and opposed to aggression in general, the United States demanded that the Japanese withdraw from China and from southeast Asia. The United States placed an embargo on aviation fuel and scrap metal for Japan, although general trade continued, and in 1941 froze Japanese assets. Faced

with the failure of negotiations, the military-dominated cabinet of General Hideki Tojo ordered a simultaneous surprise attack on the British, Dutch, and U.S. possessions in Southeast Asia and the Pacific. On December 7–8, 1941, highlighted by a surprise attack on the U.S. Pacific Fleet at Pearl Harbor, the Japanese struck all across southeast Asia. The United States declared war on Japan on December 8; honoring the Tripartite Pact, Germany and Italy declared war on the United States on December 11. World War II had now spread from Europe and Africa to the Pacific and Asia.

The war aims of Japan combined the short-term offensive with the long-term defensive. Japan planned to seize southeast Asia and the western Pacific and complete the conquest of China; taking India and Australia were additional options, depending on circumstance. The Japanese would then dig in to hold their conquests, and eventually the west would have to agree to Japan's control of Asia and the western Pacific. During the six months following December 7, the Japanese carried out much of their program, destroying western military forces throughout southeast Asia and the western Pacific. By May 1942,

779

HOLOCAUST IN THE UKRAINE

[Public notice in Kiev:] All Yids living in the city of Kiev and its vicinity are to report by 8 o'clock on the morning of Monday, September 29th, 1941, at the corner of Melnikovsky and Dokhturov Streets (near the cemetery). They are to take with them documents, money, valuables, as well as warm clothes, underwear, etc.

Any Yid not carrying out this instruction and who is found elsewhere will be shot. . . .

They started arriving while it was still dark, to be in good time to get seats in the train. With their howling children, their old and sick, some of them weeping, others swearing at each other, the Jews who lived and worked on the vegetable farm emerged on to the street. There were bundles roughly tied together with string, worn out cases made from plywood, woven baskets, boxes of carpenters' tools. . . . Some elderly women were wearing strings of onions hung around their necks like gigantic necklaces—food supplies for the journey. . . .

Then the people in charge started giving orders and shouting, making those who were sitting down stand up and moving them on, pushing the ones in the rear forward, so that some sort of straggling queue was formed. Some of the people's belongings were put down in one place, others in another; there was much pushing and shoving. . . .

At that moment they entered a long corridor formed by two rows of soldiers and dogs. It was very narrow—some four or five feet across. The soldiers were lined up shoulder to shoulder, with their sleeves rolled up, each of them brandishing a rubber club or big stick.

Blows rained down on the people as they passed through.

There was no question of being able to dodge or get away.

Brutal blows, immediately drawing blood, descended on their heads, backs and shoulders from left and right. The soldiers kept shouting: "Schnell, schnell!" laughing happily, as if they were watching a circus act; they even found ways of delivering harder blows in the more vulnerable places, the ribs, the stomach and the groin. . . .

The poor people, now quite out of their minds, tumbled out into a space cordoned off by troops, a sort of square overgrown with grass. The whole of this grass plot was scattered with articles of underwear, footwear and other clothes.

The Ukranian police . . . were grabbing hold of people roughly, hitting them and shouting:

"Get your clothes off! Quickly! Schnell!"

Those who hesitated had their clothes ripped off them by force, and were kicked and struck with knuckledusters or clubs by the Germans, who seemed to be drunk with fury in a sort of sadistic rage. . . .

[Back in Kiev] . . . A fourteen-year-old boy, the son of the collective-farm stableman, . . . [ran] into the farmyard and was telling the most frightful stories: that they were being made to take all their clothes off; that several of them would be lined up [in a quarry], one behind the other, so as to kill more than one at a time; that the bodies were then piled up and earth thrown over them, and then more bodies were laid on top; that there were many who were not really dead, so that you could see the earth moving, that some had managed to crawl out, only to be knocked over the head and thrown back into the pile. . . .

They packed the hospital patients into the gas-chambers in groups of sixty to seventy, then ran the engines for some fifteen minutes so that the exhaust gases went into the vans. Then the suffocated people were taken out and dropped into a pit. This work went on for several days, quietly and methodically. The Germans were not in a hurry, and took regular hour-long breaks for meals.

The patients in the hospital were not all mad; there were many who were simply being treated for nervous disorders. But they were all buried in the pits of Babi Yar. Most remarkable of all was that after the first horrible days of Babi Yar the destruction of all the patients in an enormous hospital went practically unnoticed and was even taken as a matter of course.[*]

[*]A. Anatoli (Kuznetsov), *Babi Yar*, trans. David Floyd (New York: Farrar, Straus, and Giroux, 1970), pp. 91, 93, 97, 105, 106, 153.

Japan controlled a vast land and water domain far larger than the area conquered by the Germans.

In the process of conquest, the Japanese dealt, as it would turn out, a heavy blow to western colonialism in Asia. Many Asians in the conquered areas greatly respected the Japanese for driving out the western imperialists and rallied around the Japanese slogan of "Asia for the Asians." Like Germany's New Order, however, Japan's administration of the conquered areas, which it called the Greater East Asia Co-Prosperity Sphere, became so brutal that most Asians came to hate the Japanese, hope for their overthrow, and plan for independence.

THE BACKGROUND TO ALLIED VICTORY

By 1942 World War II was essentially two separated, simultaneous conflicts: a European war and an Asian-Pacific war. The Axis powers, although formally allied, could not easily coordinate their military efforts. Nonetheless, Axis forces were apparently winning both wars in early 1942; Great Britain and the Soviet Union were barely hanging on against Germany, and the Chinese along with Commonwealth forces in India and Australia were struggling to hold off Japan. The United States was safe behind its protective oceans, but was

MAP 83

World War II in Asia and the Pacific. War came to this area in stages, beginning with Japan's invasion of China in 1937. Leaving the Chinese still fighting, Japan in December 1941 attacked the possessions of Great Britain, the Netherlands, and the United States. By May, 1942, the Japanese were in control of Southeast Asia and the western Pacific, threatening Australia and India. The United States defeated Japan by destroying the Japanese fleet, and after "island hopping" to within range, bombing the Japanese homeland until Japan surrendered. At the time of surrender, Japanese land forces were still in possession of large areas of Asia and the Pacific.

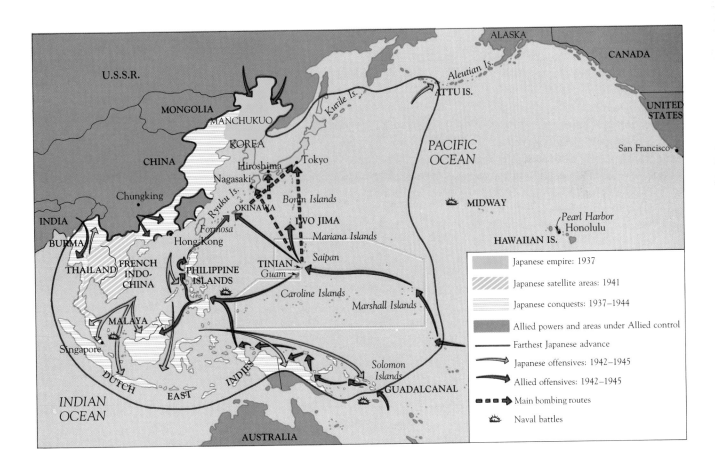

781

far removed from the areas where the war would have to be fought.

In this situation, several important factors would have to fall into place if the Allied nations were to defeat the Axis. The Allies would have to create an effective strategy, backed by a massive U.S. military buildup. The Allies also needed to take advantage of their superior military intelligence and naval technology to clear the oceans; U.S. land forces could then be brought to within striking distance of Germany and Japan. The Axis nations also needed to be greatly weakened by air bombardment. Only then would the new landing craft, which could land men and heavy equipment rapidly on a defended shore, make it possible for the western allies to land sufficient forces in the enemy heartland to join with Soviet forces in destroying the Axis.

The Alliance Against the Axis

The Allies realized that they had to forge a worldwide alliance and come to an agreement on strategic priorities if the Axis were to be beaten. From 1942 to 1945, Roosevelt, Churchill, and on some occasions Stalin met at conferences around the world to coordinate the struggle. Overcoming many differences, they agreed to fight together until all the Axis powers surrendered unconditionally, and Stalin pledged to enter the war against Japan after Germany was defeated. They decided to concentrate on defeating Germany first, since it represented the greater threat to all. However, as this decision evolved, the British and the Russians, looking at both military considerations and Europe's postwar future, argued intensely over how and when to attack Hitler; the Americans and the British also had major differences. A strategy finally developed

The Home Front. World War II produced the greatest outpouring of war material up to that time. As in World War I, women were called upon to replace men absent in the service, particularly in the armaments industry. After the war, however, most women returned to traditional domestic roles.

The War at Sea. This scene of the U.S. Pacific fleet dramatically depicts the transformation of naval technology since World War I. The string of aircraft carriers loaded with planes was the heart of the flotilla, and victories over the Japanese fleet were achieved through airpower. The U.S. navy, in conjunction with the land forces, set the stage for the final defeat of Japan through long range bombardment.

as the war progressed: The western Allies would first clear the Mediterranean and defeat Italy and then land in France and attack Germany from the west. Meanwhile, the Soviet Union would drive against Germany from the east.

"The Great Arsenal of Democracy"

The enormous war production of the United States was the backbone of the Allied war effort. Once again, the Germans had fatally underestimated the latent power of the U.S. economy. The United States not only equipped its own huge military establishment of 12 million men but supplied much of the war materials used by their allies. The United States increased its agricultural production by one-third, sending food to its allies and other nations. By 1945, U.S. military production had more than

doubled that of the combined Axis powers.

The Allied war effort was made possible by close cooperation among government, industry, and the military. The national government regulated the production, prices, and distribution of civilian and military products. As in World War I, government propaganda urged people on the home front to hate the enemy, make sacrifices, and work harder. In the western democracies, people became accustomed to a high level of government involvement in economic life. While abating somewhat after the war, such involvement became a permanent feature of life in these nations.

The Struggle for the Oceans

Another Allied move was to clear the oceans so that the power of the United

States could be brought to bear in Europe and Asia. In the Atlantic, the scene was a replay of World War I, where both sides were trying to destroy each other's shipping and deprive each other of vital supplies. Early in the war, the British navy mined the approaches to Germany, cutting off all supplies from outside Europe. With the supplies of all Europe under its control, however, Germany was less vulnerable to a naval blockade than in World War I. Great Britain, on the other hand, was as vulnerable to starvation by naval blockade as ever. During the war, Germany built a large number of long-range submarines or U-boats, capable of cruising the entire Atlantic. Submarine "wolf-packs" attacked Allied convoys on the way to Great Britain and the Soviet Union, while single U-boats cruised the South Atlantic and the coastline of the United States. With increasing success the Allies used new sonar detection techniques, the convoy system, destroyers, submarine-hunting aircraft carriers, and land-based aircraft against the submarines. By late 1943, the submarine threat was rapidly fading, and U.S. troops and military equipment were crossing in such volume that Great Britain was turning into a huge Anglo-American military base.

In the Pacific, the strategic situation was reversed. It was Japan that required the sea-lanes for vital supplies and the United States that attacked convoys with submarines and aircraft. By 1945, the Americans had succeeded in destroying the bulk of Japanese shipping, virtually severing the Japanese homeland from its empire.

The Pacific war also introduced a new era of naval warfare: carrier-based air bombardment. Opposing naval squadrons hundreds of miles apart sent out waves of dive bombers, high-altitude bombers, and torpedo planes to sink the carriers in the enemy fleet. Naval task forces now consisted of one or more aircraft carriers surrounded like queen bees with supporting craft. The support ships, including the battleships that had previously dominated naval warfare, bristled with antiaircraft batteries to protect the carriers. The U.S. navy won most of the naval battles, in part because of superior planes and better trained pilots and in part because its cryptographers had cracked the Japanese naval code.

Softening Up the Axis from the Air

To weaken the Axis before the final assault the United States and Great Britain employed strategic bombard-ment, the long-range bombardment of transportation networks, industrial sites, military concentrations, and population centers. After 1942, aided by new bombsights that allowed more accurate bombardment, U.S. and British bombers flew farther and farther into Germany and central Europe. Allied fighters protecting the bombers shot down German intercepting planes faster than they could be replaced. Although suffering substantial losses, Allied bombers became increasingly effective in destroying factories, dams, roads, canals, and railroads as German air defenses weakened. The Germans rebuilt their factories underground and maintained a high level of production, but the destruction of the transportation network above ground made it difficult to get the military supplies to the fighting fronts. The Allies also employed terror bombing, killing hundreds of thousands of civilians in massive air raids on Hamburg, Berlin, and Dresden.

With the regular air force in rapid decline, German scientists and technicians created new weapons to reassert German control of the air. Jet-propelled aircraft appeared near the end of the war, but too late to be put into combat. More effective were Germany's jet-powered V-1 "buzz bombs" and liquid-fueled V-2 rockets, which terrorized southeastern Britain. However, Germany had too few of these missiles for them to be decisive. Like the airplane and the tank in World War I, however, the jet airplane and the guided missile of World War II gave a foreboding preview of future warfare.

Strategic and terror bombardment of Japan was not effective until late 1944, when bombers began to fly over Japan from bases in the Marianas. The Japanese air force had been effectively wiped out by that time, and by the spring and summer of 1945, U.S. bombers flew at will over Japan, using incendiary bombs that consumed the wooden buildings of the Japanese cities in raging firestorms. Hundreds of thousands of Japanese perished in these raids.

ALLIED TRIUMPH

With the oceans rapidly being cleared and the Axis under increasingly heavy air bombardment, the Allies began to fight their way back. A series of amphibious landings and land campaigns in both theaters of war in 1942 and 1943 brought Allied forces closer to the heart of the Axis domains. During 1944 and 1945, it took a massive Allied effort on three land fronts to conquer Germany, but Japan was defeated by airborne devastation without an assault by land forces on its home territory.

The Conquest of the European Axis

Beginning in 1942, in conjunction with the general operations previously discussed, Allied forces mounted a series of campaigns that led to the surrender of Italy in September 1943, Germany in May 1945, and Japan in August 1945. The Russian-German war in eastern Europe was the major battle zone in World War II, pitting the best of the German armed forces against the growing military might of the Soviet Union, accompanied by bitter overtones of genocide. The Germans had conquered additional areas in southern Russia during 1942, but their army and air force remained bogged down on the thousand-mile eastern front.

The Axis occupying forces inflicted so many atrocities on civilians throughout the Soviet Union that they drove non-Russian ethnic groups originally friendly to the invaders into an alliance with the Soviet govern-ment. A swarm of guerrillas attacked German supply lines and installa-tions. As British and U.S. air raids increasingly disrupted the German economy and the transportation sys-tem, Germany could not keep its armed forces effectively supplied. In the autumn and winter of 1942–1943, Soviet forces surrounded and cap-tured a German army at Stalingrad. The Russians sustained 700,000 mil-itary and civilian casualties, but they inflicted 300,000 casualties on the Axis armed forces and put Hitler per-manently on the defensive in the east.

By 1943, the Soviet Union, bol-stered by U.S. and British aid, had created an impressive armaments in-dustry that could support an army of more than 6 million men, more than

The War in the Air. U.S. B-26 Maur-aders are here shown bombing a rail yard and power station in Charleroi, Bel-gium. Like the tank, the airplane was a new technology that transformed war-fare. Unescorted bombers in daylight often suffered heavy losses when at-tacked by faster, more maneuverable fighters. When protected by fighters or flying at night, however, as was the case for allied raids later in the war, long range bombers committed heavy de-struction that weakened Germany and completed the defeat of Japan.

Stalingrad. This cartoon depicting massive German casualties in their debacle at Stalingrad in 1942–1943 stands as a symbol of the devastating effect that the Russian front as a whole, the greatest land war in human history, had on the German war machine. Although the Germans and their allies killed an estimated 22 million Russians, the resilient Russians in their turn destroyed Germany's best air, armored, and infantry units and swept across eastern Europe to victory.

double the Germans and their allies in the east, and providing a three-to-one advantage over the Germans in artillery, tanks, and airplanes. With this superiority, the Russians now attacked all along the front. In July 1943, the Russians destroyed the core of the German armor at Kursk and rolled the Germans back. By the spring of 1944, Soviet troops had recaptured the Ukraine and pushed into Rumania and Poland. The Soviet invasion of Germany was now only a matter of time: dread of "Bolshevik" revenge for the savage Nazi reign in

the Soviet Union haunted the German high command and made all other campaigns secondary.

With the Germans fighting for their lives in the Soviet Union, the western Allies struck in the Mediterranean. In November 1942 the Americans and British made amphibious assaults on Vichy-held Morocco and Algeria and pushed eastward, joining up with British and Commonwealth forces moving westward through Libya. Caught between the pincers, masses of German and Italian troops surrendered in Tunisia in May 1943.

U.S. and British forces then conquered Sicily in July and August 1943 and landed on the Italian Peninsula in September. Never a major military power and at the mercy of the Allies, Italy surrendered. With the southern approaches to Germany open, German troops rushed into Italy and dug in across the peninsula south of Rome, preventing further Allied advance for some time. The Germans rescued Mussolini from jail and set him up as the puppet ruler of German-occupied north Italy.

In the summer and autumn of

1944 the Allies opened the crucial campaigns that were to end the war in Europe. On June 6, 1944—"D-Day"—U.S., British, and Canadian forces launched a massive landing on the Normandy coast in France, opening up a second major front. For a month, German forces held the Allies on the beaches, but in July the Americans broke out in force and German resistance collapsed in France. By autumn, German forces had withdrawn to the fortified western border of Germany. In Italy the Allies captured Rome and the central part of the peninsula, but the Germans retained control of the north.

During 1944, the Russians continued their relentless drive westward. By December, the Soviet army had cleared most of the Balkans and advanced to the outskirts of Budapest and Warsaw, despite frantic German resistance. Finland, Rumania, and Bulgaria surrendered, and Josef Tito's communist guerrillas made headway against the Germans in Yugoslavia.

By the spring of 1945, Germany was caught in a massive vise. U.S. and British forces crossed the Rhine and pressed eastward, while Soviet forces moved in from the east and captured Berlin. Hitler committed suicide in his underground bunker in Berlin, and by May 8, 1945, German forces had laid down their arms. After nearly six years the war in Europe had come to an end.

The Defeat of Japan

Although it had originally been intended that the allied forces would concentrate on Japan after Germany was defeated, secondary effort of the United States in the Pacific was sufficient to bring the Japanese close to defeat at the time of the German surrender. The tide had turned as early as the summer of 1942. The Japanese had been prevented from attacking Australia and in May the U.S. fleet had defeated and driven back a Japanese task force at the Battle of Midway, the first important reverse for the Japanese navy. By 1943, the enormous U.S. war effort was turning out enough war materiel and training enough men to press the war in the Pacific as well as in Europe. In 1943 and early 1944, in a strategy called "island hopping," U.S. forces used the new amphibious landing craft with naval and air support to capture selected islands in the central Pacific. These islands were no longer protected by the Japanese fleet, which had been driven back into Asian waters. Japanese garrisons on the remaining islands were left to starve. Meanwhile, General Douglas MacArthur worked his way along the coast of New Guinea and began the reconquest of the Philippines, in effect cutting off Japanese forces in southeast Asia from those in China and Japan.

In June and July 1944, Admiral Chester Nimitz's forces seized Saipan and Tinian in the Marianas and built airstrips from which the new B-29 bomber could begin the strategic

D-Day. On June 6, 1944 Allied forces launched the greatest sea-to-land invasion in history, crossing the English Channel from Great Britain to assault German fortifications on the coast of Normandy, France. This landing opened up the second major front which, in conjunction with the Soviet drive from the east, brought defeat to the Nazi regime in less than a year.

Hiroshima: The End and a Beginning. The incinerated and irradiated city is shown here one year after the explosion of the atomic bomb on August 6, 1945. One scarred concrete building still stands; a few new homes and gardens have sprung up amidst the weeds and rubble of the general devastation; lumber for more construction has been gathered. Despite this hopeful start and forty years of atomic peace, the shadow of the nuclear blasts that ended World War II has continued to becloud the future.

bombardment of the Japanese home islands. In the spring of 1945, the Chinese regained territory, and the British and Indians began to retake Burma. The United States needed air bases closer to Japan so that fighters could accompany the bombers over Japan. U.S. Army and Marine units, sustaining heavy casualties, captured the islands of Iwo Jima and Okinawa.

The resolute Japanese struggle to hold Iwo Jima and Okinawa, accompanied by extensive kamikaze (sui-

cide) air attacks on the U.S. navy at Okinawa made it clear that lives in the millions would be lost on both sides when Allied forces invaded Japan in late 1945 or 1946. Meanwhile, Allied scientists had created bombs from the fission of atoms that promised to unleash massive destruction. After Roosevelt's death in April 1945, President Harry Truman at the Potsdam Conference in July 1945 authorized its use. On August 6 one bomb was dropped on Hiroshima, followed on August 9 by one on Nagasaki. The bombs, creating as much damage and death as hundreds of conventional bombs, completely destroyed both cities and released radioactivity over a wide area, eventually killing 200,000 Japanese. Radioactivity kept on killing, maiming, and creating genetic defects long after the bombs were dropped. Meanwhile, the Soviet Union declared war on August 8 and invaded Manchuria and Korea. The destruction caused by both incendiary and atomic bombs and the generally bleak military situation convinced Emperor Hirohito to capitulate. On August 14, 1945, the Japanese surrendered, the formal ceremony taking place on September 2 in Tokyo Bay. World War II had ended, but the mushroom-shaped clouds over Hiroshima and Nagasaki ushered in a new era of nuclear power and the potential for nuclear devastation.

ARRANGEMENTS AT WAR'S END

World War II caused even greater carnage than World War I. An estimated 60 million people were dead, 35 million injured, and 3 million missing. Possibly 35 million civilians died from starvation and disease or perished in battles, air raids, labor and extermination camps, and deportations. At least 35 million died in Europe, including 20 million Soviet citizens, 6 million Germans, and 4 million Poles. In Asia, 20 million Chinese and 2 million Japanese perished. British and U.S. wartime losses were much lower, in combination numbering 600,000.

In addition to the casualties, 30 million Europeans were uprooted from their homes. In many nations, the ethnic majority permanently expelled ethnic minorities. Some 17 million Germans were driven out of eastern Europe, and the Soviet Union sent 2 million wartime "unreliables," most of them ethnic minorities, to Siberia. About a million of the surviving European Jews immigrated to Palestine (later Israel). The United Nations resettled a million homeless refugees in western Europe, the Western Hemisphere, and Australasia.

In addition to the lives lost, vast reaches of Europe and Asia had been physically destroyed. Most of the large cities in central and eastern Europe and in eastern Asia had been bombed and shelled into rubble. The transportation network in those areas had for the most part disappeared, and millions of acres of farmland had been damaged. The war, including both damages and war expenditures, had cost an estimated $1.5 trillion.

Settlements with Germany and Japan

Under these circumstances of death and destruction the victorious Allies were determined that Germany and Japan would never threaten the world again. Instead of a formal peace conference, as after World War I, Allied leaders worked out most issues in a series of military and foreign ministers' conferences, some as late as 1963. Some of the agreements were ratified through bilateral treaties; some de facto arrangements were not formally approved until the Helsinki meeting in 1975.

The territorial changes, as after World War I, mostly affected eastern

Europe. The Soviet Union retained the areas first acquired in 1939–1940 and in their possession at the end of the war: Estonia, Latvia, Lithuania, portions of Rumania and Finland, and the eastern half of Poland. In addition, the Soviet Union annexed a province of Czechoslovakia and the northern half of East Prussia. The total effect of these acquisitions was to move the Soviet border dramatically westward compared with 1938. Although some nations refused to acknowledge the change, Poland received the eastern one-quarter of Germany in compensation for the loss of eastern Poland. Other boundary changes were relatively minor. For Hitler's allies—Finland, Hungary, Rumania, Bulgaria, and Italy—the overall terms were not particularly harsh: some territorial adjustments, reparations payments, and limitations on their military establishments. The western boundary of Germany was set as it existed in 1937, mainly by returning Alsace-Lorraine to France. Austria was detached from Germany and occupied until 1955.

As at Versailles, the victorious powers were primarily concerned with the postwar status of Germany. During the war, they had considered permanently dismembering Germany or reducing it to a feeble agricultural region. By 1945, however, the Allies had agreed to retain Germany as a single nation, hedged about with safeguards to prevent future aggression. Germany was disarmed and divided into four occupation zones: French, British, U.S. and Soviet. The occupying forces would remain until the German people had been de-Nazified and had set up a government acceptable to all the occupying powers, presumably in three to five years.

Germany attacks U.S.S.R

Farthest Axis advance

Italy surrenders

D–Day invasion

Germany surrenders

Atomic bombs end Pacific war

Japan attacks Southeast Asia and bombs Pearl Harbor

Soviets drive west

Intensive bombing of Japan

United Nations founded

The victors were initially interested in reparations settlements and agreed that the heavily ravaged Soviet Union would receive the largest share.

One feature of the occupation zone arrangements would become a major source of trouble in the postwar years. Although Berlin was in the middle of the Soviet zone, the western allies insisted on sharing in the control of the vanquished enemy's capital city. In an awkward arrangement, Berlin was divided into four occupation zones separate from those in Germany. The western powers were to supply their three sectors in west Berlin through certain designated highways, railroads, and air corridors through the Soviet occupation zone. Western forces in Berlin were thus in a precarious military situation, cut off behind the Soviet lines.

The Nazis had caused such horror that the victorious powers were determined to punish the leaders. At Nuremburg during 1945–1946 the highest surviving Nazi leaders were put on trial for waging aggressive war and for committing crimes against humanity. Twelve were condemned to death, seven were imprisoned for terms up to life, and three were acquitted. Although some attacked the process as "victor's justice," the prec-

edent was set that brutal treatment of prisoners and noncombatants constituted a crime against humanity and that "following orders" was not a sufficient defense. Trials of lesser officials followed.

The victors also treated Japan severely. They stripped the fallen nation of its empire, reducing it to the four home islands and the Ryukyus. The western Pacific islands were transferred to the United States as a United Nations Trust Territory. The Soviet Union received the southern half of Sakhalin and the Kurile Islands; China regained Taiwan. Soviet and U.S. forces split Korea into two occupation zones until a mutually acceptable government could be installed.

Japan itself received much the same treatment as Germany. Japan's armed forces were disbanded, and Japan renounced war as an instrument of national policy. The United States would occupy Japan and administer the Ryukyu chain with its important Okinawa air base. Under the direction of General MacArthur, U.S. forces would stay until the Japanese could demonstrate they were no longer an aggressive people. Japan was allowed to retain a government purged of militarists until a new constitution

was written that would create a form of government acceptable to the United States. The emperor was to keep his throne on the condition that he renounce his claim to divinity. Japanese leaders were also tried for war crimes; seven were executed, and others imprisoned.

Creating the United Nations

Once again, as after World War I, an international organization was formed in hopes of maintaining the peace in the postwar period. In 1945, as World War II was ending, fifty-one nations replaced the League of Nations with a new organization, the United Nations (UN). It consisted of six bodies: the General Assembly, the Security Council, the Secretariat, the Economic and Social Council, the Trusteeship Council, and the International Court of Justice. The Security Council had five permanent members: France, Great Britain, the United States, the Soviet Union, and China. The council also contained six nonpermanent members elected for two-year terms by the Assembly. Although the council was created to defuse crisis situations, the permanent members could veto any action. The Economic and Social Council was to take an active role to improve the economics, social conditions, culture, education, and health of the poor areas of the world. Whether the United Nations would be any more successful than the League in forestalling the aggressive acts of major powers remained to be seen.

SUMMARY

Beginning in the 1930s, Japan, Germany, and Italy, all nations nursing grievances after World War I, began a series of aggressive acts that led to World War II. Led by Adolf Hitler, Germany flouted the Treaty of Versailles by rearming, reoccupying the Rhineland, and annexing Austria. Pursuing the general vision of expanding eastward and the particular goal of incorporating German-speaking areas, Hitler annexed Czechoslovakia and then attacked Poland in 1939. Although France and Great Britain had appeased Hitler throughout the period, the attack on Poland brought them to declare war, and World War II began.

From 1939 to 1941, Hitler's powerful army and air force overran Poland, western continental Europe, and the Balkans. He was unable to conquer Great Britain, but nonetheless turned aside to invade the Soviet Union in June 1941. Initially successful, German forces bogged down short of victory as distance, winter, and increasingly effective Russian resistance took its toll.

By 1941, Japanese aggression brought war to Asia. Japan took over Manchuria in 1931, and by the late 1930s Japan had overrun most of east China. Determined to gain control of the petroleum and rubber of southeast Asia, Japan moved into French Indochina and planned to take over British and Dutch colonies there. Confronted by the United States, Japan attacked in 1941, overrunning southeast Asia and the western Pacific by mid-1942.

Confronted by the powerful Axis states, the opponents agreed to concentrate on defeating Germany first. The United States became the main economic force behind the war, although the Soviet Union built up an impressive war machine substantially on its own. While the Soviet Union engaged Germany and its allies in a massive struggle inside the Soviet Union, the United States and Great Britain broke the German submarine blockade in the Atlantic and began a systematic aerial bombardment of German-held Europe. Meanwhile, British and U.S. forces cleared the Mediterranean, knocking Italy out of the war. In 1944, Allied forces landed on the French coast and subsequently swept forward to the western border of Germany. At the same time, a powerful drive through eastern Europe brought Soviet forces to the outskirts of Berlin. German resistance collapsed in May 1945.

Although the defeat of Japan was a secondary priority, the United States made quick headway. The Japanese fleet was driven out of the Pacific, and a series of island-hopping campaigns brought the U.S. Air Force to within striking distance of Japan by 1944. U.S. planes began a methodical incendiary bombardment of Japan, culminating in dropping two atomic bombs in August 1945. Japan immediately surrendered, and World War II was over.

To prevent future aggression the victors imposed harsh postwar treaties. They stripped Germany and Japan of their conquests and some territory and disarmed both nations. They were to occupy Germany and Japan until satisfactory, nonaggressive governments were formed, and punished war criminals. Meanwhile the United Nations was set up in hopes that it would aid in preserving world peace.

SELECTED SOURCES

Baer, George W. *The Test Case: Italy, Ethiopia, and the League of Nations.* 1976. A discussion of the failure of international peace-keeping efforts in the face of totalitarian aggression.

˙Carr, Raymond. *The Spanish Tragedy: The Civil War in Perspective.* 1977. A thoughtful analysis of the Spanish Civil War and foreign intervention.

*Clark, Alan. *Barbarosa.* 1965. A lively account of the gigantic struggle between the Soviet Union and Germany.

Costello, John. *The Pacific War.* 1981. An authoritative account of the war between the United States and Japan.

Eisenhower, Dwight D. *Crusade in Europe.* A history of the victorious Allied campaigns in western Europe, by the man who directed them.

*Monsarrat, Nicholas. *The Cruel Sea.* 1951. An enthralling novel depicting the destroyer-submarine struggle in the Atlantic. Also a motion picture. Should be seen in conjunction with the German motion picture *Das Boot.*

Rowse, A. L. *Appeasement: A Study in Political Decline, 1933–1939.* 1963. A critical look at the liberal appeasement of aggression in the 1930s.

*Smith, Bradley. *Reaching Judgment at Nuremburg.* 1979. An insightful look at the corruption of Nazism. Also a motion picture, *Judgment at Nuremburg.*

*Taylor, A. J. P. *The War Lords.* 1977. Descriptions of the men who directed World War II.

Tregaskis, Richard W. *Guadacanal Diary.* 1943. A first-hand account of jungle fighting in the Pacific.

*Young, Peter. *World War, 1939–45: A Short History.* 1966. A balanced overview.

*Available in paperback.

THE COLD WAR

I call upon Chairman Khrushchev to halt and eliminate this clandestine, reckless, and provocative threat to world peace and to stabilize relations between our two nations. I call upon him further to abandon this course of world domination and to join in an historic effort to end the perilous arms race and transform the history of man. He has an opportunity now to move the world back from the abyss of destruction—by . . . withdrawing these weapons from Cuba—by refraining from any action which will widen or deepen the present crisis—and then by participating in a search for peaceful and permanent solutions. . . .

It is difficult to settle or even discuss these problems in an atmosphere of intimidation. That is why this latest Soviet threat—or any other threat which is made either independently or in response to our actions this week—must and will be met with determination. Any hostile move anywhere in the world against the safety and freedom of peoples to whom we are committed . . . will be met by whatever action is needed.

On the evening of October 22, 1962, as an anxious American public watched their president deliver these words on television, the world stood on the brink of atomic holocaust. The two great nuclear-armed powers, the United States and the Soviet Union, faced each other in a heart-stopping confrontation over Soviet missiles in Cuba, the culmination of seventeen years of competition in the "Cold War."

The Cold War was a complex pattern of competitive, often hostile, relationships between the two major postwar powers that began in Europe as World War II came to an end. Conducted diplomatically, economically, and militarily short of atomic war, the Cold War persisted at varying levels of intensity into the 1960s. In terms of local conflicts and confrontations it spread from Europe to Asian and Caribbean nations; it also expanded as the United States and the Soviet Union competed in a global arms race that placed the world in the position where atomic annihilation could come in a matter of minutes.

CONTENTS

The Missile Era in a Cold War World. A Pershing missile undergoing tests thunders skyward, representing U.S. capacity to deliver nuclear warheads to targets in the Soviet Union. Matched by equivalent missiles in the Soviet Union, a "balance of terror" was maintained, with nuclear war kept at bay by the prudence of U.S. and Soviet leaders.

THE ONSET OF
THE COLD WAR:
EUROPE, 1945–1949

Even as they were fighting the Axis, the United States, Great Britain, and the Soviet Union were looking ahead to arranging the postwar world to suit their interests. Great Britain wished to maintain its empire and retain its imperial economic system; the United States wished to retain its spheres of influence in the western hemisphere and Asia, but also wished to construct a worldwide system of free markets; the Soviet Union, with 20 million wartime dead, was determined to dominate eastern Europe and to keep Germany militarily impotent to prevent another invasion out of the west. The U.S.S.R. was also interested in promoting Marxist interests around the world if it could do so without embroiling itself in too many difficulties.

Historians have debated heatedly about the origins and course of the Cold War. They have argued as to whether the United States employed the atomic bomb because it was necessary to use it to win the war or used it primarily to threaten the Soviet Union in the postwar period with its presence. They have also differed over whether the United States or the Soviet Union was more aggressive in bringing on and pursuing the Cold War, and whether ideological, military, or economic factors carried the most weight in framing postwar policy.

Germany, Eastern Europe, and the Mediterranean

Relationships among the victorious powers rapidly deteriorated during and after the last two wartime conferences at Yalta and Potsdam in 1945. One major issue was reparations. The United States had prospered during the war and was more interested in rebuilding Germany as a trading partner than in crushing it economically. The Soviet Union, on the other hand, had been devastated during the war and wished to rebuild its economy with postwar loans from the United States and with reparations from defeated Germany. Instead, to pressure the Russians into opening up eastern Europe, the United States cut off their Lend-Lease, refused to lend them money, and ended shipments of industrial German supplies to the Soviet Union from Allied occupation zones. The Soviet Union then proceeded to strip its occupation zone in eastern Germany of industrial materials.

The atomic bomb also harmed postwar relationships. The Soviet Union feared the U.S. weapon, but not enough to back down from defending its interests. Meanwhile, the United States presented the Baruch Plan, under which nations would stop making atomic bombs and submit to inspection by an independent international agency. Because the United States and its allies controlled the United Nations, and thus the proposed international agency, the Russians rejected the plan.

Eastern Europe was the main area of contention in the period immediately after the war, as Soviet troops occupied the area. The Soviet Union was determined to weld eastern Europe into a buffer zone of friendly nations that would protect it from future invasion. Despite pressure from the west to permit free elections and open up the area to trade with the west, the U.S.S.R. tightened the grip of communist parties in Poland, Rumania, and Bulgaria. By 1948, communist takeovers added Hungary and Czechoslovakia to the Soviet sphere. The Russians meanwhile began the integration of the economies of eastern European nations with that of the U.S.S.R. While Churchill charged that an "iron curtain" had fallen between Moscow-controlled eastern Europe and the west, Stalin told the Soviet people that they were surrounded by enemies and would have to endure privations to maintain their economic and military strength. Meanwhile, Yugoslavia, although communist, took an independent, nationalistic course under Marshall Joseph Tito.

As the U.S.S.R. consolidated its power in eastern Europe, trouble developed in the Mediterranean. Turkey, hoping for western support, refused a Russian demand in 1946 and early 1947 for joint Soviet-Turkish supervision of the waterway through Turkey connecting the Black Sea to the Aegean Sea. At the same time, Greece was embroiled in a brutal civil war between the corrupt Greek government and communist-dominated guerrillas backed by the communist regimes in the Balkans. The British, who had been aiding the Greek government to keep the Soviet Union out of the Mediterranean, pulled out in 1947 for economic reasons.

The United States Becomes a Major European Power

The developments in Greece and Turkey, as well as the unfavorable situation in eastern Europe, caused the Truman administration to work through a major change of policy concerning the role of the United States in world affairs. The traditional outlook of the United States was that its interests were best served by staying out of European issues. Only when the vital interests of the nation were threatened, as in the two world wars, had Americans gone to fight in Europe. According to this view, it was time for Americans to pull back to the western hemisphere, as they had done after World War I.

However, by 1947, President Harry Truman, a staunch anticommunist, and most of his civilian and military advisers were concluding that the Russians had a plan to destroy the "free" (noncommunist) world. The United States was the only postwar noncommunist nation that could contain the spread of communism until the people in the communist nations grew tired of Marxism and overthrew their governments. To do that, the United States must remain in Europe for the foreseeable future, actively employing its economic and military power. Once the administration adopted the containment policy, a series of dramatic policy initiatives quickly followed, requiring the administration to persuade Congress and the American people to reverse 150 years of an essentially isolationist outlook.

Unwilling for the moment to attack the Soviet Union directly, the Truman administration proposed sending military aid and advisers to any friendly government under external or internal communist threat, so they could defeat the communists through their own efforts. This policy became known as the Truman Doctrine. In March 1947, at the request of President Truman and after intense lobbying, Congress appropriated $400 million to rush military aid and ad-

visers to Greece and Turkey. Thus bolstered, the Turkish government continued to refuse the Soviet Union, and the reorganized and better-equipped Greek army became more effective against the guerrillas. When Yugoslavia cut off supplies and refuge to the guerrillas in 1949, they surrendered.

Trouble in western Europe quickly produced another major policy innovation, the Marshall Plan. By 1947, despite billions of dollars in U.S. loans, the economy of western Europe had not revived. France and Italy in particular were plagued with shortages, inflation, unemployment, and inadequate housing. Out of desperation, many French and Italians voted for socialist and communist candidates, and as a result the communists and socialists held a number of seats in the cabinets. In the eyes of the Truman administration, this situation called for more effective American economic intervention. In June 1947 Secretary of State George Marshall proposed that the nations of Europe consult with one another and with the United States to determine the amount of economic assistance they would need to rebuild their economies. The Soviet Union, suspicious of U.S. economic penetration, prevented eastern European nations from participating. Congress at first balked at the novel idea of giving money away in peacetime foreign aid instead of lending it in wartime, but in 1948 Congress created the European Recovery Program, usually referred to as the Marshall Plan, with an initial outlay of $4 billion. By 1951 Marshall Plan aid totaled over $13 billion, most of it going to Great Britain, Germany, France and Italy, whose economies recovered rapidly under its

A New World Role for the United States. President Truman addresses a joint session of Congress on March 12, 1947, calling for military aid to Greece and Turkey "against aggressive movements that seek to impose upon them totalitarian regimes." Subsequently called the Truman Doctrine, this effort to block communist expansion into the Mediterranean highlighted a general shift in U.S. foreign policy towards worldwide containment of the Soviet Union.

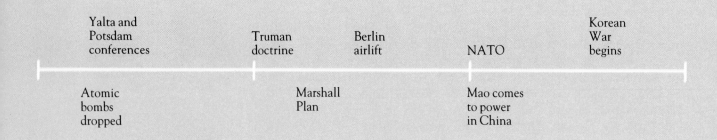

| 1945 | 1947 | 1949 | 1951 |

Yalta and Potsdam conferences

Truman doctrine

Berlin airlift

NATO

Korean War begins

Atomic bombs dropped

Marshall Plan

Mao comes to power in China

impetus. The Marshall Plan was a political success, as well, assuring the decline of communist political fortunes that had begun even before the aid plan went into effect. In both Italy and France, voters excluded communists from cabinet positions after mid-1947, and communist-led general strikes in 1947–1948 in those countries were broken by government action. Hoping for a similar success in the non-western world, Congress funded the Point Four program beginning in 1950. This program channeled millions and eventually billions of dollars into emerging non-western nations in the hope of preventing them from turning to communism.

As a major part of the containment policy, the United States and its allies combined the three western zones of occupation in Germany into a German national state as a buffer against the Soviet-controlled east. By September 1949, the Federal Republic of Germany (West Germany) was operating as a sovereign state, although formal recognition did not come until later. Western military forces remained, their role having changed from anti-German to anti-Soviet.

Of all the western actions in the early Cold War, the reestablishment of Germany had the most searing effect on the Soviet Union. After Russia's two twentieth-century experiences, the Soviet Union believed the west intended to rearm Germany and use it as the European spearhead in a general attack against the U.S.S.R. The Russians countered by organizing their zone into the German Democratic Republic (East Germany).

The main Soviet response centered on the spot where the western allies were most vulnerable: Berlin. In June 1948, the Russians announced they had closed for repairs those railroads and highways in East Germany set aside to supply western troops and the civilians in West Berlin. The western governments used the air corridors for the Berlin Airlift, or "Operation Vittles," supplying more than two million West Berliners and western troops with food, clothing, coal, and other supplies. In May 1949, the Russians conceded defeat and reopened the highways and railroads. The immediate crisis was over, but Berlin remained a trouble spot.

In the late 1940s and 1950s, Cold War tensions had come to permeate western society. As in other war situations the governments of the major powers bombarded their publics with propaganda depicting the other side

as bent on destroying all that was near and dear. The mass media, now including the new wonder of television, once again played a major role. In the totalitarian Soviet bloc, the governments carefully controlled all information received by their citizens, whereas in the open societies the ostensibly independent press and television generally followed the lead of their governments. Americans were egged on to worry about alleged "subversives," "Commie dupes," "parlor pinks," and "fellow travelers." Congress ran several investigations of alleged subversives in the United States and created legislation with such broad power to combat subversive organizations that it posed a threat to civil liberties. The executive branch created a government loyalty program designed to uncover subversives and unreliables in the federal government. Although a few pro-Soviet Americans were found, most of the accused were innocent people, many of whom lost their jobs or had their reputations tarnished. The climax of anticommunist hysteria in the United States occurred from 1950 to 1954; Senator Joseph McCarthy made the term "McCarthyism" famous by his unproven charges of subversion directed against a wide variety of Americans ranging from ordinary citizens to army generals. Finally, his colleagues and the media turned against him.

THE COLD WAR BECOMES GLOBAL, 1949–1960s

Beginning in 1949, the Cold War, born in Europe, began to assume the characteristics of a worldwide military confrontation. The United States began to encircle the Soviet Union with a ring of air bases, and both sides later threatened each other with a global network of nuclear missiles. By the 1960s, the fate of the entire world depended on the common sense and prudence of the leaders in Washington and Moscow.

The U.S.A. Surrounds the U.S.S.R.

In 1949, the Truman administration moved to a much more aggressive form of containment when it abandoned its traditional policy of unilateral action and set up a system of anti-Soviet alliances and military bases. Postwar events culminating in Czechoslovakia and Berlin convinced U.S. leaders that the Soviet Union represented a permanent aggressive menace in Europe that must be met by a permanent U.S. military presence, bolstered by an alliance system. The Truman administration set up the North Atlantic Treaty Organization (NATO), in which the United States, Canada, Iceland, Norway, Denmark, the Netherlands, Belgium, Luxemburg, Great Britain, France, Portugal, and Italy (and later Greece and Turkey) agreed to come to one an-

other's aid if attacked (see Map 84). The national armed forces of the member nations were incorporated into a unified military operation under the direction of a U.S. commander. The United States Strategic Air Command (SAC) established air bases in western Europe and in the non-NATO nations of Spain and Libya. From all these bases, U.S. B-52s could drop atomic bombs in the Soviet Union by the mid-1950s.

By 1954, the Cold War had spread to Asia. To oppose the Asian communists, the United States had already developed SAC bases in U.S.-occupied Japan and Okinawa, and in 1956 the United States organized the Southeast Asia Treaty Organization (SEATO). This alliance, although aimed at communist nations in Asia, also extended the string of SAC air bases into a global noose around the Soviet Union. The United States could bomb the U.S.S.R. from every direction, often at close range, whereas the Russians could attack the United States only at long range over the North Pole (see Map 85).

The encirclement of the Soviet Union created a series of escalating pressures in Europe. The Russians increased the size of their army in Europe until it greatly outnumbered the NATO forces opposing it. This in effect turned western European nations into hostages in a superpower confrontation, stimulating these nations to raise a restraining voice in U.S.-Soviet crises. To lessen the imbalance in ground forces, the United States pressured its reluctant NATO allies, who were caught between fear of the Soviet Union and suspicion of a rearmed Germany, to admit West Germany into NATO. Stung by the specter of a rearmed Germany, the

Soviet Union created its own military alliance system, the Warsaw Pact, integrating the armed forces of eastern Europe into a unified force under Soviet command. In addition, the Russians recognized East Germany as an independent state and admitted it into the Warsaw Pact. Although the hope of some day unifying Germany remained, from 1955 Germany was two separate nations, integrated into the military spheres of opposing superpowers.

In the early 1950s, the two superpowers also found themselves engaged in a fevered arms race, pitched to ever more destructive weapons. Five months after NATO was organized, the Russians detonated their own atomic bomb. In 1952 and 1953 both nations exploded hydrogen (thermonuclear) bombs, the first weapon that could wipe out the human race. By 1955, both superpowers were operating bombers of intercontinental range that could drop hydrogen bombs on the opponent's homeland; each bomb was capable of substantially destroying a major urban center. The U.S. Air Force, however, maintained a four to one lead over the Soviet Union in aircraft capable of delivering bombs on the enemy's homeland. The Eisenhower administration based its military policy on "massive retaliation," the concept that in the event of any Soviet attack on the United States or its allies, SAC bombers from bases around the world would destroy the Soviet Union with nuclear bombs.

During the 1950s, eastern Europe remained a Cold War trouble spot. Dissatisfaction with living conditions plus the hopes raised by more liberal policies under new Soviet leader Nikita Khrushchev led to riots and other convulsions in East Germany in 1953

1. GERMAN DEMOCRATIC REPUBLIC
2. CZECHOSLOVAKIA
3. HUNGARY

- NATO member
- Non-NATO ally
- NATO member to 1969
- Warsaw pact member
- Unrest/revolt in Eastern Europe

United States/NATO

- Missile bases: NATO
- Troops: U.S.
- Nuclear bombers: U.S.
- Naval port: U.S.
- Fleet: U.S.
- Nuclear missile submarine: U.S.

Soviet/Warsaw Pact

- Missile bases: Warsaw Pact
- Troops: Soviet
- Nuclear bombers: Soviet
- Naval port: Soviet
- Fleet: Soviet
- Nuclear missile submarine: Soviet

MAP 84

The Cold War in Europe. After World War II the division of Europe into spheres dominated by the two superpowers was intensified by the NATO and Warsaw Pact alliances and by the arms race. Rival land forces, backed up by arrays of nuclear missiles and bombers, faced each other in central Europe, while surface fleets and missile-firing submarines roamed the Atlantic and the Mediterranean. Despite, or because of, Cold War confrontations and military buildups, Europe remained at peace after 1945.

and Poland in 1956. When Hungary announced in 1956 that it would cease to be a one-party state and a member of the Warsaw pact, Soviet troops poured in to suppress the rebellion. The United States, distracted by events elsewhere and unwilling to go to war over eastern Europe, did nothing. The Soviet Union crushed the rebellion and remained supreme in eastern Europe.

By the middle of the tension-laden 1950s, the superpowers began to make sporadic attempts to negotiate their differences. Khrushchev and Eisenhower were suspicious of each other, but were also responsive to the danger and cost of the Cold War and the pressure of world opinion. They met at a summit conference in Geneva in 1955. The occupying powers agreed to end the occupation of Austria, and the Soviet Union recognized the West German government. Selected groups of Americans and Russians began to visit one another. After 1955, neither superpower believed that it could get along without summit meetings and other periodic discussions of issues, especially in times of alarm.

The Opening of the Space and Missile Age

On October 4, 1957, the Cold War escalated into a still more dangerous phase. The Russians, using a powerful new rocket, launched the first satellite into an orbit around the earth. Two months later, they launched an intercontinental ballistics missile (ICBM). The space and missile age had begun. Americans were alarmed. Having prided themselves in leading the world in science and technology, they brought heavy censure on the scientific and educational community. The Eisenhower administration poured money into scientific research in the universities, tying them more closely to the military-industrial-political complex. A U.S. satellite went up in 1958, and the National Aeronautics and Space Administration

(NASA) was created to get Americans ahead in space. Stung by Democratic charges of a "missile gap," the Eisenhower administration began a major ICBM building program and also constructed submarine-launched missiles (SLM). The United States also based intermediate-range ballistics missiles in Great Britain, Italy, and Turkey. By 1962–1963, the United States had 450 missiles and 2,000 bombers capable of striking the Soviet Union, as opposed to 50 to 100 Soviet ICBMs and 200 bombers that could reach the United States. The phrases "balance of terror"

and, later, "mutually assured destruction" (MAD) came into use.

From 1960 to 1963, the two superpowers appeared headed toward nuclear war. In May 1960, Russian forces shot down a U.S. high-altitude spy plane flying over the U.S.S.R. The embarrassment of the Eisenhower administration and the missile gap controversy aided the election of John F. Kennedy, who promised new programs to restore U.S. prestige.

A believer in the containment doctrine, President Kennedy was anxious to take a vigorous stance against the

The Great Kitchen Debate. Premier Khrushchev and Vice President Nixon debate the merits of the Soviet and U.S. ways of life at a U.S. exhibition in Moscow in 1959. Although the exchanges were sharp, at least they were talking. The late 1950s were generally a more relaxed period in the Cold War than the early 1950s and early 1960s.

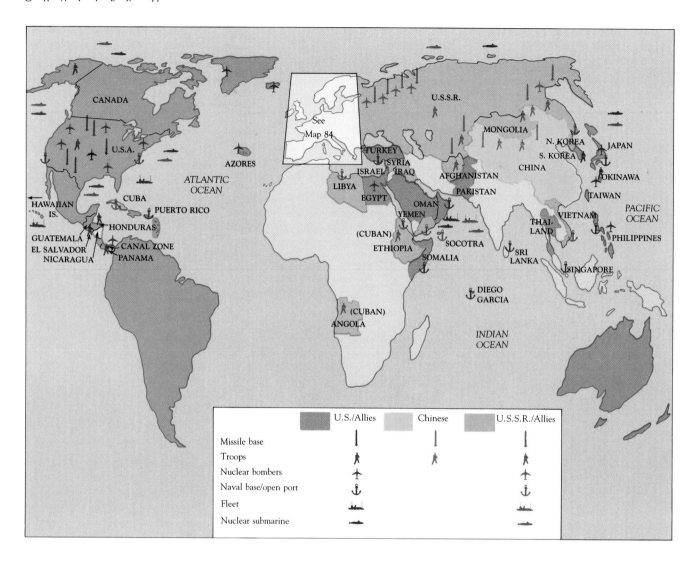

MAP 85
The Global Cold War. By the 1980s the Cold War, originally a two-superpower confrontation in Europe, had become a three-dimension adversarial system operating around the world. U.S. bomber and missile sites in North America, Europe, and Asia threatened the Soviet Union with nuclear annihilation, while missiles in the Soviet Union and missile-launching submarines off the U.S. coast promised the same to the United States. Meanwhile, guerrilla warfare involving pro- and anticommunist forces in Southeast Asia, Africa, and Latin America added another dimension to the Cold War. The hostility of the People's Republic of China to the Soviet Union added to the complexity of the situation.

Soviet Union and to demonstrate that the Democratic party was not "soft on communism." In 1961, the perennial trouble spot, Berlin, flared up into a dangerous confrontation. Khrushchev was embarrassed by Berlin, not only because it contained a western military garrison behind Soviet lines, but also because it was a source of worldwide ridicule, as tens of thousands of East Germans annually were fleeing the communist regime by crossing from East Berlin into West Berlin. The Russians therefore

authorized East Germany to put up a barrier to stop the exodus. The Berlin Wall went up in August 1961 and became, in the eyes of the west, a major symbol of communist repression. Tensions remained high in the months that followed. Additional U.S. troops and equipment were sent to Europe, and Kennedy went to West Berlin to underscore U.S. determination to protect the city, telling an excited crowd, "Ich bin ein Berliner." Although affairs later quieted down, Berlin remained a potential flashpoint, the only spot on the globe where American and Russian troops were face to face, with the possibility of an incident setting off an instant nuclear war.

Despite these events, Europe saw no major war in the forty years following the end of World War II. All nations understood the one stark ground rule of European affairs: attacking a European ally of a superpower meant worldwide atomic war. The contending powers were operating within the familiar framework of European history and western culture. The postwar confrontation was really a continuation of the European tradition of power maneuvers, although now for higher stakes because of the awesome power of nuclear weapons. No disastrous miscalculations occurred, because the leaders of each side usually had a clear idea of each other's interests, which allowed accurate estimates of the room for maneuver. As a result, Europeans spent the postwar period worrying that the leaders of the superpowers would lose perspective and destroy them, while at the same time building up the continent to an unprecedented level of prosperity.

THE SPREAD OF THE COLD WAR TO PEASANT LANDS

By 1950 the Cold War had spread from Europe to East Asia, and then to the Middle East, Latin America, and Africa. As it did, it became enmeshed in new forces: nonwestern cultures, the collapse of colonialism, and above all, the growing desire of peasants to improve their lives. Operating in less familiar contexts, both

Cold War Confrontation in Berlin. U.S. and Soviet tanks face each other on October 28, 1961, during the period of tension when the East Germans were putting up the wall sealing off East Berlin. The occupation zones in Berlin, an artificial arrangement after World War II that isolated western forces behind communist lines, continues to remain a flashpoint. In Berlin, the only spot in the world where U.S. and Soviet forces face each other directly, an incident could spark a nuclear war.

Soviet and U.S. leaders made a series of miscalculations that led to extensive guerrilla warfare, nonatomic wars, and, in Cuba, to the brink of nuclear holocaust.

Peasant Problems and Solutions

As had been true for thousands of years, most of the postwar world was made up of peasant societies. Peasants generally worked in a labor-surplus economy, and as a result were compensated meagerly for full-time work on the landlord's fields and mines and often could find only part-time work. Most peasants lacked adequate food, housing, sanitation, and health care, had little chance of enjoying education or political and civil rights, and knew little or nothing about the world outside their immediate environs. A few intrepid individuals ran away to join bandit gangs or the army or went to the slums of the big cities, but most remained where they were born, dying worn out in their thirties and forties. Many peasants assumed that circumstances would not change for their children and their children's children.

After World War II, however, the static pattern of peasant life began to change, first slowly and then more rapidly. Some of the causes were economic and technical, such as the Green Revolution in agriculture, but the two greatest agents for change were probably modern mass communications, particularly the radio, and Leninist-Maoist revolutionary theory and practice. Even the poorest peasant communities often possessed a transistor radio, and through the radio broadcasts the peasants began to get a better idea of the outside world

and how others lived. Depending on the time and place, the voice on the radio might stir up the embers of local discontent, calling for the support of the government or for throwing out the colonial masters.

Sometimes the peasants heard a Marxist voice, urging them to improve their condition by destroying their landlord oppressors, overthrowing the government that backed the landlords, and opposing the United States, the prop of the government and the landlords. As a consequence, peasants around the world became increasingly restless and more willing to take action to improve their lives.

The Marxist message to the peasants would not have been effective if it had been made by Marx himself. A European interested in the changes wrought by the Industrial Revolution, Marx envisioned Marxism triumphing in the industrial nations of the west, mainly through the mass action of the urban workers. In the early twentieth century, as western industrial nations created the welfare state to placate the workers, the vision of the circumstances in which Marxism would be victorious began to change. Lenin pulled off the first successful Marxist revolution in a peasant land, by using the tiny urban proletariat at the crucial time and place. Mao Tse-tung went much further, turning Marx on his head: Mao envisioned the peasant in both western and nonwestern cultures becoming the driving force of Marxist change, opening up the whole peasant world to the cause of Marxism. In this context of evolving Marxism, the Cold War, conducted by the leaders of the two most powerful industrial nations of the west, was increasingly fought out in the lands of the peasants.

The Cold War in East and Southeast Asia, 1940s–1960s

On October 1, 1949, the victorious communist leader in China's war, Mao Tse-tung, proclaimed the People's Republic of China. Mao's triumph in China was an early example of trends that would become increasingly important in the postwar world (see Map 86). His strength had originally risen from effective communication with the Chinese peasantry, attending to their needs while indoctrinating and organizing them to defeat the corrupt Nationalist regime of Chiang Kai-shek. As his following grew, Mao was able, with captured Japanese equipment and some Soviet help, to move from guerrilla warfare to the conventional field armies that finally destroyed Chiang Kai-shek's forces. In different ways, both of the superpowers, caught up in their own frame of reference, missed the point of the successful peasant war. The United States, seeing only the spread of communism, backed the anticommunist but repressive Chiang government and came out on the losing side. After 1949, the United States, hoping that Chiang could make a comeback from his refuge on Taiwan, refused to recognize Mao's government and blocked its membership in the United Nations, earning the enmity of the most populous nation in the world.

The Soviet Union also mishandled the Chinese situation. In the 1950s, it persisted in treating the People's Republic as an eastern European satellite, while attacking Mao's brand of Marxism. In addition, the People's Republic made the nationalistic demand that the Russians return the Chinese provinces lost to the tsars

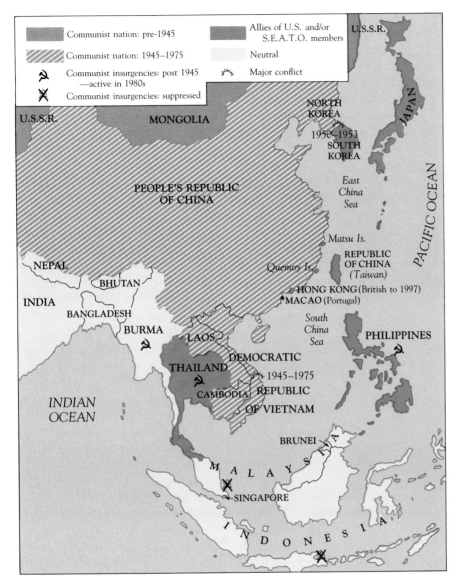

MAP 86
The Cold War in Asia. After World War II, communism spread into Asia in the context of armed struggle, despite resistance by the United States. Communist regimes came to power in China through civil war and in Vietnam, Laos, and Cambodia through civil war and through outlasting the French and the Americans. Only a major military effort, again on the part of the United States, prevented the Communists from taking over all of Korea. Communist guerrillas also were active throughout the rest of Southeast Asia; in some nations the guerrillas were eliminated, but in others they persisted, particularly in the Philippines.

during the New Imperialism. By the 1960s, these issues led to a persisting state of hostility between the two great Marxist states. The Sino-Soviet border, amidst sporadic clashes, became one of the most heavily guarded frontiers in the world, and the Russians found themselves faced with major enemies in both Europe and Asia. The Cold War had become a three-dimensional affair.

Compared with the peasant-guerrilla roots of the conflict in China, the 1950–1953 war in Korea was a European-style struggle over spheres of influence. In the postwar settlement, Korea had been divided into two occupation zones to buffer Soviet interests in Manchuria and U.S. interests in Japan. The occupation forces soon departed, however, leaving a communist dictatorship in North Ko-

rea and an anticommunist authoritarian regime in South Korea. In contrast to Europe, the United States displayed uncertainty over the extent of its sphere of influence in Asia. The U.S. umbrella definitely covered Japan, Okinawa, and the Philippines, but did it extend to noncommunist regimes in Taiwan, South Korea, and Southeast Asia?

Believing that the United States

did not intend to protect South Korea, North Korea invaded and quickly overran most of that nation in June 1950. The ensuing struggle inaugurated another pattern in the Cold War in Asia. U.S. allies in Asia were weaker than the allies of the Soviet Union; the United States would have to expend fighting men as well as military supplies, whereas the Soviet Union only needed to send supplies to keep its allies in the field. Deciding that it still wished to retain South Korea as a buffer to protect Japan, the Truman administration, with United Nations' sanction to repel aggression, rushed U.S. troops to Korea. Under the direction of General MacArthur, U.N. forces, overwhelmingly U.S. and South Korean, drove the North Koreans back, and by the autumn of 1950 were approaching the border of the People's Republic. Mao, at that time an ally of the Soviet Union, was sheltering the remnants of the North Korean air force. Fearing a retaliatory invasion, he sent masses of Chinese troops into Korea, sweeping the U.N. forces back into South Korea.

By 1951, fighting had bogged down near the original border between the two Koreas. It was clear that U.S. forces could not win a ground war against the Chinese, who could only be defeated by bombing them with conventional or possibly nuclear bombs. This made war with the Soviet Union a distinct possibility, and Truman and the Joint Chiefs of Staff decided that U.S. interests on the Asian mainland were not important enough to risk a third world war. The People's Republic was not bombed, and MacArthur was sacked when he made public protests.

The United States settled for a stalemate in Korea. In 1953, an armistice was signed, but the cease-fire line remained heavily fortified in the years that followed, with the reconstituted North Korean army facing South Korean and U.S. troops. The United States sustained 158,000 casualties and incurred heavy costs to fight the war and to maintain its military presence in Korea, whereas the Soviet Union expended a few supplies and lost not a man.

Learning from its indecision over Korea, the United States between 1954 and 1956 applied the containment policy to Asia. Trying to make Asia as stable as Europe, the United States instituted mutual defense treaties with South Korea, Taiwan, and later South Vietnam. Further, it established the Southeast Asia Treaty Organization (SEATO), a military alliance consisting of the United States, Great Britain, France, Australia, New Zealand, Thailand, and the Philippines. The Eisenhower administration now believed it had walled in "communist aggression" in Asia as well as in Europe.

Even as the wall was going up, foundations were beginning to crumble. During the 1950s, the Soviet Union and in particular the People's Republic promoted "wars of liberation," Marxist-led peasant guerrilla conflicts, in Southeast Asia. Marxist guerrillas, depending on the circumstances, struck at landlords, colonial authorities, and independent governments. The United States, seeing the Marxist leadership but not the sources of peasant unrest, sent Truman Doctrine-style military aid and advisers to the colonial masters and the authoritarian governments of the region. This aid, in combination with other factors, eliminated insurgency in some

areas, but Marxist guerrillas continued to operate in Burma, Thailand, and particularly the Philippines throughout the postwar period.

By the late 1950s and early 1960s, the Eisenhower and Kennedy administrations were becoming aware of struggles for social reform welling up in Asia, Africa, and Latin America. Although hoping to deal with the roots of peasant unrest, U.S. leaders faced a cluster of questions to which they found no completely satisfactory answer. Outside western Europe, most non-Marxist nations of the world, including many of the newly independent ex-colonies, were authoritarian states whose economy and society were based on the exploitation of peasant labor. Should the United States, the bastion of free enterprise and private property, interfere in sovereign states and force the landlords to give up part of their property to the peasants for land reform, part of their income to provide social services, and a share of their political power? What if the newly reconstructed nation ceased being an ally of the United States against the Soviet Union? Or was it better to continue to support proven allies and hope that either by force or reform they would deal with peasant unrest? What if some of these governments, even with U.S. military aid, failed to stem Marxist-led guerrillas? Should the United States send troops to fight Marxist guerrillas to save an anti-Soviet ally? Basically, how does a capitalist state conduct a Cold War in peasant lands?

Trying to respond to peasant unrest, the Eisenhower and Kennedy administrations initiated several economic assistance programs. Eisenhower set up the Inter-American Export Bank and Kennedy earmarked $1 billion dollars for ten years for the Alliance for Progress, both programs for those Latin American nations that undertook social reforms. The initiatives fizzled, however; the Latin American ruling groups did not make the necessary sacrifices, instead diverting the money to the military. The Kennedy administration created the Peace Corps, where individual Americans volunteered to bring educational and technological skills to poor nations; but this program had only a feeble impact on the key problems of the peasant world.

Despite their new interest in promoting social reform, U.S. leaders continued to put the bulk of their efforts into the old policy of military containment. Kennedy coupled to the old massive retaliation doctrine the new concept of "flexible response," which entailed building up the army, navy, and marines to fight limited wars. The United States also stepped up Truman Doctrine commitments to train and supply the armed forces of allies around the world. At the same time that its new policies were evolving, the United States had two opportunities to deal with the Cold War in lands where peasants were a significant presence: Cuba and Vietnam.

CRISES IN CUBA,
1959–1962

The Cuban episode merits some attention as a study in the pressures and perceptions that could lead to nuclear war. Cuba in the 1950s was controlled by dictator Fulgencio Batista, an ally of the U.S. government and a friend of U.S. businesses ranging

from sugar refining to gambling interests in Havana. Under Batista, Cuban urban areas maintained a relatively high standard of living, but the rural peasantry suffered from seasonal unemployment and lacked medical facilities and education. The United States, requiring only that political regimes in postwar Latin America be anticommunist, that is, support the United States in the Cold War, backed Batista.

In 1959, a young lawyer named Fidel Castro, who had made earlier attempts to overthrow Batista, gathered enough support to topple Batista's regime. Castro, who assumed dictatorial powers, also announced that he was a Marxist. Castro began to create a society based on Marxist principles, building hospitals, schools, and providing work for the unemployed; he also confiscated foreign business holdings. Castro made overtures for economic aid from the Russians and announced that Cuba would spread the gospel of Marxist revolution throughout Latin America.

The Eisenhower administration reacted vigorously. Washington could not tolerate the existence of a "communist" country in the heart of the U.S. sphere of influence in the Caribbean. Trying to make trouble for Castro at home and bring about his downfall, Eisenhower broke diplomatic relations with Cuba and reduced U.S. sugar imports. Believing that once the Cubans had a taste of communism they would be ready to rebel against it, Eisenhower authorized the CIA (Central Intelligence Agency) to recruit and train anti-Castro Cubans to invade Cuba and provide a rallying point for the Cuban population to overthrow Castro. Faced with aggressive U.S. hostility, Castro

accelerated his nationalization of U.S. business holdings in Cuba and secured economic aid from the Soviet Union.

On entering office in 1961, President Kennedy authorized the invasion force to proceed, with the understanding that the United States was not to be involved in the landing itself. In April, the anti-Castro forces bombed a Cuban air base and landed at the Bay of Pigs, but the peasants, whose lot had improved under Castro, did not rise, supporting the regime instead. Kennedy vetoed pleas for air support, and Cuban militia crushed the invasion in two days. The Bay of Pigs fiasco was a sharp blow to Kennedy's prestige. Attacked for not supporting the invasion force, he was determined to move more vigorously in the future.

The Bay of Pigs, combined with other factors, apparently led Khrushchev to consider Kennedy to be a weak leader. More ominously, it tempted Khrushchev to use Cuba to solve some of his own problems: He was criticized at home for failures in agriculture and for letting the United States get ahead in the missile race. Castro, afraid that the United States would try again to topple him, was calling for support. Khrushchev therefore arranged to send medium-range bombers and medium-range missiles secretly to Cuba. These weapons could defend Cuba by threatening destruction in the southeastern United States if Cuba were attacked. Such a move would demonstrate that Khrushchev could take a tough line, apply additional pressure to get the western powers out of Berlin, moderate the imbalance in the arms race, and provide support for a Marxist comrade.

In October 1962, U.S. spy planes discovered the missile sites under construction in Cuba, some almost complete. The Kennedy administration sprang into action. Cuba was for the United States the equivalent of Hungary for the U.S.S.R.: a direct challenge to a vital sphere of influence. At stake were U.S. leadership in Latin America and its credibility in western Europe; in addition, President Kennedy seems to have considered it a personal test. Amid a flurry of pressures, the Kennedy administration worked out the U.S. position. The missiles and bombers must go. If the Soviet Union refused to remove them voluntarily, the United States would destroy the missiles by air strike or invasion. If such an action meant a collision with the Soviet Union, the United States would go to war. Some SAC bombers were put into the air and others on fifteen-minute alert. ICBMs

were placed in a preliminary state of readiness to fire. Army units were moved into position in the Southeast and Guantánamo Bay was reinforced. Kennedy also imposed a "quarantine," a peacetime naval blockade of Cuba (by international law an act of war). Latin American nations, at a meeting of the OAS (Organization of American States), supported the blockade. While publicly throwing down the gauntlet, the Kennedy administration was careful not to back the Russians into a corner; intimations were given that in return for Soviet withdrawal the United States would promise not to again try to attack Castro, and perhaps would remove the provocative missiles from Turkey.

The decision now lay in Moscow, and for six days peace or war hung in the balance. Faced with U.S. resolve backed by U.S. nuclear superiority,

the Soviet premier ordered the Soviet ships carrying missiles to Cuba to turn back and avoid confrontation with the U.S. Navy. In an exchange of notes, Khrushchev and Kennedy agreed that the Soviet Union would remove the offending missiles and bombers and that the United States would make a public pledge not to invade Cuba. The United States later removed its missiles from Turkey. The armed forces of the two nations were ordered to stand down, and the shadow of nuclear war passed over.

THE STRUGGLE IN INDOCHINA, 1945–1975

The Cuban episode had been spectacular but relatively brief; the struggle originating in French Indochina was a grinding thirty-year war of at-

Away from the Brink of Nuclear Holocaust. A U.S. destroyer pulls alongside a Soviet freighter apparently carrying Soviet missiles out of Cuba in November 1962. The U.S. naval blockade of Cuba, although technically an act of war, was one of a series of military threats and diplomatic manueverings that persuaded the Soviet Union to withdraw its missiles from Cuba, ending a moment of Cold War crisis that threatened the world with nuclear war.

1953	1957	1960	1963	1964-75

Castro
assumes
power
in Cuba

Cuban
missile
crisis

Escalation
and termination
of war in
Indochina

Death
of Stalin

Warsaw
Pact

Sputnik

Hungarian
revolt

Berlin
wall

trition. Beginning in 1945, the Vietnamese communist Ho Chi Minh led the Vietminh, a broad coalition of Vietnamese, in a guerrilla war to expel the French. He was extremely popular in north Vietnam, which became his stronghold, while the French were stronger in the south. Ho's military leader, General Giap, wore down the French by endless guerrilla raids, while building a regular army. In 1954, the Vietnamese captured the heavily fortified French stronghold of Dien Bien Phu. Exhausted militarily and financially and with a mandate from the war-weary French people, the French government pulled out of Indochina.

At this point, the Cold War intruded into what had been predominantly an anticolonial struggle. Seeing the conflict basically in terms of the advance of communism, the United States had previously aided the French and now intervened to prevent Ho from gaining all of French Indochina. At the same time, the People's Republic and the Soviet Union rushed in to bolster Ho. At the Geneva peace talks, Laos and Cambodia were set up as independent noncommunist states, and Vietnam was divided into two districts, to be unified by an election in 1956. Ho controlled the northern half of Vietnam, and the anticommunist Ngo Dinh Diem was put into authority in the south. The United States was pleased; Ho's successes had been limited; the wall of containment had bent but not broken. During the years that followed, the election fell by the wayside; Ho transformed the north into a hardline communist dictatorship and Diem attempted to impose an authoritarian regime on the south.

In the late 1950s and early 1960s the United States found its wall of containment in Indochina rapidly being undermined. Communist guerrillas were operating in Laos, and a Marxist-dominated group had risen up in South Vietnam against the repressive government of Diem. The anti-Diem guerrillas gained the support of a large section of the peasantry, but at first received little more than cheers of support from North Vietnam and other Marxist states. Diem, however, claimed he had been attacked by Viet Cong (Vietnamese communists) from the south and also by troops from North Vietnam. He asked the United States for aid under the Truman Doctrine, as a friendly nation threatened by both inside and outside aggression.

The Eisenhower and Kennedy administrations, agreeing with Diem, sent military equipment and advisers to South Vietnam, involving the United States for the first time in a peasant guerrilla war. By 1963, the Viet Cong, supplied by the North Vietnamese with Russian and Chinese war materiel along the mountainous and jungle-covered Ho Chi Minh Trail, had gained control of large sections of South Vietnam.

During 1964–1965, two decisions transformed what had been a civil war in South Vietnam into a multination, full-scale struggle. Once again forced to prop up an ally weaker than its communist opponents, the United States believed the communist Vietnamese must be stopped or that all the southeast Asian nations would fall one by one like dominoes. After U.S. supply bases in South Vietnam and naval ships off North Vietnam were attacked, the Johnson administration sent troops to South Vietnam and began bombing the Ho Chi Minh Trail and the southern section of North Vietnam. Meanwhile, the North Vietnamese decided to send units of their army to South Vietnam to assist the Viet Cong. Formidably disciplined, the communists were ready to wage the same war of attrition against the Americans and the South Vietnam-

"NAM"

The mood was sardonic, fatalistic, and melancholy. I could hear it in our black jokes: "Hey, Bill, you're going on patrol today. If you get your legs blown off can I have your boots?" I could hear it in the songs we sang. Some were versions of maudlin country-and-western tunes like "Detroit City," the refrain of which expressed every rifleman's hope:

I wanna go home, I wanna go home,
O I wanna go home.

. . . The fighting had not only become more intense, but more vicious. Both we and the Viet Cong began to make a habit of atrocities. One of 1st Battalion's radio operators was captured by an enemy patrol, tied up, beaten with clubs, then executed. . . .
. . . We paid the enemy back, sometimes with interest. It was common knowledge that quite a few captured VC never made it to prison camps; they were reported as "shot and killed while attempting to escape." Some line companies did not even bother taking prisoners; they simply killed every VC they saw, and a number of Vietnamese who were only suspects. The latter were usually counted as enemy dead, under the unwritten

rule "If he's dead and Vietnamese, he's VC."

Everything rotted and corroded quickly over there: bodies, boot leather, canvas, metal, morals. Scorched by the sun, wracked by the wind and rain of the monsoon, fighting in alien swamps and jungles, our humanity rubbed off of us as the protective bluing rubbed off the barrels of our rifles. We were fighting in the cruelest kind of conflict, a people's war. It was not orderly campaign, as in Europe, but a war for survival waged in a wilderness without rules or laws; a war in which each soldier fought for his own life and the lives of the men beside him, not caring who he killed in that personal cause or how many or in what manner and feeling only contempt for those who sought to impose on his savage struggle the mincing distinctions of civilized warfare—that code of battlefield ethics that attempted to humanize an essentially inhuman war. According to those "rules of engagement," it was morally right to shoot an unarmed Vietnamese who was running, but wrong to shoot one who was standing or walking; it was wrong to shoot an enemy prisoner at close range, but right for a sniper at long range to kill an enemy soldier who was no more

able than a prisoner to defend himself; it was wrong for infantrymen to destroy a village with white-phosphorus grenades, but right for a fighter pilot to drop napalm on it. Ethics seemed to be a manner of distance and technology. You could never go wrong if you killed people at long range and with sophisticated weapons.*

U.S. soldiers and marines were not prepared for the ground fighting in Vietnam. They had expected to face their enemy in open battle, as in World War II and in Korea. In Vietnam, there were few battlefronts; helicopters flew in troops to spots where the enemy allegedly were concentrated and after combat flew them out again. After ten patrols up the same trail, one second of carelessness on the eleventh patrol meant sudden wounds or death from an antipersonnel mine. The enemy were nowhere and everywhere; the villagers working in the fields claimed to know nothing, but some tossed grenades into U.S. bivouacs at night. After serving for a few months, burnt-out veterans had to be spelled off with fresh, but still unprepared, troops.

*Philip Caputo, A Rumor of War (New York: Holt, Rinehart, and Winston, 1977), pp. 227–230.

ese government that had been successful against the French. They were determined to endure casualties and bombing destruction while inflicting damage on their enemies until the American public lost its will to continue the struggle. Once the Americans left, Vietnam would be united by force into a single communist state.

As the struggle in Vietnam con-

tinued, the world powers tacitly agreed to keep the conflict from triggering a devastating nuclear world war. The Soviet Union and the People's Republic would confine themselves to supplying the communist Vietnamese, while the United States would not employ nuclear weapons or bomb Russian supply ships and Chinese supply depots in North Vietnam. As

in the Korean war the United States was fighting a conventional war on the Asian mainland without the knockout punch its nuclear weapons could provide.

Unlike Korea, where regular armies fought along a well-defined battlefront, U.S. forces had to conduct anti-guerrilla operations over a wide area; the winner would be the side who could best operate in a Vietnamese peasant environment. Despite building their forces to more than 500,000 men by 1968, the Americans failed to make decisive headway in the war. The mass of South Vietnamese peasants were caught in the middle. They had little loyalty to the corrupt and repressive South Vietnamese government and none at all to the strange westerners who not only backed that government but had also supported the French. Most peasants were not interested in Marxism either, but at least the Marxists were their own kind.

At the same time, most Americans in the war had little background for understanding or respecting the people whose loyalty was essential for victory. Separated from their clients by language, culture, and physical appearance, many Americans lumped them all together as alien "gooks." Equally important, the Vietnamese communists in the long run were more effective in controlling the peasant villages through indoctrination and the terror of their daily presence than the Americans were with their resettlement programs and sporadic raids.

Beginning in 1968 the war reached its watershed. Influential elements of the U.S. public had already turned against the war, and antidraft and antiwar disruptions steadily increased.

Vietnam. In an attempt to catch an elusive enemy, U.S. forces in Vietnam transported infantry by helicopter in attempts to surprise Viet Cong and North Vietnamese units. Such attacks were designed to inflict casualties rather than capture territory, and the attacking forces were usually withdrawn afterwards. Helicopter raids were only one facet of U.S. tactics, which included patrols, defense of fixed positions, "Freefire zones," napalm strikes, and high altitude bombardment.

The administration of President Richard M. Nixon intensified aspects of the war while systematically withdrawing American troops, both policies having the object of bringing Hanoi to the negotiating table.

In 1973 both sides agreed to an armistice, and to all foreign troops leaving South Vietnam. U.S. forces departed, leaving the South Vietnamese army heavily armed and elaborately equipped. In 1975, North Vietnamese forces, which had remained in Vietnam, and the Viet Cong launched a major assault, overrunning South Vietnam in a few weeks. Meanwhile, communist units also took over in Laos and Cambodia. A major Cold War struggle had come to an end, but others continued or were yet to come.

SUMMARY

As World War II ended, the United States and the Soviet Union, the superpowers of the postwar period, became antagonists over affairs in Europe. An extended period of postwar competition known as the Cold War developed, centering initially in Europe. Beginning with the Truman administration, U.S. leaders were convinced that the Soviet Union was determined to take over as much of the world as possible for communism. In place of the traditional premise of U.S. foreign policy, staying out of European affairs, they maintained a permanent presence in Europe in order to contain communism.

In the decade that followed, the United States pursued a number of energetic policies that stabilized western Europe and the Mediterranean and brought these areas under the military protection of the United States. Fearing attack by the capitalist nations, the Soviet Union consolidated its position in eastern Europe. Both nations were involved in major confrontations over Berlin and Hungary.

The superpowers exacerbated the situation by plunging into a frightening nuclear arms race. Both nations developed hydrogen bombs that were individually capable of destroying major cities, mounting them on bombers and then on missiles, both of which had intercontinental range. The United States maintained the nuclear advantage into the 1960s, surrounding the Soviet Union with air and missile bases and maintaining a large lead in missiles and bombers.

Meanwhile the Cold War spread to Asia and the Caribbean in the context of peasant lands. In general, peasants found Marxists to be more sympathetic to their problems. Most peasant guerrilla wars to overturn the landlord-dominated governments in Asia and the Caribbean were controlled by Marxists, while the United States routinely supported those governments because they were anti-Marxist. Mao Tse-tung came to power in China with peasant support, as did Ho Chi Minh in Vietnam. Although the People's Republic eventually split with the Soviet Union, the United States became embroiled with both in the Korean War. Unwilling to bomb the Chinese and risk a nuclear war with the Soviet Union, the United States settled for a stalemate. Later, fearing the spread of communism in southeast Asia, the United States intervened in South Vietnam. As in Korea, the United States limited its military power to avoid nuclear war, and, unable to operate successfully in a peasant guerrilla war, was forced to withdraw.

The most dangerous Cold War incident occurred in Cuba, where Fidel Castro set up a peasant-backed communist state. A U.S. attempt to overthrow him backfired, and when the Soviet Union intervened to protect him against another such attempt, the United States took measures that threatened war. Although the situation was defused, the potential for atomic holocaust continued to hang over the world.

Selected Sources

The Deer Hunter. 1979. A thoughtful motion picture about the effects of the Indochina war on both Vietnamese and U.S. society.

*De Porte, Anton W. *Europe Between the Superpowers: The Enduring Balance.* 1979. An overview of Europe's precarious role in the Cold War.

*Divine, Robert A. *The Cuban Missile Crisis.* 1971. A collection of documents and analysis, giving both the U.S. and Soviet point of view.

*Gaddis, John L. *The United States and the Origins of the Cold War, 1941–1947.* 1972. Stresses Russian expansionism. Compare with Horowitz.

*Herring, George C. *America's Longest War: The U.S. and Vietnam, 1950–75.* 1979. Well-written, concise, and balanced.

*Horowitz, David. *The Free World Colossus.* rev.ed. 1971. Portrays the United States as an active counter-revolutionary force, rather than merely containing communism. Compare with Gaddis.

*LaFeber, Walter. *America, Russia, and the Cold War, 1945 to 1980.* 1980. A well-written account, giving most attention to the United States.

*Martin, Russ. *The Last Parallel.* A first-hand account of fighting in Korea.

Medvedev, Roy A. *Khrushchev.* 1982. The best biography, written by a Soviet dissident.

*Patterson, Walter C. *Nuclear Power.* 1976. A sprightly account of the interconnection of the arms race and the Cold War.

*Ulam, Adam B. *The Rivals: America and Russia Since World War II.* 1971. A balanced account by an expert on the Soviet Union.

*Available in paperback.

THE WEST AND THE NONWEST

Long years ago we made a tryst with destiny, and now the time comes when we shall redeem our pledge, not wholly or in full measure, but very substantially. At the stroke of the midnight hour, when the world sleeps, India will awake to life and freedom. A moment comes, which comes but rarely in history, when we step out from the old to the new, when an age ends, and when the soul of a nation, long suppressed, finds utterance. . . . The achievement we celebrate today is but a step, an opening of opportunity, to the greater triumphs and achievements that await us.

The eloquence of Jawaharlal Nehru (1889–1964), first prime minister of independent India, was more than political rhetoric. India's Congress party, as other colonial liberation movements across Asia and Africa, had roots that reached back well before the beginning of this century. In India as in other colonized areas, however, the climactic conflict and final victory came in the wake of World War II. The independence that resulted, as Nehru suggested, brought opportunities for economic development as well as political liberation. But in this field, the new nations would find success harder to achieve.

The following pages first survey the end of western imperial rule over much of the nonwestern world and then examine the paths to economic development taken by the new countries and their part in international affairs.

CONTENTS

THE DISMANTLING OF IMPERIALISM

The novelty and scope of the postwar liberation movement can scarcely be exaggerated. In the three decades after 1945, western nations surrendered imperial overlordship of a billion human beings, a third of the population of the earth. In a single generation, African and Asian colonies, some

The United Nations Building in New York. High hopes for the international organization are reflected in this picture of the U.N. flanked by the flags of all nations. While the United Nations has not always lived up to the aspirations of its founders, it does continue to provide a forum for contact between representatives of east and west, large nations and small ones.

going back five centuries to the beginning of European overseas empire building, were granted their independence. Dozens of new nations emerged, and the so-called third world was born.

There were precursors to the postwar independence movement, particularly in the evolution of the British Commonwealth of Nations between the world wars. The Act of Westminster, passed by the British Parliament in 1931, made official the independence of such older colonies as Australia, New Zealand, and South Africa, which had in fact been self-governing for decades. The voluntary affiliation of these nations in the Commonwealth did not in any way limit self-rule in the former colonies. Continental European powers such as France, however, seemed to be moving toward closer integration with their colonies before 1939.

The pattern of post-World War II liberation was not uniform, but important similarities existed between the various liberation struggles. Most of the anticolonial movements were led by western-educated Asian or African leaders. These charismatic popular figures understood western ways. They learned how to use European ideas, institutions, and weapons to dislodge their imperial rulers. A prime instrument in most such struggles was a strongly centralized, mass-based political party, usually built around the personality and program of the rebel leader. These national liberation parties often became the base of political power in the new nation once the westerners departed.

The changeover from colony to nation was sometimes accompanied by a good deal of bloodshed. Violence came in the course of winning independence, as in French Indochina or Algeria, or afterward, as in British India and the Belgian Congo. In many cases, however, the western powers withdrew without a struggle. Exhausted by World War II and finding it increasingly hard to justify imperialism, Europeans were frequently glad enough to get out of their colonial entanglements without a fight.

THE COLLAPSE OF COLONIALISM IN SOUTH AND SOUTHEAST ASIA

Whereas most of Asia had come under some degree of European political and economic influence, south and southeast Asia had experienced full colonial status, complete incorporation in western-ruled empires. In the Indian subcontinent and in the islands and peninsulas of southeast Asia, militant and sometimes violent mass movements proved necessary to expel western imperialists at last after World War II.

India and Pakistan

Britain's Indian empire, the jewel in Queen Victoria's crown a century earlier, was one of the first colonies to gain independence after 1945. British India did not, however, emerge as a single new country, but as several sovereign states. The most important of these were the primarily Hindu nation of India and the Muslim state of Pakistan.

The demand, first for autonomy and then for complete independence, had been growing in the Indian subcontinent since the later nineteenth century. The largest liberation movements had been organized by western-educated spokespersons for the two largest religions, the Hindus (350 million) and the Muslims (100 million). The more numerous Hindus, however, had taken the lead. The Congress party, led by Mohandas Gandhi (1869–1949), popularly called the Mahatma or "Enlightened One," had severely shaken British rule by a series of nonviolent campaigns of civil disobedience between the world wars. After World War II, the British Labor party, long opposed to imperialism, came to power and began to negotiate for Indian independence.

Both the British leaders and Gandhi hoped to free India as one nation. But religious tensions between Hindus and Muslims, long antedating the coming of the British, made postimperial union impossible. Muslims in particular feared discrimination in a unified state in which Hindus would heavily outnumber them. A virtual civil war erupted, and mass migrations took place as whole villages moved toward centers of population dominated by their coreligionists. In the end, India was liberated in 1947 as two major nations: a predominantly Hindu India filling most of the subcontinent and a divided northern state of Pakistan inhabited mostly by Muslims. The historically related island of Ceylon, renamed Sri Lanka, gained its independence the following year.

Southeast Asia

During World War II, the Japanese overran most of the mainland and islands of southeast Asia. In so doing, they conquered or expelled British, French, Dutch, and American imperial rulers. Although the Japanese

occupation proved no more popular with southeast Asians than western rule had been, the Japanese example—Asians defeating westerners—heartened the colonial peoples for the postwar liberation struggle.

The British and the French had dominated mainland southeast Asia before the war. The British controlled Burma, on India's northeastern frontier, and the long peninsula of Malaya. The French ruled or exercised a protectorate over the Indochinese states of Vietnam, Laos, and Cambodia. In the aftermath of World War II, all these areas gained their freedom—the British colonies with little conflict, the French after a long, bloody struggle in Vietnam.

The British granted independence to Burma in 1948 and to Malaya in 1957. In both former colonies, the British suppressed guerrilla movements, some communist led and others mounted by ethnic minorities. In Malaya, the guerrillas were put down before the colony was freed; in Burma, the struggle continued after the British withdrew. Perhaps the most successful of these former colonies was the great port of Singapore at the tip of the Malay Peninsula. Dominated by a thriving Chinese commercial class, Singapore became an independent and very prosperous state in 1959.

The 3,000 islands of Indonesia, sprawling over an area as large as the United States, had been a Dutch colony since the seventeenth century. In 1945, however, the Japanese ex-

Jawaharlal Nehru and Mohandas Gandhi. The leaders of India's independence movement enjoy a relaxed moment on the eve of their country's liberation in 1947. Nehru, a long-time follower of the immensely popular Mahatma, displayed a more formal style of leadership as the first prime minister of the new country.

ample and the weakness of the Netherlands after World War II encouraged Indonesians to resist the return of the Dutch. A charismatic leader named Achmed Sukarno organized and led the Indonesian Nationalist party in a revolutionary war. The Dutch hung on until 1949, when pressure by the United States compelled them to abandon the struggle.

The Philippine Islands, just north of Indonesia, was one of the first colonies to be freed after the war. The United States, which had taken the islands from Spain at the turn of the century, had promised them independence by 1944, a date that was only briefly delayed by the war. Rav-

aged by heavy fighting, the new Philippine republic was also confronted by a communist guerrilla movement that persisted into the 1980s.

A number of small Pacific island territories and some mainland and island colonies in the Caribbean Sea also achieved independence, including the mainland colonies of British Honduras and British Guiana, as well as most of the Bahamas and many islands of the Lesser Antilles. Some enclaves of western colonialism remained in both areas, however. French, British, and U.S. colonies continued in the Pacific, including the French Marquesas and Society Islands, the British Gilberts, American

Samoa, and the U.S. military outpost of Guam. In the Caribbean basin, French Guiana, the British Virgin Islands, and the U.S. dependency of Puerto Rico survived as remnants of once larger empires.

THE DECLINE OF WESTERN CONTROLS IN THE MIDDLE EAST AND NORTH AFRICA

Another important area of European colonial involvement in 1945 was the swath of territories around the eastern

MAP 87

Asia after World War II. This map depicts the results of the independence movement that swept Asia. Most Asians secured their independence from western colonial powers in the 1940s and 1950s. China was divided between two governments after the war.

Partition of India

French Vietnamese War

French Algerian War

Liberation of Burma

Liberation of Indonesia

Liberation of Malaya

Founding of Israel

Egyptian Revolution

Suez Crisis

and southern shores of the Mediterranean Sea. These two zones of the Middle East and north Africa had in common an arid, often desert terrain, a substantial Arab and Berber (in north Africa) population, and the Muslim religion. The major colonial powers in the area were, once more, the British and the French.

Despite its rather sparse population and unproductive land, the region was valued by Europeans for a number of reasons. One was its strategic location on the way to south and east Asia: By far the shortest route to the east was through the Suez Canal, which lay across Egyptian territory. Another was the growing oil production of the area, particularly in Arabia, Iran, and the smaller states around the Persian Gulf. Minority populations, particularly growing numbers of European Jews in the British mandate of Palestine and the large number of French settlers in French Algeria, were other concerns. As the cold war developed, finally, the region became an area of Soviet-American competition for influence and alliances.

The liberation movements that arose in the Middle East and north Africa, then, encountered a tangled web of western interests. Ideological and religious developments caused

further problems. These included both Israeli and Arab nationalism and a powerful Muslim religious revival. The result was a confusion of conflicts that began with the postwar independence movements of the 1940s and continued into the 1980s.

Israel, Egypt, and the Arabs

One of the most divisive events of the postwar years was the emergence of the new nation of Israel in Great Britain's Palestine mandate. This powerful little western state took shape in the heart of a region already aflame with Arab nationalism, soon to be fueled even more by the Muslim religious resurgence.

Great Britain felt a strong need to ensure good relations with the Arab states after World War II, both for their strategic location and for their oil reserves. The British had even encouraged Arab nationalism in the neighboring French mandates of Syria and Lebanon, which led to the independence of these small nations in 1946. Great Britain granted full independence to the British protectorate of Transjordan (later Jordan) in that year, and terminated its remaining supervisory relations with Iraq. There remained the British mandate

over Palestine, a region with a majority Arab population but a growing minority of Jewish immigrants from Europe.

The Jews, pouring into Palestine from the concentration camps of Hitler's Europe, were determined to establish a homeland of their own in what had, in ancient times, been the Hebrews' "promised land." To achieve this end, in the face of hostile British policy, they organized a terrorist underground and tried to force the British out. The Palestinian Arabs, equally determined to defend the land that had been theirs for centuries, called on the neighboring Arab states for help. Great Britain, caught in the middle, turned the problem over to the United Nations, which in 1947 recommended partition of Palestine between the feuding parties. Neither side was happy with this solution. When the British withdrew in 1948, the Jews, under David Ben Gurion, announced the creation of the new nation of Israel—and the neighboring Arabs promptly attacked it.

The Israelis, better equipped and trained, more unified, and supported from the beginning by the United States, defeated their Arab adversaries. More than a million Palestinian Arabs fled their villages into refugee camps in surrounding Arab states. But

819

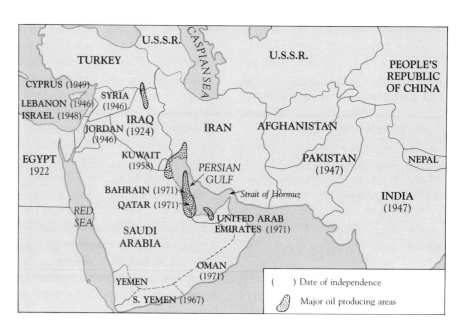

MAP 88
The Middle East after World War II. In the 1940s Great Britain and France pulled out of Cyprus and the Fertile Crescent territories they had held as League of Nations Mandates since the end of World War I. United Nations attempts to partition Palestine between the Arab and Jewish inhabitants living there, coupled with the hostility of the neighboring Arab states to the new Jewish nation of Israel, led the region into a state of continuing turmoil. Great Britain also ended its controls over the Arab states on the perimeter of the Arabian Peninsula. Persian Gulf petroleum has become a major factor in world economics and politics.

neither the Arab nations nor the displaced Palestinians regarded the issue as settled.

The history of Egypt's emergence as an independent power was also complicated and violent. Located in north Africa but historically related to the Middle East since ancient times, Egypt had fallen into Great Britain's imperial orbit in the second half of the nineteenth century. An independent kingdom since the 1920s, Egypt had nevertheless retained close treaty relations with Great Britain until the 1950s. Egypt's King Farouk, however, had done little for his country, and in 1952 he was overthrown by a military revolt. The officer who became the nation's new ruler was Gamal Abdel Nasser, one of the most aggressive and popular liberation leaders of the postwar period.

Nasser announced a number of reforms, including the distribution of land to the poor and the building of a huge dam at Aswan on the Upper Nile. He was a strong opponent of

Israel, and he suspected imperialist motives behind British and American attempts to organize an Arab alliance to keep the Russians out of the Middle East. To counter British and American influence, he sought better relations with the Soviet Union and other eastern European countries.

The Suez crisis of 1956 erupted from these simmering conflicts. The United States, resenting Nasser's turn to communist bloc countries for weapons to be used against Israel, announced it would not provide the huge amount of capital earlier promised for the Aswan Dam. Nasser struck back against the west by nationalizing the strategic Suez Canal, which had remained in British hands after their withdrawal from the rest of Egypt. Thus challenged, the British concluded a secret agreement with the Israelis and the French to retake the canal by force.

The brief conflict that followed proved in the long run a defeat for the former imperial powers. The Is-

raeli army, with the help of British and French air power, successfully overran the canal zone. The United States, shocked at this return to nineteenth-century "gunboat diplomacy" and acting in rare agreement with the Soviet Union, compelled her allies to return the canal to Egypt. Nasser, whose overthrow had been a prime goal of the expedition, actually came out of the crisis more popular with his people than ever.

The Algerian Revolution

France's colonies in north Africa included the kingdom of Morocco, the small colony of Tunisia, and the much larger colony of Algeria in between. The Arab and Berber population of these regions had become strongly nationalistic and antiimperialist between the world wars and had begun to reorganize politically. In 1956, two years after their defeat in Vietnam, the French granted independence to Morocco and Tunisia. They were, however, determined to retain control of Algeria, with its large population of French settlers and its potential oil wealth.

The consequence was a long and bloody struggle between the French and the National Liberation Front (FLN) in Algeria. The French army responded to guerrilla attacks and urban terrorism by bombing villages and torturing suspects. The French settlers organized their own terrorist group, the Secret Army, which killed many Algerians. France itself was divided over the issue, much as the

Israeli Troops in Jerusalem. The shortest of the Arab-Israeli wars that followed independence was the "Six Day War" of 1967, in which Israeli troops seized their ancient holy city of Jerusalem. This photo shows soldiers at the traditional "Wailing Wall" in that city.

821

ALGERIA IS FRANCE

No uncertainty must be allowed to remain as to our inflexible determination to preserve Algeria from the terrible destiny that some are seeking to prepare for it. France is at home here, or rather, Algeria and all her inhabitants form an integral part of France, one and indivisible. All must know, here and elsewhere, that France will not leave Algeria any more than she will leave Provence or Brittany. Whatever happens, the destiny of Algeria is French.

This means that a choice has been made. The choice is called "integration." It is to make Algeria each day more completely a province, different from the others, certainly, but fully French. *

Jacques Soustelle, French governor-general of Algeria, thus expressed the traditional French belief that France's imperial territories should be tightly integrated with France, represented in the French Chamber of Deputies and administered like the departments of mainland France. This political integration was useful to some colonial leaders, enabling them to gain valuable understanding of the French political system against which they struggled. In Algeria, however, this attitude strengthened the will of French settlers to resist liberation for the colony with the slogan "L'Algerie, c'est la France!"— "Algeria is France!"

*Jacques Soustelle before the Algerian Assembly, 1956, in Edward Behr, *The Algerian Problem* (Harmondsworth, England: Penguin Books, 1961), p. 74.

United States was to be over Vietnam in the next decade. In 1959, however, General de Gaulle, France's World War II hero, became the nation's president for the second time. Seeing the Algerian conflict as hopeless and divisive, de Gaulle began the painful process of extricating France from the struggle with the FLN. This difficult feat was not accomplished until 1962, when the Algerians at last won their independence, at a cost of perhaps a million Algerian lives.

THE DECLINE OF WESTERN EMPIRE IN SUB-SAHARAN AFRICA

North Africa, the Africa of the Mediterranean and the Sahara, was part of the Arab zone, linked by cultural and religious ties to the Middle East. Africa south of the Sahara, by contrast, was inhabited largely by black Africans. Most of sub-Saharan, black Africa had been absorbed into European overseas empires less than a century before, during the scramble for African colonies that began in the 1870s. After no more than a 100 years of western overlordship, most of these African colonies won their independence during the 1960s and 1970s.

Most of sub-Saharan Africa, as much of Asia, was ruled by the British or the French in 1945. The Portuguese and the Belgians also controlled large portions of southern Africa, and the Republic of South Africa was a rich and powerful enclave of white settler rule at the southern tip of the continent. The following sections explore the liberation struggles in each of these groups of colonies.

French and British Africa

The French controlled a wide band of colonies that ran south of the Sahara from the Atlantic east to the frontiers of Egypt and Sudan. Collectively known as French west Africa and French equatorial Africa, these colonies had been promised some degree of autonomy during World War II. By 1960, this new relationship had evolved rapidly to complete independence for all these territories.

The most successful leader of the movement for the liberation of France's black African colonies was Felix Houphouet-Boigny, a black African planter, doctor, and politician from the small but relatively prosperous colony of Ivory Coast. Houphouet-Boigny, who had served in French governments in Paris, was an experienced political leader. He and other African spokespersons organized a west African independence party and worked with liberal and socialist politicians in Paris to end French rule in the area.

This objective was achieved with minimal violence. Elections held in 1958 granted limited freedom to most of the colonies, with France retaining some political and economic control. The colony of Guinea, under the radical leader Sekou Touré, however, demanded complete independence. In 1960, the rest of French west and French equatorial Africa also secured full independence. In that year also, the French gave up their large east African island colony of Madagascar.

Great Britain's African colonies after World War II consisted of a scattering of British territories along the southern edge of French west Africa and a band of larger colonies running from north to south down the length of east central Africa. Leaders of liberation movements won independence for most of these colonial dependencies with little or no violence, though a terrorist movement did erupt in one east African colony.

The first British colony to gain independence—indeed, the first of all the black African colonies to be liberated—was the west African territory called the Gold Coast, today's Ghana. Kwame Nkrumah, the leader of Ghana's drive for self-government, had studied in both Great Britain and the United States. On his return to the Gold Coast in the early 1950s, he organized the Convention People's party (CCP), a typical mass-based African liberation party. Boycotts, strikes, and other measures speeded up the British timetable for emancipation. In 1957, the new nation of Ghana emerged. In 1960, Nkrumah became president for life, his CCP the only party in a one-party state. Other British west African colonies gained their freedom soon after, the largest

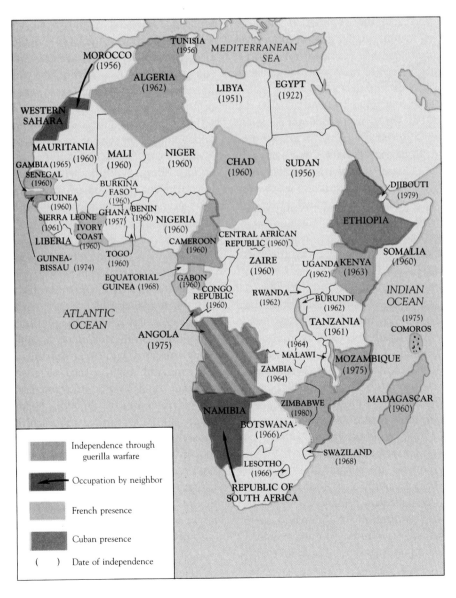

MAP 89
Africa after World War II. This map depicts the results of the independence movements in northern and central Africa in the 1950s and 1960s and in southern Africa in the 1970s. European powers departed peacefully from their overwhelmingly black colonies, but they had to be pushed out by guerrilla warfare from areas that contained a minority of white settlers. French forces remained by invitation in some former French colonies, and Cuban troops arrived in two instances to support Marxist interests in the Cold War.

FREEDOM BRINGS RESPONSIBILITIES

We prefer self-government with danger to servitude in tranquility. Doubtless we shall make mistakes, as have all other nations. We are human beings and hence fallible. But we can try also to learn from the mistakes of others so that we may avoid the deepest pitfalls into which they have fallen. Moreover, the mistakes we make will be our own mistakes, and it will be our responsibility to put them right. As long as we are ruled by others, we shall lay our mistakes at their door, and our sense of responsibility will remain dulled. Freedom brings responsibilities, and our experience can be enriched only by the acceptance of these responsibilities. *

Kwame Nkrumah, speaking three years before the Gold Coast colony gained its independence, made an argument that Gandhi had also made in demanding India's freedom. In answer to the common imperialist assertion that the colonies were not yet developed or experienced enough for independence, Nkrumah asked for his people the right to make their own mistakes, to learn through their errors, and to take responsibility for their own future.

*Kwame Nkrumah, addressing the Gold Coast Assembly, 1954, in The Autobiography of Kwame Nkrumah (Edinburgh: Thomas Nelson and Sons, 1959), p. 166.

and most important of them being Nigeria, in 1960.

Great Britain's east African holdings included Tanganyika, today's Tanzania, freed in 1961; Uganda, liberated in 1962; and Kenya, which secured its independence in 1963. Only in Kenya did the liberation movement have to resort to arms to dislodge the imperialists. Kenya had a sizable minority population of British settlers who, like the Algerian whites, strongly resisted the idea of liberation under majority black rule. Their fears were intensified by the depredations of a terrorist movement called the Mau Mau. In the end, however, Great Britain freed the colony under the leadership of Jomo Kenyatta, a British-educated Ph.D. with a wide popular following.

Zaire, Angola, and Zimbabwe

Europe's colonial territories in central and southern Africa included the huge Belgian Congo, two large Portuguese territories—Angola and Mozambique—and the British colonies of Northern and Southern Rhodesia. The struggles for independence in most of these colonies revealed the many forms that western resistance could take, as well as the numerous problems facing new nations.

The Belgian Congo, today's Zaire, was important to Belgium primarily for the valuable copper mines of its Katanga province. At the first sign of agitation for independence, the Belgian government, fearful of becoming mired in colonial wars as France and others had been, hastened to pull out of the Congo. The colony was freed in 1960, with little preparation for self-government and no strong liberation party to take over. For most of the next five years, the new nation was torn by civil war.

In contrast to Belgium's rapid pullout from the Congo, Portugal refused even to consider independence for her southern African colonies of Angola and Mozambique. Guerrilla revolts broke out in both colonies in the early 1960s. In the long struggle that followed, the autocratic Portuguese government got help from its NATO allies, whereas the Marxist leaders of the nationalist guerrilla movements received aid from European communist countries. In the end, however, it was only the overthrow of the Portuguese autocracy at home that led to independence for Angola and Mozambique in 1975.

In Angola, the struggle did not end with freedom from Portugal. The Marxist-led Angolan Liberation Movement (MPLA) was at once engulfed in a new struggle for supremacy with other nationalist guerrillas representing rival tribal alignments. Both the Republic of South Africa and the United States supported the latter, led by Dr. Jonas Savimbi, whereas Cuban military units moved in to shore up the MPLA. The resulting conflict dragged on into the 1980s.

A related armed struggle, meanwhile, broke out in neighboring Namibia. This former colony, annexed in 1949 by South Africa, had by 1966 produced a guerrilla revolt led by the South West African People's Organization (SWAPO). In the 1970s and 1980s, newly liberated Angola provided bases and support for SWAPO, while South Africa strove to suppress the guerrillas and conducted raids into Angola itself. Members of the communist bloc also supported SWAPO. Many western nations were alienated from South Africa by that nation's efforts to impose her racially discriminatory policies in Namibia.

The fates of the two Rhodesias were quite different. Both colonies had strong minorities of white settlers, like those in Kenya or Algeria. In the

Rhodesias too, these European colonists lobbied hard against any form of independence that would allow black majority rule. In 1964, however, a more democratic constitution imposed on the settlers by London led to the election of a black African president, Kenneth Kaunda, and to the creation of the new nation of Zambia.

Southern Rhodesia resisted similar efforts by London officials to impose democracy and black African rule in the colony. In 1965, its settler minority government declared its own independence under the white supremacist leader Ian Smith. South Africa supported the new regime, and Rhodesian mineral wealth and cash crops provided economic support. Despite guerrilla revolts, the hostility of neighboring countries, and pressure from Great Britain and the United States to negotiate a more democratic solution, the Smith government survived for a decade and a half. Relatively free elections were finally held, however, and a black government took over the new nation of Zimbabwe in 1980.

South Africa—The Hold-Out

By the 1980s, then, European imperial rule had ended over almost all of Africa. The single hold-out has been the Republic of South Africa at the southern tip of the continent. Here, unique circumstances have combined to preserve a powerful white minority regime, presenting the western world with a particularly painful challenge.

South Africa had been a British dominion and ultimately an independent member of the British Commonwealth of Nations. Its minority white population included Afrikaners, whose Dutch ancestors had arrived as early as the seventeenth century, and British, who had moved in during the nineteenth century. South Africa's government has been dominated by the Afrikaners, who outnumber the British, though the latter control much of the nation's modern economy. In addition, foreign firms from all other western nations, including the United States, have invested in South Africa, whose natural resources include a good percentage of the world's supplies of gold and diamonds.

The large majority of South Africans, however, are not westerners at all. Most are black Africans, including a large contingent of the once-powerful Zulu people. South Africa also has a substantial population of Indians and other south Asians. It was to maintain a white rule over this nonwhite majority that the Afrikaner government instituted the apartheid system after World War II.

The goal of apartheid (separate development) has been to keep the races apart and the European-descended peoples in control. Apartheid has consisted of a set of laws that requires each race—black Africans, Asians, and people of "mixed races"—to live, go to school, attend church, find their recreation, and otherwise spend their lives separate from the others and from the western peoples who rule them. Black and brown Africans have had to carry special passes, were prohibited from marrying whites, and often have had to travel long distances from their segregated housing to workplaces in the white community. To this system of legal separation has been added the creation of a number of black African "homelands," essen-

Jomo Kenyatta. The father of modern Kenya, Kenyatta was also a widely admired symbol of the liberation movement all across black Africa. The East African leader, who had earned a British PhD, was later imprisoned by the British for his part in the struggle. He is shown here after his release outside Nairobi in 1961.

825

| 1950 | 1955 | 1960 | 1965 | 1970 | 1975 | 1980 |

Liberation
of Kenya

Liberation
of Ghana

Liberation
of Nigeria

Zimbabwe
founded

Apartheid established
in South Africa

Liberation
of French
African
Colonies

Zambia
founded

Angola and
Mozambique
liberated

Congo Crisis

---

tially reservations where most blacks have been expected to live, though they have been able to find little work there and the land is generally poor.

Black South Africans have responded to apartheid with repeated waves of protest since the imposition of the system in the 1950s. Demonstrations have been crushed by police power, and organizations like the African National Congress (ANC) outlawed. Some black African activists have gone underground or into exile to organize guerrilla attacks on South Africa. Others, such as Nobel Peace Price winner Bishop Albert Luthuli and Winnie Mandela, wife of a long-imprisoned ANC leader, have continued to work openly for an end to racial discrimination.

In the 1980s, the crisis in South Africa has seemed to be drawing to a head. Mounting violence in the black townships and increasing western pressure for change has apparently had some effect. The threat of withdrawal of western investment capital and strains in the South African economy have encouraged the government to promise some reforms in the system, including a promise in 1986 to remove the hated pass regulations. But the black South African demand for majority rule—which would mean

black rule—still seems far from the minds of the nation's white rulers.

PATHS TO DEVELOPMENT IN THE NEW NATIONS

The new nations of Asia and Africa share much political and economic history as well as problems common to emerging nations. These common patterns have made them the core of the third world—the "underdeveloped" or "developing" parts of the globe—along with the older nations of Latin America. The primary goal for all these nations has been to build an affluent, technologically advanced society comparable to those of Europe and North America. The political and economic strategies that third-world nations have adopted to move toward this goal are discussed in this section.

Political Organization: Military Rule or One-Party State

Government in most of these new countries has taken a common form. Many of the former colonies were

granted their independence with democratic constitutions ready to hand. Virtually all were led by men who had been in the forefront of the struggle for independence. These leaders had assured their people that the object of their fight was freedom from oppression. In most cases, however, the liberal constitutions offered the liberated people did not long survive. Freedom turned out to mean emancipation from foreign rule, but not the individual rights common in many western countries. Instead, two sorts of authoritarian rule have predominated: military dictatorship and government by a single political party that tolerates no legal opposition.

A number of reasons have been put forward to explain the emergence of autocratic regimes across Asia and Africa. One is the lack of a strong sense of national loyalty and the frequency of tribal, religious, or other divisions caused by the arbitrary colonial (later national) boundaries drawn by the imperial powers in the preceding century. Another reason is the immense difficulty of the job of national development: The new nations have needed a central authority to plan, secure resources, and mobilize the people for economic growth.

826

Finally, obvious political motives should not be overlooked: Revolutionary parties or successful generals have frequently seized or retained control for the same reasons they have often done so in western history—for the sake of the power and wealth they could acquire.

The single party governing some new nations has usually been a mass-based organization. The party has sometimes had tribal or religious underpinnings, but it has typically claimed to speak for the whole people, transcending all such divisions. Party activists in each village or neighborhood would rally their neighbors to the support of party policies and programs. At the top would be the movement's maximum leader, generally hailed as the father of his country, as Sukarno was in Indonesia, Nkrumah in Ghana, or Kenyatta in Kenya. When the party's leader has been a person of ability and dedication, the country might be the better for such one-party rule; when the leader has been inefficient or tyrannical, the nation has suffered.

When these civilian parties have proved too inefficient or corrupt, the army has generally been there to replace them. Generals, colonels, and even sergeants have often seized power by force in Asia or Africa. Although offering an end to the self-serving politics of their predecessors, they have had the armed force to impose their own will on the nation. Military rulers have brought order out of chaos, as Joseph Mobutu did in Zaire or Nasser in Egypt. Often, however, they have lacked the administrative skills of the trained officials they replaced.

Under such governments, the underdeveloped countries of Asia and

---

STUDENTS AND PEASANTS

For learning of all kinds has a purpose: that purpose is to increase man's power over himself and his environment. In other words, the function of learning is . . . development. . . . A university is wasting time and effort it if ignores the society in which its student grew and learned his preliminary lessons.

The community's investment will . . . have been a bad one if the student is ill-equipped to do any of the jobs required when he is called upon to make this contribution. . . . The same is true if the graduate is unwilling to fulfill his responsibilities without demanding further privileges from the community. . . . Students eat the bread and butter of the peasants because they have promised a service in the future. If they are unable or unwilling to provide that service when the time comes, then the students have stolen from the peasants as surely as if they had carried off their sacks of wheat in the night.*

In these remarks, spoken at the inauguration of Tanzania's new Dar es Salaam University in 1970, Julius Nyerere addressed a common problem in the new nations of the third world. The children of liberation leaders tended to think that the struggle was now history, and that they, as heirs of the new elite, had no responsibilities to their countrymen. Nyerere urged that the educated few owed something to the peasant majority whose labor had paid for their education—and that economic development was as great a struggle as the independence movement itself.

*Julius K. Nyerere, "Relevance and Dar es Salaam University," in Freedom and Development/Uhuru na Maendeleo . . . Writings and Speeches, 1968–1973 (London: Oxford University Press, 1973), pp. 194–195.

Africa have turned to their fundamental task: development. In this also, however, they have encountered a host of problems.

The Difficulties and Successes of Development

The new nations of the third world have confronted an overwhelming array of difficulties. They are almost all poor countries by affluent western standards, and their growing populations mean that on a per capita basis, they are getting poorer every year. Infertile or overused soil, lack of water,

and many diseases often add to their woes.

Their goal has been economic growth, but the new countries also lack most of the requirements for industrial development. They usually have had much too little capital, far too few trained technicians, and a minimal infrastructure of roads, railways, and seaports. They might have plenty of labor available, but it is usually not skilled labor, educated in modern business techniques or familiar with machinery. They might or might not have natural resources, but they have needed foreign financial and

827

Third World Development. This huge hydroelectric dam at Itaipu in Brazil illustrates the type of large-scale development projects popular particularly during the 1960s and 1970s. More modest efforts, however, have sometimes proved more useful on the local level.

technical help to develop whatever they have.

To many of the new leaders, the key to development has seemed to be, quite simply, money. Capital for schools and roads, to build dams or factories, or to hire foreign technicians has been the first prerequisite for economic growth. But here too they have run into difficulties. The major sources of the funds they need are trade, aid, and commercial loans. All these have also proved costly to the poor nations of the third world.

Trade, for instance, usually means selling agricultural products or mineral resources to the developed countries of the west. The prices for these

commodities, however, are at the mercy of the drift of the international market and are often too low to finance large-scale development. Aid, in the form of loans or outright grants from friendly governments, has often seemed more desirable. But aid frequently has come with political strings attached in the form of accepting the political leadership or the ideological principles of the donor. It might also mean allowing foreign military bases, purchasing manufactured goods from the aid-providing nation, and other requirements. Loans from commercial banks in the west, finally, have been hard to get unless the nation has had a major resource to offer as collateral, such as oil or valuable minerals. Such loans also require high interest payments, higher still if the borrowing nation cannot pay on time and has to reschedule the loan. A last-resort source of capital, finally, has been international agencies like the International Monetary Fund. The IMF, however, loans money only under stringent conditions that although intended to make the borrowing governments more solvent, can also bring real hardship to their people.

Women in the underdeveloped world have faced particular difficulties. Traditional cultures have often bound women to home and family and made them subordinate to fathers or husbands even more rigorously than western societies have done. Women are usually "the poorest of the poor," frequently lacking education, property rights, or opportunity for employment in the modern sectors of the economy. Though they sometimes enjoy a larger share of political authority than westerners realize—in some African societies, for instance—women have more often been excluded from political power.

Despite these difficulties, there have been some significant successes in the new third-world nations during the first decades of independence. Some mammoth projects, such as the building of the Aswan High Dam in Egypt, were completed—the Aswan Dam with considerable Russian help. At a more basic level, the so-called green revolution led to the development of new strains of rice, corn, and other grains that have produced far more abundant harvests to feed the growing populations of India and southeast Asia—an achievement largely of the Ford and Rockefeller foundations. Other economic advances have

been carried through by third-world nations without any western help, sometimes even in competition with western interests. One of these has been the development of export industries along the "east Asian fringe," from Korea through Taiwan and Hong Kong to Singapore. Another has been the organization of OPEC, the oil-producing nations' cartel, through which oil-rich third-world countries like Saudi Arabia, Venezuela, and Nigeria were able to multiply the world price of petroleum several times over during the 1970s and early 1980s. There have been some remarkable political accomplishments too, such as the preservation of democratic government in India despite religious conflict, swelling population, and poverty.

Third-world nations have also had setbacks. Some committed resources to too many "prestige projects," such as airports or manufacturing plants, which were of little use to predominantly peasant populations. Third-world cities have seen uncontrollable growth that has undermined village traditions and produced slums as brutalizing as those of industrializing Europe a century earlier. Many nations abandoned subsistence agriculture to produce cash crops for export. This has brought in badly needed foreign capital to finance development, but when the prices paid for these crops has gone down, villages that had once been self-sufficient have sometimes found it impossible to earn enough to purchase food. Indeed, during the 1970s, the overall decline of commodity prices, coupled with the soaring cost of the oil that most developing nations had to import, pushed many of them to the brink of bankruptcy.

The 1970s, however, also saw some important shifts of priorities and changes of direction in third-world development. One widely heralded new trend is the turning away from big industrial projects toward the sort of "appropriate technologies" that can be cheaply applied at the village level, use local materials, and require little specialized training or expensive repair. Another new emphasis is the earmarking of aid for the poorest classes and the related effort to see that women benefit equally from education, new jobs, and other opportunities. A third apparent shift is from government-sponsored economic activity toward encouraging entrepreneurial initiatives by private citizens. The development picture, although complex and not without problems, is thus far from hopeless as the 1980s advance.

THIRD WORLD NATIONS AND SUPERPOWER CONFLICT

The leaders of the world's new nations after World War II were faced with an international problem of the first magnitude: the confrontation between the two superpowers and their allies known as the Cold War. Inevitably, pressures mounted on this recently emancipated third of the world's population to choose sides, to support either the United States or the Soviet Union in their conflict of ideologies and interests.

The difficulties of choice were real. Both sides claimed to be strongly opposed to imperialism, the United States pointing to its tradition of democratic self-government, the So-

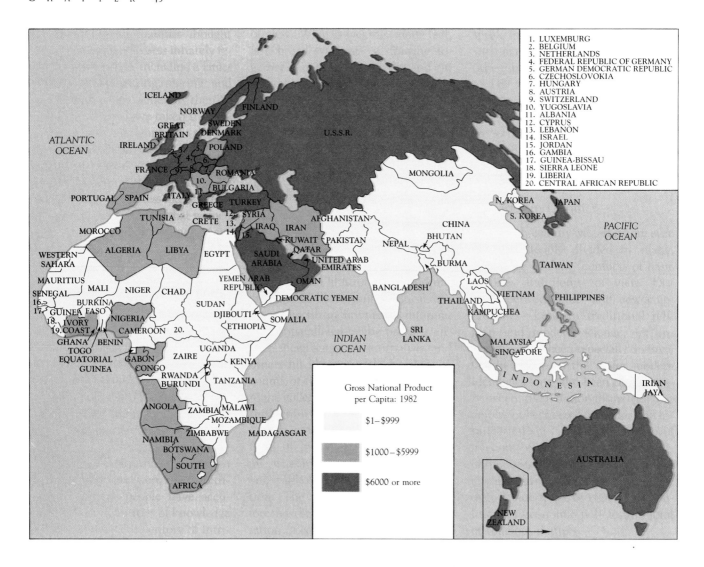

1. LUXEMBURG
2. BELGIUM
3. NETHERLANDS
4. FEDERAL REPUBLIC OF GERMANY
5. GERMAN DEMOCRATIC REPUBLIC
6. CZECHOSLOVAKIA
7. HUNGARY
8. AUSTRIA
9. SWITZERLAND
10. YUGOSLAVIA
11. ALBANIA
12. CYPRUS
13. LEBANON
14. ISRAEL
15. JORDAN
16. GAMBIA
17. GUINEA-BISSAU
18. SIERRA LEONE
19. LIBERIA
20. CENTRAL AFRICAN REPUBLIC

Gross National Product
per Capita: 1982

$1–$999

$1000–$5999

$6000 or more

MAP 90
Wealth and Poverty in Europe, Asia, and Africa in the 1980s.

viet Union expressing the Leninist view that imperialism is a form of capitalist exploitation. Both sides offered some support in the colonial struggle for freedom, Americans pressuring their allies to hasten the process of colonial emancipation, the Russians providing material support for guerrilla movements. Both sides clearly felt the need for things the new nations had to offer, from natural resources and military bases to votes in the United Nations. Both had some-

thing to offer the new nations in return, including economic and technological aid and even military support in third-world struggles. Both, finally, could punish nations that rejected their overtures by cutting off aid or by supporting their enemies.

Faced with this difficult choice, most of the new Asian and African countries declared a policy of nonalignment. This attempt at a neutral stance established the claim of the new nations to be a "third world," supporting neither the United States nor the Soviet Union in their confrontation.

This policy was formalized with the establishment of the Organization of Nonaligned States at Bandung, Indonesia, in 1955, which brought heads of Asian, African, and some Latin American states together for periodic discussions of common problems.

Third-world representatives at the United Nations also began to think and operate as a voting bloc on many issues, particularly in the General Assembly, where their numbers counted heavily.

This "neutralist" stand angered such western leaders as U.S. Secretary of State John Foster Dulles, who declared during the Eisenhower admin-

istration that neutralism was "immoral." As the years passed, leaders like Jeanne Kirkpatrick, President Reagan's United Nations ambassador, condemned the third world, not for neutrality, but for a decided tilt against the west.

There has been some substance to this charge. The leaders of former colonies have resented the colonial leg-

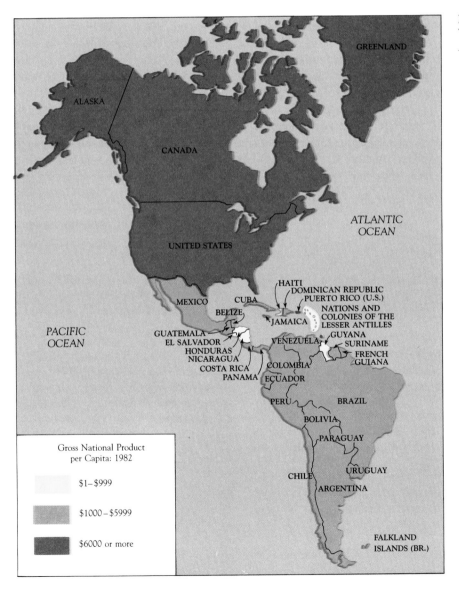

MAP 91
Wealth and Poverty in North and South America in the 1980s.

acy of such major allies as Great Britain and France. Since most of these third-world leaders had no experience of Russian imperialism, they have been less likely to be anti-Soviet. The policies of the two superpowers have also influenced some officially non-aligned states to favor the Soviet Union. The Soviet bloc has supplied at least some military aid and training, and much rhetorical support, for antiimperialist guerrillas. The United States, by contrast, has had important political and economic ties with Israel and South Africa, countries that many Asians and Africans see as surviving islands of western rule in their midst.

Some factors have favored the west. The western nations have furnished large quantities of aid to underdeveloped countries and bought their products. The United States has urged South Africa to move more rapidly toward a pluralistic society and Israel to work for peace in the Middle East. Nevertheless, some third-world na-

tions have opposed the United States on key international issues. This tilt crystallized in the 1970s into a growing demand for an economic "new deal" for the third world.

During the 1970s, a number of third-world leaders joined theorists concerned with the future of the globe in urging a new analysis of the basic divisions among nations. One conclusion was that the east-west Cold War is not the fundamental division that Washington and Moscow believe it to be. The great divide, according to this view, is the conflict between north and south, between the rich nations of the northern hemisphere and the poor nations of the tropics and the global south.

Many western liberals have been willing to agree with this analysis, but have balked at its implications. Third-world advocates also insist that the poverty of the underdeveloped nations has been caused above all by western imperial exploitation and, furthermore, that the rich nations

should make restitution for this past exploitation by offering substantial aid for third-world development. What is needed, they believe, is nothing less than a global redistribution of wealth and technology.

The moral appeal of this argument is powerful, especially when the poverty of the south is thrust forcefully on the conscience of the west, as during the great African famine of the 1980s and in face of the massive debts of many Latin American nations. Many in the wealthier nations, however, have refused to accept the historical argument that this poverty is fundamentally rooted in imperialist exploitation. The United States has particularly pressed underdeveloped countries to follow the western model of capitalist economic growth to prosper as the west has done. Entrepreneurship and incentives for private economic initiatives have seemed to be on the upswing in some third-world nations in the 1980s.

SUMMARY

A major trend of the decades after World War II was the collapse of the European overseas empires. This great liberation freed a third of the world's population from foreign rule. After their emancipation, however, the former colonies faced difficult problems of national development. They also sought viable positions in the Cold War and in their relations with the wealthier nations of the global north.

The western empires in south and

southeast Asia were dissolved with some bloodshed. Britain's Indian empire was partitioned into the new nations of India and Pakistan, a process accompanied by bloody riots pitting Hindus against Muslims. The liberation of Burma and Malaya, and particularly that of the French colonies of Indochina, were accompanied by guerrilla struggles that lasted for years. Indonesia also had to fight for its independence from the Dutch; the U.S.-

held Philippines were quickly freed, but were torn by guerrilla conflict after their liberation.

The two centers of violence in the Middle East and north Africa during this period of transition were British-ruled Palestine and French Algeria. In the Palestine mandate, the birth of Israel began a long series of battles between the new country and its Arab neighbors. In Algeria, well-established French settlers and French armed forces fought a long and bloody struggle with the Arab and Berber population before the latter won their independence.

Sub-Saharan Africa saw many colonies liberated with very little violence, though some conflicts erupted following the departure of the Europeans. France's west and equatorial African colonies and most of Britain's west and east African possessions were granted their freedom with little struggle. Farther south, Portuguese Angola and Zimbabwe—the British colony of Southern Rhodesia—were

scenes of complicated political and military clashes. South Africa dug in its heels and resisted black majority rule with the repressive system of apartheid.

The political and especially economic development of these new Asian and African nations has been more difficult than many had hoped. Economic growth has come slowly to poor nations needing everything from health care and education to basic industries and caught up in the problems of commodity markets and international loans. Nevertheless, suc-

cesses like the green revolution and new directions in development such as the trend toward "appropriate technologies" have rekindled hopes for the future.

The broader international orientation of the new nations has been toward a neutral stance in the Cold War, sometimes tilting against their former colonial rulers and the United States. Third-world demands for a global reallocation of wealth from north to south have met with little substantive response from the more developed nations of the world.

SELECTED SOURCES

*Achebe, Chinua. *Things Fall Apart*. 1981. Much-admired novel about the aftermath of African liberation.

Antonius, George. *The Arab Awakening*. 1965. Older but solid account of the sources of Arab nationalism and the Muslim resurgence.

*Dupuy, T. N. *Elusive Victory: The Arab-Israeli Wars, 1947–1974*. 1978. Thorough coverage of a controversial subject.

Emerson, R. *From Empire to Nation: The Rise of Self-Assertion of Asian and African Peoples*. 1960. Good survey of the antiimperialist movement.

Gandhi. 1984. Richard Attenborough's

epic film of the father of Indian independence and the twentieth-century prophet of nonviolent protest.

*Harrison, Paul. *Inside the Third World*. 1981. An informed reporter's account of the problems and techniques of third-world development, with many illuminating examples.

Kahin, G. M., ed. *Governments and Politics of Southeast Asia*. 1964. Collapse of western empires at this angle of Asia.

*Nkrumah, Kwame. *The Autobiography of Kwame Nkrumah*. 1959. Political life of one of the best-known of black Africa's liberation leaders.

*Paton, Alan. *Cry, the Beloved Country*.

1961. Celebrated novel of black South Africa, by one of that country's most famous writers.

Ward, Barbara. *Women in the New Asia*. 1963. Tradition and change in the lives of Asian women.

*Available in paperback.

THE CONTEMPORARY WEST

France believes that she must, for her part, change the form of our alliance without altering its substance. . .

Above all, it is a question of keeping ourselves free of any vassalage. It is true that, in many areas, we have the best reasons for associating with others. But on condition of retaining our self-determination. Thus, so far as the solidarity of the western peoples appears to us necessary; of the eventual defense of Europe, our country will remain the ally of her allies but, upon the expiration of the commitments formerly taken—that is, in 1969 by the latest—the subordination known as "integration" which is provided for by NATO and which hands our fate over to foreign authority shall cease, as far as we are concerned. . .

. . . France intends to recover, in her territory, the full exercise of her sovereignty, now impaired by the permanent presence of Allied military elements or by the habitual use being made of its air space, to terminate her participation in the "integrated" commands, and no longer to place forces at the disposal of NATO . . . [France] is prepared to reach agreement . . . regarding the military facilities to be accorded on a mutual basis in the event of a conflict in which she would join battle at [NATO's] side, and regarding the conditions governing the cooperation between her forces and theirs in the event of joint action, especially in Germany.

Thus Charles de Gaulle announced that France was withdrawing from its commitments to NATO, the western military alliance. His action was only the most spectacular incident in the weakening of the Cold War power blocs in the 1960s and after. Continuing peace and growing prosperity, signs of economic weakness in the United States and the Soviet Union, and a thaw in superpower hostilities made Europeans resistant to continued superpower domination.

Although Cold War tensions in Europe were reduced, the opposite was the case in the Middle East and Latin America. The Cold War intruded into the original Arab-Israeli conflict as some Arab states severed ties with the Soviet Union and Israel and some of Israel's Arab neighbors were supported by the United States. Cold War confrontation over the transmission of petroleum from the Persian Gulf exacerbated Middle East ten-

De Gaulle Leads the Resurgence of Europe. President Charles de Gaulle addresses the public at the time France was withdrawing its forces from NATO and in general pursuing a separate course from that of the United States. In this, and in leading France out of a draining war in Algeria, de Gaulle represented trends underway in newly prosperous Western Europe, a region anxious to be independent from close supervision by the United States and largely ready to leave its imperialist past behind.

sions. In Latin America, a movement toward genuine political democracy was overshadowed by the Cold War. Social revolutions and elections that brought Marxists to power provoked the United States to try to suppress what it deemed to be an extension of Soviet power and influence to the Western Hemisphere. The pages that follow trace the main trends in this complex period.

THE SUPERPOWERS

The two superpowers that dominated the globe during the decades after World War II, the United States and the Soviet Union, were the most powerful and productive nations in history. They differed strikingly in their political systems, the United States being one of the freest nations, the U.S.S.R. one of the most authoritarian. In military might, the two had achieved a rough parity by the 1980s, and both were far stronger militarily than any potential rival.

Despite their powerful standing, however, the superpowers, like other nations of the western world, experienced their share of economic, social, and political problems during the quarter of a century between the 1960s and the 1980s. Neither was crippled by those difficulties, but both faced sobering challenges as the century drew toward its close.

The United States from Kennedy to Reagan

U.S. history from the 1960s through the mid-1980s was marked by a conservative political mood. The 1960s, the Kennedy-Johnson years, saw a large amount of both social agitation and liberal legislation. Much more conservative policies prevailed in the 1980s, the period of Ronald Reagan's two terms in office. This period, however, also produced important political events and economic and social trends that transcended the liberal-conservative division.

The 1960s were a decade of social change in the United States comparable to the New Deal era of the 1930s or the Progressive years after 1900. At the grass roots level, demands for change were spearheaded by black Americans, whose most charismatic leader was the Rev. Martin Luther King. Although King's tactics of nonviolent civil disobedience predominated, violence often accompanied the struggle for black equality. Black advances in civil rights inspired Spanish-speaking Americans, Native Americans, poor Americans, and

The Civil Rights Revolution in the United States. Martin Luther King, Jr., Coretta King, and [far left] Ralph Abernathy and Rosa Parks lead a march in 1965 protesting racial segregation and other forms of discrimination, both in the South and throughout the nation. Although most blacks followed King and his peaceful approach based on the principles of the black churches and on Gandhi, some blacks turned to violence and to the radical teachings of Malcolm X and Stokley Carmichael.

many women to make similar demands for fairer treatment.

In Washington, Presidents Kennedy and Johnson responded with legislation that completed the structure of the U.S. welfare state begun by Franklin Roosevelt. The contribution of John Kennedy, the youngest of U.S. presidents, was largely one of dynamic political style, which kindled a renewed enthusiasm for social reform. Lyndon Johnson, a shrewd Texas politician who had served in Congress during the New Deal, pushed through a large body of liberal legislation. Civil rights and voting rights laws prohibited discrimination against blacks and other groups. The poor benefited from food stamps, school lunches, and job retraining programs. Federal funds were spent to support education, help rebuild decaying inner cities, and otherwise develop what Johnson called the Great Society. The Supreme Court under the leadership of Earl Warren actively furthered the expansion of civil rights and civil liberties, overturning generations of entrenched social practice.

The later 1960s and the 1970s, however, was a discouraging and bewildering time for many Americans. In 1968, Richard Nixon was elected president, apparently with a mandate to slow down social change and to end the Vietnam war, but antiwar protest and social unrest continued into the early 1970s. Nixon further undermined national self-esteem through his complicity in what became known as the Watergate affair. The repressive and duplicitous tactics that Nixon employed against social and antiwar activists and even against leaders of the Democratic party led to the conviction of many of his subordinates for illegal actions and to

WHICH PATH TO BLACK EQUALITY?

I cite these various revolutions, brothers and sisters, to show you that you . . . [can't] have a peaceful revolution. You don't have a turn-the-other-cheek revolution. The only kind of revolution that is nonviolent is the Negro revolution. It's the only revolution in which the goal is the desegregated lunch counter . . . and the desegregated toilet. . . . That's no revolution. Revolution is based on land. Land is the basis for freedom, justice, and equality. . . .

Revolution is bloody, revolution is hostile, revolution knows no compromise, revolution overturns and destroys everything that gets in its way. . . . Whoever heard of a revolution where they lock arms . . . singing "We shall overcome?" . . . A revolutionary wants land so that he can set up his own nation, an independent nation. [*]

* * *

Our defense is to meet every act of violence toward a Negro with the fact that there are thousands of others who will present themselves in his place as potential victims. . . . This dynamic unity, this amazing self-respect, this willingness to suffer, and this refusal to hit back will soon cause the oppressor to become ashamed of his own methods.

. . . we need not follow the "do-nothingism" of the complacent or the hatred and despair of the black na-

tionalist. There is the more excellent way of love and non-violent protest. I'm grateful to God that, through the Negro church, the dimension of nonviolence entered our struggle. . . . if our white brothers . . . refuse to support our nonviolent efforts, millions of Negroes, out of frustration and despair, will seek solace and security in black nationalist ideologies, a development that will lead inevitably to a frightening racial nightmare. [**]

Here Malcolm X and Martin Luther King, Jr. outline different options for blacks in their efforts to obtain equality in the United States. The black civil rights movement was the largest of a series of social protest movements that transformed U.S. society in the 1960s and early 1970s. Most blacks followed King, but riots in the cities, attacks on freedom marchers in the South, and King's assassination were examples of the violence that such profound social changes could engender.

[*] X, Malcolm. *Malcolm X Speaks.* George Breitman, editor, (New York: Pathfinder, 1965), p. 9.
[**] King quoted in Stephen B. Oates, *Let the Trumpet Sound: The Life of Martin Luther King, Jr.* (New York: Harper and Row, 1982), p. 106; "Letter from a Birmingham Jail," quoted in Lerone Bennett, Jr., *What Manner of Man: A Biography of Martin Luther King, Jr.* (Chicago: Johnson, 1976), p. 150.

Nixon's own resignation under fire in 1974, an unhappy first in U.S. political history.

The decline of social activism, the disgrace of President Nixon, and the failure of U.S. policy in Vietnam all

contributed to a darker mood of self-doubt and malaise in the United States during the 1970s. In addition, a combination of factors, including soaring international petroleum prices and accelerating inflation, made the U.S.

economy, which had boomed in the sixties, decline sharply.

Following the election of President Ronald Reagan in 1980, the United States seemed to embark on a new direction and to recover much of its lost self-confidence. The oldest man ever elected to the White House and one of the most conservative, Reagan, a former actor, was a skilled public speaker and an immensely popular personality who had an instinct for expressing the hopes and fears of a majority of the U.S. public.

Not all of the conservative policies he launched succeeded: His early determination to balance the budget, for example, was soon abandoned in favor of a huge armaments program that doubled the size of the national debt. Reagan was, however, successful in cutting or abolishing government spending for a series of social programs. He also appointed many conservative officials, including federal judges who would perpetuate his influence into later years. In addition, he took a strongly anticommunist position in international affairs, an attitude that proved popular with many Americans. Finally, the economy, after a deep early recession, improved in the middle 1980s.

The Soviet Union from Khrushchev to Gorbachev

The Soviet Union exhibited more domestic stability during the quarter century after 1960 than at any time since the establishment of the Soviet state in 1917. Still, the Russians also had their problems during these decades.

From the 1960s to the 1980s, Communist party leaders continued to dominate the U.S.S.R., and government planners continued to manage the economy. Nevertheless, the leadership did change, and the economy revealed trends and currents that sometimes escaped the control of the bureaucrats. The most apparent change was from the relatively crude and heavy-handed Soviet leadership style of the Khrushchev era in the 1960s to the more sophisticated tactics of Mikhail Gorbachev in the 1980s.

The violent politics of the Stalinist dictatorship declined drastically after Stalin's death in 1953. Nikita Khrushchev's famous "secret speech" attacking Stalin's tyranny was followed by the release of many political prisoners and a weakening of the power of the secret police. When Khrushchev himself was forced to resign in 1964, following the failure of his agriculture policies and his retreat before Kennedy in the Cuban missile crisis, he suffered no worse fate than enforced retirement. The Soviet Union remained a one-party state, lacking the basic civil liberties enjoyed by many in the west, but no Russian ruler since Stalin has exercised his dictatorial power.

Party leader Leonid Brezhnev dominated the Soviet state for almost two decades. Politically, he supported career men in the party and in the state bureaucracy. Under Brezhnev, persecution of dissenters was resumed, but labor camps, internal exile, or commitment to mental institutions replaced the more rigorous Stalinist punishments. Soviet heavy industry continued to grow and living standards slowly improved. Agricultural production on the collective farms remained low, however, a perennial problem in the Soviet Union. A vigorous armaments program brought the U.S.S.R. to a position of rough nuclear equality with the United States.

The emergence of Gorbachev as head of the Communist party and the nation in 1985 signaled a more subtle and flexible style of Soviet leadership. Gorbachev's earliest efforts were directed to the removal of political deadwood inherited from the Brezhnev years and toward greater efficiency and productivity in the Russian economy. The new leader's problems, however, remained substantial. The strain of improving Russia's domestic production while keeping up military spending was considerable. Gorbachev had to deal with both the short- and long-term consequences of the nuclear disaster at Chernobyl, low agricultural output, and the renewed military competitiveness of the United States under Reagan.

WESTERN AND EASTERN EUROPE

The history of postwar Europe reflected the changed geopolitical situation, where a region that had once dominated the globe now took second place to the two superpowers. Europe's position was crucial, however. There was great material progress, particularly in western Europe, a key factor in creating resistance to the power of the superstates.

Economic Resurgence

One of the most striking features of European life has been the high general level of prosperity over the decades since World War II. An im-

MAP 92
European Economic and Political Developments. This map shows the economic division between western and eastern Europe that to a major degree reflects its Cold War political division. Europe also continued to display its long history of ethnic and religious strife: Protestant-Catholic conflict in Northern Ireland; Basque separatism in Spain; Croatian and Albanian unrest in Yugoslavia.

portant element in this economic resurgence was the integration of the economies of the western European nations under the aegis of the European Economic Community (EEC), or Common Market, and of eastern Europe under COMECON (see Map 92).

The EEC, founded in 1957 and expanded in the 1970s and 1980s, was a customs union that reduced competition among its members and turned all of western Europe into an open market area for European producers. The Common Market combined with the new technology generated by the recent war and with the increased demand created by a postwar "baby boom" to stimulate rapid economic growth. Europe, prostrate in 1945, was by 1965 a major competitor of the United States.

COMECON, founded in 1949 by the Soviet Union, assigned industrial and agricultural priorities to each nation. Its objective was to integrate the state-run economies of Russia's new satellites with one another and with that of the Soviet Union. First intended as a support system for the Russian economy, which had been devastated during the war, the organization contributed to the economic growth of eastern Europe as a whole.

During the late 1970s and the early 1980s, both western and eastern Europe suffered from the same global economic decline that affected the United States. Escalating petroleum prices hurt many European economies, though Great Britain in particular profited from the exploitation of North Sea petroleum. Unemployment rose to unprecedented levels, even in such wealthy and productive nations as West Germany. Heavy indebtedness to western banks, meanwhile, pushed such east bloc countries as Poland to the brink of economic collapse. Neither the conservative remedies applied by Prime Minister Margaret Thatcher of Great Britain nor the socialist policies of France's President François Mitterand brought the hoped-for rapid re-

839

covery in the 1980s. In addition, both Europe and the United States faced formidable competition for world markets from a vast array of consumer goods from the "Asian Rim" of Japan, South Korea, Hong Kong, and Singapore.

Political Trends in Western Europe

Perhaps the most impressive characteristic of the political life of western Europe in the second half of the twentieth century was the revitalization of democratic political institutions. The claim of the European totalitarians of the interwar years that democracy was doomed proved false. Free elections and civil liberties flourished. This democratic renaissance not only took place in established democracies such as Great Britain, France, and the Scandinavian nations, but also in former totalitarian states like West Germany and Italy. The struggle for political freedom was also successful in old-fashioned authoritarian states in southern Europe, including Spain, Portugal, and Greece.

Within this framework of electoral politics and free debate, a spectrum of parties ranging from conservative to socialist competed vigorously for the right to guide the destinies of the nations. Between 1949 and 1969, West Germany's conservative Christian Democratic party, headed for many years by the aging anti-Nazi and anticommunist Konrad Adenauer, led that nation's return to prosperity and political respectability. France's wartime leader Charles de Gaulle, restored to power for a decade between 1958 and 1969, brought that nation stability and a measure of its former self-confidence. British politics in the 1980s was dominated by Margaret Thatcher, who struggled to reverse Great Britain's long economic decline by again making British products competitive in the world.

Major socialist leaders included Great Britain's Labor party leader Clement Attlee in the later 1940s, Willy Brandt, anti-Stalinist former mayor of West Berlin who led West Germany's Social Democrats to victory in 1969, and Olaf Palme, whose efforts helped make Sweden perhaps the most socialist of western European nations. Nationalization of some major industries and a wide array of social legislation marked their regimes, making them the prime architects of the developed welfare state in the democratic west. Under their guidance, public health, public housing, government pensions, and other social services for all citizens became facts of life in western Europe, even under communist governments.

By contrast with the success of the middle-range political parties, both communists on the left and old-fashioned authoritarian regimes of the right either changed their stripes or faded from the scene during the postwar decades. Communist parties remained strong in such nations as Italy and France, but they were unable to win power on the national level. Some west European Communist parties were forced by the need of political survival to establish a position independent of the Soviet Union, condemning that nation for intervention in the affairs of other nations. Authoritarian Spain and Portugal, meanwhile, were transformed into democracies after the deaths of old-line dictators Franco and Salazar, while a military junta, the reign of "the colonels," was replaced by a democratic regime in Greece. Spain in the 1980s, with a democratic king, Juan Carlos—who had faced down right-wing military rebels gun in hand—and a socialist prime minister, provided a striking example of the flexibility, variety, and vitality of political life in the democratic west.

Strains in the Western Alliance

Western European economic and political revival led to a weakening of the western alliance after 1960. This diminished unity took the form of a series of challenges to U.S. leadership or dissent from U.S. policies.

An early dissenter was President de Gaulle of France, whose distrust of what he saw as Anglo-American predominance and diminished U.S. concern for protecting Europe led him to take his nation out of NATO in the 1960s. By creating an independent nuclear force for France, opening diplomatic relations and negotiating with Soviet Russia, and trading with the People's Republic of China, de Gaulle made it clear that France, although remaining a U.S. ally, was in no sense a puppet of Washington.

Great Britain and West Germany remained perhaps the closest European allies of the United States. By the 1980s, however, even these nations voiced disapproval of some of President Reagan's more militantly anticommunist policies. The deployment of new nuclear missiles in NATO nations and U.S. pressure on Nicaragua and Libya stirred mass demonstrations in the cities of western Europe.

Many western Europeans saw little likelihood of an invasion by the Soviet Union and her Warsaw Pact al-

Men in
Space

Civil rights
struggle in
United States

France pulls
out of NATO

U.S.-Chinese
rapprochement

Beginning
of Détente

Six-Day
War

Men on
the Moon

SALT I

"Yom Kippur"
war in
Middle East

lies. Nevertheless, the sheer massiveness of Soviet military power dictated that the North Atlantic Treaty Organization would continue to operate to maintain a prudent balance of power on the continent. Conflict over NATO, however, seemed to point to a future redefinition of the alliance, and of Europe's role in it.

Unrest in Eastern Europe

Similar strains appeared in eastern Europe, fueled by resentment of continuing Russian hegemony over the Soviet satellites. Although some of this opposition took more violent forms than was the case in western Europe, successful dissent from superpower leadership was much less common in the east.

As Stalin had crushed violent outbreaks in East Germany in 1953 and Khrushchev in Hungary in 1956, so Brezhnev sent Russian troops into insurgent Czechoslovakia in 1968. The regime of a reform-minded communist leader, Alexander Dubček, in Prague, had restored a measure of civil liberties and began to develop a freer economy and closer ties to western nations, all anathema to the Soviet Union. In the spring of 1968, Warsaw Pact troops led by the Russians occupied the nation, replaced Dubček, and reestablished closely controlled relations between Czechoslovakia and the Soviet Union.

Defiance of communist authority in Poland in 1980 and 1981 was also suppressed, though this time without overt Russian intervention. During those years, the noncommunist Polish labor union Solidarity struggled for a liberalization of that nation's political and economic system. In this case, Wojciech Jaruzelski, a tough Polish general, came to the rescue of the demoralized Communist party leadership, suppressing the maverick union and imposing martial law.

Dissenting policies, however, were tolerated in some eastern European nations, particularly in economic matters, as long as the communist governments retained control over their populations and remained loyal to the Soviet Union. For example, not all the satellite states followed the Soviet model of massive state planning and collectivization of agriculture, and not all accepted Soviet guidance of their economic development. Rumania's communist leaders insisted on their right to develop the Rumanian economy as they saw fit, including a larger industrial sector than the Russians proposed. Poland did not socialize the bulk of its private peasant farms. Hungarian "goulash communism" fostered an unlikely combination of state ownership of the means of production with managerial responsiveness to free market forces.

In foreign policy too, some east bloc nations proved surprisingly independent of Soviet control. Yugoslavia, which had rejected Stalin's overlordship as early as 1948, remained the only European communist state to break from the Soviet orbit entirely. Albania became a supporter of the People's Republic of China in the ideological struggle between that nation and the Soviet Union for the leadership of worldwide communism. Rumania at times voted against the U.S.S.R. in the United Nations. Eastern European nations also signed trade agreements with capitalist nations, borrowed western technology, and took out heavy loans from banks in western Europe and the United States. The Iron Curtain became more and more porous in the 1970s and the 1980s, but all eastern European nations remained reliable members of the Warsaw Pact.

841

THE RISE AND FALL OF DÉTENTE

Another factor contributing to Europe's restlessness under the old superpower-dominated alliance system was the reduced threat of U.S.-Soviet nuclear combat. A key feature of western international relations from the 1960s to the 1980s was the attempt at an armed truce in the Cold War known by the French diplomatic term *détente*. Also called "peaceful coexistence" or "competitive coexistence," détente centered around the two superpowers' search for ways of living together in a dangerous world.

By the unwritten terms of détente, neither side would sacrifice its major interests or its ideological convictions, but would avoid open conflict and would seek to expand areas of peaceful interaction and cooperation. Détente rose to prominence in the 1960s, in the last days of Kennedy and Khrushchev. It sank into disarray in the 1980s, during the Reagan years and the confused period in the Soviet Union between the decline of Brezhnev and Gorbachev's ascendancy.

Economic and Diplomatic Rapprochement

Perhaps the tensest moment in the Cold War was the Cuban crisis of 1962, in which the United States and the U.S.S.R. nearly went to war over the presence of Soviet nuclear missiles in Castro's Cuba. Coming away from this confrontation with a healthy awareness of the dangers of mutual annihilation exacerbated by the Cold War, President Kennedy and Chairman Khrushchev took prudent steps to ease tensions.

An early move in this campaign of improved diplomatic relations, or rapprochement, was the installation of the "hot line," a direct telephone hookup that linked the White House with the Kremlin, enabling U.S. and Russian leaders to make instant contact in any future crisis. Another important step was the test ban treaty of 1963, the first of a series of agreements intended to curb the danger of nuclear war.

Economic relations between the superpowers also improved during the 1960s and 1970s. Trade agreements opened up large markets for U.S. business. Repeated failures of Russian grain harvests in particular provided a valuable market for U.S. farmers, whose main problem was overproduction. U.S. tourists also began to visit the Soviet Union in large numbers. In addition, cultural and sports exchange programs brought each nation's scientists and other thinkers to the other. Members of the Kirov ballet travelled to the United States in exchange for U.S. jazz groups; hockey teams exchanged visits.

An even more dramatic easing of Cold War tensions came a decade after the first beginnings of détente, when in the 1970s the United States began the process of extending diplomatic recognition to the People's Republic of China. This step was a pragmatic one for both U.S. President Richard Nixon and Chairman Mao Tse-Tung of the People's Republic. The United States was just emerging from its divisive and unsuccessful war in Vietnam. The People's Republic was coming out of its Cultural Revolution, a period of violent and costly conflict within the Chinese Communist party itself. The Chinese feared that closer relations between the United States and the U.S.S.R., both outspoken foes, could leave the People's Republic dangerously isolated between the two hostile superpowers. Some U.S. leaders saw closer ties with the People's Republic as a way of outflanking the Russians, leaving the Soviet Union in an uncomfortable position between the NATO alliance in the west and the People's Republic in the east.

As a result, then, the United States agreed to allow the Nationalist government of Taiwan—the only "China" the United States had recognized since 1949—to be expelled from the United Nations and replaced by the People's Republic in 1971. The following year, President Nixon himself flew to Peking for talks with Chinese leaders. More formal diplomatic relations and growing economic ties followed through the 1970s and into the 1980s.

Thermonuclear Accommodation

The most feared aspect of the Cold War was the peril of mutual nuclear annihilation posed by the accumulation of atomic weaponry on both sides. To reduce this terrible danger, the superpowers negotiated a series of international agreements during the 1960s and 1970s.

The Nuclear Test Ban Treaty of 1963, mentioned earlier, was an agreement, signed by more than 100 nations, to refrain from testing unclear weapons in the atmosphere, under water, or in space. The Nuclear Nonproliferation Treaty, signed by almost 100 nations, committed its signatories not to add to the common danger by developing nuclear weapons of their own.

In the next decade, President Nixon and Chairman Brezhnev signed the

Détente. At the conclusion of the apparently successful SALT II Conference in Vienna on June 18, 1978, Soviet President Leonid Brezhnev plants one of his famous kisses on the cheek of U.S. President Jimmy Carter.

Strategic Arms Limitation Treaty (SALT) of 1972. The SALT treaty put limitations on the number of ICBMs, ABMs, and nuclear missile-firing submarines the two superstates could deploy. Subsequent agreements during the 1970s forbade large underground tests, deployment of missiles on the bottom of the sea, and other potentially dangerous advances in the arms race.

Pioneering in space was another area of accomplishment during the period of détente. In 1961 Soviet cosmonaut Yuri Gagarin was the first human to orbit the earth, followed one year later by U.S. astronaut John Glenn. In 1969 Neil Armstrong was the first person to stand on the moon. By the 1970s the Soviet Union was constructing space platforms, and the United States was sending manned

shuttles back and forth between earth and orbits in space. The United States was also launching space probes deep into the solar system to bring back information about other planets. At the height of détente, U.S. astronauts and Soviet cosmonauts even embarked on a joint space mission. Much of this space activity, however, particularly the space platforms and the shuttles, plus various types of spy and "killer" satellites, were aspects of the arms race rather than vehicles of scientific investigation.

The Arms Race Continues

Although discussions on nuclear arms limitation continued throughout the 1970s and into the 1980s, the nuclear arms race also went on, revealing the fragility of the spirit of détente.

Détente. At the conclusion of the apparently successful SALT II Conference in Vienna on June 18, 1978, Soviet President Leonid Brezhnev plants one of his famous kisses on the cheek of U.S. President Jimmy Carter. The SALT II agreement was a high point in the period of relaxed tensions that had begun in the 1960s, leading to hopes that the Cold War might be fading out. A year later, however, new points of conflict cropped up, the United States did not ratify the treaty, and adversarial Cold War postures returned.

Men on the Moon. Beginning in 1957, there were major breakthroughs in the exploration of space, led by U.S. and Soviet scientists and engineers. Manned and unmanned satellites were placed into orbit around the earth, space probes explored the planets of the solar system, and, most exciting to the general populace, the United States put a man on the moon in 1969. Neil Armstrong was the first man to step onto the moon's surface. Here astronaut Jim Irwin salutes for the camera in 1971.

A number of nations had from the first refused to be bound by the test ban and nonproliferation treaties. France, the People's Republic of China, India, Pakistan, Israel, and other powers saw the development of nuclear weaponry as essential to their national interests, in some cases to their survival. France and the People's Republic openly joined the "nuclear club" of the United States, the Soviet Union, and Great Britain by building nuclear arsenals during the 1960s and 1970s.

The two superstates, meanwhile, enhanced their already awesome nuclear stockpiles by building weapons systems not forbidden by treaty. Examples included multiple indepen-

dently targeted re-entry vehicles (MIRVs), which were single rockets bearing a number of separately targeted nuclear bombs; cruise missiles, which could slip in under enemy radar defenses to strike at targets; and neutron bombs, designed to kill humans with minimum damage to property.

Through the 1970s, Brezhnev's Russia engaged in an extensive nuclear arms buildup. In the 1980s, the United States under President Reagan responded with an equally massive program of arms construction. Reagan also urged the building of an elaborate space-based system of defenses against nuclear attack, the strategic defense initiative (SDI), pop-

ularly known as "Star Wars." Gorbachev objected to SDI, partly because it would be very costly for the Soviet Union to match it and partly because he saw it as fundamentally offensive, not defensive, in character. A thoroughly protected superpower, opponents of SDI asserted, would no longer be deterred by fear of retaliation from launching a nuclear strike on other powers.

The Fading of Détente

Even during the 1960s and 1970s, when some thought the Cold War was winding down, the spirit of détente had distinct limitations. During the 1980s, the conflict heated up once more, and some of the carefully constructed machinery of peaceful co-existence seemed to be coming apart.

In the later 1970s, the Soviet Union, perhaps emboldened by the success of its long arms buildup and by the apparent weakness of the United States after the fall of Vietnam in 1975, adopted more aggressive tactics in international affairs. The Soviet Union offered overt aid to guerrilla groups in Africa, even arranging the dispatch of Cuban troops to help the victorious Marxist rebels in Angola and to shore up the Marxist government of Ethiopia. In 1979, the Soviet Union sent its own troops into neighboring Afghanistan to rescue its client government, which was crumbling under the pressure of Muslim rebels. In the early 1980s, Soviet aid arrived for the Sandinista government in Nicaragua, which in turn supported the guerrilla revolt in El Salvador. In Europe itself, the Polish government's suppression of the liberal labor union Solidarity was carried out partly because of strong Russian disapproval of the new movement.

After Ronald Reagan's election, U.S. foreign policy also became more aggressive. Supported by a large peacetime armaments program, Reagan's charges that the Soviet Union was an "evil empire" reminded America's allies of some of the heated rhetoric of the earlier days of the Cold War, including Khrushchev's claim that "we will bury you."

Reagan's militance took more concrete forms. He deployed a new generation of nuclear weapons to NATO bases in Europe in the teeth of Russian—and considerable allied—opposition. The United States raided Libya, a Soviet ally. It deployed U.S. troops in Honduras, on the Nicara-

guan frontier, to put pressure on the Sandinista government. It furnished covert support for guerrilla movements fighting Marxist regimes in Nicaragua, Angola, and Afghanistan.

The renewal of U.S. commitment to the Cold War was made easier by Russia's weakness during the early 1980s. Reagan's first years in the presidency coincided with the death of Brezhnev and his two ailing successors. The accession of Gorbachev, a younger and more vigorous leader, ended this period of indecisiveness in the Kremlin. A meeting between Reagan and Gorbachev renewed hopes for a revival of the spirit of accommodation, particularly in future arms talks. Nevertheless, with problems such as the future of Nicaragua or the strategic defense initiative still unsolved, a true restoration of détente seemed unlikely in the remaining years of the decade.

THE MIDDLE EAST: ISRAEL AND PETROLEUM

Among the legacies of western imperialism, no more difficult tangle of problems existed than that centered around the Middle East, the new nation of Israel, and the politics of petroleum. Here again, local problems interacted with the Cold War to shape the history of another region on the fringe of the western world.

Israel: A Western Society in the East

The state of Israel, founded in 1948, was in many ways part of the western

world, established and governed largely by Jews from Europe and North America who were imbued with western ideas of democracy. Israel, however, was geographically not in Europe or the Americas but in Asia, surrounded by Muslim nations. The new Jewish state also included substantial numbers of Arabs among its own population. The hostility of Israel's Arab neighbors and the doubtful loyalty of the new nation's non-Jewish citizens posed serious problems for this western people established in a nonwestern part of the world.

Arab-Israeli tension in the decades following Israel's establishment was punctuated by a series of open conflicts. The Israeli refusal to acquiesce in the creation of a separate Palestinian state matched the intransigent Arab denial of the right of Israel itself to exist. Some Europeans saw Israel as a bastion of old-fashioned western imperialism operating under the cloak of Zionism. Others sought to cement their own relations with the petroleum-rich Middle East by rejecting the United States' determined support for the Jewish homeland.

Into this complicated Middle Eastern situation intruded the imperatives of the Cold War. The Soviet Union tended to see that nearby region as a natural sphere of Russian influence. It offered technological and military aid to Arab governments committed to the destruction of Israel, including at various times Egypt, Syria, and Iraq. The United States, on the other hand, committed itself to full military and economic support of Israel. That nation, aware of the historic mistreatment of Jews in the Soviet Union under both tsarist and communist regimes, became an ally of the United States in the Cold War.

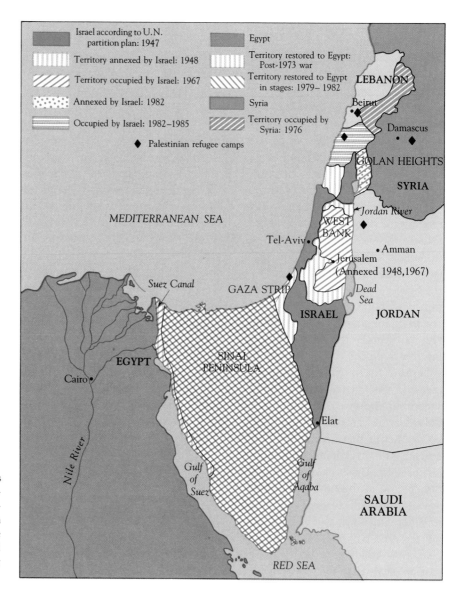

MAP 93
The Arab-Israeli Conflict. Two basic concepts are set out here: Israel's expansions and annexations from 1948 to 1982, and its occupations of, and subsequent withdrawals from the Sinai and southern Lebanon. The future of the West Bank and the Gaza Strip, still under Israeli occupation and partly settled by Israelis, has been in doubt.

Israel, the Arabs, and the Cold War

All the foregoing elements contributed to the post-1956 Arab-Israeli wars. These included the quick Israeli victory of 1967, the less clear-cut clash of 1973, and Israel's Lebanon incursion in 1982 (see Map 93).

The 1967 Arab-Israeli conflict, sometimes called the Six Day War, was triggered by the threats of Egypt's Gamal Abdel Nasser to take over a key waterway between Israel and the Red Sea from United Nations administrators. Israel's preemptive strike against Egypt and its allies Syria and Jordan was a smashing success. The Israelis seized much Arab territory, including the large Sinai Peninsula from Egypt, eastern Jerusalem and the west bank of the Jordan River from Jordan, and a strategic area, the Golan Heights, from Syria.

One consequence of this humiliating defeat of the leading Arab states was the decision of some Palestinian exiles to turn to guerrilla raids and terrorist strikes to dislodge Israel from Arab lands. Under the leadership of

Yasir Arafat, the Palestinian Liberation Organization (PLO) was to be a thorn in the side of Israel and its allies for the next two decades.

The 1973 war between Israel and Egypt was not a clear-cut triumph for either side. The Israelis beat back Syrian attacks on the Golan Heights but Egyptian forces, mobilized slowly and carefully by Nasser's successor, Anwar Sadat, succeeded in crossing the Suez Canal and knifing into the Sinai. With this achievement to his credit, Sadat later offered peace and diplomatic recognition to Israel in return for recovering the Sinai. The resulting settlement, brokered by President Carter in 1978, did not provide for an independent Palestinian state and left Egypt isolated in the Arab world. The peace settlement did, however, mark a break in the solid front of Arab states against Israel. Furthermore, Egypt, formerly a Russian client, now became an ally of the United States.

In 1982, Israel invaded her northern neighbor, Lebanon, which had become the major base for PLO terrorist attacks on Israel. The Israeli army rapidly fought its way to Beirut. Efforts to establish Israeli allies in power in Beirut failed, however. In 1985 Israeli forces withdrew, leaving Israel's implacable foe Syria as the strongest force in Lebanon.

The Geopolitics of Petroleum

Another aspect of the Middle Eastern situation that was at least as important to the west as the fate of Israel was the huge petroleum production of that region. Most western European nations, Japan, and even the relatively petroleum-rich United States depended for much of their supply of this essential power source on such Middle Eastern petroleum producers as Saudi Arabia, Iran, Iraq, and the smaller Arab states of the Persian Gulf. The Soviet Union, with ample petroleum of its own, also took an interest in the region, partly be-

cause of the Middle East's vast reserves of petroleum and partly to maintain pressure on its western adversaries. To further the latter aim, the Soviet Union established an Indian Ocean naval squadron with access to ports in South Yemen and Ethiopia.

The United States, concerned about maintaining access to Middle East petroleum, tried to maintain close ties with such conservative Middle Eastern states as Saudi Arabia and Iran, even while supporting Israel. The overthrow of the shah of Iran, a strong U.S. ally, by Muslim fundamentalists led by the Ayatollah Khomeini was a major setback for U.S. interests in the area. The United States compensated militarily for this setback by closer relations with Egypt after it made peace with Israel and by the establishment of a U.S. naval base in the northern reaches of the Indian Ocean, within striking distance of the Persian Gulf.

The petroleum of the Middle East

The Continuing Arab-Israeli Conflict. During the 1973 war, Israeli troops prepare to counterattack across the canal. Since 1948, a series of conflicts in the Middle East have kept that region in constant turmoil, with no end in sight.

847

had other effects on western nations. Arab petroleum producers were leaders in the Organization of Petroleum Exporting Countries (OPEC), the petroleum producers' cartel, which boosted petroleum prices to unprecedented levels during the 1970s. The rise in petroleum prices was a major cause of the economic recession that gripped the west in the later 1970s and the 1980s. The inability of OPEC nations to control production combined with decreased demand brought on a petroleum glut in the 1980s temporarily and broke the power of the "oil sheiks." No industrialized nation, however, communist or capitalist, could afford to ignore the long-term importance of Middle East petroleum.

LATIN AMERICA

The Latin American nations, like the states of eastern and western Europe and the two superpowers themselves, underwent significant social and economic changes during the second half of the twentieth century, which provided a foundation for conflicting political developments. These included the installation of "personalist" authoritarian government and military rule, some dramatic revolutions, and, as in Europe, an impressive revival of democracy by the 1980s. All these tendencies, however, were significantly affected by the pressures generated by the continuing Cold War.

Demographic, Economic, and Social Trends

Latin America escaped the ravages of World War II, but not that of the Great Depression of the preceding decade. Earlier gains were undermined by the collapsing commodity prices of the 1930s, and many South and Central American leaders put economic growth at the top of their list of priorities after the war. Unfortunately, fundamental economic, social, and demographic facts of Latin American life made such progress very difficult.

Despite a disturbingly high infant mortality rate, the population of Latin America grew much more rapidly than that of the rest of the western world in the postwar period. In the 1970s, for instance, Latin American populations were growing at a rate of 2.7 percent per year, as contrasted with a growth rate of 0.9 percent for North America and 0.6 percent for Europe. Latin America was also a rapidly urbanizing area, as the countryside was unable to sustain this increased population and hundreds of thousands of impoverished people flooded the cities. In 1930, south of the Rio Grande, only a single city had a population of more than a million; in the 1980s, there were twenty-two cities.

A large proportion of Latin Americans remained very poor. As in the nineteenth century, many Latin Americans were peasant laborers on the estates of wealthy landowners. Increasing numbers fled the farms, only to become slum-dwelling factory workers, miners, or transportation workers laboring at low wages in the new industries run by progressive Latin American business persons and encouraged by progressive political leaders. Still others remained both landless and unemployed, surviving as best they could. The continuing miseries of the great majority of Latin Americans contributed to the turbulent politics of the region.

Political leadership in these southern republics had traditionally been vested in two groups: an old aristocracy of large landowners and a newer business and professional elite. Both of these powerful groups were oriented toward Europe and North America, areas to which they exported Latin American raw materials and agricultural products and from which they imported consumer goods. Progressive political leaders from the 1930s onward encouraged domestic industry and even nationalized foreign holdings in South and Central American nations. Latin America as a whole, however, continued to lag behind the rest of the west in industrial development and to depend heavily on fluctuating commodity prices and foreign loans to finance the little growth that was achieved.

Economically less developed and burdened with poverty and excess population, the Latin American region was even more vulnerable than North America and western Europe to the economic downturn of the 1970s and 1980s. Declining prices for the region's resource exports, including the petroleum of Mexico and Venezuela during the petroleum glut of the 1980s, were a substantial blow to development hopes. Development loans, coming due when the Latin Americans could least afford to pay them, pushed such major Latin American nations as Mexico and Brazil to the verge of bankruptcy.

Against this background of hope for development and less hopeful realities, the politics of postwar Latin America often took a violent turn. Among the political solutions sought

1974   1977   1980   1983   1986

Oil Embargo   Camp David Accords   Soviets in Afghanistan   Reagan-Gorbachev Era

Rightest coups in Latin America   Sandinistas come to power in Nicaragua   Unrest in Poland   Civilian government ascendant in South America

were old-fashioned personalist authoritarianism, military and revolutionary rule, and a resurgence of political democracy.

Personalist Authoritarianism: The Peróns

Charismatic leaders have been a tradition in Latin American politics. Perhaps the most effective recent example is that of Juan Perón and his wife Evita, whose powerful personal rule held sway in Argentina for almost a decade and whose continuing legend is a factor in Argentian politics today. Juan Perón was an army officer and part of the military junta who ruled Argentina in the 1940s. Perón, however, found a personal following among poverty-striken urban industrial workers, particularly in Buenos Aires. Winning their support with social reforms and higher wages, he rode this popularity to dictatorial power in postwar Argentina. In this process, Evita Perón, a former actress beloved by the Argentine masses, proved an essential asset, championing women's interests and those of the very poor.

The personalist dictatorship of the Peróns collapsed in the 1950s. They had aroused the hatred of the traditional elites and of such powerful institutions as the church and the army. Also, in their concern for the urban laboring classes, their principal political supporters, they had neglected the peasantry, whose loyalty to the dynamic duo had worn thin. Evita died in 1952, widely mourned by her adoring followers. Juan was overthrown by the military and fled into exile.

The Perón legend, however, lived on. The Perónist party remained a powerful force in Argentina politics for the next twenty years. Juan Perón himself was briefly restored to power in the later 1970s, and his second wife, Isabelita, headed the government for a few years after his death. Personalist authoritarianism still functioned in the later twentieth century.

Castroite Revolution and Military Dictatorship

Two other approaches to the problems of Latin American society were the old expedient of rule by a military junta and the revolutionary solution exemplified by Cuba under the leadership of Fidel Castro. Both played important parts in the postwar history of Latin America.

Military rule dated back to the rise of backcountry *caudillos* or military strong men, in the nineteenth century, to be replaced in the twentieth by a more professional officer caste. During the decades after 1945, cliques of army officers ruled a number of Latin American nations. They brought stability and order and sometimes economic progress, measured in such broad terms as gross national product and foreign exports. Usually, however, they also upheld the traditional landholding and business classes, doing little to improve the lot of the peasants or factory workers.

It was to those latter groups that Fidel Castro's revolutionary transformation of Cuba was calculated to appeal. After his successful political revolution and defiance of the United States—the "octopus of the North" to many Latin Americans—Castro set out to make Cuba a model communist state in the New World. He succeeded in establishing a wide range of social services for the Cuban people, including public housing, education, and medical care. His efforts, however, were undermined by his failure to diversify the Cuban economy or to increase the sugar production on which Cuba, as in earlier years, had to rely for export revenues. Caught in the grip of the U.S. economic embargo, he therefore turned increasingly from dependence on the U.S. market to dependence on Soviet-bloc customers to buy this basic commodity. Politically, furthermore, the totalitarian power structure created by the Castroites seemed to many observers to be no great improvement over the dictatorships that had preceded it.

As a militant communist, Castro also attempted to export his revolutionary solution to other Latin American nations (see Map 94). Cuban military advisers joined with insurgent groups in Central America and parts of South America in the 1960s and later decades. Most of these efforts failed in the face of the response of local authorities and U.S. counterrevolutionary measures, particularly training government forces in counterinsurgency techniques. The United States also employed direct military intervention in 1984, overthrowing

MAP 94
Recent Political Trends in South America. Two major trends are depicted here: Leftist guerrilla warfare based in the countryside was sporadic in northwestern South America since the 1960s. Sponsored by Castro in the 1960s in Venezuela, Colombia, and Bolivia, leftist peasant guerrilla warfare was most recently manifested by indigenous groups in Peru. In the other trend, in the 1960s and 1970s leftist guerrillas were active in the cities of the industrialized nations. Such terrorism was one cause for the series of coups that brought in repressive military regimes in Brazil, Uruguay, Argentina, and Chile.

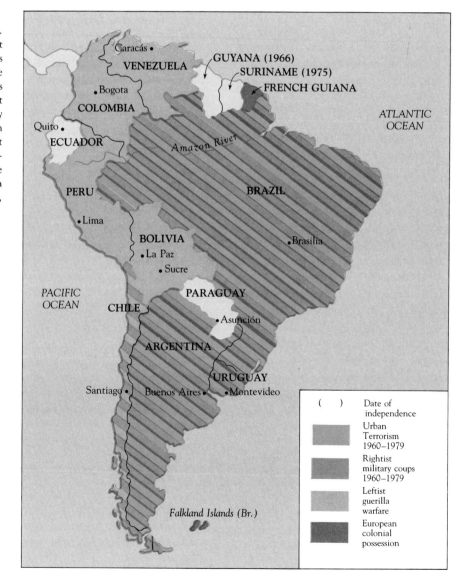

Castro's ally, the Marxist government of Grenada.

The Movement Toward Representative Government

Though the large majority of Latin American nations had been nominal republics for more than 150 years by 1980, real democracy had been much rarer in the region. Even radically democratic documents such as the Mexican Constitution of 1917 had often been followed by the political predominance of privileged minorities or single parties. Personalist dictatorships, military juntas, and, more recently and less commonly, revolutionary regimes like that of Castro's Cuba had controlled political life in the region. In the early 1980s, however, a renewed enthusiasm for democracy seemed to be gathering momentum in Central and South America.

Some Latin American states had established representative institutions well before the 1980s. These included small but relatively prosperous Costa Rica in Central America and petroleum-rich Venezuela in South America. Mexico, where a single party had governed for half a century, nevertheless, held regular and relatively free elections.

During the 1980s, citizens of a number of other Latin American nations defied traditional elites and rejected revolutionary solutions in favor of democratic institutions to help them solve their problems. Electoral democracy replaced military rule in several nations ranging from Ecuador and Peru to such major powers as Argentina and Brazil. In tiny El Salvador, the people rejected both a right-wing military elite and a left-wing

guerrilla movement to elect a liberal president, Napoleon Duarte.

Democracy still faced many problems. Only time would tell whether the new movements would have success in dealing with underlying social and economic problems. Nevertheless, there seemed to be genuine vitality in some of the new democratic regimes.

Social Revolution and the Cold War

The Cold War conflict divided the rest of the west and also had its im-

---

A REVOLUTIONARY CREDO

Why does our government have to be . . . isolated, and threatened by destruction and death?

They want, simply, to destroy our revolution in order to continue exploiting the other nations of Latin America. . . . they want to destroy us, because we have had the desire to liberate ourselves economically. They want to destroy us because we have desired to do justice. They want to destroy us because we have concerned ourselves with the humble of our land, because we have cast our lot with the poor of our country. . . .

Revolutions are remedies—bitter remedies, yes. But at times revolution is the only remedy that can be applied to evils even more bitter. . . . The Cuban revolution is already a reality for the history of the world. . . .

What is the outcome of a situation in which misery and hunger lead year by year to more misery and hunger? Can there be any other outcome than that of revolution? . . . This revolu-

tion, in the situation of present-day Latin America, can only come by the armed struggle of the peoples. . . .

We want to convert our work to wealth and welfare for our own people and for other peoples. . . . Our country, our people, and our future are important, but still more important are our 230 million Latin American brothers!*

Fidel Castro here gives the Marxist viewpoint on revolution and social change and on the United States' reaction to it. He stresses economic improvement, not political freedom. Castro also expresses his conviction about the inevitable triumph of Marxism, first in Cuba, later throughout the rest of Latin America.

*Fidel Castro, *Labor Day Address About the Destiny of Cuba*, May 1, 1960. (Havana: Cooperative Obera de Publicidad, 1966), pp. 14, 16–17, 21; *Fidel Castro Speaks*. Edited by Martin Kenner and James Petras. (New York: Grove Press, 1969), pp. 151, 159.

---

pact on Latin American affairs during the postwar period. Particularly in Central America and the Caribbean, Cold War concerns interacted with indigenous efforts at social revolution to produce a volatile and dangerous political situation.

The massive U.S. influence—economic, political, social, and military—had generated extensive anti-Yankee sentiment in Latin America throughout the twentieth century. During the decades after World War II, furthermore, many Latin American radicals and revolutionaries turned to the communist regimes in Russia, the People's Republic of China, and after 1962 Castro's Cuba for inspiration, arms, and other aid. By allying themselves with these Cold War antagonists of the United States, Latin American revolutionaries risked —and sometimes suffered from —U.S. intervention to suppress their efforts at social revolution. The United States thus sometimes found itself opposing attempts at genuine social change primarily because of real or assumed ties between Latin American nations seeking change and the communist bloc.

In Guatemala in the 1950s and in Chile in the 1970s, U.S. support for local anticommunist elements led to the overthrow of leftist governments. In Chile, which had an established tradition of democracy and socialism, the freely-elected Marxist government of Salvador Allende was top-pled, with at least U.S. approval and covert support of a military clique that subsequently became a byword for political brutality in the Americas.

In Nicaragua, in 1978–1979, the broad-based Sandinista guerrilla movement overthrew the dictatorial regime of the Somoza family, which had close ties to the United States. President Jimmy Carter initially recognized and offered aid to the new Sandinista government, which apparently had no overt ties to the Soviet Union, but Ronald Reagan strongly opposed the Sandinista regime after his election in 1980. The Reagan administration was convinced that the Sandinistas were in fact working closely with Cuba and the Soviet Union and were themselves supporting guerrilla activities in nearby El Salvador. During the 1980s, the United States, as it had in Cuba, applied a number of economic sanctions against Nicaragua. In addition, it sponsored an anti-Sandinista guerrilla movement in Nicaragua, while supporting El Salvador's efforts to suppress the leftist guerrillas in that country.

The Sandinistas in Nicaragua, like Castro in Cuba, offered a combination of state socialism and social services for the people. This was accompanied by increasing political repression, as the most radical leftists in the Sandinista leadership gained control of the government. As with Cuba, however, U.S. opposition— and Soviet support—appeared to be determined as much by the politics of the reheated Cold War as by the nature of the Nicaraguan social revolution itself.

Revolution in Central America. Communist guerrillas in El Salvador, many of them mere boys, move out of a town they have temporarily captured. Poverty and misery throughout Latin America brought on many forms of revolution and guerrilla warfare, many of them led by Marxist elements. The United States actively opposed Marxist movements in strategic Central America, orchestrating military pressure against the Marxist regime in Nicaragua and communist guerrillas in El Salvador.

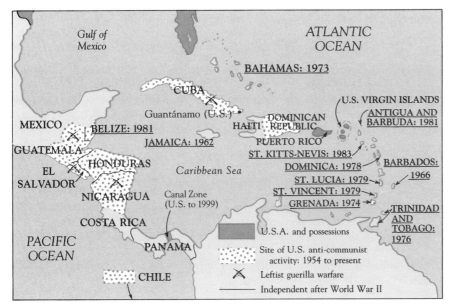

MAP 95

The Caribbean and Central America after World War II. Two major developments have marked this area. Many colonies held by Great Britain became independent, although those held by the French and the Dutch kept their association with the governing nation. At the same time, the United States pursued an active policy of intervention in areas it considered to be associated with its Cold War rival, the Soviet Union. In Grenada, the two developments came together.

SUMMARY

Postwar history in the west focused on the relations between the two superpowers, the United States and the Soviet Union, and on their respective allies in western and eastern Europe. These relations were largely governed by the rise and fall of détente within the larger framework of the Cold War. Middle East conflicts and developments in Latin America were also affected by the Cold War.

The United States grew more truly democratic as a result of the social reforms of the 1960s. Economic decline, the failure of the Vietnam venture, and the political scandals of the Nixon administration led to the election of President Reagan in the 1980s and a new stress on national self-confidence. The Soviet Union during this period achieved political stability, slow economic growth, and military parity with the United States.

Europe, meanwhile, recovered economically under the aegis of the Common Market and COMECON. Democracy flourished in western Europe and led to some challenges to U.S. leadership. In eastern Europe, much less autonomy was tolerated, but some loosening of Soviet hegemony of the region did occur.

The 1960s and 1970s saw an effort at détente, or peaceful coexistence, in the Cold War. Economic, social, and cultural contacts, diplomatic negotiations, and some steps toward limitation of nuclear arms contributed to hopes for an easing, if not an end, to superpower conflict. However, the arms race continued, and during the early 1980s détente faded rapidly.

Conflicts between Israel and its Arab neighbors and the global importance of Arab petroleum made the Middle East an area of concern during this period. Supporting Israel, yet courting Arab states like Saudi Arabia and Egypt and trying to protect the petroleum supplies of the Persian Gulf, the United States in particular followed a difficult path in this part of Asia.

Latin America continued to suffer from poverty and the rule of traditional elites during the postwar decades. Personalist dictatorships and revolutionary regimes were two responses to these problems. Political democracy seemed to be on the rise in this area in the 1980s, but the Cold War increasingly intruded into social upheaval in Central America.

SELECTED SOURCES

Banks, O. *Faces of Feminism.* 1982. A comparison of the U.S. and British feminist movements. Should be read in conjunction with G. W. Lapidus, *Women, Work and Family, in the Soviet Union.* 1982.

Dupuy, T. N. *Elusive Victory: The Arab-Israeli Wars, 1947–1974.* 1978. Comprehensive, detailed survey, excluding only the Lebanon incursion of the early 1980s.

*Edmunds, Robin. *Soviet Foreign Policy: The Brezhnev Years.* 1983. An insightful, brief account.

Fejto, F. A. *A History of People's De-mocracies: Eastern Europe Since Stalin.* 1973. Trans. D. Weissart. A survey of the varieties of Communism in Eastern Europe.

*Keen, Benjamin, and Mark Wasserman. *A Short History of Latin America.* 2nd ed. 1984. One half of the book covers twentieth century Latin America. Excellent bibliography.

*Laquer, Walter. *Europe Since Hitler.* Rev. ed. 1982. A description of economic, social, political, and cultural developments in Europe from 1945 to the beginning of the 1980s.

*Larson, Thomas B. *Soviet-American Rivalry.* 1981. An examination of major contemporary differences.

*Leuchtenburg, William. *A Troubled Feast.* Updated ed. 1983. A lively and concise survey of the United States after World War II.

Mowart, R. C. *Creating the European Community.* 1973. The creation of Europe's unique economic institutions in the years after World War II.

*O'Neill, William. *Coming Apart.* 1971. A spirited account of the United States in the turbulent 1960s.

*Available in paperback.

Some Principal Emperors, Kings, and Popes

Roman Empire

Augustus	27 B.C.–A.D. 14	Commodus	180–193
Tiberius	14– 37	Septimius Severus	193–211
Caligula	37– 41	Caracalla	211–217
Claudius	41– 54	Elagabalus	218–222
Nero	54– 68	Severus Alexander	222–235
Vespasian	69– 79	Philip the Arab	244–249
Titus	79– 81	Decius	249–251
Domitian	81– 96	Valerian	253–260
Trajan	98–117	Gallienus	260–268
Hadrian	117–138	Aurelian	270–275
Antoninus Pius	138–161	Diocletian	284–286
Marcus Aurelius	161–180		

West

Maximian	286–305
Constantius	305–306
Constantine	308–337
Maxentius	307–312
Constantine II	337–340
Constans	337–350
Constantius II	351–361
Julian	360–363
Jovian	363–364
Valentinian	364–375
Gratian	375–383
Valentinian II	383–392
Theodosius	394–395

East

Diocletian	284–305
Galerius	305–311
Maximius	308–313
Licinius	308–324
Constantine	324–337
Constantius II	337–361
Julian	361–363
Jovian	363–364
Valens	364–378
Theodosius	379–395

Carolingian Kingdom

Pepin, Mayor of the Palace	680–714
Charles Martel, Mayor of the Palace	715–741
Pepin the Short, Mayor of the Palace	741–751
Pepin the Short, King	751–768
Charlemagne and Carloman, Joint Kings	768–771
Charlemagne, King	771–814
Charlemagne, Emperor	800–814
Louis the Pious, Emperor	814–840

West Franks

Charles the Bald	840–877	Charles	855–863
		Lothar II	855–869
Louis II the Stammerer	877–879		
		East Franks	
Louis III	879–882	Louis the German	840–876
Carloman	879–884		
		Carloman	876–880
Lotharingia		Louis	876–882
Lothar	840–855	Charles the Fat	884–887
Louis II	855–875		

Roman Empire—Continued

West		East	
Honorius	395–423	Arcadius	393–408
		Theodosius II	408–450
Valentinian III	425–455	Marcian	450–457
		Leo	457–474
Romulus	475–476	Zeno	474–491
		Anastasius	491–518
		Justin	518–527
		Justinian	527–565

Holy Roman Empire

Saxons

Henry the Fowler	919– 936
Otto I	962– 973
Otto II	973– 983
Otto III	983–1002

Salians

Conrad II	1024–1039
Henry III	1039–1056
Henry IV	1056–1106
Henry V	1106–1125
Lothar II	1125–1137

Hohenstaufens

Frederick I Barbarossa	1152–1190
Henry VI	1190–1197
Philip of Swabia	1198–1208
Otto IV (*Welf*)	1198–1215
Frederick II	1215–1250
Conrad IV	1250–1254

Luxemburg, Hapsburg, and Other Dynasties

Rudolf of Hapsburg	1273–1291
Adolph of Nassau	1292–1298
Albert of Austria	1298–1308
Henry VII of Luxemburg	1308–1313
Ludwig IV of Bavaria	1314–1347
Charles IV	1347–1378
Wenceslas	1378–1400
Rupert	1400–1410
Sigismund	1410–1437

Hapsburgs

Frederick III	1440–1493
Maximilian I	1493–1519
Charles V	1519–1556
Ferdinand I	1556–1564
Maximilian II	1564–1576
Rudolf II	1576–1612
Matthias	1612–1619
Ferdinand II	1619–1637
Ferdinand III	1637–1657
Leopold I	1658–1705
Joseph I	1705–1711
Charles VI	1711–1740
Charles VII	1742–1745
Francis I	1745–1765
Joseph II	1765–1790
Leopold II	1790–1792
Francis II	1792–1806

The Papacy

Leo I	440– 461
Gregory I	590– 604
Nicholas I	858– 867
Silvester II	999–1003
Leo IX	1049–1054
Nicholas II	1058–1061
Gregory VII	1073–1085
Urban II	1088–1099
Paschal II	1099–1118
Alexander III	1159–1181
Innocent III	1198–1216
Gregory IX	1227–1241
Boniface VIII	1294–1303
John XXII	1316–1334
Gregory XI	1370–1378
Martin V	1417–1431
Eugenius IV	1431–1447
Nicholas V	1447–1455
Pius II	1458–1464
Alexander VI	1492–1503
Julius II	1503–1513
Leo X	1513–1521
Adrian VI	1522–1523
Clement VII	1523–1534
Paul III	1534–1549
Paul IV	1555–1559
Pius V	1566–1572
Gregory XIII	1572–1585
Pius VII	1800–1823
Gregory XVI	1831–1846
Pius IX	1846–1878
Leo XIII	1878–1903
Pius X	1903–1914
Benedict XV	1914–1922
Pius XI	1922–1939
Pius XII	1939–1958
John XXIII	1958–1963
Paul VI	1963–1978
John Paul I	1978
John Paul II	1978–

ENGLAND

Anglo-Saxons

Alfred the Great	871– 900
Ethelred the Unready	978–1016
Canute (*Danish*)	1016–1035
Harold I	1035–1040
Hardicanute	1040–1042
Edward the Confessor	1042–1066
Harold II	1066

Normans

William the Conqueror	1066–1087
William II	1087–1100
Henry I	1100–1135
Stephen	1135–1154

Angevins

Henry II	1154–1189
Richard I	1189–1199
John	1199–1216
Henry III	1216–1272
Edward I	1272–1307
Edward II	1307–1327
Edward III	1327–1377
Richard II	1377–1399

Houses of Lancaster and York

Henry IV	1399–1413
Henry V	1413–1422
Henry VI	1422–1461
Edward IV	1461–1483
Edward V	1483
Richard III	1483–1485

Tudors

Henry VII	1485–1509
Henry VIII	1509–1547
Edward VI	1547–1553
Mary I	1553–1558
Elizabeth I	1558–1603

Stuarts

James I	1603–1625
Charles I	1625–1649
Charles II	1660–1685
James II	1685–1688
William III and Mary II	1689–1694
William III alone	1694–1702
Anne	1702–1714

Hanoverians (from 1917, Windsors)

George I	1714–1727
George II	1727–1760
George III	1760–1820
George IV	1820–1830
William IV	1830–1837
Victoria	1837–1901
Edward VII	1901–1910
George V	1910–1936
Edward VIII	1936
George VI	1936–1952
Elizabeth II	1952–

FRANCE

Capetians

Hugh Capet	987– 996
Robert II the Pious	996–1031
Henry I	1031–1060
Philip I	1060–1108
Louis VI	1108–1137
Louis VII	1137–1180
Philip II Augustus	1180–1223
Louis VIII	1223–1226
Louis IX	1226–1270
Philip III	1270–1285
Philip IV	1285–1314
Louis X	1314–1316
Philip V	1316–1322
Charles IV	1322–1328

Valois

Philip VI	1328–1350
John	1350–1364
Charles V	1364–1380
Charles VI	1380–1422
Charles VII	1422–1461
Louis XI	1461–1483
Charles VIII	1483–1498
Louis XII	1498–1515
Francis I	1515–1547
Henry II	1547–1559
Francis II	1559–1560
Charles IX	1560–1574
Henry III	1574–1589

Bourbons

Henry IV	1589–1610
Louis XIII	1610–1643
Louis XIV	1643–1715
Louis XV	1715–1774
Louis XVI	1774–1792

Post 1792

Napoleon I, Emperor	1804–1814
Louis XVIII (*Bourbon*)	1814–1824
Charles X (*Bourbon*)	1824–1830
Louis Philippe (*Bourbon-Orléans*)	1830–1848
Napoleon III, Emperor	1851–1870

SPAIN

Ferdinand and	1479–1516
Isabella	1479–1504

Hapsburgs

Philip I	1504–1506
Charles I (Holy Roman Emperor as Charles V)	1506–1556
Philip II	1556–1598
Philip III	1598–1621
Philip IV	1621–1665
Charles II	1665–1700

Bourbons

Philip V	1700–1746
Ferdinand VI	1746–1759
Charles III	1759–1788
Charles IV	1788–1808
Ferdinand VII	1808
Joseph Bonaparte	1808–1813
Ferdinand VII (restored)	1814–1833
Isabella II	1833–1868
Amadeo	1870–1873
Alfonso XII	1874–1885
Alfonso XIII	1886–1931
Juan Carlos I	1975–

ITALY

Victor Emmanuel II	1861–1878
Humbert I	1878–1900
Victor Emmanuel III	1900–1946
Humbert II	1946

AUSTRIA AND AUSTRIA-HUNGARY

(Until 1806 all except Maria Theresa were also Holy Roman Emperors.)

Maximilian I, Archduke	1493–1519
Charles I (Emperor as Charles V)	1519–1556
Ferdinand I	1556–1564
Maximilian II	1564–1576
Rudolf II	1576–1612
Matthias	1612–1619
Ferdinand II	1619–1637
Ferdinand III	1637–1657
Leopold I	1658–1705
Joseph I	1705–1711
Charles VI	1711–1740
Maria Theresa	1740–1780
Joseph II	1780–1790
Leopold II	1790–1792
Francis II	1792–1835
Ferdinand I	1835–1848
Francis Joseph	1848–1916
Charles I	1916–1918

PRUSSIA AND GERMANY

Hohenzollerns

Frederick William the Great Elector	1640–1688
Frederick I	1701–1713
Frederick William I	1713–1740
Frederick II the Great	1740–1786
Frederick William II	1786–1797
Frederick William III	1797–1840
Frederick William IV	1840–1861
William I	1861–1888
Frederick III	1888
William II	1888–1918

RUSSIA

Ivan III	1462–1505
Basil III	1505–1533
Ivan IV the Terrible	1533–1584
Theodore I	1584–1598
Boris Godunov	1598–1605
Theodore II	1605
Basil IV	1606–1610

Romanovs

Michael	1613–1645
Alexius	1645–1676
Theodore III	1676–1682
Ivan IV and Peter I	1682–1689
Peter I the Great alone	1689–1725
Catherine I	1725–1727
Peter II	1727–1730
Anna	1730–1740
Ivan VI	1740–1741
Elizabeth	1741–1762
Peter III	1762
Catherine II the Great	1762–1796
Paul	1796–1801
Alexander I	1801–1825
Nicholas I	1825–1855
Alexander II	1855–1881
Alexander III	1881–1894
Nicholas II	1894–1917

I N D E X

N

S

ACKNOWLEDGMENTS—*continued*

771 Michihiko Hachiya, *Hiroshima Diary*, translated by Warner Wells (Chapel Hill: University of North Carolina Press, 1955), pp. 31–32.

780 Excerpts from A. Anatoli (Kuznetsov), *Babi Yar*, translated by David Floyd. (New York: Farrar, Straus & Giroux, 1970), pp. 91, 93, 97, 105, 106, 153. Copyright © 1970 by Farrar, Straus & Giroux, Inc. Reprinted by permission of Farrar, Straus & Giroux, Inc.

795 Address by President John F. Kennedy, October 22, 1962, in David L. Larson, ed., *The "Cuban Crisis" of 1962*. (Boston: Houghton, Mifflin, 1963), p. 44–45.

810 From Philip Caputo, *A Rumor of War* (New York: Holt, Rinehart, and Winston, 1977), pp. 227–30. Copyright © 1977 by Philip Caputo. Reprinted by permission of Henry Holt and Company.

815 Jawaharlal Nehru addressing the Indian parliament, August 14, 1947, in Michael Brecher, *Nehru: A Political Biography* (London: Oxford University Press, 1961), p. 137.

835 De Gaulle Press Conference, September 9, 1965, *Speeches and Press Conferences*, No. 228 (New York: French Embassy, 1965); De Gaulle to President Johnson, March 7, 1966, "Report of the Subcommittee on Europe of the House Committee on Foreign Affairs, The Crisis in NATO" (Washington, GPO, 1966), p. 7 reprinted in Arthur L. Funk, ed. *Europe in the Twentieth Century* (Homewood, Ill.: Dorsey, 1968), pp. 427–28.

A-1–A-4 D. Kagan, S. Ozment, and F. Turner, *The Western Heritage* (New York: Macmillan, 1983), pp. i–iv. Reprinted with permission of Macmillan Publishing Company from *The Western Heritage* by D. Kagan, S. Ozment, and F. Turner. Copyright © 1983 by Macmillan Publishing Company.

PHOTO CREDITS

382 Scala/Art Resource, N.Y.; **385** Giraudon/Art Resource, N.Y.; **392** The Bettmann Archive; **395** The Bettmann Archive; **396** Saskia/Art Resource, N.Y.; **398** The Bettmann Archive; **400** SEF/Art Resource, N.Y.; **406** Historical Pictures Service, Chicago; **407** The Granger Collection; **408** The Granger Collection; **409** Brown Brothers; **412** The Granger Collection; **416** The Granger Collection; **419** The Bettmann Archive; **420** Art Resource, N.Y.; **424** Giraudon/Art Resource, N.Y.; **429** The Wallace Collection; **430** National Gallery of Art, Washington, Samuel H. Kress Collection; **434** The Bettmann Archive; **438** Culver Pictures, Inc.; **439** The Bettmann Archive; **442** The Fotomas Index; **444** Photographie Bulloz; **448** Giraudon/Art Resource, N.Y.; **452** John Trumball, *Surrender of Lord Cornwallis at Yorktown*. (Detail). Copyright Yale University Art Gallery; **454** Mansell Collection; **457** The Granger Collection; **458** Michael Holford; **462** The Granger Collection; **466** National Portrait Gallery, London; **469** The Granger Collection; **474** The Granger Collection; **480** Giraudon/Art Resource, N.Y.; **482** Photographie Bulloz; **487** Giraudon/Art Resource, N.Y.; **489** Photographie Bulloz; **491** The Bettmann Archive; **496** Photographie Bulloz; **499** Brown Brothers; **500** Giraudon/Art Resource, N.Y.; **504** The Granger Collection; **506** Photographie Bulloz; **511** Giraudon/Art Resource, N.Y.; **518** The Bettmann Archive; **523** The Granger Collection; **524** The Bettmann Archive; **527** The Bettmann Archive; **531** The Bettmann Archive; **536** The Bettmann Archive; **541** The Granger Collection; **544** Mansell Collection; **545** Brown Brothers; **549** Giraudon/Art Resource, N.Y.; **551** The Granger Collection; **554** Giraudon/Art Resource, N.Y.; **556** Mansell Collection; **558** Photographie Bulloz; **564** Photographie Bulloz; **566** Bibliothèque Nationale, Paris; **567** The Granger Collection; **572** The Fotomas Index; **577** (top) The Granger Collection; **577** (bottom) Culver Pictures, Inc.; **580** Bibliothèque Nationale, Paris; **584** The Fotomas Index; **585** The Bettmann Archive; **590** Historical Pictures Service, Chicago; **594** H. Roger Viollet; **596** The Bettmann Archive; **600** The Granger Collection; **604** Photographie Bulloz; **607** Photo Researchers, Inc.; **610** Hulton Picture Library, The Bettmann Archive; **613** The Bettmann Archive; **616** Hulton Picture Library, The Bettmann Archive; **618** Hulton Picture Library, The Bettmann Archive; **622** Historical Pictures Service, Chicago; **623** The Bettmann Archive; **628** Photographie Bulloz; **632** E. T. Archive; **634** Photographie Bulloz; **640** The Bettmann Archive; **641** The Bettmann Archive; **644** Giraudon/Art Resource, N.Y.; **647** The Granger Collection; **650** The Bettmann Archive; **654** Mansell Collection; **657** Church Missionary Society Archives, London; **660** Mansell Collection; **662** Culver Pictures, Inc.; **663** The Bettmann Archive; **666** Historical Pictures Service, Chicago; **669** Michael Holford; **671** Historical Pictures Service, Chicago; **677** (top) The Bettmann Archive; **677** (bottom) Brown Brothers; **679** Historical Pictures Service, Chicago; **682** "The Assault," by H. de Groux, Musee de la Guerre, Paris, DR.; **685** (top) Imperial War Museum, London; **685** (bottom) L'Illustration; **689** Brown Brothers; **691** Imperial War Museum, London; **695** Historical Pictures Service, Chicago; **704** Elliott Erwitt, Magnum Photos, Inc.; **707** Ford Motor Co.; **709** Erich Hartmann, Magnum Photos, Inc.; **714** Dick Davis, Photo Researchers, Inc.; **716** Brown Brothers; **718** B. Barbey, Magnum Photos, Inc.; **720** Mary Evans Picture Library/Photo Researchers, Inc.; **724** Art Resource, N.Y.; **728** Peter Marlow, Magnum Photos, Inc.; **733** The Granger Collection; **736** Toledo Museum of Art; **741** Hans Namuth, Photo Researchers, Inc.; **743** Martha Swope; **745** Elliott Erwitt, Magnum Photos, Inc.; **747** Rocky Widner/Retna Ltd.; **752** The Bettmann Archive; **754** Brown Brothers; **760** The Bettmann Archive; **763** Brown Brothers; **765** Wide World Photos, Inc.; **770** E. T. Archive; **775** The Bettmann Archive; **777** UPI/Bettmann Newsphotos; **782** Hulton Picture Library/Bettmann Archive; **783** U.S. Navy; **785** U.S. Air Force; **786** Historical Pictures Service, Chicago; **787** The Bettmann Archive; **788** UPI/Bettmann Newsphotos; **794** Walt Johnson, The Picture Group, Inc.; **797** Wide World Photos, Inc.; **801** AP/Wide World Photos, Inc.; **803** AP/Wide World Photos, Inc.; **808** AP/Wide World Photos, Inc.; **811** Phillip Jones Griffiths, Magnum Photos, Inc.; **814** Arthur Tress, Photo Researchers, Inc.; **817** AP/Wide World Photos, Inc.; **821** Cornell Capa, Magnum Photos, Inc.; **825** Ian Berry, Magnum Photos, Inc.; **828** Morrison Knudsen Engineers; **834** Elliott Erwitt, Magnum Photos, Inc.; **836** Bob Adelman, Magnum Photos, Inc.; **843** Bettmann Newsphotos; **844** The Granger Collection; **847** Micha Bar-Am, Magnum Photos, Inc.; **852** C. Steele-Perkins, Magnum Photos, Inc.

ABOUT THE AUTHORS

Richard D. Goff (Ph.D.: Duke) is Professor of History at Eastern Michigan University where he has taught survey courses in Western and World Civilization. In 1983 he received a distinguished faculty service award from the university. Among his publications is *The Twentieth Century: A Brief Global History*, published by Knopf.

George H. Cassar (Ph.D.: McGill) is Professor of History at Eastern Michigan University where he has taught survey courses in Western Civilization, and courses in European and Military History. He is a recent recipient of the Faculty Award for Research and Publication from Eastern Michigan University. His publications include *The French and the Dardanelles, Kitchener: Architect of Victory, The Tragedy of Sir John French,* and *Beyond Courage: The Canadiens at the Second Battle of Ypres*.

Anthony Esler (Ph.D.: Duke) is Professor of History at the College of William and Mary. He has written on a variety of topics, including the history of youth movements and global history. His most recent book is *The Human Venture: A World History*, published by Prentice-Hall.

James P. Holoka (Ph.D.: Michigan) is Professor of Foreign Languages at Eastern Michigan University where he has taught Classics and Humanities for twelve years. He is a recipient of a Rackham Prize Fellowship as well as an excellence in teaching award from Eastern Michigan University. He is the author of numerous publications in such journals as *Classical World, Transactions of the American Philological Association,* and *Classical Philology*.

James C. Waltz (Ph.D.: Michigan State) is Professor and former Chairman of History at Eastern Michigan University where he has taught survey courses in Western Civilization and courses in Ancient, Medieval, Renaissance, and Reformation History. He is a recipient of an N.E.H. Fellowship for residents for college teachers (University of Chicago). He is the author of many articles and book reviews in *The Muslim World* and other publications.